MW01493085

Data Quality

Also available from ASQ Quality Press:

Quality Experience Telemetry: How to Effectively Use Telemetry for Improved Customer Success
Alka Jarvis, Luis Morales, and Johnson Jose

Linear Regression Analysis with JMP and R
Rachel T. Silvestrini and Sarah E. Burke

Navigating the Minefield: A Practical KM Companion
Patricia Lee Eng and Paul J. Corney

The Certified Software Quality Engineer Handbook, Second Edition
Linda Westfall

Introduction to 8D Problem Solving: Including Practical Applications and Examples
Ali Zarghami and Don Benbow

The Quality Toolbox, Second Edition
Nancy R. Tague

Root Cause Analysis: Simplified Tools and Techniques, Second Edition
Bjørn Andersen and Tom Fagerhaug

The Certified Six Sigma Green Belt Handbook, Second Edition
Roderick A. Munro, Govindarajan Ramu, and Daniel J. Zrymiak

The Certified Manager of Quality/Organizational Excellence Handbook, Fourth Edition
Russell T. Westcott, editor

The Certified Six Sigma Black Belt Handbook, Third Edition
T. M. Kubiak and Donald W. Benbow

The ASQ Auditing Handbook, Fourth Edition
J.P. Russell, editor

The ASQ Quality Improvement Pocket Guide: Basic History, Concepts, Tools, and Relationships
Grace L. Duffy, editor

To request a complimentary catalog of ASQ Quality Press publications,
call 800-248-1946, or visit our website at http://www.asq.org/quality-press.

Data Quality

Dimensions, Measurement, Strategy, Management, and Governance

Dr. Rupa Mahanti

ASQ Quality Press
Milwaukee, Wisconsin

American Society for Quality, Quality Press, Milwaukee 53203
© 2018 by ASQ
All rights reserved. Published 2018
Printed in the United States of America
24 23 22 21 20 19   5 4 3 2 1

Library of Congress Cataloging-in-Publication Data

Names: Mahanti, Rupa, author.
Title: Data quality : dimensions, measurement, strategy, management, and
  governance / Dr. Rupa Mahanti.
Description: Milwaukee, Wisconsin : ASQ Quality Press, [2019] | Includes
  bibliographical references and index.
Identifiers: LCCN 2018050766 | ISBN 9780873899772 (hard cover : alk. paper)
Subjects: LCSH: Database management—Quality control.
Classification: LCC QA76.9.D3 M2848 2019 | DDC 005.74—dc23
LC record available at https://lccn.loc.gov/2018050766

ISBN: 978-0-87389-977-2

Publisher: Seiche Sanders
Sr. Creative Services Specialist: Randy L. Benson

ASQ Mission: The American Society for Quality advances individual, organizational, and community excellence worldwide through learning, quality improvement, and knowledge exchange.

Attention Bookstores, Wholesalers, Schools, and Corporations: ASQ Quality Press books, video, audio, and software are available at quantity discounts with bulk purchases for business, educational, or instructional use. For information, please contact ASQ Quality Press at 800-248-1946, or write to ASQ Quality Press, P.O. Box 3005, Milwaukee, WI 53201-3005.

To place orders or to request ASQ membership information, call 800-248-1946. Visit our website at http://www.asq.org/quality-press.

 Printed on acid-free paper

Quality Press
600 N. Plankinton Ave.
Milwaukee, WI 53203-2914
E-mail: authors@asq.org

ASQ   The Global Voice of Quality®

Table of Contents

List of Figures and Tables

Foreword: The Ins and Outs of Data Quality

We—meaning corporations, government agencies, nonprofits; leaders, professionals, and workers at all levels in all roles; and customers, citizens, and parents—have a huge problem. It is "data," that intangible stuff we use every day to learn about the world, to complete basic tasks, and to make decisions, to conduct analyses, and plan for the future. And now, according to *The Economist*, "the world's most valuable asset."

The problem is simple enough to state: too much data are simply wrong, poorly defined, not relevant to the task at hand, or otherwise unfit for use. Bad data makes it more difficult to complete our work, make basic decisions, conduct advanced analyses, and plan. The best study I know of suggests that only 3% of data meet basic quality standards, never mind the much more demanding requirements of machine learning.

Bad data are expensive: my best estimate is that it costs a typical company 20% of revenue. Worse, they dilute trust—who would trust an exciting new insight if it is based on poor data! And worse still, sometimes bad data are simply dangerous; look at the damage brought on by the financial crisis, which had its roots in bad data.

As far as I can tell, data quality has always been important. The notion that the data might not be up to snuff is hardly new: computer scientists coined the phrase "garbage in, garbage out" a full two generations ago. Still, most of us, in both our personal and professional lives, are remarkably tolerant of bad data. When we encounter something that doesn't look right, we check it and make corrections, never stopping to think of how often this occurs or that our actions silently communicate acceptance of the problem.

The situation is no longer tenable, not because the data are getting worse—I see no evidence of that—but because the importance of data is growing so fast! And while everyone who touches data will have a role to play, each company will need a real expert or two. Someone who has deep expertise in data and data quality, understands the fundamental issues and approaches, and can guide their organization's efforts. Summed up, millions of data quality experts are needed!

This is why I'm so excited to see this work by Rupa Mahanti. She covers the technical waterfront extremely well, adding in some gems that make this book priceless. Let me call out five.

First, "the butterfly effect on data quality" (Chapter 1). Some years ago I worked with a middle manager in a financial institution. During her first day on the job, someone made a small error entering her name into a system. Seems innocent enough. But by the end of that day, the error had propagated to (at least) 10 more systems. She spent most of her first week trying to correct those errors. And worse, they never really went away— she dealt with them throughout her tenure with the company. Interestingly, it is hard to put a price tag on the "cost." It's not like the company paid her overtime to deal with the errors. But it certainly hurt her job satisfaction.

Second, the dimensions of data quality and their measurement. Data quality is, of course, in the eyes of the customer. But translating subjective customer needs into objective dimensions that you can actually measure is essential. It is demanding, technical work, well covered in Chapters 3 and 4.

Third, is data quality strategy. I find that "strategy" can be an elusive concept. Too often, it is done poorly, wasting time and effort. As Rupa points out, people misuse the term all the time, confusing it with some sort of high-level plan. A well-conceived data quality strategy can advance the effort for years! As Rupa also points out, one must consider literally dozens of factors to develop a great strategy. Rupa devotes considerable time to exploring these factors. She also fully defines and explores the entire process, including working with stakeholders to build support for implementation. This end-to-end thinking is especially important, as most data quality practitioners have little experience with strategy (see Chapter 5).

Fourth, the application of Six Sigma techniques. It is curious to me that Six Sigma practitioners haven't jumped at the chance to apply their tools to data quality. DMAIC seems a great choice for attacking many issues (alternatively, lean seems ideally suited to address the waste associated with those hidden data factories set up to accommodate bad data); Chapter 6 points the way.

Fifth, "myths, challenges, and critical success factors." The cold, brutal reality is that success with data quality depends less on technical excellence and more on soft factors: resistance to change, engaging senior leaders, education, and on and on. Leaders have to spend most of their effort here, gaining a keen sense of the pulse of their organizations, building support when opportunity presents itself, leveraging success, and so on. Rupa discusses it all in Chapter 7. While there are dozens of ways to fail, I found the section on teamwork, partnership, communication, and collaboration especially important—no one does this alone!

A final note. This is not the kind of book that you'll read one time and be done with. So scan it quickly the first time through to get an idea of its breadth. Then dig in on one topic of special importance to your work. Finally, use it as a reference to guide your next steps, learn details, and broaden your perspective.

Thomas C. Redman, PhD, "the Data Doc"
Rumson, New Jersey
October 2018

Preface

I would like to start by explaining what motivated me to write this book. I first came across computers as a sixth-grade student at Sacred Heart Convent School in Ranchi, India, where I learned how to write BASIC programs for the next five years through the tenth grade. I found writing programs very interesting. My undergraduate and postgraduate coursework was in computer science and information technology, respectively, where we all were taught several programming languages, including Pascal, C, C++, Java, and Visual Basic, were first exposed to concepts of data and database management systems, and learned how to write basic SQL queries in MS-Access and Oracle. As an intern at Tata Technologies Limited, I was introduced to the concepts of the Six Sigma quality and process improvement methodology, and have since looked to the DMAIC approach as a way to improve processes. I went on to complete a PhD, which involved modeling of air pollutants and led to my developing a neural network model and automating a mathematical model for differential equations. This involved working with a lot of data and data analysis, and thus began my interest in data and information management. During this period, I was guest faculty and later a full-time lecturer at Birla Institute of Technology in Ranchi, where I taught different computer science subjects to undergraduate and postgraduate students.

Great minds from all over the world in different ages, from executive leadership to scientists to famous detectives, have respected data and have appreciated the value they bring. Following are a few quotes as illustration.

In God we trust. All others must bring data.

—W. Edwards Deming, statistician

It is a capital mistake to theorize before one has data.

—Sir Arthur Conan Doyle, Sherlock Holmes

Where there is data smoke, there is business fire.

—Thomas C. Redman, the Data Doc

Data that is loved tends to survive.

—Kurt Bollacker, computer scientist

If we have data, let's look at data; if all we have are opinions,
let's go with mine!

—Jim Barksdale, former CEO of Netscape

I joined Tata Consultancy Services in 2005, where I was assigned to work in a data warehousing project for a British telecommunications company. Since then, I have played different roles in various data-intensive projects for different clients in different industry sectors and different geographies. While working on these projects, I have come across situations where applications have not produced the right results or correct reports, or produced inconsistent reports, not because of ETL (extract, transport, load) coding issues or design issues, or code not meeting functional requirements, but because of bad data. However, the alarm that was raised was "ETL code is not working properly." Or even worse, the application would fail in the middle of the night because of a data issue. Hours of troubleshooting often would reveal an issue with a single data element in a record in the source data. There were times when users would stop using the application because it was not meeting their business need, when the real crux of the problem was not the application but the data. That is when I realized how important data quality was, and that data quality should be approached in a proactive and strategic manner instead of a reactive and tactical fashion. The Six Sigma DMAIC approach has helped me approach data quality problems in a systematic manner. Over the years, I have seen data evolving from being an application by-product to being an enterprise asset that enables you to stay ahead in a competitive market.

In my early years, data quality was not treated as important, and the focus was on fixing data issues reactively when discovered. We had to explain to our stakeholders the cost of poor data quality and how poor data quality was negatively impacting business, and dispel various data quality misconceptions. While with compliance and regulatory requirements, the mind set is gradually changing and companies have started to pay more attention to data, organizations often struggle with data quality owing to large volumes of data residing in silos and traveling through a myriad of different applications. The fact is that data quality is intangible, and attaining data quality requires considerable changes in operations, which makes the journey to attaining data quality even more difficult. This book is written with the express purpose of motivating readers on the topic of data quality, dispelling misconceptions relating to data quality, and providing guidance on the different aspects of data quality with the aim to be able to improve data quality.

The only source of knowledge is experience.

—Albert Einstein

I have written this book to share the combined data quality knowledge that I have accumulated over the years of working in different programs and projects associated with data, processes, and technologies in various industry sectors, reading a number of books and articles, most of which are listed in the Bibliography, and conducting empirical research in information management so that students, academicians, industry professionals, practitioners at different levels, and researchers can use the content in this book to further their knowledge and get guidance on their own specific projects. In order to address this mixed community, I have tried to achieve a balance between technical details (for example, SQL statements, relational database components, data quality dimensions measurements) and higher-level qualitative discussions (cost of data quality, data quality strategy, data quality maturity, the case made for data quality, and so on) with case studies, illustrations, and real-world examples throughout. Whenever I read a book on a particular subject, from my student days to today, I find a book containing a balance of concepts and examples and illustrations easier to understand and relate to, and hence have tried to do the same while writing this book.

INTENDED AUDIENCE

- Data quality managers and staff responsible for information quality processes

- Data designers/modelers and data and information architects

- Data warehouse managers

- Information management professionals and data quality professionals—both the technology experts as well as those in a techno-functional role—who work in data profiling, data migration, data integration and data cleansing, data standardization, ETL, business intelligence, and data reporting

- College and university students who want to pursue a career in quality, data analytics, business intelligence, or systems and information management

- C-suite executives and senior management who want to embark on a journey to improve the quality of data and provide an environment for data quality initiatives to flourish and deliver value

- Business and data stewards who are responsible for taking care of their respective data assets

- Managers who lead information-intensive business functions and who are owners of processes that capture data and process data for other business functions to consume, or consume data produced by other business process

- Business analysts, technical business analysts, process analysts, reporting analysts, and data analysts—workers who are active consumers of data

- Program and project managers who handle data-intensive projects

- Risk management professionals

This book in divided into eight chapters. Chapter 1, "Data, Data Quality, and Cost of Poor Data Quality," discusses data and data quality fundamentals. Chapter 2, "Building Blocks of Data: Evolutionary History and Data Concepts," gives an overview of the technical aspects of data and database storage, design, and so on, with examples to provide background for readers and enable them to familiarize themselves with terms that will be used throughout the book. Chapter 3, "Data Quality Dimensions," and Chapter 4, "Measuring Data Quality Dimensions," as the titles suggest, provide a comprehensive discussion of different objective and subjective data quality dimensions and the relationships between them, and how to go about measuring them, with practical examples that will help the reader apply these principles to their specific data quality problem. Chapter 5, "Data Quality Strategy" gives guidance as to how to go about creating a data quality strategy and discusses the various components of a data quality strategy, data quality maturity, and the role of the chief data officer. Chapter 6, "Data Quality Management," covers topics such as data cleansing, data validation, data quality monitoring, how to ensure data quality in a data migration project, data integration, master data management (MDM), metadata management, and so on, and application of Six Sigma DMAIC and Six Sigma tools to data quality. Chapter 7, "Data Quality: Critical Success Factors (CSFs)," discusses various data quality myths and challenges, and the factors necessary for the success of a data quality program. Chapter 8, "Data Governance and Data Quality," discusses data governance misconceptions, the difference between IT governance and data governance, the reasons behind data governance failures, data governance and data quality, and the data governance framework.

In case you have any questions or want to share your feedback about the book, please feel free to e-mail me at rupa.mahanti0@gmail.com.

Alternatively, you can contact me on LinkedIn at https://www.linkedin.com/in/rupa-mahanti-62627915.

Rupa Mahanti

Acknowledgments

Writing this book was an enriching experience and gave me great pleasure and satisfaction, but has been more time-consuming and challenging than I initially thought. I owe a debt of gratitude to many people who have directly or indirectly helped me on my data quality journey.

I am extremely grateful to the many leaders in the field of data quality, and related fields, who have taken the time to write articles and/or books so that I and many others could gain knowledge. The Bibliography shows the extent of my appreciation of those who have made that effort. Special thanks to Thomas C. Redman, Larry English, Ralph Kimball, Bill Inmon, Jack E. Olson, Ted Friedman, David Loshin, Wayne Eckerson, Joseph M. Juran, Philip Russom, Rajesh Jugulum, Laura Sebastian-Colemen, Sid Adelman, Larissa Moss, Majid Abai, Danette McGilvray, Prashanth H. Southekal, Arkady Maydanchik, Gwen Thomas, David Plotkin, Nicole Askham, Boris Otto, Hubert Österle, Felix Naumann, Robert Seiner, Steve Sarsfield, Tony Fisher, Dylan Jones, Carlo Batini, Monica Scannapieco, Richard Wang, John Ladley, Sunil Soares, Ron S. Kenett, and Galit Shmueli.

I would also like to thank the many clients and colleagues who have challenged and collaborated with me on so many initiatives over the years. I appreciate the opportunity to work with such high-quality people.

I am very grateful to the American Society for Quality (ASQ) for giving me an opportunity to publish this book. I am particularly thankful to Paul O'Mara, Managing Editor at ASQ Quality Press, for his continued cooperation and support for this project. He was patient and flexible in accommodating my requests. I would also like to thank the book reviewers for their time, constructive feedback, and helpful suggestions, which helped make this a better book. Thanks to the ASQ team for helping me make this book a reality. There are many areas of publishing that were new to me, and the ASQ team made the process and the experience very easy and enjoyable.

I am also grateful to my teachers at Sacred Heart Convent, DAV JVM, and Birla Institute of Technology, where I received the education that created the opportunities that have led me to where I am today. Thanks to all my English teachers, and a special thanks to Miss Amarjeet Singh through whose efforts I have acquired good reading and writing skills. My years in PhD research have played a key role in my career and personal development, and I owe a special thanks to my PhD guides, Dr. Vandana Bhattacherjee and the late Dr. S. K. Mukherjee, and my teacher and mentor Dr. P. K. Mahanti, who supported me during this period. Though miles way, Dr. Vandana Bhattacherjee and Dr. P. K. Mahanti still provide me with guidance and encouragement, and I will always be indebted to them. I am also thankful to my students, whose questions have enabled me think more and find a better solution.

Last, but not least, many thanks to my parents for their unwavering support, encouragement, and optimism. They have been my rock throughout my life, even when they were not near me, and hence share credit for every goal I achieve. Writing this book took most of my time outside of work hours. I would not have been able to write the manuscript without them being so supportive and encouraging. They were my inspiration, and fueled my determination to finish this book.

1

Data, Data Quality, and
Cost of Poor Data Quality

THE DATA AGE

Data promise to be for the twenty-first century what steam power was for the eighteenth, electricity for the nineteenth, and hydrocarbons for the twentieth century (Mojsilovic 2014). The advent of information technology (IT) and the Internet of things has resulted in data having a universal presence. The pervasiveness of data has changed the way we conduct business, transact, undertake research, and communicate.

What are *data*? The *New Oxford American Dictionary* defines data first as "facts and statistics collected together for reference or analysis." From an IT perspective, data are abstract representations of selected features of real-world entities, events, and concepts, expressed and understood through clearly definable conventions (Sebastian-Coleman 2013) related to their meaning, format, collection, and storage.

We have certainly moved a long way from when there was limited capture of data, to data being stored manually in physical files by individuals, to processing and storing huge volumes of data electronically. Before the advent of electronic processing, computers, and databases, data were not even collected on a number of corporate entities, events, transactions, and operations. We live in an age of technology and data, where everything—video, call data records, customer transactions, financial records, healthcare records, student data, scientific publications, economic data, weather data, geospatial data, asset data, stock market data, and so on—is associated with data sources, and everything in our lives is captured and stored electronically. The progress of information technologies, the declining cost of disk hardware, and the availability of cloud storage have enabled individuals, companies, and governments to capture, process, and save data that might otherwise have been purged or never collected in the first place (Witten, Frank, and Hall 2011). In today's multichannel world, data are collected through a large number of diverse channels—call centers, Internet web forms, telephones, e-business, to name a few—and are widely stored in relational and non-relational databases. There are employee databases, customer databases, product databases, geospatial databases, material databases, asset databases, and billing and collection databases, to name a few. Databases have evolved in terms of capability, number, and size. With the widespread availability and capability of databases and information technology, accessing information has also become much easier than it used to be with a physical file system. With databases, when anyone wants to know something, they instinctively query the tables in the database to extract and view data.

This chapter starts with a discussion on the importance of data and data quality and the categorization of data. The next sections give an overview of data quality and how data quality is different, the data quality dimensions, causes of bad data quality, and the cost of poor data quality. The chapter concludes with a discussion on the "butterfly effect of data quality," which describes how a small data issue becomes a bigger problem as it traverses the organization, and a summary section that highlights the key points discussed in this chapter.

ARE DATA AND DATA QUALITY IMPORTANT? YES THEY ARE!

The foundation of a building plays a major role in the successful development and maintenance of the building. The stronger the foundation, the stronger the building! In the same way, data are the foundation on which organizations rest in this competitive age. Data are no longer a by-product of an organization's IT systems and applications, but are an organization's most valuable asset and resource, and have a real, measurable value. Besides the importance of data as a resource, it is also appropriate to view data as a commodity. However, the value of the data does not only lie with the data themselves, but also the actions that arise from the data and their usage. The same piece of data is used several times for multiple purposes. For example, address data are used for deliveries, billing, invoices, and marketing. Product data are used for sales, inventory, forecasting, marketing, financial forecasts, and supply chain management. Good quality data are essential to providing excellent customer service, operational efficiency, compliance with regulatory requirements, effective decision making, and effective strategic business planning, and need to be managed efficiently in order to generate a return. Data are the foundation of various applications and systems dealing in various business functions in an organization.

Insurance companies, banks, online retailers, and financial services companies are all organizations where business itself is data centric. These organizations heavily rely on collecting and processing data as one of their primary activities. For example, banking, insurance, and credit card companies process and trade information products. Other organizations like manufacturing, utilities, and healthcare organizations may appear to be less involved with information systems because their products or activities are not information specific. However, if you look beyond the products into operations, you will find that most of their activities and decisions are driven by data. For instance, manufacturing organizations process raw materials to produce and ship products. However, data drive the processes of material acquisition, inventory management, supply chain management, final product quality, order processing, shipping, and billing. For utility companies, though asset and asset maintenance are the primary concern, they do require good quality data about their assets and asset performance—in addition to customer, sales, and marketing data, billing, and service data—to be able to provide good service and gain competitive advantage. For hospitals and healthcare organizations, the primary activities are medical procedures and patient care. While medical procedures and patient care by themselves are not information-centric activities, hospitals need to store and process patient data, care data, physician data, encounter data, patient billing data, and so on, to provide good quality service. New trends in data warehousing, business intelligence, data mining, data analytics, decision support, enterprise resource planning, and customer relationship management systems draw attention to the fact that data play an ever-growing and important role in organizations.

Large volumes of data across the various applications and systems in organizations bring a number of challenges for the organization to deal with. From executive-level decisions about mergers and acquisition activity to a call center representative making a split-second decision about customer service, the data an enterprise collects on virtually every aspect of the organization—customers, prospects, products, inventory, finances, assets, or employees—can have a significant effect on the organization's ability to satisfy customers, reduce costs, improve productivity, or mitigate risks (Dorr and Murnane 2011) and increasing operational efficiency. Accurate, complete, current, consistent, and timely data are critical to accurate, timely, and unbiased decisions. Since data and information are the basis of decision making, they must be carefully managed to ensure they can be located easily, can be relied on for their currency, completeness, and accuracy, and can be obtained when and where the data are needed.

DATA QUALITY

Having said that data are an important part of our lives, the next question is "is the quality of data important?" The answer is "yes, data quality is important!"

However, while good data are a source of myriad opportunities, bad data are a tremendous burden and only present problems. Companies that manage their data effectively are able to achieve a competitive advantage in the marketplace (Sellar 1999). On the other hand, "bad data can put a company at a competitive disadvantage," comments Greengard (1998). Bad data, like cancer, can weaken and kill an organization. To understand why data quality is important, we need to understand the categorization of data, the current quality of data and how is it different from the quality of manufacturing processes, the business impact of bad data and cost of poor data quality, and possible causes of data quality issues.

CATEGORIZATION OF DATA

Data categories are groupings of data with common characteristics. We can classify the data that most enterprises deal with into five categories (see Figure 1.1):

1. Master data

2. Reference data

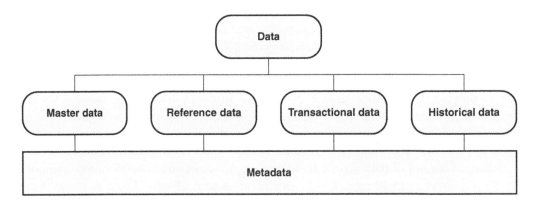

Figure 1.1   Categories of data.

3. Transactional data

4. Historical data

5. Metadata

Master Data

Master data are high-value, key business information that describes the core entities of organizations and that supports the transactions and plays a crucial role in the basic operation of a business. It is the core of every business transaction, application, analysis, report, and decision. *Master data* are defined as the basic characteristics of instances of business entities such as customers, products, parts, employees, accounts, sites, inventories, materials, and suppliers. Typically, master data can be recognized by nouns such as *patient*, *customer*, or *product*, to give a few examples. Master data can be grouped by places (locations, geography, sites, areas, addresses, zones, and so on), parties (persons, organizations, vendors, prospects, customers, suppliers, patients, students, employees, and so on), and things (products, parts, assets, items, raw materials, finished goods, vehicles, and so on). Master data are characteristically non-transactional data that are used to define the primary business entities and used by multiple business processes, systems, and applications in the organization. Generally, master data are created once (Knolmayer and Röthlin 2006), used multiple times by different business processes, and either do not change at all or change infrequently.

Master data are generally assembled into master records, and associated reference data may form a part of the master record (McGilvray 2008a). For example, state code, country code, or status code fields are associated reference data in a customer master record, and diagnosis code fields are associated reference data in a patient master record. However, while reference data can form part of the master data record and are also non-transactional data, they are not the same as master data, which we will discuss in more detail in the "Reference Data" section.

Errors in master data can have substantial cost implications. For instance, if the address of a customer is wrong, this may result in correspondence, orders, and bills sent to the wrong address; if the price of a product is wrong, the product may be sold below the intended price; if a debtor account number is wrong, an invoice might not be paid on time; if the product dimensions are wrong, there might be a delay in transportation, and so on. Therefore, even a trivial amount of incorrect master data can absorb a significant part of the revenue of a company (Haug and Arlbjørn 2011).

Reference Data

Reference data are sets of permissible values and corresponding textual descriptions that are referenced and shared by a number of systems, applications, data repositories, business processes, and reports, as well as other data like transactional and master data records. As the name suggests, reference data are designed with the express purpose of being referenced by other data, like master data and transactional data, to provide a standard terminology and structure across different systems, applications, and data stores throughout an organization. Reference data become more valuable with widespread reuse and referencing. Typical examples of reference data are:

- Country codes.

- State abbreviations.

- Area codes/post codes/ZIP codes.

- Industry codes (for example, Standard Industrial Classification (SIC) codes are four-digit numerical codes assigned by the US government to business establishments to identify the primary business of the establishment; NAICS codes are industry standard reference data sets used for classification of business establishments).

- Diagnosis codes (for example, ICD-10, a medical coding scheme used to classify diseases, signs and symptoms, causes, and so on).

- Currency codes.

- Corporate codes.

- Status codes.

- Product codes.

- Product hierarchy.

- Flags.

- Calendar (structure and constraints).

- HTTP status codes.

Reference data can be created either within an organization or by external bodies. Organizations create internal reference data to describe or standardize their own internal business data, such as status codes like customer status and account status, to provide consistency across the organization by standardizing these values. External organizations, such as government agencies, national or international regulatory bodies, or standards organizations, create reference data sets to provide and mandate standard values or terms to be used in transactions by specific industry sectors or multiple industry sectors to reduce failure of transactions and improve compliance by eliminating ambiguity of the terms. For example, ISO defines and maintains currency codes and country codes as defined in ISO 3166-1. Currency codes and country codes are universal, in contrast to an organization's internal reference data, which are valid only within the organization. Reference data like product classifications are agreed on in a business domain.

Usually, reference data do not change excessively in terms of definition apart from infrequent amendments to reflect changes in the modes of operation of the business. The creation of a new master data element may necessitate the creation of new reference data. For example, when a company acquires another business, chances are that they will now need to adapt their product line taxonomy to include a new category to describe the newly acquired product lines.

Reference data should be distinguished from master data, which represent key business entities such as customers in all the necessary detail (Wikipedia Undated "Reference Data") (for example, for customers the necessary details are: customer number, name, address, date of birth, and date of account creation). In contrast, reference data usually consist only of a list of permissible values and corresponding textual descriptions that help to understand what the value means.

Transactional Data

Transactional data describe business events, and comprise the largest volume of data in the enterprise. Transaction data describe relevant internal or external events in an organization, for example, orders, invoices, payments, patient encounters, insurance claims, shipments, complaints, deliveries, storage records, and travel records. The transactional data support the daily operations of an organization. Transactional data, in the context of data management, are the information recorded from transactions.

Transactional data record a "fact" that transpired at a certain point in time. Transactional data drive the business indicators of the enterprise and they depend completely on master data. In other words, transaction data represent an action or an event that the master data participate in. Transaction data can be identified by verbs. For example, customer *opens* a bank account. Here *customer* and *account* are master data. The action or event of *opening* an account would generate transaction data.

Transaction data always have a time dimension, and are associated with master and reference data. For example, order data are associated with customer and product master data; patient encounter data are associated with patient and physician master data; a credit card transaction is associated with credit card account and customer master data. If the data are extremely volatile, then they are likely transaction data.

Since transactions use master data and sometimes reference data, too, if the associated master data and reference data are not correct, the transactions do not fulfill their intended purpose. For example, if the customer master data are incorrect—say, the address of the customer is not the current address or the customer address is incorrect because of incorrect state code in the customer record—then orders will not be delivered.

Historical Data

Transactional data have a time dimension and become historical once the transaction is complete. Historical data contain significant facts, as of a certain point in time, that should not be altered except to correct an error (McGilvray 2008a). They are important from the perspective of security, forecasting, and compliance. In the case of master data records, for instance, a customer's surname changes after marriage, causing the old master record to be historical data.

Not all historical data are old, and much of them must be retained for a significant amount of time (Rouse Undated [1]). Once the organization has gathered its historical data, it makes sense to periodically monitor the usage of the data. Generally, current and very current data are used frequently. However, the older the data become, the frequency at which the data are needed becomes lesser (Inmon 2008). Historical data are often archived, and may be held in non-volatile, secondary storage (BI 2018).

Historical data are useful for trend analysis and forecasting purposes to predict future results. For example, financial forecasting would involve forecasting future revenues and revenue growth, earnings, and earnings growth based on historical financial records.

Metadata

Metadata are data that define other data, for example, master data, transactional data, and reference data. In other words, metadata are data about data. *Metadata* are structured information labels that describe or characterize other data and make it easier to retrieve, interpret, manage, and use data. The purpose of metadata is to add value to the data they describe, and it is important for the effective usage of data. One of the common uses of metadata today is in e-commerce to target potential customers of products based on an analysis of their current preferences or behaviors.

Metadata data can be classified into three categories (see Figure 1.2):

- Technical metadata

- Business metadata

- Process metadata

Technical metadata are data used to describe technical aspects and organization of the data stored in data repositories such as databases and file systems in an organization, and are used by technical teams to access and process the data. Examples of technical

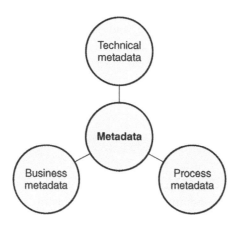

Figure 1.2   Metadata categories.

metadata include physical characteristics of the layers of data, such as table names, column or field names, allowed values, key information (primary and foreign key), field length, data type, lineage, relationship between tables, constraints, indexes, and validation rules.

Business metadata describe the functionality—nontechnical aspects of data and how data are used by the business—that adds context and value to the data. Business metadata are not necessarily connected to the physical storage of data or requirements regarding data access. Examples include field definitions, business terms, business rules, privacy level, security level, report names and headings, application screen names, data quality rules, key performance indicators (KPIs), and the groups responsible and accountable for the quality of data in a specific data field—the data owners and data stewards.

Process metadata are used to describe the results of various IT operations that create and deliver the data. For example, in an extract, transform, load (ETL) process, data from tasks in the run-time environment—such as scripts that have to be used to create, update, restore, or otherwise access data, and so on, start time, end time, CPU seconds used, disk reads/source table read, disk writes/target table written, and rows read from the target, rows processed, rows written to the target—are logged on execution. In case of errors, this sort of data helps in troubleshooting and getting to the bottom of the problem. Some organizations make a living out of collecting and selling this sort of data to companies; in that case the process metadata become the business metadata for the fact and dimension tables. Collecting process metadata is in the interest of businesspeople who can use the data to identify the users of their products, which products they are using, and what level of service they are receiving (Wikipedia Undated "Metadata").

Audit trail metadata are a particular type of metadata, usually stored in a record and protected from alteration, that capture how, when, and by whom the data were created, accessed, updated, or deleted (McGilvray 2008a). Audit trail metadata are used for tracking security breaches and compliance issues, and forensic and litigation purposes. Examples of audit trail metadata include timestamp, which is the date and time when the action was performed, and user and device information associated with the action performed, and description of the action (for example, creation, deletion, modification, printing).

Metadata are generally associated with any discipline, operation, or activity that uses data, owing to the fact that metadata enable and improve the understanding and use of the data that they describe. While business metadata, technical metadata, process metadata, and audit trail metadata are the most common categories of metadata, it could be suggested that there are other types of metadata that make it easier to locate, retrieve, interpret, use, and manage data. The label for any metadata may not be as important as the fact that they are being deliberately used to support data goals (McGilvray 2008a).

The quality of reference data impacts the quality of master data records as well as transactional data records as it forms a part of both transactional and master data records. The quality of master data impacts the quality of transactional data. The quality of metadata impacts the quality of master data, transactional data, reference data, and historical data.

DATA QUALITY: AN OVERVIEW

Data quality is the capability of data to satisfy the stated business, system, and technical requirements of an enterprise. Data quality is an insight into or an evaluation of data's fitness to serve their purpose in a given context. Data quality is accomplished when a business uses data that are complete, relevant, and timely. The general definition of data quality is "fitness for use," or more specifically, to what extent some data successfully serve the purposes of the user (Tayi and Ballou 1998; Cappiello et al. 2003; Lederman et al. 2003; Watts et al. 2009). From a business perspective, data quality is all about whether the data meet the needs of the information consumer (Scarisbrick-Hauser and Rouse 2007).

Redman (2001) comes to the following definition based on Joseph Juran (Juran and Godfrey 1999): "Data are of high quality if they are fit for their intended uses in operations, decision-making, and planning. Data are fit for use if they are free of defects and possess desired features."

Table 1.1 illustrates the desired characteristics for data that make them fit for use.

From an assessment perspective, data quality has two aspects: intrinsic data quality and contextual data quality. *Intrinsic data quality* is based on the data elements themselves, independent of the context in which they are used. Examples include the accuracy, representation, and accessibility of the data (Fisher et al. 2003, Strong et al. 1997, Jarke et al. 2000). For example, data elements such as age, salary, and product dimensions should have a numerical value and cannot be less than zero; the customer name should be spelled correctly. *Contextual data quality* relates to the individuals' perceptions of data quality, which are influenced by contextual factors such as the purpose for which the data are used or the decision to be derived from the data, the timing of use, and organizational factors and characteristics of the information consumer, usually a business

Table 1.1	Characteristics of data that make them fit for use.
Free of defects	**Desired features**
Correct	Contextual
Complete	Pertinent
Valid	Comprehensive
Reliable	Easy to read
Consistent	Unambiguous
Unique	Easy to understand
Current	Right level of detail

user. In other words, intrinsic data quality relates to the objective, unchangeable aspects of the data, whereas contextual data quality brings to bear a task-person interaction with respect to data elements such that the data quality is more relevant for the current task than for a different task; this exemplifies the task-person interaction perspective. When an individual opines a data element as more relevant for the current task than for a different task, this exemplifies the task-person interaction perspective. For instance, consider a sales report (that is, showing item codes, quantities, cost, and selling prices) where some of the "selling price" values are missing. For decisions regarding the "shelf placement" of products, a manager would need to know which products have the potential to generate higher profits, and the report with missing selling price data would be "incomplete" for this decision task. Yet, for making inventory decisions (that is, reordering, stocking, and so on) this report would be "complete" since the "quantity" data are available for all products. This example illustrates the contextual, task-dependent nature of data quality. For example, when two different individuals assess the accuracy of the same data element differently, this reflects differences in their respective psychologies.

Data quality does not have a one-size-fits-all template—not even within an organization—and neither does it equate to zero defects. Perfection is practically unattainable in data quality, as with the quality of manufacturing products and services. In truth, it is also unnecessary, since at some point improving data quality becomes more costly than leaving it alone (Maydanchik 2007). Data quality depends on the context in which data are used and their conformance to valid requirements, and not on their creation only. To attain an acceptable level of data quality, the business user or data steward/data owner needs to be identified, and the degree of conformance must then be set after consultation with him or her. The required degree of conformance represents the data quality threshold, the minimum confidence level in the data, and the maximum tolerance level for errors. Data quality is then established by knowing whether the minimum acceptable level has been not attained, attained, or exceeded. The Six Sigma DMAIC (define, measure, analyze, improve, and control) methodology can be utilized to measure and improve data quality as well as maintain data quality and prevent data quality issues. The application of Six Sigma DMAIC methodology to data quality is discussed in detail in Chapter 6, "Data Quality Management."

HOW IS DATA QUALITY DIFFERENT?

The quality of a manufactured product, for example, a camera or bricks, depends on the manufacturing production process and machinery by which the product is designed and produced. Likewise, the quality of information depends on the business processes, databases, software design, data, and software production processes involved in producing the information. Once a manufactured product is purchased by a customer, it is no longer available for the next customer to buy. Once raw materials are used to build that product, they are not available to be used in the next manufacturing cycle. However, data or information do not deplete and are never consumed once used. Data and information are reusable. If the data or information are wrong, they will be used again and again—with negative results (McGilvray 2008b).

Unlike manufactured products, which are tangible and have physical characteristics like size, color, weight, texture, and so on, data do not have tangible characteristics like weight, texture, or color that allow quality to be easily assessed. Characteristics of data include data type, format, field length, and key constraints. While data themselves are intangible, data are captured and stored in particular forms (data values with meaningful formats, data fields of defined sizes) in relation to other pieces of data (data models, fields in an application), and these days largely through systems (databases and applications) designed to perform particular functions (Sebastian-Coleman 2013). Data are embedded in these systems. The way the system is set up will establish a set of requirements for how data are formatted, how keys must be defined, and how data sets can be maintained. Their expression can change as they move from system to system or from use to use, but data always have some shape, and that shape can be understood in relation to the system in which they exist. The quality of data depends to a large extent on how they are presented in these systems and how well people are able to understand the context and conventions of their presentation. To understand the significance of the presentation of data, we need to understand the systems in which they are captured and stored and from which they are accessed. Data quality measurement also depends on these things. For instance, systems can store date data in any of the following formats:

- Month/day/year

- Year/month/day

- Day/month/year

Users need to understand the format that is used by the system they are accessing in order to correctly interpret the data. Data quality is a function of imperceptible properties called *data quality dimensions*. For example, a data element "age" has to be a number greater than 0.

Physical manufacturing processes take limited amounts of raw materials that are transformed through a series of processes into a unique final product. That product's attributes and criteria can be compared to discrete specifications for its intended use, such as the amount of usable storage on a DVD, the number of carats in a piece of gold jewelry, or the melting temperature of a screw. In this analogy, data are the raw material, and information products are the results. Yet, in contrast to real raw materials, data can be used multiple times, and contrary to real resulting manufactured products, the output of information processes can be reused and repurposed in ways that the original owners never dreamed, let alone prepared for. While a manufacturing product needs to conform to specifications and a one-size-fits-all template applies, data do not have a one-size-fits-all template and depend on the context in which they are used. Attempting to monitor compliance to specifications requires that all those specifications are known beforehand, and this is often not the case with data. Further, because data have no physical properties, they are much harder to measure. It is easier to measure the quality of manufactured product than the quality of data because a manufacturing product has physical characteristics. For example, you can measure the size using a measuring tape. Data quality can, however, be measured in an objective way using data quality dimensions. Data quality dimensions are intangible characteristics of data that can be measured or assessed against a set of defined standards in order to determine the quality of data. Some examples of data quality dimensions are accuracy, completeness, consistency, uniqueness, and timeliness.

DATA QUALITY DIMENSIONS

Enterprise data must conform to the various dimensions of data quality to be fit for operational and analytical use. Wang and Strong (1996) define a data quality dimension as "a set of data quality attributes that represent a single aspect or construct of data quality." Data quality dimensions provide a means to quantify and manage the quality of data. When defining data quality measures, one should endeavor to focus on the dimensions that are meaningful and pertinent for the business, with maximum return on investment. On the other hand, measuring all the different dimensions of data quality gives the complete picture. Some commonly used data quality dimensions are completeness, accuracy, timeliness, conformity, and consistency. We will discuss data quality dimensions in detail in Chapter 3, "Data Quality Dimensions" and Chapter 4, "Measuring Data Quality Dimensions."

CAUSES OF BAD DATA QUALITY

Data quality issues can be found at all levels and within all the components of information, including definition, content, and presentation (Scarisbrick-Hauser and Rouse 2007). Data issues can sneak into every phase of the data life cycle, starting from initial data creation and procurement/collection through various touch points like Internet, call centers, sensors, mailings, and branch offices, to name a few, to data processing, transfer, and storage, to archiving and purging. Thus, data quality is impacted by activities in all of the phases in the data life cycle. Figure 1.3 shows the data life cycle.

The manner in which data quality degrades as it is transferred across systems and interfaces reminds me of the game Chinese Whispers. Chinese Whispers (also known

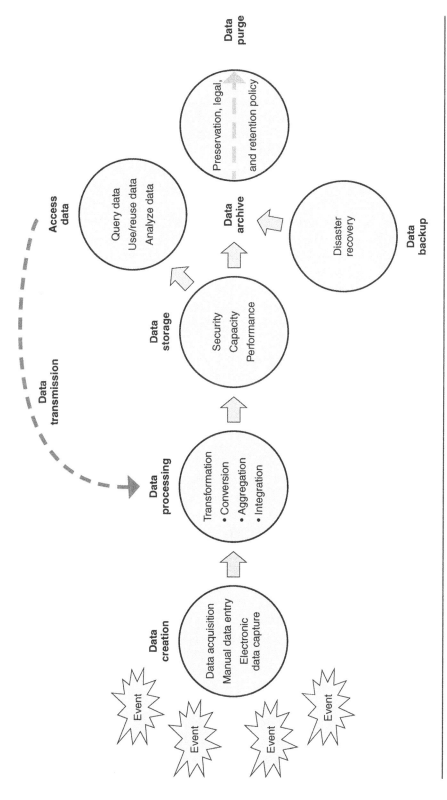

Figure 1.3   The data life cycle.

as the Telephone Game) is a game played around the world in which one person whispers a message to another, which is passed through a line of people until the last player announces the message to the entire group. As the message is passed from one player to another, inaccuracies are introduced, and typically grow with every exchange, so the statement announced by the last player differs and deviates considerably, and often comically, from the one articulated by the first player. I will explain this using an example.

Say, today is June 25, 2010. Tina logs into a retail website to open an online account. She enters her name, date of birth as "12-06-1992" in the "day-month-year" format, and contact information (physical address, contact phone number, and e-mail ID), and submits the online form. Tina's date of birth is June 12, 1992. Tina's details are stored in the customer database after they pass the initial validation process. Various downstream applications access the customer database and populate other databases and reports. One application process, say A1, extracts the data from the customer data and populates the data in a downstream database, say database system 2. However, database system 2 stores the data in "month-day-year" format. The date of birth for Tina is stored as "12-06-1992" in database system 2. However, as per database system 2, Tina's birth date is December 6, 1992, which is not correct. The application process A1 has introduced a defect. The marketing process M1 uses data in database system 2 to calculate Tina's age and populate the marketing database on the first day of every month. If the age of the customer is less than 18, the marketing flag is marked as "N," which means certain products and promotions will not be mailed to the customer. So, when the marketing process runs on July 1, 2010, Tina's age is populated as 17.5 and the marketing flag is marked as "N."

Poor data quality can be caused by the following processes (Figure 1.4 summarizes the causes of bad data quality).

Manual Data Entry

Manual data entry can give rise to data issues, as human beings are susceptible to errors. The computing principle of "garbage in, garbage out" (GIGO) applies to data entry as well. In spite of considerable automation in data architecture these days, data are still typed into web forms and other user interfaces by people. Eighty-four percent of businesses cite mistakes at the point of entry as a significant barrier to achieving more accurate customer information (Parker 2007). A competent data entry clerk has an average error rate of 2 to 4 percent. By contrast, the error rate on the web is 10 to 15 percent since it is members of the public that are entering the data (Reid and Catterall 2005). People enter incorrect information, provide incomplete information, choose wrong options and incorrect entries in a list, and enter correct information in the wrong textbox. This can be done by mistake, or because they simply don't have the information, or due to time constraints, or to safeguard their privacy. For example, many people enter junk e-mail addresses and incorrect telephone or cell phone numbers in web-based forms to avoid receiving spam e-mails and advertising calls. How many times have you entered a phantom telephone number or an incomplete address or just the initials of your name, or just not bothered to choose the right title from the list box because a default title was

Figure 1.4   Causes of bad data quality.

already available in a web form for promotions or for downloading a document from a website that requires you to provide personal information before you can download? If there is nothing at stake for the people who key in the data, and the data are not mandatory to complete the transaction, there will be a natural inclination to resort to garbage values or leaving the fields blank. Examples of fields in which people generally do not disclose correct information are age, marital status, phone number (this includes home phone number, work phone number, and mobile phone number), e-mail address, annual income, annual expenses, educational level, and race.

There are instances when a person providing the information may have difficulty keying in the information. For example, in a water utility company, there were a number of data quality issues discovered in the data extracted from an above-ground and below-ground asset closure forms database that a technician needed to fill in after fixing the problem with the asset. One of the root causes behind the incomplete, incorrect, and inconsistent information in the forms was the difficulty in entering information in the handheld device that the technicians used. The interface was extremely small and not user friendly. The technicians would find it extremely frustrating and difficult to choose the correct options and key in the data, resulting in bad data in the database.

Another case where an individual purposely enters wrong information is when the entry enables a person to obtain a benefit by keying in incorrect data. Some examples from the real world illustrate this:

- A person enters different names and e-mail addresses to get one-time promotions repetitively.

- An individual gets a $10 e-gift card when he completes an electronic survey. However, the quality of information provided is highly suspect as the driving factor to take the survey is the gift card, and not the individual's interest in taking the survey.

- A bank gives branch bank employees a commission for selling term loan and term deposit products to new customers, as well when an existing customer does a top-up at the branch. In the case of a term loan, a top-up means additional funds being assigned to the term loan and in the case of a term deposit, top-up means a customer depositing additional funds in the term deposit. The bank employee can do a top-up to get his commission and then reverse the top-up after a few days.

- The Association of Certified Fraud Examiners noted in their 2006 *Report to the Nation* (ACFE Report) different methods that employees use to generate fraudulent payments. As a by-product of employees introducing incorrect or invalid data, there was an increase in inappropriate disbursements, and the report provided the details about the costs associated with these fraudulent payments.

Also, there are times when the field to enter certain information is not provided, which results in people entering this information in the available fields, resulting in incorrect data getting stored in the database, or misfielded data. For instance, I have come across situations when I have had to enter my permanent address details in a form on a US bank website, but there has been no textbox to enter my state details; in this case the state happens to be an Indian state, and the list box provided only had the US state codes listed, so I had to enter the state code in the textbox provided for entering city information. I was also not able to submit the form without selecting one of the US state codes in the list box, and hence had to select one arbitrarily and then submit the form. In this case, the fields storing the state code and city information would have wrong information. It is worth noting that according to the Data Warehousing Institute, 76% of all errors, across sectors and setting, result from "data entry" (CFH 2006).

Inadequate Validation in the Data Capture Process

Data capture is not always implemented in many transactional systems with well-thought-out validation, for example, at the field type level where a numeric field should not be accepting other characters, or at the next level where the semantics of the field dictate whether the data is good or not. Consider telephone number entry, for example. At the form level, where validation may need to be made on the back end with another table, if I enter a customer name, can I find and have the person validate whether that name and address, and maybe a phone number, match before typing the rest of the data in? A lack of validation checks causes erroneous data to enter a system. Inadequate data validation processes may fail to catch data entry errors in the case of automated data entry through online forms and screens.

Aging of Data/Data Decay

Data decay, or *aging of data*, is data degradation over time, resulting in bad data quality. This proves that data are subject to the same laws of physics as physical objects in the universe, that is, over the course of time, data will also degenerate. While all of the values stored in the database were once correct, with the progress of time, most of them may become stale and inaccurate. This is because, while some data elements like date of birth of a person, gender, place of birth, and social security number never change, other data elements like marital status, telephone number, address, title, job function, designation, passport number, or nationality change over time. The tricky part is that every data element has a different expiration date. For instance, while change in nationality or passport is less frequent, telephone number or address can change more frequently. The death date for an individual will only be updated once, as a person dies only once.

There are also certain databases where data degenerate less rapidly than in others. Now let's consider an above-ground asset database in a water utility company. A boiler is one of the above-ground assets. However, the location of the boiler is unlikely to change over the years. So, there are databases where degradation of data occurs, but at a very, very slow rate, whereas in the case of a customer database, because of the changing nature of the customer base, the data quality deteriorates more rapidly (Inmon 2009). Two percent of records in a customer file become obsolete in one month because customers die, divorce, marry, and move (Eckerson 2002). According to Gartner Group's Beth Eisenfeld, customer data degrade at a rate of 2% per month, which translates to almost a quarter of the entire customer database annually (Alshawi et al. 2011). You can expect 25 to 30 percent of your organization's contact data to go bad each year under normal circumstances (Neubarth 2013). So, if your organization's customer database has 12 million customer contact records, then more than 3 million to 4 million customer contact records will be obsolete annually. That is a huge number! This equates to not being able to contact 3 million to 4 million customers, causing a lot of returned correspondence and wasted postage.

According to Salesforce.com, about 70% of customer relationship management (CRM) data "goes bad," or becomes obsolete, annually:

- 60% of people change job functions within their organization every year.

- 20% of all postal addresses change every year.

- 18% of all telephone numbers change every year.

Reliance on end users to submit and update their data depends on the incentive of those users to actually change their information. This information usually lags and is often incomplete and reduces the value of the data (Thorp Undated).

Data have a shelf life and require continuous maintenance. To ensure that data are current, it's important to set guidelines for how often each field should be updated. In some cases, you may be able to tell that a record has been updated recently but you're unable to tell which field was updated. If a particular data field on a data record is critical for your business, while other fields are not, depending on your requirement, you may want to formulate a way to identify which field was modified. For instance, say the customer's address was updated in the customer address table in the customer relational database. There are several ways to keep track of this change:

- *Option 1.* One way to do this is by expiring the existing record and inserting a new record with the updated information. By comparing the old record and the new record, one is able to say which field or fields were changed in the table.

- *Option 2.* The customer's address update date could be tracked separately from the rest of the record.

- *Option 3.* A comments field can be included in the table to state what field or fields were updated; in this case it would be the customer's address.

Inefficient Business Process Management and Design

Lack of a standard process to address business requirements and business process improvements, poorly designed and implemented business processes that result in lack of training, coaching, and communication in the use of the process, and unclear definition of subprocess or process ownership, roles, and responsibilities have an adverse impact on data quality.

In a case study involving call centers, findings revealed that call center agents were traditionally incentivized by the speed of answering, that is, the number of calls they could answer in one working shift, and the completeness of each form on screen. With this focus, call center agents did not understand the importance of the quality of the data that they were entering. Previously within the company, customer data were collected via the call center but not used for data mining and customer analysis. Hence, little concern was given to the quality of the data collected, meaning that it did not really matter that default codes were input into the system as long as the call center agent answered more calls in a working shift and each form was completed fully (though each free text field may have only had an "a," "b," or "c" entered). The bad data quality only came to light when the data were needed for data mining, for analysis of the effectiveness and efficiency of various marketing campaigns (Reid and Catterall 2005).

We will use an example of a business process improvement project in a financial services organization to illustrate the bad data quality resulting from lack of training.

One of the process steps in the to-be business process involved capturing the data attributes for eligible and ineligible transactions for electronic processing using a third-party tool, in a spreadsheet stored in a secure shared file location on a server. An eligibility checklist containing eligibility and ineligibility criteria was defined to determine transactions eligible and ineligible for electronic processing. The following data attributes were to be captured in the spreadsheet once the eligibility criteria were assessed and electronic identification number was created for transactions lodged electronically:

- *Transaction date.* The date when the transaction was processed.

- *Transaction ID.* Unique number to identify the transaction.

- *Transaction eligible (Yes/No).* Would have the value "Yes" for transactions eligible for electronic processing and the value "No" for transactions ineligible for electronic processing and hence manually processed.

- *Electronic identification number.* A system-generated number for transactions processed electronically. Data were captured only for transactions eligible for electronic processing.

- *Ineligibility reason.* Reason stating the ineligibility criteria. Data were captured only for ineligible transactions.

The data in the spreadsheet would be used by the management quarterly to provide information to the third-party tool vendor so it could enhance the features and capabilities of the tool to be able to process the transactions currently not eligible for electronic processing and hence improve efficiency and reduce cost, as manual processing was more time-consuming, error prone, and less cost-effective. However, due to roles and responsibilities not being clearly defined and no proper training being organized, the spreadsheet was not being populated correctly and consistently. This was only discovered at the end of the first quarter when management requested the data, and the ineligibility reason data field was not populated for most of the ineligible transaction records entered in the spreadsheet.

Data Migration

Data migration or conversion projects can lead to data problems. Data migration generally involves the transfer of data from an existing data source to a new database or to a new schema within the same database. Much of the data does not land in the new database, and some of the data changes considerably in the new database or the new schema in the same database.

Data migration projects deal with the migration of data from one data structure to another data structure, or data transformed from one platform to another platform with modified data structure. Figure 1.5 shows a high-level view of the data migration process. The new system to which data need to be migrated is built on new architectures and data models and does not synchronize with the old data lying in the source system.

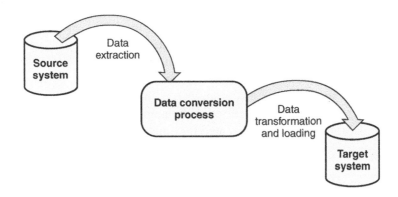

Figure 1.5   Data migration/conversion process.

An example of a data conversion project is migrating data from a legacy data system to a relational database management system. Legacy systems in corporations that were created in different generations create major stumbling blocks for migrating data to integrated application systems (Scarisbrick-Hauser and Rouse 2007). During the production years, source data can become corrupted in a way that is not always visible in the legacy applications. Every system is made of three layers: database, business rules, and user interface. As a result, what users see is not what is actually stored in the database. This is particularly true for older "legacy" systems (Maydanchik 2007). Legacy systems rarely have complete specifications, and the embedded business rules and changes are not documented well, if documented at all. There is usually a huge gap between the legacy data model and actual legacy data. The legacy system stores and uses data in a manner in which it should not be used. For instance, the date of birth of a customer is appended to the name of the customer and stored in a single field in the legacy system as there is no separate field for capturing the date of birth. The business rules defined in the legacy system deal with the data quality issues so that the output is as desired. However, since these embedded business rules are not formally documented anywhere, the data conversion project does not implement business rules to deal with the data quality issues, resulting in bad data. The data conversion mappings based solely on the legacy model do not take into account the gaps between the legacy data model and actual legacy data, resulting in a lot of errors in the target system.

Some bad data records are dropped and not transformed. Others are altered by the transformation routines. Such "mutation" errors are much more challenging to identify and correct after data conversion. Even worse, bad data records impact conversion of many correct data elements.

Data Integration

Data integration is at the core of enterprise information management. *Data integration* processes bring together and combine data from numerous heterogeneous source systems into a new technology application. Figure 1.6 illustrates a high-level view of

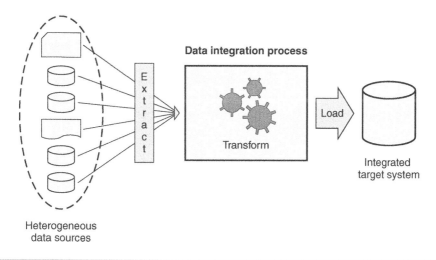

Figure 1.6 Data integration process.

data integration. At the least, it involves physical movement of data from one or more applications to another application. The process of data integration involves combining conflicting data through the use of conflict resolution business rules to resolve data discrepancies.

Differences in application design and formats and usage of information necessitate the manipulation of data through transformations as a part of the integration process. Mapping specifications are used to transform the data from the source systems and load them into the target applications. For example, say the customer number in the source system is stored as a nine-digit number, but is stored as a 10-character string in the target data system. The mapping specification to handle this would include transformation rules to convert the customer number to *string* data type and append a "0" as a prefix to the customer number to satisfy the requirements of the target application.

The quality of the target data depends on the robustness of the data mapping specifications and conflict resolution business rules and how well these rules cover all the business scenarios and data discrepancy scenarios; wrong data mapping specifications and incorrect conflict resolution rules can cause introduction of data quality issues into the target data systems.

Data Cleansing Programs

Data cleansing is the process of correcting the erroneous data elements. Data cleansing programs, while resolving old data quality issues, might introduce new data quality issues. In the old days, the data set was relatively smaller and cleansing was done manually and was rather safe. However, with the vast amount of data that are collected nowadays, manual cleansing is no longer a feasible option. The new methodologies and tools use automated data cleansing rules to make corrections en masse (Maydanchik 2007).

Automated data cleansing algorithms are implemented by computer programs, which will inevitably have bugs. Bugs in these algorithms are very dangerous because they often impact thousands or millions of records.

Another problem is that data quality specifications sometimes do not reflect actual data requirements, leading to quality issues. For example, the requirement is to store the gender data element for a customer in the customer database as follows:

- If male, store "M"

- If female, store "F"

- If not known, store "UKNWN"

However, if the above is not captured clearly, it could result in population of values like "Male" for a male customer, "Female" for a female customer, or "Not Known" or "Unknown" for customers whose gender is not known, causing data quality issues. Also, as companies are capturing and storing more and more data, certain data, such as personally identifiable information (PII), personal health information (PHI), and payment card industry (PCI) data, are sensitive and need to be protected. Personally identifiable information is a data field or combination of data fields that can be used to identify an individual. *Data anonymization* is the process of removing PII from a data set so that individuals described by the data cannot be identified. Examples of PII include social security number, employee number, home address, and date of birth. However, incorrect security solution requirements may result in the wrong data elements getting masked or encrypted, or correct data elements not meeting masking or encryption solution requirements, resulting in data errors or corruption. Additionally, technical or coding errors made during masking or encryption may also inadvertently corrupt the data.

Organizational Changes

Organizational changes like corporate mergers and acquisitions, globalization, restructuring or reorganization, or external changes increase the probability of data quality errors. We will discuss each of them in this section.

Corporate Mergers and Acquisitions. Data consolidation after company mergers and acquisitions can lead to a lot of data duplication and inconsistencies, resulting in data quality issues. This is because individual companies have their own IT systems, database systems, data definitions, and models and standards, and store data at different levels of granularity, so merging of companies and globalization does not lead to an immediate merging of IT systems and data. This often results in accidental deletion or duplication of data records. When the merging of the IT systems and data happens, it happens under excessively tight deadlines, and is often not planned, which results in people taking shortcuts to make it happen, and knowingly or unknowingly compromising data quality. Loss of expertise when key people quit halfway through the project worsens matters. Cultural clashes between the IT departments of the companies involved in the merger or acquisition, where each have their own version of truth and offer resistance to change, result in integration and data consistency issues.

Say for instance, Bank 1 acquires Bank 2. Both Bank 1 and Bank 2 have different applications and database systems. Both the banks have their own standards for defining and modeling their key business entities (such as customers, accounts, employees, and so on), resulting in problems in integrating the data. The grain of data for certain entities stored in Bank 1's database is different from the grain of data for certain entities stored in Bank 2's database. An example of different standards is as follows. Customer gender is stored as "F" for female and "M" for male in the customer database of Bank 1, but is stored as "2" for female and "1" for male in the customer database of Bank 2. Bank 1 stores the customer address data differently from how Bank 2 stores customer address data, resulting in problems matching data for the same customer.

Globalization. The mantra is "Go global!" With the formulation of trade agreements, the barriers between countries have been broken, and more and more companies are diversifying and growing their businesses by expanding into global markets. While globalization can do wonders for a company's bottom line, it adds another dimension of complexity and can wreak havoc on currency, date, address, telephone numbers, and other data elements already in place, resulting in data quality issues that were not prevalent at the domestic level. When a company goes global, the branches in the different countries have to communicate with each other proficiently, and they have to manage data that come in different formats, and reflect different cultural behaviours. For instance, in the United States the date is stored in the month/day/year format, whereas in India and in the United Kingdom it is stored in the day/month/year format. For example, in the United States, "04/06/2015" would represent April 6, 2015, while in the United Kingdom it would represent June 4, 2015.

Each country has a different currency. While global companies have an official "base" currency that is usually dependent on the company's headquarters location, issues related to currency that generally arise are as follows:

- How frequently will the system convert exchange rates?

- Will the exchange rate type be a floating rate, fixed rate, buy rate, sell rate, forward rate, spot rate, or something different?

- What currency or currencies are used for financial reporting purposes?

On a domestic level, absence of the country in an address would not pose a problem; however, on an international level it would be a major data quality issue. The same goes for the data item "telephone number." Prior to a company going global, the country code in the telephone number would not have been mandatory, but post-globalization the telephone numbers without a country code would be a data quality issue. This would also require a change in the data model to capture information not required on the domestic level.

In addition, different countries have different legal requirements where data are concerned. Each country will have different rules concerning what data can be stored, how they can be stored (encryption requirements), how long they can or should be stored (retention requirements), and so on, which can lead to data quality issues if careful attention and consideration are not given to all of these parameters.

Reorganization. Reorganization or restructuring leads to changes in organization structures, often leading to changes and reductions in staff. When staff who have knowledge about the detailed working of the IT systems leave, their knowledge is lost and everything goes haywire, and there is negative impact on data quality.

External Changes. External changes also cause hurriedly deployed patches to existing systems: tax law changes, regulatory requirements (such as financial reporting requirements, compliance requirements, global data protection regulations for protecting sensitive data, and privacy regulations), accounting changes such as those experienced in recent years, the Y2K problem, the Euro conversion, and on and on. This rapid evolution has meant that systems have been developed hastily and changed aggressively. This is done with few useful standards for development and control (Olson 2003). In the face of aggressive schedules, something has to give, and what generally gives is quality, especially data quality.

Each batch feed carries huge volumes of data, and any problem in it causes a big mess further magnified by future feeds. In real-time interfaces, data are propagated at a great speed, leaving no time for data validation and letting bad data enter the system.

System Upgrades

System upgrades introduce data quality problems. It is usually assumed that the data comply with what is theoretically expected of them. However, in reality, data are inaccurate and are massaged into a form acceptable to the previous version. System upgrades expose these data inaccuracies. The upgraded system is designed and tested against what data are expected to be, and not what they really are. Once the upgrades are implemented, everything goes haywire (Maydanchik 2007).

Data Purging

Data purging is a process that permanently erases and removes old data from a storage space or database to make space for new data. This is done once the retention limit of the old data is reached and the data are obsolete and hence no longer necessary. However, data purging may accidentally impact the wrong data, or purge some relevant data, purge more data than intended, or purge less data than intended, resulting in data quality consequences. The risk increases when erroneous data are present in the database, resulting in data being purged when they should not have been purged. For example, say the purging strategy is to purge all patient data from the database for patients who have expired three years prior. In the case where the death date has been populated for an otherwise living patient and the death date is three or more than three years old, it would satisfy the purging criteria. This would result in permanently losing the patient record, which should have been retained. Another aspect is whether all instances of the same data set have been deleted. For example, a patient record has been deleted from the patient database but is still residing in the encounter database, thus resulting in data integrity and data consistency issues.

Multiple Uses of Data and Lack of Shared Understanding of Data

Data quality depends on the context in which the data are used. Data that are fit for one purpose may not be fit for another purpose. Usually, data are captured or acquired, generated, processed, and stored in databases to meet the specific business requirements of a department, division, or operating group in an organization. The process or application for producing those data is designed for that specific purpose, and the data are good enough to meet those business requirements. However, as time goes by, other departments or groups need to use those data for a different purpose but have no understanding of the primary work flow processes that produced the data in the first place. When they discover that the data do not meet their requirements, they declare that the data quality is bad. For example, missing customer address data would not have any effect on the sales report, but would certainly have an adverse impact on billing. Similarly, missing bank employee data would not impact a sales report; however, missing bank employee data will certainly impact the commission report, which contains the names of the employees who sold a new product to a customer and are hence eligible for commission. Missing bank employee data in the latter case means that an eligible employee does not get his or her commission.

Another example of context-dependent data quality is, for example, if you were to encounter the value "400033" in the ZIP code field of a customer address table, you might consider the value incorrect. Within the context of a US-based customer, this ZIP code would undoubtedly be wrong. But if we expand the context to include Indian customers, the value is entirely possible, and could be associated with a customer in the city of Mumbai.

Companies use data as a shared resource in multiple business processes, such as procurement, production, marketing, or sales processes. When creating, using, and processing and manipulating data, however, each business process and business function follows its own needs, interpreting data according to its own semantics (Ofner et al. 2012). As a result, data are often used across boundaries of business processes and business units in an uncoordinated way, which has negative effects on the quality of data (Levitin and Redman 1998; Redman 2004).

The lack of a shared understanding of the uses and value of data among those carrying out the same tasks and among those performing different tasks can lead to creation of bad data (Vosburg and Kumar 2001). Tayi and Ballou (1998) point out that the data gatherer and initial user may be fully aware of the nuances of meaning of the various data items, but that does not hold true for all of the other users. Where those performing the same tasks have a different understanding of the data being processed, inconsistencies are inevitable. For example, if the marketing services department members differ on whether abbreviations are to be used in customer master data, inconsistent entry is the result. Locating these data becomes difficult for customer support representatives because they cannot be sure if they are using the wrong abbreviation, or if the data have not been entered. The result of this lack of shared understanding is duplicate records; when the customer support representatives cannot find the record that they are looking for, a new record is requested (Vosburg and Kumar 2001).

Loss of Expertise

Data-intensive projects generally involve at least one person who understands all the nuances of the application, process, and source and target data. These are the people who also know about all the abnormalities in the data and the workarounds to deal with them, and are the experts. This is especially true in the case of legacy systems that store and use data in a manner it should not be used. The knowledge is not documented anywhere and is usually inside the minds of the people. When the experts leave, with no one having a true understanding of the data, the data are not used properly and everything goes haywire.

Here is another example that emphasizes how the loss of expertise creates havoc with data. In the list of applications maintained and supported by a data warehousing group in a healthcare company, there was an application, say application A, that needed to be run every day. If the application was not run for a day, the data pertaining to that day would be lost and irrecoverable. As a result of reorganization, a lot of employees in the group got laid off, and the employee who was handling application A also got laid off. The application failed for a couple of days in sequence; however, since the new person who had taken over the support job did not understand the consequences of not fixing the problem and ensuring that the application ran on the same day, he delayed looking into the issue as he had other high-priority tasks in hand. The application was not run for two consecutive days, and as a result, data were lost.

Lack of Common Data Standards, Data Dictionary, and Metadata

Lack of common data standards across various business divisions and metadata leads to data quality issues. Metadata are very valuable to the business because they facilitate the understanding of data. Without this understanding, the data would be useless. Very few organizations have standard methods to record an address or name, or have the defined domains of the list of cities. There is no enterprise-wide data dictionary. The problem of business definition inconsistency across enterprise environments is often attributed to the absence of an enterprise-wide data dictionary. For example, one department uses the term *customer*, and another department uses the term *client*. Are they talking about the same thing?

Lack of data entry standards can lead to people entering data in different ways. For example, the Electronic Health Record (EHR) does not standardize how blood pressure should be entered, nor is it made into a mandatory field. Some providers enter the blood pressure as a numeric value, others key it in as text, while still others may document it elsewhere in notes (ONCHIT 2013).

Consider a banking environment that operates multiple lines of business such as branch offices, home loans, personal loans, and investment banking. Each line of business may manage a customer independently and maintain a fully separate and independent set of customer information. Due to the variances in data entry standards and data controls implemented by applications in each line of business, the customer information may be recorded differently in each application (IBM 2007). As a result, multiple downstream applications that use customer data may end up interpreting the four customer records as four different customers, thereby impacting business decisions made using the data.

Business Data Ownership and Governance Issues

Important data assets may have several providers or producers and numerous consumers who are often oblivious of one another, and data quality often is not in the immediate interest of the data providers. There is no clearly defined ownership, stewardship, transparency, and accountability, with limited or inconsistent governance across functional and business units. This leads to bad data quality. When there is no transparency and no one is accountable for data quality, the resultant data are either incomplete, not current, inaccurate, unreliable, inconsistent, or a combination of some or all of these. Most companies have some kind of problems associated with data ownership; the ownership definitions may be inadequate or the attitudes toward data ownership are negative. When data ownership issues are not clear, the data quality suffers (Silvola et al. 2011). The data steward is the person who holds data producers/providers accountable to the terms of their data quality metrics to satisfy the needs of the business process. When conflicts between a producer/provider and its consumers arise, the data steward is responsible for mediating the situation by working with both parties to identify an appropriate solution (Blosser and Haines 2013).

Data Corruption by Hackers

Data quality can be greatly compromised by data being corrupted by hackers. Hackers can not only corrupt data but can steal or delete data too.

As stated by FBI Director James Comey in March 2017:

> It's not just even the loss of data. Increasingly, we are worried about the corruption of data. Think about the harm someone could do by an intrusion at a blood bank and changing blood types, an intrusion at a financial institution and changing just a few digits in the holdings of an institution.

Chris Young, speaking on corruption of data at a 2017 RSA conference stated, "Weaponized data is the next threat vector challenging all of us in cybersecurity."

Serious problems can result if hackers gain control of a database and then alter it to suit their needs. For example, at the same RSA conference mentioned above, TrapX Security showed how medical devices were infected with malware. Compromised medical machines can be manipulated to give inaccurate or deadly results. Hackers can corrupt GPS data to perform a number of nefarious actions. At the lowest level, hackers learned how to spoof GPS data to play Pokemon Go and pretend they were in exotic places when they were not (Mierzejewski 2017).

If the data are PII, PHI, or PCI, in addition to data quality being compromised, organizations will face loss of customer confidence, reputational damage, or regulatory actions resulting from breaches of inadequately protected sensitive data. For example, the European Commission proposed the General Data Protection Regulation in 2012, which will result in the imposition of fines up to 2% of a company's annual global turnover for failure to safeguard consumers' private information (European Commission 2012).

COST OF POOR DATA QUALITY

To understand the importance of data quality, we need to understand the impacts and implications of bad quality data. Poor-quality data have negative effects on business users, which are seen in lower customer satisfaction, increased operating costs, loss of revenue, inefficient and faulty decision-making processes, wasted time, inferior performance, loss of credibility, and lower employee job satisfaction (Redman 1998; Vosburg and Kumar 2001; Pipino et al. 2002; Kahn et al. 2002). The existence of poor data quality means analysis and key performance indicators used to guide the enterprise's strategy and appraise its decisions are potentially flawed. Poor data quality is a key reason for 40% of all business initiatives failing to attain their targeted benefits. Data quality affects overall labor productivity by as much as a 20% (Friedman and Smith 2011). A survey performed by the Data Warehouse Institute demonstrates similar results, with respondents claiming that poor data quality has led to lost revenue (54%), extra costs (72%), and decreases in customer satisfaction (67%) (Eckerson 2002). The business costs of bad data quality include irrecoverable costs, rework of products and services, workarounds, and lost and missed revenue; these may be as high as 10% to 25% of revenue or total budget of an organization. Furthermore, as much as 40% to 50% or more of the typical IT budget may actually be spent in "information scrap and rework" (English 1999). Information scrap and rework includes all costs associated with hunting and tracking down information, redundant or incorrect or incomplete data entry, correcting and verifying data, compensating alienated customers, and penalties and fines for noncompliance.

There are many regulatory, legal, and contractual implications in working with data that is not fit for its intended purpose (Jugulum 2014). Erroneous financial data cause organizations to restate financial earnings and suffer the associated consequences with regulatory agencies and shareholders. Data quality issues with customer account information impact an organization's ability to segment customers and offer customized service. For example, poor customer data contribute to millions of wasted dollars in poorly targeted sales and marketing campaigns. A large proportion of loyalty programs have suffered from bad contact data. More than 70% of organizations running these programs reported problems, with inaccurate customer information (34%) the chief cause (Adamson 2014). The lack of accurate and complete information about a customer's true relationship with the organization in terms of products purchased and their propensity to purchase other products places future business opportunities at risk. For example, a lack of knowledge of the customer relationship may result in missed sales or marketing opportunities. Alternatively, there is a higher risk of under-promoting or over-promoting products. Third, a lack of understanding of customer characteristics from a historical viewpoint impacts the organization's ability to mature and enhance their suite of products to meet customer needs (Scarisbrick-Hauser and Rouse 2007).

Since data are created and used in all daily operations, data are crucial inputs to virtually all decisions, and data implicitly delineate common terms in an enterprise, data constitute a substantial contributor to organizational culture. Thus, poor data quality can have adverse impacts on the organizational culture (Levitin and Redman 1998; Ryu et al. 2006).

The Institute of International Finance and McKinsey & Company (2011) cite one of the key factors in the global financial crisis that began in 2007 as inadequate information technology (IT) and data architecture to support the management of financial risk. This highlights the importance of data quality and leads us to conclude that the effect of poor data quality on the financial crisis cannot be ignored. During this crisis, many banks, investment companies, and insurance companies lost billions of dollars, causing some to go bankrupt. The impacts of these events were significant and included economic recession, millions of foreclosures, lost jobs, depletion of retirement funds, and loss of confidence in the industry and in the government (Jugulum 2014). There is an industry consensus that data quality was the biggest factor in under-prediction of (insurance industry) losses in 2005 (Ernst and Young 2008).

A 2002 survey on credit risk data performed by PricewaterhouseCoopers suggested that a significant percentage of the top banks were found wanting in credit risk data management. Areas of actual concern included counterparty data repositories, counterparty hierarchy data, common counterparty identifiers, and consistent data standards (Inserro 2002).

Another more serious data quality problem involves a report in 2003 about the federal General Accounting Office (GAO) being incapable of determining the number of H-1B visa holders working in the United States. The GAO was missing fundamental data, and its systems were not integrated. This presented a key challenge to the Department of Homeland Security, which tried to track all visa holders in the United States (Adelman et al. 2005).

Poor data quality can also have serious health risks. The *Journal of the American Medical Association* reports that as many as 98,000 people in the United States die from medical errors, despite increased focus on attempts to reduce errors (Weise 2005). In one incident, a young mother in the United Kingdom died of breast cancer because her cancer diagnosis and ensuing treatment were delayed. The cause of the delay was an error in the hospital's patient record, which listed her house number as "16" instead of "1b." As a result, the patient never received the hospital's letters, and missed crucial medical appointments (*The Daily Mail* 2011). Another incident relates to the 2003 case of heart transplant patient Jesica Santillan, where inaccurate information regarding blood typing resulted in a botched heart–lung transplant, which not only led to the girl's death, but also prevented other critically ill patients from receiving needed donated organs. A woman underwent a double mastectomy after being advised that she had breast cancer. After the surgery she was informed that the laboratory had swapped her lab results with another patient and that she never had cancer (Grady 2003).

Government Accountability Office (GAO) reports indicate that the Department of Defense (DoD) also suffers from the use of poor-quality data in its measurement and analysis infrastructure (GAO 2009). The consequences of this can be significant:

- Data and information reported to program offices are often inconsistent or incomplete. These data are further reported to oversight organizations, stored in repositories, and used as input for future assessments and resolutions.

- Flawed data adversely influence the development of acquisition policy and processes.

The DoD Guidelines on Data Quality Management describe the cost impacts of poor data quality:

> . . . the inability to match payroll records to the official employment record can cost millions in payroll overpayments to deserters, prisoners, and "ghost" soldiers. In addition, the inability to correlate purchase orders to invoices is a major problem in unmatched disbursements. In the DoD, resultant costs, such as payroll overpayments and unmatched disbursements, may be significant enough to warrant extensive changes in processes, systems, policy and procedure, and AIS data designs.

Marsh (2005) summarizes the findings from several such surveys, which indicate that:

- "88 percent of all data integration projects either fail completely or significantly overrun their budgets."

- "75 percent of organizations have identified costs stemming from dirty data."

- "33 percent of organizations have delayed or canceled new IT systems because of poor data."

- "Less than 50 percent of companies claim to be very confident in the quality of their data."

- "Only 15 percent of companies are very confident in the quality of external data supplied to them."

- "According to Gartner, bad data is the number one cause of CRM system failure."

- "Organisations typically overestimate the quality of their data and underestimate the cost of errors."

Poor data quality in both the planning and execution phases of business initiatives is a primary reason for 40% of all business initiatives failing to achieve their targeted benefits (Friedman and Smith 2011). Bad-quality data is one of the culprits behind the failure of crucial information-intensive projects. High-profile IT projects, like enterprise resource planning (ERP), customer relationship management (CRM) implementation, e-business, and business intelligence/data warehousing implementations, get delayed or even fail due to unforeseen data quality issues. Data quality problems make it challenging, if not impossible, to generate business value from business applications as they involve substantial integration of data. In fact, poor data quality can cripple large, high-profile projects (Hempfield 2011). According to a study published by the Gartner Group (Gartner Report 2006), almost 70% of CRM failures were attributed to issues with data reliability (Kaila and Goldman 2006; Alshawi et al. 2011). In 1996 Fleet Bank (now part of Bank of America) attempted to implement a $38 million CRM project that never reached its original objectives and led to dismissals after three years of failure (Eckerson 2002). A company can spend $10 million on a customer relationship management (CRM) system but not get a return on investment because the data are bad, says Tim Waggoner, chief technology officer at Group 1 Software Inc., a data quality software vendor in Lanham, Maryland (Betts 2002). Industry estimates for enterprise resource planning (ERP) and data warehouse implementations show that these projects fail or go over budget 65 to 75 percent of the time (DataFlux Corporation 2003). In almost every instance, project failures, cost overruns, and long implementation cycles are due to the same problem—a fundamental misunderstanding about the quality, meaning, or completeness of the data that are essential to the initiative (Fisher 2009; Mahanti 2014).

A straightforward approach to analyzing the degree to which poor data quality impedes business success involves categorizing business impacts associated with data errors within a classification scheme as follows (Loshin 2011a) and summarized in Figure 1.7:

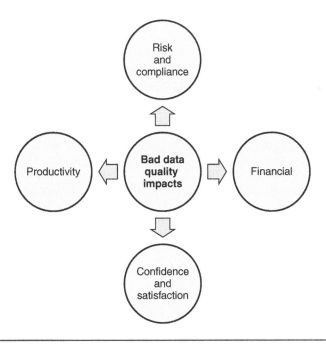

Figure 1.7   Bad data quality impacts.

- Financial impacts, such as increased operating costs, customer attrition, decreased sales and revenues, missed opportunities, overpayments, scrap and rework, reduction or delays in cash flow, or increased penalties, fines, or other charges, and low benefit realization.

- Confidence and satisfaction-based impacts, such as customer, employee, vendor, or supplier satisfaction, as well as decreased organizational trust, loss of credibility, low confidence in forecasting, inconsistent operational and management reporting, and delayed or improper decisions (Loshin 2011a) and increase in customer complaints.

- Productivity impacts such as increased workloads, decreased throughput, increased rework, increased processing or turnaround time, or decline in end product quality.

- Risk and compliance impacts associated with credit assessment, investment risks, competitive risk, health risk, capital investment and/or development, information integration risk, fraud, and leakage, and compliance with government regulations and industry regulations (for example, HIPAA, Sarbanes-Oxley, BASIL I, BASIL II, GDPR, to name a few), industry expectations, or self-imposed policies (such as privacy policies).

Some widely known financial statistics relating to data quality cited from existing literature are as follows:

- Poor data across businesses and the government cost the US economy $3.1 trillion a year (Zeiss 2013).

- The literature (Redman [1998] and Haug and Arlbjorn [2011]) suggests that in a large corporation the impact of poor data quality can range between 8 percent and 12 percent of revenue, with an average being 10 percent (Jugulum 2014).

- Informally 40% to 60% of the expense of the service organization may be consumed as a result of poor data (Redman 1998).

- The Data Warehousing Institute (TDWI) estimates that data quality problems cost US businesses more than $600 billion a year (Eckerson 2002).

- Ovum, a global analyst firm, estimated that "poor data quality costs US businesses at least 30% of revenues—a staggering $700 billion per year" (Sheina 2010).

- The Data Warehousing Institute (TDWI) estimates that poor-quality customer data costs US businesses a staggering $611 billion a year in postage, printing, and staff overhead (Eckerson 2002).

- A global financial institution invested in a company thought to be creditworthy. It ended up losing more than one-half billion dollars

($500 million+) because differences in the definitions of risk codes across its business units led to the wrong decisions (English 2004).

- A major bank lost over $200 million because changes in the credit rating information received from its credit bureau caused it to send out preapproved credit cards to thousands of individuals who were not creditworthy (English 2004).

- According to research published by Gartner, some individual organizations estimate that they "lose as much as $100 million annually due to poor data" (Gartner 2010).

- Wrong price data in retail databases alone costs US consumers $2.5 billion annually (English 2000).

- Research from Experian Data Quality shows that inaccurate data have a direct impact on the bottom line of 88% of companies, with the average company losing 12% of its revenue (Davis 2014).

- Research from Experian Data Quality shows that 75% of businesses are wasting 14% of revenue due to poor data quality. This equates to a staggering £197.788M in wasted revenue across UK businesses (Adamson 2014).

- An insurance company lost hundreds of thousands of dollars annually in mailing costs (postage, returns, collateral, and staff to process returns) due to duplicate customer records (Hempfield 2011).

- One company spent more than $100,000 in labor costs identifying and correcting 111 different spellings of the company AT&T (DataFlux Corporation 2003).

- The US Insurance Data Management Association separately estimated bad data to cost between 15 and 20 percent of corporations' operating revenue (Tay 2011).

- According to a report from Experian QAS, UK companies are throwing away £1 in every £6 of budget spent thanks to poor-quality data (Burns 2012).

- A financial company absorbed a net loss totalling more than $250 million when interest rates changed dramatically, all because the company database was lacking in quality and simple updates (Huang et al. 1999).

- An AT Kearny study showed that 30% of data reported by grocers were erroneous. They also estimated that the consumer packaged goods industry is losing $40 billion in annual sales due to bad product data. This study found 43% of invoices included errors leading to unnecessary price reductions (Dyche and Levy 2006).

- A study by the Automotive Aftermarket Industry Association (AAIA) found that trading partners sharing product data were forced to manually enter it. The AAIA estimated that manual rework like this, combined with the lost sales, costs the automotive industry $2 billion a year (Dyche and Levy 2006).

- Research conducted by Capgemini, a global consulting firm, found that poor data cost the UK economy £67 billion per year—£46 billion in the private sector and £21 billion in the public sector (Capgemini 2008).

- Libor rate discrepancies, for which several banks were fined hundreds of millions in 2012 and 2013, were the result of inconsistencies in data between the relevant systems (Experian 2015).

- In March 1997, a UK bank discovered it lost around £90 million ($145 million) due to data errors in a computer model that caused inaccurate valuation of a risk manager's investment positions (English 1999).

- A UK engineering company stock lost 13% of its value in April 1997 because a data error caused profits to be overstated. Some costs that had been written off as they were incurred continued to be carried in the balance sheet (English 1999).

- A European company learned through a data audit that it was not invoicing 4% of its orders. For a company with $2 billion in revenues, this meant that $80 million in orders went unpaid (English 1999).

- A study (Ferriss 1998) found out that "Canadian automotive insurers are taking a major hit from organized and computer-literate criminals who are staging crashes and taking advantage of dirty data in corporate databases." The study found out that in one case several insurance firms lost $56 million to one fraud ring.

- Poor data costs the Department of Defense (DoD) and federal government billions of dollars per year: an estimated $13 billion for the DoD and $700 billion for the federal government (English 2009).

- It is reported that more than $2 billion of US federal loan money had been lost because of poor data quality at a single agency (Wang et al. 1995; Pandey 2014).

- According to the Gartner Group, poor data quality drains a company on average $8.2 million annually in squandered resources and expenses for operational inefficiencies, missed sales, and unrealized new opportunities (Dun & Bradstreet 2012).

- According to a 2009 Gartner survey of 140 companies, almost a quarter of all respondents reported that bad data were costing them more than

$20 million every year, while 4% put the figure as high as $100 million (Friedman 2009).

- NBC News reported that "dead people still eat!" Because of outdated information in US government databases, food stamps continued to be sent to recipients long after they died. Fraud from food stamps costs US taxpayers billions of dollars (Huang et al. 1999).

- A survey of 599 companies conducted by PricewaterhouseCoopers estimated that poor data management costs global businesses more than $1.4 billion per year in billing, accounting, and inventory glitches alone. Much of that cost is due to the accuracy component of data quality (Olson 2003).

- Erroneous pricing data in retail databases alone cost US consumers $2.5 billion each year (English 2000; Fan et al. 2009).

- Sixty-five percent of organizations admit to losing revenue, and on average, in Australia, it is estimated that 6% of revenue is wasted due to poor address data (Parker 2007; Dynamic Markets 2005).

- An information services firm lost $500,000 annually and alienated customers because it repeatedly recalled reports sent to subscribers due to inaccurate data (Hempfield 2011).

- A telecommunications firm lost $8 million a month because data entry errors incorrectly coded accounts, preventing bills from being sent out (Nguyen Undated).

- A global chemical company discovered it was losing millions of dollars in volume discounts in procuring supplies because it could not correctly identify and reconcile suppliers on a global basis (Nguyen Undated).

- GS1, the company that is responsible for bar coding and product identification systems, released a report that found bad data cost grocery retailers $675 million in lost sales every year (Forbes, 2014).

- It is estimated that incorrect data in the retail business cost $40 billion annually, and at the organizational level costs are approximately 10% of revenues (Snow 2008; Batini et al. 2009; Redman 2001).

The costs of poor data quality are astronomical. Data generated by one business process are typically consumed by several downstream business processes, often very far from the point of entry. As bad data move through a process, the cost of correcting the bad data increases, just as it does in manufacturing. Quality professionals use the phrase "1:10:100" to describe the increasing cost impact of correcting a product as it moves through different stages (Insurance Data Management Association Undated). This is the same as the Sirius Decisions 1-10-100 rule formulated by W. Edwards Deming: it costs about $1 to verify a record as it is entered, about $10 dollars to fix it later, and $100 if nothing is done, as the consequences of the errors are felt over and over again. Figure 1.8 depicts an inverted pyramid to show the increasing costs: Prevention cost:Correction cost:Failure cost in the ratio of 1:10:100. The different currency symbols—dollar ($), euro (€), pound (£), and yen (¥) have been used to indicate the different cost measurement units, but are certainly not limited to these.

While some costs, such as additional expenses, lost employees, and lost customers and clients, are relatively easy to spot and quantify, other costs, such as bad decisions, damaged reputation of a brand, lack of trust and confidence, low morale, low predictability, lost opportunity, emotional quotient, are more difficult to measure, but even more important. The latter category of costs is unknown, and many are almost certainly unknowable. Thus, the second key is to acknowledge that Dr. Deming's famous observation that "the most important costs (of quality in manufacturing) are unknown and unknowable" extends to data as well (Redman 2012).

For example, criminal identification systems determine if a person has a criminal record. This information is typically used by judges (to decide whether the individual has to be punished, and how) and by organizations (to decide whether to hire the individual). These systems are critical because, in some way, our future may be influenced by the quality of the data and the procedures used to recover them. Although a high-quality application is used to access the data, the identification is based on several attributes, and sophisticated algorithms are used to match them, it turns out that erroneous deductions can be obtained when bad-quality data are present in the system (Bobrowski et al. 1970). It has been found that 50% to 80% of computerized criminal records in the United States are inaccurate, incomplete, or ambiguous (Tayi 1998; Bobrowski et al. 1970). This poor-quality data may result in sending innocent people to jail or not hiring them (Bobrowski et al. 1970).

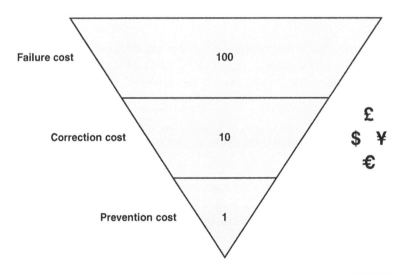

Figure 1.8   Prevention cost:Correction cost:Failure cost.
Source: Adapted from Ross (1993).

An example of where the emotional quotient is involved is mail sent from a hospital to a dead patient to keep medical appointments since their expiry date was not populated in the hospital's database. The letters were intercepted by his widow, who had not come to terms with her husband's death. In another instance, a bank denied a customer a credit card only because his date of birth was stored in its customer database incorrectly and the age derived from the date of birth was less than 16, and hence he was considered not eligible to hold a credit card. Here, the bank loses a customer because of incorrect data, though the bank is completely unaware of that fact.

Quite a few companies have gone out of business because of bad data quality. Below are a few instances:

- *National Westminster Bank.* This British bank had to dispose of its equities businesses in February 1998, taking a pre-tax loss of around $1.77 billion (£1.01 billion), according to *The Financial Times*, February 25, 1998. The failure stemmed from losses of over $150 million (£90 million) caused by incorrectly pricing its derivatives over a two-year period, according to *The Times,* March 14, 1997 (English 1999).

- *Oxford Health Plans Inc.* In 1997 Oxford Health Plans disclosed that computer glitches that occurred while trying to convert to a new computer system, and the resulting inaccurate data, caused it to overestimate revenues and underestimate medical costs. Other information quality problems caused overbilling of its customers at the same time. Estimating a third-quarter loss of up to $69.3 million, its stock dropped 62%; the actual loss was even greater. The New York State Insurance Department fined Oxford $3 million for violations of insurance laws and regulations and ordered Oxford to pay $500,000 to customers that it had overcharged, according to the *Wall Street Journal*, December 24, 1997. Oxford is struggling for survival. Its stock price as of October 8, 1998 was around $8—only 9% of its all-time high value of around $89. Oxford lost money in 1998, and the consensus of stock market analysts was that it would lose money in 1999 as well (English 1999).

THE BUTTERFLY EFFECT ON DATA QUALITY

When you throw a stone into water, water gets displaced, and the ripples travel outward in increasingly larger circles.

Data are highly vulnerable to the "butterfly effect." The concept of the butterfly effect comes from the science of chaos theory, which defines the term as the sensitive dependence on initial conditions in which a small change in one state of a deterministic nonlinear system can result in large differences in a later state (Boeing 2016; Wikipedia Undated "Butterfly Effect"). The term *butterfly effect* refers to the way the fluttering of a butterfly's wings, which is in itself a trivial event, can have a major impact on weather, which is a complex system. When butterflies sit on flowers to suck nectar, pollens stick to their wings. The fluttering of the butterfly wing in itself represents an insignificant change in the initial state of the system; however, it has a ripple effect as it starts a sequence of events: pollens sticking to the butterfly's wings start moving through the air, which causes a gazelle to sneeze, which in turn triggers a stampede of gazelles, which raises a cloud of dust, which partially blocks the sun, which results in change in the atmospheric temperature, which in due course alters the path of a hurricane on the other side of the world (Walker 2011). Just like a small butterfly and the action of flapping its wings—which is indeed a very minor activity—can wreak havoc on the other side of the world, a small data issue in an upstream system can cause significant issues further downstream. Data issues often begin with a small error—misspelled product codes or wrong date formats or erroneous account numbers in one part of the organization—but propagate across systems in an exponential manner; the butterfly effect can produce disastrous results. This is because corporate data are not static, and the enterprise data world comprises numerous databases linked by innumerable IT systems, applications, and real-time and batch data feeds. Staring from the point of entry, data flow continuously as they are collected and processed at different locations and in different formats. As data travel through the enterprise, they impact different systems and business processes. The more interconnected systems are in the organization, the greater is the impact of data quality errors. The data error has gone viral! Hence, the impacts of data quality errors are costly and far-reaching.

We will illustrate the butterfly effect on data quality with two real-world scenarios.

Scenario 1. Consider a postal code reference table that stores the state and the corresponding postal codes. One record had the wrong postal code stored for a particular state. Since different software processes and applications use the reference table to populate the state code from the postal codes in the absence of a state code in the input data, a large number of customer records ended up with the wrong state code. As the data flowed to downstream systems, a large number of customer records in different target databases and reports had incorrect address data, which resulted in mail bouncing back and communications not reaching the customers. This had the following adverse impacts:

- Disgruntled customers/loss of customers

- Mailing costs

- Failed marketing campaigns

- Loss of revenue

It must be understood that in the postal code reference table, the incorrect data by themselves have little impact, and it is a small defect to fix. However, as these data are propagated to other systems, the cumulative effect of a wrong value in multiple records is drastic.

Scenario 2. The different customer statuses such as solvent, deceased, bankrupt, active, sound, inactive, and so on, are stored in a customer status reference table in a financial institution's data warehouse. Every time the business defines a new status, this status needs to be inserted into the customer status reference table.

Depending on the statuses, the organization determines whether the customer is eligible for certain products. The processes that populate the customer status in the primary tables in the data warehouse use the reference table to map the customer status to that in the source file or source table. In case a match is not found for a customer, a value of 9999 is populated for the customer status for that customer.

It so happened that a new status was defined by the business. However, due to a process discrepancy, the new status was not inserted into the customer reference table. The source files containing customer and status information have an average of 1000 customers with the new status every day. However, since the process that populated the customer status in the primary tables in the data warehouse could not find a match, a value of 9999 (as per the business rule) was populated for the customer status for all 1000 customers having the new status. Since 30 different downstream processes use the source customer status information from the data warehouse, and populate downstream tables or reports after massaging that information, there were at least 32 different tables and reports containing wrong data/information. Also, since this was noticed only after 10 days—when an eligible customer credit card application was rejected—there were approximately 100,000 customer records with wrong customer status information.

Figure 1.9 shows the butterfly effect of bad data as data travel through the data systems in the organization.

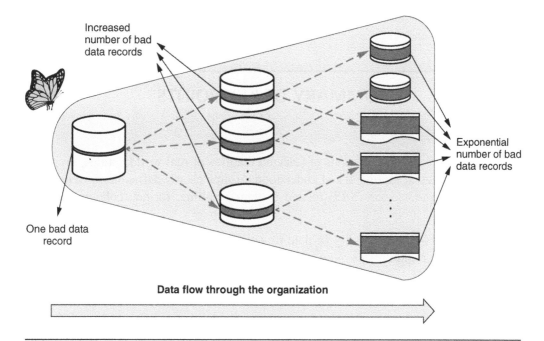

Figure 1.9   Butterfly effect on data quality.

CONCLUSION

Quality is a certain level of excellence and is not universal, not an absolute, and not a constant, but a relative degree. The same applies in the case of data quality too. The *degree* of data quality excellence that should be attained and sustained is driven by the criticality of the data, the business need, and the cost and time necessary to achieve the defined degree of data quality. The costs in time, resources, and dollars to achieve and sustain the desired quality level must be balanced against the return on investment and benefits derived from that degree of quality. The questions to ask are:

- Is it necessary to fix the small percentage—say five percent data issues?

- What are the minimum data quality thresholds that are acceptable?

- Is the data quality level to be achieved worth the time, effort, and money spent in attaining it?

You do not need to have zero percent data issues. There are acceptable percentages of data issues, and they need to be acknowledged and accepted. In other words, you do not need 100% data quality. There is a point where data are good enough. The minimum acceptable quality level differs from data set to data set based on the criticality of the data in question, and can be determined by evaluating the data within their context of use. Once acceptable data quality is achieved, ongoing monitoring must be maintained for critical data to ensure that the quality doesn't degrade because of new business processes, changes in existing business processes, new applications, system changes, database structure changes, and so on.

SUMMARY OF KEY POINTS

Key Terms

data—Abstract representations of selected features of real-world entities, events, and concepts, expressed and understood through clearly definable conventions (Sebastian-Coleman 2013) related to their meaning, format, collection, and storage.

data quality—The capability of data to satisfy the stated business, system, and technical requirements of an enterprise.

data quality dimensions—Set of data quality attributes that represent a single aspect or construct of data quality (Wang and Strong 1996). Data quality dimensions provide a means to quantify and manage the quality of data. Examples: completeness, accuracy, consistency, timeliness, and so on.

Categories of Data

- Master data

- Reference data

- Transactional data

- Historical data

- Metadata

  - Technical metadata

  - Business metadata

  - Process metadata

Cost of Poor Data Quality—Business Impacts

- Financial impacts (such as increased operating costs, fines, and so on)

- Confidence and satisfaction-based impacts (such as decreased organizational trust, customer dissatisfaction, and so on)

- Productivity impacts (such as increased workloads, decreased throughput, and so on)

- Risk and compliance impacts (such as investment risks, competitive risk, and so on)

Prevention cost:Correction cost:Failure cost = 1:10:100

Causes of Bad Quality Data

- Manual data entry

- Aging of data/data decay

- Inadequate validation in the data capture process

- Inefficient business process management and design

- Multiple uses of data and lack of shared understanding of data

- Lack of common data standards, data dictionary, and metadata

- Business data ownership and governance issues

- Loss of expertise

- Organizational changes

- – Corporate mergers and acquisitions
- – Globalization
- – Reorganization
- – External changes
- Data migration
- Data integration
- Data cleansing programs
- Data purging
- System upgrades
- Data corruption by hackers

2

Building Blocks of Data: Evolutionary History and Data Concepts

INTRODUCTION

In Chapter 1 we established that both data and data quality are important, and data are an organization's most valuable asset. In order to assess, improve, and maintain data quality, it is necessary to understand the fundamental concepts related to data, their relation to real-world entities, their structure, characteristics, organization, and storage in organizations. It has been a long journey from data being handwritten and stored in leaves and parchments in the ancient times to the present day, with data being stored digitally in computer systems in databases and data warehouses with the advancement of technologies. This chapter starts with a discussion about the evolution of data collection, data structures, and storage over this period of time, and the inception of the database, relational database, and data warehouse. This is followed by a discussion about databases, data models, normalization, database schema, relational databases, data warehousing, and data hierarchy, followed by a summarization of commonly used data-related terminology to be used throughout the book.

EVOLUTION OF DATA COLLECTION, STORAGE, AND DATA QUALITY

Before the advent of computers and electronic processing, collection, organization, processing, and maintenance of data on corporate entities, events, transactions, and operations were performed manually. Use of data in the form of records has been in existence since ancient Egyptian times, with trade being the major driver in keeping detailed records due to the need to track transactions. In the thirteenth and fourteenth centuries the need for recording as well as retrieving and updating data led to the development of double-entry bookkeeping (Lake and Crowther 2013). In essence, before the electronic processing era, important data like financial and medical/heathcare data were manually stored in physical paper files and paper registers and organized in filing cabinets. Retrieval of information from these paper files and registers was a time-consuming and tedious exercise as it would require locating the right file in stacks of files and then searching for the information within the file. Paper-based system indexes were developed to ease and speed the retrieval of data. Some libraries, especially those that used comprehensive indexing systems, in a way represented what data stores signify today. The production of reports from the data was a manual and time-consuming exercise and prone to errors. However, in the mid-nineteenth century, these problems were mitigated when manual calculators came into existence and were used to assist in the process of producing reports.

With the advent of electronic processing, electronic capture and storage of data became rampant. "Punch card" technology was invented by Herman Hollerith in 1890 to tabulate 1890 census data, and was extensively used at the end of the nineteenth century. In the very early years of computers, punch cards were used for input, output, and data storage. Punch cards offered a quick way to punch in data, and to retrieve it. In 1890 Herman Hollerith adapted the punch cards used for weaving looms to act as the memory for a mechanical tabulating machine (Foote 2017). The tabulating machines of those times gave way to the IBM machines of modern times. Punch cards were replaced by paper tapes. However, storage was very expensive and restricted. With the introduction and use of magnetic tape, it was possible to hold very large volumes of data cheaply. With magnetic tape, there were no major constraints on the format of the record of data. With magnetic tape, data could be written and rewritten. However, data could be retrieved in a sequential manner only; that is, in order to access 1% of the data, 100% of the data had to be physically accessed and read (Inmon et al. 2008). In addition, magnetic tape was susceptible to wear and tear, rendering the tape useless after a certain length of time.

In the early 1950s the foremost computer programs were developed, with coding languages and algorithms being the primary focus. COBOL was the first nonproprietary programming language used for coding. During this time computers were basically giant calculators, and data were considered as the by-product. The electronic computer empowered the first revolution in database technologies by permitting high-speed and random access to vast volumes of data. In 1956 IBM introduced hard disk drives, which permitted direct access to data (Lake and Crowther 2013). However, hard disk drives had comparatively low capacity and were more expensive compared to tape systems. By 1961, the systems had become more economical, and there was a potential to add extra drives to the system. The benefit of a disk drive was that one could go right to a file record, facilitating real-time transaction processing. This forms the basis of processing for almost all commercial computer systems. At the same time, operating systems were developed to allow multiple users and multiple programs to be active simultaneously (Lake and Crowther 2013). This capability eliminated some of the constraints imposed by the tight scheduling needed on single-process machines.

In 1960 Charles W. Bachman, an industrial researcher, developed the first database management system, known as the Integrated Database Store (IDS). The term *database* was coined in the early 1960s "to capture the sense that the information stored within a computer could be conceptualized, structured, and manipulated independently of the specific machine on which it resided" (Committee on Innovations in Computing and Communications 1999). In the 1960s IBM also developed their first database management system, known as Information Management System (IMS), written for NASA's

Apollo space program. Both of these database systems are known as the precursors of navigational databases. A database, as a collection of information, can be organized so a database management system can access and extract specific information (Foote 2017). By the mid-1960s, as computers became more technologically advanced, faster, and more flexible, and started gaining popularity, several kinds of general-use database systems became available. As a result, customers demanded that a standard be developed, in turn leading to Bachman forming the Database Task Group. The Database Task Group took accountability for the design and standardization of a language called COmmon Business Oriented Language (COBOL). The Database Task Group presented this standard in 1971, which also came to be known as the "CODASYL (COnference on DAta SYstems Languages) approach." The CODASYL approach was an extremely complex and complicated system and could not be used without considerable training. The CODASYL approach was reliant on a "manual" navigation technique using a linked data set, which formed a large network. Searching for records could be accomplished by one of three techniques (Foote 2017):

- Using the primary key (also known as the CALC key)

- Moving relationships (also called sets) from one record to another

- Scanning all records in sequential order

Over a period of time, the CODASYL approach lost its attractiveness as simpler, user-friendly systems entered the marketplace. In the first database systems known as *pre-relational databases*, the physical organization of the data on the disk determined the manner in which the data could be retrieved and navigated. Relationships between data items—for example, relationships between employees and payrolls were predefined in the same structure of the database. There was little ability for ad hoc querying, and sophisticated programmers could only hope to extract data from such a system using complex programming. In 1970 Edgar F. Codd wrote a paper entitled "A Relational Model of Data for Large Shared Data Banks" in which he proposed substituting pre-relational databases with databases represented by a tabular structure (that is, tables containing rows and columns, which Codd called *relations*). This concept would become the relational database management system (DBMS). Records would not be stored in a free-form list of linked records, as in the CODASYL model, but instead used a "table with fixed-length records." The relations could be accessed by means of a high-level non-procedural (or declarative) language. Instead of writing algorithms to access data, this approach only needed a predicate that identified the desired records or combination of records (Danielsen 1998).

In 1973 Michael Stonebraker and Eugene Wong (both then at UC Berkeley) made the decision to research relational database systems. The project was called INGRES (Interactive Graphics and Retrieval System), and successfully demonstrated that a relational model could be efficient and practical. INGRES worked with a query language known as QUEL, and coerced IBM into developing SQL in 1974, which was more advanced (SQL became ANSI and OSI standards in 1986 and 1987). SQL quickly replaced QUEL as the more functional query language (Foote 2017).

Following the advancements in technology in the areas of processors, computer memory, computer storage, and computer networks, the sizes, capabilities, and performance of databases and their respective database management systems have grown in orders of magnitude. In the 1980s several other relational DBMS (RDBMS) products emerged (for example, Oracle, Informix, and DB2). The relational database revolution in the early 1980s resulted in improved access to the valuable information contained deep within data.

However, databases modeled to be efficient at transactional processing were not always optimized for complex reporting or analytical needs. In large corporations it was usual for numerous decision support environments to function autonomously. However, though the different decision support environments served different users, they often required the same stored data. The process of sourcing, cleaning, and integrating data from various sources, usually from long-term existing operational systems, also known as *legacy systems*, was typically, in part, replicated for each environment. In fact, the need for systems offering decision support functionality preceded the first relational model and SQL. Market research and television ratings magnate ACNielsen provided clients with something called a "data mart" in the early 1970s to enhance their sales efforts (Kempe 2012). Bill Inmon, considered by many people the father of data warehousing, first began to discuss the principles of the data warehouse, and even coined the term in the 1970s. But the concept and practice of data warehousing as known today only dawned in the late 1980s. In principle, the data warehousing concept was intended to deliver an architectural model for the flow of data from operational systems to decision support environments. Barry Devlin and Paul Murphy published an article, "An Architecture for a Business Information System," in the *IBM Systems Journal* in 1988, in which they coined the term *business data warehouse*. Inmon's approach to data warehouse design focuses on a centralized data repository modeled to the third normal form. Although the original data warehouse concept was introduced by Bill Inmon, the technology advanced as a result of Ralph Kimball's dimensional modeling concept for data warehouse design. Inmon's work focused on large centralized data warehouses and Kimball's work focused on integrated systems of smaller data marts have had a considerable influence on today's architectures. The evolution of today's data warehousing was also motivated by users' need for real-time access to information for decision-making purposes, by developments in the technology, and the progression of cloud computing. Data warehousing depends heavily on concrete enterprise integration. Whether an organization follows Inmon's top-down, centralized view of warehousing, Kimball's bottom-up, star schema approach, or a mixture of the two, integrating a warehouse with the organization's overall data architecture remains a key principle (Kempe 2012).

Data warehousing has exposed atrocious data quality problems that become apparent when an organization makes an effort to integrate disparate data. The fact that these data quality problems had not surfaced until data warehouses came into the picture and became dominant is not because data quality had suddenly gone downhill. Data quality problems have been masked by bad business and systems practices over the years (English 1999). The earliest computing technology did not enable data sharing. As a consequence, all early application development methodologies were created to overcome this technology limitation. That limitation resulted in building isolated applications and islands of information independent of or only loosely interfaced with other systems, applications, and databases. In other words, systems operated in a siloed fashion. Data quality problems have been masked by layer upon layer of interface programs in which inconsistent data from one application "transformed" into usable data structure and values is required by another application area. However, the validity of this approach is seriously challenged as the weight of those layers of interfaces consumes the time and resources of information systems organizations to maintain them (English 1999).

The evolution of the field of data management overlaps significantly with data quality management (DQM) and total data quality management (TDQM). The concept of data quality management within the world of data management developed in the 1980s in step with the technological ability to access stored data in a random fashion (Wikipedia Undated "Data Management").

DATABASE, DATABASE MODELS, AND DATABASE SCHEMAS

Databases have evolved since their inception in the 1960s, beginning with hierarchical and network databases, through the 1970s, with object-oriented databases, through the 1980s, with relational databases, through the 1990s, with more-sophisticated relational database technologies evolving, and with NoSQL and cloud databases originating in the latter part of the 2000s such that today we have SQL and NoSQL databases and cloud databases. A *database* can be described as a structured collection of interrelated data that are organized and stored in computer systems in such a way as to facilitate efficient retrieval. The database structure is attained by appropriately organizing the data with the aid of a database model.

A *database model* is a type of data model that determines the logical structure of a database and fundamentally determines in which manner data can be stored, organized, and manipulated (Wikipedia Undated "Database Model"). Some of the common database models include relational models, hierarchical models, flat-file models, object-oriented models, entity relationship models, and network models.

A *database schema* is the structure in a database management system that holds the physical implementation of a data model. Technically speaking, a database schema is the skeletal structure that describes the structure of exactly how the data are stored, and is itself stored by the DBMS for reference. It includes all implementation details, such as data field names, data types, data sizes, constraints, and indices, as well as primary keys and/or foreign keys. A database schema does not have data in it.

When discussing databases, you must distinguish between the *database schema*, which is the logical blueprint of the database, and the *database instance*, which is a snapshot of the data in the database at a particular point in time. A database schema is generally static, since it is difficult to modify the structure of a database once it is operational. However, database instances can change over time. The database model is prepared first, and the database schema is followed by that.

RELATIONAL DATABASE

A *relational database* is a digital database based on the *relational model* of data, as proposed by Edgar F. Codd in 1970 (Codd 1970). A relational database is made up of tables. A software system used to maintain relational databases is a *relational database management system* (RDBMS). The *relational model*—the theoretical basis of relational databases—is a framework of structuring data using relations ("relational tables" or "tables"), which are grid-like tabular structures consisting of columns and rows. The relational model organizes data into one or more tables of columns and rows, with a unique identification or key (also known as the *primary key*) identifying each row. In other words, the primary key (PK) is the unique identifier for each row in a table. Rows are also called *records* or *tuples*. A record is a horizontal object in the table. Named columns of a table are also called *field names*. Generally, each table/relation represents an entity (such as a customer, employee, or product). The rows represent instances of that particular type of entity, and the columns represent values attributed to that instance. A column is a vertical object in a table that contains all information associated with a specific attribute in a table. Often, the tables are organized into *data domains* or *subject areas* containing tables with related content (Sebastian-Coleman 2013). For example, all the tables relating to a customer and containing customer-related data would fall under the *customer* data domain or subject area.

An *entity* is any object in the system that we want to model and store data about. Entities are usually familiar concepts, either tangible or intangible, such as persons, places, objects, phenomena, or events that have relevance to the database. *Attributes* are characteristics or features of an entity. An entity occurrence is an *instance* of an entity (Scottish Qualification Authority 2007). For example, in the customer entity, the information about each individual customer detail is an entity occurrence. An entity occurrence can also be referred to as a *record*.

A *relationship* is an association or link between entities, with an attribute or set of attributes establishing the link. A relationship is established by a foreign key in one entity linking to the primary key in another entity (Scottish Qualification Authority 2007).

Figure 2.1a shows the layout of a relational table, and Figure 2.1b shows a table containing customer data.

In brief, there are four main elements in a relational database:

- *Field name*. Field name is also known as the *column name*, which represents attributes of entities, depending on the level of granularity of the data.

- *Field*. Field is also known as a *column*, which represent attribute values of entities. The field is the basic unit of data in a database and stores attribute values of a particular data type. Fields are combined to construct a record. A *domain* is a set or range of allowable values for a field. A field is also known as an *attribute*.

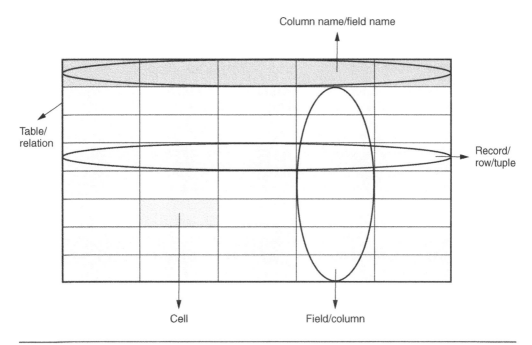

Figure 2.1a   Layout of a relational table.

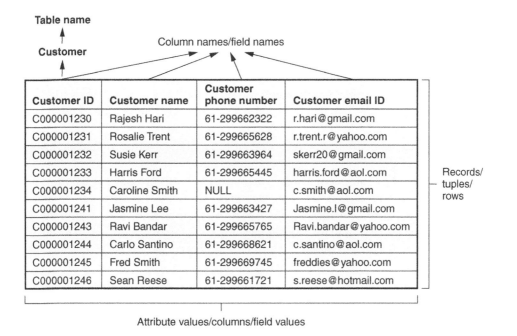

Figure 2.1b   Table containing customer data.

- *Record.* Record is also known as a *row*, and represents a particular instance of an entity. A record is composed of fields and contains all the data about one particular entity.

- *Table.* Table is also known as a *relation* or *relational table*, which represent an entity. A set of records and fields that hold the data makes a table.

In the relational model, a *primary key* (PK) is a single column, or a set of columns, that can be used to uniquely identify a row of data (or records) in a given table. Sometimes, a single column is not sufficient to uniquely identify a record in a table, in which case more than one column is required for this purpose. When a primary key consists of a set of columns, then it is called a *composite primary key*. No two rows in the table may contain matching data in the primary key columns. It must be kept in mind that what is an adequate primary key in one scenario may not uniquely identify data instances in another, and hence all the scenarios must be taken into account while defining the primary key. For example, a customer ID can uniquely differentiate a customer from another customer in the customer table but would not be able to uniquely identify orders as multiple orders can be associated with a single customer. A *natural key* is an attribute or set of attributes that already exist in the real world and can uniquely identify a record. For example, social security number in the case of US residents is a natural key. Natural keys can be used as primary keys if there are no privacy or security restrictions to using them and if the values never change. Sometimes, there can be several natural keys that can be declared as the primary key, and all these natural keys are called *candidate keys*. A *surrogate key* is any column or set of columns in a relational table that does not have a business meaning but can be used to uniquely identify records in the table, and which can be declared as the primary key instead of the natural key.

In the relational model, a *foreign key* (FK) is a column or a set of columns from one relational table whose values must match another relational table's primary key. This creates a link between the two tables. Foreign keys are used when defining relationships between tables. We illustrate relationships, primary key, and foreign key using the *customer* and *order* relational tables containing customer and order details, respectively, as shown in Figure 2.2.

The customer table has four fields: customer ID, customer name, customer phone number, and customer e-mail ID. The customer ID is the primary key in the customer table; that is, no two rows in the customer table can have the same customer ID value. The order table has four fields: order ID, customer ID, order date, and order value. The customer ID field in the order table should match with the customer ID field in the customer table. The customer ID field in the customer table is a primary key, whereas the customer ID field in the order table is the foreign key, and serves as a link between the two tables. This eliminates repetitive data input, and diminishes the possibility of error.

There is a one-to-many relationship between customer and order; that is, a customer can place many orders. The information in foreign key columns does not have to be unique. Matching information can appear in multiple rows, as in the example order table where a customer can place several orders. For this reason, relationships are often

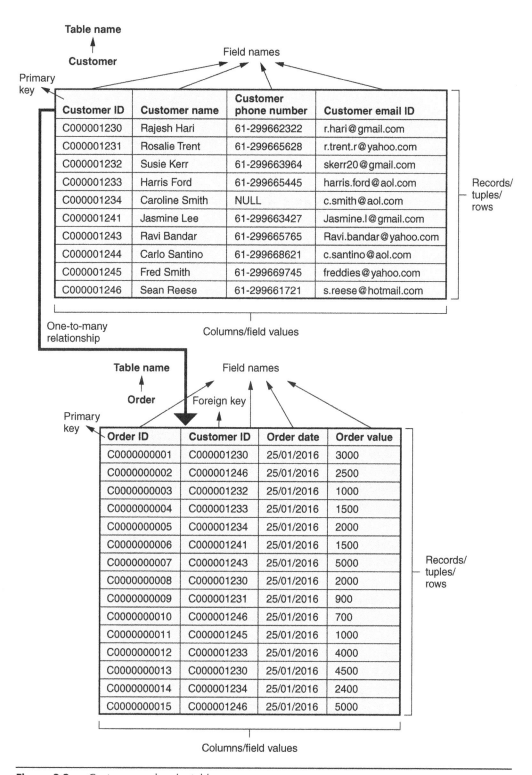

Figure 2.2 *Customer* and *order* tables.

called "one-to-many links," as one value in the primary key of a table may link to many rows in the related tables.

Structured query language (SQL) is a relational database query and manipulation language. Virtually all relational database systems use SQL for querying and extracting data from the database and maintaining the database by performing actions such as inserts, updates, and deletions. The command and flexibility of SQL allows for the creation, modification, truncation, and deletion of databases and tables, and the manipulation and query of data.

DATA MODELS

A *data model* is an abstract representation of the database. A data model organizes data elements and data objects and standardizes how they relate to one another and to properties of the real-world entities at different levels of abstraction. Different types of data models depict data at different levels of abstraction. The three basic styles of data model are as shown in Figure 2.3a:

- Conceptual data models

- Physical data models

- Logical data models

Conceptual data models present the entities that are represented in the database and identify the highest-level relationships between the different entities. Attributes and key structures do not form a part of the conceptual data model.

Logical data models present the entities and relationships within and among them, with detail about all attributes for each entity and key structure (the attributes needed to define a unique instance of an entity and attributes to identify the relationship between different entities), expressed independently of a particular database management product

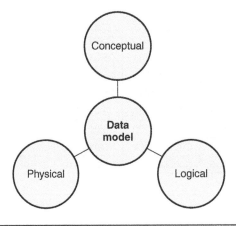

Figure 2.3a   Data model—basic styles.

or storage technology. Relationships between entities can be optional or mandatory. They differ in terms of cardinality (one-to-one, one-to-many, many-to-many) (Sebastian-Coleman 2013). Logical data models are often diagrammatic in nature and are typically used in business processes that seek to capture things of importance to an organization and how they relate to one another. Once validated and approved, the logical data model can serve as the foundation for the physical data model to build on and lead to the design of a database.

Physical data models represent the way the model will be built in the database and how data are physically stored in a database. They describe the physical characteristics of the data elements that are required to set up and store actual data about the entities represented. A physical database model displays all table structures, including column name, column data type, column constraints, primary key, foreign key, and relationships between tables. The physical data model will not be the same for different RDBMSs. For example, the data type for a column may be different between Microsoft Access, Teradata, and Netezza. During the life cycle of a project, the physical data model naturally derives from a logical data model, although it may be reverse-engineered from a given database implementation.

In Figure 2.3b we depict the conceptual, logical, and physical versions of a single data model. The conceptual model shows the entities *customer* and *order* and the relationship, that is *customer places order* at a high level without any display of attri-

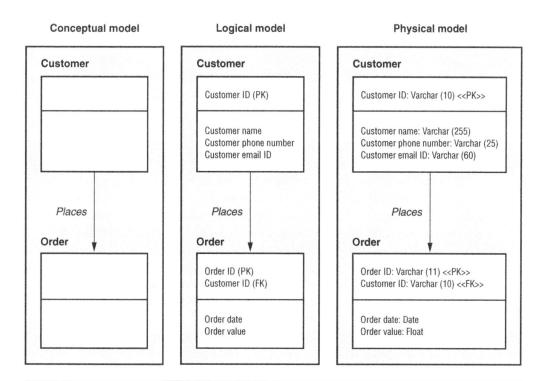

Figure 2.3b   Conceptual, logical, and physical versions of a single data model.

Table 2.1   Comparison of conceptual, logical, and physical model.

Characteristics	Conceptual	Logical	Physical
Entity names	✓	✓	
Entity relationships	✓	✓	
Attributes		✓	
Key structure (primary key and foreign key)		✓	✓
Table names			✓
Table structure			✓
Column names/field names			✓
Field specification			✓
Data types			✓

Source: Adapted from 1Key Data (Undated).

butes involved. The *logical model* is a progression of the *conceptual model*, with *customer* and *order* attributes displayed along with the primary keys (PKs) and foreign keys (FKs). The *physical model* replaces entity names with table names, and attributes with field names or column names, along with data specifications (data types and length). Table 2.1 compares the conceptual model, logical model, and physical model.

In addition to models that differ by levels of abstraction, there can also be models of data with consumer-facing views of the data. Technically, a *view* is a data set generated through a query that produces a virtual table. At its simplest, a view can have exactly the same structure as a physical table. Views can also be used to display a subset of data from a table, to aggregate data within a table, or combine data from multiple tables (Sebastian-Coleman 2013).

A data set can be modeled in a number of different ways. In order to understand the data and make sense out of them, the data require context and structure. Data models provide a means of understanding this context (Sebastian-Coleman 2013) and logically structure the data. In doing so, they create both context and interrelationships between the data by translating business process and business logic into a structural representation. If data stakeholders find that models are understandable representations of data, then they can become a primary means of defining data (Sebastian-Coleman 2013).

For most databases as well as data-driven applications, data models are crucial and are needed for data management. The conceptual model gives a high-level view of the data entities involved and business requirements regarding the data to the business, while logical models enable data stakeholders to be aware of what data elements reside in the data asset, in addition to the relationships. The physical data model is more detailed than the logical data model and relates to physical representation of the data, movement of data within the database, and data access. The main purpose of data modeling behind database construction is to make sure that entities, attributes, attribute structure, and the relationships between the entities are completely and correctly represented. This is because data models use easily understood pictorial representations and commonplace language and hence can be used to communicate with the end users as well as the developers. The physical data model has enough detail and can be used by developers as a plan for building a physical database. The information that is in the data model could be used to identify relational tables, field or column names, relationships, primary keys, foreign keys, and constraints. If a database is created without appropriate and careful planning, it could result in a database that omits attributes, thus leading to results being incomplete, inaccurate, and inconsistent. This could result in rendering data not fit for purpose and/or not serving the requirement of business users or data consumers. Hence, data modeling approaches (that is, modern data modeling tools and standards) should be used to model data in a standard and consistent fashion.

NORMALIZATION

Normalization, also known as *data normalization*, is a refinement process and a systematic approach of restructuring data in a database such that there is no data redundancy (that is, eliminating unnecessary duplication) and the data dependencies are logical (that is, all related data elements are stored together). Normalization also helps eliminate insertion, update, and deletion anomalies. It was first proposed by Edgar F. Codd as a fundamental part of his relational model.

An unnormalized relation, also known as an *unnormalized form* (UNF) or *non-first normal form* (NF2) (Kitagawa and Kunii 1989), can be described as being a simple database data model (organization of data in a database) lacking the efficiency of database normalization. An unnormalized data model will suffer the pitfalls of data redundancy, where multiple values and/or complex data structures may be stored within a single field/attribute (Studytonight Undated), or where fields may be replicated within a single table (a way of subverting the first normal form rule of one value per field/attribute) (Wikipedia Undated "Unnormalized Form").

DATA WAREHOUSE

Bill H. Inmon, the father of data warehousing, defines *data warehouse* as follows:

> A data warehouse is a collection of integrated, subject-oriented, non-volatile, and time variant databases where each unit of data is specific to some period of time. Data warehouses can contain detailed data, lightly summarized data, and highly summarized data, all formatted for analysis and decision support. (Inmon 2005)

The book *The Data Warehouse Toolkit* gives a more abridged definition:

> A data warehouse is a copy of transaction data specifically structured for query and analysis. (Kimball 1996)

Both definitions place emphasis on the data warehouse's analysis focus, and highlight the historical nature of the data found in a data warehouse. A *data warehouse* (DW) is also known as an *enterprise data warehouse* (EDW) and is a trusted source for integrated enterprise data.

Data warehousing is interesting in that it is a source of information used by the business to make strategic decisions, but it does not truly create any data (Geiger 2004). Data warehousing involves the capture and integration of data from multiple heterogeneous sources. Figure 2.4 shows different data sources that can feed data into a data warehouse. The data in the enterprise data warehouse usually cover a wide range of subject areas or data domains (for example, employee, customer, event, product, sales, and so on) depending on the organization's business process domain. Data quality problems in data warehouses can be due to faulty acquisition of data in the source systems, flawed delivery processes, interpretation issues due to faulty design of the data warehouse itself, or a combination of some or all of these.

Data in a data warehouse are sourced from disparate sources, as illustrated in Figure 2.4. All the data sources from which the data warehouse sources data have their own methods of storing data. While some of the data sources may be cooperative, others might be noncooperative. Diversities among the data sources may contribute to data quality problems if not properly taken care of. A source that offers any kind of unsecured access can become unreliable and ultimately contribute to poor data quality. Different data sources have different issues that can impact data quality adversely. For example, data from legacy data sources do not have metadata that describe the data. Also, a particular field may hold more than one data element; this is known as *data overloading.*

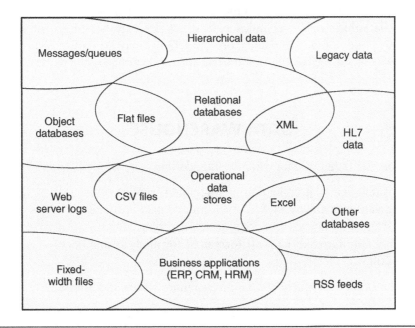

Figure 2.4   Possible sources of data for data warehousing.

Warehouse data can be designed according to different meta models (star schemas, snowflake schemas, hierarchy, fact/dimension) that mandate differing degrees of normalization. In all the cases, data are understood in terms of tables and columns. The warehouse's data model provides a visual representation of the data content of a data warehouse (Sebastian-Coleman 2013). The design of the data model for the data warehouse has an influence on the quality of data residing in the data warehouse. A flawed schema adversely affects the data warehouse data quality. Dimensional modeling is a design technique for databases intended to support end user queries in a data warehouse. It is oriented around understandability and performance (Kimball and Ross 2002; Wikipedia Undated "Dimensional Modeling"). Dimensional models should be designed in collaboration with subject matter experts and data governance representatives from the business (Kimball Group Undated).

Dimensional Modeling, Fact, Dimensions, and Grain

Dimensional modeling always uses the concepts of facts (measures) and dimensions (context) (Wikipedia Undated "Dimensional Modeling"). *Facts* are measurements from business processes and are generally (but not always) numeric values that can be aggregated, and *dimensions* are groups of hierarchies and descriptors that define the facts. Dimensional modeling involves four key steps (Kimball Group Undated):

- *Selection of the business processes.* Business processes correspond to the operational activities performed in your company. Each company will have its own set of business processes. Processing a loan application is an example of a business process in a bank; processing an insurance claim is an example of a business process in an insurance company; processing a customer order is an example of a business process in a retail store. Choosing the business process is essential because it outlines a specific design target and allows the grain, dimensions, and facts to be declared.

- *Declaring the grain.* The declaration of grain is a crucial step in dimensional design and must occur before choosing dimensions or facts because every candidate dimension or fact must be consistent with the grain. The grain institutes precisely what a single fact table row represents. Each one of the proposed fact table grains results in a separate physical table; different grains should not be mixed in one fact table.

- *Identification of the dimensions.* Dimensions provide the "who, what, where, when, why, and how" context with respect to the business process event. Dimension tables contain the descriptive attributes used for filtering and grouping the facts. Dimension tables are generally wide, flat denormalized tables with a number of low-cardinality text attributes. With the grain of a fact table firmly established, all the possible dimensions can be identified. Attributes can be added to an existing dimension table by creation of new columns. Whenever possible, a dimension should be single valued when linked with a given fact row. Every dimension table has a single primary key column. This primary key is embedded as a foreign key in any related fact table where the dimension row's descriptive context is exactly correct for that fact table row.

- *Identification of the facts.* A single fact table row has a one-to-one relationship to a measurement event as defined by the fact table's grain. Thus, the design of the fact table is based on a physical, observable event or activity and is not subjective to current or future reporting requirements. Within a fact table, only facts that are consistent with the declared grain are acceptable. For example, in a retail sales transaction, the quantity of a product sold and its extended price are good facts; however, the store manager's salary is not permissible. In addition to numeric measures, a fact table always contains foreign keys for each of its associated dimensions, as well as optional degenerate dimension keys and date/time stamps. Fact tables are the key target of calculations and dynamic aggregations arising from queries. Dimensions can be added to an existing fact table by creating new foreign key columns, presuming they do not alter the grain of the fact table. Facts consistent with the grain of an existing fact table can be added by creation of new columns.

Star Schema, Snowflake Schema, and OLAP Cube

The *star schema* and the *snowflake schema* are dimensional modeling techniques that provide a means to organize data marts or entire data warehouses using relational databases. Both the star schema and snowflake schema use *dimension tables* to describe data aggregated in a *fact table* and typically consist of fact tables linked to associated dimension tables via primary/foreign key relationships. Star schema and snowflake schema are similar at heart: a central fact table, with the dimension tables surrounding the central fact table.

Figure 2.5 shows the design of a star schema. Figure 2.6 shows a simplified star schema in a relational database for sales, which has product, time, and customer dimension tables connected to a central sales fact table. In this scenario, the *sales* fact table contains only four columns with IDs from the dimension tables, namely product, time, customer, and address, instead of eight columns for time data, 10 columns for product data, and 13 columns for customer data. Thus, the size of the fact table is significantly reduced. In addition, when you must add or modify a column, you make only a single change in the dimension table instead of making many changes in the fact table.

The dimensional tables in a star schema are not normalized. The dimensional tables in a snowflake schema are normalized. The process of normalizing dimension tables is called *snowflaking*. In other words, a snowflake schema is a star schema with fully normalized dimensions. A *hierarchy* is a set of levels having many-to-one relationships between each other, and the set of levels jointly makes up a *dimension* or a *tree*. A *tree* shows a hierarchical relationship. In a relational database, the different levels of

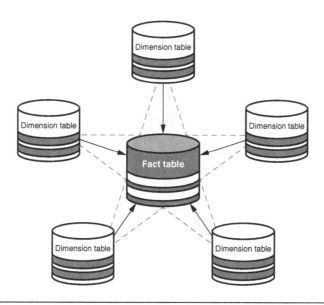

Figure 2.5　Star schema design.

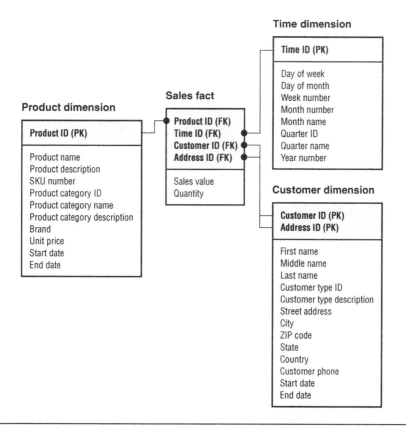

Figure 2.6　Star schema example.

a hierarchy can be stored in a single table (as in a star schema) or in separate tables (as in a snowflake schema). Snowflake schemas will use less space than a star schema to store dimension tables as normalization results in fewer redundant records. Query writing is more complex in snowflake schema than in star schema. Normalization and query complexity are the fundamental differences between star and snowflake schemas. Denormalized data models increase the likelihood of data integrity problems and also pose complications to future modifications and maintenance as well.

Figure 2.7 shows the design of a snowflake schema, and Figure 2.8 shows a snowflake schema in a relational database for sales, which has product, time, and customer dimensions that have been snowflaked into additional dimensions and a central sales fact table. The time dimension table has been snowflaked into *month* and *quarter dimension* tables. The customer dimension has been snowflaked into *address* and *customer type dimension*s. The *product dimension* has been snowflaked into *product category dimension*.

An *online analytical processing* (OLAP) *cube* is a dimensional structure used for storing multidimensional data and implemented in a multidimensional database, and

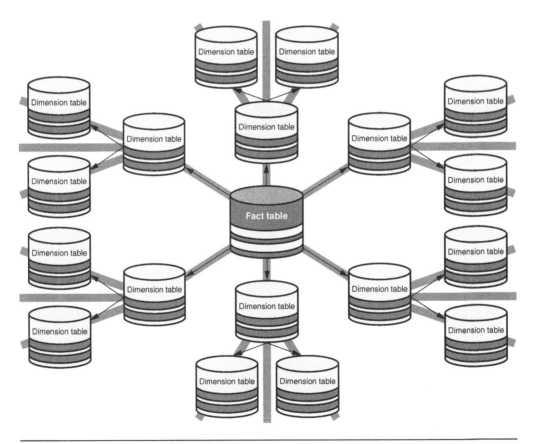

Figure 2.7   Snowflake schema design.

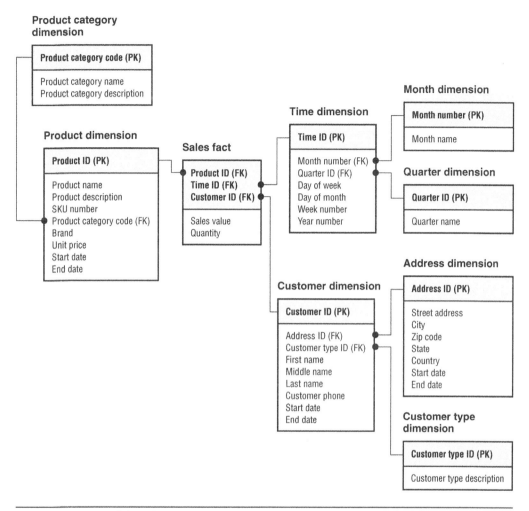

Figure 2.8   Snowflake schema example.

is optimized for advanced analytics. It can be equivalent in content to, or more often derived from, a relational star schema (Kimball Group Undated). An OLAP cube contains facts and dimensions, but it is accessed through *multidimensional expression* (MDX) languages that have more analytic capabilities than SQL, such as XMLA. An OLAP cube can have more than three dimensions, in which case it is known as a *hypercube*. An OLAP cube is often the final step in the deployment of a dimensional data warehouse system, or may exist as an aggregate structure based on a more atomic relational star schema (Kimball Group Undated).

There are two approaches to designing a data warehouse: top-down design and bottom-up design. The top-down design approach creates dimensional data marts that are specialized—sometimes, local databases for explicit groups of users—only after the creation of the complete data warehouse. In the bottom-up approach, the data marts are created first and then the data marts are combined into one all-inclusive data warehouse. The design approach an organization chooses would depend on factors like the organization's strategic business objectives, nature of the business, budget and time factors, and the extent of dependencies between various business functions or departments. Building a complete data warehouse is a costly and time-consuming venture. The top-down design approach is suitable if the organization has sufficient budget and time to invest and there are a lot of interdependencies such that the data marts cannot be built in isolation. The bottom-up approach is suitable if budget is a constraint, quick wins are desirable, and data marts for business functions and departments can be built in isolation.

Data marts are essentially specialized, sometimes local databases or custom-built data warehouse offshoots that store data related to individual business units or specific subject areas.

An enterprise data warehouse integrates data from multiple source systems, enabling a central view across the enterprise. A *source system* is a transactional system, business application, or data store that provides data to another system (Sebastian-Coleman 2013). However, the term *source system* is relative. As we discussed in Chapter 1, enterprise data are not static, and the enterprise data world comprises numerous databases linked by innumerable IT systems, applications, and real-time and batch data feeds. Starting from the point of entry, data flow continuously through various systems. A system that sources data from one system may be a source system for another downstream system. A system that receives data from one or more data sources is a *target system*. It is important to make a distinction between *originating data system* or *system of data origin*, where the data were created originally, and *immediate upstream source system* or *direct source system*, from where the target system sources data. Noting the originating data system and immediate upstream system is especially important in case of data warehouse to ensure traceability and enhance credibility since a data warehouse sources data from multiple sources and acts as a source of truth for various business units and downstream applications (for example, reporting, analytics applications, decision-making applications, and so on). Sometimes, data in the target system are directly sourced from the originating data system without any intermediate systems, in which case the originating data system is the same as the immediate upstream source system.

For the purposes of this book, a *data warehouse* is a large database that sources and integrates data from multiple disparate data sources and provides a centralized view across the entire enterprise. Figure 2.9 shows the structure of a data warehouse.

A data warehouse is populated through a sequence of steps that:

1. Extract all required data from homogeneous or heterogeneous data sources and make them accessible for further processing *(extract)*. Each data source may use different data organization or representation formats. Source data may be in relational databases, object databases, Excel, XML, COBOL copybooks (in legacy systems), and so on. Since different data sources have different data formats, the extraction process must convert the data into a format suitable for further transformation.

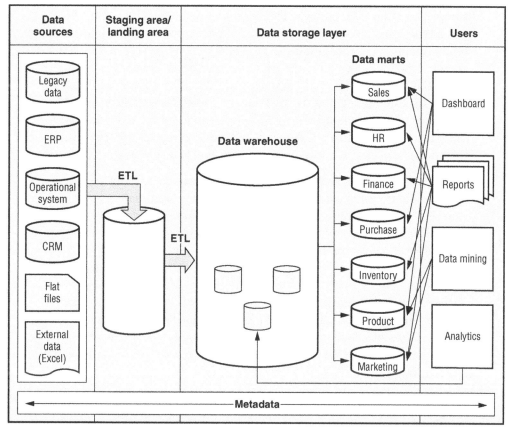

Figure 2.9   Data warehouse structure.

2. Modify the extracted data. This step involves application of a set of rules to transform the extracted data before the data are loaded into the target. This includes data format conversion, joining data from several sources, generating aggregates, sorting, deriving new calculated values, and applying advanced validation rules (*transform*).

3. Place the extracted and transformed data into the target (*load*).

This process is symbolized by the abbreviation ETL, for *extract, transform,* and *load*. A data warehouse's architecture consists of the following components:

*   *Staging area*. The staging area, or *landing zone* or *area*, is a transitional storage area used for data processing during the extract, transform, and load (ETL) process. The data staging area sits between the data source(s) and the data target(s), which are often data warehouses, data marts, or other data repositories (Oracle Corp. Undated; Wikipedia Undated "Staging (Data)"). Data staging areas are often transient in nature, with their contents being erased prior to running an ETL process or immediately following successful

completion of an ETL process. There are staging area architectures, however, that are designed to hold data for extended periods of time for archival or troubleshooting purposes (Wikipedia Undated "Staging (Data)"). Staging areas can be implemented in the form of tables in relational databases, text-based flat files (or XML files) stored in file systems, or proprietary formatted binary files stored in file systems (Ponniah 2001). Though the source systems and target systems supported by ETL processes are often relational databases, the staging areas that sit between data sources and targets need not also be relational databases (Kimball 1998; Wikipedia Undated "Staging (Data)").

- *The Data Storage Layer.* Once data have been extracted from the source systems and transformed by the ETL process, they are usually loaded and stored in one logically centralized single repository: a *data warehouse*, also known as a *primary data warehouse* or *corporate data warehouse*. The data warehouse can be directly accessed, but it can also be used as a source for creating data marts. Metadata repositories store information on sources, access procedures, data staging, users, data mart schemas, and so on. It acts as a centralized storage system for all the data being summed up (Golfarelli Undated). Though in Figure 2.9 the data storage layer shows the data warehouse and the data marts, depending on the architecture, the data storage layer can have a data warehouse, data mart, or operational data store, a combination of two of these, or all of these.

The data warehouse metadata (Kimball and Ross 2002) (also known as *metadata*) (Inmon 2005) are necessary for the interpretation of data stored in a data warehouse. The metadata describe the data model and state the ETL transformations and the data quality rules.

As seen in the data warehouse architecture, data undergo multistep processing, starting from extraction from different heterogeneous sources, storage in a transitional storage area, called a *staging area*, transformation and integration as per business rules, and loading into targets. Flaws in the design and implementation process for data warehouse staging and ETL processes can result in bad data quality.

THE DATA HIERARCHY

Data are collections of facts, such as numbers, words, measurements, observations, or descriptions of real-world objects, phenomena, or events and their attributes. Data are *qualitative* when they contain descriptive information, and *quantitative* when they contain numerical information. The data may represent real-world atomic phenomena, in which case they are *elementary data*, or may be obtained from a collection of elementary data by applying some aggregation function to them, in which case they are *aggregated data*.

At the most granular level is the *data element*, which is the most basic unit of data and the smallest named unit in the database that has meaning for the user and defined for processing. The data element represents an attribute or collection of attributes of a real-world entity. Characteristics of data elements include data type, length, and/or precision (precision usually comes into play in the case of numeric data values), formats and default values (if applicable), domain (that is, a set or a range of values) if applicable, and constraints. These characteristics, along with the description of the data element, form the metadata for the data elements, and are applicable for all instances of the data element, that is, all the values that the data element can have. Any change made to a data element affects all objects derived from that data element. In addition, any change to any attribute automatically changes the data element on which it is based, and, therefore, all other attributes derived from that data element (IBM Undated).

A *record* is a collection of related data element values, and records the occurrence of an entity. A *file* or *table* is a collection of records. Database and file systems are collections of tables and files, respectively. The data hierarchy for a database is illustrated in Figure 2.10. While databases are widely used to store data in organizations, not all data are stored in databases. Data can be stored in spreadsheets, paper files, and so on, and we use the term *data store* to refer to the broad class of storage systems including databases.

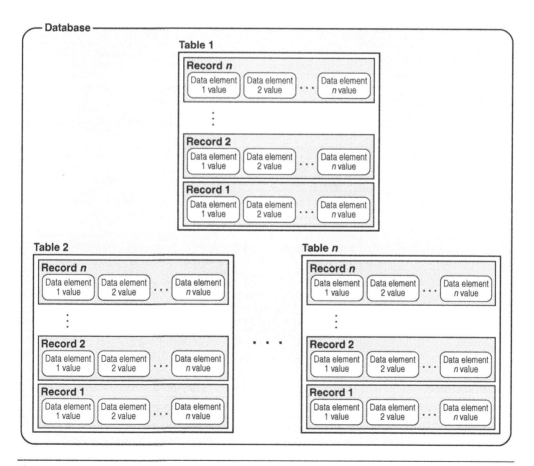

Figure 2.10   Data hierarchy in a database.

COMMON TERMINOLOGIES IN A NUTSHELL

Table 2.2 summarizes the common terminologies referred to throughout this book.

Table 2.2 Common terminologies.	
Terminology	**Description**
Entity	An object in the system that we want to model and store data about. Entities are usually familiar concepts, either tangible or intangible, such as persons, places, objects, or things, phenomena or events that have relevance to the database.
Attributes	Characteristics or features of an entity.
Data element/data field/ field/column/data item	The most basic unit of data defined for processing and measurement, which represents an attribute of a real-world entity. Technically, *data elements* describe the logical unit of data, fields are the actual storage units, and data items are the individual instances of the data elements. In practice, all three terms may be used interchangeably (PC Magazine Undated). Data fields are also referred to as *attributes*.
Domain	A set or range of allowable values for a data element or field.
Data record/tuple/record	A set of data elements or field values describing attributes of an entity in a table or file and corresponding to an occurrence of an entity in a table or file.
Relation/table/relational table	A two-dimensional structure made up of rows (tuples or records) and columns (fields) that stores data about a real-world entity, with each record uniquely identified by a primary key.
Primary key (PK)	A single column, or a set of columns that can be used to uniquely identify a record in a given relational table.
Foreign key (FK)	A single column or a set of columns from one relational table whose values must match another relational table's primary key.
Normalization	A refinement process and a systematic approach of restructuring data in a database such that there is no data redundancy and the data dependencies are logical (that is, all related data elements are stored together).
Data set	A collection of data in the form of records (rows and columns) used to accomplish a task and that can be measured. The data could have been extracted from files or tables.
Database	A structured collection of interrelated data that are organized and stored in computer systems in such a way as to facilitate efficient retrieval.
Relational database	A database in which all data are stored in relational tables.
Data warehouse	A centralized set of data collected from different sources.
Metadata	Data that describe other data by providing information like data type, length, textual description, and other characteristics of the data.

Continued

Table 2.2	*Continued.*
Terminology	**Description**
Elementary data	Data that represent real-world atomic phenomena (Batini and Scannapieco 2006).
Aggregated data	Data obtained from a collection of elementary data by applying some aggregation function to them (Batini and Scannapieco 2006).
Data model	An abstract model that organizes data elements and data objects and standardizes how they relate to one another and to properties of the real-world entities at different levels of abstraction.
Database schema/schema	A description of the structure of exactly how the data are stored and is itself stored by the DBMS for reference. It includes all implementation details, such as data types, constraints, and foreign or primary keys.
Source system	A transactional system, business application, or data store that provides data to another system (Sebastian-Coleman 2013).
Target system	A system that receives data from one or more data sources.
Data mart	Specialized, sometimes local databases or custom-built data warehouse offshoots, or a subset of a data warehouse, that store data related to individual business units or specific subject areas. While data warehouses have an enterprise-wide depth, a data mart pertains to a single business function.

SUMMARY

This chapter discussed the evolution of data from ancient times, when limited data were physically stored, to the present age, which is characterized by massive amounts of data stored digitally. As the data management encoding process moved from the highly controlled and defined linear process of transcribing information to tape to a system allowing for the random updating and transformation of data fields in a record, the need for a higher level of control over what exactly can go into a data field (including type, size, and values) became evident (DAMA International 2010). Advancements in hardware and technology have enabled storage of massive amounts of data, which has brought with it data quality issues.

The data element or data item is the basic unit of data that can be used for processing purposes; data elements build into records, which in turn build into files or tables, which in turn build into databases and data stores. Understanding of data concepts at different levels of abstraction, and how data relate to the real-world entities, data models, and metadata (that is, data about data), provides the foundation to measure, analyze, improve, maintain, and control the quality of data.

3

Data Quality Dimensions

INTRODUCTION

In Chapter 1, we discussed the importance of data quality, causes of bad data, and impacts of poor data quality. In the second chapter, the fundamental concepts related to data, their relation to real-world entities, databases, database schemas, data models, and data warehouses were discussed. Now that we have established that data quality is important and understand data at different levels of abstraction, we need to be able to define a way to manage data quality. In order to be able to assess, improve, maintain, and control the quality of data, the data quality needs to be measured. Quantification of data quality is essential for data quality management.

Data quality has been defined as fitness for use or purpose for a given context or specific task at hand. Despite the fact that fitness for use or purpose does capture the principle of quality, it is abstract, and hence it is a challenge to measure data quality using this holistic construct or definition. To be able to assess such a construct, we need to operationalize it into measurable variables (Kenett and Shmueli 2016).

When people talk about data quality, they usually relate to data accuracy only and do not consider or assess other important data quality dimensions in their quest to achieve better-quality data. Undeniably, data are normally considered of poor quality if erroneous values are associated with the real-world entity or event, such as incorrect ZIP code in an address, or wrong date of birth, incorrect title or gender for people, incorrect phone numbers or e-mail IDs in contact information, incorrect product specifications of products in a retail store, and so on. However, data quality is not one-dimensional. While accuracy is definitely an important characteristic of data quality and therefore should not be overlooked, accuracy alone does not completely characterize the quality of data. Data quality has many more attributes than the evident characteristic of data accuracy. Data quality is multidimensional as well as hierarchical, and hence is complex. There are other substantial dimensions, like completeness, consistency, currency, timeliness, and so on, that are essential to holistically illustrate the quality of data, which is a multidimensional concept. Hence, to measure data quality, one needs to measure one or more of the dimensions of data quality, depending on the context, situation, and task the data are to be used for. In short, data quality dimensions enable us to operationalize data quality. Data quality is also related to different levels of organizational data: at the lowest level are data elements, data values, or data fields; at higher levels are data records, then data sets, then database tables, in an increasing order of hierarchy, and, finally, data stores across the enterprise at the highest level of the hierarchy. With the increasing levels of data hierarchy, the quantification of data quality also becomes more complex, as shown in Figure 3.1.

The management axiom "what gets measured gets managed" (Willcocks and Lester 1996) applies to data quality, and in this light, data quality dimensions signify a fundamental management element in the data quality arena. Six Sigma, a quality control program developed in 1986 by Motorola, also stresses the use of measurements to assess and maintain quality. *Data quality* (DQ) *dimension* is a term used by information management professionals to describe an attribute/characteristic of data element(s) that can be measured or gauged against well-defined standards in order to determine, analyze, improve, and control or keep track of the quality of data. The data quality dimensions can be used to quantify the levels of data quality of data elements/fields, data records, data sets, database tables, and data stores, and can be used to identify the gaps and opportunities for data quality improvement across different systems within the organization. Data elements can relate to master data, reference data, or transactional data.

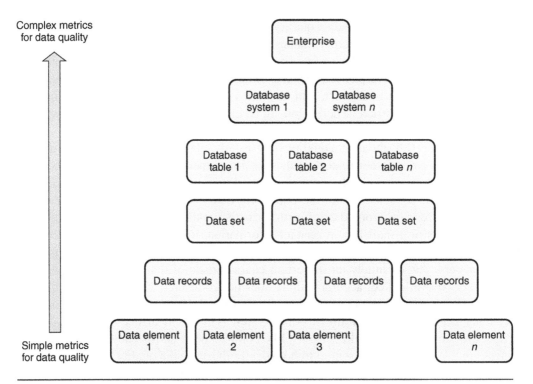

Figure 3.1 Data hierarchy and data quality metrics.
Source: Adapted from Loshin (2001), Elmasri and Navathe (2007), and Redman (1996).

Both data quality and schema quality dimensions are important. Data of low quality deeply influence the quality of business processes, while a schema of low quality, for example, an unnormalized schema in the relational model, results in potential redundancies and anomalies during the life cycle of the data usage. Data quality dimensions can be considered more relevant in real-life applications and processes than schema dimensions (Batini et al. 2009).

Each data quality dimension captures a particular measurable aspect of data quality. In other words, the dimensions represent the views, benchmarks, or measures for data quality issues that can be understood, analyzed, and resolved or minimized eventually. The more commonly used data quality dimensions include accuracy, completeness, timeliness, currency, integrity, uniqueness, and consistency, although many other dimensions have been proposed in the literature, as described in the next sections. Some of the dimensions are subjective or qualitative, while others are objective and quantitative. Also, there are relationships and overlaps among the data quality dimensions.

A DQ dimension is *different* from, and should not be confused with, other dimension terminologies, such as those used in (DAMA 2013):

- Other aspects of data management, for example, a data warehouse dimension or a data mart or data cube dimension

- Physics, where a dimension refers to the structure of space or how material objects are located in time

Measuring all the different dimensions of data quality gives a holistic picture of the health of your data. However, there will be certain situations where one or more data quality dimensions may not be pertinent, or the cost of measuring some data quality dimensions may override the benefits. When defining data quality measures, one should therefore endeavor to focus on the data quality dimensions that are meaningful and pertinent to the business and facilitate maximum return on investment.

Understanding data quality dimensions is the first step toward measuring and analyzing the current state of data quality, and defining and implementing strategies to improve and manage data quality. The ability to segregate data issues by dimensions or taxonomy, and analysis of these issues along those data quality dimensions, empowers the following:

- Enabling of analysts and developers in conjunction with the business users to define processing logic to implement improvement techniques using data quality tools to fix the data quality issues and enhance the quality of the existing data

- Unearthing possible opportunities to improve the underlying business processes, IT systems, and the various touchpoints that capture, produce, transfer, transform, and access the data

This chapter provides a literature overview of data quality dimensions and provides definitions for the common data quality dimensions, which users can choose to adopt when embarking on the journey to analyze and improve the quality of the data in their organization. Several examples have been used to explain the various concepts and characteristics, with the following intent:

- Provide context so there can be a common understanding among information technology workers, business stakeholders, and researchers

- Assist the reader to be able to relate data quality dimensions to the data elements that they are working on

DATA QUALITY DIMENSIONS—CATEGORIES

Data quality can be measured along the lines of different data quality dimensions. Data quality is an expansive, umbrella term for the different data quality dimensions of a particular piece or set of data and for how data enters and flows through the enterprise.

Different researchers have approached and categorized data quality dimensions in a different fashion. In 1996, Wand and Wang noted that there was no general agreement on data quality dimensions. Even today, the key data quality dimensions are not universally agreed on among data quality professionals. In this section, we will briefly discuss the approaches to data quality dimensions by some leading researchers: Thomas C. Redman, Larry English, Yang W. Lee, Leo L. Pipino, James D. Funk, Richard Y. Wang, Diane M. Strong, and David Loshin.

In their 1985 research article on data quality, Ballou and Pazer divided data quality into four dimensions: accuracy, completeness, timeliness, and consistency. They are of the opinion that the accuracy dimension is the easiest to gauge as it is simply a matter of analyzing the difference between the correct value and the actual value used.

In his book, *Data Quality for the Information Age* (1996), Thomas C. Redman approaches data quality dimensions from the following three perspectives:

- Data modeling

- Data value

- Data presentation

Data modeling dimensions correspond to conceptual schema or schema dimensions. Data value dimensions refer explicitly to values, independently of the internal representation of data; data presentation dimensions relate to data format. In this approach, a data item is defined in an abstract way, as a representable triple: a value, from the domain of an attribute, within an entity (Sebastian-Coleman 2013). Redman recognizes 27 individual data quality dimensions that are closely tied to an understanding of data structure. The first set of dimensions relates to the conceptual schema view or data model. Redman discusses 15 characteristics related to the data model and cuts these characteristics down to the following dimensions: content, level of detail, composition, consistency, and reaction to change. These characteristics are interconnected and reflect the choices that sometimes need to be made when developing a model.

Redman also presents eight dimensions related to data presentation. Seven dimensions relate to data formats: appropriateness, interpretability, portability, format precision, format flexibility, ability to represent null values, and efficient use of storage. The eighth, representational consistency, relates to physical instances of data being in solidarity with their formats. Redman clinches his description of dimensions with an acknowledgment that consistency of entities, values, and presentation can be understood in terms of constraints. Different types of constraints apply to different types of consistency (Sebastian-Coleman 2013; Redman 1996).

In his book, *Data Quality: The Field Guide* (2001), Redman expands this grouping of data quality dimensions to include 55 dimensions across seven categories of quality. The new categories include characteristics of the data quality environment (data accessibility, privacy, commitment, and improvement) in addition to those associated with the data model, data values, and data representation. This second formulation still provides for dimensions of quality to be associated with aspects of the data model, including a new category for architecture. However, it does not retain "quality of the conceptual view" as a separate category. The dimensions linked with the data model are entrenched in the categories of quality of content and architecture (Sebastian-Coleman 2013; Redman 2001).

In his book, *Improving Data Warehouse and Business Information Quality* (1999), Larry English classifies information quality characteristics into two broad categories:

- Information content, or inherent quality characteristics

- Information presentation, or pragmatic quality characteristics

Inherent or *static*, *quality characteristics* are quality characteristics that are inherent in the data. English presents nine inherent quality characteristics: definitional conformance, completeness of values, validity or business rule conformance, accuracy to a surrogate source, accuracy to reality, precision, non-duplication, equivalence of redundant or distributed data, and concurrency of redundant or distributed data. *Definitional conformance* is the consistency of the meaning of the actual data values with their data definition. English's recognition of the importance of data definition is similar to Redman's recognition of the importance of the model in providing data context (Sebastian-Coleman 2013).

Pragmatic quality characteristics, also known as *dynamic quality characteristics*, relate to how intuitive the data are in their presented format and how well the data support specific business processes and facilitate knowledge workers in achieving their objectives. While inherent quality characteristics are independent of the processes that use the data, pragmatic quality characteristics are associated with the human–machine interface; that is, presentation quality characteristics are applicable only to the interaction of people and data. English presents six pragmatic characteristics associated with data presentation and specific uses of data (Sebastian-Coleman 2013): accessibility, timeliness, contextual clarity, derivation integrity, usability, "rightness," or fact completeness.

In his book, *Information Quality Applied* (2009), English revisits and clarifies the earlier set of information quality characteristics. In his reformulation, he distinguishes between content characteristics and presentation characteristics (rather than inherent and pragmatic characteristics) and includes 12 additional dimensions, for a set of 27 all told (Sebastian-Coleman 2013).

In his book, *The Practitioner's Guide to Data Quality Improvement* (2010), David Loshin classifies data quality dimensions into the following three categories:

- Intrinsic

- Contextual

- Qualitative

Loshin recognizes 16 data quality dimensions across these three categories. Loshin identifies a total of 38 characteristics; 23 characteristics across the intrinsic dimensions and 15 characteristics across the contextual dimensions. The intrinsic dimensions are focused on data values and their measurement, without essentially assessing the context of those values. These dimensions describe structure, formats, meanings, and enumeration of data domains (Loshin 2010a). Loshin presents four intrinsic dimensions: accuracy, lineage, structural consistency, and semantic consistency.

Accuracy refers to the degree to which data values agree with an identified source of correct information; *lineage* measures the historical sources of data; *structural consistency* refers to the consistency in the representation of similar attribute values in the same data set and across the data sets associated with related tables, and *semantic consistency* refers to the extent to which similar data objects and attributes across the enterprise data sets share consistent names and meanings, the contextual data quality dimension (Loshin 2010a). Consistency refers to the presentation formats, presentation completeness for data elements including *null* value representations, and rules for data entry, editing, and importation.

Contextual dimensions relate to the relationship between data items. Loshin presents six contextual dimensions: completeness, timeliness, currency, consistency, reasonableness, and identifiability.

Qualitative dimensions are focused on how well the information meets defined expectations; however, these dimensions are subjective, and there is less clarity around the ability to measure these dimensions. Loshin recognizes six qualitative dimensions: authoritative sources, trust, anonymity/privacy, quality indicator, edit and imputation, standards and policies. Loshin notes that dimensions take on different levels of importance to different organizations (Loshin 2001).

Wang et al. (1995) summarize the most commonly cited data quality dimensions (Haug et al. 2011), depicted in Figure 3.2.

The dimensions used to assess data quality are grouped into four general categories (Wang and Strong 1996), as follows:

- *Intrinsic data quality.* Intrinsic data quality indicates that data have
  quality in their own right (Wang and Strong 1996). Intrinsically good data
  are accurate, correct, and objective, and come from a reputable source
  (Sebastian-Coleman 2013). Individual dimensions related to intrinsic

Accuracy	25	Flexibility	5	Sufficiency	3	Informativeness	2
Reliability	22	Precision	5	Useableness	3	Level of detail	2
Timeliness	19	Format	4	Usefulness	3	Quantitativeness	2
Relevance	16	Interpretability	4	Clarity	2	Scope	2
Completeness	15	Content	3	Comparability	2	Understandability	2
Currency	9	Efficiency	3	Conciseness	2		
Consistency	8	Importance	3	Freedom from bias	2		

Figure 3.2   Commonly cited data quality dimensions.
Source: Wang et al. (1995), Haug et al. (2011).

data quality are accuracy, objectivity, believability, and reputation. *Accuracy* means that the data need to be accurate (free from errors), and *objectivity* means that data should be without partiality, that is, data should be free from bias and judgment. While these two dimensions seem to be easy to understand, the dimensions *believability* and *reputation* are not as apparent. These dimensions are not about the data themselves, but they denote the source of the data, either the respondents or the fieldwork provider; respondents need to be real and authentic, while the fieldwork provider should be trustworthy and serious (Tress 2017).

- *Contextual data quality.* Contextual data quality alludes to the requirement that data quality must be considered within the context of the corresponding task at hand, understood largely as the extent to which data are relevant to the task of the data consumer. The focus of contextual data quality is the data consumer's task, not the context of representation itself. As the context of the task at hand can change with time and business need and regulatory requirements, to name a few, attaining high contextual data quality is not always easy. Individual dimensions related to contextual data quality are relevancy, value-added, timeliness, completeness, and amount of information. Most of the contextual data quality dimensions require thorough planning before setting up and conducting the research. In contrast, it is difficult to improve contextual data quality once it has been collected (for example, reminders to improve completeness) (Tress 2017; Sebastian-Coleman 2013).

- *Representational data quality.* Representational data quality refers to the format of the data (concise and consistent representation) and the degree to which one can derive meaning from them (interpretability and ease of understanding) (Tress 2017). The category is "based on the direct usability of data" (Fisher et al. 2011). Wang and Strong (1996) describe representational consistency as data that are continuously presented in an identical format, consistently represented and formatted, as well as compatible with data that were presented beforehand. Individual dimensions related to representational data quality are interpretability, ease of understanding, concise representation, and consistent representation.

- *Accessibility data quality.* Accessibility data quality highlights the significance of the roles and permissions required to access systems. Related dimensions are accessibility and access security. *Accessibility* is the extent to which data are available or obtainable, as well as the ease with which they can be made available to the data consumer, while *access security* is about restricting and controlling access. If data cannot be accessed, a data consumer cannot assess other quality aspects of the data like accuracy, uniqueness, completeness, and so on. The system must also be protected to avoid misappropriation of data.

In other words, high-quality data should be intrinsically good, contextually appropriate for the task at hand, clearly represented (Tress 2017), and easily and securely accessible to the data consumer. *Intrinsic data quality* mainly depends on selecting the right data source, *contextual data quality* on planning the study thoroughly, *representational data quality* on collecting the data in the right way, and *accessibility data quality* on reporting the data correctly. Representational DQ and accessibility DQ emphasize the importance of the role of systems (Tress 2017).

Redman's stress on the conceptual view or data model differentiates his classification in a noteworthy manner from Wang and Strong's classification. The model provides context for understanding the data that are incorporated within it. What can be perceived as qualities intrinsic to the data must also be understood as constructs of the model (Redman 1996; Sebastian-Coleman 2013). There is an important difference between English's formulation and those of Wang and Strong and Redman: English's emphasis on a preliminary assessment of the information quality environment (data definition and standards, specifications, and information architecture) points to the idea that metadata and other explicit knowledge of data are critical to using it successfully (Sebastian-Coleman 2013).

At present there are no consistent definitions for the data quality dimensions. The different definitions for the various dimensions offered by different researchers are presented in Appendix A of this book.

DATA QUALITY DIMENSIONS

This section discusses the different data quality dimensions that can be used in an organization to gauge the quality of their data in terms of conformance to specification, fitness for use, or delivering the right data at the right time to the required stakeholders. The data quality dimensions help us relate to the different perspectives from which data quality can be approached. Figure 3.3 summarizes the various data quality dimensions.

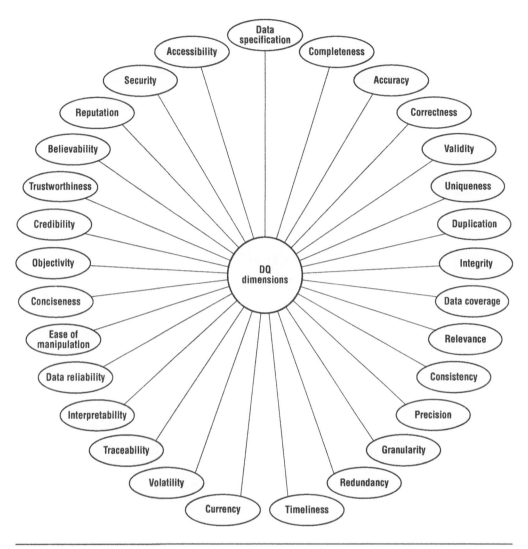

Figure 3.3   Data quality dimensions.

The schema quality dimensions *data specifications* and *granularity* have been discussed in brief. While schema quality dimensions are not properties of the data themselves, they have an impact on the structure, representation, and data type and have an impact on the quality of the data in the long run. Schema is to data as foundation is to a building; the foundation of a building has a huge bearing on the strength and quality of the building. Similarly, schema quality has a bearing on the quality of the data it is designed to hold. For instance, if you have not included a field in a table to represent an important attribute, you will not be able to capture and store values related to this attribute in the table, which in turn will render your data as incomplete.

Wherever possible, I have provided context and examples to explain the nuances related to the various data quality dimensions. Detailed instructions for measuring data quality dimensions, with examples, can be found in Chapter 4, "Measuring Data Quality Dimensions."

Data Specifications

Data specifications are a measure of the existence, completeness, quality, and documentation of data standards, data models (McGilvray 2008a), data definitions, and metadata. Data specifications are important because they provide the standard against which to compare the results of the other data quality dimensions.

A *data model* is a formal organized representation of real-world entities, focused on the definition of an object and its associated attributes and relationships between the entities. Data models should be designed consistently and coherently. They should not only meet requirements, but should also enable data consumers to better understand the data. Entity and attribute names used in the model should be clear and reflective of the entity and attributes. Class words should be used consistently, abbreviations should be kept to a minimum, all relationships should be captured correctly, and the model should be available and understandable (Sebastian-Coleman 2013; English 1999). The data model, however, is mostly concerned with the structure of the representation and not necessarily all the details associated with the values or content in that structure. Data model quality comprises the following characteristics: content, level of detail, composition, consistency, and reaction to change (Redman 1996). These characteristics are interrelated and reflect the choices that sometimes need to be made when developing a model: what to include, what to leave out, and the reasons for doing so. In terms of content, the model needs to be comprehensive and contain only required entities and attributes (Sebastian-Coleman 2013). Entities and attributes that serve no business purpose and that will never be populated or used should not be included in the model. *Level of detail* includes attribute granularity (the number and coverage of attributes used to represent a single concept) and precision of attribute domains (the level of detail in the measurement or classification scheme that defines the domain) (Sebastian-Coleman 2013). *Composition* includes characteristics of naturalness (the idea that each attribute should have a simple counterpart in the real world and that each attribute should bear on a single fact about the entity), identifiability (each entity should be distinguishable from every other entity), homogeneity, and minimum necessary redundancy (model normalization). *Model consistency* refers to both the semantic consistency of the components of the model and the structural consistency of attributes across entity types. The final dimensions of the model include *robustness* (its ability to accommodate changes without having to change basic structures) and *flexibility* (the capacity to change to accommodate new demands) (Sebastian-Coleman 2013).

Data definition quality is the extent to which the data definition accurately describes the meaning of the real-world entity type or fact type the data represent and meets the need of all information users to understand the data they use (English 1999).

Data standards govern the definition of data to enable consistent and quality information definition. *Data standards quality* measures the degree to which data are defined consistently, accurately, clearly, and understandably (English 1999).

Metadata are often called data about data (National Information Standards Organization 2007), such as type of asset, author, date created, usage, and file size. Metadata is structured information that describes, traces, or otherwise makes it easier to retrieve, use, or manage an information resource. *Metadata quality* is the extent to which metadata are informative, include a clear statement of the conditions and terms of use, use content standards, and perform the core bibliographic functions of discovery, use, provenance, currency, authenticity, and administration (National Information Standards Organization 2007; Park 2009).

Completeness

Completeness is the most basic dimension in the family of data quality dimensions. *Completeness* is the measure of whether data are present or absent. In a relational database "data present" equates to non-blank values in a data field in a table; "data absent" implies *null* or blank values in a data field in the table. Sometimes, values such as "unknown" or "not applicable" are also used to represent missing data.

The typical questions to ask are:

- Is all the necessary information available?

- Are critical data values missing in the data records?

- Are all the data sets recorded?

- Are all mandatory data items recorded?

In some cases, missing data or information is immaterial. However, in cases where the missing data or information is crucial to a particular business process or for the task at hand, completeness becomes a matter of concern.

In order to characterize completeness, it is important to understand why the value is missing (Scannapieco et al. 2005). A value can be missing in any of the following scenarios:

- *Scenario 1.* The value exists but is not known (that is, known unknown).

- *Scenario 2.* The value does not exist at all.

- *Scenario 3.* The existence of the value is not known (Scannapieco et al. 2005), (that is, unknown unknown.)

- *Scenario 4.* The attribute is not applicable.

- *Scenario 5.* The value is only populated under specific conditions.

In the case where a value is missing because it exists but is not known, then this is definitely a case of data incompleteness. For example, if the contact telephone number is missing for an organizational customer, then it is definitely a case of missing data as the organization would definitely have a land line number. However, if the value is missing because it does not exist at all, it means that the data is not incomplete. For example, if the contact number for an individual customer is missing because he does not have one, then it does not mean incomplete or missing data. In a case where the existence of a value is not known, further investigations or root cause analysis need to be carried out to understand whether the missing value is legitimate. The trade-off between cost and benefit needs to be assessed before any such investigation is embarked upon. If the value is missing because the attribute is not applicable, this means that there is no issue in terms of completeness. In the fifth scenario, where a value is only populated under certain conditions, the data incompleteness will apply only if the conditions are satisfied and the data is missing. For example, consider a patient record having data fields for patient name, address, birth date, and expiry date. The expiry date will only be populated for patients who have passed away.

Figure 3.4 illustrates the first three scenarios. The table in Figure 3.4 stores customer contact information: customer name, customer type (individual/organization/trust), customer ID (unique number/set of characters by which one customer is distinguished from another), and telephone number. The customer type "individual" is stored using a single character "I," "organization" is stored using the character "O," and "trust" is stored using the character "T" in the customer type data field for individual, organization, and trust customers, respectively.

In Figure 3.4 we can see that out of seven records, only three of the records have telephone numbers populated. Since the first record does not have a telephone number populated because a telephone number does not exist for the customer, the data record or attribute is not incomplete. The fifth record in the data set in Figure 3.4 corresponds to PTC Private Ltd., and the associated customer type value for this customer indicates that PTC Private Ltd. is an organizational customer. Since an organizational customer would have a contact telephone number, a *null* value for telephone number for PTC Private Ltd. indicates the scenario where data exist but is not known, hence, the fifth record is incomplete. The third and fourth records correspond to individual customers,

Customer ID	Customer name	Customer type	Telephone number	
C000001234	Caroline Smith	I	NULL	◄—— Not existing
C000001235	James Word	I	+61-299666789	
C000001236	Raj Ayeppa K. Gopala	I	NULL	◄—┐ Not known if
C000001237	Tina Conlon	I	NULL	◄—┘ value exists
C000001238	PTC Private Limited	O	NULL	◄—— Exists but value not known
C000001239	SBT Trust	T	+61-299663158	
C000001240	Rita Summer Darcy	I	+61-299666765	

Figure 3.4 Customer contact data set completeness.

and the existence of a value is not known, hence, data completeness cannot be confirmed without further analysis.

When missing data are due to nonavailability of information, this does not represent a lack of completeness. For example, if the data from the various source systems are populated on a monthly basis on the second day of the month into the tables in the data warehouse, and the data are not present in the data warehouse on the first day of the month, this will not be classed as missing data in the data warehouse table.

For example, in a product table, all product IDs should have product names associated with them. A product ID is a unique identification code that is assigned to a particular product. No two different products can have the same product ID. A product ID should always be associated with a product name from a data completeness perspective, as a product ID by itself does not have a meaning. So if a product ID or product name is missing in a data set containing a product ID and product name combination, it means that *the value exists but is unknown.* Also, a product ID field in the table containing product information should not be blank or have *null* values. To illustrate an example of data incompleteness we use the data set having two data elements: product ID and product name as shown in Figure 3.5. Product IDs P000002 and P000004 have *null* values for product name, whereas the product name values for product IDs P000007 and P000008 are blank. Out of the eight records, all of which have product ID values, two records have *null* values for product name and two records have a blank value for the product name. Hence, four records have a missing product name value.

To illustrate another example of data incompleteness where "the value exists but is unknown," we consider the residential address data set shown in Figure 3.6. Address data should typically have a unit/house/apartment number, apartment name, street number, street name, city, ZIP/postal code, state, and country for the address data to be complete. The residential address data set shown in Figure 3.6 has the following data fields:

- Address ID—a unique number/set of characters that distinguishes one address record from another address record and acts as a primary key

Product ID	Product name
P000001	Small mug
P000002	NULL
P000003	Small plate
P000004	NULL
P000005	Medium mug
P000006	Large plate
P000007	
P000008	

Blank values

Figure 3.5   Incompleteness illustrated through a data set containing product IDs and product names.

Address ID	Street address line 1	Street address line 2	City	ZIP code	State	Country
A000000001230	12024	Swallow Falls Ct.	Silver Spring	NULL	MD	USA
A000000001231	80	Waldo Avenue	Jersey City	07306	NJ	USA
A000000001232	50	Garisson Avenue	Jersey City	NULL	NJ	USA
A000000001233	12100	Sweet Clover Dr.	Silver Spring	20904	MD	United States
A000000001234	3300	Major Denton Dr	Beltsville	NULL	Maryland	United States
A000000001235	11317	Cherry Hill Road	Beltsville	NULL	Maryland	United States
A000000001236	514	S. Magnolia St.	Orlando	NULL	FL	USA
A000000001237	25	Bedford Street	New York	10014	NY	USA
A000000001238	18	Midland Rd	Edison	NULL	NJ	USA
A000000001239	306	Clinton Avenue	Plainfield	NULL	NJ	USA

Exists but value not known or unknown knowns

Figure 3.6   Residential address data set having incomplete ZIP code data.

- Street address line 1—contains the apartment number or unit number or house number or house name
- Street address line 2—contains the street number and street name
- City
- ZIP code
- State
- Country

The data set in Figure 3.6 has a total of ten US residential address records, of which seven records do not have ZIP codes. Since an address should always have a ZIP code or postal code, this is a case of "value exists but is unknown." Hence, out ten records, for only three records is the ZIP code complete.

However, missing data does not always mean that data are incomplete. For example, consider a table that stores customer information like customer name, customer type (individual/organization/trust), date of birth, customer ID, and gender (see data set in Figure 3.7). The birth date and gender values missing for a record that belongs to an organization customer type or a trust customer type is perfectly fine, as an organization or trust can have neither a date of birth nor gender associated with it. This is an example of an *inapplicable attribute*. However, both of these values have to be present for individual customers for data completeness.

The data set in Figure 3.7 has a total of seven customer records, of which five records relate to individual customers, one record relates to an organizational customer, and one

Customer ID	Customer name	Customer type	Date of birth	Gender
C000001234	Caroline Smith	I	25/12/1975	F
C000001235	James Word	I		M
C000001236	Raj Ayeppa K. Gopala	I	06/30/1989	M
C000001237	Tina Conlon	I	29/07/1970	F
C000001238	PTC Private Limited	O		
C000001239	SBT Trust	T		
C000001240	Rita Summer Darcy	I		

Applicable attribute missing value

Inapplicable attribute missing values

Applicable attributes missing values

Figure 3.7   Customer data—applicable and inapplicable attributes.

record relates to a trust customer. The second record in the table is an individual customer whose date of birth is missing. The last record in the table also relates to an individual customer. The date of birth and the gender value are missing for this customer. Since the fifth and sixth records relate to organization and trust customers, respectively, the missing values for date of birth and gender are legitimate, as these attributes are inapplicable attributes in the cases of organizations and trusts. However, the second record and last record are examples of data incompleteness.

From a measurement perspective, *completeness* is the fraction of stored data compared to the potential of "100% complete." It should be noted that the values "N/A" or "not applicable" or "null" or "unknown" may equate to data not being present and need to be investigated to determine whether data are really missing, before defining rules needed to discover "hidden blanks" within an attribute. The definition of "100% complete" depends on the population being measured, attribute applicability, special conditions, and whether the data elements are optional or mandatory.

Optional data missing is fine as far as data completeness is concerned. For example, a customer's middle name is optional, so a record can be considered complete, even if a middle name is not available.

The percentage of data missing/present can not only be measured at the data item/element level but also measured in a record, data set, or database. Pipino identified three types of completeness (Pipino et al. 2002).

- *Schema completeness* is defined as the extent to which entities and attributes are not missing from the schema (Pipino et al. 2002). This is essentially at a data model level when one is designing database tables.

- *Column completeness* is defined as the extent of values not missing in a column of a table.

- *Population completeness* amounts to evaluating missing values with respect to a reference population or data set. A reference data set must contain all values. However, reference population data values are rarely available; instead, the total number of records in the reference data set is much easier to obtain. There are also cases in which the reference population data are available, but only periodically (for example, when a census is performed) (Scannapieco et al. 2005).

Missing customer records might have a huge impact: lost opportunities, additional costs, customer dissatisfaction, and so on. For example, consider a scenario where an application sources new customer records from a text file and then populates a customer table in the database once every day at 10 p.m. Ideally, the total number of records in the table should be equal to the number of records before the application ran to populate new customer records (the table load) plus the total number of customer records in the text file. Say the customer table contained 10,000 customer records. After the daily run, the table contained 10,100 customer records. However, the text file used to load the table had 120 customer records, which means 20 customer records are missing and analysis needs to be done to fix the issue. In this case, the text file containing the 120 records is the *reference population* or *data set*. Measuring completeness at the data set level often requires a reference data set that is considered an authoritative source of data and is 100% complete.

Completeness of crucial information is extremely important, as missing data are not only a cost issue but are also a massive lost opportunity issue, and that is why this measure is very important. Let us walk through an example to understand the massive impact of incomplete/missing data elements. All of us know that address information is crucial for communication purposes, and an incomplete address is as good as not having one at all. As demonstrated through the residential address data set in Figure 3.6, the ZIP code did not have any values for 7 out of 10 records. However, without the ZIP code, mailing to customers would not be possible. If there were a total of 100,000 records, of which only 30,000 records had the ZIP codes recorded, then the ZIP code data would be 70% incomplete. If an advertising campaign were being conducted by a retail clothing store, in which booklets would be sent to addresses to attract new customers with a success rate of 1% lead to sales ratio, in the absence of ZIP codes, the booklets would only be able to be sent to 30,000 customers. If the average order value was $200 per lead, 1% of 70,000 addresses would be 700 new customers bringing in 700 × $200 worth of revenue, that is, $140,000 in sales. Capturing ZIP codes for 20,000 addresses would result in an increase in dispatch of booklets to 20,000 additional addresses. This would lead to 200 × $200 or $40,000 worth of additional sales, which is a significant increase in revenue that would be attained by population of ZIP codes. Say, as per statistics and historical data, a customer spends around $2000 in their lifetime, then the extra sales from the additional e-mails would generate 200 × $2000 or $400,000 over the lifetime of these customers. It is important to carry out a cost versus benefit analysis for capturing the missing data to confirm whether the effort will be worthwhile. For example, optional data add little business value, but their capture, population, and storage can be a costly and time-consuming endeavor; in such cases an effort to capture the missing data is not worth pursuing.

Conformity or Validity

Conformity, or *validity*, means the data comply with a set of internal or external standards or guidelines or standard data definitions, including metadata definitions. Comparison between the data items and metadata enables measuring the degree of conformity.

The questions to contemplate in this category are:

- Should data values conform to specific formats? If so, do all the values need to conform to those formats?

- Do the data match the rules or syntax of their definition, referred to as *metadata*?

- What data are not stored in a standard format?

- What data values are out of range?

Why Do We Need to Define a Format or Standard, and Why Do Data Need to Conform to Them? Sustaining conformance to explicit formats is imperative in data representation, presentation, aggregate reporting, searching, matching, and establishing key relationships. We will further explain the need for data conformity using one of the most commonly used data elements or items: "Name." For example, a person's name can be recorded in many different ways. We will use different names to show the variety of different ways that the same name can be recorded, if there are no standard definitions, as illustrated in Figure 3.8.

In the first example, that is, Name scenario 1, the person has a first name, middle name, and last name, and this name can be stored in at least six different ways. In the second example, that is, Name scenario 2, the person has only a first name and last name, and the name in this scenario can be recorded in at least four different ways. In the third example, that is, Name scenario 3, the person has a first name only and it can be recorded in two ways. In the last example, that is, Name scenario 4, the person has first name, middle name, a third name, and a last name that can be recorded in at least eight different ways. The larger the number of components in the name, the greater is the possibility of recording the name in different ways. Without predefined standards, formats, or naming conventions in place, the same person could be recorded differently in the same table more than once at different times, resulting in duplication. Since individual name information is one of the key data used to distinguish one individual from another, this could lead to duplicate records stored in the tables, resulting in repeated contact, double mailing, and so on, all of which would cost an organization both time and money. Establishing firm standards reduces the risk of duplicating the same information.

For example, individuals/people's names should be stored using the formatting conventions shown in Figure 3.9. To elaborate the definition/format rules illustrated in Figure 3.9, if a person's full name consists of a first name, middle name, and last name, or less, all characters of the name should be recorded instead of initials only. The words in the name should be separated by a single blank. However, if a person's full name has

Name scenario 1: Different representations of the name—"Rita Summer Darcy"

Rita Summer Darcy

Rita S. Darcy

Rita Darcy

Rita S Darcy

R. S. Darcy

R S Darcy

Name scenario 2: Different representations of the name—"Tina Conlon"

Tina Conlon

T. Conlon

T Conlon

Conlon, Tina

Name scenario 3: Different representations of the name—"Cardin" being the first name

Cardin

Cardin LNU

Name scenario 4: Different representations of the name—"Raj Ayeppa Kandarpa Gopala"

Raj Ayeppa Kandarpa Gopala

Raj Gopala

R. A. K. Gopala

Raj A. K. Gopala

Raj A. Gopala

Raj Ayeppa K. Gopala

Raj Ayeppa Gopala

R. Gopala

Figure 3.8 Different representations of an individual's name.

- If no Last Name is present, "LNU" should be used in place of the last name.
- If no First Name is present, "FNU" should be used in place of the first name.
- If there are no additional names between the First Name and Last Name, then the name should be recorded as follows:

  <First Name> <1 space> <Last Name>
- If the name has a First Name, Middle Name, and Last Name, then the name should be recorded as follows:

  <First Name> <1 space> <Middle Name> <1 space> <Last Name>
- If the name has more words than the First Name, Middle Name, and Last Name, then the name should be recorded as:

  <First Name> <1 space> <Second Name> <1 space> <Third Name Initials> <.> <1 space> <Fourth Name Initials> <.> <1 space> <Fifth Name Initials> <.> <1 space> . . . <1 space> <Last Name>

Figure 3.9 Name format.

more words than first name, middle name, and last name, the first name, the second name in the full name, and the last name should be displayed in full, but the names in between the second and last name would have the initials followed by a dot character. For example, the full name "Raj Ayeppa Kandarpa Gopala" would be stored in the database table as "Raj Ayeppa K. Gopala." "Rita Summer Darcy" would be stored as "Rita Summer Darcy." "Tina Conlon" would be recorded as "Tina Conlon," and "Cardin" would be recorded as "Cardin LNU."

Examples where data may need to conform to formats are:

- For designations, an organization may have an internal list of titles to use, and the data must conform to one of these values.

- Formats could also apply to department names, product names, and so on.

- For external conformity, addresses and industry codes are good examples. For example, in the United Kingdom, all addresses may need to be matched to Royal Mail's Postal Address File. For industry codes, data conformity may require organizations to follow the standard industry SIC codes and their descriptions.

- In other cases, the data might need to comply with standard data definitions defined by the organization or accepted worldwide.

Some standard data definitions involve the following parameters:

- *Data type.* This indicates the type of the element, for example, integer, whole numbers, Boolean value, character, string, date, and so on. For example:

  - The "Y" or "N" flag data element is a single-character field.

  - Customer names are strings.

  - Date of birth is a date field.

  - Order quantity is an integer.

- *Size.* This refers to the length of the data element. For example:

  - The length of a "Y" or "N" flag data field is 1.

- *Format.* This alludes to specific patterns in the data. For example:

  - An e-mail ID needs to have an "@" character followed by the domain.

  - Date values are usually represented in one of the following formats:

    - mm/dd/yyyy

    - dd/mm/yyyy

    - yyyy/mm/dd

    - yyyy/dd/mm

For a particular database system, a decision needs to be made on the format; for example, the date needs to be stored in the agreed on format across all date fields, in all records in all tables, in the database systems.

Generally, a set format is usually defined for identification codes such as customer IDs, department IDs, job codes, designation codes, account IDs, employee IDs, and so on, and data need to abide by the predefined formatting rules.

Say, for an employee table that stores employee information, the following list illustrates the data definition standards for one of the data elements/data fields: *employee ID:*

1. The employee ID should be a string field.

2. The employee ID needs to start with the letter "E" followed by eight digits.

3. The length of the employee ID should be nine characters.

4. The field should not have leading or trailing spaces.

5. Except for the starting letter "E," no alphabetic or special characters are allowed.

- Line item 1 defines the data type of the data element *employee ID.*

- Line item 3 defines the size of the data element *employee ID.*

- Linc itcms 2, 4, and 5 define the format of the data element *employee ID*

Taking the above standards and guidelines into consideration, Table 3.1 shows the data values that are valid and invalid, with an explanation when the value is not valid.

- *Range.* This parameter range defines the minimum, maximum, or the possible set of allowable values that a data element can have. For example, the *interest rate* data field can be in a range of 0 to 100. The *salary* data field or *age* field cannot have a negative value. Their values are always greater

Table 3.1	Valid and invalid values for employee ID.	
Employee ID	**Valid?**	**Explanation**
"E00009102"	✓	Satisfies all the data definition standard criteria.
"E9102"	X	Does not satisfy data definition standard criteria 2 and 3.
9102	X	Does not satisfy data definition standard criteria 1, 2, and 3.
"E-9102"	X	Does not satisfy data definition standard criteria 2, 3, and 5.
"000009102"	X	Does not satisfy data definition standard criterion 2.
"9102EMP"	X	Does not satisfy data definition standard criteria 2, 3, and 5.
"E0009102 "	X	Does not satisfy data definition standard criteria 2 and 4.

than zero. *Month* can have a value of 1 to 12. A customer's gender can have either of the following values: "F" or "M."

– Female: "F"

– Male: "M"

Range is also known by the term *domain*. The domain, or range of values, is sometimes represented using the set theory notation as follows:

{M,F}

Standards/formats are defined for the customer data set attributes, namely, Customer ID, Customer Name, Customer Type, Date of Birth, and Gender in Figure 3.10. We will use the data set in Figure 3.11 to illustrate conformity.

Let us have a look at the data set in Figure 3.11 to see whether the data values stored comply with the standards set in Figure 3.10:

- All values of *Customer ID* in the data set conform to the defined format and are valid.

- Except for *SBT Trust*, which does not end with the word *Limited*, all other values for customer name are recorded as per the format.

Formats defined to ensure data conformity for customer data set attributes:.

- Customer ID should be recorded as follows:
  a. The customer ID should be a string field.
  b. The customer ID needs to start with the letter "C" followed by 9 digits.
  c. The length of the customer ID should be 10 characters.
  d. The field should not have leading or trailing spaces.
  e. Except for the starting letter "C" no alphabetic or special characters are allowed.
- Customer name should be recorded as follows:
  a. Individuals/people's names should be stored using the format defined in the Name Format conventions in Figure 3.9.
  b. Organization or trust names should be the full name and end with the word *Limited*.
- Date of birth should be recorded in the yyyy/mm/dd format.
- Gender should be recorded as a single character: "F" for female and "M" for male, respectively.
- Customer type should be recorded as a single character as follows:

Customer type	Recorded value
Individual	I
Organization	O
Trust	T

Note: Date of birth and gender only apply to individual customer types.

Figure 3.10   Standards/formats defined for the customer data set in Figure 3.11.

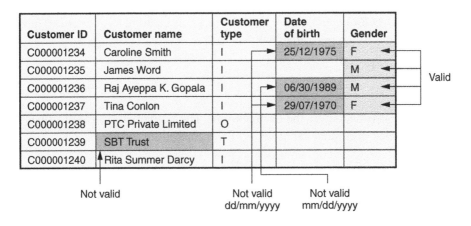

Customer ID	Customer name	Customer type	Date of birth	Gender	
C000001234	Caroline Smith	I	25/12/1975	F	
C000001235	James Word	I		M	
C000001236	Raj Ayeppa K. Gopala	I	06/30/1989	M	Valid
C000001237	Tina Conlon	I	29/07/1970	F	
C000001238	PTC Private Limited	O			
C000001239	SBT Trust	T			
C000001240	Rita Summer Darcy	I			

Not valid   Not valid   Not valid
dd/mm/yyyy   mm/dd/yyyy

Figure 3.11   Customer data set—conformity as defined in Figure 3.10.

- None of the records where *Date of Birth* is an applicable attribute have a valid date of birth. The first and fourth records in the data set shown in Figure 3.11 have a date of birth value, but recorded in the dd/mm/yyyy format. The third record has the date of birth recorded in the mm/dd/yyyy format.

- All the applicable records, that is, *individual* customer records (except for the last record, which has no value recorded for gender), have the gender value recorded as per the defined guidelines.

- The *Customer Type* data element is populated as per the defined guidelines for all the records.

Attaining the acceptable conformity is part of the data quality improvement process. Conformity against internal standards can be improved by restricting applications and systems to allow only those values that are valid to be entered, and including validation rules to check conformance to standards. To avoid errors resulting from manually keying in the data values, a dropdown list can be used to select values. For external conformity standards, using data capture software and batch software containing industry standard reference files (Actuate 2010) and using a reference table to look up values are good ways to ensure conformance to external standards.

Uniqueness

The *Uniqueness* data quality dimension is representative of the fact that there should be no duplicate records captured for the same entity or event in the same data set or table. Uniqueness is also referred to as *non-duplication*.

The questions to ask are:

- Does a data set have repetitions of the same data objects?

- Is there a solitary observation of a data record?

- Are any individual pieces of data from the data set logged more than once?

- Are there numerous unnecessary representations of the same data objects within one data set?

- What data records are replicated?

Each data record should be unique, otherwise the risk of retrieving out-of-date information increases.

For example, in the customer data set in Figure 3.12, there are seven customer records, of which three customers were registered as the following:

- Elizabeth King

- Beth King

- Eli King

All three are, in fact, the same person, but the last record has the most recent details. Now, this situation poses the risk that a customer service representative might access outdated information under Elizabeth King or Beth King and will not be able to get in touch with the customer. The inability to maintain a single representation for each entity across systems also leads to data inconsistency.

Cardinality. *Cardinality* refers to the uniqueness of the data values that are contained in a particular column (also known as a *field* or *attribute*) of a database table. Cardinality can be described at three levels: high, medium, and low (Southekal 2017):

- *High cardinality*. High cardinality means that a database table column, field, or attribute contains a large proportion of unique values. Examples of fields with high cardinality are identification codes (product identification numbers, social security numbers, tax identification numbers, passport

Customer ID	Customer name	Customer type	Date of birth	Gender	Mobile number
C000001234	Caroline Smith	I	25/12/1975	F	
C000001237	Tina Conlon	I	29/07/1970	F	
C000001250	Elizabeth King	I	30/08/1984	F	+61-450980780
C000001251	John Hudson	I	21/10/1968	M	+61-405676453
C000001252	Eli King	I	30/08/1984	F	+61-450980780
C000001253	James Song	I	10/08/1978	M	+61-478765432
C000001254	Beth King	I	30/08/1984	F	+61-478765151

Latest contact detail

Duplicate records for the same person

Figure 3.12   Customer data set—uniqueness.

numbers, employee identification numbers, company registration numbers), e-mail addresses, and phone numbers.

- *Medium cardinality.* Medium cardinality means that a database table column, field, or attribute contains some values that are repeated. Examples include postal codes, country, and state.

- *Low cardinality,* Low cardinality means that a data table column, field, or attribute contains a large proportion of duplicate values. This occurs in the case of attributes that have a very small set of possible predefined values. Low cardinality values include status flags, Boolean values, and gender (Southekal 2017). For example, gender can only be either "male" or "female."

Figure 3.13 shows an employee data set containing the following data elements:

- Employee ID, the employee identification number, which is the primary key

- Employee name

- Social security number

Since each employee ID should be associated with only one social security number, the social security number field and employee ID should have unique values in the data set. If a duplicate value is found in either of these columns, this would indicate a data quality issue and would need investigation.

In the employee data set shown in Figure 3.13 we see that the social security number "122-17-9870" has been assigned to two employees—"Jo Lee" with an employee ID of "E00000952" and "Lisa Strong" with an employee ID of "E00000956"—which is not possible, and hence this needs to be investigated. In this case, at least one of the employees, Jo Lee or Lisa Strong, has an incorrect social security number. We notice, however, that each employee has a unique employee identification number (ID), hence, employee ID is unique.

In enterprise databases or tables, all three types of cardinality—high, medium, and low—coexist. For example, in a database table that stores customer bank account information, the "account number" column will have very high cardinality, while the

Employee ID	Employee name	Social security number	
E00000952	Jo Lee	122-17-9870 ◄	
E00000953	Mark Young	155-76-5432	
E00000954	Lance Seaton	142-19-8765	Duplicate values
E00000955	Brent Morton	111-76-7890	
E00000956	Lisa Strong	122-17-9870 ◄	

Figure 3.13   Employee data set to illustrate uniqueness.

customer gender column will have low cardinality (as the column will likely only have "Male" and "Female" as values). Another example of high cardinality is the nine-digit Data Universal Numbering System (DUNS) issued by Dun & Bradstreet that uniquely identifies a business entity in the United States.

Typically, in database tables, primary key columns have high cardinality to prevent duplicate values from being entered and to be able to distinguish between records.

Duplication

The data quality dimension *uniqueness* is the inverse of the assessment of the data quality dimension *duplication*, and vice versa. In this book, we will be referring to both these terms interchangeably from a data quality dimension perspective.

Redundancy

Data redundancy is the extent to which data are replicated and captured in two different systems in different storage locations.

The question to ask is:

- Is the same data replicated and stored in more than one system?

Redundancy is a thoughtful and strategic mechanism that enterprises use for backup and recovery purposes (Southekal 2017). However, since there is a considerable cost associated with redundancy, the desire is to keep it to a minimum. The need for redundancy and the extent of redundancy are driven by the business value and criticality of the data, and the risk and cost to the enterprise if they are lost. Factors like reputation, customer dissatisfaction, and compliance, regulatory, and legal requirements—and the equivalent cost to the enterprise—also need to be taken into consideration. In cases where the business value of the data and the cost if the data are lost is much higher than the cost associated with redundancy, then redundancy is a necessity.

Redundancy versus Duplication. Redundancy should not be confused with duplication. *Duplication* occurs when the records for the same entity or event are captured more than once in the same table within one database in the same system, whereas in the case of *redundancy,* the records for the same entity or event are captured more than once in different IT systems. While redundancy is a desired and acceptable attribute, duplication is not at all acceptable and should not occur.

Consistency

Data consistency means that data values are identical for all instances of an application, and data across the enterprise should be in sync with each other. The format and presentation of data should be consistent across the whole data set relating to the data entity.

The questions to ask are:

- Is there a solitary representation of data?

- Do different data sources or multiple data environments provide contradictory information about the same underlying data object?

- What data values give contradictory information?

- Are the data stored in the same format across different data tables and systems?

- Are values uniform across all data sets and data sources?

- Do mutually dependent attributes appropriately mirror their estimated consistency?

- Is there different information about the same underlying data object in various environments?

Some examples of data inconsistency are:

- An employee status is *deceased*, *retired*, or *terminated*, but the employee's pay status is still active.

- There are sales registered for a particular month, but no orders registered in that month.

- Orders are registered against a product code that is not present in the master product list.

- Customer complaints have been registered against a customer whose customer details show that the customer status is not active.

- An account has been closed, but account statements are still being sent to the customer.

- A credit card has been closed, but the card billing status shows "due."

- The number of employees in a department exceeds the number of employees in the organization.

Data values in one data set should be consistent with the data values in other data sets. In the field of databases (Silberschatz et al. 2006) it typically means that the same data that reside in different data stores should be considered to be equivalent. Equivalency means that the data have equal value and the same meaning. This is essential for reconciling between different systems and applications. Reconciliation between different systems and applications becomes difficult in the case of data inconsistencies across different data sources. *Data synchronization* is the process of making data equal.

Within multinational organizations, identical data rarely reside in only one database or table, but are very often shared across systems and business units. When identical data are shared across sources, it is imperative to ensure that data consistency standards are met. At first, it would be easy to assume that if data are accurate across all systems, then consistency would follow as a natural consequence, but that is not necessarily the case. While data may be accurate in the individual systems, data values may still be inconsistent because of different representations or formats.

Say an organization has two databases. Let us call them DB1 and DB2. Let's look at the data sets in Figure 3.14, which shows the address data elements stored in the tables in databases DB1 and DB2.

Comparison of the data in the data sets stored in database DB1 and database DB2 reveals the following:

- Both of the data sets have the same data stored in them.

- The values in the data fields *street address line 1*, *city*, and *ZIP code* are in sync across the two the data sets.

- However, the value in the data fields *street address line 2*, *state*, and *country* are represented differently across the two data sets, and hence they are not in sync with each other; this is an instance of data inconsistency.

As per the conformity standards defined for database DB1, data fields in tables in database DB1 should be recorded as the full name. However, the conformity standards defined for database DB2 require the data elements to be recorded in the abbreviated form, where possible. Therefore, if the *state* data field has a value "New York" in tables in database DB1, the value would be recorded as "New York", while the tables in DB2 would have the value "NY" for the state data field. If we examine the data values for all the data elements in the databases in Figure 3.14, they conform to their respective defined standards. However, they are inconsistent across the databases DB1 and DB2. To ensure data consistency across databases, the data values should have the same format, in this case the full form or abbreviated form, that is, either "Maryland" or "MD," "United States of America" or "USA," "Avenue" or "Ave," "Court" or "Ct."

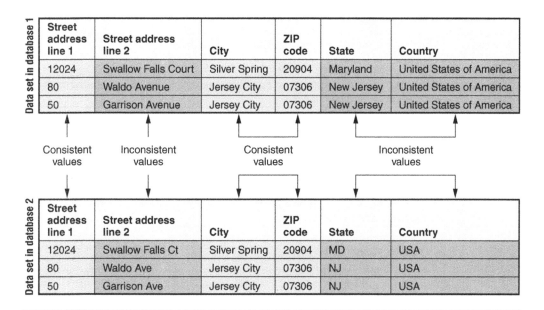

Figure 3.14 Data set in database DB1 compared to data set in database DB2.

Another common example of data consistency is the *name* field. A person's name can be recorded differently in different tables in different databases, causing data inconsistency. Earlier in this chapter, we saw various representations of a name belonging to one individual. Say an organization has four databases—DB1, DB2, DB3, and DB4—containing individual customer data as shown in Figures 3.15, 3.16, 3.17, and 3.18, respectively. The formatting guidelines for the data element *customer name* in each of the four databases are illustrated in Table 3.2.

Let us examine the data sets from databases DB1, DB2, DB3, and DB4 as shown in Figures 3.15, 3.16, 3.17, and 3.18, respectively. Comparison of the data in the data sets stored in database DB1, database DB2, database DB3, and database DB4 reveals the following:

- The data sets from the different databases have the same customer data stored in them.

- The values in the data fields *customer ID* and *customer type* are in sync across all four data sets.

- The following three values in the data field *customer name* are in sync across all four data sets:

  - Caroline Smith

  - James Word

  - Tina Conlon

Table 3.2	Individual customer name formatting guidelines for databases DB1, DB2, DB3, and DB4.
Database	**Individual customer name formatting guidelines**
DB1	\<First Name> \<1 space> \<Second Name> \<1 space> \<Last Name>
	If the full name consists of more than three names, ignore names between the second name and last name.
DB2	\<First Name> \<1 space> \<Last Name>
	If the full name contains of more names between the first name and last name, ignore them.
DB3	\<First Name> \<1 space> \<Second Name Initial> \<.> \<1 space> \<Last Name>
	If the full name consists of more than three, names ignore names between the second name and last name, with the second name replaced by the second name initial and period.
DB4	\<First Name> \<1 space> \<Second Name> \<1 space> \<Third Name Initial> \<.> \<1 space> \<Last Name>.
	If the full name consists of more than four names, ignore names between the third name and last name, with the third name replaced by the third name initial and period.

Customer ID	Customer name	Customer type
C000001234	Caroline Smith	I
C000001235	James Word	I
C000001236	Raj Ayeppa Gopala	I
C000001237	Tina Conlon	I
C000001240	Rita Summer Darcy	I

Figure 3.15   Customer name data set from database DB1.

Customer ID	Customer name	Customer type
C000001234	Caroline Smith	I
C000001235	James Word	I
C000001236	Raj Gopala	I
C000001237	Tina Conlon	I
C000001240	Rita Darcy	I

Figure 3.16   Customer name data set from database DB2.

Customer ID	Customer name	Customer type
C000001234	Caroline Smith	I
C000001235	James Word	I
C000001236	Raj A. Gopala	I
C000001237	Tina Conlon	I
C000001240	Rita S. Darcy	I

Figure 3.17   Customer name data set from database DB3.

Customer ID	Customer name	Customer type
C000001234	Caroline Smith	I
C000001235	James Word	I
C000001236	Raj Ayeppa K. Gopala	I
C000001237	Tina Conlon	I
C000001240	Rita Summer Darcy	I

Figure 3.18   Customer name data set from database DB4.

- The following value in the data field *customer name* is in sync only in databases DB1 and DB4 as shown below:

Database	Customer name value
DB1	Rita Summer Darcy
DB2	Rita Darcy
DB3	Rita S. Darcy
DB4	Rita Summer Darcy

- The following value in the data field *customer name* is represented differently in each of the four databases as shown below:

Database	Customer name value
DB1	Raj Ayeppa Gopala
DB2	Raj Gopala
DB3	Raj A. Gopala
DB4	Raj Ayeppa K. Gopala

In all the databases, the name values meet the defined conformity standards for the individual databases. However, when we compare the values across the databases, some of the name values fail to match, even though they belong to the same person. To enforce and ensure data consistency, enterprise-wide formatting rules or naming conventions should be decided on, and the values should be stored in the predefined format in all the tables and databases across the enterprise. However, there will be exceptions to the rule, and enterprise-wide definitions may not always be possible, specifically in multinational companies spread across different geographies.

Consistency may be defined in the following contexts.

Record Level Consistency. Record level consistency is consistency between one set of attribute values and another attribute set within the same record. An example illustrating inconsistency follows. A data set has the following data fields:

- First name

- Middle name

- Last name

- Full name

The value in the *full name* field should be a concatenation of *first name*, *middle name*, and *last name*, with a space or blank character separating them as shown below:

Full Name = <First Name> < 1 space> <Middle Name> <1 space> <Last Name>

If an individual does not have a middle name, then the full name should be a concatenation of the first name and last name:

Full Name = <First Name> <1 space> <Last Name>

Let us examine the name data set in Figure 3.19 to find out whether the values are consistent.

Figure 3.20 shows the *full name* field values after concatenating the *first name*, *middle name*, and *last name* data elements for each of the records from the name data set in Figure 3.19. A comparison of the *full name* field values and full name obtained after concatenation reveals the following:

- The first, fifth, and sixth records in the data set are not consistent.

- The second, third, and fourth records in the data set are consistent.

Another common inconsistency issue that we find is inconsistencies between different date data elements. Common examples are:

- Date of expiry, date of admission, procedure date, or consultation date cannot precede the date of birth for a patient in a patient's record.

Full name	First name	Middle name	Last name
Mona Lisa Ray	Mona		Ray
Isabella Justin	Isabella		Justin
Raul Arnold Clint	Raul	Arnold	Clint
Mary Sutherland	Mary		Sutherland
Rosie Marie Ford	Rosie	M.	Ford
Mina Katie Smith	Mina	K	Smith

Inconsistent values

Figure 3.19 Name data set to illustrate intra-record consistency.

Full name	Concatenation of first name, middle name, and last name
Mona Lisa Ray	Mona Ray
Isabella Justin	Isabella Justin
Raul Arnold Clint	Raul Arnold Clint
Mary Sutherland	Mary Sutherland
Rosie Marie Ford	Rosie M. Ford
Mina Katie Smith	Mina K. Smith

Figure 3.20 Full name field values and values after concatenating first name, middle name, and last name.

- In a medical insurance database, the policy start date cannot precede the date of birth of the customer. Also, the policy termination date cannot precede the date of birth or policy start date of the customer.

- In a banking database, the account closed date or account modification date cannot precede the account opening date, which in turn cannot precede the application date.

- In an employee database, the employee start date cannot exceed the employee end date, or the leave end date cannot precede the leave start date.

- In a customer complaint data set, the issue resolution date cannot be prior to the issue reported date.

- In a credit card database, the credit card start date cannot be later than the credit card expiration date.

Cross Record Consistency. *Cross record consistency* is consistency between one set of attribute values and another attribute set in different records. Cross record inconsistencies can occur between tables in the same database or different databases.

Cross record consistency increases with organizations having heterogeneous and autonomous data sources. Data sources may conflict with each other at three different levels (Anokhin 2001):

- *Schema level.* Sources are in different data models or have different schemas within the same data model.

- *Data representation level.* Data in the sources are represented in different formats or different measurement systems.

- *Data value level.* There are factual discrepancies between the sources in data values that describe the same objects.

Cross record consistency has been illustrated in the address and name consistency across data sets in different databases in the examples shown earlier.

Temporal Consistency. *Temporal consistency* is consistency between one set of attribute values and the same attribute set within the same record at different points in time.

To illustrate temporal consistency, we will examine a data set containing the data fields *full name*, *first name*, *middle name*, and *last name* at different points in time. The full name as defined earlier must be a concatenation of *first name*, *middle name*, and *last name*, with a space or blank character separating them. For example, say on January 2, 2016, the name data set contained the records shown in Figure 3.21.

If you look at Figure 3.21, all the records are consistent, with *full name* being a concatenation of *first name*, *middle name*, and *last name*, with a space/blank character separating them.

Isabella Justin got married on October 10, 2016, and her last name changed to "Cole" and full name changed to "Isabella Cole." Mary Sutherland got married on October 12,

Full name	First name	Middle name	Last name
Isabella Justin	Isabella		Justin
Raul Arnold Clint	Raul	Arnold	Clint
Mary Sutherland	Mary		Sutherland

Figure 3.21   Name data set as per January 2, 2016.

Full name	First name	Middle name	Last name
Isabella Cole	Isabella		Cole
Raul Arnold Clint	Raul	Arnold	Clint
Mary Reeds	Mary		Sutherland

Figure 3.22   Name data set as per October 15, 2016.

2016, and her last name changed to "Reeds" and full name changed to "Mary Reeds." On October 15, 2015, the data set had the information as shown in Figure 3.22.

A quick look at the data sets in Figure 3.21 and Figure 3.22 reveals that the first two records are consistent. However, if we look at the third record, we see that though the *full name* field reflects "Mary Reeds," the *last name* field contains "Sutherland," hence, this record is inconsistent.

It must be noted that consistency does not imply accuracy or correctness. Data values for different data elements may be consistent across different data sets across different databases but still be inaccurate or incorrect if they do not represent the real-world event, object, situation, or phenomenon in question correctly, or are not free from error. However, when data values are inconsistent, in most cases at least one of the values is incorrect.

Integrity

Integrity refers to the relationships between data entities or objects, the validity of data across the relationships, and ensures that all data in a database can be traced and connected to other related data.

The questions to ask are:

- What data are missing vital relationship linkages?

- Are the relationship linkages between the data sets valid linkages?

Data relationships should follow the same rules applicable to real-world entities and objects. Relationship cardinality defines the number of ways in which entities or objects can be linked to one another. There are three fundamental cardinality relationships (Duncan and Wells 1999; Adelman et al. 2005; Sebastian-Coleman 2013):

- *One-to-one.* An entity is related to another entity only once. The one-to-one relationship is applicable in both directions. Examples of a one-to-one relationship are:

  – An individual in the United States can have only one social security number, and one social security number can belong to only one person.

  – A country can have only one capital city, and the capital city can only belong to one country.

  – An employee can have only one employee identification number, and an employee identification number can belong to only one employee.

- *One-to-many.* The first entity is related to many instances of a second entity, but any instance of the second entity can only be related to one of the first entity. Examples of a one-to-many relationship are:

  – A date of birth can belong to many individuals, but an individual can have only one date of birth.

  – A ZIP code can be belong to several addresses, but an address can have only one ZIP code.

  – A joining date can apply to several employees, but an employee can have only one date of joining.

  – Each client can place several orders, but one order can be associated with only one client.

- *Many-to-many.* An entity can be related to another entity countless times in both directions. Examples of a many-to-many relationship are:

  – A teacher can teach several subjects, and a subject can be taught by many teachers.

  – A customer can buy several products, and one product can be bought be several customers.

  – A student can enroll in several course subjects, and a subject can be enrolled in by several students.

Relationship cardinality is also understood in terms of *optionality*. Two entities may have a mandatory relationship (they must be related at least once) or an optional relationship (they do not have to be related at all). There are three optionality relationships (Adelman et al. 2005):

- *One-to-one.* Each entity has a mandatory relationship with the other. If an entity exists, it must be related to a second entity. For example, an employee cannot exist without an employee identification number, and an employee identification number must be associated with an employee.

- *One-to-zero.* The first entity has a mandatory relationship with the second, but the second entity has an optional relationship with the first. For example, a customer can place zero, one, or many purchase orders, but an order cannot exist without a customer.

- *Zero-to-zero.* Two entities have a completely optional relationship. Zero-to-zero is the equivalent of two people walking down the street without knowing each other and not even looking at each other.

The failure to link interrelated records together may in effect cause duplication across different systems. As great value is derived from analyzing connectivity and relationships, the inability to link related data instances together hinders this valuable analysis.

The term *referential integrity* is used to define an explicit relationship between tables. Each table in a database must have a primary key. A *primary key* is a column or a set of columns in a table that define what constitutes a unique data record and help distinguish one row of data from another row of data in a table. In relational databases, tables often also contain foreign keys. A *foreign key* represents data in another table for which it is the primary key (Sebastian-Coleman 2013). Referential integrity asserts that for any foreign key relationship, every foreign key in table B that refers to a primary key in table A must exist in table A (SAS 2012). A foreign key in one table (called the *child table*) represents data in another table (called the *parent table*) for which it is the primary key. In other words, the primary key in the parent table is the foreign key in the child table. Records in a child table that do not have corresponding references in the parent table are called *orphan records.* On the other hand, records in a parent table that do not have corresponding references in the child table are called *childless parent records.* If all records in the child table do have references in the parent table, then referential integrity exists between the two tables. This relationship is sometimes called the *inheritance rule.* Foreign key relationships always represent an expectation about the data. It is expected that any value present in the foreign key column will be present in the table for which it is the primary key. If the value is not present in the parent table, then the expectation has not been met (Sebastian-Coleman 2013).

For example, in a customer database there should be a valid customer, customer contact details, and a relationship between them. If there is customer order relationship data without a customer, then that data is not valid, and are considered orphaned records. This is illustrated in the tables in Figure 3.23. In Figure 3.23 there are two tables: *customer* table and *order* table. The customer table has all unique customer information. The order table has information about orders placed by customers. A customer can place zero or more orders. Therefore, there is a one-to-many relationship between a customer and an order, with the customer table being the parent table. Hence, an order should be always associated with a customer already present in the customer table. Order ID is the primary key in the order table; customer ID is the primary key in the customer table, and the foreign key in the order table.

If we look at the records in the customer and order tables in Figure 3.23, we see that customer IDs "C000001241," "C000001244," and "C000001246," have placed

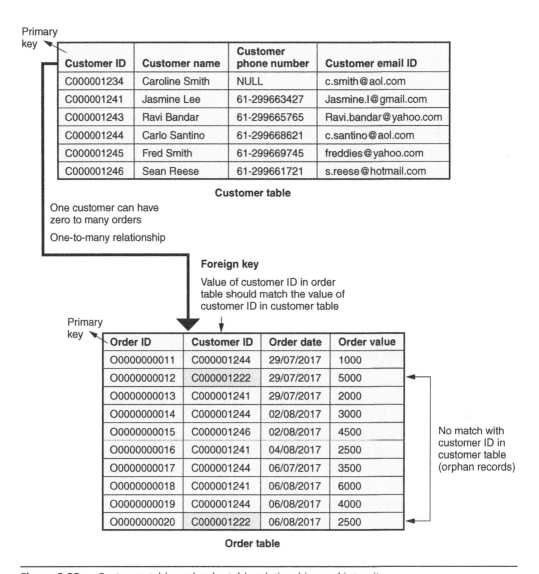

Figure 3.23   Customer table and order table relationships and integrity.

three, four, and one orders, respectively, and these customer IDs are present in the customer table. Hence, the one-to-many relationship between a customer and order is satisfied. However, the customer with customer ID "C000001222" has placed two orders identified by order IDs "O0000000012" and "O0000000020," but the customer information for customer ID is not there in the customer table, and hence a linkage is missing between the customer table and order table. The order records corresponding to "O0000000011" and "O0000000020" are orphan records. Because integrity represents the internal consistency and completeness of a data set, it encompasses these other dimensions (Sebastian-Coleman 2013).

An individual in the United States can and should have only one social security number. In other words, a particular social security number can be associated with one and only one individual. Also, a social security number cannot exist by itself without being associated with an individual. Hence, there is a *one-to-one mandatory* relationship between a social security number and an individual. If the same social security number were assigned to two different US residents, this would violate the "one-to-one" relationship between an individual and their social security number. We will use the employee data set that was used to demonstrate uniqueness of employee IDs and social security numbers to illustrate data integrity and violation of data integrity (see Figure 3.24). An employee ID should have a one-to-one mandatory relationship with a social security number. If we look at the data set records in Figure 3.24, we see that the first and fifth records belong to two different individuals with two different employee IDs but have the same social security number. In the sixth record, the employee ID "E00000957" does not have a social security number assigned. Therefore, the first, fifth, and sixth records violate data integrity. However, the second, third, and fourth records have no problems with data integrity as the one-to-one mandatory relationship is satisfied.

Examples of data integrity issues include:

- The price of a product is not in the master price list, but the product is showing as available for sale.

- A customer has ordered a product, and the order table has the order details with the customer ID, but the corresponding customer details are not present in the customer master table in the database.

- Payroll information for a particular employee is generated and is present in the payroll table, but the corresponding employee details are missing in the employee table.

- Account transactions have been captured in the account transaction table, but the corresponding account information is missing in the account table.

- A utility company has work order information for a particular asset, but the corresponding asset details are missing in the asset master table that stores details about all assets in the utility company.

Employee ID	Employee name	Social security number
E00000952	Jo Lee	122-17-9870
E00000953	Mark Young	155-76-5432
E00000954	Lance Seaton	142-19-8765
E00000955	Brent Morton	111-76-7890
E00000956	Lisa Strong	122-17-9870
E00000957	Neil Ford	

Integrity violated

Figure 3.24   Employee data set illustrating data integrity.

Accuracy

Accuracy refers to how well the data stored in a system reflect reality. It is the degree to which data correctly describe the real-world object, entity, situation, phenomenon, or event being described. It is a measure of the correctness of the content of the data (which requires an authoritative source of reference to be identified and available). Incorrect spellings of products, people, vendor names, or addresses can impact operational and analytical applications.

The questions to ask are:

- Do data objects precisely characterize the real-world values they are expected to represent and the real-life entities they model?

- How closely do the data correctly capture what they were designed to capture?

- Do the data accurately represent reality or a verifiable source?

In his book *Data Quality: The Accuracy Dimension* (2003), Jack Olson elucidated that data accuracy refers to whether data values are correct. To be correct, a data value must be both the true value and must be represented in a consistent and unambiguous form. Olsen stated form and content as the two characteristics of data accuracy.

Form. Form dictates how a data value is represented. Olson clarified that form is important because it eliminates ambiguities about the content, and he used his date of birth (December 13, 1941) as an example of how one cannot always tell the representation from the value. If a database was expecting birth dates in United States representation (that is month/day/year format, where the month is followed by the day), a value of 12/13/1941 would be correct, 12/14/1941 would be inaccurate because it's the wrong value, and 13/12/1941 would be inaccurate because it's the wrong form since it's in the European representation (that is day/month/year format, where the day is followed by the month).

For example, the date February 5, 1944, in United States representation would have the value 02/05/1944, whereas in the European representation it would have the value 05/02/1944, which could be misunderstood as May 2, 1944. Because of this ambiguity, a user would not know whether a birth date was invalid or just erroneously represented. Thus, in order for a data value to be accurate, the data should comply with a set of internal or external standards or standard data definitions. In the case of *date*, it should be established whether the date values in the system should follow the United States representation or European representation. Hence, conformity, or validity, is the related dimension of accuracy. It should be noted that if a data element is invalid, it is not accurate. Conformity does not guarantee accuracy. A data element may be valid but not accurate. However, if a data element is accurate, then it is valid too.

Content. As for content, Olson explained that two data values can be both accurate and unambiguous yet still cause issues. This is a common challenge with free-form text, such as a city name or state names. The data values for city "ST Louis" and "Saint Louis" may both refer to the same city, but the recordings are inconsistent, and thus at least one of them is inaccurate. The state names "New South Wales" and "NSW" both refer to the same state, but since the recordings are inconsistent, at least one of them is not accurate. Consistency is a part of accuracy, according to Olson, because inconsistent values cannot be correctly aggregated and compared. Since a lot of data usage comprises comparisons and aggregations at different levels, inconsistencies create an opportunity for the inaccurate usage of data.

How to Measure Accuracy. Accuracy is measured by whether the data values match with an identified source of correct information (such as reference data). There are different sources of correct information: a database of record, a similar corroborative set of data values from another table, dynamically computed values, or perhaps the result of a manual process (Loshin 2008). For example, an accuracy rule might specify that for financial institutions, the SIC code attribute must have a value that is accurate according to the industry SIC codes. If those data are available as a reference data set, an automated process can be put in place to verify the accuracy. In the absence of automation, a manual process may be instituted to determine the accuracy of the attribute. However, this is a tedious and time-consuming endeavor.

Conformity versus Accuracy. *Data conformity* means that the data value is in the set of possible accurate values, and is represented in an unambiguous and consistent way. It means that the value has the potential to be accurate. It does not mean that the value *is* accurate. To be accurate, it must also be the correct value (Olson 2003).

Defining all values that are valid for a data element is useful because it allows invalid values to be easily spotted and rejected from the database (Olson 2003). However, we often mistakenly think values are accurate because they are valid. For example, if a data element is used to store the date of birth of a person in United States representation, a value of "NSW" or "15/10/1988" is invalid. A value of "12/12/1988" would be valid but inaccurate if "12/12/1988" is not the real date of birth of the person.

Correctness

Correctness is the characteristic of the data being free of errors or mistakes. Correctness is closely related to accuracy. While you can have a degree of accuracy, with correctness, that is not the case. Correctness has a Boolean nature: a data element can either be correct or incorrect. A data element cannot be partially correct; there cannot be a degree of correctness (Southekal 2017).

To illustrate with an example, if an electronic transaction occurred at 11:30:05 a.m.:

- The recorded time "11:30 a.m." is correct as well as accurate.

- The recorded time "11:30:05 a.m." is correct but more accurate than the first recording.

- The recorded time "12:00 p.m." is neither correct nor accurate.

Another example is:

- "Eiffel Tower is located in Paris" is correct and accurate.

- "Eifel Tower is in France" is correct but is accurate to a lesser degree than the first observation.

- "Eifel Tower is in Europe" is correct but is accurate to an even lesser degree than the second observation.

- "Eifel Tower is in South Africa" is neither correct nor accurate.

Thus, we see that data that are accurate to a greater or lesser degree are certainly correct. Thus, for data to be accurate, it has to be correct. If data is not correct, then it cannot be accurate to any degree.

Granularity

Granularity refers to the extent to which the data are represented by constituent parts (Sebastian-Coleman 2013) or the degree to which data elements can be subdivided.

The questions to ask are:

- Can the data element be subdivided?

- If the data element is subdivided, will the constituent parts provide meaningful information?

For example, a customer name generally consists of a first name and a last name and sometimes a middle name too, as shown in Figure 3.25. A system that stores first name, middle name, and last name as multiple data elements or fields has a finer grain than a system that stores the first name, middle name, and last name in a single data field or data element, as shown in the example in Table 3.3.

In the example of postal address, at the coarsest level of granularity the entire postal address is stored in one data field, at the next finer level of granularity, postal address is decomposed into the different fields—*street address, city, state, ZIP code,* and *country,* and at the next finer level, in addition to the former fields, the street address is further subdivided into *unit/apartment number, street address line 1,* and *street address line 2,* as shown in Figure 3.26 and Table 3.4.

Atomic grain refers to the lowest level at which data are captured by a given business process. *High granularity* means a minute, sometimes atomic grade of detail, often at the level of the transaction. *Low granularity* zooms out into a summary view of data and transactions (HIMSS 2017). The finer the granularity of the data, the greater are the overheads in terms of data input and storage.

Data stored at a lower level generally offer a different meaning from aggregated, summarized, and manipulated collections of data at a higher level. For example, a single closing account balance across all products and brands in a bank at the end of each

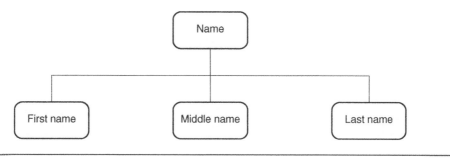

Figure 3.25   Name granularity.

Table 3.3	Coarse granularity versus fine granularity for name.
Coarse granularity	**Fine granularity**
Name = Rita Summer Darcy	First name = Rita
	Middle name = Summer
	Last name = Darcy

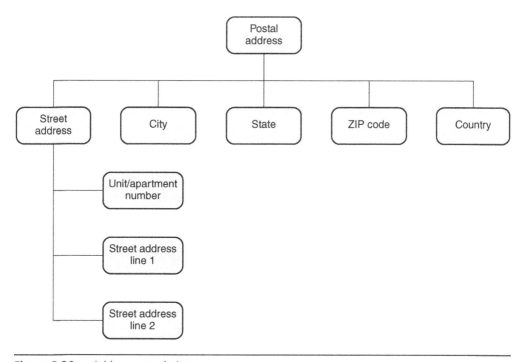

Figure 3.26   Address granularity.

Table 3.4	Postal address at different levels of granularity.
Granularity	**Postal address**
Coarse granularity	Postal address = #2, 80 Everest Avenue, Silver Spring, MD 20904, USA
Fine granularity	Street address = #2, 80 Everest Avenue
	City = Silver Spring
	State = MD
	ZIP code = 20904
	Country = USA
Finer granularity	Unit/apartment number = #2
	Street address line 1 = 80
	Street address line 2 = Everest Avenue
	City = Silver Spring
	State = MD
	ZIP Code = 20904
	Country = USA

month has the lowest level of granularity. A closing account balance by product and by brand at the end of each week has a greater level of granularity. A closing account balance by customer at the end of each week has an even greater level of granularity. A closing account balance for each account at the end of each day has the highest level of granularity, as a customer can have many accounts. Data may be required at a different level or grain depending on the audience, business needs, and reporting requirements. Having data at the lowest level of grain enables you to summarize and aggregate the data at a higher level and have different "slices and dices" of data. It also provides ease and flexibility in data assessment and processing. However, it requires considerable effort and data processing logic to grind coarse grains of data, for example address and name, into finer levels. In certain cases, like the closing account example, it is impossible to derive an account level closing balance from the aggregated account balance data.

Granularity is an important aspect, and should be given careful consideration while designing the tables in a data warehouse, especially the fact and dimension tables. An appropriate level of granularity must be defined to enable distinctive properties to become visible. Data should be stored at a granularity level fine enough to provide the maximum level of usefulness.

Precision

Precision can be defined as the resolution or degree of fineness of the measurement and thoroughness or detail of description for a data element, for example, the correct number of decimal digits to the right of the decimal point.

The question to ask is:

* Are data stored with the requisite amount of detail required by the business?

A measurement made to the nearest millimeter is certainly more precise than one made to the nearest centimeter, which in turn is more precise than one made to the nearest meter. The precision required would depend on the context of use. Precise locational data may measure a location to a fraction of a unit. Precise attribute information may stipulate the characteristics or features in great detail. However, it is important to understand that precise data, even though meticulously measured, may still be inaccurate.

In older data systems there was a limit on the number of significant digits that could be shown for floating-point values. In these systems the screen display of a value with more significant digits than the allowed limit showed either a truncated or rounded value, neither of which was a representation of the true value. If the values were too big or too small, the value would be either displayed incorrectly or not appear at all (Loshin 2001).

The level of precision and the margin for error allowed vary significantly by their applications and context of use, and should be predefined prior to data storage. The level of precision or detail mirrored in the data should be smaller than the margin of error. For some data elements for which the magnitude of expected change is large, even relatively large measurement errors may be perfectly acceptable, while for some data elements, even a slight degree of change is important, and even reasonable levels of measurement error would be deemed unacceptable. Engineering projects such as road and utility construction require extremely precise information measured to the millimeter or tenth of an inch. However, demographic analyses of marketing or electoral trends can often make do with less precision, say to the closest ZIP code or precinct boundary (Foote and Huebner 1995). Another example where the level of precision can be an issue is in environmental data, where measurement of air quality only records concentrations in parts per thousand, whereas known contaminants can cause serious illness when found in concentrations of parts per million.

We will illustrate a situation where there is a greater level of detail needed. The data set shown in Figure 3.27 contains the employee ID, employee name, and the number of years of experience, and is to be used by management to determine who would best qualify for a promotion to the one vacant position, based on their years of experience. If we look at the records in the data set in Figure 3.27, we find that all the employees have five years recorded in the experience column, and hence it is not possible to select an employee based on their years of experience. However, if the data set had a greater level of detail, as shown in the data set in Figure 3.28, then management could easily see that Brent Morton has the most experience in terms of time spent with the organization.

Precision and granularity are different concepts, but they are sometimes thought to be synonymous. Precision refers to how fine the data are in a given field or data element, or the degree of detail in the data element. Data in different systems might have the same level of granularity or be of the same grain but have different degrees of precision or detail. For example, the concept of address status might be represented in one database system (DB1) as *valid* or *invalid*, as shown in the address data set in Figure 3.29.

Employee ID	Employee name	Experience in years
E00000952	Jo Lee	5
E00000953	Mark Young	5
E00000954	Lance Seaton	5
E00000955	Brent Morton	5
E00000956	Lisa Strong	5

Lesser precision

Figure 3.27   Employee data set with *experience in years* recorded values having less precision.

Employee ID	Employee name	Experience in years
E00000952	Jo Lee	5.5
E00000953	Mark Young	5.25
E00000954	Lance Seaton	5.75
E00000955	Brent Morton	5.9
E00000956	Lisa Strong	5.1

Greater precision

Figure 3.28   Employee data set with *experience in years* recorded values having greater precision.

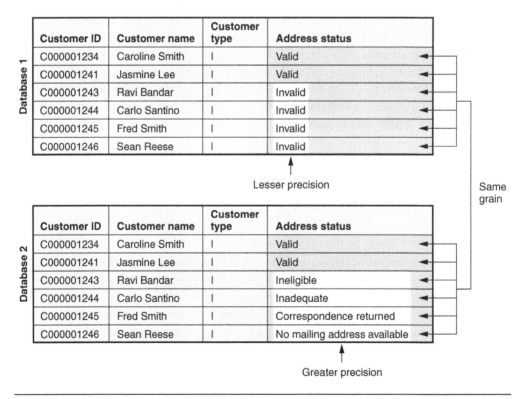

Database 1

Customer ID	Customer name	Customer type	Address status
C000001234	Caroline Smith	I	Valid
C000001241	Jasmine Lee	I	Valid
C000001243	Ravi Bandar	I	Invalid
C000001244	Carlo Santino	I	Invalid
C000001245	Fred Smith	I	Invalid
C000001246	Sean Reese	I	Invalid

Lesser precision

Same grain

Database 2

Customer ID	Customer name	Customer type	Address status
C000001234	Caroline Smith	I	Valid
C000001241	Jasmine Lee	I	Valid
C000001243	Ravi Bandar	I	Ineligible
C000001244	Carlo Santino	I	Inadequate
C000001245	Fred Smith	I	Correspondence returned
C000001246	Sean Reese	I	No mailing address available

Greater precision

Figure 3.29   Address data set in database DB1 and database DB2.

In another database system (DB2) address status includes a set of values such as *valid, ineligible, inadequate, correspondence returned, no mailing address available,* and so on, as shown in Figure 3.29. Both systems would have the same data granularity (one attribute to represent address status), but within that attribute, the set of valid values offers different degrees of precision.

Highly precise data can be extremely difficult and expensive to collect. Therefore, cost–benefit analysis needs to be undertaken prior to any data collection exercise, and the trade-offs need to be considered before embarking on a journey to ensure high precision. It must be noted that high precision does not indicate high accuracy, nor does high accuracy imply high precision.

Ease of Manipulation

Ease of manipulation can be defined as the extent to which the data are easy to manipulate for different tasks. This involves modification, concatenation, aggregation, and customization of data elements in data sets or tables, and joining with other data elements.

Conciseness

Conciseness is the extent to which data are compactly represented without being overwhelming (that is, brief in presentation, yet complete and to the point) (Wang and Strong 1996). Concise data are data that are compact and well formatted on the one hand, but also clear, self-descriptive, and complete on the other hand (Zaveri et al. 2012). Concise data are easy to understand because they do not have complicated structures and formats. Hence, conciseness can also be defined as the extent to which data have simple structures and formats.

The questions to contemplate in this category are:

- Are data concisely presented?

- Are data complete?

- Are data unambiguous and self-descriptive?

- Are the data formats and structures complicated?

Well-presented and succinct information can enhance ease of operation (Lee 2014).

Objectivity

Objectivity can be defined as the extent to which the data are unbiased, unprejudiced, and impartial (Pipino et al. 2002). Objectivity reflects the extent to which data represent reality without distortion by personal feelings, bias, ulterior motives, or prejudices. Interpretation and analysis of data, results in introduction of bias, and hence, untouched data is of higher quality. Objectivity is the extent to which the data reflect the facts without being distorted by the personal feelings or prejudices of the data provider. The applicability of the objectivity dimension is considerably influenced by the type of data and the data capturer. For instance, date of birth, gender, and product dimensions can be captured without judgment or bias. The objectivity of other types of information, like comments and descriptions, might be influenced by individuals' judgmental interpretations or preferences, either on purpose or unintentionally. The information capturer can be subjective or objective. Subjective sources include human beings. Objective information capturers such as sensors, electronic instruments, and automated processes are free of the biases inherent in human judgment, and data quality depends only on how well sensors are calibrated (Rogova and Bosse 2010). Objectivity overlaps with the concept of accuracy. There is a direct relationship between the data quality dimension of objectivity and believability. Objectivity promotes believability. As the judgment of information being biased or not is dependent on customers and reliable sources of information, it is also tightly coupled with the reputation dimension (Lee 2014).

Data Coverage

Data coverage can be defined as the extent of the availability and comprehensiveness of the data when compared to the total data universe or population of interest (McGilvray 2008a).

The questions to contemplate in this category are:

- Is the scope of the data defined?

- Do the available data support multiple business functions?

- Are known sources of data in scope documented?

The more the data coverage, the greater is the ability of the data to suit multiple applications, business processes, and functions. Reference and master data have high coverage as they are usually shared in the enterprise, while transactional data have less data coverage as they are specific to one line of business or function (Southekal 2017). Data coverage is important in analytics and decision-making systems. The key is to determine whether decisions are based on data that represent relevant representation as a whole or that are too small to be extrapolated.

Relevance

Relevance can be defined as the extent to which the data content and coverage are relevant for the purpose for which they are to be used, and the extent to which they meet the current and potential future needs.

The questions to contemplate in this category are:

- Is the data coverage relevant for the purpose?

- Do the data meet business users' needs?

- Do the data have the sufficient depth and breadth for the purpose?

To assess the relevance of the data, it is essential to understand the value contributed by the data in question; the value is characterized by the degree to which the data serve to address the purposes for which they are sought after by consumers and users. The purpose might be a need to answer a business user query, or a need for a solution to a problem, reporting requirements, and so on. For data to be relevant, they have to have the appropriate coverage. For example, in a multinational retail business, if the business need is to assess consumers' behavior based on a few parameters like age, gender, geography, occupation, and annual income in a database, but the *annual income* data element is not captured in any table in the database, and data are available only for North American consumers, then the relevance threshold is not satisfied, and this should be addressed by modifying the structure of the database and its tables to include additional fields to capture the annual income information.

Measuring relevance involves identification of the target population or the user groups and their requirements. The data in question may have multiple uses and users, and both of these may change over time. New needs may arise that require new data. Users might change jobs or move to new business units. Hence, there should be processes in place to identify users and the uses they make of the data.

Relevance is an important dimension, as if data are not relevant, their value drops significantly, even if the data are accurate, valid, precise, current, consistent, complete, and timely.

Interpretability

Interpretability can be defined as the extent to which the user can easily understand and properly use and analyze the data. It relates to the availability of adequate supplementary information, metadata, and support necessary to enable users to appropriately utilize and construe the data in hand.

The questions to contemplate in this category are:

- How easy is it to understand and interpret the data?

- Are supplementary information, metadata, and documentation available?

- Are standard terminologies and classifications used?

The appropriateness of the definitions of concepts, variables, classifications, and terminology underlying the data, and information describing the limitations of the data, if any, largely determines the degree of interpretability. Different user groups might have different levels of familiarity and understanding of the data, as well as different degrees of technical expertise. Depending on the range of the target user groups using the data, attention needs to be given to metadata (data about data) presentation in stratums of increasing detail. Definitional and procedural metadata assist in interpretability; thus, it is important that these metadata are comprehensible. Use of standard concepts, terminologies, and classifications makes it easier to interpret data.

Believability, Credibility, and Trustworthiness

Believability is defined as the extent to which the data are regarded as being trustworthy and credible by the user. Believability can be seen as expected accuracy (Naumann 2002). While *accuracy* refers to the preciseness or closeness with which data or information about the real world is captured by an information system, *believability* refers to trusting information without checking.

Credibility is defined as the extent to which the good faith of a provider of data or source of data can be relied on to ensure that the data actually represent what the data are supposed to represent, and that there is no intent to misrepresent what the data are supposed to represent (Chisholm 2014).

Trustworthiness is defined as the extent to which the data originate from trustworthy sources. Trustworthiness can be assessed on the basis of several parameters:

- *Whether or not data can traced to the source.* It is difficult to trust data from unknown sources.

- *Whether data are sourced from an authoritative source or provider with a known control environment and track record.* Data originating from an authoritative source or a provider with a known control environment and track record can be trusted more than data not originating from an authoritative source.

- *The number of complaints or data issues reported.* The greater the number of complaints or data issues, the less the data are trustworthy.

- *The number of requests for the data.* A greater number of requests for the data is indicative that the data are of high quality and can be trusted.

- *The degree to which reports on data quality statistics are published.* Missing or incomplete reports indicate underlying data quality issues, and hence data can be trusted to a lesser capacity than when reports on data quality statistics are complete.

The credibility, trustworthiness, and believability of data values, data records, or data sets is essentially the credibility and trustworthiness of the agent or provider who provided those values. The believability of data depends on their origin or data sources, and consequent processing history (updates or modifications) or lineage. One's knowledge, experience, and degree of uncertainty in the related data (Fisher et al. 2011; Samitsch 2015) and domain experience are known to have an influence on believability. Tagging the source or origin of the data as a value in a new data element indicative of the origin or source of the data helps improve believability. Agarwal and Yiliyasi (2010) consider the data quality dimension *believability* to be connected with the social media challenges of spam and freshness of information, and thereby an important dimension for organizations analyzing social media data. Believability is hence an important quality dimension for forecasts and predictive analytics, which by nature cannot be verified in advance.

Reputation

Reputation is defined as the extent to which the data are highly regarded in terms of their source or content. The reputation of a *data set* is the opinion that people have about a database or data set and its data. Happenings in the past are a determinant of how a database or data set is regarded. For example, data issues in the past can result in a low regard for the database in question, whereas high quality of data can result in high regard for the database. The reputation of data is built over time, and both data and data sources can build reputation (Wang and Strong 1996).

Time-Related Dimensions (Timeliness, Currency, and Volatility)

Things change with time, and data are not different. Time has an impact on data. *Time-related data quality dimensions* are about the time lag between an event taking place and data being captured and made available to consumers, the prospect of data elements being influenced by time, and the degree to which data represent reality at a particular point in time. The principal time-related dimensions are:

- Timeliness

- Currency, or freshness

- Volatility

The questions to ask are:

- What is the time difference between the occurrence of the real-world event or phenomena and the capture of data for the same?

- What is the time difference between the occurrence of the real-world event or phenomena and the availability of the related data to the business user?

- Are the data accessible when needed?

- Are the data appropriately up-to-date for the specific task in hand?

- How current are the data at the time of release?

- Is the data update frequency acceptable to meet the business requirements?

Timeliness refers to whether the data are available when they are expected and needed. Data should be captured as swiftly as possible after the occurrence of an event or activity and be available for the intended use as quickly as possible to support business needs and decisions. The acceptable time lag between occurrence of an event and availability of the related data depends on the context of use. For example, online availability of item stock must be instantaneously available to inventory management, but a four-hour delay could be adequate for clearing vendor invoices in the vendor invoice clearing system

(Southekal 2017). The timeliness dimension is driven by the fact that it is possible to have current data that do not serve any purpose because they are late for a specific usage (Batini et al. 2009). One way to ensure timeliness of data is to measure the time lag or gap from the request for a data element to the point where it is available for use. Recording the date and timestamp when the data record was first recorded and modified also helps in determining the timeliness of the data at the time of accessing the data.

Timeliness measurement implies that not only are data current, but they are also in time for a specific usage. Therefore, a possible measurement consists of (Scannapieco et al. 2005):

- A currency measurement

- A check of whether data are available before the planned usage time

Currency is the degree to which the data are up-to-date for the business requirement or task in question. Data currency may be measured as a function of the expected frequency rate at which different data elements are expected to be refreshed, as well as by verifying that the data are up-to-date (Loshin 2001; Loshin 2006).

Volatility measures the frequency with which data vary over time. The more volatile the data, the lesser is its currency. The relevance of the concept of currency depends on volatility (Batini et al. 2009): currency is significant for data that are highly volatile, while currency is considerably less important for data that are less volatile and is not at all relevant for nonvolatile or static data. Some data attributes such as an individual's date of birth, maiden name, gender, and place of birth are static and never change over time. These data have the lowest value in a given metric scale for volatility as they do not change at all, and are considered nonvolatile, or stable, data. Such data represent "permanent" characteristics. Nonvolatile data are not affected by time, hence, they are always current.

However, there are data elements that can change over time, which are called *time variant* or *volatile* data. The concept of currency (the degree to which data are up-to-date) is extremely critical for volatile data. Typical examples of volatile data include a customer's address, annual income, marital status, or change in surname, the age of a person, passport number, automobile license, and so on. Not all data age in a uniform fashion. Some data may age differently than others. Some data attributes, like automobile license and passport number, age naturally, while for others, change is triggered by a particular event, for example, promotion being a trigger for change in annual income, or marriage triggering a change in surname of the married woman. It must also be noted that some of these attributes change more frequently than others. For example, a short-term tourist visa validity is one year, while a long-term tourist visa validity may range from three to ten years depending on the country. On the other hand, there are time-variant data that are highly volatile. A good example of highly volatile data is stock quotes due to the fact that stock quote values remain valid for very short time intervals. Currency is more important for highly volatile data than low-volatile data, as the more volatile the data, the lesser the duration they will stay current.

Timeliness impacts accuracy. Timeliness should be a component of service-level agreements (SLAs) and identify such criteria as acceptable levels of data latency, frequency of data updates, and data availability. Timeliness can then be measured against these defined SLAs and shared as part of the data quality metrics (Couture 2016).

Accessibility

Data accessibility is the ease with which the existence of data and/or metadata (data about data) can be determined and the suitability of the form or medium through which the data can be quickly and easily accessed and retrieved. As data users are more and more removed from any personal experience with the data, metadata that contains information about the data would help users in gauging the pertinence of the data for the intended decisions.

Questions to contemplate in this category are:

- Are the data available for access and use?

- If the data are available, how can the data be accessed?

- Are the data easily accessible?

Data accessibility refers to how easy or difficult it is to locate, access, obtain, and view data within a database from the storage repository (database or file storage) in the system. In the case of data stored in tables in a relational database, accessibility is the ability of the user to query the data he needs when he needs it. Data accessibility is very important from a business perspective, especially if business stakeholders need to quickly obtain and analyze data. The ability to effectively search, retrieve, and use data at all times for business operations can be considered a key characteristic of good data quality. Technically, there are two main ways data are accessed in the IT system (Southekal 2017):

- In random access, retrieval of data happens anywhere on the disk.

- In sequential access, each segment of data has to be read sequentially until the requested data are found. Sequential files are usually faster to retrieve than random access, as they require fewer seek operations.

The accessibility of information is influenced by practical factors like time-of-day and week-dependent network congestion, worldwide distribution of servers, high concurrent usage, denial-of-service attacks, or planned maintenance interruptions (Naumann 2002).

Data accessibility alone is not sufficient, as there is little or no benefit attained if the underlying data are incomplete, or do not conform to the format, or if there are problems with other data quality dimensions. This is reinforced by the statement "Even with Forrester's insight that a 10% increase in data accessibility will result in more than $65 million in additional net income, senior executives still crave direct attribution of improved data quality to a more profitable bottom line" (Myler 2017).

Security

Data security is the extent to which access to data is restricted and regulated appropriately to prevent unauthorized access.

Questions to ask are:

- Are the data protected against unauthorized access?

- How well are data protected against unauthorized access?

- What are the measures or mechanisms used to secure data?

- Is there an adequate data security policy in place?

The more sensitive the data, the greater the measures that need to be taken to guard against unauthorized access and cyber threats such as hacking, scams, or malware. Data need to be secured while at rest (that is, while residing in data storage or a data repository) or in motion (for example, during data transfer between systems). This dimension is extremely important for financial institutions and health organizations due to privacy and safety regulations, and in the case of personally identifiable information (PII). With the General Data Protection Regulation (GDPR) coming into play in May 2018, this dimension is gaining more prominence. This is because GDPR enhances data security and breach notification standards, and applies to the handling of the personal data of all European Union (EU) data subjects: customers, employees, and prospects.

Traceability

Traceability, also known as *lineage*, is the extent to which data can be verified with respect to their origin, history, first inserted date and time, updated date and time, and audit trail by means of documented recorded identification.

The questions to ask are:

- Can the data element be traced to its source system?

- Is the source of the data recorded?

- When was the data first recorded?

- Are the data derived?

- When was the data record last modified?

Data related to their origin, history, first inserted date and time, and updated date and time should be captured in the metadata of the data elements. In the case where data travels between intermediate systems, the metadata need to capture the immediate upstream system name.

Why Is Traceability or Lineage Important? With large quantities of data coming from multiple heterogeneous sources, including external sources, the need to track data as they are consumed, transformed, and moved via the different data pipelines through a number of systems in the organization, is imperative for its effective use. In organizations, data stored in data warehouses or used in downstream systems for reporting purposes are sourced from multiple sources at different frequencies. Sometimes, the data flow through several intermediate systems before getting stored in data warehouses, and before traveling further down to data marts, downstream systems, and reports. During the travel of data through the different systems, data elements usually get transformed and consolidated.

Figure 3.30 illustrates how data are stored in different source systems and the pathways through which data travel through the organization through intermediate systems, data warehouse, data marts, downstream systems, and reports. Without the ability to trace the data to upstream systems and the originating source, it is very difficult to diagnose data quality issues. Hence, there should be data fields and metadata to facilitate tracing the data back to the system from where the data are populated. Each system should have the immediate upstream system name from where the data are sourced, and relevant date parameters; date of record creation, timestamp or date when the event occurred, date when the entity was created, and date of modification are a few examples. Good lineage helps in tracking data from the target back to the original sources.

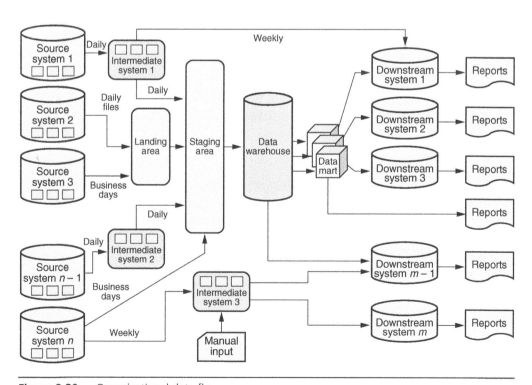

Figure 3.30 Organizational data flow.

Data Reliability

Data reliability refers to the completeness, relevance, accuracy, uniqueness, and consistency of the data set for the intended purposes of use, and the ability to trace the data to a trustworthy source. In other words, data are considered to be reliable if they are:

- *Complete.* The critical data elements in each record are populated appropriately for the intended purposes of use and are not missing.

- *Relevant.* Relevant records are present and data attributes in the data set are sufficient for the intended purposes, and no relevant data attribute is missing. For example, if the intended data are used by a multinational retail business to build their marketing strategy based on the results of consumer predictive analytics using gender, age group, occupation, annual income range, and geography, but the annual income attribute is missing in the data set, and data corresponding to North American geography are missing, then the data are not relevant for the intended purposes of use.

- *Accurate.* The critical data element values reflect the real-world entity, phenomena, or activity that they are supposed to model or represent.

- *Unique.* There is no duplication of data records or identifiers for a particular entity or event.

- *Consistent.* This refers to the need to obtain and use data that are clear and well defined enough to yield similar results in similar analyses. For example, if data are entered at multiple sites, inconsistent interpretation of data entry rules can lead to data that, taken as a whole, are unreliable (GAO 2009).

- *Timely.* The data are available for use by business users as per the agreed SLA on timeliness.

- *Traceable.* The data can be traced back to the source system.

Data do not need to be completely error free or perfect to meet the reliability benchmark. It means that any errors found are within a tolerable range, that is, the associated risks have been assessed and the errors are not significant enough to cause a reasonable person, aware of the errors, to doubt a finding, conclusion, or recommendation based on the data (GAO 2009). In other words, data reliability is the level of confidence that the business user can have in the data.

For example, for the purposes of assessing consumer behavior, the following seven age groups have been considered:

- 18–27

- 28–35

- 36–42

- 43–50

- 51–58

- 59–65

- 66+

If the date of birth has been wrongly recorded for 20% of the customer records, but they still fall into the same age group, even if the incorrect date of birth was recorded, then, for the purposes of predicting consumer behavior, the age group data values are still adequate for the purposes of use and hence considered reliable.

HOW TO USE DATA QUALITY DIMENSIONS

Use of data quality dimensions varies depending on the business requirements, the context in which the data are used, and the industry involved. Loshin (2001) notes that dimensions take on different levels of importance to different organizations. Before attempting to use data quality dimensions, an organization needs to agree on the quality threshold, definitions, standards, and business rules against which the data need to be assessed. Different data quality dimensions require different data quality rules to be created in order for a measure to be processed. These rules need to be developed based on the data quality dimensions, organizational requirements for the data, and the impact on an organization if data does not comply with these rules. Some examples of organizational impacts are as follows:

- Incorrect or missing or outdated e-mail (DAMA International 2013) and physical addresses would have a significant impact on any marketing campaigns.

- Inaccurate personal details may lead to missed sales opportunities (DAMA International 2013), wasted mailing costs, and/or a rise in customer complaints and increased customer dissatisfaction.

- Inaccurate address details can lead to products getting shipped to the wrong locations.

- Wrong product measurements can lead to significant transportation issues, for example, the product will not fit into a truck. Conversely, too many trucks may have been ordered for the size of the actual load.

- Incorrect material details can put a stop to the production process.

- Incorrect asset valuation data or information can cause financial losses.

- Inconsistent financial data or information may have a regulatory impact.

Data generally only have value when they support a business process or organizational decision making. The agreed-on data quality rules should take account of the value that data can provide to an organization, the criticality of the data, and the frequency of use of the data. If it is identified that data have a very high value in a certain context, then this may indicate that more-rigorous data quality rules are required in this context (DAMA International 2013).

While choosing the appropriate dimensions for the context of their use, the data analyst must take care to consider all the relevant dimensions of data quality that apply to the situation to ensure subsequent appropriate measurements of data quality. For example, measuring timeliness is often considered important, as is completeness of the data. By measuring both and prioritizing their importance, the organization has appropriate data quality information on which to base decisions regarding timeliness versus completeness trade-off (Ballou and Pazer 1995). Trade-offs are sometimes required, where, for example, complete data are not available in a time frame acceptable to the data user, and therefore the user could decide to use the incomplete data set. If completeness is important for the context of use, then the user would have to wait until the complete data set is available for use. Data consumers may need to decide which is more important for the context in which they use the data.

Depending on the underlying data in question, different data quality dimensions require different standards, techniques, processing logic, tools, and technologies to measure them. Thus, different amounts of time, effort, and resources may be involved in completing the assessments in relation to the different data quality dimensions. It is best to start with a dimension or set of dimensions that are most meaningful for the situation at hand and choosing the ones that fit your needs and would have the maximum return on investment (ROI). The choice of data quality dimensions also varies with business requirements, organizational impacts of bad data quality, level of risk, and industry. The trade-off between cost and benefit needs to be taken into account when choosing the set of data quality dimensions to be used for a particular data element, data set, or database table.

DATA QUALITY DIMENSIONS: THE INTERRELATIONSHIPS

Data quality dimensions are interconnected to each other, and dependencies and correlations exist between them. This section discusses some of the relationships and positive and negative correlations between the data quality dimensions. If one dimension is considered more significant than the others for a specific application, then the choice of favoring it may imply negative consequences for the other ones (Batini et al. 2009). The choice would depend on the results of a cost–benefit value evaluation.

Data completeness and data duplication/uniqueness are two of the most noticeable data quality dimensions. Issues related to either of these dimensions in the data sets become quickly and easily evident to users and can have a negative impact on the believability and reliability dimensions as users lose trust and confidence in the data repository or database that holds the related data sets.

Accessibility and security are inversely associated dimensions. As an example, time-consuming security features like authorized access permissions, login user ID, or passwords that are incorporated to restrict data access make the data more secure but make it more difficult for users to get access to information they need for making decisions. Increasing security probably decreases accessibility (Fischer et al. 2011). Accessibility is important, since, if consumers cannot access the data by any means, there is no way that they would be able to evaluate how good or bad the data are. Since unauthorized access might result in unwanted, unregulated updating, insertion, or deletion of data, which have a negative impact on completeness, correctness, accuracy, consistency, uniqueness, integrity, and believability, data security has a positive correlation with the data quality dimensions of completeness, correctness, accuracy, uniqueness, integrity, consistency, and believability.

Traceability, or lineage, has a positive impact on the believability data quality dimension. Traceability enables the users to trace the data back to their origin and provides information about data record entry and modification, and these features encourage consumers to trust the data. The data coverage dimension may possibly have a positive impact on the relevance dimension. The reputation of the data might prevent people from considering how accurate the data are (Samitsch 2015).

The more current the data, the more likely the data are accurate. So, the currency, or freshness, dimension has a positive relationship with data accuracy. On the other hand, greater volatility has an inverse relationship with currency and accuracy, as the greater the frequency at which data values change over time, the lesser is the accuracy and currency.

Having complete, valid, accurate, nonduplicate, and consistent data in the data repositories and data storage involves capturing data and ensuring that they are accurate, valid, unique, consistent, and complete. Several tasks need to be performed, including validation checks, and all these activities take considerable time. On the other hand, having timely data would result in lower quality in terms of accuracy, validity, uniqueness, consistency, and completeness. Therefore timeliness has an inverse relationship with the data quality dimensions of accuracy, validity, uniqueness, consistency, and completeness. Sometimes, a trade-off needs to be made, depending on which dimension is more important to the application or business need. Timeliness can be favored over other data quality dimensions like accuracy, completeness, or consistency in the case of most web applications because as the time constraints are often extremely rigid for web data, it is possible that such data are lacking with respect to other quality dimensions. For instance, a list of courses published on a university website must be timely, though there could be accuracy or consistency errors, and some fields specifying courses could be missing (Batini et al. 2009). On the other hand, for billing and financial processes, the accuracy, completeness, and consistency dimensions are more important compared to timeliness.

DATA QUALITY DIMENSIONS SUMMARY TABLE

The different data quality dimensions have been summarized in Table 3.5.

Table 3.5   Data quality dimensions—summary table.

Data quality dimension	Definition
Accessibility	The ease with which the existence of data can be determined and the suitability of the form or medium through which the data can be quickly and easily retrieved
Accuracy	The extent to which data is the true representation of reality, the features of the real-world entity, situation, object, phenomenon, or event, that they are intended to model
Believability	The extent to which the data are regarded as being trustworthy and credible by the user
Credibility	The extent to which the good faith of a provider of data or source of data can be relied on to ensure that the data actually represent what the data are supposed to represent, and that there is no intent to misrepresent what the data are supposed to represent (Chisholm 2014)
Trustworthiness	The extent to which the data originate from trustworthy sources
Timeliness	The time expectation for accessibility of information (Loshin 2001)
Currency	The extent to which the stored data values are sufficiently up-to-date for intent of use despite the lapse of time
Volatility	The frequency at which the data elements change over time
Correctness	The extent to which the data are free from errors
Precision	The extent to which the data elements contain sufficient level of detail
Reliability	Whether the data can be counted on to convey the right information (Wand and Wang 1996)
Consistency	The extent to which the same data are equivalent across different data tables, sources, or systems
Integrity	The extent to which data are not missing important relationship linkages (Faltin et al. 2012)
Completeness	The extent to which the applicable data (data element, records, or data set) are not absent
Conformance/validity	The extent to which data elements comply to a set of internal or external standards or guidelines or standard data definitions, including data type, size, format, and other features
Interpretability	The extent to which the user can easily understand and properly use and analyze the data
Security	The extent to which access to data is restricted and regulated appropriately to prevent unauthorized access

Continued

Table 3.5	*Continued.*
Data quality dimension	**Definition**
Conciseness	The extent to which the data are compactly represented (Pipino et al. 2002)
Reputation	The extent to which the data are highly regarded in terms of their source or content (Pipino et al. 2002)
Uniqueness	The extent to which an entity is recorded only once and there are no repetitions. *Duplication* is the inverse of uniqueness
Duplication	The extent of unwanted duplication of an entity. *Uniqueness* is the inverse of duplication
Cardinality	The uniqueness of the data values that are contained in a particular column—known as an *attribute*—of a database table
Relevance	The extent to which the data content and coverage are relevant for the purpose for which they are to be used and the extent to which they meet the current and potential future needs
Ease of manipulation	The extent to which the data are easy to manipulate for different tasks (Pipino et al. 2002)
Objectivity	The extent to which the data are unbiased, unprejudiced, and impartial (Pipino et al. 2002)
Traceability/Lineage	The extent to which data can be verified with respect to the origin, history, first inserted date and time, updated date and time, and audit trail by means of documented recorded identification
Data Specification	A measure of the existence, completeness, quality, and documentation of data standards, data models, business rules, metadata, and reference data (McGilvray 2008a)
Data coverage	The extent of the availability and comprehensiveness of the data when compared to the total data universe or population of interest (McGilvray 2008a)
Granularity	The extent to which data elements can be subdivided
Redundancy	The extent to which data are replicated and captured in two different systems in different storage locations

SUMMARY

This chapter discussed the different data quality dimensions, with examples, with an aim to provide guidance to practitioners, enabling them to isolate the set of data quality dimensions best suited for dealing with their current operational or business problem or need.

One must also keep in mind that one data quality dimension by itself is seldom able to provide the complete picture of data quality. For example, completeness of data that do not conform to standards and are not accurate, conformance of data to standards that are inaccurate, and accessibility to data that are not satisfactorily unique, complete, timely, and accurate are not worth much and will probably not serve any purpose.

Similarly, consistency of data across multiple sources that are not accurate would not be of value.

Although the list of data quality dimensions presented in this chapter is comprehensive, and some of them—such as accuracy, completeness, consistency, uniqueness, time-related dimensions, and conformity—are commonly and widely used in different industry sectors, there is no one-size-fits-all data quality dimension or combination of data quality dimensions that can be applied in all situations. Depending on context, situation, the data themselves (master data, transactional data, reference data), business need, and the industry sector, different permutations and combinations of data quality dimensions would need to be applied.

Also, there is nothing stopping you from defining your own data quality dimensions if there are characteristics and aspects of data that are important for your organization to define, measure, and manage, but not covered by the existing data quality dimensions found in the literature. There are many other aspects that may be specific to an industry (for example, conformance to industry data standards), a corporation (associated with internal information policies), or even a line of business (Loshin 2010a), or compliance rules or regulations, for that matter. Not-for-profit organizations may have different constraints and different productivity measures. Government agencies may have different kinds of collaboration and reporting oversight (Loshin 2010a). These organizations might need to define new characteristics and measures for data quality.

4

Measuring Data Quality Dimensions

MEASUREMENT OF DATA QUALITY

You cannot manage what you cannot measure! Measurement is the first phase in moving away from the world of perceptions, myths, misconceptions, assumptions, politics, and emotions and moving into the world of facts and figures. Measurement exposes the hidden truths and thus is essentially the first step toward diagnosing and fixing data quality. With data quality being so broad, and with the huge amounts of data and data elements that organizations have and continue to capture, store, and accumulate—thanks to the capabilities of digitization—measurement feels overwhelming. The myth that data need to be 100% error free makes things even more difficult. However, data do not need to be 100% error free, and though data quality is broad, the various data quality dimensions make measurement an achievable exercise. Neither do all data quality dimensions need to be measured for data, nor do all data elements need to be subject to measurement. Only those data elements that drive significant benefits should be measured for quality purposes.

In Chapter 3 we discussed in detail the various data quality dimensions and how each one contributes to the overall data quality picture. We also explored the interrelationships among the different data quality dimensions. In this chapter we will focus on how to measure each of the data quality dimensions. Measurement can be objective when it is based on quantitative metrics, or subjective when it is based on qualitative assessments by data administrators and users.

Measurement of data quality dimensions for a data set involves understanding the data set as a whole, as well as understanding the constituent data elements, the context of data use, and the characteristics of the data elements, such as size, data type, and default values. Metadata are the first input to the process of measuring and assessing data quality and include foundational information necessary to comprehend common-sense assumptions about data, thus providing a starting point for defining expectations related to data quality (Sebastian-Coleman 2013). In the absence of metadata or inadequate metadata, subject matter experts need to be consulted to get an understanding of the data. When measuring data quality dimensions, it is also imperative to contemplate the data granularity level at which they are applicable so that the measurements are practically useful. In studying data quality dimensions, we observe that some dimensions (for example, data coverage, timeliness) are applicable at higher granularity levels, such as the data set level, whereas some dimensions like completeness can be applicable at lower levels of data granularity, namely, the data element level, as well as higher levels of data granularity, such as the data record or data set levels. Further, we observe that granularity may depend on the type of the dimension.

Data quality dimensions that are related to characteristics of the data themselves—for example, completeness, accuracy, consistency, uniqueness, integrity, and validity—are primarily defined on the data element and/or data record level. In this case, measurement generally involves objectively comparing data values stored in the data set against business rules to measure the data quality dimensions. *Data profiling*, also called *data discovery* or *data auditing*, is a process for capturing statistics that help understand the data available in an organization, provide a picture of the current state of its data assets, and provide some useful characteristics of the underlying data. It provides information about the quality of the organization's data—the relative strengths and weaknesses. Data profiling is often part of a broader data quality management effort, including master data management, data migration, data integration, data warehouse implementation, or an information asset management initiative. On the other hand, the data quality dimensions that deal with the usage of data that contribute to users' judgment about the data's fitness for use—like interpretability, accessibility, and credibility—may be defined on any arbitrary abstraction of data elements, records, or data sets.

In this chapter we consider three data granularity levels when measuring data quality:

- *Data element.* An attribute of a real-world entity that can be measured.

- *Data record.* A collection of attributes (represented by data elements) that represent a real-world entity occurrence.

- *Data set.* A data set is a collection of data in the form of records (rows and columns) extracted from data files or database tables for accomplishing a task, and that can be measured.

This chapter starts with a discussion of subjective and objective data quality dimension measurement. This is followed by sections on what data to target for measurement, the role of metadata in data quality measurement, and some basic data quality statistics. This is followed by sections that elaborate the steps involved in measuring different data quality dimensions, with examples. The next sections discuss the different data profiling options: manual, spreadsheets, SQL scripts, and data profiling tools. The chapter concludes with a discussion of the pros and cons of the different data profiling options.

DATA QUALITY DIMENSIONS MEASUREMENT: SUBJECTIVE VERSUS OBJECTIVE

Subjective data quality measurements evaluate data quality from the viewpoint of data collectors, custodians, and data consumers (Pipino et al. 2002) and could adopt a comprehensive set of data quality dimensions that are defined from the perspective of the data consumers (Wang and Strong 1996). The assessment is focused on the management perspective and concentrates on whether the data are fit for use. During this process, questionnaires, interviews, and surveys can be developed and used to assess these dimensions. Objective assessments can be task-independent or task-dependent (Pipino et al. 2002). Task-independent metrics reflect states of the data without the contextual knowledge of the application, and can be applied to any data set, regardless of the tasks at hand. Task-dependent metrics, which include the organization's business rules, company and government regulations, and constraints provided by the database administrator, are developed in specific application contexts (Pipino et al. 2002). During this process, software can be applied to automatically measure data quality according to a set of data quality rules. Dimensions developed from a database perspective can be used for objective assessment (Cappiello et al. 2003).

We also classify each metric as being objectively (quantitatively) or subjectively (qualitatively) assessed. Objective metrics are those that can be quantified, or for which a concrete value can be calculated. For example, for the *completeness* dimension, the metrics such as schema completeness or attribute completeness can be quantified. On the other hand, subjective dimensions are those that cannot be quantified but depend on the users' perspective of the respective dimension and are measured indirectly via surveys. For example, metrics belonging to dimensions such as objectivity or conciseness depend strongly on the user and can only be qualitatively measured. Table 4.1 summarizes the data quality dimensions and their measurement criteria.

WHAT DATA SHOULD BE TARGETED FOR MEASUREMENT?

Typically, organizations have large amounts of data stored in different systems, and these systems have data stored in files or tables in a large number of data elements. It is not practical to measure data quality dimensions for all available data assets, data sets, and data elements due to measurement costs, time, and effort. Not all data sets and data elements stored in an organization have the same level of importance and business value. Some are more important than others. Since analyzing all the data assets is an extremely expensive and time-consuming exercise, selecting the right data sets and data elements for profiling or measurement is very important to ensure maximum benefit.

Data profiling project selection can be made based on the following:

1. *Data sets matching with business priorities.* The business stakeholders or data owners need to be queried regarding the key issues faced by the business due to poor-quality data. Short feedback surveys and analysis of customer complaint reports can reveal the key issues. The data assets relating to at least one of the key issues that the business is encountering due to data quality issues should be targeted for profiling purposes. For example, OFWAT, the Water Services Regulation Authority, has designed a service incentive mechanism (SIM) to improve the level of service that water companies provide, which is based on the number of complaints and unwanted contacts a company

Table 4.1	Data quality dimensions and measurement.	
Data quality dimension	**Measurement**	**Usage/data value**
Accessibility	Subjective	Usage
Accuracy	Objective	Data value
Believability	Subjective	Usage
Credibility	Subjective	Usage
Trustworthiness	Subjective	Usage
Timeliness	Objective	Data
Currency	Objective	Usage
Volatility	Objective	Usage
Reliability	Objective and subjective	Data value and usage
Consistency	Objective	Data value
Integrity	Objective	Data value
Completeness	Objective	Data value
Conformance/validity	Objective	Data value
Interpretability	Subjective	Usage
Security	Objective	Usage
Conciseness	Subjective	Usage
Reputation	Subjective	Usage
Uniqueness	Objective	Data value
Relevance	Objective	Data value
Ease of manipulation	Subjective	Usage
Objectivity	Subjective	Usage
Traceability/lineage	Objective and subjective	Usage
Data coverage	Objective	Data value

receives. So, one of the key business priorities in the UK water companies is assessing and improving the quality of customer complaint data (Mahanti 2015).

When analyzing the issue or defect reported, it is not sufficient to look at physical counts and percentages. It is necessary to assess the impact scope of that defect—how far will that data reach across the organization and cause issues. Depending on the impact, the defect might or might not be a business priority. For example, in the case of a missing value in a transactional-type record, the issue is likely to be localized to that transactional process. The transaction can feed into downstream systems and cause knock-on problems, and there may be an underlying defect that has affected many more transactions in the past. But in terms of issue scope, the issue is confined to that transaction (Jones 2012). However, if a defect is in the master data or reference data—for example, the supplier address is incorrect, or issuance of an incorrect customer status code—such data issues could affect thousands of transactions and have a cascading effect.

2. *Criticality of data based on business need.* The data owners/data stewards need to be questioned as to which data sources, data sets, and data elements are critical, that is, where bad data quality would adversely impact operations, regulatory reporting, or decision making, and so on. Exactly which data are critical for an organization's most important business processes depends on the industry, even the specific company (Mahanti 2015). For instance, with capital markets, reference data on customers, security, and transactions make up about 40 percent of the information used in every trade. These data typically come from numerous internal and third-party sources, are rarely updated, and are not generated as part of the transactions that a firm's operational systems are designed to handle. Yet poor-quality reference data are an enormous cost that can drag down performance in the securities industry (Bell and Davis 2006). On the other hand, for the water utilities industry sector, the quality of the asset data is critical as asset performance management essentially depends on the accuracy and correctness of the asset data (Mahanti 2015).

3. *Bottom-line financial benefits.* The underlying data should have a measurable impact on the business processes or financial bottom line. The cost of poor-quality data to the effectiveness of the most critical business processes, the cost of maintaining high-quality information for those processes, and the net benefit to the organization from maintaining data quality for those processes need to be determined before commencing data profiling. Since all data quality issues do not have the same impact on business results, trying to address all of an organization's data quality challenges can be overwhelming and inefficient (IBM Software 2012). A data profiling exercise should not be embarked upon without knowing the potential benefits to the business, or the impact. For example, if the aim is to increase sales, quality of customer data and/or product data would be a focus (Mahanti 2015).

4. *What types of projects are the data being used for?*

   - *Data conversion or migration projects.* Data conversion or migration projects involve migration of data from one data structure to another data structure, or transformed from one platform to another platform with a modified data structure. An example of a data conversion project is migrating data from a legacy data system to a relational database management system. The quality of the source data needs to be assessed before the migration or conversion starts. During the production years, source data can become corrupted in a way that is not always visible in the legacy applications. Therefore, it can be necessary to develop data profiling applications that provide insight into their data quality. Also, target data need to be profiled to check whether the conversion was successful (Mahanti 2015) and that all the data have been migrated completely and correctly.

   - *Data integration projects.* Data integration projects often fail due to poor data quality. Performing a data profiling exercise and fixing data issues before starting a data integration project will ensure smooth implementation of data integration projects. As Lee Edwards, data architect at Ford Financial Europe, explained, "It costs 100 times more to repair a problem with an actual integration interface than if the issue is identified before coding begins" (Trillium Software 2007).

* *Enterprise resource planning (ERP) and data warehouse implementations.* Industry estimates for ERP and data warehouse implementations show that these projects fail or go over budget 65% to 75% of the time (DataFlux Corporation 2003). In fact, according to a META Group survey, data quality is the number one challenge that companies are facing as they implement their data warehouses. META Group program director John Ladley estimates that when building a data warehouse, 10% to 20% of the raw data used are corrupt or incomplete in some way (Shepard 1997). In almost every instance, project failures, cost overruns, and long implementation cycles are due to the same problem—a fundamental misunderstanding about the quality, meaning, or completeness of the data that are essential to the initiative. These are problems that should be identified and corrected prior to beginning the project. And by identifying data quality issues at the front end of a data-driven project, one can drastically reduce the risk of project failure (Mahanti 2015).

  According to Kimball et al. (2008), data profiling is performed several times and with varying intensity throughout the data warehouse development process. A light profiling assessment, as opposed to a detailed profiling assessment, should be carried out as soon as candidate source systems have been identified right after the acquisition of the business requirements for the Data Warehousing/Business Intelligence (DW/BI). The purpose of a light profiling assessment is to get clarity at an early stage whether the right data are available at the right level of detail and so that anomalies can be handled subsequently without spending too much time and effort in the profiling exercise. If the right data or the right grain of the data are not available, the project might have to be canceled. More-detailed profiling is done prior to the dimensional modeling process in order to see what it will require to convert data into the dimensional model, and the profiling process extends into the ETL system design process to establish what data to extract and which filters to apply. Data profiling is also conducted during the data warehouse development process after data have been loaded into staging, the data marts, and so on. Doing so at these points in time helps assure that data cleaning and transformations have been done correctly according to requirements (Kimball et al. 2008).

* *Customer relationship management (CRM) system implementations.* A CRM system works on building more profitable relationships with

customers, and typically focuses on name and address data. According to Gartner, bad data are the number one cause of CRM system failure (Marsh 2005). Some common data quality issues are transposition of letters, comma reversal of names, duplicate customer records, outdated addresses, and missing state/county codes or postal/ZIP codes, among other errors. To ensure successful deployment of CRM systems, every CRM deployment should begin with profiling of name, address, and e-mail address data, and any other contact information needed for a strong relationship with your customer, followed by data standardization (Walker 2011). High-quality customer data are essential if enterprises are to successfully deploy and maintain increasingly integrated operational and analytical CRM systems and maintain a meaningful set of customer metrics (Mahanti 2015).

CRITICAL DATA ELEMENTS

Once data domains, data systems, and data sets have been targeted for a data quality measurement exercise, the right data elements or the critical data elements need to be identified. It should be understood that many data values are captured and stored for dubious reasons (they were part of a purchased data model, or retained from a data migration project), but they may not be necessary to achieve any business objectives. Assessing the quality of such data is a waste of time and effort (Mahanti 2015). For example, consider a data profiling exercise that involves measuring the quality of data required for the company's direct marketing campaign. The next question is what data does one need to execute a direct marketing campaign? It would essentially require customer contact data such as names, addresses, e-mail addresses, and so on. The right data source containing customer contact data and the right data elements/fields holding the customer names, addresses, and e-mail addresses should be selected. However, fields recording comments or data elements that have no business value in the customer contact data set need not be assessed (Mahanti 2015).

In this chapter we will discuss how to measure the different data quality dimensions for critical data elements. But what is a critical data element? A *critical data element* can be defined as a data element that supports critical business functions or processes or enterprise obligations and will cause customer dissatisfaction, pose a compliance risk, and/or have a direct financial impact if the data quality is not up to the mark along one or more data quality dimensions. Customer dissatisfaction and regulatory impact can have an adverse effect on finances. For example, a failure to comply with regulations may cause businesses to pay penalty charges. Disgruntled customers may take their businesses elsewhere, causing loss of revenue. In general, financial impacts may be penalty costs, lost opportunities costs, increases in expenses, or decreases in revenue and profit. Thus, the cost associated with the data element or group of data elements or data entity with respect to different data quality dimensions can be used to determine criticality. For example, inaccurate name and address data elements in most customer-centric organizations like financial services, telecommunications, utilities, or retail companies can result in huge mailing costs, hence, address data are highly critical. One way to go about understanding the critical data entities and the related data elements is by understanding the important enterprise obligations that depend on data quality and mapping the data dependencies, that is, the critical data entities and associated data elements needed to obtain information for each obligation. Data elements that are critical for one enterprise obligation may not be critical for another enterprise obligation. For example, enterprise obligations in a retail company may include sales reporting and consumer behavior trend reporting. While customer age, annual income, and occupation might be critical data elements for consumer behavior trend reporting, they are not critical data elements for sales reporting. On the other hand, there might be data elements that are critical for most enterprise obligations. Enterprise obligations might vary by industry sector or type of business. The following factors can be used to determine the criticality of data elements:

- Number of enterprise obligations that the data elements are used for

- Cost associated with the data elements

- Risks associated with the data elements

- Number of departments, teams, or users using the data

In addition to the above, certain data and information are extremely sensitive and can be classified as critical from the perspective of data security. Examples of such data and information are social security numbers, protected health information (PHI), debit card numbers, credit card numbers, security PIN numbers, passcodes, and passport numbers.

METADATA AND DATA QUALITY MEASUREMENT

Metadata are the first input to the process of measuring data quality. Data element values or records used to represent real-world entity occurrences by themselves have no meaning and are out of context, with no relation to other things. Consider the following data element value examples:

- *C000000345*. Is this value an identification number? Is it a customer identification number? Is it an employee identification number or product identification number, or is it something else?

- *APRIL*. Is "APRIL" the month of April? Is it the first name or last name of an individual? Is it a product name or a product brand, or something else entirely?

- *WINTER*. Is this the name of the season? Is it the first name or last name of an individual? Or is it the name of a retail store or a product brand, or is it something else not related to any of these options?

- *10000.* Does 10000 represent the account balance? Is it the weekly, fortnightly, monthly, or annual income of an individual? Is it the order quantity for a particular order placed by a customer, or is it the cost of the order, or is it the unit price for a product, or is it total number of units sold? Is it the monthly utility bill amount? Or does the figure represent something else that is not in any way related to any of the mentioned alternatives?

- *10/11/1989.* This clearly represents a date value, but what kind of date does it represent? There are innumerable choices: date of birth, account opening date, start date, complaint reported date, resolution date, billing date, or date when the customer placed an order, to name a few. Also, does the date 10/11/1989 represent November 10, 1989, or October 11, 1989?

For all the above, the data values do not have any context associated with them. In the absence of any description or metadata (data about data), it is not possible to determine what these data values represent, and hence it is impossible to assess their quality.

Now consider the following record, which has seven fields. However, only five of the fields have values, and two fields do not have any values. Without column names, and in the absence of any description, it is impossible to tell what the record relates to and to measure the quality of the data element values and record. There is no information that tells us about the data. In other words, there is no metadata (that is, data about data). Without metadata, data have no identifiable meaning—it is merely a collection of digits, characters, or bits.

| C000000345 | APRIL | | WINTER | 10/10/1989 | 10000 | |

Now let us add column names to the above record, as shown below.

Customer ID	First name	Middle name	Last name	Birth date	Annual income	Gender
C000000345	APRIL		WINTER	10/10/1989	10000	

While column names do give some insight into what the data values represent, they do not give the complete picture. For example, in the above example, what constitutes a valid customer ID? What date format applies to the *birth date* field? What is the set of values that represent gender?

Metadata give data meaning by providing documentation such that data can be understood, used by information professionals and business users, and more readily consumed by your organization. Ideally, metadata describe what data are intended to represent (definition of terms and business rules), how the data affect this representation (conventions of representation, including physical data definition—format, field sizes, data types, and so on—system design, and system processing), the limits of that representation (what the data do not represent), what happens to the data in systems (provenance, lineage, data chain, and information life cycle events), how data are used, and how they *can* be used (Sebastian-Coleman 2013). Standard database metadata include table names and their definitions and descriptions, and information related to columns present in the table, including primary key and foreign keys. Information about columns includes column names, column definitions and description, column sizes and data types, whether the columns can have null values or not, data formats, domain of values, and default values for columns and constraints, if applicable.

Even if the metadata do not contain explicitly formulated expectations, metadata include foundational information necessary to comprehend commonsense assumptions about data, thus providing a starting point for defining expectations related to data quality. Dimensions of data quality focus on measuring data's representational effectiveness (how well people understand what they represent), characteristics of their presentation, and their suitability for particular purposes. The better defined each of these is, the clearer the expectations about data, and therefore, the clearer the criteria for measurement (Sebastian-Coleman 2013).

DATA QUALITY: BASIC STATISTICS

By measuring some basic statistics as shown below, you can learn a fair bit about your data and data elements. This holds true for all types of data, specifically for numeric data:

- **Minimum** value of data elements, based on the ordering properties
- **Maximum** value of data elements, based on the ordering properties
- **Minimum length** for string data
- **Maximum length** for string data
- **Range**, which the is range of values between minimum and maximum values
- **Mean**, providing the average value (for numeric data)
- **Median**, providing the middle value (if applicable)
- **Standard deviation**, for numeric data element values
- **Patterns**, format patterns for a particular data element
- **Null count or percentage**, count or percentage of *null* values

Example 4.0. To illustrate basic statistics, we will use an example of a customer data set of a financial organization that contains the customer's annual income. These data are used for analysis to determine whether the customer is eligible for certain financial products. Let's take a look at some basic statistics from the annual income column in the customer database shown in Table 4.2.

The statistics captured in Table 4.2 show some potential problems with the annual income data. The minimum value for annual income is a negative number of –200, which is not a possible value, as annual income can only have

Table 4.2	Statistics for annual income column in the customer database.
Statistics	**Value**
Minimum	−200
Maximum	500000
Mean	150000
Median	212123.657
Standard deviation	391567.768
Null count	2000
Count of rows	50000
Null percentage	4%

values of zero or greater than zero. In other words, the minimum value of annual income can only be zero. There are 2000 null values, which means that the annual income is missing for 2000 customers. The standard deviation value and median value are unexpectedly large numbers. All these statistics are indicative of possible issues with the annual income data.

With these statistics we have begun the process of data discovery; however, business and data quality rules need to be defined for in-depth measurement of the different aspects of data quality.

DATA QUALITY DIMENSIONS: MEASUREMENT

This section focuses on how to measure the different data quality dimensions. When measuring data quality dimensions, it is important to understand *what you are measuring*. This includes an understanding of what the data set is used for, the definition and descriptions of the data set, the context of use, the definitions of the data elements involved that the data set is made of, how the data elements are being used, the set or range of values that a data element can hold (maximum, minimum, or set of values) if applicable, length and precision, formats, and constraints for populating the data elements, if applicable. Metadata provide a starting point to help in understanding the above. However, in the absence of metadata, or in situations where metadata are not sufficient to understand the data, subject matter experts need to be consulted.

Measuring Completeness

The data quality dimension *completeness* is a measure of whether data are present or absent. In order to measure the degree of data completeness, it is necessary to define what missing data means and what missing values equate to (for example, *null*, spaces, blanks, or hidden blanks, unknown or not applicable, and so on). Completeness can be measured at three levels:

- Data element

- Data record

- Data set

Completeness is usually measured as a percentage, and is the proportion of the stored data versus the potential of 100% complete.

Measuring Data Element Completeness. Following are the steps outlined to measure completeness at a data element level:

1. For each critical data element, determine whether the data element is a mandatory or inapplicable attribute, or an attribute that is populated only under certain conditions. Usually, optional attributes are not critical. Mandatory attributes would always have values, whereas inapplicable attributes or attributes populated only under certain conditions would have values populated only under certain business scenarios or when certain criteria or conditions are satisfied.

Determine the business scenarios or conditions under which the data elements will not be populated. For example, consider a data set that contains bank account creation transactions and has employee ID, account type, account ID, and account creation date fields. For instance, if an account is opened online, then employee ID will not be populated for these transactions. This is a valid business scenario and not a case of data incompleteness. Business subject matter experts who have knowledge about business functions or processes would be best positioned to provide information about what constitutes a valid business scenario.

2. Determine how missing values are represented in the data set. Metadata sometimes specify default values for data elements. While blanks, spaces, and *null* values equate to missing data values, sometimes certain values like Unknown, Not applicable, NA, and N/A are also equivalent to missing values. This can be evaluated by performing data analysis and finding out the number of times each value for a particular data element occurs in a data set. If a particular value has an inordinately high occurrence, further analysis needs to be conducted to understand the reason behind its high occurrence. The value may be legitimate in the case of a one-to-many relationship, or in cases of inapplicable attributes or indicative values, or when values are not populated under certain conditions. On the other hand, the value may be a manifestation of hidden blank values. Performing this exercise helps us distinguish between legitimate and illegitimate missing data values.

3. For *mandatory* attributes, the percentage of completeness can be calculated using the following formula:

Data element completeness % = ((Total number of values that should be populated for the data element − Total number of *null* values − Total number of blanks or spaces − Total number of hidden blanks) / Total number of values that should be populated for the data element) × 100

For *inapplicable* attributes, the percentage of completeness can be calculated using the following formula:

> Data element completeness % = ((Total number of data values that should be populated for the data element – Total number of invalid *null* values – Total number of invalid blank or space values – Total invalid hidden blanks) / Total number of data values that should be populated for the data element) × 100

The *Total number of data values that should be populated for the data element* in the denominator is representative of the potential for 100% completeness. The definition of 100% completeness depends on the population under measurement and whether the attributes are mandatory, optional, or inapplicable attributes, or where attributes are only populated under certain conditions. In the case of mandatory attributes, 100% completeness usually equates to the total number of records in the data set under measurement. In the case of inapplicable attributes or where attributes are populated with values only under certain conditions, business rules need to define what represents 100% completeness.

> **Example 4.1.** We will illustrate how to calculate completeness of mandatory attributes using the example of an employee data set of a US-based company. The data set contains information about employees who joined the company in January 2017. The employee data has three critical data elements: Employee ID, Employee Name, and Social Security Number, as shown in Table 4.3.
>
> There are 30 records in the data set. An employee should always have an employee ID, a name, and social security number. Hence, all the data elements in this data set are mandatory attributes and should have a non-blank value assigned to them.
>
> The data set in Table 4.3 shows that:
>
> 1. Employee ID is populated for each record, and each value has just one occurrence.
>
> Applying the formula for completeness, the completeness % for the Employee ID data element is:
>
> > (Total number of values that should be populated (30) – Total number of null values (0) – Total number of blanks or spaces (0) – Total number of hidden blanks (0) / Total number of values that should be populated (30)) × 100
>
> = ((30 – 0 – 0 – 0) / 30) × 100
>
> = (30 / 30) × 100
>
> = 100%
>
> Hence, the employee ID data element is 100% complete.

Table 4.3	Employee data set for Example 4.1.	
Employee ID	**Employee name**	**Social security number**
E00000952	Jo Lee	122-17-9870
E00000953	Mark Young	155-76-5432
E00000954	Lance Seaton	142-19-8765
E00000955	Brent Morton	111-76-7890
E00000956	Lisa Strong	122-17-9870
E00000957	Neil Ford	NULL
E00000958	James Worth	143-14-1422
E00000959	Fredrick Ashton	abc de
E00000960		151-77-7654
E00000961	Harry Fielding	132-11-8775
E00000962	Silver Rhodes	UNKWN
E00000963	Rodger Rome	UNKWN
E00000964	Ray Bridgeford	152-12-9431
E00000965	Gretta Collins	UNKWN
E00000966	Philip Montana	UNKWN
E00000967	Monica Sutton	132-11-8775
E00000968	Augustus Edward	UNKWN
E00000969	Leonardo Napoli	UNKWN
E00000970	Raj Kumar Singh	UNKWN
E00000971	Joseph Forrest	163-13-4325
E00000972		143-17-7884
E00000973	Nicholas Emerson	UNKWN
E00000974	Mona Sinha	UNKWN
E00000975	Lovissa Wu	NULL
E00000976	Gianna King	UNKWN
E00000977	George Anton	143-17-7884
E00000978	Deep Seth	NULL
E00000979	Farah Hong	181-14-9893
E00000980	Harish Kant Patel	133-12-7545
E00000981	Rose Baxter	UNKWN

2. Employee Name has "blanks" or "spaces" for two records. There are no *null* or hidden blanks for Employee Name.

   Applying the formula for completeness, the completeness % for the Employee Name data element is:

(Total number of values that should be populated (30) –
Total number of *null* values (0) – Total number of blanks or
spaces (2) – Total number of hidden blanks (0) / Total
number of values that should be populated (30)) × 100

= ((30 – 0 – 2 – 0) / 30) × 100

= (28 / 30) × 100

= 93.33%

3. The social security number occurrences are summarized in Table 4.4.

Analysis of the social security number value occurrences reveals the following:

1. Out of 30 records in the data set, 10 social security number values have only one occurrence.

2. Three social security number values have two occurrences.

3. There are three *null* occurrences.

4. There are 11 occurrences of the value "UNKWN." The value "UNKWN" actually stands for "value unknown" and is a manifestation of a hidden blank.

Table 4.4	Social security number occurrences for Example 4.1.
Social security number	**Count**
111-76-7890	1
122-17-9870	2
132-11-8775	2
133-12-7545	1
142-19-8765	1
143-14-1422	1
143-17-7884	2
151-77-7654	1
152-12-9431	1
155-76-5432	1
163-13-4325	1
181-14-9893	1
abc de	1
NULL	3
UNKWN	11

Hence, completeness % for the Social Security Number data element is:

(Total number of values that should be populated (30) – Total number of *null* values (3) – Total number of hidden blanks (11) / Total number of values that should be populated (30)) × 100

= ((30 – 3 – 11) / 30) × 100

= (16 / 30) × 100

= 53.33%

Hence, the Social Security Number data element is 53.33% complete.

Example 4.2. We will illustrate how to calculate completeness of inapplicable attributes with the customer data set shown in Figure 4.1 below. The customer data set contains customer data for seven customers who enrolled online in the last month, and has seven data records. The business need is to determine individual, trust, and organizational customers who have enrolled in the last month so as to advertise certain products to the targeted population. Only individual customers whose age is greater than 60 are to be targeted for this requirement. The data set has five data elements: Customer ID, Customer Name, Customer Type, Date of Birth, and Gender.

From a business requirement perspective, *gender* is not a critical attribute from a data completeness analysis viewpoint as the advertising is irrespective of gender; hence, we will not be measuring the completeness percentage for this data element. However, customer ID, customer name, customer type, and date of birth are critical attributes. While customer ID, customer name, and customer type are mandatory attributes, date of birth is an inapplicable attribute for organization and trust customers. The mandatory attributes should be populated for all the records in the data set. However, inapplicable attributes will only be

Customer ID	Customer name	Customer type	Date of birth	Gender
C000001234	Caroline Smith	I	25/12/1975	F
C000001235	James Word	I		M
C000001236	Raj Ayeppa K. Gopala	I	06/30/1989	M
C000001237	Tina Conlon	I	29/07/1970	F
C000001238	PTC Private Limited	O		
C000001239	SBT Trust	T		
C000001240	Rita Summer Darcy	I		

Inapplicable attribute missing values

Applicable attributes missing values

Figure 4.1 Customer data set for Example 4.2.

The business rules to determine whether a customer is an individual, trust, or organization is as follows:

    1. If the customer is an individual, then the data element, customer type = I

    2. If the customer is an organization, then the data element, customer type = O

    3. If the customer is a trust, then the data element, customer type = T

The business rules to determine whether the data element Date of Birth should be populated is as follows:

    1. If the data element Customer Type = I, then the date of birth should be populated.

    2. If the data element Customer Type = O, then the date of birth should not be populated.

    3. If the data element Customer Type = T, then the date of birth should not be populated.

Figure 4.2   Business rules for date of birth completeness for Example 4.2.

populated where applicable. Figure 4.2 shows the set of business rules for analyzing the data set for the completeness of the Date of Birth data element.

Analysis of the customer data set reveals the following:

1. Customer ID is populated for each record, and each value has just one occurrence.

   Applying the formula for completeness, the completeness % for the Customer ID data element is:

   (Total number of values that should be populated (7) – Total number of *null* values (0) – Total number of blanks or spaces (0) – Total number of hidden blanks (0) / Total number of values that should be populated (7)) × 100

   $= ((7 - 0 - 0 - 0) / 7) \times 100$

   $= (7 / 7) \times 100$

   $= 100\%$

2. Customer name is populated for each record, and each value has just one occurrence.

   Applying the formula for completeness, the completeness % for the Customer Name data element is:

   (Total number of values that should be populated (7) – Total number of *null* values (0) – Total number of blanks or spaces (0) – Total number of hidden blanks (0) / Total number of values that should be populated (7)) × 100

   $= ((7 - 0 - 0 - 0) / 7) \times 100$

   $= (7 / 7) \times 100$

   $= 100\%$

Table 4.5	"Customer type" counts for Example 4.2.
Customer type	**Count**
I	5
O	1
T	1

3. Customer type is populated for each record, and the occurrence of each value is shown in Table 4.5.

   Though the customer type value "I" has five occurrences, it is a legitimate value indicating individual customers, and not a hidden blank.

   Applying the formula for completeness, the completeness % for the Customer Type data element is:

   (Total number of values that should be populated (7) – Total number of *null* values (0) – Total number of blanks or spaces (0) – Total number of hidden blanks (0) / Total number of values that should be populated (7)) × 100

   $= ((7 - 0 - 0 - 0) / 7) \times 100$

   $= (7 / 7) \times 100$

   $= 100\%$

4. The data element Date of Birth is an inapplicable attribute in the cases of organizations or trusts, and hence will not have a value for organizational and trust customers. The Date of Birth data element will only be populated for individual customers. Following the business rules defined in Figure 4.2, the date of birth will not be populated for customers "PTC Private Ltd" and "SBT Trust." The date of birth should be populated for all the other five records as all the other records belong to individual customers.

   Therefore, the total number of date of birth values that should be populated = 5

   The total number of date of birth values that are populated for individual customers = 3 (Rita Summer Darcy and James Word are individual customers, but the date of birth value is missing for them).

   Applying the formula for completeness, the completeness % for the Date of Birth data element is:

(Total number of values that should be populated (5) –
Total number of invalid *null* values (0) – Total number of invalid
blanks or spaces (2) – Total number of invalid hidden blanks (0) /
Total number of values that should be populated (5)) × 100

$= ((5 - 0 - 2 - 0) / 5) \times 100$

$= (3 / 5) \times 100$

$= 60\%$

Measuring Record Completeness. Record completeness can be measured by computing the percentage of records that have all critical data elements populated with a non-blank value and these non-blank values are not hidden blanks. Following are the steps outlined to measure record completeness:

1. Determine all the critical data elements in the data sets that should have a value.

2. For each critical data element in the data set, perform steps 1, 2, and 3 of the steps outlined to measure completeness at the *data element level*.

3. Determine the number of records in the data set that have all the critical data elements populated with a non-blank value (the non-blank values are not hidden blanks). If for a record, even one critical data element that should have a value is not populated with a non-blank value, the record is considered to be incomplete.

   Record completeness % =

   (Number of records in the data set that have all the critical data elements populated with a non-blank value and no hidden blanks) × 100 / (Number of records in the data set that should have values for critical data elements)

   Alternatively, record completeness % =

   (Number of records in the data set that should have values for critical data elements) – (Number of records in the data set that do not have values for critical data elements) × 100 / (Number of records in the data set that should have values for critical data elements)

Example 4.3. Let us illustrate record level completeness using the employee data set of the US-based company from Example 4.1, which we used to illustrate data element completeness. The employee data set had three critical mandatory data elements: Employee ID, Employee Name, and Social Security Number. For the data set to have 100% completeness, all the records should have non-blank values that are not hidden blank values for all the data elements in the data set. If even one data element in a data record has a missing value (that is, *nulls*, blanks/spaces, or hidden blanks), the record is considered incomplete. The incomplete records are highlighted in the employee data set shown in Figure 4.3.

Employee ID	Employee name	Social security number
E00000952	Jo Lee	122-17-9870
E00000953	Mark Young	155-76-5432
E00000954	Lance Seaton	142-19-8765
E00000955	Brent Morton	111-76-7890
E00000956	Lisa Strong	122-17-9870
E00000957	Neil Ford	NULL
E00000958	James Worth	143-14-1422
E00000959	Fredrick Ashton	abc de
E00000960		151-77-7654
E00000961	Harry Fielding	132-11-8775
E00000962	Silver Rhodes	UNKWN
E00000963	Rodger Rome	UNKWN
E00000964	Ray Bridgeford	152-12-9431
E00000965	Gretta Collins	UNKWN
E00000966	Philip Montana	UNKWN
E00000967	Monica Sutton	132-11-8775
E00000968	Augustus Edward	UNKWN
E00000969	Leonardo Napoli	UNKWN
E00000970	Raj Kumar Singh	UNKWN
E00000971	Joseph Forrest	163-13-4325
E00000972		143-17-7884
E00000973	Nicholas Emerson	UNKWN
E00000974	Mona Sinha	UNKWN
E00000975	Lovissa Wu	NULL
E00000976	Gianna King	UNKWN
E00000977	George Anton	143-17-7884
E00000978	Deep Seth	NULL
E00000979	Farah Hong	181-14-9893
E00000980	Harish Kant Patel	133-12-7545
E00000981	Rose Baxter	UNKWN

Incomplete records

Figure 4.3 Employee data set—incomplete records for Example 4.3.

Analysis of the data set reveals the following:

1. Out of 30 records in the data set, two records have blanks or spaces for the Employee Name data element, though the employee ID and social security number values are populated for these records. Since these two records do not have non-blank values for Employee Name, these two records are incomplete.

2. Three records have *null* values for the social security number, though the Employee ID and Employee Name data elements have non-blank values.

3. 11 records have a hidden blank value of "UNKWN" for the Social Security Number data element. The Employee ID and Employee Name data elements for these records have a non-blank value.

The number of records that are incomplete = 2 + 3 + 11 = 16 (Refer to Figure 4.3 for the incomplete records).

Record completeness % =

(Number of records in the data set that should have values for critical data elements (30)) – (Number of records in the data set that do not have values for critical data elements (16)) × 100 / (Number of records in the data set that should have values for critical data elements (30))

= (30 – 16) × 100 / 30

= 14 × 100 / 30

= 46.67%

Example 4.4. Let us illustrate record completeness using the customer data set (Figure 4.1) used in Example 4.2 to illustrate data element completeness. The customer data set has five data elements—Customer ID, Customer Name, Customer Type, Date of Birth, and Gender—of which only the first four are critical. The first three data elements are mandatory attributes, and the fourth and fifth data elements are inapplicable attributes in the case of organizational and trust customers. For a record to qualify as complete, Customer ID, Customer Name, and Customer Type should be populated with non-blank values. The date of birth is an inapplicable attribute for organization and trust customers, that is, Customer Type has the value "O" or "T," so, in the case of records where the customer is an organization or trust, the record will be considered as complete if the Customer ID, Customer Name, and Customer Type data elements are populated with non-blank values. However, if a record contains information for an individual customer (that is, Customer Type = I), for the record to qualify as complete, in addition to Customer ID, Customer Name, and Customer Type data elements being populated with non-blank values, the Date of Birth data element should also be populated with non-blank values.

Analysis of the data set reveals the following:

1. Out of the seven records in the customer data set, the first four records contain individual customer information (Customer Type = I) and have non-blank values populated for all the critical data elements, namely, Customer ID, Customer Name, Customer Type, and Date of Birth. Hence, the first four records are complete for the context in which the data are to be used.

2. The fifth and the sixth records contain customer information for organizational customer "PTC Private Ltd" (that is, customer type = O) and trust customer "SBT Trust" (that is, customer type = T), respectively. The Customer ID, Customer Name, and Customer Type data elements are populated with non-blank values for these records. Since the Date of Birth data element is an inapplicable attribute for organizational and trust customers, it will not be populated for these records. Hence, the fifth and sixth records are also complete.

3. The seventh record in the customer data set contains individual customer information (Customer Type = I) and have non-blank values populated for the critical data elements, namely, Customer ID, Customer Name, and Customer Type. However, since the Date of Birth data element, which is an applicable attribute in this case, is blank, this record is incomplete.

Hence,

Total number of complete records = 6

Total number of incomplete records = 1

Applying the formula for record completeness,

Record completeness % =

(Number of records in the data set that have all the critical data elements populated with non-blank values and no hidden blanks (6)) × 100 / (Number of records in the data set that should have values for critical data elements (7))

= 6 × 100 / 7

= 85.7%

Measuring Data Set Completeness. Data set completeness can be measured by computing the proportion of records that are present in the data set versus the total number of records that should have been there in the data set. When measuring completeness at the data set level, there is often a need for a reference data set that is considered to be the authoritative source of such data. If a reference data set is not available, then at the least, the count of the number of records that should be present in the data set should be available in order to determine the data set completeness.

Data set completeness % =

Number of records present in the data set × 100 / Number of records in the reference data set

For example, consider the employee data set of the US-based company who joined the company in the month of January 2017. We had used this data set (Table 4.3) in Example 4.1 to illustrate data element completeness and record completeness. This data set had 30 records indicating that 30 new employees joined the company. For this data set to be complete at a data set level, the number of employees that actually joined the company should also be 30. Let us have a look at the reference data set in Table 4.6. If we

Table 4.6 Employee reference data set.

Employee ID	Employee name	Social security number
E00000952	Jo Lee	122-17-9870
E00000953	Mark Young	155-76-5432
E00000954	Lance Seaton	142-19-8765
E00000955	Brent Morton	111-76-7890
E00000956	Lisa Strong	181-18-6770
E00000957	Neil Ford	142-32-9834
E00000958	James Worth	183-14-1422
E00000959	Fredrick Ashton	125-18-7633
E00000960	Joanna Cory	151-77-7654
E00000961	Harry Fielding	132-11-8775
E00000962	Silver Rhodes	131-22-3241
E00000963	Rodger Rome	162-13-4697
E00000964	Ray Bridgeford	144-12-9431
E00000965	Gretta Collins	155-28-9823
E00000966	Philip Montana	119-63-5348
E00000967	Monica Sutton	125-13-4070
E00000968	Augustus Edward	143-18-7642
E00000969	Leonardo Napoli	191-15-6534
E00000970	Raj Kumar Singh	173-24-5432
E00000971	Joseph Forrest	163-13-4325
E00000972	James Hutch	143-17-7884
E00000973	Nicholas Emerson	184-81-6542
E00000974	Mona Sinha	172-23-6548
E00000975	Lovissa Wu	142-43-3564
E00000976	Gianna King	187-22-6591
E00000977	George Anton	161-79-5450
E00000978	Deep Seth	193-14-6542
E00000979	Farah Hong	181-14-9893
E00000980	Harish Kant Patel	133-12-7545
E00000981	Rose Baxter	182-18-5370
E00000982	Richard Hills	182-17-7659
E00000983	Raschid Bangeni	123-15-7132

have a look at the reference data set and compare it with the employee data set on which we were performing our analysis, we find that the last two records in the reference data set are missing from the employee data set for newly joined employees in the month of January 2017. The reference data set as seen in Table 4.6 has 32 records.

The data set completeness % of the employee data set is

Data set completeness % = Number of records present in the data
set (30) × 100 / Number of records in the reference data set (32)

= 30 × 100 / 32

= 93.75%

Measuring Uniqueness

As defined in Chapter 3, the uniqueness data quality dimension is representative of the fact that there should be no duplicate records captured for the same entity or event in the same data set or table. Uniqueness is the inverse of the assessment of duplication.

Uniqueness is usually measured in a percentage, and is the proportion of the number of entities, objects, events, or their attributes as assessed in the real world versus the number of records of entities, objects, or attributes in the data set.

Uniqueness can be measured at two levels:

- Data element

- Data record

Measuring Uniqueness at the Data Element Level. Data element level uniqueness is generally measured for data elements that have high cardinality, that is, attributes that have a high degree of uniqueness, for example, social security numbers and passport numbers. Data elements with medium or low cardinality are bound to have a degree of duplication, and therefore there is no business value in measuring the uniqueness of such elements.

Following are the steps outlined to measure uniqueness at the data element level:

1. For each critical data element, determine whether the data element is a high, medium, or low cardinality attribute.

2. For critical elements having high cardinality, determine the number of occurrences of each data value.

3. Determine how missing values are represented in the data set as explained in the "Measuring Data Element Completeness" section of this chapter. Missing value occurrences are excluded from the uniqueness calculation.

4. Find out the number of times each value for a particular data element occurs in the data set.

5. Find out the number of unique values, excluding manifestations of missing values. Note: manifestation of missing values includes hidden blanks too.

6. Find out the number of values for the data element, excluding manifestations of missing values in the data set.

The formula for calculating the uniqueness % is as follows:

$$\text{Uniqueness \%} = \text{(Number of unique values of a data element in the data set, excluding manifestations of missing values} \times 100 \text{ / (Number of values for the data element in the data set, excluding manifestation of missing values)}$$

Example 4.5. We will illustrate uniqueness at the data element level using the employee data set we used in Example 4.1. We will use the employee data set of a US-based company who joined the company in January 2017 to illustrate uniqueness at the data element level (see Table 4.7). Each employee should have a unique employee ID, that is, no two employees can have the same employee ID. The same applies to the social security number. However, two employees can have the same name.

Applying the steps outlined to measure uniqueness at the data element level: In the employee data set, all the data elements, namely, Employee ID, Employee Name, and Social Security Number are critical.

The data elements Employee ID and Social Security Number have high cardinality.

The number of occurrences of each value for data element Employee ID is shown in Table 4.8. Since each data value has one occurrence, data element employee ID has 100% uniqueness.

The number of unique values of the data element Employee ID, excluding manifestations of missing values and hidden blanks, is 30. The total number of Employee ID values in the data set is 30. Applying the formula for uniqueness:

$$\text{Uniqueness \%} = \text{(Number of unique values of a data element in the data set, excluding manifestations of missing values (30))} \times 100 \text{ / (Number of values for the data element in the data set, excluding manifestation of missing values (30))}$$

$$= 100\%$$

Now let us evaluate the uniqueness of the data element Social Security Number. The social security number value occurrences are summarized in Table 4.9.

The missing values for social security number are represented by *null* values and the value "UNKWN." There are three occurrences of NULL and 11 occurrences of the value "UNKWN." The total number of values for the Social Security Number data element in the data set is 30, of which the total number of missing values and hidden blanks is 14. So, for the purpose of calculation of the

Table 4.7	Employee data set showing duplication of social security number (highlighted in the same shade) for Example 4.5.	
Employee ID	**Employee name**	**Social Security number**
E00000952	Jo Lee	122-17-9870
E00000953	Mark Young	155-76-5432
E00000954	Lance Seaton	142-19-8765
E00000955	Brent Morton	111-76-7890
E00000956	Lisa Strong	122-17-9870
E00000957	Neil Ford	NULL
E00000958	James Worth	143-14-1422
E00000959	Fredrick Ashton	abc de
E00000960		151-77-7654
E00000961	Harry Fielding	132-11-8775
E00000962	Silver Rhodes	UNKWN
E00000963	Rodger Rome	UNKWN
E00000964	Ray Bridgeford	152-12-9431
E00000965	Gretta Collins	UNKWN
E00000966	Philip Montana	UNKWN
E00000967	Monica Sutton	132-11-8775
E00000968	Augustus Edward	UNKWN
E00000969	Leonardo Napoli	UNKWN
E00000970	Raj Kumar Singh	UNKWN
E00000971	Joseph Forrest	163-13-4325
E00000972		143-17-7884
E00000973	Nicholas Emerson	UNKWN
E00000974	Mona Sinha	UNKWN
E00000975	Lovissa Wu	NULL
E00000976	Gianna King	UNKWN
E00000977	George Anton	143-17-7884
E00000978	Deep Seth	NULL
E00000979	Farah Hong	181-14-9893
E00000980	Harish Kant Patel	133-12-7545
E00000981	Rose Baxter	UNKWN

Table 4.8	Number of occurrences of employee ID values for Example 4.5.
Employee ID	**Number of occurrences**
E00000952	1
E00000953	1
E00000954	1
E00000955	1
E00000956	1
E00000957	1
E00000958	1
E00000959	1
E00000960	1
E00000961	1
E00000962	1
E00000963	1
E00000964	1
E00000965	1
E00000966	1
E00000967	1
E00000968	1
E00000969	1
E00000970	1
E00000971	1
E00000972	1
E00000973	1
E00000974	1
E00000975	1
E00000976	1
E00000977	1
E00000978	1
E00000979	1
E00000980	1
E00000981	1

Table 4.9	Number of occurrences of social security number values for Example 4.5.
Social security number	**Count**
111-76-7890	1
122-17-9870	2
132-11-8775	2
133-12-7545	1
142-19-8765	1
143-14-1422	1
143-17-7884	2
151-77-7654	1
152-12-9431	1
155-76-5432	1
163-13-4325	1
181-14-9893	1
abc de	1
NULL	3
UNKWN	11

percentage of uniqueness, the total number of values is 16. The total number of unique social security number values is 13.

Applying the formula for uniqueness,

Uniqueness % = (Number of unique values of a data element in the data set, excluding manifestations of missing values (13)) × 100 / (Number of values for the data element in the data set excluding manifestation of missing values (16))

= 81.25%

Measuring Uniqueness at the Data Record Level. In order to measure uniqueness at the data record level, business rules or logic need to be defined to outline what constitutes a unique record and what constitutes a duplicate record to determine whether more than one record represents the same facts. Definition of these rules requires an accurate understanding of the entities and the characteristics captured in the data set, and what the data in the data set represent. This could be determined either from a different, and perhaps more reliable, data set or a relevant external comparator.

Following are the steps outlined to measure uniqueness at the data record level:

1. Find the total number of records in the data set.

2. Define the business rules as to what constitutes a duplicate record and what constitutes a unique record.

3. Using the business rules and the reference data set, determine the number of times the same record occurs in the data set.

4. Find the number of unique records in the data set.

Record uniqueness can be calculated using the following formula:

Record uniqueness % = (Number of unique values of a data record in the data set) × 100 / (Total number of records in the data set)

Example 4.6. We will illustrate uniqueness at the data record level using the employee data set we used in Example 4.1. We will use the employee data set of a US-based company who joined the company in January 2017 to illustrate uniqueness at the data record level. In order to measure uniqueness at the data record level, we use the reference data set shown in Table 4.10. The reference data set has 28 records, whereas the employee data set has 30 records, as shown in Table 4.11.

Applying the steps outlined to measure uniqueness at the data record level:

1. The total number of records in the data set is 30.

2. Define the business rules as to what constitutes a duplicate record and what constitutes a unique record.

   The business rules for identifying a unique record in the employee data set are as follows:

   • *Rule 1.* If two or more employee records in the data set have the same names or preferred names (when compared with the reference data set) and the same social security numbers, then these are duplicate records.

   • *Rule 2.* If two employee records have the same social security number, and one record has a preferred name as recorded in the reference data set and the other record has the employee name as recorded in the reference data set, then these records are duplicate records.

   • *Rule 3.* If two or more employee records have same social security number and the employee name is not populated for all of them or only one of them, then these records are duplicate records.

   • *Rule 4.* No two or more records should have the same employee number.

3. Applying the business rules defined in the previous step, we find the following:

   • Applying rule 1, none of the employee records in the data set have the same names or preferred names and the same social security numbers.

Table 4.10   Employee reference data set for Example 4.6.

Employee ID	Employee name	Preferred name	Social security number
E00000952	Jo Lee	Lisa Strong	122-17-9870
E00000953	Mark Young	Mark Young	155-76-5432
E00000954	Lance Seaton	Lance Seaton	142-19-8765
E00000955	Brent Morton	Brent Morton	111-76-7890
E00000957	Neil Ford	Neil Ford	126-43-6083
E00000958	James Worth	James Worth	143-14-1422
E00000959	Fredrick Ashton	Fred Ashton	118-41-3412
E00000960	Sita Hari	Sita Hari	151-77-7654
E00000961	Harry Fielding	Harry Fielding	132-11-8775
E00000962	Silver Rhodes	Silver Rhodes	151-23-6545
E00000963	Rodger Rome	Rodger Rome	141-11-9826
E00000964	Ray Bridgeford	Ray Bridgeford	152-12-9431
E00000965	Gretta Collins	Gretta Collins	135-24-9843
E00000966	Philip Montana	Philip Montana	121-98-3215
E00000967	Monica Sutton	Monica Sutton	132-12-8775
E00000968	Augustus Edward	Augustus Edward	132-43-5634
E00000969	Leonardo Napoli	Leonardo Napoli	121-34-7865
E00000970	Raj Kumar Singh	Raj Kumar Singh	113-75-6547
E00000971	Joseph Forrest	Joseph Forrest	163-13-4325
E00000973	Nicholas Emerson	Nic Emerson	163-89-5438
E00000974	Mona Sinha	Mona Sinha	185-32-6572
E00000975	Lovissa Wu	Diana Song	129-31-5678
E00000976	Gianna King	Gianna King	146-13-3577
E00000977	George Anton	George Anton	143-17-7884
E00000978	Deep Seth	Deep Seth	171-52-5398
E00000979	Farah Hong	Farah Hong	181-14-9893
E00000980	Harish Kant Patel	Harish Kant Patel	133-12-7545
E00000981	Rose Baxter	Rose Baxter	127-33-2198

Table 4.11	Employee data set for Example 4.6.	
Employee ID	**Employee name**	**Social security number**
E00000952	Jo Lee	122-17-9870
E00000953	Mark Young	155-76-5432
E00000954	Lance Seaton	142-19-8765
E00000955	Brent Morton	111-76-7890
E00000956	Lisa Strong	122-17-9870
E00000957	Neil Ford	NULL
E00000958	James Worth	143-14-1422
E00000959	Fredrick Ashton	abc de
E00000960		151-77-7654
E00000961	Harry Fielding	132-11-8775
E00000962	Silver Rhodes	UNKWN
E00000963	Rodger Rome	UNKWN
E00000964	Ray Bridgeford	152-12-9431
E00000965	Gretta Collins	UNKWN
E00000966	Philip Montana	UNKWN
E00000967	Monica Sutton	132-11-8775
E00000968	Augustus Edward	UNKWN
E00000969	Leonardo Napoli	UNKWN
E00000970	Raj Kumar Singh	UNKWN
E00000971	Joseph Forrest	163-13-4325
E00000972		143-17-7884
E00000973	Nicholas Emerson	UNKWN
E00000974	Mona Sinha	UNKWN
E00000975	Lovissa Wu	NULL
E00000976	Gianna King	UNKWN
E00000977	George Anton	143-17-7884
E00000978	Deep Seth	NULL
E00000979	Farah Hong	181-14-9893
E00000980	Harish Kant Patel	133-12-7545
E00000981	Rose Baxter	UNKWN

- Applying rule 2, the following records are duplicates and occur twice:

Employee ID	Employee name	Social Security number
E00000952	Jo Lee	122-17-9870
E00000956	Lisa Strong	122-17-9870

- Applying Rule 3, the following records are duplicates and occur twice:

Employee ID	Employee name	Social Security number
E00000972		143-17-7884
E00000977	George Anton	143-17-7884

- None of the records in the data set have the same employee number.

- While the social security number "132-11-8775" is shared by two employees in Table 4.11, the duplication is at one data element (that is, social security number) level only and not at data record level.

4. Hence, out of the 30 records, there are two duplicate records. Thus, there are 28 unique records.

   Applying the formula for record level uniqueness,

   Record uniqueness % = (Number of unique values of a data record in the data set (28)) × 100 / (Total number of records in the data set (30))

= 28 × 100 / 30

= 93.33 %

Measuring Validity

Validity, also known as *conformity*, is a measure of whether the data comply with a set of internal or external standards or guidelines or standard data definitions, including metadata definitions. Hence, in order to measure the data validity, it is necessary that a set of internal or external standards, guidelines, standard data definitions, including metadata definitions, range, format, and syntax, that the data elements need to comply with, exists. Business rules need to be defined to assess conformance of the data elements and data record. Validity can be measured at two levels:

- Data element
- Data record

Validity is usually measured in a percentage and is the proportion of the stored data versus the potential of 100% validity.

Measuring Data Element Validity. Following are the steps outlined to measure validity at the data element level.

For each critical data element in the data set:

1. Review the standards, definitions, format, range, and syntax that the data elements need to conform to. Define the business rules, if needed, for comparison between the data and definitions for the data element.

2. Determine whether there are any missing values. This is explained in the "Measuring Data Element Completeness" section of this chapter. Missing value occurrences are excluded from the validity calculations.

3. Determine whether the critical data element values are valid or not by comparing the values with the standards, definitions, format, range, and syntax defined in step 1.

4. Find out the number of values for the data element, excluding manifestations of missing values in the data set.

5. Find the number of valid values (values that conform to the data definitions and standards).

6. Find the number of invalid values (values that do not conform to the data definitions and standards).

The formula for calculating the data element validity % is as follows:

$$\text{Validity \%} = \text{(Number of valid values of a data element in the data set, excluding manifestations of missing values} \times 100 / \text{(Number of values for the data element in the data set, excluding manifestation of missing values)}$$

Alternatively,

$$\text{Validity \%} = \text{(Number of values for the data element in the data set, excluding manifestation of missing values} - \text{Number of invalid values of a data element in the data set, excluding manifestations of missing values)} \times 100 / \text{(Number of values for the data element in the data set, excluding manifestation of missing values)}$$

$$\text{Invalidity \%} = \text{(Number of invalid values of a data element in the data set, excluding manifestations of missing values)} \times 100 / \text{(Number of values for the data element in the data set, excluding manifestation of missing values)}$$

Example 4.7. We will illustrate validity at the data element level using the employee data set we used in Example 4.1. We will use the employee data set of a US-based company who joined the company in January 2017 to illustrate validity at the data element level. In the employee data set all three data elements, that is, Employee ID, Employee Name, and Social Security Number, are critical data elements.

The metadata for the data elements Employee ID, Employee Name, and Social Security Number are as per Figure 4.4.

Measuring Employee ID Validity

Step 1. As shown in Figure 4.4, the following list illustrates the data definition standards for the data element/data field Employee ID that employee ID data values should satisfy in order for them to be valid:

1. The employee ID should be a string field.

2. The employee ID needs to start with the letter "E" followed by eight digits.

3. The length of the employee ID should be nine characters.

4. The field should not have leading or trailing spaces.

5. Except for the starting letter "E," no alphabetic or special characters are allowed.

6. Employee ID cannot have *null* or blank values.

The first step is to review the metadata, which shows that:

- Item 1 defines the data type of the data element Employee ID.

- Item 3 defines the size of the data element Employee ID, that is, an employee ID having less than nine characters or more than nine characters will be invalid.

- Items 2, 4, and 5 define the format of the data element Employee ID. Any violation of the formatting requirements will result in the employee ID being invalid.

- Item 6 indicates that an employee ID should always be present; it cannot be blank.

Step 2. The next step is to determine whether there are any missing values, including hidden blanks. There are no missing values or hidden blanks for the data element Employee ID in the data set in Table 4.12.

Step 3. On comparing the data values with the data definition standards reviewed in step 1, we find that all the Employee ID data values satisfy all the data definitions set in step 1, as follows:

1. All the values are string values, that is, the data type is a string.

2. All the values start with the letter "E" and are followed by eight digits.

Employee ID:

The employee ID is an alphanumeric identifier used to uniquely identify a staff member.

1. The employee ID should be a string field.
2. The employee ID needs to start with the letter "E," followed by eight digits.
3. The length of the employee ID should be nine characters.
4. The field should not have leading or trailing spaces.
5. Except for the starting letter "E," no alphabetic or special characters are allowed.
6. Employee ID cannot have *null* or blank values.

Employee Name:

The employee name is the legal name of the employee as recorded on his or her birth certificate.

1. The employee name should be a string field.
2. The length of the employee name should not exceed 255 characters.
3. The field should not have leading or trailing spaces.
4. The employee name should have one of the following formats:

    <First Name> <1 space> <Middle Name> <1 space> <Last Name>

    If an individual has more than one name in between the first name and last name, then the full name should be a concatenation of the first name, second name, and last name.

    <First Name> <1 space> <Second Name> <1 space> <Last Name>

    If an individual does not have a middle name, then the full name should be a concatenation of the first name and last name.

    <First Name> <1 space> <Last Name>

5. No special characters are allowed in the Employee Name field.

Social Security Number:

In the United States, a social security number (SSN) is a nine-digit number issued to US citizens, permanent residents, and temporary (working) residents under section 205(c)(2) of the Social Security Act, codified as 42 USC § 405(c)(2) (Wikipedia Undated "Social Security Number").

1. The social security number should be a string field.
2. The length of the social security number should be 11 characters.
3. The social security number should have the following format:

    XXX-XX-XXXX

    where X is a number or digit.

    Thus, the social security number values should have a group of three digits followed by the "-" character, followed by a group of two digits, which are in turn followed by the "-" character, which is in turn followed by a group of four digits.

4. The Social Security Number data element should not have any leading or trailing spaces.
5. There should be no special characters in the Social Security Number data element, other than the "-" character, as specified in the format in rule 3.
6. Numbers with all zeros in any digit group are not allowed in a social security number.
7. Numbers with 666 or 900–999 in the first digit group are never allocated.

Figure 4.4   Metadata for data elements Employee ID, Employee Name, and Social Security Number for Example 4.7.

Table 4.12 Employee data set for Example 4.7.

Employee ID	Employee name	Social security number
E00000952	Jo Lee	122-17-9870
E00000953	Mark Young	155-76-5432
E00000954	Lance Seaton	142-19-8765
E00000955	Brent Morton	111-76-7890
E00000956	Lisa Strong	122-17-9870
E00000957	Neil Ford	NULL
E00000958	James Worth	143-14-1422
E00000959	Fredrick Ashton	abc de
E00000960		151-77-7654
E00000961	Harry Fielding	132-11-8775
E00000962	Silver Rhodes	UNKWN
E00000963	Rodger Rome	UNKWN
E00000964	Ray Bridgeford	152-12-9431
E00000965	Gretta Collins	UNKWN
E00000966	Philip Montana	UNKWN
E00000967	Monica Sutton	132-11-8775
E00000968	Augustus Edward	UNKWN
E00000969	Leonardo Napoli	UNKWN
E00000970	Raj Kumar Singh	UNKWN
E00000971	Joseph Forrest	163-13-4325
E00000972		143-17-7884
E00000973	Nicholas Emerson	UNKWN
E00000974	Mona Sinha	UNKWN
E00000975	Lovissa Wu	NULL
E00000976	Gianna King	UNKWN
E00000977	George Anton	143-17-7884
E00000978	Deep Seth	NULL
E00000979	Farah Hong	181-14-9893
E00000980	Harish Kant Patel	133-12-7545
E00000981	Rose Baxter	UNKWN

3. The length of all the employee ID data values is nine characters.

4. None of the data values have leading or trailing blank spaces.

5. Except for starting with the letter "E," no other alphabetic or special characters are in any of the data values.

6. None of the employee ID fields have *null* or blank values.

Step 4. The number of values for the data element Employee ID, excluding manifestations of missing values (including hidden blanks), in the data set is 30. Note: There are no manifestations of missing values for the Employee ID data element in the data set in Table 4.12.

Step 5. The number of valid employee ID values (values that conform to the data definitions and standards) is 30.

Step 6. The number of invalid employee ID values is zero.

Applying the formula for calculating the employee ID validity %,

$$\text{Validity \%} = \text{(Number of valid values of a data element in the data set, excluding manifestations of missing values (30))} \times 100 / \text{(Number of values for the data element in the data set, excluding manifestation of missing values (30))}$$

$$= 30 \times 100 / 30$$

$$= 100\%$$

Alternatively,

$$\text{Validity \%} = \text{Number of values for a data element in the data set, excluding manifestation of missing values (30)} - \text{Number of invalid values of a data element in the data set, excluding manifestations of missing values (0)} \times 100 / \text{(Number of values for the data element in the data set, excluding manifestation of missing values (30))}$$

$$= 30 \times 100 / 30$$

$$= 100\%$$

$$\text{Invalidity \%} = \text{(Number of invalid values of a data element in the data set, excluding manifestations of missing values (0))} \times 100 / \text{(Number of values for the data element in the data set, excluding manifestation of missing values (30))}$$

$$= 0 \times 100 / 30$$

$$= 0\%$$

Measuring Employee Name Validity

Step 1. As shown in Figure 4.4, the following list illustrates the data definition standards for the data element/data field Employee Name that employee name data values should satisfy in order for them to be valid:

1. The employee name should be a string field.

2. The length of the employee name should not exceed 255 characters.

3. The field should not have leading or trailing spaces.

4. The employee name should have one of the following formats:

   <First Name> <1 space> <Middle Name> <1 space> <Last Name>

   If an individual has more than one name in between the first name and last name, then the full name should be a concatenation of the first name, second name, and last name.

   <First Name> <1 space> <Second Name> <1 space> <Last Name>

   If an individual does not have a middle name, then the full name should be a concatenation of the first name and last name.

   <First Name> <1 space> <Last Name>

5. No special characters are allowed in the employee name field.

The first step is to review the metadata, which show that:

- Item 1 defines the data type of the data element Employee Name.

- Item 2 defines the size of the data element Employee Name.

- Items 3 and 4 outline the formatting requirements of the data element Employee Name.

Step 2. The next step is to determine whether there are any manifestation of missing values. There are two missing values in the form of blanks for the data element Employee Name in the data set in Table 4.12.

Step 3. On comparing the data values with the data definition standards set in step 1, we find that all the employee name data values satisfy all the data definitions set in step 1 as follows:

1. All the values are string values, that is, the data type is a string.

2. All the values have either of the below formats:

   <First Name> <1 space> <Middle Name> <1 space> <Last Name>

   <First Name> <1 space> <Last Name>

3. Counting the number of characters in the employee name data values, the length of none of the employee ID data values exceeds 255 characters.

4. None of the data values have leading or trailing blank spaces.

Step 4. The number of values for the data element Employee Name, excluding manifestations of missing values, in the data set in Table 4.12 is 28. Note: There are two missing values in form of blanks for the Employee Name data element in the data set in Table 4.12.

Step 5. The number of valid employee name values (values that conform to the data definitions and standards) is 28.

Step 6. The number of invalid employee name values is zero.

Applying the formula for calculating the employee name validity %,

$$\text{Validity \%} = \text{(Number of valid values of a data element in the data set, excluding manifestations of missing values (28))} \times 100 \, / \, \text{(Number of values for the data element in the data set, excluding manifestation of missing values (28))}$$

$= 28 \times 100 \, / \, 28$

$= 100\%$

Alternatively,

$$\text{Validity \%} = \text{(Number of values for a data element in the data set, excluding manifestation of missing values (28)} - \text{Number of invalid values of a data element in the data set, excluding manifestations of missing values (0))} \times 100 \, / \, \text{(Number of values for the data element in the data set, excluding manifestation of missing values (28))}$$

$= 28 \times 100 \, / \, 28$

$= 100\%$

$$\text{Invalidity \%} = \text{(Number of invalid values of a data element in the data set, excluding manifestations of missing values (0))} \times 100 \, / \, \text{(Number of values for the data element in the data set, excluding manifestation of missing values (28))}$$

$= 0 \times 100 \, / \, 28$

$= 0\%$

Measuring Social Security Number Validity

Step 1. As shown in Figure 4.4, the following list illustrates the data definition standards for the data element/data field Social Security Number that social security number data values should satisfy in order for them to be valid.

1. The social security number should be a string field.

2. The length of the social security number should be 11 characters.

3. The social security number should have the following format:

   XXX-XX-XXXX

   where X is number or digit.

   Thus, the social security number values should have a group of three digits followed by the "-" character, followed by a group of two digits, which are in turn followed by the "-" character, which is in turn followed by a group of four digits.

4. The Social Security Number data element should not have any leading or trailing spaces.

5. There should be no special characters in the Social Security Number data element other than the "-" character, as specified in the format in item 3.

6. Numbers with all zeros in any digit group are not allowed in a social security number.

7. Numbers with 666 or 900–999 in the first digit group are never allocated.

The first step is to review the metadata, which show that:

- Item 1 defines the data type of the data element Social Security Number.

- Item 2 defines the size of the data element Social Security Number.

- Items 3, 4, 5, 6, 7, and 8 outline the formatting requirements of the data element Social Security Number.

Step 2. The next step is to determine whether there are any manifestations of missing values. There are three *null* values, and 11 hidden blanks manifested by the value "UNKNWN," for the data element Social Security Number in the data set in Table 4.12. Hence, there are 14 missing social security number values in the data set.

Step 3. On comparing the data values with the data definition standards set in step 1, we find that except for the data value "abc de," all the rest of the social security number data values in the data set satisfy all the data definitions set in step 1.

The value "abc de" does not conform to items 2, 3, 4, and 5.

Step 4. The number of values for the data element Social Security Number, excluding manifestations of missing values, in the data set in Table 4.12 is 16. Note: There are 14 missing values, including *null* values and hidden blanks, for the Social Security Number data element in the data set.

Step 5. The number of valid social security number values (values that conform to the data definitions and standards) is 15.

Step 6. The number of invalid social security number values is 1.

Applying the formula for calculating the employee name validity %,

> Validity % = (Number of valid values of a data element in the data set, excluding manifestations of missing values (15)) × 100 / (Number of values for the data element in the data set, excluding manifestation of missing values (16))

$= 15 \times 100 / 16$

$= 93.75\%$

Alternatively,

> Validity % = (Number of values for a data element in the data set, manifestation of missing values (16) – Number of invalid values of a data element in the data set, excluding manifestations of missing values (1)) × 100 / (Number of values for the data element in the data set, excluding manifestation of missing values (28))

$= 15 \times 100 / 16$

$= 93.75\%$

> Invalidity % = (Number of invalid values of a data element in the data set, excluding manifestations of missing values (1)) × 100 / (Number of values for the data element in the data set, excluding manifestation of missing values (16))

$= 1 \times 100 / 16$

$= 6.25\%$

Measuring Data Record Validity. Data record validity is measured by defining business rules regarding what constitutes a valid data record, and determining the count of data records that comply with the defined business rules. This usually comprises the validity of all the individual critical data elements.

1. Determine the validity of critical data elements for each data record as defined in the "Measuring Data Element Validity" section in this chapter.

2. Define business rules for data record validity.

3. Determine whether the records are valid or invalid based on the business rules defined in step 2.

4. Find the total number of data records in the data set.

5. Compute the total number of valid records and total number of invalid records.

6. Record validity can be calculated using the following formula:

Record validity % = (Number of valid data records in the data set) × 100 / (Total number of records in the data set)

Alternatively,

Record validity % = (Total number of records in the data set – Number of invalid data records in the data set) × 100 / (Total number of records in the data sct)

Record invalidity % = (Number of invalid data records in the data set) × 100 / (Total number of records in the data set)

Example 4.8. We will illustrate validity at the data record level using the employee data set we used in Example 4.1. We will use the employee data set of a US-based company who joined the company in January 2017 to illustrate validity at the data record level. In the employee data set, all three data elements, that is, Employee ID, Employee Name, and Social Security Number, are critical data elements.

Step 1. As illustrated in Example 4.6, all the populated values for the data elements Employee ID and Employee Name are valid. All the populated values for social security number, except one, are valid.

Step 2. The business rule for identifying valid and invalid records is as follows.

A data record is considered invalid if:

- Data values for one or more critical data elements are missing, including hidden blanks.

- Data values for one or more critical data elements are invalid.

Step 3. Based on the business rules defined in step 2, the records are marked as *valid* or *invalid*, with the reason stated under "Explanation," as shown in Table 4.13.

Step 4. The total number of records in the data set is 30.

Step 5. The total number of valid records as per Table 4.13 is 13, and the total number of invalid records is 17.

Step 6. Applying the formula for record validity,

Record validity % = (Number of valid data records in the data set (13)) × 100 / (Total number of records in the data set (30))

= 13 × 100 / 30

= 43.33%

Table 4.13	Valid and invalid records for Example 4.8.			
Employee ID	**Employee name**	**Social security number**	**Valid or invalid**	**Explanation**
E00000952	Jo Lee	122-17-9870	Valid	Data values for all data elements are valid and complete
E00000953	Mark Young	155-76-5432	Valid	Data values for all data elements are valid and complete
E00000954	Lance Seaton	142-19-8765	Valid	Data values for all data elements are valid and complete
E00000955	Brent Morton	111-76-7890	Valid	Data values for all data elements are valid and complete
E00000956	Lisa Strong	122-17-9870	Valid	Data values for all data elements are valid and complete
E00000957	Neil Ford	NULL	Invalid	The social security number data element value is missing
E00000958	James Worth	143-14-1422	Valid	Data values for all data elements are valid and complete
E00000959	Fredrick Ashton	abc de	Invalid	The social security number data element value is invalid
E00000960		151-77-7654	Invalid	The employee name data element has blanks
E00000961	Harry Fielding	132-11-8775	Valid	Data values for all data elements are valid and complete
E00000962	Silver Rhodes	UNKWN	Invalid	The social security number data element value is UNKWN, which is a representation of a hidden blank
E00000963	Rodger Rome	UNKWN	Invalid	The social security number data element value is UNKWN, which is a representation of a hidden blank
E00000964	Ray Bridgeford	152-12-9431	Valid	Data values for all data elements are valid and complete

Continued

Table 4.13	*Continued.*			
Employee ID	**Employee name**	**Social security number**	**Valid or invalid**	**Explanation**
E00000965	Gretta Collins	UNKWN	Invalid	The social security number data element value is UNKWN, which is a representation of a hidden blank
E00000966	Philip Montana	UNKWN	Invalid	The social security number data element value is UNKWN, which is a representation of a hidden blank
E00000967	Monica Sutton	132-11-8775	Valid	Data values for all data elements are valid and complete
E00000968	Augustus Edward	UNKWN	Invalid	The social security number data element value is UNKWN, which is a representation of a hidden blank
E00000969	Leonardo Napoli	UNKWN	Invalid	The social security number data element value is UNKWN, which is a representation of a hidden blank
E00000970	Raj Kumar Singh	UNKWN	Invalid	The social security number data element value is UNKWN, which is a representation of a hidden blank
E00000971	Joseph Forrest	163-13-4325	Valid	Data values for all data elements are valid and complete
E00000972		143-17-7884	Invalid	The employee name data element has blanks.
E00000973	Nicholas Emerson	UNKWN	Invalid	The social security number data element value is UNKWN, which is a representation of a hidden blank
E00000974	Mona Sinha	UNKWN	Invalid	The social security number data element value is UNKWN, which is a representation of a hidden blank
E00000975	Lovissa Wu	NULL	Invalid	The social security number data element value is missing.

Continued

Table 4.13	*Continued.*			
Employee ID	**Employee name**	**Social security number**	**Valid or invalid**	**Explanation**
E00000976	Gianna King	UNKWN	Invalid	The social security number data element value is UNKWN, which is a representation of a hidden blank
E00000977	George Anton	143-17-7884	Valid	Data values for all data elements are valid and complete
E00000978	Deep Seth	NULL	Invalid	The social security number data element value is missing
E00000979	Farah Hong	181-14-9893	Valid	Data values for all data elements are valid and complete
E00000980	Harish Kant Patel	133-12-7545	Valid	Data values for all data elements are valid and complete
E00000981	Rose Baxter	UNKWN	Invalid	The social security number data element value is UNKWN, which is a representation of a hidden blank

Alternatively,

Record validity % = (Total number of records in the data set (30) – Number of invalid data records in the data set (17)) × 100 / (Total number of records in the data set (30))

$$= (30 - 17) \times 100 / 30$$

$$= 13 \times 100 / 30$$

$$= 43.33\%$$

Record invalidity % = (Number of invalid data records in the data set (17)) × 100 / (Total number of records in the data set (30))

$$= 17 \times 100 / 30$$

$$= 56.67\%$$

Measuring Accuracy

Accuracy is the degree to which data correctly represent the real-world object, entity, situation, phenomena, or event being described. It is a measure of the correctness of the content of the data (which requires an authoritative source of reference to be identified and available). Accuracy of data can only be achieved by either:

- Assessing the data against the real-world entity, event, or phenomena that they represent.

- Assessing the data against an authoritative reference data set that is a substitute for the real-world entity, event, or phenomena, and that has been validated for accuracy. The authoritative data set may be third-party reference data from sources that are considered trustworthy and of the same chronology. Validating addresses for accuracy is often done by comparing them with the postal databases of the respective countries.

Business rules need to be defined to assess accuracy. In order to correctly define business rules to measure data accuracy, it is necessary to understand the grain and representation of the data in both the data set whose accuracy needs to be measured and in the reference data set against which accuracy is assessed. Business rules for assessing accuracy would differ based on the grain, format, and representation of the data and business rules. For example, there are three different data sets whose accuracy needs to be assessed against a reference data set. All these data sets store the customer name, among other customer attributes.

- In the reference data set, the customer's first name, middle name, and last name are stored in different data elements, say, First Name, Middle Name, and Last Name.

- In the first data set, the customer's full name, consisting of the first name, middle name, and last name, separated by spaces, is stored in a single data element, say, Full Name.

- In the second data set, the customer's full name, consisting of only the first and the last name, separated by a space, is stored in a single data element, say, Full Name.

- In the third data set, the customer's first name, middle name, and last name are stored in different data elements, say, First Name, Middle Name, and Last Name.

The business rules for comparing the customer names with those in the reference data set would differ for all three data sets.

For the first data set, the full name values in the data set need to be compared against a concatenation of the first name, middle name, and last name, separated by spaces, from the reference data set. If the middle name is not populated or has blank values, the full name in the data set needs to be compared against a concatenation of the first name and last name, separated by a space, from the reference data set.

For the second data set, the full name in the data set needs to be compared against a concatenation of the first name and last name, separated by a space, from the reference data set.

For the third data set, the value resulting from the concatenation of the first name, middle name, and last name, separated by spaces, in the data set needs to be compared against a concatenation of the first name, middle name, and last name, separated by spaces, from the reference data set. If the middle name is not populated or has blank values, the value resulting from the concatenation of the first name and last name, separated by a space, in the data set needs to be compared against a concatenation of the first name and last name, separated by a space, from the reference data set.

Accuracy can be measured at two levels:

- Data element

- Data record

Accuracy is usually measured in a percentage, and is the proportion of the stored data versus the potential of 100% accuracy.

Measuring Accuracy at the Data Element Level. Data element accuracy is measured by comparing the data element with the available domain of values for the same data element in the reference data set. Following are the steps outlined to measure accuracy at the data element level.

For each critical data element in the data set:

1. Determine whether there are any missing values. This is explained in the "Measuring Data Element Completeness" section of this chapter. Missing value occurrences are excluded from the accuracy calculations.

2. Determine the matching data elements between the data set and the reference data set. While sometimes, data element names in both sets are the same or similar, there are times when it is difficult to determine which data element in the reference data set needs to be matched with the data element in the data set, either because there are more than one data element with similar names or because the data element names in the data set and those in the reference data set are not comparable. In such cases, matching data elements can be determined by studying the data definitions and metadata of the data elements. Ideally, the metadata for matching data elements should be similar. It is good practice to study the metadata of the data elements when matching data elements, even when the names are very similar.

3. Look up the data element values—excluding missing values and hidden blank values in the data set—in the set of values for the corresponding data

element in the reference data set. If the value is present in the set of values in the corresponding data element in the reference data set, then the data element value is accurate, otherwise it is inaccurate.

4. Find the number of values for the data element, excluding manifestations of missing values and hidden blanks, in the data set.

5. Compute the total number of accurate values for the data element and the total number of inaccurate values for the data element.

The formula for calculating the data element accuracy % is as follows:

Accuracy % = (Number of accurate values of a data element in the data set, excluding manifestations of missing values) × 100 / (Number of values for the data element in the data set, excluding manifestation of missing values)

Alternatively,

Accuracy % = (Number of values for a data element in the data set, excluding manifestation of missing values – Number of inaccurate values of the data element in the data set, excluding manifestations of missing values) × 100 / (Number of values for the data element in the data set, excluding manifestation of missing values)

Inaccuracy % = (Number of inaccurate values of a data element in the data set, excluding manifestations of missing values) × 100 / (Number of values for the data element in the data set, excluding manifestation of missing values)

Example 4.9. We will illustrate accuracy at the data element level using the employee data set we used in Example 4.1. As discussed before, in the employee data set, all three data elements, that is, Employee ID, Employee Name, and Social Security Number, are critical data elements. In order to measure accuracy at the data element level, we use the reference data set as shown in Table 4.14 and the employee data set shown in Table 4.15.

Measuring Employee ID Accuracy

Step 1. Scanning through the Employee ID data element values, we can see that there are no missing values and no hidden blanks.

Step 2. The Employee ID data element in the employee data set needs to be compared with the equivalent data element Employee ID in the reference data set. Since the names are an exact match, we will skip browsing the metadata of these data elements.

Step 3. Comparing each employee ID value in the employee data set with the employee ID values in the reference data set, we find that except for the following employee ID

Table 4.14	Reference employee data set for Example 4.9.		
Employee ID	**Employee name**	**Preferred name**	**Social security number**
E00000952	Jo Lee	Lisa Strong	122-17-9870
E00000953	Mark Young	Mark Young	155-76-5432
E00000954	Lance Seaton	Lance Seaton	142-19-8765
E00000955	Brent Morton	Brent Morton	111-76-7890
E00000957	Neil Ford	Neil Ford	126-43-6083
E00000958	James Worth	James Worth	143-14-1422
E00000959	Fredrick Ashton	Fred Ashton	118-41-3412
E00000960	Sita Hari	Sita Hari	151-77-7654
E00000961	Harry Fielding	Harry Fielding	132-11-8775
E00000962	Silver Rhodes	Silver Rhodes	151-23-6545
E00000963	Rodger Rome	Rodger Rome	141-11-9826
E00000964	Ray Bridgeford	Ray Bridgeford	152-12-9431
E00000965	Gretta Collins	Gretta Collins	135-24-9843
E00000966	Philip Montana	Philip Montana	121-98-3215
E00000967	Monica Sutton	Monica Sutton	132-12-8775
E00000968	Augustus Edward	Augustus Edward	132-43-5634
E00000969	Leonardo Napoli	Leonardo Napoli	121-34-7865
E00000970	Raj Kumar Singh	Raj Kumar Singh	113-75-6547
E00000971	Joseph Forrest	Joseph Forrest	163-13-4325
E00000973	Nicholas Emerson	Nic Emerson	163-89-5438
E00000974	Mona Sinha	Mona Sinha	185-32-6572
E00000975	Lovissa Wu	Diana Song	129-31-5678
E00000976	Gianna King	Gianna King	146-13-3577
E00000977	George Anton	George Anton	143-17-7884
E00000978	Deep Seth	Deep Seth	171-52-5398
E00000979	Farah Hong	Farah Hong	181-14-9893
E00000980	Harish Kant Patel	Harish Kant Patel	133-12-7545
E00000981	Rose Baxter	Rose Baxter	127-33-2198

Table 4.15   Employee data set for Example 4.9

Employee ID	Employee name	Social security number
E00000952	Jo Lee	122-17-9870
E00000953	Mark Young	155-76-5432
E00000954	Lance Seaton	142-19-8765
E00000955	Brent Morton	111-76-7890
E00000956	Lisa Strong	122-17-9870
E00000957	Neil Ford	NULL
E00000958	James Worth	143-14-1422
E00000959	Fredrick Ashton	abc de
E00000960		151-77-7654
E00000961	Harry Fielding	132-11-8775
E00000962	Silver Rhodes	UNKWN
E00000963	Rodger Rome	UNKWN
E00000964	Ray Bridgeford	152-12-9431
E00000965	Gretta Collins	UNKWN
E00000966	Philip Montana	UNKWN
E00000967	Monica Sutton	132-11-8775
E00000968	Augustus Edward	UNKWN
E00000969	Leonardo Napoli	UNKWN
E00000970	Raj Kumar Singh	UNKWN
E00000971	Joseph Forrest	163-13-4325
E00000972		143-17-7884
E00000973	Nicholas Emerson	UNKWN
E00000974	Mona Sinha	UNKWN
E00000975	Lovissa Wu	NULL
E00000976	Gianna King	UNKWN
E00000977	George Anton	143-17-7884
E00000978	Deep Seth	NULL
E00000979	Farah Hong	181-14-9893
E00000980	Harish Kant Patel	133-12-7545
E00000981	Rose Baxter	UNKWN

values, all the other employee ID values in the employee data set are also present in the reference data set:

- E00000956

- E00000972

Hence, all the employee ID values except for the above two values are accurate.

Step 4. The total number of employee ID values in the data set is 30.

Step 5. In step 3, we discovered that all the employee ID values except for "E00000956" and "E00000972" are accurate. Hence, 28 employee ID values are accurate in the employee ID data set.

Step 6. Two employee ID data values are inaccurate.

Applying the formula for calculating the data element accuracy %,

> Accuracy % = (Number of accurate values of a data element in the data set, excluding manifestations of missing values (28) × 100 / (Number of values for the data element in the data set, excluding manifestation of missing values (30))

= 28 × 100 / 30

= 93.33%

Alternatively,

> Accuracy % = (Number of values for a data element in the data set, excluding manifestation of missing values (30) − Number of inaccurate values of the data element in the data set, excluding manifestations of missing values (2)) × 100 / (Number of values for the data element in the data set, excluding manifestation of missing values (30)

= (30 − 2) × 100 / 30

= 93.33%

> Inaccuracy % = (Number of inaccurate values of a data element in the data set, excluding manifestations of missing values (2)) × 100 / (Number of values for the data element in the data set, excluding manifestation of missing values (30))

= 2 × 100 / 30

= 6.67%

Measuring Employee Name Accuracy

Step 1. Scanning through the Employee Name data element values in the employee data set, we can see that there are two blanks, that is, two employee names are missing.

Step 2. The Employee Name data element in the employee data set (Table 4.15) needs to be compared with the equivalent data element Employee Name in the reference data set (Table 4.14). Even though the names are an exact match, since there is another data element, Preferred Name, that is very close to Employee Name, we will have to look at the description/metadata of these data elements to be sure as to which data element in the reference data set should be used for the purpose of matching Employee Name.

Following are the data definitions for the data elements in question:

- *Employee Name:* Employee name is the legal name of the employee.

- *Preferred Name:* Preferred name is the preferred name of the employee, which the employee uses for communication purposes.

Step 3. Comparing each employee name value in the employee data set with the employee name values in the reference data set, we find that, except for the employee name value "Lisa Strong," all the other employee name values in the employee data set are also present in the reference data set.

Hence, all the employee name values except for the value "Lisa Strong" are accurate.

Step 4. The total number of employee name values, excluding missing values, in the data set is 28.

Step 5. In step 3, we discovered that all the employee name values except for "Lisa Strong" are accurate. Hence, 27 employee name values are accurate in the Employee data set.

Step 6. One employee name data value is not accurate.

Applying the formula for calculating the data element accuracy %,

> Accuracy % = (Number of accurate values of a data element in the data set, excluding manifestations of missing values (27) × 100 / (Number of values for the data element in the data set, excluding manifestation of missing values (28))

$$= 27 \times 100 / 28$$

$$= 96.43\%$$

Alternatively,

> Accuracy % = (Number of values for a data element in the data set, excluding manifestation of missing values (28) – Number of inaccurate values of the data element in the data set, excluding manifestations of missing values (1)) × 100 / (Number of values for the data element in the data set, excluding manifestation of missing values (28)

$$= (28 - 1) \times 100 / 28$$

$$= 96.43\%$$

Inaccuracy % = (Number of inaccurate values of a data element in the data set, excluding manifestations of missing values (1)) × 100 / (Number of values for the data element in the data set, excluding manifestation of missing values (28))

= 1 × 100 / 28

= 3.57%

Measuring Social Security Number Accuracy

Step 1. The first step is to determine whether there are any missing social security number values, including hidden blanks. There are three *null* values and 11 hidden blanks manifested by the value "UNKNWN" for the data element Social Security Number in the employee data set. Hence, there are 14 missing social security number values in the data set (Table 4.15).

Step 2. The next step involves looking for the matching data element for the Social Security Number data element in the reference data set (Table 4.14). The reference data set has a data element Social Security Number, which can be used for matching social security number values in the employee data set (Table 4.15).

Step 3. Comparing each social security number value in the employee data set with the social security number values in the reference data set, we find that, except for the social security number value "abc de," all the other social security number values in the employee data set are also present in the reference data set.

Hence, all the social security number values except for the value "abc de" are accurate.

Step 4. The total number of social security number values, excluding missing values, in the data set is 16.

Step 5. In step 3, we discovered that all the social security number values, except for "abc de," are accurate. Hence, 15 social security number values are accurate in the employee data set.

Step 6. One social security number data value is not accurate.

Applying the formula for calculating the data element accuracy %,

Accuracy % = (Number of accurate values of a data element in the data set, excluding manifestations of missing values (15) × 100 / (Number of values for the data element in the data set, excluding manifestation of missing values (16))

= 15 × 100 / 16

= 93.75%

Alternatively,

> Accuracy % = (Number of values for a data element in the data set, excluding manifestation of missing values (16) – Number of inaccurate values of the data element in the data set, excluding manifestation of missing values (1)) × 100 / (Number of values for the data element in the data set, excluding manifestation of missing values (16)

$= (16 - 1) \times 100 / 16$

$= 15 \times 100 / 16$

$= 93.75\%$

> Inaccuracy % = (Number of inaccurate values of a data element in the data set, excluding manifestations of missing values (1)) × 100 / (Number of values for the data element in the data set, excluding manifestation of missing values (16))

$= 1 \times 100 / 16$

$= 6.25\%$

Measuring Accuracy at the Data Record Level. Data record accuracy can be measured by comparing all the critical data elements in a record with the corresponding record elements in the reference data set. If all critical data element values for a particular data set record have a one-to-one match with the corresponding data element values in a matching record in the reference data set, then the record is considered to be accurate. Following are the steps outlined to measure accuracy at the data record level:

1. Determine the critical elements in the data set.

2. For each critical data element, determine the matching data element in the reference data set as described in step 2 of the "Measuring Accuracy at the Data Element Level" section in this chapter.

3. Define business rules for defining data record accuracy, to compare the data element values for each critical data element for a particular record against the corresponding data element or data elements in a parallel record in the reference data set. If one or more critical data element values do not match or are missing, the record is considered inaccurate.

4. Apply the business rules for each record in the data set.

5. Compute the total number of accurate records in the data set and the total number of inaccurate records in the data set.

6. Find the total number of records in the data set. This should be the sum of the number of accurate records and inaccurate records in the data set. That is,

> Number of records in the data set = Number of accurate records in the data set + Number of inaccurate records in the data set

The formula for calculating the data record accuracy % is as follows:

$$\text{Accuracy \%} = \frac{(\text{Number of accurate records in the data set}) \times 100}{(\text{Number of records in the data set})}$$

Alternatively,

$$\text{Accuracy \%} = \frac{(\text{Number of records in the data set} - \text{Number of inaccurate records in the data set}) \times 100}{(\text{Number of records in the data set})}$$

$$\text{Inaccuracy \%} = \frac{(\text{Number of inaccurate records in the data set}) \times 100}{(\text{Number of records in the data set})}$$

Example 4.10. We will illustrate accuracy at the data record level using the employee data set we used in Example 4.1. In order to measure accuracy at the data record level, we use the reference data set as shown in Table 4.16.

Step 1. The first step is determining the critical elements in the employee data set. As discussed earlier in this chapter, the employee data set consists of three data elements—Employee ID, Employee Name, and Social Security Number, and all of these are critical.

Step 2. As described in Example 4.8 where we determined the matching data elements in the data set and the reference data set, the following table shows the mapping between the data elements in the data set whose record accuracy we need to measure and the reference data set.

Employee data set—data element	Reference data set—data element
Employee ID	Employee ID
Employee Name	Employee Name
Social Security Number	Social Security Number

Step 3. The business rules for establishing data record level accuracy are as follows.

For each data record in the employee data set:

- *Rule 1.* Using the employee ID value in the employee data set, search for the corresponding employee ID value in the reference data set. If a record with a matching employee ID value is not found in the reference data set, then the data record is not accurate. If the employee ID value is missing for a particular record, then mark the record as inaccurate.

  In other words, if

Table 4.16   Employee reference data set for Example 4.10.

Employee ID	Employee name	Preferred name	Social Security number
E00000952	Jo Lee	Lisa Strong	122-17-9870
E00000953	Mark Young	Mark Young	155-76-5432
E00000954	Lance Seaton	Lance Seaton	142-19-8765
E00000955	Brent Morton	Brent Morton	111-76-7890
E00000957	Neil Ford	Neil Ford	126-43-6083
E00000958	James Worth	James Worth	143-14-1422
E00000959	Fredrick Ashton	Fred Ashton	118-41-3412
E00000960	Sita Hari	Sita Hari	151-77-7654
E00000961	Harry Fielding	Harry Fielding	132-11-8775
E00000962	Silver Rhodes	Silver Rhodes	151-23-6545
E00000963	Rodger Rome	Rodger Rome	141-11-9826
E00000964	Ray Bridgeford	Ray Bridgeford	152-12-9431
E00000965	Gretta Collins	Gretta Collins	135-24-9843
E00000966	Philip Montana	Philip Montana	121-98-3215
E00000967	Monica Sutton	Monica Sutton	132-12-8775
E00000968	Augustus Edward	Augustus Edward	132-43-5634
E00000969	Leonardo Napoli	Leonardo Napoli	121-34-7865
E00000970	Raj Kumar Singh	Raj Kumar Singh	113-75-6547
E00000971	Joseph Forrest	Joseph Forrest	163-13-4325
E00000973	Nicholas Emerson	Nic Emerson	163-89-5438
E00000974	Mona Sinha	Mona Sinha	185-32-6572
E00000975	Lovissa Wu	Diana Song	129-31-5678
E00000976	Gianna King	Gianna King	146-13-3577
E00000977	George Anton	George Anton	143-17-7884
E00000978	Deep Seth	Deep Seth	171-52-5398
E00000979	Farah Hong	Farah Hong	181-14-9893
E00000980	Harish Kant Patel	Harish Kant Patel	133-12-7545
E00000981	Rose Baxter	Rose Baxter	127-33-2198

Employee ID$_{\text{Employee data set}}$ is not missing, *and*

Employee ID$_{\text{Employee data set}}$ = Employee ID$_{\text{Reference data set}}$,

then proceed to Rule 2, otherwise, mark the record as inaccurate.

- *Rule 2.* If a matching employee ID is found while executing rule 1 for a data record, compare the employee name and social security number values for that record with the employee name and social security number values in the corresponding record in the reference data set. If the values for both of these data elements match, then mark the record as accurate. If either the social security number or employee name value does not match the record, then mark the record as inaccurate.

In other words, *if*

Employee ID$_{\text{Employee data set}}$ = Employee ID$_{\text{Reference data set}}$

and if

Employee name$_{\text{Employee data set}}$ = Employee name$_{\text{Reference data set}}$

and

Social security number$_{\text{Employee data set}}$ = Social security number$_{\text{Reference data set}}$,

then mark the employee data set record as accurate

else mark the employee data set record as inaccurate.

Step 4. Applying the business rules defined in step 3, the records have been marked as accurate or inaccurate, with the reason stated under Explanation, in Table 4.17.

Step 5. The total number of accurate records as per Table 4.17 is 11, and the total number of inaccurate records is 19.

Step 6.

Number of records in the data set = Number of accurate records in the data set + Number of inaccurate records in the data set

= 11 + 19

= 30

Applying the formula for record accuracy,

Accuracy % = (Number of accurate records in the data set (11)) × 100 / (Number of records in the data set (30))

= 11 × 100 / 30

= 36.67%

Table 4.17	Accurate versus inaccurate records for Example 4.10.			
Employee ID	**Employee name**	**Social security number**	**Accurate or inaccurate**	**Explanation**
E00000952	Jo Lee	122-17-9870	Accurate	Matching employee ID value found in reference data set and a matching record containing the same employee name and social security number values found in the reference data set.
E00000953	Mark Young	155-76-5432	Accurate	
E00000954	Lance Seaton	142-19-8765	Accurate	
E00000955	Brent Morton	111-76-7890	Accurate	
E00000956	Lisa Strong	122-17-9870	Inaccurate	No matching employee ID value *E00000956* found in the reference data set.
E00000957	Neil Ford	NULL	Inaccurate	Though matching employee ID and employee name values found in reference data set, social security number is missing and hence cannot be matched with the social security number value in the reference data set.
E00000958	James Worth	143-14-1422	Accurate	Matching employee ID value found in reference data set and a matching record containing the same employee name and social security number values found in the reference data set.
E00000959	Fredrick Ashton	abc de	Inaccurate	Though matching employee ID and employee name values found in reference data set, social security number in the reference data set is *118-41-3412* and does not match with the social security number value in the employee data set.
E00000960		151-77-7654	Inaccurate	Though matching employee ID and social security number values found in reference data set, employee name is missing and hence cannot be matched with the employee name value in the reference data set.

Continued

	Employee name	Social security number	Accurate or inaccurate	Explanation
Table 4.17	*Continued.*			
Employee ID	**Employee name**	**Social security number**	**Accurate or inaccurate**	**Explanation**
E00000961	Harry Fielding	132-11-8775	Accurate	Matching employee ID value found in reference data set and a matching record containing the same employee name and social security number values found in the reference data set.
E00000962	Silver Rhodes	UNKWN	Inaccurate	Though matching employee ID and employee name values found in reference data set, social security number has hidden blank value of *UNKWN* and hence cannot be matched with the social security number value in the reference data set.
E00000963	Rodger Rome	UNKWN	Inaccurate	
E00000964	Ray Bridgeford	152-12-9431	Accurate	Matching employee ID value found in reference data set and a matching record containing the same employee name and social security number values found in the reference data set.
E00000965	Gretta Collins	UNKWN	Inaccurate	Though matching employee ID and employee name values found in reference data set, Social Security number has hidden blank value of *UNKWN* and hence cannot be matched with the social security number value in the reference data set.
E00000966	Philip Montana	UNKWN	Inaccurate	
E00000967	Monica Sutton	132-11-8775	Inaccurate	Though matching employee ID and employee name values found in reference data set, social security number in the reference data set is *132-12-8775* and does not match with the social security number value in the employee data set.

Continued

Employee ID	Employee name	Social security number	Accurate or inaccurate	Explanation
E00000968	Augustus Edward	UNKWN	Inaccurate	Though matching employee ID and employee name values found in reference data set, social security number has hidden blank value of *UNKWN* and hence cannot be matched with the social security number value in the reference data set.
E00000969	Leonardo Napoli	UNKWN	Inaccurate	
E00000970	Raj Kumar Singh	UNKWN	Inaccurate	
E00000971	Joseph Forrest	163-13-4325	Accurate	Matching employee ID value found in reference data set and a matching record containing the same employee name and social security number values found in the reference data set.
E00000972		143-17-7884	Inaccurate	No matching employee ID value *E00000972* found in the reference data set.
E00000973	Nicholas Emerson	UNKWN	Inaccurate	Though matching employee ID and employee name values found in reference data set, social security number has hidden blank value of *UNKWN* and hence cannot be matched with the social security number value in the reference data set.
E00000974	Mona Sinha	UNKWN	Inaccurate	
E00000975	Lovissa Wu	NULL	Inaccurate	Though matching employee ID and employee name values found in reference data set, social security number is missing and hence cannot be matched with the social security number value in the reference data set.

Table 4.17 Continued.

Continued

Table 4.17	*Continued.*			
Employee ID	**Employee name**	**Social Security number**	**Accurate or inaccurate**	**Explanation**
E00000976	Gianna King	UNKWN	Inaccurate	Though matching employee ID and employee name values found in reference data set, social security number has hidden blank value of *UNKWN* and hence cannot be matched with the social security number value in the reference data set.
E00000977	George Anton	143-17-7884	Accurate	Matching employee ID value found in reference data set and a matching record containing the same employee name and social security number values found in the reference data set.
E00000978	Deep Seth	NULL	Inaccurate	Though matching employee ID and employee name values found in reference data set, social security number is missing and hence cannot be matched with the social security number value in the reference data set.
E00000979	Farah Hong	181-14-9893	Accurate	Matching employee ID value found in reference data set and a matching record containing the same employee name and social security number values found in the reference data set.
E00000980	Harish Kant Patel	133-12-7545	Accurate	
E00000981	Rose Baxter	UNKWN	Inaccurate	Though matching employee ID and employee name values found in reference data set, social security number has hidden blank value of *UNKWN* and hence cannot be matched with the social security number value in the reference data set.

Alternatively,

$$\text{Accuracy \% = (Number of records in the data}$$
$$\text{set (30) } - \text{Number of inaccurate records in the data set}$$
$$(19)) \times 100 \, / \, (\text{Number of records in the data set (30))}$$

$$= 11 \times 100 \, /30$$

$$= 36.67\%$$

$$\text{Inaccuracy \% = (Number of inaccurate records in the data}$$
$$\text{set (19)) } \times 100 \, / \, (\text{Number of records in the data set (30))}$$

$$= 19 \times 100 \, / \, 30$$

$$= 63.33\%$$

Measuring Consistency

As defined in Chapter 3, *data consistency* means that data values are identical for all instances of an application, and data across the enterprise should be in sync with each other. Consistency can be measured at three levels:

- Record consistency

- Cross-record consistency

- Data set consistency

Please note that if values are consistent, it does not definitely mean that the values are accurate. However, if values are not consistent, then it definitely indicates that at least one of the values, if not all, are inaccurate and/or invalid.

Consistency is usually measured as a percentage, and is the proportion of the stored data versus the potential of 100% consistency.

Measuring Record Consistency. *Record consistency* is the consistency between the related data elements in the same record in one data set, and can be measured at two levels:

1. Data element combinations, where data elements are related to one other.

2. Record level—if one or more data element combinations are inconsistent, the record is inconsistent.

Measuring Consistency for Data Element Combinations in the Records in the Same Data Set. Data element combination consistency can be measured using the following steps:

1. Determine the data elements in the data set that have a relationship and need to be consistent. This can be done by studying the data elements and data in the data set to understand the nature of the data, and consulting a business user or subject matter expert.

2. Outline the business rules defining the relationship between the related data elements.

3. Apply the business rules to the related data elements in each record in the data set to determine whether the data element values are consistent.

4. For each data element combination, find the number of consistent data element combination values.

5. Find the total number of data element combination values in the data set. This should be the sum of the number of consistent data element combination values and the number of inconsistent data element combination values in the data set. That is,

$$\text{Number of data element combination values in the data set} = \text{Number of consistent data element combination values in the data set} + \text{Number of inconsistent data element combination values in the data set}$$

The formula for calculating the data element combination consistency % is as follows:

$$\text{Consistency \%} = (\text{Number of consistent data element combination values in the data set}) \times 100 / (\text{Number of data element combination values in the data set})$$

Alternatively,

$$\text{Consistency \%} = (\text{Number of data element combination values in the data set} - \text{Number of inconsistent data element combination values in the data set}) \times 100 / (\text{Number of data element combination values in the data set})$$

$$\text{Inconsistency \%} = (\text{Number of inconsistent data element combination values in the data set}) \times 100 / (\text{Number of data element combination values in the data set})$$

Example 4.11. We will illustrate data element level consistency using a random sample customer data set (related to individual customers only) of a utility company extracted from their database, as shown in Table 4.18. The customer data set has the following data elements: Customer ID, Title, Full Name, Date of Birth, First Name, Middle Name, Last Name, Gender, Customer Start Date, and Customer End Date, and contains 15 records. Figure 4.5 shows the data definitions of the data elements.

Step 1. Study the data to determine which data elements have relationships with one another and should be consistent.

Studying the data, we discover the following:

- Title and Gender should be consistent.

- Date of Birth and Customer Start Date should be consistent.

Table 4.18   Sample customer data set for Example 4.11.

Customer ID	Title	Full name	Date of birth	First name	Middle name	Last name	Gender	Customer start date	Customer end date
C000000345	Miss	Neil Reid	07/30/1965	Neil		Reid	Male	07/30/1989	12/12/9999
C000000346	Mrs	Maria Rome Ray	12/11/1978	Maria	Rome	Ray	Female	10/10/1978	12/12/9999
C000000347	Mr.	Brent Cart Lee	10/08/1959	Brent	Cart	Lee	Male	11/13/1988	12/12/9999
C000000348	Mr.	Carol More	11/15/1971	Carol		More	Female	10/20/2000	12/11/1995
C000000349	Mr.	Ryan Cole	12/14/1983	Ryan	Harris	Cole	Male	08/25/2001	12/12/9999
C000000350	Miss	Keith Edward	11/14/1990	Keith	John	Edward	Male	11/12/1980	12/12/9999
C000000351	Mrs	Sita Johnson	10/20/1984	Sita		Johnson	Female	10/10/1992	12/12/9999
C000000352	Lord	John E. King	07/30/1972	John	Edward	King	Male	04/25/1996	12/12/9999
C000000353	Mrs	Monica Ford	07/24/1983	Monica	Summer	Ford	Male	07/30/2004	12/12/9999
C000000354	Lord	Richard Sutton	12/14/1960	Richard		Sutton	Male	11/10/1988	10/01/2005
C000000355	Miss	Rosie Smith	12/14/1986	Rosie		Smith	Female	10/05/2007	12/12/9999
C000000356	Miss	Carly Hart	12/14/1945	Carly		Hart	Female	12/10/1997	12/12/9999
C000000357	Mrs	Sienna Ross	12/14/1960	Sienna		Ross	Female	10/18/1998	12/12/9999
C000000358	Mr	Deep Kumar Singh	12/14/1964	Deep	K.	Singh	Male	12/18/1988	12/12/9999
C000000359	Mr	Edmond Travers	07/30/1976	Edmond		Travers	Male	07/30/1995	12/12/9999

Data element name	Data definition
Customer ID	• Customer ID is a unique identifier for identifying a customer. • Customer ID should be recorded as follows: a. The customer ID should be a string field. b. The customer ID needs to start with the letter "C" followed by nine digits. c. The length of the customer ID should be 10 characters. d. The field should not have leading or trailing spaces. e. Except for the starting letter "C," no alphabetic or special characters are allowed. • Customer ID is a mandatory data element.
Title	• Title is a word prefixing a person's name (for example, Mr, Mrs, Miss). The full list of possible title values can be found under the "Title" column in Table 4.19. • Title is a mandatory data element. • Title should be recorded as follows: a. The title should be a string field with a maximum of 30 characters b. The field should not have leading or trailing spaces. c. No numeric or special characters are allowed.

Full name	• Full name is the legal name of the individual.
	
	• Full name is a string field with a maximum length of 255 characters.
	
	• No numeric or special characters except for spaces and "." are allowed.
	
	• Full name is a mandatory data element.
	
	• Full name should be stored in the following format:
	
	   – If no last name is present, "LNU" should be used in place of the last name.
	
	   – If no first name is present, "FNU" should be used in place of the first name.
	
	   – If there are no additional names between the first name and last name, then the name should be recorded as follows:
	
	      <First Name> <1 space> <Last Name>
	
	   – If the name has a first name, middle name, and last name, then the name should be recorded as follows:
	
	      <First Name> <1 space> <Middle Name> <1 space> <Last Name>
	
	   – If the name has more words than the first name, middle name, and last name, then the name should be recorded as follows:
	
	      <First Name> <1 space> <Second Name> <1 space> <Third Name Initials> <.> <1 space> <Fourth Name Initials> <.> <1 space> <Fifth Name Initials> <.> <1 space>.........<1 space> <Last Name>

Date of birth	• Date of birth is the birth date of the individual as reported on their birth certificate or other appropriate document. • Date of birth uses a date data type. • Date of birth has the following format: mm/dd/yyyy, for example, 12/14/1989, where mm is the month (in the example, 12), dd is the day of the month (in the example, 14), and yyyy is the year (in the example, 1989). • Date of birth is a mandatory data element.

Figure 4.5   Customer data—data definitions for Example 4.11.   *Continued*

Data element name	Data definition
First name	• First name is the first name of the individual. • First name is a string field with a maximum length of 255 characters. • No numeric or special characters except for spaces are allowed. • If no first name is present, "FNU" should be used in place of the first name. • First name is a mandatory data element.
Middle name	• Middle name is the middle name of the individual, and is the name between the first and last name. • If there is more than one name between the first and the last names, then the second name should be stored, followed by the initials, followed by the "." character. • Middle name is an optional field.
Last name	• Last name is the last name of the individual. • Last name is a string field with a maximum length of 255 characters. • No numeric or special characters except for spaces are allowed. • If no last name is present, "LNU" should be used in place of the last name. • Last name is a mandatory data element.
Gender	• Gender is the individual's sex, and is the biological distinction between male and female. • Gender has a string data type and a maximum length of six characters. • The permissible values are as per the table below: | Permissible values	Definition
M	Male
F	Female | • Gender is a mandatory data element.
Customer start date	• Customer start date is the date when the customer was registered. • Customer start date uses a date data type • Customer start date has the following format: mm/dd/yyyy. • Customer start date is a mandatory data element
Customer end date	• Customer end date is the date when the customer ceased to be a customer. • Customer end date uses a date data type. • Customer end date has the following format: mm/dd/yyyy. • For an existing customer, the customer end date should be recorded as "12/12/9999." • Customer end date is a mandatory data element.

Figure 4.5   *Continued.*

- Customer Start Date and Customer End Date should be consistent.

- Date of Birth and Customer End Date should be consistent.

- Full Name should be consistent with the First Name, Middle Name, and Last Name.

Table 4.19	Title and gender mappings for Example 4.11.
Title	**Gender**
Miss	F
Mrs	F
Mr	M
Master	M
Lord	M
Lady	F
Dr	M or F
Ms	F
Madam	F
Judge	M or F
Sir	M
Father	M
Brother	M
Mother	F
Sister	F

Step 2. Define the rules for consistency of each data element combination.

Title and gender consistency business rules. The valid title and gender mappings for title and gender consistency are documented in Table 4.19. Please note that the titles "Dr." and "Judge" are applicable to both females and males.

Date of birth and customer start date consistency business rules. The date of birth and customer start date should adhere to the following business rules to be consistent:

The customer start date cannot precede the customer's date of birth. Also, the customer needs to be at least 18 years of age on the date of registration. That is,

$$\text{Date of birth} < \text{Customer start date}$$

$$\text{and Customer start date} - \text{Date of birth} \geq 18 \text{ years}$$

Customer start date and customer end date consistency business rule. The customer start date and customer end date should adhere to the following business rule to be consistent:

The customer end date cannot precede the customer start date. That is,

$$\text{Customer start date} \leq \text{Customer end date}$$

Date of birth and customer end date consistency business rules. The date of birth and customer end date should adhere to the following business rules to be consistent:

> The customer end date cannot precede the customer's date of birth. Also, since the customer needs to be at least 18 years of age at the time of registration, the difference between the customer's end date and the customer's date of birth needs to be at least 18 years. That is,

$$\text{Date of birth} < \text{Customer end date}$$

$$\text{and Customer end date} - \text{Date of birth} \geq 18 \text{ years}$$

Full name, first name, middle name, and last name consistency business rules. For the full name to be consistent with the first name, middle name, and last name, the following business rules apply:

> The value in the full name field should be a concatenation of first name, middle name, and last name, with a space or blank character separating them:

$$\text{Full Name} = <\text{First Name}> < \text{1space}>$$
$$<\text{Middle Name}> <\text{1 space}> <\text{Last Name}>$$

> If an individual does not have a middle name, then the full name should be a concatenation of the first name and last name:

$$\text{Full Name} = <\text{First Name}> <\text{1 space}> <\text{Last Name}>$$

Step 3. *Title and Gender data element combination.* Applying the defined business rule to the data elements—Title and Gender, Table 4.20 shows the consistent and inconsistent values.

Step 4. *Title and Gender data element combination.* Table 4.20 shows that out of 15 value pairs, four title and gender combination values are inconsistent and the other 11 are consistent.

Step 5. *Title and Gender data element combination.* Step 5 involves computation of the total number of data element combination values in the data set. This should be the sum of the number of consistent data element combination values and the number of inconsistent data element combination values in the data set. That is,

$$\begin{aligned}\text{Number of data element combination values in the} \\ \text{data set} = \text{Number of consistent data element combination} \\ \text{values in the data set (11)} + \text{Number of inconsistent data} \\ \text{element combination values in the data set (4)}\end{aligned}$$

$$= 15$$

Applying the formula for calculating the data element combination consistency %,

Table 4.20	Title and gender—inconsistent and consistent values for Example 4.11.		
Customer ID	**Title**	**Gender**	**Consistent/inconsistent**
C000000345	Miss	Male	Inconsistent
C000000346	Mrs	Female	Consistent
C000000347	Mr	Male	Consistent
C000000348	Mr	Female	Inconsistent
C000000349	Mr	Male	Consistent
C000000350	Miss	Male	Inconsistent
C000000351	Mrs	Female	Consistent
C000000352	Lord	Male	Consistent
C000000353	Mrs	Male	Inconsistent
C000000354	Lord	Male	Consistent
C000000355	Miss	Female	Consistent
C000000356	Miss	Female	Consistent
C000000357	Mrs	Female	Consistent
C000000358	Mr	Male	Consistent
C000000359	Mr	Male	Consistent

Consistency % = (Number of consistent data element combination values in the data set (11)) × 100 / (Number of data element combination values in the data set (15))

= 11 × 100 / 15

= 73.33%

Alternatively,

Consistency % = (Number of data element combination values in the data set (15) – Number of inconsistent data element combination values in the data set (4)) × 100 / (Number of data element combination values in the data set (15))

= (15 – 4) × 100 / 15

= 11 × 100 / 15

= 73.33%

Inconsistency % = (Number of inconsistent data element combination values in the data set (4)) × 100 / (Number of data element combination values in the data set (15))

= 4 × 100 / 15

= 26.67%

Since step 1 ("Determine the data elements in the data set that have a relationship and need to be consistent. This can be done by studying the data elements and data in the data set to understand the nature of the data and consulting a business user or subject matter expert") and step 2 ("Outline the business rules to define the relationship between the related data elements") have already been covered in the earlier section, we will not be repeating them for each relationship. Instead, we will skip to steps 3 through 5 to discuss the following relationships:

- *Date of Birth and Customer Start Date data element combination*

- *Customer Start Date and Customer End Date data element combination*

- *Date of Birth and Customer End Date data element combination*

- *Full Name, First Name, Middle Name, and Last Name data element combination*

Step 3. *Date of Birth and Customer Start Date data element combination.* Applying the defined business rules to the data elements Date of Birth and Customer Start Date, Table 4.21 shows the consistent and inconsistent values.

Step 4. *Date of Birth and Customer Start Date data element combination.* Table 4.21 shows the date of birth and customer start date value combinations that are consistent and inconsistent. There are 11 consistent values and four inconsistent values.

Step 5. *Date of Birth and Customer Start Date data element combination.* Step 5 involves computation of the total number of data element combination values in the data set. This should be the sum of the number of consistent data element combination values and the number of inconsistent data element combination values in the data set. That is,

$$\text{Number of data element combination values in the data set} = \text{Number of consistent data element combination values in the data set (11)} + \text{Number of inconsistent data element combination values in the data set (4)}$$

$$= 15$$

Applying the formula for calculating the data element combination consistency %,

$$\text{Consistency \%} = \text{(Number of consistent data element combination values in the data set (11))} \times 100\ /\ \text{(Number of data element combination values in the data set (15))}$$

$$= 11 \times 100\ /\ 15$$

$$= 73.33\%$$

Table 4.21	Consistent and inconsistent values (date of birth and customer start date combination) for Example 4.11.			
Customer ID	**Date of birth**	**Customer start date**	**Consistent/ inconsistent**	**Explanation**
C000000345	07/30/1965	07/30/1989	Consistent	Customer's date of birth precedes customer start date, and their difference is greater than 18 years
C000000346	12/11/1978	10/10/1978	Inconsistent	Customer start date cannot precede the customer's date of birth
C000000347	10/08/1959	11/13/1988	Consistent	Customer's date of birth precedes customer start date, and their difference is greater than 18 years
C000000348	11/15/1971	10/20/2000	Consistent	Customer's date of birth precedes customer start date, and their difference is greater than 18 years
C000000349	12/14/1983	08/25/2001	Inconsistent	Customer's date of birth precedes customer start date, but their difference is less than 18 years
C000000350	11/14/1990	11/12/1980	Inconsistent	Customer start date cannot precede the customer's date of birth
C000000351	10/20/1984	10/10/1992	Inconsistent	Customer's date of birth precedes customer start date, but their difference is less than 18 years
C000000352	07/30/1972	04/25/1996	Consistent	Customer's date of birth precedes customer start date, and their difference is greater than 18 years
C000000353	07/24/1983	07/30/2004	Consistent	Customer's date of birth precedes customer start date, and their difference is greater than 18 years
C000000354	12/14/1960	11/10/1988	Consistent	Customer's date of birth precedes customer start date, and their difference is greater than 18 years

Continued

Table 4.21	Continued.			
Customer ID	**Date of birth**	**Customer start date**	**Consistent/ inconsistent**	**Explanation**
C000000355	12/14/1986	10/05/2007	Consistent	Customer's date of birth precedes customer start date, but, their difference is less than 18 years
C000000356	12/14/1945	12/10/1997	Consistent	Customer's date of birth precedes customer start date and their difference is greater than 18 years
C000000357	12/14/1960	10/18/1998	Consistent	Customer's date of birth precedes customer start date and their difference is greater than 18 years
C000000358	12/14/1964	12/18/1988	Consistent	Customer's date of birth precedes customer start date and their difference is greater than 18 years
C000000359	07/30/1976	07/30/1995	Consistent	Customer's date of birth precedes customer start date and their difference is greater than 18 years

Alternatively,

Consistency % = (Number of data element combination values in the data set (15) – Number of inconsistent data element combination values in the data set (4)) × 100 / (Number of data element combination values in the data set (15))

= (15 – 4) × 100 / 15

= 11 × 100 / 15

= 73.33%

Inconsistency % = (Number of inconsistent data element combination values in the data set (4)) × 100 / (Number of data element combination values in the data set (15))

= 4 × 100 / 15

= 26.67%

Now we return again to step 3 for further analysis of the other relationships.

Step 3. *Customer Start Date and Customer End Date data element combination).* Applying the defined business rule to the data elements Customer Start

Date and Customer End Date, Table 4.22 shows the consistent and inconsistent values.

Step 4. *Customer Start Date and Customer End Date data element combination.* Table 4.22 shows that 14 out of 15 customer start date and customer end date value combinations are consistent. One customer start date and customer end date value combination is not consistent.

Table 4.22			Consistent and inconsistent values (customer start date and customer end date combination) for Example 4.11.	
Customer ID	Customer start date	Customer end date	Consistent/ inconsistent	Explanation
C000000345	07/30/1989	12/12/9999	Consistent	Customer start date precedes customer end date
C000000346	10/10/1978	12/12/9999	Consistent	Customer start date precedes customer end date
C000000347	11/13/1988	12/12/9999	Consistent	Customer start date precedes customer end date
C000000348	10/20/2000	12/11/1995	Inconsistent	Customer start date does not precede customer end date
C000000349	08/25/2001	12/12/9999	Consistent	Customer start date precedes customer end date
C000000350	11/12/1980	12/12/9999	Consistent	Customer start date precedes customer end date
C000000351	10/10/1992	12/12/9999	Consistent	Customer start date precedes customer end date
C000000352	04/25/1996	12/12/9999	Consistent	Customer start date precedes customer end date
C000000353	07/30/2004	12/12/9999	Consistent	Customer start date precedes customer end date
C000000354	11/10/1988	10/01/2005	Consistent	Customer start date precedes customer end date
C000000355	10/05/2007	12/12/9999	Consistent	Customer start date precedes customer end date
C000000356	12/10/1997	12/12/9999	Consistent	Customer start date precedes customer end date
C000000357	10/18/1998	12/12/9999	Consistent	Customer start date precedes customer end date
C000000358	12/18/1988	12/12/9999	Consistent	Customer start date precedes customer end date
C000000359	07/30/1995	12/12/9999	Consistent	Customer start date precedes customer end date

Step 5. *(Customer Start Date and Customer End Date data element combination.* Step 5 involves computation of the total number of data element combination values in the data set. This should be the sum of the number of consistent data element combination values and the number of inconsistent data element combination values in the data set. That is,

Number of data element combination values in the data set =
Number of consistent data element combination values
in the data set (14) + Number of inconsistent data
element combinations values in the data set (1)

= 15

Applying the formula for calculating the data element combination consistency %,

Consistency % = (Number of consistent data element
combination values in the data set (14)) × 100 / (Number of
data element combination values in the data set (15))

= 14 × 100 / 15

= 93.33%

Alternatively,

Consistency % = (Number of data element combination values
in the data set (15) − Number of inconsistent data element
combination values in the data set (1)) × 100 / (Number of
data element combination values in the data set (15))

= (15 − 1) × 100 / 15

= 14 × 100 / 15

= 93.33%

Inconsistency % = (Number of inconsistent data element
combination values in the data set (1)) × 100 / (Number of
data element combination values in the data set (15))

= 1 × 100 / 15

= 6.67%

Now we return again to step 3 for further analysis of the other relationships.

Step 3. *Date of Birth and Customer End Date Data Element Combination.* Applying the defined business rules to the data elements Date of Birth and Customer End Date, Table 4.23 shows the consistent and inconsistent values.

Table 4.23	Consistent and inconsistent values (date of birth and customer end date combination) for Example 4.11.			
Customer ID	Date of birth	Customer end date	Consistent/ inconsistent	Explanation
C000000345	07/30/1965	12/12/9999	Consistent	Customer's date of birth precedes customer end date, and their difference is greater than 18 years
C000000346	12/11/1978	12/12/9999	Consistent	Customer's date of birth precedes customer end date, and their difference is greater than 18 years
C000000347	10/08/1959	12/12/9999	Consistent	Customer's date of birth precedes customer end date, and their difference is greater than 18 years
C000000348	11/15/1971	12/11/1995	Consistent	Customer's date of birth precedes customer end date, and their difference is greater than 18 years
C000000349	12/14/1983	12/12/9999	Consistent	Customer's date of birth precedes customer end date, and their difference is greater than 18 years
C000000350	11/14/1990	12/12/9999	Consistent	Customer's date of birth precedes customer end date, and their difference is greater than 18 years
C000000351	10/20/1984	12/12/9999	Consistent	Customer's date of birth precedes customer end date, and their difference is greater than 18 years
C000000352	07/30/1972	12/12/9999	Consistent	Customer's date of birth precedes customer end date, and their difference is greater than 18 years
C000000353	07/24/1983	12/12/9999	Consistent	Customer's date of birth precedes customer end date, and their difference is greater than 18 years
C000000354	12/14/1960	10/01/2005	Consistent	Customer's date of birth precedes customer end date, and their difference is greater than 18 years
C000000355	12/14/1986	12/12/9999	Consistent	Customer's date of birth precedes customer end date, and their difference is greater than 18 years

Continued

		Customer	Consistent/	
Customer ID	**Date of birth**	**end date**	**inconsistent**	**Explanation**
C000000356	12/14/1945	12/12/9999	Consistent	Customer's date of birth precedes customer end date, and their difference is greater than 18 years
C000000357	12/14/1960	12/12/9999	Consistent	Customer's date of birth precedes customer end date, and their difference is greater than 18 years
C000000358	12/14/1964	12/12/9999	Consistent	Customer's date of birth precedes customer end date, and their difference is greater than 18 years
C000000359	07/30/1976	12/12/9999	Consistent	Customer's date of birth precedes customer end date, and their difference is greater than 18 years

Table 4.23 *Continued.*

Step 4. *Date of Birth and Customer End Date data element combination.* Table 4.23 shows that all 15 date of birth and customer end date value combinations are consistent.

Step 5. *Date of Birth and Customer End Date data element combination.* Step 5 involves computation of the total number of data element combination values in the data set. This should be the sum of the number of consistent data element combination values and the number of inconsistent data element combination values in the data set. That is,

Number of data element combination values in the data set = Number of consistent data element combination values in the data set (15) + Number of inconsistent data element combination values in the data set (0)

= 15

Applying the formula for calculating the data element combination consistency %,

Consistency % = (Number of consistent data element combination values in the data set (15)) × 100 / (Number of data element combination values in the data set (15))

= 15 × 100 / 15

= 100%

Alternatively,

Consistency % = (Number of data element combination values in the data set (15) – Number of inconsistent data element combination values in the data set (0)) × 100 / (Number of data element combination values in the data set (15))

= (15 – 0) × 100 / 15

= 15 × 100 / 15

= 100%

Inconsistency % = (Number of inconsistent data element combination values in the data set (0)) × 100 / (Number of data element combination values in the data set (15))

= 0 × 100 / 15

= 0%

Now we return again to step 3 for further analysis of the last relationship.

Step 3. *(Full Name, First Name, Middle Name, and Last Name data element combination.* Applying the defined business rules to the data elements Full Name, First Name, Middle Name, and Last Name, Table 4.24 shows the consistent and inconsistent names.

Step 4. *Full Name, First Name, Middle Name, and Last Name data element combination.* Table 4.24 shows that of 15 full name, first name, middle name, and last name data value combinations, 10 are consistent and 5 are inconsistent.

Step 5. *Full Name, First Name, Middle Name, and Last Name data element combination.* Step 5 involves computation of the total number of data element combination values in the data set. This should be the sum of the number of consistent data element combination values and the number of inconsistent data element combination values in the data set. That is,

Number of data element combination values in the data set = Number of consistent data element combination values in the data set (10) + Number of inconsistent data element combinations values in the data set (5)

= 15

Table 4.24 Consistent and inconsistent values (full name, first name, middle name, and last name data element combination) for Example 4.11.

Full name	First name	Middle name	Last name	Concatenated value	Consistent/ inconsistent	Explanation
Neil Reid	Neil		Reid	Neil Reid	Consistent	
Maria Rome Ray	Maria	Rome	Ray	Maria Rome Ray	Consistent	
Brent Cart Lee	Brent	Cart	Lee	Brent Cart Lee	Consistent	
Carol More	Carol		More	Carol More	Consistent	
Ryan Cole	Ryan	Harris	Cole	Ryan Harris Cole	Inconsistent	The middle name is missing in the full name
Keith Edward	Keith	John	Edward	Keith John Edward	Inconsistent	The middle name is missing in the full name
Sita Johnson	Sita		Johnson	Sita Johnson	Consistent	
John E. King	John	Edward	King	John Edward King	Inconsistent	The middle name "Edward" has been abbreviated to "E." in the full name
Monica Ford	Monica	Summer	Ford	Monica Summer Ford	Inconsistent	The middle name is missing in the full name
Richard Sutton	Richard		Sutton	Richard Sutton	Consistent	
Rosie Smith	Rosie		Smith	Rosie Smith	Consistent	
Carly Hart	Carly		Hart	Carly Hart	Consistent	
Sienna Ross	Sienna		Ross	Sienna Ross	Consistent	
Deep Kumar Singh	Deep	K.	Singh	Deep K. Singh	Inconsistent	Middle name is "K." in concatenated value but "Kumar" in the full name
Edmond Travers	Edmond		Travers	Edmond Travers	Consistent	

Applying the formula for calculating the data element combination consistency %,

> Consistency % = (Number of consistent data element combination values in the data set (10)) × 100 / (Number of data element combination values in the data set (15))

= 10 × 100 / 15

= 66.67%

Alternatively,

> Consistency % = (Number of data element combination values in the data set (15) – Number of inconsistent data element combination values in the data set (10)) × 100 / (Number of data element combination values in the data set (15))

= (15 – 5) × 100 / 15

= 10 × 100 / 15

= 66.67%

> Inconsistency % = (Number of inconsistent data element combination values in the data set (5)) × 100 / (Number of data element combination values in the data set (15))

= 5 × 100 / 15

= 33.33%

Table 4.25 summarizes the consistency and inconsistency results for all the different data element value combinations in the customer data set.

Table 4.25   Consistency results for different data element combinations for Example 4.11.

Data element combinations	Consistency %	Inconsistency %
Title and gender should be consistent.	73.33	26.67
Date of birth and customer start date should be consistent.	73.33	26.67
Customer start date and customer end date should be consistent.	93.33	6.67
Date of birth and customer end date should be consistent.	100	0
Full name should be consistent with the first name, middle name, and last name.	66.67	33.33

Measuring Consistency at the Record Level in the Same Data Set. Record
level consistency in the same data set can be measured using the following steps:

1. Determine the data elements in the data set that have a relationship and
    need to be consistent. This can be done by studying the data elements and
    data in the data set to understand the nature of the data, and by consulting
    a business user.

2. Outline the business rules for defining the relationship between the related
    data elements.

3. Apply the business rules to the related data elements in each record in the
    data set to determine whether the data element values are consistent.

    For each data record, determine whether any of the data element values are
    inconsistent. If any of the data element values are inconsistent in the data
    record, then the record is considered inconsistent. If all the data element
    values that have a relationship are consistent as per the defined business
    rules, then the data record is considered consistent.

4. Compute the total number of consistent records and the total number of
    inconsistent records in the data set.

5. Find the total number of records in the data set. This should be the sum
    of the number of consistent records and the number of inconsistent
    records in the data set. That is,

    > Number of records in the data set = Number of consistent records
    > in the data set + Number of inconsistent records in the data set

    The formula for calculating the record consistency % is as follows:

    > Consistency % = (Number of consistent records in
    > the data set) × 100 / (Number of records in the data set)

    Alternatively,

    > Consistency % = (Number of records in the
    > data set − Number of inconsistent records in the
    > data set) × 100 / (Number of records in the data set)

    > Inconsistency % = (Number of inconsistent records in
    > the data set) × 100 / (Number of records in the data set)

Example 4.12. We will make use of the customer data set shown in Example
4.11 (Table 4.18) to measure record level consistency. The first three steps used
to measure consistency for data element combinations in the records in the
same data set can also be used to measure record level consistency, and since
these steps have already been executed in Example 4.10, Table 4.26 provides a
holistic picture of which records are consistent and inconsistent, and the reason
for inconsistency.

Table 4.26 Record level consistency/inconsistency for Example 4.12.

Customer ID	Title	Full name	Date of birth	First name	Middle name	Last name	Gender	Customer start date	Customer end date	Consistent/ inconsistent	Number of data element combinations not consistent	Reason for inconsistency
C000000345	Miss	Neil Reid	07/30/1965	Neil		Reid	Male	07/30/1989	12/12/9999	Inconsistent	1	Title is "Miss" but gender is male.
C000000346	Mrs	Maria Rome Ray	12/11/1978	Maria	Rome	Ray	Female	10/10/1978	12/12/9999	Inconsistent	1	Customer Start Date precedes the customer's date of birth.
C000000347	Mr	Brent Cart Lee	10/08/1959	Brent	Cart	Lee	Male	11/13/1988	12/12/9999	Consistent	0	
C000000348	Mr	Carol More	11/15/1971	Carol		More	Female	10/20/2000	12/11/1995	Inconsistent	2	Title is "Mr" but gender is female. Customer End Date precedes Customer Start Date.
C000000349	Mr	Ryan Cole	12/14/1983	Ryan	Harris	Cole	Male	08/25/2001	12/12/9999	Inconsistent	2	The Full Name is not concatenation of First Name, Middle Name, and Last Name. The difference between Date of Birth and Customer Start Date is less than 18 years.
C000000350	Miss	Keith Edward	11/14/1990	Keith	John	Edward	Male	11/12/1980	12/12/9999	Inconsistent	3	The Full Name is not concatenation of First Name, Middle Name, and Last Name. Title is "Miss" but gender is male. Customer Start Date precedes the Customer's Date of Birth.
C000000351	Mrs	Sita Johnson	10/20/1984	Sita		Johnson	Female	10/10/1992	12/12/9999	Inconsistent	1	The difference between Date of Birth and Customer Start Date is less than 18 years.
C000000352	Major	John E. King	07/30/1972	John	Edward	King	Male	04/25/1996	12/12/9999	Inconsistent	1	The Full Name is not concatenation of First Name, Middle Name, and Last Name.
C000000353	Mrs	Monica Ford	07/24/1983	Monica	Summer	Ford	Male	07/30/2004	12/12/9999	Inconsistent	2	Title is "Mrs" but gender is male. The Full Name is not concatenation of First Name, Middle Name, and Last Name.
C000000354	Lord	Richard Sutton	12/14/1960	Richard		Sutton	Male	11/10/1988	10/01/2005	Consistent	0	
C000000355	Miss	Rosie Smith	12/14/1986	Rosie		Smith	Female	10/05/2007	12/12/9999	Consistent	0	
C000000356	Miss	Carly Hart	12/14/1945	Carly		Hart	Female	12/10/1997	12/12/9999	Consistent	0	
C000000357	Mrs	Seinna Ross	12/14/1960	Seinna		Ross	Female	10/18/1998	12/12/9999	Consistent	0	
C000000358	Mr	Deep Kumar Singh	12/14/1964	Deep	K.	Singh	Male	12/18/1988	12/12/9999	Inconsistent	1	The Full Name is not concatenation of First Name, Middle Name, and Last Name.
C000000359	Mr	Edmond Travers	07/30/1976	Edmond		Travers	Male	07/30/1995	12/12/9999	Consistent	0	

Step 4. From Table 4.26, we find that the number of consistent records is six, and the number of inconsistent records is nine.

Step 5. The total number of records in the customer data set is the sum of the consistent and inconsistent records, that is,

$$6 + 9 = 15$$

Applying the formula for record level consistency,

Consistency % = (Number of consistent records in the data set (6)) × 100 / (Number of records in the data set (15))

$$= 6 \times 100 / 15$$

$$= 40\%$$

Alternatively,

Consistency % = (Number of records in the data set (15) – Number of inconsistent records in the data set (9)) × 100 / (Number of records in the data set (15))

$$= (15 - 9) \times 100 / 15$$

$$= 6 \times 100 / 15$$

$$= 40\%$$

Inconsistency % = (Number of inconsistent records in the data set (9)) × 100 / (Number of records in the data set (15))

$$= 9 \times 100 / 15$$

$$= 60\%$$

Measuring Cross-Record Consistency. *Cross-record consistency* is the consistency between the records of different data sets, and can be measured using the following steps:

1. Determine the critical data elements in the data sets that need to be consistent with each other, and understand the relationship between the data stored in the data sets. The related data records across the data sets might have a one-to-one, one-to-many, or many-to-many relationship between them.

2. Outline the business rules for determining consistency between the data elements across the data sets identified in step 1.

3. Apply the business rules to the related data elements in each record in the data sets to determine whether the data element values are consistent. If

one or more of the business rules are not satisfied, then the records in the data sets are considered inconsistent. If all the business rules are satisfied for the pair of records across the data sets, then the records are considered to be consistent.

4. Compute the total number of consistent records across the data set and the total number of inconsistent records across the data set.

The formula for calculating the data record consistency % is as follows:

$$\text{Consistency \%} = \frac{(\text{Number of consistent records in the data set}) \times 100}{(\text{Number of consistent records in the data set} + \text{Number of inconsistent records in the data set})}$$

Alternatively,

$$\text{Consistency \%} = \frac{(\text{Number of records in the data set} - \text{Number of inconsistent records in the data set}) \times 100}{(\text{Number of consistent records in the data set} + \text{Number of inconsistent records in the data set})}$$

$$\text{Inconsistency \%} = \frac{(\text{Number of inconsistent records in the data set}) \times 100}{(\text{Number of consistent records in the data set} + \text{Number of inconsistent records in the data set})}$$

Example 4.13. We will illustrate calculation of cross-record consistency between claim data set and customer data set extracts of a medical insurance company. The customer data and claim data are captured in different data sources. The customer data set extract has the following data elements: Customer ID, Customer Name, Date of Birth, Policy Number, Customer Start Date, and Customer End Date. The claim data set has the following data elements: Customer ID, Customer Name, Doctor Name, Date of Illness, Claim Submission Date, Illness Category, and Illness Description. Tables 4.27a and 4.27b show the sample customer and claim data sets that we will use to illustrate cross-record consistency.

Step 1. The first step involves determining the critical data elements that need to be consistent across the data sets. The data elements that need to be consistent across the data sets are as follows:

1. The customer ID in the claim data set should be consistent with the customer ID in the customer data set.

2. The customer name in the claim data set should be consistent with the customer name in the customer data set.

3. The date data elements in the claim data set should be consistent with the date data elements in the customer data set.

Table 4.27a	Customer data table for Example 4.13.				
Customer data					
Customer ID	**Customer name**	**Birth date**	**Policy number**	**Customer start date**	**Customer end date**
A00001234	Brian Kerr	23/12/1994	P01234A	19/09/2017	12/12/1999
A00001235	Kylie Hart	14/12/1958	P01234A	10/11/1981	12/12/1999
A00001236	Mona Mary Lee	10/08/1967	P01234A	11/06/1989	12/12/1999
A00001239	Greg Trent Nerd	21/11/1967	P01111A	16/04/1999	12/12/1999
A00001240	Ash Heather Ray	10/08/1974	P01234A	10/03/1998	12/12/1999
A00001241	Kent John Seth	17/01/1972	P01234A	12/10/1989	12/12/1999
A00001243	John Port Hill	10/05/1962	P01111A	22/04/1986	21/12/1999
A00001245	Ria Lia Singh	12/08/1945	P01234A	17/08/1970	12/12/1999
A00001246	Mitch Haris Wild	18/03/1960	P01111A	11/04/1988	12/12/1999
A00001247	Fionna Wu	12/10/1964	P01234A	11/07/1994	12/12/1999

A customer can place several claims; however, a claim can be related to only one customer, hence there is a one-to-many relationship between the customer and claim data sets.

Step 2. In this step, we will define the business rules for consistency between data elements across the data sets. For a particular customer, following are the business rules for the related records to be considered consistent:

1. The customer ID in a data record in the claim data set should have the same value as the customer ID in the corresponding record in the customer data set.

2. The customer name in a data record in the claim data set should have the same value as the customer name in the corresponding record in the customer data set.

3. The illness start date value in the claim data set should be greater than the customer start date in the customer data set.

4. The illness start date value in the claim data set should be less than the customer end date in the customer data set.

5. The illness start date value in the claim data set should be greater than the birth date in the customer data set.

6. The claim submission date value in the claim data set should be greater than the customer start date in the customer data set.

Table 4.27b Claim data table for Example 4.13.

Claim data

Customer ID	Claim ID	Customer name	Doctor name	Illness start date	Illness end date	Claim submission date	Illness description
A00001234	L000001234	Brian Kerr	Connor Young	10/09/2017	12/09/2017	18/09/2017	Eye redness
A00001235	L000001235	Kylie Hart	Rashmi Singh	11/09/2017	11/09/2017	18/09/2017	Cough
A00001236	L000001236	Mona Mary Lee	Nora Ford	15/09/2017	15/09/2017	18/09/2017	Migraine
A00001239	L000001237	Greg Nerd	Maria Smith	14/09/2017	14/09/2017	18/09/2017	Fever
A00001240	L000001238	Ash Ray	Rashmi Singh	14/09/2017	14/09/2017	18/09/2017	Stomach upset
A00001241	L000001239	Kent John Seth	Connor Young	16/09/2017	16/09/2017	18/09/2017	Eye irritation
A00001243	L000001240	John Port Hill	Nora Ford	16/09/2017	18/09/2017	18/09/2017	Abdomen pain
A00001245	L000001241	Ria Lia Singh	John Forest	10/09/2017	10/09/2017	18/09/2017	Chest pain
A00001246	L000001242	Mitch Wild	Charles Holt	11/09/2017	11/09/2017	18/09/2017	Sore throat
A00001247	L000001243	Fionna Wu	Connor Young	12/09/2017	12/09/2017	18/09/2017	Low vision

7. The claim submission date value in the claim data set should be less than the customer end date in the customer data set.

8. The claim submission date value in the claim data set should be greater than the birth date in the customer data set.

9. The illness end date value in the claim data set should be greater than the customer start date in the customer data set.

10. The illness end date value in the claim data set should be less than the customer end date in the customer data set.

11. The illness end date value in the claim data set should be greater than the birth date in the customer data set.

Step 3. Applying the business rules for consistency across the records in the data sets, the consistent and inconsistent records have been marked with an explanation, as shown in Tables 4.28a and 4.28b.

Step 4. From Table 4.28, we find that the total number of consistent records is six, and total number of inconsistent records is four.

Applying the formula for calculating the data record consistency %,

Consistency % = (Number of consistent records in the data set (6) × 100 / (Number of consistent records in the data set (6) + Number of inconsistent records in the data set (4))

= 6 × 100 / 10

= 60%

Table 4.28a	Customer data and claim data inconsistency/consistency for Example 4.13.				
Customer data					
Customer ID	**Customer name**	**Birth date**	**Policy number**	**Customer start date**	**Customer end date**
A00001234	Brian Kerr	23/12/1994	P01234A	19/09/2017	12/12/1999
A00001235	Kylie Hart	14/12/1958	P01234A	10/11/1981	12/12/1999
A00001236	Mona Mary Lee	10/08/1967	P01234A	11/06/1989	12/12/1999
A00001239	Greg Trent Nerd	21/11/1967	P01111A	16/04/1999	12/12/1999
A00001240	Ash Heather Ray	10/08/1974	P01234A	10/03/1998	12/12/1999
A00001241	Kent John Seth	17/01/1972	P01234A	12/10/1989	12/12/1999
A00001243	John Port Hill	10/05/1962	P01111A	22/04/1986	21/12/1999
A00001245	Ria Lia Singh	12/08/1945	P01234A	17/08/1970	12/12/1999
A00001246	Mitch Haris Wild	18/03/1960	P01111A	11/04/1988	12/12/1999
A00001247	Fionna Wu	12/10/1964	P01234A	11/07/1994	12/12/1999

Table 4.28b Customer data and claim data inconsistency/consistency for Example 4.13.

Claim data

Customer ID	Claim ID	Customer name	Doctor name	Illness start date	Illness end date	Claim submission date	Illness description	Consistent/ inconsistent	Explanation
A00001234	L000001234	Brian Kerr	Connor Young	10/09/2017	12/09/2017	18/09/2017	Eye redness	Inconsistent	Illness start date < Customer start date Illness end date < Customer start date
A00001235	L000001235	Kylie Hart	Rashmi Singh	11/09/2017	11/09/2017	18/09/2017	Cough	Consistent	All business rules satisfied
A00001236	L000001236	Mona Mary Lee	Nora Ford	15/09/2017	15/09/2017	18/09/2017	Migraine	Consistent	All business rules satisfied
A00001239	L000001237	Greg Nerd	Maria Smith	14/09/2017	14/09/2017	18/09/2017	Fever	Inconsistent	Customer names across the data sets do not match
A00001240	L000001238	Ash Ray	Rashmi Singh	14/09/2017	14/09/2017	18/09/2017	Stomach upset	Inconsistent	Customer names across the data sets do not match
A00001241	L000001239	Kent John Seth	Connor Young	16/09/2017	16/09/2017	18/09/2017	Eye irritation	Consistent	All business rules satisfied
A00001243	L000001240	John Port Hill	Nora Ford	16/09/2017	18/09/2017	18/09/2017	Abdomen pain	Consistent	All business rules satisfied
A00001245	L000001241	Ria Lia Singh	John Forest	10/09/2017	10/09/2017	18/09/2017	Chest pain	Consistent	All business rules satisfied
A00001246	L000001242	Mitch Wild	Charles Holt	11/09/2017	11/09/2017	18/09/2017	Sore throat	Inconsistent	Customer names across the data sets do not match
A00001247	L000001243	Fionna Wu	Connor Young	12/09/2017	12/09/2017	18/09/2017	Low vision	Consistent	All business rules satisfied

Alternatively,

Consistency % = (Number of records in the data set (10)
– Number of inconsistent records in the data set (4)) ×
100 / (Number of consistent records in the data set (6)
+ Number of inconsistent records in the data set (4))

= 6 × 100 / 10

= 60%

Inconsistency % = (Number of inconsistent records in the
data set (4)) × 100 / (Number of consistent records in the data
set (6) + Number of inconsistent records in the data set (4))

= 4 × 100 / 10

= 40%

Measuring Data Set Consistency. Data set consistency is usually measured between the source system and target systems, for example, data flowing from source systems to tables in a data warehouse. Data set inconsistencies happen either because there was a failure in loading and the table was only partially loaded, or reloading did not happen from the last checkpoint, causing data in the target system to be inconsistent with the source.

Scenario 1. In this case, all data records in the source are directly loaded into the target table, and the target table is truncated and loaded with the source data, without any selection or exclusion criteria, in order for the source and target data sets to be consistent after a data load.

Number of records in the source = Number of
records in the target + Number of rejected records

Data set inconsistency % = Absolute value of (Number of
records in the source – Number of records in the target – Number
of rejected records) × 100 / Number of records in the source

Example 4.14. In a banking database for a US-based company, the currency conversion data, from US dollars to different currencies, are loaded from a source file into a downstream database table on a daily basis, which is then used by the system for reporting purposes. The downstream database table only stores the currency conversion data for one particular day, and the table is truncated and populated at 6 a.m. daily. Say, for a particular day, the number of records loaded into the target table is 30, and the number of records in the source is 30, and the number of rejected records is zero. Since the number of rejected records is zero, applying the formula above, the number of data records in the source must be the same as the number of data records loaded into the target. In this case, the number of records in the source is 30 and the number of records loaded into the target is also 30, hence, the data sets are consistent.

Applying the formula for data inconsistency,

> Data set inconsistency % = Absolute value of (Number of records in the source (30) – Number of records in the target (30) – Number of rejected records (0)) × 100 / Number of records in the source (30)

> = 0%

Hence, on the data set level, 100% consistency applies.

Scenario 2. However, in most cases, the data in the target table will be an incremental load. In this case, the number of records loaded into the target in a particular execution will be used for data set consistency assessment purposes. In the case where the data in the target table are sourced from multiple data sources, and the frequency of load is daily or less (for example, weekly, fortnightly), the date of load and source system codes are used to determine the number of records loaded into the table for a particular load run. If the data in the target table are sourced from only one data source, the date of load can be used to determine the number of records.

> Number of records in the source = Number of records in the target in a particular execution + Number of rejected records

> Data set inconsistency % = Absolute value of (Number of records in the source – Number of records in the target in a particular execution – Number of rejected records) × 100 / Number of records in the source

Example 4.15. A banking database sources the information-related accounts created by employees for different products each day on five business days from six source files, which are stored in secure server locations. Each source file contains an extract of all account creation and the employee information for specific product types, for example, loan products, deposit products, and so on, for the previous business day from the respective source database tables. Therefore, the data stored in the target table in the data warehouse on day T will have data for $T - 1$ day. The target table has source system identifier and date of account creation columns to facilitate the calculation of the number of records loaded from a particular source system into the target on a particular business day.

On September, 22, 2017, the number of records in the source file that contained account creation data for source 1, September, 21, 2017, was 100. The number of records in the target table corresponding to source 1 and date of account creation September 21, 2017, is 105. The number of rejected records is zero.

Applying the formula for data set inconsistency,

> Data set inconsistency % = Absolute value of (Number of records in the source (100) – Number of records in the target in a particular execution (105) – Number of rejected records (0)) × 100 / Number of records in the source (100)

= Absolute value of (100 – 105 – 0) × 100 / 100

= Absolute value of (–5) × 100 / 100

= 5 × 100 / 100

= 5%

Scenario 3. Where certain selection criteria are used to load only selected records from the source into the target for a particular execution, the following formulas can be used to assess data set consistency:

> Number of source records that should be loaded into the target as per selection criteria = Number of records in the target in a particular execution + Number of rejected records

> Data set inconsistency % = Absolute value of (Number of source records that should be loaded into the target as per selection criteria – Number of records in the target in a particular execution – Number of rejected records) × 100 / Number of source records that should be loaded into the target as per selection criteria

Example 4.16. In a hospital database, the incremental mother/baby delivery information is sourced from a source system and loaded into a target table in the data warehouse on a daily basis. Every day at 7 a.m., data for the previous day are loaded into the target table, and the data extract from the source table is selected based on the date. On September 24, 2017, the number of records extracted from the source table based on the date selection criteria is 50, and the number of records loaded into the target table is 45, and no records have been rejected.

Applying the formula for data set inconsistency,

> Data set inconsistency % = Absolute value of (Number of source records that should be loaded into the target as per selection criteria (50) – Number of records in the target in a particular execution (45) – Number of rejected records (0)) × 100 / Number of source records that should be loaded into the target as per selection criteria (50)

= Absolute value of (50 – 45 – 0) × 100 / 50

= Absolute value of (5) × 100 / 50

= 10%

Measuring Integrity

Integrity refers to the relationships between data entities or objects, and the validity of data across the relationships, and ensures that all data in a database can be traced and connected to other data. Data integrity, or the extent to which data integrity is lacking, can be measured at the record level between data sets by finding the number of records across the data sets that are missing the necessary relationship linkages or in which the relationships that exist are not valid. Data integrity is usually measured in a percentage, and is the proportion of the stored data versus the potential of 100% integrity.

Data integrity is measured at the record level between data sets, and can be assessed using the following steps:

1. Determine the relationships and linkages between the data stored in the data sets. The related data records across the data sets might have a one-to-one, one-to-many, or many-to-many relationship between them.

2. Outline the business rules for determining missing linkages.

3. Outline the business rules for determining valid and invalid relationships.

4. Apply the business rules defined in step 2 and step 3 to determine the missing linkages and valid and invalid relationships.

5. Count the number of records with missing linkages using the business rules defined in step 2.

6. Count the number of records that have valid relationships and the number of records that have invalid relationships using the business rules defined in step 3.

The formula for calculating the data integrity % is as follows:

$$\text{Integrity \%} = \frac{(\text{Number of records that have valid relationships}) \times 100}{(\text{Number of records with missing linkages} + \text{Number of records that have valid relationships} + \text{Number of records that have invalid relationships})}$$

Alternatively,

$$\text{Lack of integrity \%} = \frac{(\text{Number of records with missing linkages} + \text{Number of records that have invalid relationships}) \times 100}{(\text{Number of records with missing linkages} + \text{Number of records that have valid relationships} + \text{Number of records that have invalid relationships})}$$

Example 4.17. We will illustrate how to calculate integrity using the customer order relationship captured in the customer and order data sets extracted from the customer and order tables, respectively, as shown in Tables 4.29 and 4.30. The customer table stores customer information for all the customers, and has one record stored for each customer. Each customer is identified by a unique identifier called the customer ID. The order table stores details of orders placed by

Table 4.29   Customer sample data set for Example 4.17.

Customer ID	Customer name	Customer phone number	Customer email ID
C000001234	Caroline Smith	NULL	c.smith@aol.com
C000001241	Jasmine Lee	61-299663427	jasmine.l@gmail.com
C000001243	Ravi Bandar	61-299665765	ravi.bandar@yahoo.com
C000001244	Carlo Santino	61-299668621	c.santino@aol.com
C000001245	Fred Smith	61-299669745	freddies@yahoo.com
C000001246	Sean Reese	61-299661721	s.reese@hotmail.com

Table 4.30   Order sample data set for Example 4.17.

Order ID	Customer ID	Order date	Order value
O0000000121	C000001244	25/07/2017	3000
O0000000122	C000001234	25/07/2017	2500
O0000000123	C000001243	25/07/2017	1000
O0000000124	C000001222	25/07/2017	1500
O0000000125	C000001241	25/07/2017	2000
O0000000126	C000001245	25/07/2017	1500
O0000000127	C000001246	25/07/2017	5000
O0000000128	C000001247	25/07/2017	1200
O0000000129	C000001243	25/07/2017	500
O0000000130	C000001245	25/07/2017	1000

a customer. A customer can place zero or more orders. Each order is identified by a unique order number called order ID. The order table has the following fields: order ID, customer ID, order date, and order value. The customer table has the following fields: customer ID, customer name, customer phone bumber, and customer e-mail ID. The link between the customer and order tables is the customer ID field.

For the purpose of assessing integrity, we have extracted only the customer records from the customer table corresponding to the customers that have placed one or more orders, that is, a customer ID can be found in the order table. The sample order table extract is the extract of all orders placed by customers on July 25, 2017.

Step 1. Step 1 involves determining the relationships and linkages between the order and customer information. An order, uniquely identified by an order ID, should be associated with only one customer, identified by the customer ID. However, a customer can place many orders. Thus, there is a one-to-many relationship between the customer and order information. An order cannot exist without a customer.

Step 2. This step involves the establishment of business rules for determining missing linkages. The business rules are defined as follows:

1. Each order ID should have a corresponding customer ID in the order table extract. If a customer ID is missing for an order ID in the order table extract, then the linkage is missing.

2. Each customer ID in an order record in the order table extract can be mapped to a customer ID in the customer table extract. If for a customer ID in an order record, the same customer ID cannot be found in the customer table extract, then the linkage is missing.

Step 3. This step involves the establishment of business rules for determining valid and invalid relationships. The business rules are as defined following:

1. An order ID in the order table can be associated with only one customer ID. If the same order ID is associated with more than one customer ID, then the relationship is not valid.

2. A customer ID in the customer table and order table can be associated with zero, one, or more than one order ID in the order table. This is a valid relationship.

Step 4. This step involves applying the business rules defined in step 2 and step 3 to determine the missing linkages and valid and invalid relationships. Applying the business rules, each record has been marked as to whether the customer order relationship is a valid or invalid relationship. In the case of missing linkages, applicable records have been similarly marked. As seen in Table 4.31, none of the relationships are invalid.

Step 5. As per Table 4.31, the number of order records that have missing linkages is two.

Step 6. As per Table 4.31, the number of records that have valid relationships is eight.

The number of records that do not have valid relationships is zero.

Applying the formula for calculating the data integrity %,

Integrity % = (Number of records that have valid relationships
(8)) × 100 / (Number of records with missing linkages (2)
+ Number of records that have valid relationships (8) +
Number of records that have invalid relationships (0))

= 8 × 100 / ((2 + 8 + 0)

= 8 × 100 / 10

= 80%

Table 4.31   Customer–Order relationship–integrity for Example 4.17.

Order ID	Customer ID	Order date	Order value	Integrity?	Explanation
O0000000121	C000001244	25/07/2017	3000	Valid relationship	Order ID linked to a customer ID that can be found in the customer table extract
O0000000122	C000001234	25/07/2017	2500	Valid relationship	Order ID linked to a customer ID that can be found in the customer table extract
O0000000123	C000001243	25/07/2017	1000	Valid relationship	Order ID linked to a customer ID that can be found in the customer table extract
O0000000124	C000001222	25/07/2017	1500	Missing linkage	Matching customer ID value "C000001222" cannot be found in customer table extract
O0000000125	C000001241	25/07/2017	2000	Valid relationship	Order ID linked to a customer ID that can be found in the customer table extract
O0000000126	C000001245	25/07/2017	1500	Valid relationship	Order ID linked to a customer ID that can be found in the customer table extract
O0000000127	C000001246	25/07/2017	5000	Valid relationship	Order ID linked to a customer ID that can be found in the customer table extract
O0000000128	C000001247	25/07/2017	1200	Missing linkage	Matching customer ID value "C000001247" cannot be found in customer table extract
O0000000129	C000001243	25/07/2017	500	Valid relationship	Order ID linked to a customer ID that can be found in the customer table extract
O0000000130	C000001245	25/07/2017	1000	Valid relationship	Order ID linked to a customer ID that can be found in the customer table extract

Alternatively,

$$\text{Lack of integrity \%} = (\text{Number of records with missing linkages (2)} + \text{Number of records that have invalid relationships (0)}) \times 100 / (\text{Number of records with missing linkages (2)} + \text{Number of records that have valid relationships (8)} + \text{Number of records that have invalid relationships (0)})$$

$$= 2 \times 100 / (2 + 8 + 0)$$

$$= 2 \times 100 / 10$$

$$= 20\%$$

Measuring Volatility

Volatility is the measure of the frequency at which data values change over time. Volatility is essentially measured at a data element level for a single data element or a group of data elements. As data elements represent attributes of real-world entities, phenomena, or events, it is essential to understand the nature of the attribute and whether the attribute value changes over time at regular intervals, or the change is triggered by a particular event or different events, or the attribute value never changes. If the attribute value never changes, the data element is considered nonvolatile, or has zero volatility. Examples of such attribute values are an individual's date of birth, place of birth, and gender, which, once captured correctly, should never change. Examples of attributes that change after fixed intervals of time (on a yearly basis) are annual compensation and age. Changes in certain attributes are almost continuous. For example, atmospheric temperature is one such example. Examples of attributes whose change is triggered by events are the name of an individual, their address, and marital status. A name of an individual can change when he or she gets married or divorced. Marital status changes when a person gets married or divorced. Address change can be triggered by a number of events, like expiry of a lease and no renewal of the lease, change of job location, marriage, and so on. In cases where data element value changes are triggered by events, it is only possible to estimate the average data volatility based on the historical data. While assessing volatility, it is important to understand how the data are represented and the grain of the data. For example, the attribute *marital status* is stored and represented by a single data element. However, an address is usually a composite of data elements: street address, city, ZIP code, and country. When assessing volatility, changes in one or more of these data elements need to be assessed together.

Why Is Assessing Data Volatility Important? The frequency at which the data values change, that is, *volatility*, is the measure of the time for which data element values remain accurate and current and will serve business purposes. Data volatility helps in defining how frequently updates need to be scheduled to ensure that data are fit for business purposes. However, when scheduling updates, in addition to using the average frequency at which the data values change for an attribute, the number of entities that are out of date, the number of business processes that use the data attribute, and the resulting impact in terms of lost opportunities, decrease in revenue, increase in cost, customer dissatisfaction, compliance, and so on, also need to be taken into consideration. In other words, cost versus benefit needs to be assessed.

To illustrate the importance of determining or estimating volatility, we will take the example of a data set containing addresses for all the customers of a retail store. The retail store data repository has customer details for 100,000 customers, and it is found that an address changes with an average frequency of six months for 40,000 customers. Thus, for 40% of customers, *customer* being the entity, the estimated average period of time that the address remains current is six months. After six months, if addresses are not updated, the addresses for 40% of the customers will not be current; that is, these addresses are no longer accurate and hence not fit for the given purpose. Now let us consider the impact of addresses that are not current.

A promotional campaign being conducted by a retail clothing store—in which booklets will be sent to addresses to attract customers—has a success rate of 1% lead to sales ratio. In the absence of current address data, the promotional booklets would only be able to be sent to 60,000 customers. If the average order value is $200 per lead, 1% of 40,000 addresses is 400 customers, bringing in 400 × $200 worth of revenue, that is, $80,000 in sales. If the cost of mailing the booklet is $3 per address, then for 40,000 addresses, the wasted mailing cost is 40,000 × $3, that is, $120,000.

Since the addresses are used by a number of business processes, the address data are updated regularly in the data repository.

Steps in Estimating Volatility

Step 1. Determine the critical business data attributes for which volatility needs to be assessed.

Step 2. For each critical business data attribute, map the business data attribute to a data element or a group of data elements in the data repository.

Step 3. Understand the nature of each critical business data attribute, and what brings about change in those attributes.

Step 4. Understand how each critical business data attribute is represented in the data set, and the grain of the data.

Step 5. Define business rules, if needed, for extracting the data that will be used for estimating the volatility. For example, to assess the change in marital status in a data set that has the individual's name, date of birth, gender, and marital status, since only individuals over 18 can be married or divorced, we would only extract records from the data set where the individual's age is greater than or equal to 18 as determined by their date of birth.

Step 6. Determine the difference in time between the old attribute values and new attribute values for a particular entity. This can only be possible if the history of records is maintained.

Step 7. Compute the average difference in time. The average value is the estimated value of volatility.

Example 4.18. Consider an address data set containing the following data elements: Customer ID, Address ID, Street Address, City, ZIP Code, State, Country, Created Date, and Expiry Date, as shown in Table 4.32:

The data set has date parameters, Created Date and Expiry Date, which keep track of the history of the records.

Step 1. The first step is determining the critical business data attributes for which volatility needs to be assessed. In this case, Address is the critical business data attribute.

Step 2. In this step, we need to map the business data attribute Address to the data elements in the data set. The following group of data elements is mapped to Address:

- Street Address

- City

- ZIP Code

- State

- Country

Steps 3 and 4. Steps 3 and 4 comprise understanding the nature of the attribute/attributes, what brings about change in those attributes, how the attribute is represented in the data set, and the grain of the data.

The street address, city, ZIP code, state, and country constitute the address that is associated with a customer. Each customer is uniquely identified by a customer ID. Each customer has a unique address ID associated with it. Every address has a created date, that is, the start date, and an expiry date, or end date, associated with it. An address that is current has a maximum date of "12/12/9999" assigned to the Expiry Date data element. Every time a customer moves from one address to another, which can be triggered by expiry of a lease that is not renewed or because of a change in job location, and so on, the former address record associated with a customer is expired, with the expiry date value updated to the last date that the customer lived at the former address, and a new address record is created with a maximum date of "12/12/9999" assigned to the Expiry Date data element, and the Created Date data element is assigned the date value corresponding to when the customer moved to the new address, that is, their current address.

Step 5. As observed in the data set, a customer who has lived at multiple addresses has multiple records associated with it. So, we will only extract those records for which the cardinality for customer ID is more than 1. This will result in an extract as shown in Table 4.33.

Table 4.32 Address data set for Example 4.18.

Customer ID	Address ID	Street address	City	ZIP code	State	Country	Created date	Expiry date
C000000511	A00001052	45 Logan Avenue	Jersey City	07306	NJ	USA	12/12/2015	29/06/2016
C000000511	A00001053	23 Corbin Avenue	Jersey City	07306	NJ	USA	30/06/2016	12/12/9999
C000000512	A00001054	274 Sip Avenue	Jersey City	07306	NJ	USA	21/02/2016	12/12/9999
C000000513	A00001055	10 Henry Street	Jersey City	07306	NJ	USA	15/01/2016	28/07/2016
C000000513	A00001056	54 Magnolia Avenue	Jersey City	07306	NJ	USA	29/07/2016	12/12/9999
C000000514	A00001057	119 Chestnut Avenue	Jersey City	07306	NJ	USA	25/08/2015	12/12/9999
C000000515	A00001058	81 Waldo Avenue	Jersey City	07306	NJ	USA	29/09/2015	12/12/9999
C000000516	A00001059	50 Garisson Avenue	Jersey City	07306	NJ	USA	10/06/2016	12/12/9999
C000000517	A00001060	210 Palisade Avenue	Jersey City	07306	NJ	USA	12/10/2016	10/03/2017
C000000517	A00001061	513 Palisade Avenue	Jersey City	07306	NJ	USA	11/03/2017	12/12/9999
C000000518	A00001062	143 Highland Avenue	Jersey City	07306	NJ	USA	14/11/2016	11/05/2017
C000000518	A00001063	148 Bidwell Avenue	Jersey City	07306	NJ	USA	12/05/2017	12/12/9999
C000000519	A00001064	77 Sherman Avenue	Jersey City	07306	NJ	USA	24/02/2016	12/12/9999
C000000520	A00001065	239 Clinton Avenue	Jersey City	07306	NJ	USA	11/11/2015	25/03/2016
C000000520	A00001066	257 Harisson Avenue	Jersey City	07306	NJ	USA	24/03/2016	12/12/9999

Table 4.33   Customers who have lived in multiple addresses for Example 4.18.

Customer ID	Address ID	Street address	City	ZIP code	State	Country	Created date	Expiry date
C000000511	A00001052	45 Logan Avenue	Jersey City	07306	NJ	USA	12/12/2015	29/06/2016
C000000511	A00001053	23 Corbin Avenue	Jersey City	07306	NJ	USA	30/06/2016	12/12/9999
C000000513	A00001055	10 Henry Street	Jersey City	07306	NJ	USA	15/01/2016	28/07/2016
C000000513	A00001056	54 Magnolia Avenue	Jersey City	07306	NJ	USA	29/07/2016	12/12/9999
C000000517	A00001060	210 Palisade Avenue	Jersey City	07306	NJ	USA	12/10/2016	10/03/2017
C000000517	A00001061	513 Palisade Avenue	Jersey City	07306	NJ	USA	11/03/2017	12/12/9999
C000000518	A00001062	143 Highland Avenue	Jersey City	07306	NJ	USA	14/11/2016	11/05/2017
C000000518	A00001063	148 Bidwell Avenue	Jersey City	07306	NJ	USA	12/05/2017	12/12/9999
C000000520	A00001065	239 Clinton Avenue	Jersey City	07306	NJ	USA	11/11/2015	25/03/2016
C000000520	A00001066	257 Harisson Avenue	Jersey City	07306	NJ	USA	24/03/2016	12/12/9999

Table 4.34	Difference in time between old address and current address for Example 4.18.		
Customer ID	Old address created date	Current address created date	Difference in days
C000000511	12/12/2015	30/06/2016	201
C000000513	15/01/2016	29/07/2016	196
C000000517	12/10/2016	11/03/2017	150
C000000518	14/11/2016	12/05/2017	179
C000000520	11/11/2015	24/03/2016	134

Step 6. This step involves determining the difference in time between the old address and new address for the customers whose address has changed. This can be accomplished by subtracting the created date value of the old address and the created date value of the current address for a particular customer, as shown in Table 4.34.

Step 7. The average time difference = (201 + 196 + 150 + 179 + 134) / 5

= 172 days

= 6 months, approximately

Thus, the estimated value of volatility is six months.

Measuring Currency

Data currency refers to whether a data attribute value is still up-to-date, or not outdated. In order to determine whether critical data attribute values in the data set are still current requires comparing the data attribute values with a reference data set, with both data sets having date parameters to indicate when the data record was created or updated. This can, however, be a time-consuming exercise. The volatility measure gives a good indication of whether the data attributes are current or not. For example, if the estimated value of volatility of address data is six months and there has been no change in the customer address for, say, two years, it is good practice to compare the address with a reference data set to determine whether the address data values are still current. Thus, data currency can be measured as a function of the expected frequency rate at which different data elements are expected to be refreshed (Loshin 2010a).

Measuring Timeliness

Timeliness is the velocity with which data are dispatched to or made available to the business users. Timeliness is the measure of the time interval between the time when the data came into existence and when the data are delivered to the user. When measuring timeliness, three time components come into play:

1. *Occurrence time.* The time when the real-world event being recorded occurred, or when the entity or the related attribute value(s) for the entity came into existence.

2. *Data provided time.* The time when the data related to the event, entity, or phenomena were provided or obtained.

3. *Data delivery time.* The time when the data related to the event, entity, or phenomena became available to the business users. In the case of a database, this is the time when the data are entered into the database. In the case of data stored in files, it is the time when the data files are made available at a location accessible by the user.

Timeliness can be measured in units of time using the following formula:

$$\text{Timeliness} = (\text{Data delivery time} - \text{Data provided time}) + (\text{Data provided time} - \text{Occurrence time}) \qquad [\text{Formula 4.1}]$$

The above formula applies when there is a time lag between the time when the activity, event, or phenomena took place and when the event was captured or recorded. This is common in the case of manual transactions, where there is usually a difference between the time the event occurred or when entity was created and the time when the related information was obtained.

In the case where there is no time lag between the time when the activity, event, or phenomena took place, or when the entity was created, and when the related information was obtained, for example, an electronic transaction, the following formula for timeliness applies. In this case, the event occurrence time and the event capture or event recording time are the same.

$$\text{Timeliness} = \text{Data delivery time} - \text{Occurrence time}$$
$$\textit{or Data provided time} \qquad [\text{Formula 4.2}]$$

A closer look at the first timeliness formula reveals that timeliness is the difference between the data delivery time and the occurrence time, as the data provided time gets nullified, so formula 4.1 is essentially the same as formula 4.2. However, the time difference between each of the different time components in formula 4.1 helps quantify different time lag components.

For example, 10 babies were born on July 24, 2015, but details were provided to the data entry operator on July 25, 2015, and the data were populated in the database on July 26, 2015.

$$\text{Timeliness} = (\text{Data delivery time } (07/26/2015) -$$
$$\text{Data provided time } (07/25/2015)) + (\text{Data provided time}$$
$$(07/25/2015) - \text{Occurrence time } (07/24/2015))$$

$$= 1 \text{ day} + 1 \text{ day}$$

$$= 2 \text{ days}$$

Also, in a large organization, data usually have to pass through a number of intermediate systems before they become available in the form of a report or are loaded into a downstream system accessible to the business user.

In such cases, the timeliness can be defined as

$$\text{Timeliness} = (\text{Data delivery time}_{\text{System } n} - \text{Data delivery time}_{\text{System } n-1})$$
$$+ (\text{Data delivery time}_{\text{System } n-1} - \text{Data delivery time}_{\text{System } n-2}) + \ldots$$
$$+ (\text{Data delivery time}_{\text{System } 2} - \text{Data delivery time}_{\text{System } 1})$$
$$+ (\text{Data delivery time}_{\text{System } 1} - \text{Data provided time})$$
$$+ (\text{Data provided time} - \text{Occurrence time})$$

In the case where the data capture time and occurrence time are the same, the above formula can be replaced by the following formula:

$$\text{Timeliness} = (\text{Data delivery time}_{\text{System } n} - \text{Data delivery time}_{\text{System } n-1})$$
$$+ (\text{Data delivery time}_{\text{System } n-1} - \text{Data delivery time}_{\text{System } n-2}) + \ldots$$
$$+ (\text{Data delivery time}_{\text{System } 2} - \text{Data delivery time}_{\text{System } 1})$$
$$+ (\text{Data delivery time}_{\text{System } 1} - \text{Data provided time} / \text{Occurrence time})$$

Figure 4.6 illustrates the different systems through which data flow before they are available to the user in the form of reports. In this figure there is a lag between the time when the event occurred and when the data were provided or obtained. As we can see, there is a delay as data flow from the source system, through the intermediate systems, to the staging area, to the data warehouse, and from the data warehouse to the downstream system, and are finally made available in the form of reports.

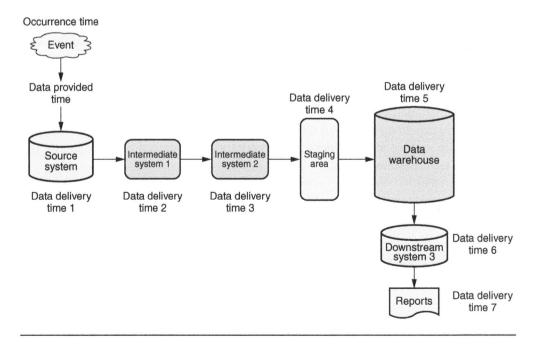

Figure 4.6 Data flow through systems where data are captured after the occurrence of the event.

Figure 4.7 also illustrates the different systems that data flow through before they are available to the user in the form of reports. The only difference between Figure 4.6 and Figure 4.7 is that there is no lag between the time when the event occurred and when the data were provided or obtained in Figure 4.7. As we can see, there is still a delay as data flow from the source system, through the intermediate systems, to the staging area, to the data warehouse, and from the data warehouse to the downstream system, and are finally made available in the form of reports.

There is usually a service level agreement (SLA) that defines the maximum time lag, that is, the time from when the related data came into being and the time when the data should be available for use. During design, time delays between the occurrence and procurement of data, volumes, processing times, and dependencies need to be taken into consideration, and these factors need to be taken into account when preparing the SLA. The greater the volume of data, the more time that is required to load the data into the target systems.

To illustrate how dependencies can impact the timing of the availability of data, we will consider the scenario of a financial services company in which account creation and account modification data are captured in two different source systems on a daily basis and populated in the same table in the data warehouse. Source system 1 stores the account creation data, and source system 2 stores the account modification data. The account modification data for all accounts for a particular business day are available in source system 2 at 11 p.m. at night for the same business day. The account creation data for a particular business day are available in source system 1 at 2 a.m. on the following

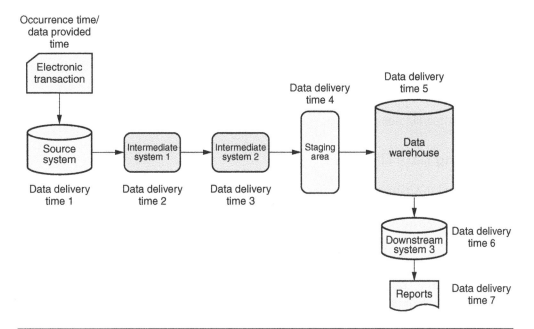

Figure 4.7   Data flow through systems where data are captured at the same time as the occurrence of the event

business day. Since modifications can be made to an account only after an account is created, but nonetheless can happen on the same day as when the account was created, it is necessary for the account creation data to be populated into the data warehouse before the account modification data are populated, even though the account modification data are available in the source system before the account creation data are available.

The formula for timeliness can be applied at three levels:

- *Data element.* For example, a customer acquires a new mobile phone number on June 10, 2016, and provides details of the updated mobile number on the same day, that is, on June 10, 2016, and the data are updated in the customer contact table on June 11, 2016. This indicates a delay of one day. Since the service level agreement for changes mandates updating two days from the day the data are provided by the customer, this time lag does not breach the timeliness constraint.

- *Data record.* For example, a customer moves to a new address on July 29, 2016, and provides details of the updated address on July 30, 2016. The old address is expired, and a new address record is entered in the customer address table on August 2, 2016. The service level agreement mandates updating two days from the day the data are provided by the customer. Since the time lag is three days from the day the customer provided the data, this time lag breaches the timeliness constraint.

- *Data set.* To illustrate data set timeliness, we will consider the example of an account creation data set that contains information on all the accounts created on a particular business day. The data for all the accounts created on a particular business day are available for loading into the source system by 6 p.m. on the same business day. However, the data set is entered and stored in the account table in the source system at 2 a.m. the following day. Hence, the time lag is eight hours. Since the service level agreement mandates that account creation data be delivered in the source system table within one day, this time lag does not breach the timeliness constraint.

Measuring Data Lineage

As discussed in Chapter 3, *data lineage* is the ability to trace data to their origins. It is essentially a link between the source and target data sources and systems. Data lineage can be measured by determining whether the information required to trace the data (data elements and data records) back to their source are present or not. Typically, this would include recording the following parameters:

- *Originating data source.* This parameter records the historical origin of the data element or record. If all the data elements corresponding to a record in a table in the target system are sourced from tables in a single source, a separate data element—the source system identifier—can be captured as a data element in the table itself; however, if the same record in the target table contains data elements sourced or derived from difference sources, the metadata for the data elements need to capture the source information.

- *Immediate upstream data source.* If data travel between several data systems, the downstream system needs to record the immediate upstream data system information. If there are no intermediate systems, the immediate upstream data source would be the same as the originating data source. If all the data elements corresponding to a record in a table in the target system are sourced from tables in the same upstream system, a separate data element, the upstream system identifier, can be captured as a data element in the table itself; however, if the same record in the target table contains data elements sourced or derived from difference sources, the metadata for the data elements need to capture this piece of information.

- *Date and time of origination.* This parameter records the date and time when a data record was first created. This corresponds to the date and time when the record was created or stored in the system (that is, the *run time*). This parameter is especially important when data are stored in files, and data need to be traced back to a particular file.

- *Date and time of modification.* This parameter records the date and time when a data record was last modified.

Measuring Data Coverage

Data coverage can be defined as the extent of the availability and comprehensiveness of data when compared to the total data universe or population of interest (McGilvray 2008a). In order to measure data coverage, the scope of the data needs to be determined. The known sources of coverage need to be documented. This includes the sources for which data corresponding to the population of interest are present, the sources for which data are not present in the population of interest (under-coverage), and the sources for which data are present, but do not correspond to the population of interest (over-coverage).

Data coverage can be measured in a percentage, and is the proportion of the stored data of interest versus the potential total data universe.

Steps in measuring data coverage are as follows:

1. Determine the scope of the data needed to fulfill the business requirement.

2. Determine the sources of under-coverage and over-coverage.

3. Determine the existing coverage of the data of interest defined by the scope in step 1, and find the number of records in the population of interest.

4. Determine the estimated number of records not available in the population of interest.

Data coverage % = The number of records in the present population defined by the scope × 100 / The number of estimated records not available in the population of interest + The number of records in the present population defined by the scope

Example 4.19. For example, consider employee reporting for a multinational company spread across five countries: the United States, Canada, UK, India, and France. The organization has five business units—Consulting, Human Resources, Operations, Finance, Research and Development—and each business unit has four departments. In order to determine whether the data in the data repository have adequate coverage for employee reporting purposes, we need to understand the scope of reporting. That is, at which level is the employee reporting needed—for a particular department, for a particular business unit, for all business units within a particular geography, or for the entire organization? The scope of reporting would be a determinant of the size of the potential total universe of the data of interest. If the scope of reporting includes reporting for the consulting business unit across all five countries, but the data stored are for only the business units in the United States and Canada, this is an example of under-coverage—as the data for the consulting business unit are not present for the UK, India, and France—and over-coverage—as the data for all the other business units for the United States and Canada not required for the present scope of reporting are present in the data repository. The number of records in the present population of interest, that is, the number of employee records in the consulting business unit of the United States and Canada is 1500, and the number of estimated records in the total population of interest, that is, the number of employee records in the consulting business unit of the UK, India, and France is 3500.

Applying the formula for data coverage,

Data coverage % = The number of records in the present population defined by the scope (1500) × 100 / The number of estimated records not available in the population of interest (3500) + The number of records in the present population defined by the scope (1500)

= 1500 × 100 / (3500 + 1500)

= 1500 × 100 / 5000

= 30%

Measuring Relevance

As defined in Chapter 3, *relevance* is the extent to which the data content and coverage are relevant for the purpose for which they are to be used, and the extent to which they meet the current and potential future needs. Hence, in order to measure relevance, we need to measure data coverage as outlined in the "Measuring Data Coverage" section. In addition, what needs to be determined are the attributes needed for the intended purpose, mapping these attributes to the data set in question, and then checking whether the values stored in the data elements actually represent what you think you are measuring. The intended purpose may be a reporting need, or data may be needed for predictive analytics, or any other business requirement.

Hence, measuring relevance consists of two components:

1. Measuring data coverage

2. Measuring the relevance of the data

A data element is relevant if it can be mapped to the intended purpose, and the values held in the data element serve to address the purposes for which they are sought by consumers and users. The relevance of the data can be measured in a percentage, and is the proportion of the relevant data elements versus the total number of data elements required for the intended purpose.

Steps in measuring the relevance of the data are as follows:

1. Determine and map the data elements in the data set to the business requirements.

2. For each of the mapped data elements, analyze the values in a sample of data to determine whether the values represent what they are supposed to represent. If the mapped data element has values that represent what they are supposed to represent and are relevant for the task at hand, it is a relevant data element.

3. Count the number of relevant data elements as established in step 2.

Relevance of the data % = (Number of relevant data elements / Total number of data elements needed for the intended purpose) × 100

Example 4.20. For example, in a multinational retail business, the business need is to assess consumers' behavior based on a few parameters like age, gender, geography, occupation, and annual income. The data set has the following fields:

1. Customer ID

2. Customer Name

3. Date of Birth

4. Gender

5. Street Address

6. City

7. Postal Code

8. State

9. Country

10. Occupation

The data set has 10,000 records, and the Country field contains the values for the United States and Canada, that is, the North American geography. If the total estimated population for other geographies is 20,000, then,

Data coverage % = The number of records in the present population defined by the scope (10,000) × 100 / The number of estimated records not available in the population of interest (20,000) + The number of records in the present population defined by the scope (10,000)

= 10,000 × 100 / (20,000 + 10,000)

= 10,000 × 100 / 30,000

= 33.33%

Step 1. To determine the relevance of data, the first step is to determine and map the data elements in the data set to the business requirements. As per the business requirements, the age, gender, geography, occupation, and annual income details are needed:

- The age can be derived from the Date of Birth data element.

- The gender can be obtained from the values stored in the Gender data element.

- The geography can be derived from the values in the Country data element.

- The occupation can be mapped to the Occupation data element.

- The annual income details cannot be mapped to any data element in the data set.

The total number of data elements needed for the business requirement is five.

Step 2. The next step is to determine that the values represent what they are supposed to represent. Let us have a look at the sample data in Table 4.35 to ascertain whether this is so. A quick scan reveals that the values represent what they are supposed to represent. For example, Country has valid country values, Gender has valid gender values, the Date of Birth field has date values, and Occupation has relevant occupations stored, respectively.

Step 3. Therefore, the number of relevant data elements is four.

Table 4.35   Sample data set for Example 4.20.

Customer ID	Customer name	Date of birth	Gender	Street address	City	Postal code	State	Country	Occupation
C000008121	Tina Renega	30/01/1991	F	3176 Kelly Drive	Greenville	24945	West Virginia	USA	Software development
C000008122	Brett Ford	23/04/1987	M	81 Waldo Avenue	Jersey City	07306	New Jersey	USA	Accountant
C000008123	Ron Kerr	15/11/1976	M	50 Garrison Avenue	Jersey City	07306	New Jersey	USA	Artist
C000008124	Karthik Sangvi	17/10/1975	M	4458 Albert Street	Kitchener	N2L 3V2	Ontario	Canada	Investment banker
C000008125	Dora West	24/11/1982	F	4625 Sunset Drive	Pine Bluff	71601	Arkansas	USA	Human resource manager
C000008126	Sebastian Carter	12/07/1970	M	816 Dundas Street	Toronto	M2N 2G8	Ontario	Canada	Project officer
C000008127	Lauren Richter	19/12/1979	F	12024 Swallow Falls Court	Silver Spring	20904	Maryland	USA	Software development
C000008128	Miranda Harris	21/11/1967	F	970 Drummond Street	Newark	07102	New Jersey	USA	Accountant
C000008129	Hunter Lee	10/10/1983	M	95 Kuhl Avenue	Atlanta	30329	Georgia	USA	Plumbing
C000008130	Veleta Carlton	28/05/1985	F	3110 Sampson Street	Aurora	80014	Colorado	USA	Software development

Applying the formula for calculating the relevance of the data set,

$$\text{Relevance of the data \% = (Number of relevant}$$
$$\text{data elements (4) / Total number of data elements}$$
$$\text{needed for the intended purposes (5))} \times 100$$

$= 4 / 5 \times 100$

$= 80\%$

Measuring Accessibility

As defined in Chapter 3, *accessibility* is the ease with which the existence of data and/or metadata (data about data) can be determined, and the suitability of the form or medium through which the data can be quickly and easily accessed and retrieved. Since accessibility is not a measure of the data content or representation quality, it cannot be quantified in the same manner as other data quality dimensions like accuracy, completeness, validity, consistency, and uniqueness. In order to assess data accessibility, we need to define different metrics and organize surveys of the target audience. The survey questionnaire would have a mix of subjective and objective questions. In this section, we will provide some guidelines regarding the metric parameters and the questions and their responses that can be used to assess accessibility.

While the metric parameters provide a means for objective measurement, question responses are based on options. Responses vary from user to user. The answers to the questions are rated using a Likert-type scale with an even number of rating points unless there is a clear need to have a neutral point in the scale. A four-point scale along the following lines is preferred unless there is a strong reason to use more scale points:

1 = Completely unacceptable

2 = Marginally unacceptable

3 = Marginally acceptable

4 = Completely acceptable

Table 4.36 shows the mapping between the scale points and accessibility.

Following are two different accessibility scenarios.

Scenario 1. Business users are able to request direct access to the data repository containing the desired data, and on getting access rights, able to retrieve the data themselves. In this case, business users have the knowledge of the technology required to retrieve the data and are proficient enough to write program codes, procedures, or queries to retrieve the right data.

Scenario 2. Business users do not have direct access to the data repository; in this case, the data need to be retrieved from the repository and provided to the users in an acceptable format.

Table 4.36   Mapping between the scale points and accessibility.

Scale points	Accessibility level
1 = Completely unacceptable	Low
2 = Marginally unacceptable	Slightly low
3 = Marginally acceptable	Slightly high
4 = Completely acceptable	High

The parameters for assessing accessibility would differ depending on which accessibility scenario applies. Following are the different metric parameters and questions to measure for accessibility for each scenario.

Scenario 1. The users themselves write queries or code to retrieve the data. The metric parameters to be used to evaluate accessibility in this scenario are defined as follows:

- *Access request elapsed time.* The elapsed time between an access request to the data repository/database containing the required data and when the user is able to access the data.

- *Query elapsed time.* The queries or codes have to be run or executed, and the resulting output is the data needed by the user. There is usually a time lapse between the execution of the code or query and query results, and this needs to be measured, too, and factored into the assessment of accessibility. Query elapsed time varies depending on the volume of data, the number of users accessing the tables, the number of queries being run, and the database servers.

- *Access frequency.* The frequency at which data need to be accessed and retrieved from the database or data repository. The data might need to be retrieved on a daily, fortnightly, monthly, quarterly, yearly, or ad hoc basis.

While an access request to the data repository is a one-time event, execution of codes or queries to retrieve the data is usually a more frequent activity. Depending on the frequency at which data need to be retrieved from the database, a time lapse between the execution of the code or query and query results could affect the accessibility score. That is, if users need to access the data less frequently, say, once per year, a longer query lapse time might be more acceptable compared to users needing access to the data more frequently, say, on a daily basis.

The following questions should be used in addition to the above metric parameters:

- Is the ease with which the database/data repository (where the data resides) can be identified acceptable?

- Is the time required to get access to the database/data repository acceptable?

- Are the processes required to request access to the data repository/database acceptable?

- Is the process required to request access to the database/data repository easily achievable?

- Once access to the databases/data repository has been granted, is the ease with which data can be located in the database/data repository acceptable?

- Is the time taken to retrieve the data from the data repository/database acceptable?

Scenario 2. The user does not have direct access to the data. The metric parameters to be used to evaluate accessibility in this scenario are defined as follows:

- *Data request response time.* This is the response time between the request for data and when the user is provided with the data in the acceptable format. In the case where the request for data has been raised through an e-mail to the authorized team/person, the data request response time would be the time elapsed between the time the mail was sent by the user and when the data are made available to the user. In the case of a request raised through a system or tool, the data request response time would be the time elapsed between the time when the request was raised by the business user and when the data are made available to the user.

- *Data request frequency.* The frequency at which data need to be requested.

The following questions should be used in addition to the above metric parameters:

- Is the ease with which the data can be located acceptable?

- Is the time required to receive the data after a request has been raised for the needed data acceptable?

- Are the processes required to request data acceptable?

- Is the process required to request data easily accessible?

Survey questionnaires should be designed using the respective metric parameters and questions designed for the applicable scenario, and survey should be conducted with the target user population directly after they access the data. In addition, any key accessibility issues not covered by the questions in the questionnaire should be captured by the evaluator. The points for questions whose responses are scaled as per Table 4.37 (for Accessibility Scenario 1) are averaged using the number of questions. The resulting scores for all the users are summed up and are averaged over the number of users responding to the survey. Alternatively, the points for questions whose responses are scaled as per Table 4.37 are summed and averaged across the number of users responding to the survey. The sums of the average responses are then averaged using the number of questions whose responses are scaled. The metric parameter values for each metric

Table 4.37   Accessibility questionnaire response for Example 4.21.

ID	Questions	User 1	User 2	User 3	User 4	User 5	User 6	Sum	Average
1	What is the time lapse between request for access and actual access (access request elapsed time) in days?	3	4	4	5	3	4	23	3.83
2	What is the time lapse between the execution of the code/query and query results (query lapse time) in minutes?	2	1	1.5	1.5	1.5	1	8.5	1.42
3	What is the access frequency (for example, daily, weekly, fortnightly, monthly, quarterly, yearly)?	Weekly	Daily	Daily	Daily	Daily	Daily	N/A	N/A
4	Is the ease with which the database/data repository (where the data resides) can be identified acceptable?	4	4	4	4	4	4	24	4
5	Is the time required to get access to the database/data repository acceptable?	3	3	3	4	3	4	20	3.33
6	Are the processes required to request access to the data repository/database acceptable?	3	3	3	4	3	4	20	3.33
7	Is the process required to request access to the database/data repository easily attainable?	4	4	4	4	4	4	24	4
8	Once access to the databases/data repository has been granted, is the ease with which data can be located in the database/data repository acceptable?	3	3	4	4	4	4	22	3.67
9	Is the time taken to retrieve the data from the data repository/database acceptable?	4	4	4	4	4	4	24	4

parameter are averaged over the number of user responses. The points are rounded to the nearest integer value and then mapped using the table to determine the level of accessibility.

Example 4.21. The financial operations department in a bank has a team of six employees who requested and got access to the corporate data warehouse a few days earlier. The employees in this department access and retrieve customer account information stored in different tables in the corporate data warehouse for analysis and reporting purposes.

This example corresponds to scenario 1, and a survey was conducted using the questions illustrated in scenario 1. The responses are captured in Table 4.37, and the results in the table will be used to determine the level of accessibility. Questions 1, 2, and 3 are related to the metric parameters; questions 4, 5, 6, 7, 8, and 9 are assessed using the 4-point Likert scale. The "Sum" column represents the sum of the responses for each question, where applicable, for the six users.

The "Average" column represents the average value for each question, where applicable, for the six users, and is calculated using the following formula:

$$\text{Average} = \text{Sum} / 6$$

From Table 4.37, we deduce the following:

- The average access request elapsed time = 3.83 days = 4 days, approximately.

- The average query lapse time = 1.42 minutes = 5 minutes, approximately.

- Most of the users need to access the database on a daily basis.

- The average score for questions 4, 5, 6, 7, 8, and 9 for all users = $(4 + 3.33 + 3.33 + 4 + 3.67 + 4) / 6 = 3.72 = 4$, approximately.

- Using the mapping table (Table 4.36), we find that the value 4 corresponds to a high level of accessibility; hence, we conclude that the data accessed by the financial operations team has high accessibility.

Measuring Data Security

Data security is the extent to which access to data is restricted and regulated appropriately to prevent unauthorized access. The data security requirements depend on how sensitive the data are, as well as the privacy and confidentiality requirements for the data. For example, personally identifiable information (PII) data, patient data, and customer financial data are highly confidential, and hence they need to be secured well. Data that are open for public use have less rigid security requirements.

While security is not an inherent characteristic of data, it can be achieved at the data element, data record, data set, or database level by restricting access. Data security can be imposed by encrypting or masking the data values, or hiding the data from view.

In this section, we will lay down a few guidelines to help determine how secure your data are. Following are a few questions that can help you assess how secure your data and/or data systems are:

1. Do systems reside in a locked facility?

2. Are adequate malware protection and antivirus software installed?

3. Are all accounts and resources accessing database systems protected by strong passwords that are automatically enforced by the system?

4. Are passwords changed at least once every 90 days for nonsensitive data?

5. Are passwords changed at least once every month for sensitive data?

6. Is the maximum number of unsuccessful database log-in attempts enforced?

7. Are successful log-in attempts to database systems audited?

8. Are unsuccessful log-in attempts to database systems audited?

9. Are serious or unusual errors audited?

10. Are accounts removed or disabled upon loss of eligibility?

11. Do user accounts have the least possible level of privilege that allows them to perform their function?

12. Are user accounts reviewed for eligibility at defined intervals?

13. Are systems protected by strong firewalls?

14. Is there an adequate security policy in place?

15. Is there a role access model in place that allows different levels of access depending on the role the user plays?

16. Are vulnerability assessment and penetration testing a part of the security plan and conducted at regular intervals?

17. Are sessions locked or closed after some reasonable period?

18. Are data transferred through secure channels?

19. Are sensitive data masked or encrypted?

20. Are data destroyed if no longer needed?

If the answers to all of the above questions are "Yes," then your data and data systems are highly secure. If the answer to any of the above questions is "No," the associated risks and impacts need to be assessed, and, depending on the risk involved, steps and measures need to be taken to eliminate the risks.

Measuring Data Reliability

As discussed in Chapter 3, *data reliability* refers to the completeness, relevance, accuracy, uniqueness, and consistency of the data set for the intended purposes of use, and the ability to trace the data to a trustworthy source. The ultimate aim of measuring data reliability is to ascertain whether the data can be used for the intended purposes. Data reliability measurement is important if the data to be analyzed are intended to materially support your findings, conclusions, or recommendations. Hence, when assessing data reliability, it is essential to understand the purpose for which the data are to be used and what the quality requirements are in terms of accuracy, completeness, relevance, uniqueness, and consistency for the intended purpose.

In order to measure the reliability of data, a combination of objective and subjective assessment is used. Following are the key steps in measuring data reliability:

1. *Assess the risk related to data reliability. Risk* is the likelihood that using data of questionable reliability could have significant negative consequences on the decisions made by the business users on the basis of those data. The risk measurement would involve understanding the following aspects:

   • *The data in the context of the final report and the extent of the role the data will play.* The following questions need to be taken into consideration while trying to find the role of the data:

     – Will the data be used to influence legislation or policy with significant impact?

     – Will the data be used for significant decisions by individuals or organizations?

     – Will the data form the basis for numbers that are likely to be widely quoted and publicized?

     – Will the data form the basis of a regulatory or compliance project?

     If the answer to one or more of the above questions is "Yes," then the risk associated with data reliability is significantly high, and hence there should a high level of confidence in the data.

   • *Nature of engagement.* The following aspects need to be considered while considering the nature of engagement:

     – Is the engagement concerned with a sensitive or controversial subject?

     – Does the engagement involve external stakeholders who have taken positions on the subject?

     – Is the overall engagement risk medium or high?

     – Does the engagement have unique factors that strongly increase risk?

If the answer to one or more of the above questions is "Yes," then the risk associated with data reliability is significantly high, and hence there should a high level of confidence in the data.

- *Will the audit depend on the data alone for important decisions?* If the data are the sole source of information leading to findings and recommendations, a more extensive assessment may be necessary than when you have strong corroborating evidence (GAO 2009). Corroborating evidence is autonomous evidence that supports information in a database or is derived from one. Such evidence, if existing, can be found in alternative databases or expert views. Corroborating evidence is exclusive to each review.

- *Will the data be summarized or will detailed information be necessary?* Although the underlying data elements from which the summary data have been aggregated still need to be assessed, the presentation of more-detailed information may require a deeper assessment. If you plan to report detailed information, then the assessment should focus on whether the data are reliable at the level you plan to report (GAO 2009). For example, in a financial organization, if consolidated reporting is required on total asset values and total liabilities, then the assessment required would not be as in-depth as when the reports are needed at the product category level. If the account information needs to be presented at an account level, then assessment needs to be even more rigorous.

- *Is it imperative to have precise data?* If the data play a significant role in the final decision making, or the data alone form the basis of important decisions, the data need to be more reliable. The greater the risk associated with the engagement, the greater is the requirement from a reliability perspective. Also, if detailed information or precise data are needed, the risk is considerably higher as the data quality thresholds need to be higher with the allowable margin for errors being lesser, as opposed to scenarios where summarized data or less-precise data are acceptable where the risk is considerably lower. The larger the magnitude of the risks, the greater would be the need in terms of level of confidence in the data.

2. *Identify the attributes required for the intended purposes.*

3. *Identify whether the data elements in the data set are relevant.* This can be achieved by comparing the data elements/data fields in the data set with the attributes identified in step 2. What needs to be determined is:

   - Are the data elements in the data set sufficient?

   - Are the identified data elements relevant?

- Do the data stored in the data elements actually represent what you think you are measuring?

- Are any data elements in the data set missing that would affect the desired outcome? If the data elements in the data set are not sufficient enough to drive the desired outcome or not relevant, then it would fail the reliability test and the problem would need to be rectified by sourcing the missing data elements.

4. *Determine whether data are sourced from trustworthy source(s).* Trustworthy sources play an important role in the stakeholders' level of confidence in the data and the extent to which they are to be tested for reliability purposes. If the sources are known to be highly trustworthy and have a good reputation, the data quality assessment in terms of completeness, consistency, accuracy, and uniqueness is less rigorous as compared to when data are sourced from less trustworthy sources. On the other hand, data from sources having very low trustworthiness could result in stakeholders rejecting the data, especially if the associated risks determined in step 1 are high.

5. *Define and apply data quality business rules for analyzing the data* Record-level data give the greatest opportunity to analyze the data and ability to conduct a more comprehensive data reliability measurement. Business rules need to be defined for the following:

- *Are any values of the key data elements missing?* For example, if in a financial organization, the calculation of employee bonuses is based on the number of loan accounts and loan amounts created by them, it is essential that values are not missing for any of these attributes.

- *The relationship of one data element to another.* For example, date of account modification cannot precede the date of account creation, as an account needs to be created before any modifications can be made to it.

- *Whether data coverage is sufficient.* Are there enough data to support findings and conclusions?

- *Whether data values are accurate.* The level of accuracy or preciseness and whether a deviation would have an impact would depend on the purposes for which the data are used.

- *Whether the data set has erroneous duplicates.* The data set needs to be assessed for duplicates at a record level or attribute/data element level.

In addition to the analysis along the above line items, the timeliness of the data and ability to trace the data back to the source system also needs to be taken into consideration.

With summary level data, it is necessary to understand the business rules, code, and queries that are used to derive the data. Since summary level data are usually an aggregate of granular data, validating summary level data would require obtaining the code used to derive the records. This will allow a greater ability to see whether the correct criteria or rules were used in providing you with the records, decreasing the chance of missing records.

The associated risks would drive the rigor of the business rules required to assess the data quality along the above lines. The outcome of the data quality assessment and the associated risks would essentially drive the decision as to whether the data are reliable enough to be used for the intended purposes.

6. *Review system controls.* The system controls are controls imposed by the system that can reduce, to an acceptable level, the risk that a significant mistake could occur and remain undetected and uncorrected. The question to ask is what checks are performed before data are stored in the system?

   Examples of such controls are completeness checks, zero-balance checks, limit and range checks, sign checks, and validity checks. If a transaction contains errors or fails to meet established criteria, it is rejected. A computer record of rejected transactions should be available from the control group responsible for reviewing output (Morgan and Waring 2004). If rigorous checks are performed before data are stored in the system, the likelihood of erroneous or junk data is considerably less than in systems that do not have any controls or inadequate checks or controls. This is because systems with insufficient controls routinely accept bad data and reject fewer erroneous transactions. For the purposes of assessing data reliability, review should be limited to evaluating the specific controls that can most directly affect the reliability of the data in question.

Figure 4.8 shows a high-level diagram of the factors that play a role in data reliability assessment.

The strength of corroborating evidence and the degree of risk can suggest different data reliability decisions. If the corroborating evidence is strong and the risk is low, the data are more likely to be considered sufficiently reliable for the intended purposes. If the corroborating evidence is weak and the risk is high, the data are more likely to be considered not sufficiently reliable. If data quality assessment does not raise any questions and answers all issues in the review of existing documentation, then the data are more likely to be considered sufficiently reliable for the intended purpose (GAO 2009).

Data reliability measurement can result in any of the following reliability decisions (GAO 2009):

- Sufficiently reliable data

- Not sufficiently reliable data

- Data of undetermined reliability

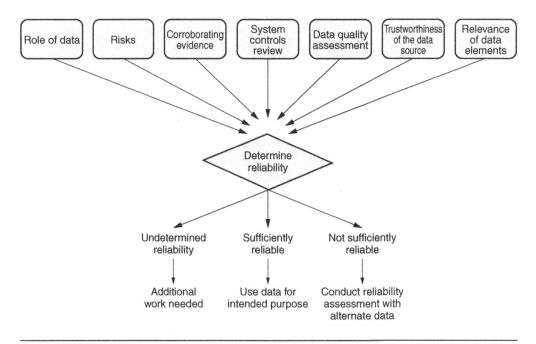

Figure 4.8   Data reliability measurement factors.

Data are considered *sufficiently reliable* when the data quality assessment results provide assurance of the following:

- The likelihood of significant errors or incompleteness is minimal.

- The use of the data would not lead to an incorrect or unintentional message (GAO 2009) or drive incorrect decisions.

A decision that the data are reliable does not automatically mean that the data are completely free of errors. There may still be some problems or uncertainties about the data, but they would be minor given the intended use of the data. Sufficiently reliable data can be used for the intended purposes. Errors are considered acceptable in the circumstance that associated risks have been assessed and it has been concluded that the errors are not substantial enough to cause a reasonable person, aware of the errors, to doubt a finding, conclusion, or recommendation based on the data (GAO 2009).

Two factors need to be taken into consideration while assessing errors in a data file:

- The proportion of the data that are erroneous.

- The magnitude of the error

For example, in a given data set, 5% of records have the incorrect date of birth. However, the dates are off by an average of 10 days, and since the data are used for calculating the age value, depending on what the data are to be used for, 10 days may not compromise reliability.

Data are considered to be *not sufficiently reliable* when the results reveal the following:

- Significant errors or incompleteness in some or all of the key data elements

- Using the data would probably lead to an incorrect or unintentional message.

If data are not sufficiently reliable, evidence from other sources needs to be sought, including alternative computerized data—the reliability of which would also need to be assessed—or original data in other forms, such as surveys, case studies, or expert interviews.

Data are considered to be of *undetermined reliability* when you are not able to determine whether the data are sufficiently reliable. This can happen if one or more of the following factors are present (GAO 2009):

- Limited or no access to a data source

- Time limitations

- A wide range of data that cannot be examined with current resources

- The deletion of original computer files

- Insufficient documentation about the data

- Lack of access to needed documents

In such cases, an attempt is made to garner as much information as possible, by contacting data owners or users or by looking for corroborating evidence, before concluding that the data are of undetermined reliability. Finding sufficient corroborating evidence, for example, may enable you to determine that the data are reliable enough for your purposes.

Measuring Ease of Manipulation

As defined in Chapter 3, *ease of manipulation* is the extent to which the data are easy to manipulate for different tasks such as modification, sorting, reformatting, classification, and aggregation, customization of data elements in data sets or tables, and joining with other data elements.

Ease of manipulation of a data set can be measured by subjective assessment. The assessment is carried out by conducting a survey where users are asked to rate the ease with which data can be manipulated on a scale of 0 to 1, where 0 indicates the lowest score, indicating that the data are very difficult to manipulate and 1 indicating that the data are extremely easy to manipulate. A fractional value of 0.5 indicates that ease of manipulation is medium. Fractional values closer to 1 indicate greater ease of manipulation and fractional values closer to 0 indicate that manipulating data for different tasks is difficult. The overall ease of manipulation rating is the average rating across all users participating in the survey.

Table 4.38	User rating for data quality dimension "ease of manipulation."
User	**Ease of manipulation rating**
User 1	0.6
User 2	0.5
User 3	0.6
User 4	0.8
User 5	0.7
User 6	0.6
User 7	0.8
User 8	0.7
User 9	0.8
User 10	0.9

Thus,

$$\text{Overall ease of manipulation rating} = \frac{\sum_{i=1}^{n} \text{Ease of manipulation rating}_i}{n}$$

where n is the number of users participating in the survey.

Table 4.38 shows the results of a survey conducted to assess the ease of manipulation of customer data. The responses of 10 users are shown in Table 4.38.

Applying the formula above, the overall ease of manipulation rating is as follows:

$$\text{Overall ease of manipulation rating} =$$
$$\frac{0.6 + 0.5 + 0.6 + 0.8 + 0.7 + 0.6 + 0.8 + 0.7 + 0.8 + 0.9}{10}$$
$$= \frac{7.0}{10}$$
$$= 0.7$$

Measuring Conciseness

As discussed in Chapter 3, *conciseness* is the extent to which data are compactly represented without being overwhelming (that is, brief in presentation, yet complete and to the point) (Wang and Strong 1996). Conciseness can be measured by subjective assessment by conducting a survey where users are asked to rate the subjective criteria shown in Table 4.39 on a scale of 0 to 1, with 0 indicating the least satisfactory rating and 1 indicating the most satisfactory rating. Values between 0 and 1 but closer to 0 represent lesser satisfaction than values closer to 1.

Table 4.39	Conciseness criteria.
Conciseness criteria ID	**Conciseness criteria**
C1	Data are compact and well formatted on the one hand, but also clear, self-descriptive, and complete on the other hand
C2	Data have simple structures and formats

Table 4.40	User rating for data quality dimension "conciseness."		
	C1	**C2**	**Conciseness rating per user**
User 1	0.7	0.8	0.75
User 2	0.6	0.5	0.55
User 3	0.7	0.7	0.70
User 4	0.7	0.6	0.65
User 5	0.8	0.7	0.75
User 6	0.8	0.8	0.80
User 7	0.6	0.7	0.65
User 8	0.7	0.7	0.70
User 9	0.6	0.7	0.65
User 10	0.75	0.75	0.75

The conciseness rating per user is the average rating of the two conciseness criteria:

$$\text{Conciseness rating per user} = \frac{C1 + C2}{2}$$

The overall conciseness rating is the average conciseness rating for all users that responded to the survey:

$$\text{Overall conciseness rating} = \frac{\Sigma_{i=1}^{n}\left[(C1 + C2)/2\right]_i}{n}$$

where n is the number of users participating in the survey.

Table 4.40 shows the results of a survey conducted to assess the conciseness of customer data. The responses of 10 users for the two conciseness criteria are shown in Table 4.40. The last column displays the conciseness rating for the corresponding user, which is the average of the two conciseness criteria ratings.

The overall conciseness rating is the average of the conciseness ratings for all the users:

$$\text{Overall conciseness rating} =$$

$$\frac{0.75 + 0.55 + 0.70 + 0.65 + 0.75 + 0.80 + 0.65 + 0.70 + 0.65 + 0.75}{10}$$

$$= \frac{6.95}{10}$$

$$= 0.695$$

$$\approx 0.70$$

Measuring Objectivity

As defined in Chapter 3, *objectivity* can be defined as the extent to which the data are unbiased, unprejudiced, and impartial. Objectivity can be assessed using the parameters shown in Table 4.41.

Each of the objectivity parameters is given a rating between 0 and 1 as per the guidelines shown in Table 4.42.

Fractional values closer to 1 indicate higher objectivity than fractional values closer to the value 0. The overall objectivity rating for a particular user is the average of all six objectivity parameters, that is,

$$\text{Objectivity rating per user} = \frac{OP1 + OP2 + OP3 + OP4 + OP5 + OP6}{6}$$

The overall objectivity rating is the average objectivity rating for all users that responded to the survey:

$$\text{Overall objectivity rating} =$$

$$\frac{\Sigma_{i=1}^{n}\left[(OP1 + OP2 + OP3 + OP4 + OP5 + OP6)/6\right]_i}{n}$$

where n is the number of users participating in the survey.

Table 4.41	Objectivity parameters.
Objectivity parameter ID	**Objectivity parameter**
OP1	Is the information source authentic?
OP2	Does the publisher have a personal impact on the data provided?
OP3	Can the data be affected due to the organization sponsors or policy?
OP4	Is the accountability of information or data clearly defined?
OP5	To what extent are independent sources available for confirmation of facts?
OP6	To what extent do processes for data collection, processing, and dissemination ensure objectivity?

Table 4.43 shows the results of a survey conducted to assess the objectivity of customer data. The responses of five users for the six objectivity criteria are shown in Table 4.43. The last column displays the objectivity rating for the corresponding user, which is the average of the six objectivity criteria ratings.

The overall objectivity rating is the average of the objectivity ratings for all the users:

$$\text{Overall objectivity rating} = \frac{0.91 + 0.9 + 0.9 + 0.86 + 0.86}{5}$$

$$= \frac{4.43}{5}$$

$$= 0.886$$

$$\approx 0.89$$

Table 4.42   Objectivity parameter rating guidelines.

Objectivity parameter ID	Objectivity parameter	Possible answers	Rating
OP1	Is the information source authentic?	Yes	1
		No	0
OP2	Does the publisher have a personal impact on the data provided?	Yes	0
		No	1
OP3	Can the data be affected due to the organization sponsors or policy?	Yes	0
		No	1
OP4	Is the accountability of information or data clearly defined?	Yes	1
		No	0
OP5	To what extent are independent sources available for confirmation of facts?	Values between 0 and 1 0 = Lowest 1 = Highest	User rating between 0 and 1
OP6	To what extent do processes for data collection, processing, and dissemination ensure objectivity?	Values between 0 and 1 0 = Lowest 1 = Highest	User rating between 0 and 1

Table 4.43   Survey results for objectivity.

	OP1	OP2	OP3	OP4	OP5	OP6	Objectivity rating per user
User 1	1	1	1	1	0.75	0.75	0.91
User 2	1	1	1	1	0.75	0.75	0.9
User 3	1	1	1	1	0.7	0.7	0.9
User 4	1	1	1	1	0.6	0.6	0.86
User 5	1	1	1	1	0.6	0.6	0.86

Measuring Interpretability

Interpretability can be defined as the extent to which the user can easily understand and properly use and analyze the data. Interpretability can be assessed by conducting a survey where users are asked to rate the subjective criteria in Table 4.44 on a scale of 0 to 1, with 0 indicating the least satisfactory rating and 1 indicating the most satisfactory rating. Values between 0 and 1 but closer to 0 represent lesser satisfaction than values closer to 1.

The interpretability rating per user is the average rating of all seven interpretability criteria, that is,

$$\text{Interpretability rating per user} = \frac{IC1 + IC2 + IC3 + IC4 + IC5 + IC6 + IC7}{7}$$

The overall interpretability rating is the average interpretability rating for all users that responded to the survey:

$$\text{Overall interpretability rating} = \frac{\sum_{i=1}^{n}\left[(IC1 + IC2 + IC3 + IC4 + IC5 + IC6 + IC7)/7\right]_i}{n}$$

where n is the number of users participating in the survey.

Table 4.45 shows the results of a survey conducted to assess the interpretability of customer data. The responses of 10 users for the seven interpretability criteria are shown in Table 4.45. The last column displays the interpretability rating for the corresponding user, which is the average of the six interpretability criteria ratings.

The overall interpretability rating is the average of the interpretability ratings for all the users:

Table 4.44	Interpretability criteria.
Interpretability criteria ID	**Interpretability criteria**
IC1	Metadata (that is, data about data) are present in increasing amount of detail.
IC2	Metadata are comprehensible.
IC3	Data definitions are clear.
IC4	Standard concepts, terminologies, and classifications are used.
IC5	Supplementary information and documentation are available.
IC6	Adequate support is available for users to properly use and interpret the data.
IC7	Formats are conducive to correct interpretation.

Table 4.45			Survey results for interpretability.					
	IC1	**IC2**	**IC3**	**IC4**	**IC5**	**IC6**	**IC7**	**Interpretability rating per user**
User 1	0.8	0.75	0.8	0.9	0.75	0.8	0.8	0.8
User 2	0.75	0.75	0.7	0.8	0.75	0.75	0.75	0.75
User 3	0.7	0.6	0.6	0.75	0.7	0.8	0.75	0.7
User 4	0.75	0.7	0.75	0.8	0.7	0.7	0.9	0.76
User 5	0.8	0.75	0.8	0.75	0.6	0.8	0.75	0.75
User 6	0.6	0.75	0.7	0.8	0.7	0.8	0.8	0.74
User 7	0.8	0.7	0.7	0.6	0.7	0.8	0.9	0.74
User 8	0.9	0.8	0.8	0.7	0.7	0.7	0.8	0.77
User 9	0.8	0.7	0.75	0.8	0.7	0.75	0.7	0.74
User 10	0.75	0.8	0.8	0.75	0.7	0.8	0.8	0.77

$$\text{Overall interpretability rating}$$

$$= \frac{0.8 + 0.75 + 0.7 + 0.76 + 0.75 + 0.74 + 0.74 + 0.77 + 0.74 + 0.77}{10}$$

$$= \frac{7.52}{10}$$

$$= 0.752$$

$$\approx 0.75$$

Measuring Believability, Credibility, and Trustworthiness

Believability is defined as the extent to which the data are regarded as being trustworthy and credible by the user. *Credibility* is defined as the extent to which the good faith of a provider of data or source of data can be relied on to ensure that the data actually represent what the data are supposed to represent, and that there is no intent to misrepresent what the data are supposed to represent (Chisholm 2014). *Trustworthiness* is defined as the extent to which the data originate from trustworthy sources.

Credibility can be assessed by conducting a survey where users are asked to rate the subjective criteria in Table 4.46 on a scale of 0 to 1, with 0 indicating the least satisfactory rating and 1 indicating the most satisfactory rating. Values between 0 and 1 but closer to 0 represent lesser satisfaction than values closer to 1.

Since ratings are based on the judgment and experience of the users, it is generally recommended to have a credibility survey conducted with expert users.

Fractional values closer to 1 indicate higher credibility than fractional values closer to the value 0. The overall credibility rating is the average credibility rating.

Table 4.46	Credibility criteria.
Credibility criteria ID	**Credibility criteria**
CC1	The good faith of the data provider can be relied on to ensure that the data represent what they are supposed to represent.
CC2	The good faith of the data provider can be relied on to ensure that there has been no intent to misinterpret the data.
CC3	There is a guarantee that data are protected from unauthorized modification.

Table 4.47	Trustworthiness parameters.
Trustworthiness parameter ID	**Trustworthiness parameter**
TP1	Are the data sourced from an authoritative source or provider with a known control environment and track record?
TP2	Can data be traced to the source?
TP3	Number of complaints or issues reported on the data in last six months?
TP4	Number of requests issued for the data in the last six months?
TP5	What is the degree to which reporting on data quality statistics is published?

The credibility rating per user is the average rating of all three credibility criteria, that is,

$$\text{Credibility rating per user} = \frac{CC1 + CC2 + CC3}{3}$$

The overall credibility rating is the average credibility rating for all users that responded to the survey:

$$\text{Overall credibility rating} = \frac{\Sigma_{i=1}^{n}\left[(CC1 + CC2 + CC3)/3\right]_i}{n}$$

where n is the number of users participating in the survey.

Trustworthiness can be assessed using the parameters in Table 4.47.

Each of the trustworthiness assessment parameters is given a rating between 0 and 1 as per the guidelines in Table 4.48.

Fractional values closer to 1 indicate higher trustworthiness than fractional values closer to the value 0. The overall trustworthiness rating is the average trustworthiness rating.

Table 4.48	Trustworthiness parameter ratings guidelines.		
Trustworthiness parameter ID	**Trustworthiness parameters**	**Possible answers**	**Rating**
TP1	Are the data sourced from an authoritative source or provider with a known control environment and track record?	Yes	1
		No	0
		Do not know	0
TP2	Can data be traced to the source?	Yes	1
		No	0
TP3	Number of complaints or issues reported on the data in last six months?	0	1
		Greater than 0 but less than or equal to 3	0.75
		Greater than 3 but less than or equal to 5	0.50
		Greater than 5 but less than or equal to 10	0.25
		Greater than 10	0
TP4	Number of requests issued for the data in the last six months?	0	0
		Greater than 0 but less than or equal to 3	0.25
		Greater than 3 but less than or equal to 5	0.50
		Greater than 5 but less than or equal to 10	0.75
		Greater than 10	1
TP5	What is the degree to which reporting on data quality statistics is published?	Not at all reported	0
		Reported intermittently and incomplete to a greater degree	0.25
		Reported more or less periodically and incomplete to a greater degree, or reported intermittently and incomplete to a lesser degree	0.50
		Reported more or less periodically and incomplete to a lesser degree	0.75
		Reported periodically and complete	1

The trustworthiness rating is the average rating of all five trustworthiness assessment parameters, that is,

$$\text{Trustworthiness rating} = \frac{TP1 + TP2 + TP3 + TP4 + TP5}{5}$$

Trustworthiness of data is usually assessed and established by a third-party organization or by data auditors.

The overall trustworthiness rating is the average trustworthiness rating for all users that respond to the survey:

$$\text{Overall trustworthiness rating} = \frac{\Sigma_{i=1}^{n}\left[(TP1 + TP2 + TP3 + TP4 + TP5)/5\right]_i}{n}$$

where n is the number of users participating in the survey.

The overall believability rating is the average of the overall credibility rating and overall trustworthiness rating:

$$\text{Overall believability rating} =$$
$$\frac{\text{Overall credibility rating} + \text{Overall trustworthiness rating}}{2}$$

Table 4.49 shows the results of a survey conducted to assess the credibility of customer data. The responses of five expert users for the three credibility criteria are shown in Table 4.49. The last column displays the credibility rating for the corresponding user, which is the average of the three credibility criteria ratings.

Applying the formula above, the overall credibility rating is as follows:

$$\text{Overall credibility rating} = \frac{0.77 + 0.78 + 0.7 + 0.73 + 0.77}{5}$$
$$= \frac{3.75}{5}$$
$$= 0.75$$

Table 4.50 shows the results based on the trustworthiness parameters, with the responses of one data auditor.

$$\text{Overall trustworthiness rating} = \frac{TP1 + TP2 + TP3 + TP4 + TP5}{5}$$
$$= \frac{1 + 1 + 0.75 + 0.75 + 0.5}{5}$$
$$= \frac{4}{5}$$
$$= 0.8$$

Table 4.49	Survey results for credibility.			
	CC1	**CC2**	**CC3**	**Credibility rating per user**
User 1	0.75	0.8	0.75	0.77
User 2	0.8	0.75	0.8	0.78
User 3	0.75	0.6	0.75	0.7
User 4	0.75	0.7	0.75	0.73
User 5	0.8	0.7	0.8	0.77

Table 4.50	Trustworthiness parameter ratings.		
Trustworthiness parameter ID	**Trustworthiness parameters**	**Answers**	**Rating**
TP1	Are the data sourced from an authoritative source or provider with a known control environment and track record?	Yes	1
TP2	Can data be traced to the source?	Yes	1
TP3	Number of complaints or issues reported on the data in last six months?	Greater than 0 but less than or equal to 3	0.75
TP4	Number of requests issued for the data in the last six months?	Greater than 5 but less than or equal to 10	0.75
TP5	What is the degree to which reporting on data quality statistics is published?	Reported more or less periodically and incomplete to a greater degree, or reported intermittently and incomplete to a lesser degree	0.50

Applying the formula for overall believability rating,

$$\text{Overall believability rating} = \frac{0.75 + 0.8}{2}$$

$$= \frac{1.55}{2}$$

$$= 0.775$$

$$\approx 0.78$$

Assessing Reputation

Reputation is defined as the extent to which the data are highly regarded in terms of their source or content, and can be assessed by obtaining possible evidence of the data provider's track record over a period of time. One way of assessing the reputation of a data source is by conducting a survey in the community or by questioning other

Table 4.51	Reputation parameters.
Reputation parameter ID	**Reputation parameters**
RP1	The data source provides accurate data consistently.
RP2	Data source issues, when found, are resolved quickly.
RP3	The data source is recommended by other reputed data producers.

members who can help to determine the reputation of a source, or by questioning the person who published a data set (Zaveri 2012).

Table 4.51 lists some parameters or subjective criteria that can be used to gauge the reputation of the data source. Users can be asked to rate the subjective criteria on a scale of 0 to 1, with 0 indicating the least satisfactory rating and 1 indicating the most satisfactory rating. Values between 0 and 1 but closer to 0 represent lesser satisfaction than values closer to 1. Since reputation builds over time, it is recommended to ensure that the survey community consists of consumers who have known the data source for a considerable period of time.

Fractional values closer to 1 indicate higher reputation than fractional values closer to the value 0. The overall reputation rating is the average reputation rating.

The reputation rating is the average rating of all three reputation assessment parameters, that is,

$$\text{Reputation rating} = \frac{RP1 + RP2 + RP3}{3}$$

The overall reputation rating is the average reputation rating for all users that responded to the survey:

$$\text{Overall reputation rating} = \frac{\Sigma_{i=1}^{n}\left[(R1 + R2 + R3)/3\right]_{i}}{n}$$

where n is the number of users participating in the survey.

HOW TO CONDUCT DATA PROFILING

Companies can basically use one of following options for examining the quality of their data assets, depending on the number of data elements or fields in the data set and the volume of data.

Manual Data Profiling

The old-fashioned way of solving data quality problems with source data was to engage a team of database professionals to manually analyze the data and unearth any issues

(Mahanti 2015), and then make necessary corrections. Earlier in this chapter we used manual data profiling to show how we can measure completeness, accuracy, uniqueness, consistency, validity, consistency, integrity, and volatility for different data sets. Manual data profiling is a feasible approach if the data set is small in terms of breadth and length, that is, it has very few data elements/fields/columns, as well as very few rows or records.

However, thanks to the digital revolution, most organizations have vast amounts of data, usually stored in large database systems, with thousands of columns and millions (or billions) of records. Also, an organization generally has multiple data stores. With today's large databases and large number of data stores, manual data profiling can take years, several people, and a big budget, and still be error prone. It is not practically plausible to compare the thousands of attributes and millions of values necessary to uncover the relationships. This approach generally works best for a one-time analysis of a small sample of data. With a relatively small reference data set, which you scan quickly to discover anomalies, manual data profiling is usually the best option.

Data Profiling Using Spreadsheets

Another way of conducting data profiling is to analyze the data using spreadsheets. Excel formulas, pivot tables, and macros are typically used for data analysis. You can also use functions to generate some statistical measures, such as a correlation coefficient. Commonly used functions that help in data profiling are:

- Vlookup(). This function searches a value in a table and returns a corresponding value; it can be useful in measuring the accuracy of a data element or data record by comparing a value with the corresponding value in the reference data set.

- If(). This is one of the most useful functions in Excel. It lets you use conditional formulas, which are calculated one way when a certain thing is true, and another way when it is false. For example, you may want to mark each sale as "high" or "low." If a sale is greater than or equal to $5000, then it needs to be marked "high," otherwise, it is "low."

- SUM(). This function can be used to calculate the sum of two or more values in different cells.

- AVERAGE(). This function can be used to calculate the average of two or more values in different cells.

- MAX(). This function can be used to get the largest number in the set of numbers stored in different cells.

- MIN(). This function can be used to get the smallest number in the set of numbers stored in different cells.

- LEN(). This function tells you about the length of a cell, that is, number of characters, including spaces and special characters.

- CONCATENATE(). This function can be used to concatenate the values in two or more cells into one cell.

The pivot table is a summary table that lets you perform operations like count, average, sum, standard deviation, or other calculations according to the reference feature you have selected. In other words, it converts a data table into an inference table, which helps in making decisions. This option is feasible only if a few data elements or fields need to be analyzed. However, like manual data profiling, this approach also is not at all practical, especially with today's large databases.

SQL Scripts for Profiling Data

Another approach to understanding the source data is to write queries, typically SQL queries, against data stored in tables in databases. *SQL* (structured query language) is a language used to retrieve and manipulate data in a relational database. Relatively simple SQL queries can be used to imitate some of the facets of column profiling, such as cardinality, minimum, maximum, and average statistics. Generating a value frequency distribution may provide a large amount of profiling information, especially when it comes to cardinality, sparseness, or outlier identification. Cross-table redundancy analysis can be easily programmed as well. However, cross-column analysis may be computationally complex (Loshin 2004). Understanding the data very well is critical for data profiling using SQL to be successful (Mahanti 2015).

For purposes of profiling using SQL, the SELECT statement can be used to extract or read data from the tables in a relational database. SQL statements are not case-sensitive. The general form of the SQL SELECT statement is as follows:

SELECT *Column names*

FROM *Table name*

<WHERE *Condition*

ORDER BY *Column names>*

The WHERE condition and ORDER BY column names are optional.

The WHERE clause filters rows that meet certain criteria and is followed by conditions or a set of conditions that return either true or false.

ORDER BY allows sorting by one or more columns. The default sort order is ascending, that is, low to high or A to Z. The keyword DESC denotes descending, that is, reverse order. If the ORDER BY clause is not used, records will not be returned in a specific order.

When all columns are to be selected from a table, then *column names* in the select statement can be replaced by * as follows:

SELECT *

FROM *Table name*

Table 4.52 summarizes some of the SQL statements and clauses that can be used when analyzing data or looking for data anomalies in relational database tables using SQL.

Table 4.52	SQL statement and clauses.	
SQL statement and clauses	**Description**	**Syntax**
SELECT MIN statement	SELECT MIN returns the minimum value for a column in the table.	SELECT MIN (column-name) FROM table-name
SELECT MAX statement	SELECT MAX returns the maximum value for a column in the table.	SELECT MAX (column-name) FROM table-name
SELECT COUNT statement	SELECT COUNT returns a count of the number of data values in a column in the table.	SELECT COUNT (column-name) FROM table-name
SELECT SUM statement	SELECT SUM returns the sum of the data values of a column in a table.	SELECT SUM (column-name) FROM table-name
SELECT AVG statement	SELECT AVG returns the average of the data values of a column in a table.	SELECT AVG (column-name) FROM table-name
SELECT DISTINCT statement	SELECT DISTINCT operates on a single column and returns only distinct values, and eliminates duplicate records from the results. DISTINCT can be used with aggregate functions like COUNT, AVG, MAX, and so on.	SELECT DISTINCT column-name FROM table-name
SQL WHERE IN clause	WHERE IN returns values that match values in a list or subquery, and is a shorthand for multiple OR conditions. This can be useful in comparing data element values from reference data sets.	SELECT column-names FROM table-name WHERE column-name IN (values)
SELECT IS NULL clause	NULL is a special value that signifies "no value."	SELECT column-names FROM table-name WHERE column-name IS NULL

Continued

Table 4.52   *Continued.*

SQL statement and clauses	Description	Syntax
SELECT IS NOT NULL clause	NOT NULL would return values. This clause is useful in assessing data element completeness.	SELECT column-names FROM table-name WHERE column-name IS NOT NULL
SQL WHERE AND clause	WHERE conditions can be combined with an AND clause. A WHERE clause with AND requires that two conditions are true.	SELECT column-names FROM table-name WHERE condition1 AND condition2
SQL WHERE OR clause	A WHERE clause with OR requires that at least one of the two conditions is true.	SELECT column-names FROM table-name WHERE condition1 OR condition2
SQL WHERE NOT clause	A WHERE clause with NOT refutes the specified condition.	SELECT column-names FROM table-name WHERE NOT condition
SQL WHERE BETWEEN clause	WHERE BETWEEN returns values that fall within a given range. WHERE BETWEEN is shorthand for ≥ AND ≤. BETWEEN operator is inclusive: begin and end values are included. This is useful when columns in a table can have a range of values but have a defined minimum or maximum value.	SELECT column-names FROM table-name WHERE column-name BETWEEN value1 AND value2
SQL WHERE LIKE statement	WHERE LIKE determines if a character string matches a pattern. Use WHERE LIKE when only a fragment of a text value is known. WHERE LIKE supports wildcard match options like: %, *, ?, and _ depending on the SQL and database technology. % and * are used for multiple character matches. ? and _ are used for single character matches.	SELECT column-names FROM table-name WHERE column-name LIKE value

Continued

Table 4.52   *Continued.*

SQL statement and clauses	Description	Syntax
SQL GROUP BY clause	The GROUP BY clause groups records into summary rows, and returns one record for each group. The GROUP BY clause can group by one or more columns. The GROUP BY clause typically also involves aggregates: COUNT, MAX, SUM, AVG, and so on.	SELECT column-names FROM table-name WHERE condition GROUP BY column-names
SQL HAVING clause	HAVING works on summarized group records from the GROUP BY results and returns only those groups that meet the HAVING criteria. HAVING needs a GROUP BY clause to be present. WHERE and HAVING can be in the same query.	SELECT column-names FROM table-name WHERE condition GROUP BY column-names HAVING condition
SQL Alias	An *alias* is an alternative name, usually an abbreviated version of a table or column name. Complex queries with aliases are generally easier to read and are useful with JOINs and aggregates: SUM, COUNT, and so on. An alias only exists for the duration of the query.	SELECT column-name AS alias-name FROM table-name alias-name WHERE condition
SQL JOIN	An SQL JOIN combines records from two tables by locating related column values in the two tables. INNER JOIN is the same as JOIN; the keyword INNER is optional.	SELECT column-names FROM table-name1 INNER JOIN table-name2 ON column-name1 = column-name2 WHERE condition Note: The keyword INNER is optional
SQL LEFT JOIN	LEFT JOIN or LEFT OUTER JOIN performs a join starting with the first (left-most) table and then any matching second (right-most) table records.	SELECT column-names FROM table-name1 LEFT JOIN table-name2 ON column-name1 = column-name2 WHERE condition

Continued

Table 4.52   *Continued.*

SQL statement and clauses	Description	Syntax
SQL RIGHT JOIN	RIGHT JOIN or RIGHT OUTER JOIN performs a join starting with the second (right-most) table and then any matching first (left-most) table records.	SELECT column-names FROM table-name1 RIGHT JOIN table-name2 ON column-name1 = column-name2 WHERE condition
SQL FULL JOIN	FULL JOIN or FULL OUTER JOIN returns all matching records from both tables whether the other table matches or not.	SELECT column-names FROM table-name1 FULL JOIN table-name2 ON column-name1 = column-name2 WHERE condition
SQL self JOIN	A self JOIN is a regular join, but the table is joined with itself rather than another table, and self JOIN is useful for comparisons within a table.	SELECT column-names FROM table-name T1 JOIN table-name T2 WHERE condition

Almost all the data quality dimensions that can be measured objectively require a count of the total number of data records stored in a database table. The following SQL query format can be used to obtain the total number of records in a database table:

SELECT COUNT(*) FROM <table name>

For example, if the table name is *employee*, then

SELECT COUNT(*) FROM employee

would return the total number of records in the employee table.

The number of occurrences of each value in a particular column can be obtained by using the following SQL format:

SELECT column name, COUNT(column name) FROM <table name>

GROUP BY column_name

For another example, if the table name is *employee*, then in order to get the count of occurrences of a distinct social security number, we can use the following query:

SELECT social_security_number, count(social_security_number) as SSN_Count FROM Employee

GROUP BY social_security_number

As seen in Example 4.1, missing values for the Social Security Number data element were represented by NULL and UNKWN. The following query can be used to obtain the count of missing values:

SELECT social_security_number, count(social_security_number) as SSN_Count FROM Employee

WHERE social_security_number = 'UNKWN' OR social_security_number is NULL

GROUP BY social_security_number

Ideally, the social security number values in the social security column in the employee table should be unique, and each employee should have a social security number, meaning the social security number cannot be missing. The above query would provide even a single occurrence of a social security number. For the purposes of detecting violation of uniqueness, it would be good to be able to see the maximum number of occurrences of a particular social security number, in cases where the number of occurrences is greater than one. The following query would achieve this result. The "having count(*)>1" clause only returns social security numbers that have occurred more than once. The "order by 2 DESC" orders the results in descending order, with the maximum number of occurrences at the top and minimum number at the bottom.

SELECT social_security_number, count(social_security_number) as SSN_Count FROM Employee

GROUP BY social_security_number

having count(*)>1

ORDER BY 2 DESC

To calculate the completeness percentage of the Social Security Number data element in the employee table, the following SQL query can be used:

SELECT (COUNT(E.social_security_number) / (SELECT COUNT(*) FROM Employee E)) * 100.00

as "SSN_percentage"

FROM Employee E

WHERE E.social_security_number is NOT NULL and
E.social_security_number <> 'UNKWN';

While analyzing completeness on the data element level, there are certain conditions or circumstances when a data element is not populated. In such cases the SQL query includes a WHERE clause for counting the total number of data values, which should be populated as follows:

SELECT COUNT(*) FROM <table name>

WHERE <condition>

Consider Example 4.2, where the need is to find whether date of birth is populated for individual customers. If the data are stored in the customer table, and the customer type for individual customers is represented by "I," in order to find the count of records where date of birth should be populated, the following SQL query can be used:

SELECT COUNT(date_of_birth) FROM customer

WHERE customer_type = 'I'

MIN, MAX, AVG, and SUM can help perform some quick sanity checks. For example, the date of birth for an individual customer cannot be in the future, and a customer has to be at least 18 years of age. Applying the MAX function on the date of birth column using the following SQL query would show us the maximum date value stored in the date of birth column, and by looking at this value we can determine if the date of birth value is a possible option.

SELECT MAX(Date_of_Birth) AS Max_DOB

FROM Customer

WHERE date_of_birth is NOT NULL

Another example showing the usage of the MAX, MIN, and AVG functions is applied to the annual income column.

SELECT MIN(Annual_Income) AS Minimum_Income, MAX(Annual_
Income) AS Max_Income, AVG(Annual_Income)

FROM Customer

WHERE customer_type = 'I'

Certain data elements like status and flag fields can have a set of values. This can be found from the metadata. For example, as in Example 4.11, the table contains the metadata for the customer data set. The gender column can have either of the two values "M" or "F."

The SQL WHERE NOT IN clause can be used to find out if the gender column has any value other than M or F:

SELECT distinct Gender

FROM Customer

WHERE Gender NOT IN ('M', 'F')

If the gender column has any values other than M or F, the above query will return those values. To obtain statistics on the number of invalid values for gender, the following query can be used:

SELECT DISTINCT Gender, count(Gender) AS GenderCount

FROM Customer

WHERE Gender NOT IN ('M', 'F')

GROUP BY Gender

SQL wildcards can be used for pattern matching. Earlier in this chapter, the format for social security number (SSN) was defined as

XXX-XX-XXXX

WHERE X is a number/digit.

Thus, the social security number values should have a group of three digits followed by the "-" character, followed by a group of two digits, which are in turn followed by the "-" character, which are in turn followed by a group of 4 digits.

The wildcard character "_" can be used to discover Social Security number (SSN) values in the employee table that do not match the above format. The below query will return any SSN values that do not follow the XXX-XX-XXXX format. However, since the wildcard "_" does not distinguish between numeric, alphabetic, or alphanumeric characters, if the SSN has alphabetic or alphanumeric characters, the results of the following query will not distinguish or isolate those anomalies:

SELECT social_security_number, COUNT (social_security_number)
FROM employee

WHERE social_security_number NOT LIKE '___-__-____'

Subqueries are useful when data from one table need to be matched with another table, usually a reference table. The following query will only return employee ID values from the employee table for which there are matching values in the reference table: employee_ref

SELECT employee_id FROM Employee WHERE employee_Id in
(SELECT employee_id FROM employee_ref)

The following query can be used to extract employee ID, employee name, and social security number values from the employee table for which there are matching records in the reference table—employee_ref. If any of the columns—employee ID, employee name, or social security number do not match at a record level with a record in the employee_ref table, then the query result will not contain that record.

SELECT e.employee_id, e.employee_name, e.social_security_number

FROM employee e, employee_ref ref

WHERE e.employee_id = ref.employee_id

AND e.employee_name = ref.employee_name

e.social_security_number = ref.social_security_number

SQL Joins. SQL joins are useful for making a comparison between tables or within the same table. SQL joins help unearth inconsistencies and reference integrity issues.

Consider Example 4.17, where the customer ID in the order data set should be linked to the customer ID in the customer data set. The following query will return all records from the order table, and the corresponding customer ID and customer name from the customer table. If an order exists in the order table with no corresponding customer details in the customer table, NULL values will be returned for ParentCustomerId and Customer_Name along with the order details. The order records that have NULL values for ParentCustomerId are the orphan records.

SELECT O.Order_ID, O.Order_Date, O.Customer_ID as OrderCustomerId, C.Customer_ID as ParentCustomerId, C.Customer_Name

FROM Order O LEFT JOIN customer C

ON O.customer_id = C.customer_id

On the other hand, a right join, as shown in the query below, would return customer records and the corresponding order records if a match were found on customer_id. If no match was found on customer_id in the order table, then customer details would be returned from the customer table but NULL values would be populated against the order details for that customer.

SELECT O.Order_ID, O.Order_Date, O.Customer_ID as OrderCustomerId, C.Customer_ID as ParentCustomerId, C.Customer_Name

FROM Order O RIGHT JOIN customer C

ON O.customer_id = C.customer_id

The above examples give a glimpse of how one can do some simple data profiling functions using SQL.

All the data profiling approaches discussed so far—manual data profiling, spreadsheets, and SQL scripts—are dependent on a combination of documentation and individual knowledge, and are focused on selected aspects of a data source. However, the above approaches are often time-consuming and incomplete, as analysis tends to be concentrated in known areas of the data. To overcome these shortcomings, data profiling tools should be used (Mahanti 2015).

Use of a Data Profiling Tool

Data sets have grown in size and complexity to the point where human analysis is not enough. There need to be computer-based and automated methods to process the massive volumes of data (Kantardzic 2011). The expansion of data has promoted the growth of new technologies and disciplines requiring new tools and approaches (Howles 2014). Data profiling tools comprise a new category of software that offers a fast, accurate, and automated way to understand data. But, while some of the functionality can be deployed internally, the vendor tools provide some specific benefits that make them worth the cost. Effective data profiling tools collect, aggregate, and examine data from multiple sources for the purpose of gathering statistics (count, sum, mean, median, frequency, variation, and so on) and details (structure, content, format, classifications, and so on) about them. However, these tools need to be integrated into the organization's software environment and configured with metadata, assertions, and rules in accordance with the organization's business user's expectations. Also, they are most effective in the hands of professionals who understand the data, the context, and the technology.

Data profiling incorporates a collection of analysis and assessment algorithms that, when applied in the proper context, will provide empirical insight into what potential issues exist within a data set (Loshin 2010a). Data profiling can be conducted at different structural levels, and data profiling techniques can be grouped into categories, as shown in Figure 4.9.

Column or Attribute Profiling. *Column profiling*, also known as *attribute profiling*, is the most basic form of data profiling and provides statistics about the columns or attributes in the data set by analyzing the values contained in each column. Column profiling deduces detailed characteristics for each column, including data type and size, range of values, frequency and distribution of values, cardinality, and null and uniqueness characteristics, as shown in Table 4.53. In this technique, analysis performed for one column is independent of all other columns contained in the data set.

The metadata include properties or characteristics for each column of the data set that describe what a valid value is within that column. The metadata, which contains a property list for each column, is actually a set of rules involving only that particular column. The objective of column profiling is to unearth data content quality issues. The more complete the metadata, the greater are the opportunities for unearthing bad data values. Data values within a column that violate the rules are invalid and/or inaccurate values. For example, if the annual income value is less than 0, it is both invalid and inaccurate, as annual income cannot take a negative value. Say that the date column needs to comply with the mm/dd/yyyy format. If the date column has the value 13/13/2000, then it is both invalid and inaccurate. However, not all inaccurate values are found through this process. Values that are invalid or inaccurate, but for which you do not have

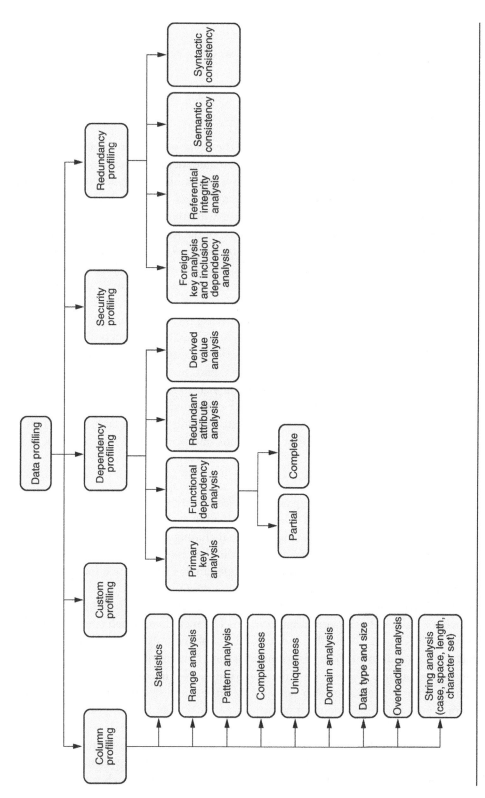

Figure 4.9 Data profiling techniques.

Table 4.53	Column profiling.		
Analysis category	**Profile**	**Data types**	**Description**
Completeness (missing column values)	Column NULL ratio profile	All data types	Percentage of *null* values in the selected column.
	Column blank ratio profile	String	Percentage of blank values in the selected column.
	Column zero ratio profile	Numeric	Percentage of zero values in the selected column. For example, the account balance column having a high percentage of zero values may be indicative of a problem.
String length	Column length distribution profile	String	Count and percentages of distinct lengths of string values in the selected column.
	Minimum string length	String	Minimum length in the selected column.
	Maximum string length	String	Maximum length in the selected column.
	Average string length	String	Average length in the selected column.
Space analysis	Leading spaces	String	Count and percentages of leading spaces in the selected column.
	Trailing spaces	String	Count and percentages of trailing spaces in the selected column.
	Maximum spaces between words	String	Count and percentages of the number of spaces between words in the selected column.
Case analysis	Upper case	String	Count and percentage of upper case letters in the selected column.
	Lower case	String	Count and percentage of lower case letters in the selected column. Certain column values, for example, those holding abbreviations need to be upper case. The count and percentage of lower case letters would be indicative of a problem.
Character set analysis	Character set profile	String	Count and percentage of invalid characters as defined by the metadata.
Cardinality/ uniqueness/ duplication	Column value distribution profile	All data types	Frequency of values in the selected column. This would indicate the cardinality of the column.
Pattern analysis	Column pattern profile	String/date	Set of patterns that cover the specified percentage of values in the column.
	Format evaluation	String/date	Count and percentage of values in the column matching the format specified by the metadata.

Continued

Table 4.53	*Continued.*		
Analysis category	**Profile**	**Data types**	**Description**
Statistics	Minimum	All data types	Minimum value, based on the ordering properties of the data set.
	Maximum	All data types	Maximum value, based on the ordering properties of the data set.
	Mean	Numeric	Average value. It is a measure of the central tendency.
	Median	Numeric	The middle value. It is a measure of the central tendency. In the case where the data distributions are skewed, the median is a much better measure of central tendency than the mean.
	Mode	All data types	Most frequent value in the data set.
	Standard deviation	Numeric	Standard deviation is a measure of dispersion. A high standard deviation indicates the data points are spread over a wide range of values.
Range analysis	Column range profile	All data types	Scans values to determine whether they are subject to a total ordering, and determines whether the values are constrained within a well-defined range (Loshin 2010a).
Domain analysis		All data types	Domain analysis is validation of the distribution of values for a given data element against the conceptual value domain. Basic examples of this include validating attributes such as gender or address attributes such as valid states or provinces within a specified region, or flags, status, or indicator fields that can take restricted values.
Overloading analysis*		All data types	Overloading analysis attempts to determine if the column is used for recording more than one business fact and is used for multiple purposes.

*Column overloading can be commonly found in legacy systems, though it was usually not a part of the original application design. However, as changes occurred in an application, the need for new columns arose. Creating new columns meant that record or segment lengths needed to be longer, which meant that databases needed to be unloaded and reloaded, and that application programs not related to the change needed to be modified or at least recompiled (Olsen 2003). To avoid these expensive disruptions, the fields that had unused bit capacity to handle the new information were overloaded rather than create new columns.

a test or rule, are not found. If the date column has the value 24/11/2000, it is invalid, but its accuracy is indeterminable. However, if the data column has the value 10/10/2000, it is valid but may or may not be accurate.

From a computational angle, column profiling is comparatively simple, requiring a scan through the entire table and a count of the number of occurrences of each distinct value within each column. In principle, this can be implemented using hash tables that map each value that appears in the column to the number of times that value appears (Loshin 2010a).

Dependency Analysis. *Dependency analysis*, also known as *dependency profiling* or *intra-table analysis* or *intra-file analysis* (McGilvray 2008a), analyzes data across records in a data set—by comparing the data values stored in every column with the values in every other column—and infers relationships that exist between the columns within the data set. Dependency analysis covers multiple columns in a data set simultaneously, and identifies column similarities and correlation between column values.

Dependency analysis involves cross-column analysis that is much more computationally intensive than column profiling. Profiling tools performing dependency analysis use algorithms to look for hidden relationships between attribute values. These algorithms require multiple scans through the table, with intermediate results managed with complex data structures. The algorithm involves recursion, and hence the results of each iterative scan should be cached to support each subsequent iteration. Some of the algorithms are reasonably simple, while others involve complex statistical models and pattern recognition techniques. For modern databases, the return on investment from using more-sophisticated pattern recognition techniques to identify data quality rules often quickly diminishes. On the other hand, sophisticated dependency profiling is often the best way to identify data quality rules in "legacy" databases with unknown schemas (Maydanchik 2007).

While dependencies between two attributes (sometimes referred to as *binary relationships*) are the simplest to identify and use, more than two attributes often participate in the relationship (Maydanchik 2007). A dependency relationship can be a functional dependency or a derived relationship. Dependency profiling identifies primary keys. In addition to discovering functional dependencies and primary keys, dependency analysis can unearth data structure quality problems.

Dependency analysis can be categorized into the following four categories:

- Derived value analysis

- Redundant attribute analysis

- Functional dependency analysis

- Primary key analysis

Derived Value Analysis. *Derived value analysis* looks for columns in a data set whose values are calculated as functions of other columns within the same record. As an example, a purchase order line item total should equal the quantity of items ordered multiplied by the unit cost of the items (Loshin 2010a).

Redundant Attribute Analysis. If differently named columns in the same data set contain the same values, then attributes are redundant. *Redundant attribute analysis* looks for redundant attributes in the same data set.

Functional Dependency Analysis. *Functional dependency analysis* determines whether the values in one column (the *dependent* column) in a data set are dependent on the values in another column or set of columns (the *determinant* columns) in the same data set, that is, whether there are embedded relationships in the data set. If a column in a data set is functionally dependent on another column or set of columns in the same data set, a value in one column can be uniquely determined based on the values in another column or column set. Functional dependencies usually arise naturally from real-world facts that the data elements in the data set refer to, and are applicable universally. For example, age would naturally be derived from the date of birth; the state would be functionally dependent on the city and ZIP code. However, there are certain cases where relationships would be defined by rules set by business and not universal. For example, if an account status is closed or suspended, then the account is an exception account for specific regulatory reporting purposes, but if the account status is open, then it has a non-exception status. The data mart table has columns to capture account status and exception status. In this case too, we have a functional dependency where the value of the exception status column is driven by the value in the account status column, but this dependency is not universal.

$X \rightarrow Y$, that is, whenever two records have the same X values, then they also have the same Y values, where X is an attribute or a set of attributes.

For example:

- ZIP code, city $\rightarrow$ State

- Date of birth $\rightarrow$ Age

- Account status $\rightarrow$ Exception status

There can be two types of functional dependencies:

- *Complete.* A functional dependency is said to be *complete* if all values in a column show a functional dependency on values in another column or set of columns in the data set. A complete functional dependency appears with 100% of the values matching. A complete functional dependency is also known as *exact functional dependency.* For example, there is a complete functional dependency between ZIP code, city, and state, that is, the state can be derived from the ZIP code and city.

- *Partial.* A functional dependency is said to be *partial* if the values in one column and another column or set of columns do not satisfy functional dependency criteria in a defined percentage of rows, and holds true only for a subset of records in the data set. Partial functional dependency is also known as *approximate functional dependency.* For example, an individual's title can often indicate gender. For example, the titles "Mr.," "Master," or "Lord" indicate *male*, whereas the titles "Miss," "Mrs," or "Lady" indicate *female*. However, the title "Dr." or "Justice" can indicate either a male or female. Therefore, gender has an approximate functional dependency on an individual's title. An approximate dependency appears with a certain percentage of values satisfying the function parameters.

Primary Key Analysis. *Primary key analysis* examines a collection of column values across each record to determine the candidate primary keys. There is a need to uniquely differentiate the entity occurrence in a data set. If the set of data elements or columns are already established as primary key, then profiling can be used to validate that the key is unique across each record in the table. This in turn helps in validating the uniqueness of records or uncovering duplicates. *Uniqueness analysis* reviews all records in the data set to ensure that no exact duplicates exist (Loshin 2001). Columns that have a high degree of uniqueness, which can be measured in a percentage, as well as at least one foreign key candidate, make the best primary key candidates.

Dependency analysis can discover the absence of a relationship between columns where the expectation is to find one, or unearth relationships between columns or identify business rules between columns where one does not have expectations to find them, or didn't know they existed. Dependency analysis can also expose null occurrences; often, the presence of nulls (as well as defaults) is triggered by conditions associated with other column values within the same instance (Loshin 2010a). Certain column values can restrict the appearance of another column value. For example, if the customer has a customer type column value of *organization* or *trust*, then the date of birth column will have null values. It must be noted that dependencies between columns change over time as data are extended, altered, or merged with other data sets. The ability to discover all the relationships depends on the power of the algorithm used to uncover these relationships.

Redundancy Analysis. *Redundancy analysis*, also known as *cross-table profiling* or *cross-file profiling*, examines content, relationships, and intersections across two or more data sets (tables). Redundancy analysis determines overlapping or identical sets of values, identifies duplicate values, or indicates foreign keys across different data sets (tables). Data are compared between data sets (tables) to determine which columns contain overlapping or identical sets of values. All values corrupting data integrity should be identified. Redundancy analysis iteratively reviews how the values within sets of columns in different tables potentially intersect and overlap. Reviewing the cardinality of the columns and the degree to which column data sets overlap across tables suggests dependencies across tables, relationships, and redundant storage, as well as opportunities for identification of data value sets that are mapped together (Loshin 2010a). Some key capabilities of redundancy analysis are:

- Foreign key analysis and inclusion dependency analysis

- Referential integrity analysis

- Syntactic consistency

- Semantic consistency

Foreign Key Analysis and Inclusion Dependency Analysis. Columns or fields that have a high percentage of values matching those contained in a primary or natural key are best suited for foreign keys. When viewing the prospective foreign key candidate columns for a particular primary or natural key, mark the columns that have the highest paired-to-base percentage. A percentage of 100% indicates that every value within the paired column exists within the base column (primary key or natural key column) (IBM 2011).

A column qualifies as a foreign key candidate if the majority (for example, 98% or higher) of its frequency distribution values match the frequency distribution values of a primary key column. After you select a foreign key, the system performs a bidirectional test (foreign key to primary key, primary key to foreign key) of each foreign key's referential integrity and identifies the number of referential integrity violations and "orphan" values (keys that do not match).

An *inclusion dependency* is defined as the existence of columns in one data set whose values must be a subset of the values in the corresponding columns in another data set, that is, if X is a column or a set of columns in one data set and Y is the corresponding column or set of columns in another data set, then the inclusion dependency, $X \subseteq Y$, means that all the values in the column or set of columns represented by X in the data set should be contained in the column or set of columns represented by Y in the other data set. X is referred to as the *dependent* and Y is called the *referenced*. Inclusion dependency analysis helps in the discovery of foreign keys.

Referential Integrity Analysis. *Referential integrity analysis* compares the values of columns in two data sets (tables) to determine orphan values as well as childless parents. Identification of orphaned records is indicative of a foreign key relationship that is violated because a child entry exists in the child table when a corresponding record does not exist in the parent table. For example, there is a parent–child relationship between the customer and order tables, hence an order cannot exist without a customer. The customer ID, which uniquely identifies a customer in the customer table (parent table), is a foreign key in the order table (child table). For example, if an order placed by a customer exists in the order table, but the customer cannot be found in the customer table, this is an instance of the foreign key relationship being violated.

Syntactic Consistency. If it is known that two data set attributes (or columns) are intended to represent the same set of values, this is a process for ensuring that the value sets share the same format specification (that is, are syntactically compatible) (Loshin 2010a). The process evaluates columns that are expected to take values from the same data domain and checks consistency with the domain rules. This can expose any disagreement of syntactic form among common columns (Loshin 2010a).

Semantic Consistency. *Semantic consistency*, also known as *synonym analysis*, is the process of determining that two (or more) columns in different data sets that share the same value set and refer to the same concept have the same name or are mapped to the same conceptual data element. Conversely, this process can explore value sets that are intended to represent the same concept but have values that occur in one column but not others (non-overlapping values) (Loshin 2010a).

Security Profiling. *Security profiling* profiles user data to determine who (or what roles) have access to the data and what they are authorized to do with the data (add, update, delete, and so on). Large organizations have hundreds, sometimes thousands, of applications that are in turn accessed by thousands of employees. Usually, different roles are defined in an application to give users different levels of access to different data objects within the application depending on their job description and the business units they are associated with. However, people change roles, move to different departments or business units, leave companies, or go on extended leave, which requires their access permissions to be revoked or suspended. It is important that user data are profiled to determine that users have the correct level of access to required applications, and that access has not been accorded to users who are not entitled to it. Determining which application user data to target for security profiling would be governed by the following factors:

- The criticality of the application in terms of the business function it supports

- The risk rating of the application

- The size of the user base for the application

Custom Profiling. Data profiling can be custom programmed to check complex business rules unique to a business (Kimball 2004). *Custom profiling* involves defining business and data rules for analyzing data tailored to meet specific business requirements of the organization; for example, verifying that all the preconditions have been met for granting approval of a major funding initiative.

In case the metrics provided by the tool are not sufficient or do not produce results in a suitable format, custom profiling scripts can be used to produce the desired metrics in the required format. In other words, custom profiling provides flexibility not built into the standardized tools.

Some vendor data profiling tools are IDQ Analyzer by Informatica, DQ Analyzer by Ataccama, InfoSphere Information Analyzer by IBM, Information Steward by SAP, and Ab Initio Data Profiler by Ab Initio. Data profiling technology vastly improves the scope and depth of data analysis in the following ways (Trillium Software 2007):

- Through automation of traditional analysis techniques it is not uncommon
  to see analysis time cut by 90% while still providing a better understanding
  (Business Data Quality 2010). The interface that provides the summarization
  of the profiling functions gives the end client a visual representation of the
  potential data quality issues. Automation and the ability to run in batch
  mode removes manual intervention, facilitating features such as scorecard
  and dashboard monitoring, which in turn provide continuous evaluation of
  data quality.

- Analysts are no longer limited to working just with sample data. Sometimes, the smallest anomalies can have the greatest impact. Most of the tools provide some sort of drill-down mechanism allowing the analyst the opportunity to review the records that are potentially flawed.

- Allowing assessment of rules that govern data that cannot easily be discerned via manual coding and inspection, for example, pattern generation, dependency testing, or join analysis. Dependency analysis, which exposes functional dependencies within a single table, is a bit more complicated to implement and is a capability that contributes significantly to different kinds of applications. Because of its complexity, this capability distinguishes more-advanced products from the more parochial ones.

- These tools work with a wide variety of data sources and have inbuilt connectors or third-party connections that enable connectivity/access to the data in the data sources.

The open source data quality market is still in its infancy, but a few vendors offer adequate data profiling software, according to Gartner. A handful of open source data quality products on the market are adequate for basic data profiling, according to Friedman. Talend, one of the most advanced open source vendors, offers Talend Open Profiler. Other open source tools available on the market are Ataccama DQ Analyzer, and CloverETL Data Profiler. Open source data quality software could be a good fit for companies looking for an inexpensive way to conduct data profiling. However, open source data quality's low price tag is offset by a number of factors, like lack of business user–friendly interfaces, lesser functionality, and limited vendor support (Kelly 2009).

Choice of a data profiling tool would essentially depend on the organization's requirements and the capabilities of the tool to meet those requirements. Some features to look for in a data profiling tool are the tool's ability to handle multiple heterogeneous data sources such as flat files, XML, COBOL, spreadsheets, relational databases, non-relational databases, and so on, the number of data sources that the tool can handle, the level of detail in the data profiling report, and ease of use (Mahanti 2015). Table 4.54 shows the pros and cons of the different data profiling options.

SUMMARY

Measurement of data quality with respect to the relevant data quality dimensions helps in establishing the current state of the data quality and the extent to which the data are good or bad. In this chapter, we have used objective and subjective measures to gauge the different data quality dimensions. It is to be understood that determining critical data based on business needs and impacts and measuring the data quality using the appropriate data quality dimensions is the first step in the journey toward better-quality data. Since data quality is very broad and an organization has a very large number of data elements stored in different systems, if you are set on measuring everything, you are

Table 4.54	Data profiling options—pros and cons.				
	Manual	**Spreadsheets**	**SQL scripts**	**Open source**	**Data profiling tools**
Data	• Small data set (few columns and minimal rows)	• Data set with limited number of data elements	• Large relational databases	• Multiple, heterogeneous large data sources	• Multiple, heterogeneous large data sources
Pros	• Inexpensive • Simplicity	• Inexpensive • Ease of use	• Relatively inexpensive • Supports column profiling, cross-table redundacy, value frequency distribution	• Inexpensive • Automated	• Can unravel hidden, unknown data issues • User-friendly • Automated
Cons	• Large data sets cannot be handled	• Time-consuming • Good knowledge of data required • Number of rows limited to that supported by the spreadsheet	• Time-consuming • Supports only one data source • Appropriate skills required • Good knowledge of data required	• Limited support • Limited features • Not user-friendly • Tool knowledge required	• Integration • Costly • Tool knowledge required

Source: Mahanti 2015.

probably doomed to failure; it is not possible to measure every aspect or dimension of the data quality of a data set, but only the most relevant data quality dimensions depending on the context of use. Selecting the right data assets and data elements is a must to ensure maximum benefit, and should be based on the criticality of the data, business needs, impacts and priorities, financial benefits, and the types of projects the data assets will be used for. It is a good practice to profile data before embarking on data-intensive initiatives like enterprise resource planning (ERP), customer relationship management (CRM), data migration, data integration, master data management, or data warehouse implementations, and so on.

Not all data quality dimensions are equally important for all purposes. Depending on what you want out of your data, you may decide to prioritize some data quality dimensions over the others. For example, data security is not important for address data elements, but is important for sensitive data like customer financial information, social security numbers, or patient health data. Hence, when assessing the quality of a data set containing social security numbers, you would assess data security, but you would not do the same for a data set containing address data elements. While measuring data quality, one should remember that the "one size does not fit all" approach holds true, and the measurement strategy is driven by the criticality of the data, business needs, the context of use, and the best cost–benefit ratio.

In this chapter, we have also discussed the different ways one can go about profiling data, namely, manual profiling, Excel spreadsheets, SQL queries, and data profiling tools. Measurement is not the end of your data quality journey, but it is definitely an integral part. Data quality dimensions such as completeness, uniqueness, conformity, integrity, accuracy, consistency, timeliness, and coverage can be used as key performance indicators. The results of measurement need to be evaluated to determine whether there is a data quality issue that needs further analysis and rectification or the data reflect a valid business scenario, and hence the metadata (information about data) need updating.

5

Data Quality Strategy

INTRODUCTION

The success of software systems like enterprise resource planning (ERP) systems, customer relationship management (CRM) systems, data warehouses, and master data repositories is highly dependent on the quality of the data that feed into them. Building and maintaining these systems costs millions of dollars. However, if the data in these systems are not reliable or of good quality, these systems will not be used by the users, which would lead to these systems being initially underused and eventually in the course of time, discarded. To appreciate the full benefit of their investments in enterprise computing systems and information systems, organizations need to have a comprehensive understanding of the present quality of their data, which data are most critical and have the highest business value, how to measure data quality, how to cleanse the data, how to monitor data quality once the data are cleaned, and how to keep the data clean. In order to be successful and stay ahead of their competitors, organizations need to approach the problem of managing data quality in a strategic manner rather than a tactical way.

This chapter begins with a discussion on data quality strategy and high-level formulation of a data quality strategy. This is followed by sections that compare the terms *data strategy* and *data quality strategy* and discuss the importance of data quality strategy. The next sections discuss data quality maturity and the data quality maturity model. This is followed by sections that discuss data strategy preplanning and the phases involved in data quality strategy formulation, the characteristics of a good data quality strategy, and implementation of the data quality strategy. This is followed by sections that discuss who drives the data quality strategy and the chief data officer role, and present some useful data quality strategy tips.

WHAT IS A DATA QUALITY STRATEGY?

Before defining a data quality strategy lets first understand the term *strategy*. The term *strategy* evolved from the Greek word *stratēgia*, which means an "art of troop leader; office of general, command, generalship" (Liddell and Scott 2007). *Strategy* is a high-level, long-term plan devised to achieve one or more goals under conditions of uncertainty. Enterprise goals drive a strategy. When defining the strategy, it is important to understand and establish the current state, or *as-is* state, define the desired future state, or *to-be* state, to be achieved, and assess the gap between the current state and future state. Strategy generally involves defining actions to address the gaps in order to realize the goals, and organizing resources to implement the activities necessary to achieve these goals.

In the context of enterprise data, enterprise goals will determine what data are critical, how the data are used, and the level of quality needed. Actions are the processes created and improved to manage the data. Resources are the people, systems, technology, financing, and the data itself. A *data quality strategy* describes a framework and a *roadmap* to address the data quality issues and provides steps to improve data quality to an acceptable level. A data quality strategy should outline the current state of data assets or current data maturity and the future desired state or future desired data maturity, and the gap between the current and future state, and provide recommendations for closing the gap. In the case of an enterprise-wide data quality strategy, establishing the current state would require a data maturity assessment to be carried out across different business units in the organization to understand how data are currently managed and to identify the challenges faced in the different business areas regarding data gathering and management. A gap analysis will also need to be undertaken to determine the gap between the current state and the desired future state, and the obstacles to be overcome and actions to be implemented to attain the future state.

As discussed in Chapter 7, "Data Quality: Critical Success Factors (CSFs)," one of the critical success factors of a data quality program or initiative is a robust data quality strategy. No two organizations are the same, and there is no one-size-fits-all approach when it comes to designing a data quality strategy. The organization's data profile and current data maturity need to be taken into consideration when designing the data quality strategy. It is essential to construct the right data quality strategy to ensure that it provides value for the organization.

On a high level, a data quality strategy formulation process would require defining the problem statement and pain points, establishing the current state and defining the future state, determining the gap between the current and future state, and proposing recommendations and initiatives and defining a roadmap with timelines to implement initiatives to achieve the future state, as shown in Figure 5.1. We will discuss in detail how to create a data quality strategy later in this chapter.

DATA STRATEGY VERSUS DATA QUALITY STRATEGY

Laura Sebastian-Coleman states that "The difference between a data strategy and a data quality strategy can also be purely semantic." An organization's data strategy or data management strategy must also be a data *quality* strategy since the purpose of data management overall should be to ensure the existence and availability of high-quality data for the organization. The discussion that follows refers specifically to *data*

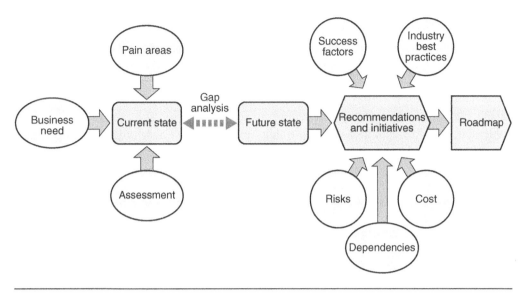

Figure 5.1   Data quality strategy formulation—high-level view.

quality strategy in order to highlight activities related to the assessment, measurement, and improvement of data (Sebastian-Coleman 2013).

WHY IS A DATA QUALITY STRATEGY IMPORTANT?

Organizations have large volumes of data that relate to different domains or subject areas, for example, party, location, and assets, which are typically the broad subject areas. The large volume of data brings with it a number of challenges to be dealt with. Different business units and departments in organizations capture and maintain similar data in silos within their systems for business processing, which results in duplication of data, inconsistencies, and data integrity issues. During the last few decades, many organizations have invested in the deployment of ERP, CRM, and data warehouses, but have failed at some point in their journey to achieve expectations and reap benefits because of poor data quality and the absence of a data quality strategy to improve and manage data and data quality.

The chaos that exists without a data strategy is not always obvious, but there exist plenty of pointers that are manifestations of the reigning confusion: dirty data, inconsistent data, the inability to integrate, poor performance (Adelman et al. 2005), duplicate data, data silos, missing data, timeliness issues, little or no accountability for data, disgruntled users who are fed up with performance and data quality issues, failure incidents, and an overall feeling that all is not as it should be.

Without a data quality strategy, data initiatives—which should have been a part of the strategy—are addressed piecemeal or as department silos without assessing the enterprise-level implications, the risks, and alignment with the organization's strategic objectives. This results in implementation of suboptimized solutions and introduction of initiatives and programs that may have an adverse effect on the overall enterprise, resulting in inconsistencies or development of systems that cannot be easily integrated.

Without a data quality strategy, the IT department in the organization has no guiding principle when it comes to making crucial decisions, including which projects to pursue, what methodologies and procedures to adopt, and what tools and technologies to implement. Not having a data quality strategy increases the risk of allowing individuals in each department or business unit of the organization to develop their own methods for using, manipulating, and managing the available data as they deem fit. The absence of a strategy gives a blank check or a free pass to those who want to pursue their own agendas, including attachment to certain technologies or Machiavellian aspirations to power. This includes those who want to try a new DBMS, new technologies (often unproven), and new tools that may or may not be appropriate for the company's data landscape and might or might not have the necessary capabilities or functionalities to meet the organization's current and future business needs (Adelman et al. 2005). This type of environment provides no checks or validation for those who might pursue a strategy that has no hope for success.

The strength of the data quality strategy components is that they help you identify focused, tangible goals within each individual discipline area. A data quality strategy is a roadmap for addressing both current and future data quality requirements, and enables the delivery of the best possible solution as the organization's needs grow and evolve. When new requirements arise and gaps become visible, the component framework provides a method for identifying the changes needed across your company's various data management capability and technology areas (Levy 2018). However, it is important to keep in mind that a data quality strategy does not address each and every unforeseen data requirement. The key elements of a data quality strategy, which we will be discussing in detail later in this chapter, are depicted in Figure 5.2.

DATA QUALITY MATURITY

Data quality and the level of maturity or sophistication of data quality practices varies greatly depending on the organization. In most organizations the approach to data quality management is reactive and in silos, often spurred by a reporting issue or when data quality does not meet functional application needs. The data analysts often analyze the data in the source systems only to reveal that the quality does not meet the functional requirements of the business application. For example, the marketing strategy of a bank is to promote a new credit card product for its existing customers who have a sound financial status, which is identified by certain values in the Financial Status data field in the customer status table in the data warehouse. However, since the Financial Status data field is blank for 50% of the customer records in the customer status table, and 20% of the customers have more than one financial status, there is a gap between the existing and required data quality maturity to generate a meaningful report that can be used by

Figure 5.2   Key elements of a data quality strategy.

the marketing team to identify the customers eligible for the new credit card product, and hence eligible to receive the communication for the promotion. It is very important to understand an organization's current data quality maturity when developing a data quality strategy, as unless you are able to nail down the current state, you will not be able to lay out the roadmap to reach the future state.

DATA QUALITY MATURITY MODEL

A key prerequisite of producing data that are ready for analysis and good enough for decision making is that the data must be of good quality—accuracy, validity, reliability, completeness, currency, timeliness, absence of duplication, integrity, and consistency being the most important data quality dimensions. However, over the years it has come to light that organizations differ on the definition of good data quality, and that these definitions fit their maturity in analytics and data science.

Maturity models represent a distinct class of models dealing entirely with organizational and information systems related to change and development processes (Becker et al. 2010; Crosby 1979; Gibson and Nolan 1974; Mettler 2010; Nolan 1973). Maturity models consist of a structured set of constructs serving to describe certain aspects of maturity of a design domain (Fraser et al. 2002). The concept of maturity is often understood according to the definition of Paulk et al. (1993), who consider maturity to be the "extent to which a process is explicitly defined, managed, measured, controlled, and effective."

The maturity model analogy is also suitable in the data domain for two reasons. First, the maturity model has a set of structured levels, with each level in the model building on top of the others, and it is impossible to jump to a higher level before conquering the lower ones. Each of the levels takes into account the people, processes, and technology surrounding data management. Second, moving to higher levels cannot be accomplished by technology alone, but also involves people, processes, and organizational thinking. The term *maturity* relates to the extent of formality and optimization of processes, from ad hoc and informal practices, to formally defined steps, to managed result metrics, to active optimization of the processes.

The data quality maturity model is modeled after the capability maturity model (CMM) developed by the Software Engineering Institute at Carnegie Mellon University. The CMM has been applied to many application domains, including software development, programmer development, IT service management processes, and project management domains. However, the CMM does not address the maturity of an organization in relation to the management of data and their quality. The data quality maturity model defines five levels of maturity, ranging from an initial or chaotic level where practices and policies are ad hoc, to the highest level, in which processes and practices lead to continuous measurement, assessment, improvement, and optimization. The progression from the bottom level to the top level of maturity is characterized by changes in people, processes, behaviors, attitudes, tools, and technology. For people, there is increasing ownership with increasing levels of maturity. There is a marked difference in attitudes and perceptions with a shift from data quality being viewed less as a cost, at lower data maturity levels, to more as a return on investment, with progression toward higher levels of maturity. For processes, with increasing levels of data maturity, data quality becomes a part of the standard business practices and is monitored rather than being looked at on an ad hoc basis for quick fixes. From a tools and technology perspective, an increasing level of maturity is characterized by a transition from manual ways of doing things to enterprise-wide, sophisticated data quality tools managing data. As you move from lower to higher levels of maturity, there is a gradual reduction of risks, and greater benefits to be reaped from data quality management practices. The level of maturity varies dramatically among organizations, with different organizations being at different levels of maturity.

The data quality maturity model can be used as benchmarking tool to assess the organization's current data maturity and determine where you want to see your organization in terms of data maturity in the next year or two.

Level 1: The Initial or Chaotic Level

The *initial*, or *chaotic*, level is the lowest level in the data quality maturity model. As the name suggests, chaos reigns at this level. This level is characterized by an absence of standards, rules, policies, and strategies related to data management. There is no or limited understanding or even awareness of data quality problems, their impact and possible solutions, or data management practices among the enterprise business users, partially because they see no advantage for themselves in taking steps to cleanse the data. Data quality is viewed as a cost rather than a return on investment (ROI). Data are perceived to be an application by-product, part of the IT environment, and, as such, the IT department's problem (Kisubika 2011). Business does not take any ownership of the data.

Data are usually managed manually, using spreadsheets or ad hoc routines. Identical or related data may exist in multiple files and databases, using multiple data formats (known and unknown), and stored redundantly across multiple systems (under different names and using different data types) (Mullins 1997). For example, an organization may have a customer database containing customer data, but comparable data may also exist in the billing and marketing database. This state is further complicated by most organizations being in denial about the quality and importance of enterprise data.

There is no apparent method to this madness (Mullins 1997), and in general, chaos rules with little or no effort to record what exists. At the initial level, the processes used for ensuring data quality are largely ad hoc, uncontrolled, reactive, and chaotic, triggered by data quality issues or incidents raised by users or business units that are acute and need immediate attention. Most of the effort is spent in reacting to data quality issues; changes are made on the fly and often require significant rollback and rework (Loshin 2010a). Generally, no root cause analysis is conducted. The environment is quite unstable, with limited or no documentation and no sharing of data quality issues and experiences, making it a challenge to trace back to the sources of the introduction of flawed data and to determine the quick fix. Hence, if a similar problem arises another time, it is difficult to repeat the fix. Fixes are quick, one-time fixes on a must-do basis, to solve the immediate problem at hand, and most likely will not address any long-term improvement in the information or the processes. The success and quality of the data are highly dependent on the skills of IT professionals, namely, programmers, analysts, and developers, in correcting data flaws. There are no established processes for root cause analysis and managed remediation.

There are no data-specific roles defined in the organization at this level. Within the entire organization, no individual, team, department, or business unit claims responsibility for data. Often, there is no central data management group; instead, new data structures are created, and changes are made, by the development teams as and when the need arises (Mullins 1997). The risks are extremely high and the benefits from data management are very low in the level 1 organization.

Level 2: The Repeatable Level

At level 2, organizations have some knowledge of the impact of bad data quality, and recognize the need for new processes that improve the quality of data, but this is not uniform throughout the enterprise. At the repeatable level, there is some elementary organizational management and information sharing, augmented by some process discipline, mostly in identifying good practices and endeavoring to reproduce them in similar situations, enabling some ability to repeat success (Loshin 2010a). To tackle the problem of data quality in the initial phases of an application's life cycle, application developers analyze the underlying data, implement simple controls to standardize data types and formats, check on mandatory data fields that cannot have null values, and validate attribute values where possible. These activities, as well as data quality fixes, happen in localized regions or departmental or business unit silos and not at the enterprise level, and hence lack the holistic perspective. Some technology components and tactical tools are in use at the departmental or business unit level, but they may not be standardized and synchronized across the enterprise. Level 2 is characterized by nonintegrated, disparate point solutions.

To move from level 1 to level 2 on the data maturity scale, an organization must commence adhering to a data management policy and establish standards. The policy should dictate how and when data structures are created, modified, and managed. While organizations at level 2 follow some kind of data management policy, they generally have yet to regulate the policy. Instead, they rely on a central person or group to understand the issues and implement the data structures of the organization reliably and consistently (Mullins 1997). This manifests itself in the emergence of a stronger data management role than in level 1 by the creation of a database administrator (DBA) function.

The success of level 2 organizations depends on the expertise of the DBAs responsible for managing the technical aspects of data. Although the differences between the business and technical aspects of data are usually (not always) understood at some level, there is less effort made to document and capture the business meaning of data, and there is no metadata (data about data) management at this level. Little (or no) differentiation between the logical and physical models of data is made. Level 2 organizations will begin to institute database administration practices such as managed schema change (maintaining records of the change) and reactive performance monitoring and tuning (Mullins 1997) depending on the level of escalation. There is still no data-specific role within the business at this level.

There is an introductory level of governance, with limited documentation of processes, plans, standards, and practices (Loshin 2010a). The rate of adoption of data management practices varies across different departments and business units. Some concerns about the impacts of poor data quality lead to introductory efforts in business evaluation and identification of gross-level measures. However, at this level, the typical business user generally waits for problems to occur instead of taking proactive steps to prevent them, and data quality problems are still perceived to be solely the IT department's responsibility (Kisubika 2011).

Level 3: The Defined Level

Organizations at level 3 fully understand the value of good-quality data as a driver for improved enterprise performance, and are proactive in their data quality efforts. At this level, data management begins to play a crucial role within an organization, as data go from being an unappreciated commodity and application by-product to an enterprise asset that assists organizations in making improved business decisions. Movement from the *repeatable* level (level 2) to the *defined* level (level 3) on the data capability maturity scale in an organization is characterized by the documentation and institutionalization of a data management policy by a structured team of data quality practitioners as a core constituent of their application development life cycle. The policy is enforced and testing is done to ensure that data quality requirements are being met (Mullins 1997). There is a movement from project-level information management, with departmental silos of data, to a coordinated enterprise information management approach.

Data quality is driven by the business. As business users feel the pain of data quality issues intensely, in both operational and decision-making situations, data quality progressively becomes part of the IT project charter. Level 3 organizations usually understand the business meaning of data and have created a *data administration* function to augment the database administration function. Level 3 organizations have a stated policy that "data are treated as a corporate asset," even if they do not entirely comprehend what that means (Mullins 1997).

The success of the level 3 organization typically hinges on the interaction between the data administration and database administration functions, and appropriate utilization of tools. Although level 1 and level 2 organizations may have the necessary tools, they usually do not apply them in a correct or consistent fashion. Tools are used by level 3 organizations to create data models, to automate DBA steps initiated by level 2 organizations (for example, schema migrations), and to begin proactively monitoring and tuning database performance (Mullins 1997).

At the *defined* level, a structured team of data quality practitioners begins to document good practices, which include an established set of data governance policies, processes for defining data quality expectations, technology components, and processes and services for implementing data quality validation, assurance, and reporting. Once these are documented and can be made available across the organization, there emerges a degree of consistent use (Loshin 2010a). Data quality tools are acquired for profiling, standardizing, and cleansing and used on a project-by-project basis, but housekeeping is typically performed "downstream," that is, by the IT department or data warehouse teams. Levels of data quality are considered good enough for most tactical and strategic decision making. At this level of maturity, the organization's culture still does not fully promote data as an enterprise-wide asset, but key steps are being taken. Department managers and IT managers are starting to communicate data administration and data quality guidelines, but compliance is not monitored or enforced. Decision makers are beginning to discuss the concept of "data ownership" (Kisubika 2011).

Level 4: The Managed Level

At level 4, data are considered and treated as a strategic and corporate asset, and the data quality process becomes part of an enterprise information management program. Data quality comes to be a major concern of the IT department and a primary business responsibility. A formalized data quality process is in place at this stage. At the *managed* level, the data quality program generously incorporates business impact analysis, linking data quality to business issues and process performance, and with the capability to express data quality expectations and measure conformance to those expectations. These measurements form the foundation of clearly defined criteria for performance in regard to meeting business goals. Metrics composed of these weighted measurements are used in gauging statistical process control at different service levels. Measured performance attributes can be used to evaluate the overall system performance against success criteria (Loshin 2010a).

Sophisticated tools and mature technologies with greater capabilities are utilized to manage metadata, data quality, and databases, and are implemented more widely across the enterprise at the managed level. Data quality management is proactive, with data quality issues unearthed early in the information life cycle. This is achieved by regular measurement and monitoring of data quality and conducting data quality audits of production data in relation to different data quality dimensions (accuracy, completeness, validity, consistency, integrity, and so on) at an enterprise level and across multiple systems. Continuous improvement feedback loops are in operation, with the outputs of root cause analysis feeding back into the feedback process, resulting in greater reliability and predictability of results. Remediation is overseen by well-documented procedures. The majority of data cleansing and data standardization operations are carried out either at the data integration layer or directly at the data source. Data quality functionality generally progresses in a staggered way from cleansing the most crucial data sets or areas of high business impact, for example, customer and address information, to less crucial ones or areas where the business impact is relatively less. Data are shared across the enterprise, and the overall performance against quality expectations is foreseeable.

Rigorous yet malleable data quality processes make incorporating new data sources straightforward, and data quality functionality is introduced beyond business intelligence and data warehousing programs; it is built into major business applications and therefore enables confident operational decision making. Multiple data stewardship roles are established within the organization to work jointly on business rules, data definitions, and metrics. The data quality champion, as part of a formalized data governance activity, establishes and communicates clear data quality mandates and policies, which are constantly monitored using metrics-based data quality dashboards (Kisubika 2011).

An organization can move to level 4 only when it institutes a managed metadata (data about data) environment. This enables the data management group (data administrator and database administrator) to catalog and maintain metadata for corporate data structures. It also provides the application development and end user staff access to what data exist where within the organization (along with definitions, synonyms, and so on). The data management group is involved (at some level) in all development efforts to provide assistance in the cataloging of metadata and reduction of redundant data elements (in logical models always; in physical models as appropriate for performance and project requirements) (Mullins 1997).

The success of the level 4 organization depends on the ability of senior management to see data as a strategic asset.

Level 5: The Optimized Level

Organizations at level 5, or the *optimized* level, run advanced enterprise information management programs for their data and information assets with the same meticulousness they handle other tangible and intangible assets like finances, products, machines, raw materials, and so on.

At this stage data management becomes a business process and is no longer just a technological tool. At level 5, data quality becomes an ongoing strategic initiative and is an indispensable part of all business processes, and is firmly embedded in the DNA of the enterprise. Rigorous processes are in place to keep data quality as high as possible through ongoing housekeeping exercises, continuous monitoring of quality levels, and by attaching quality metrics to the compensation plans of data stewards and other employees (Bitterer 2007).

Data are enriched in real time by third-party providers with additional credit, demographic, sociographic, household, geospatial, or market data. Also, any unstructured mission-critical information, such as documents and policies, becomes subject to data quality controls (Kisubika 2011).

Confidence levels or data quality thresholds are defined and associated with data crucial for decision making and related metadata. Data quality indicators are also defined for data that are known to have issues, usually in a data warehouse. Objective aspects (completeness, accuracy, currency, timeliness, and so on) and subjective aspects (believability, credibility, interpretability, and so on) are measured, monitored, and assessed against the data quality thresholds. This enables data stewards to get a holistic picture of the state of data quality in terms of objective measurements and subjective opinions. Any variations or discrepancies discovered from data quality monitoring and audits are resolved immediately. Data quality rules are sufficient for confident real-time business process automation, enabling the organization to transfer some decision-making to the business process itself (Kisubika 2011). The value of high-quality information is demonstrated by significant returns on investment (Bitterer 2007).

The data quality maturity governance framework is in place such that enterprise-wide performance measurements can be used for identifying opportunities for improved systemic data quality. The ability to assess success and identify causes for process variation may suggest actions to adapt standards, policies, and processes for incremental or fundamental quality improvements. Strategic improvements and continuous process monitoring of the data life cycle using dashboards are applied throughout the organization (Loshin 2010a).

The level 5 organization uses the practices evolved in the lower levels of data maturity, that is, levels 1 through 4, to continually improve data access, data quality, and database performance. At this level, no changes are made in data repositories in the production environment without prior analysis by the data management organization and documentation within the metadata repository.

According to Gartner, only a few organizations have mature data quality initiatives, and levels 1 and 2 are still the most common among Gartner clients, implying that many organizations are still struggling with data quality as an enterprise-wide problem (Bitterer 2007). Between 75% and 80% of all organizations analyzed are said to be on the two lowest levels. Only a few companies worldwide have reached level 5 by embracing ongoing data quality initiatives, taking care of data quality processes and metrics, assessing impact, and managing information as an enterprise-wide asset through information management approaches (Kisubika 2011). Figure 5.3 shows the different phases of a data quality maturity model.

SCOPE OF A DATA QUALITY STRATEGY

The scope of a data quality strategy should be determined by the business drivers and business goals. The scope should always account for changing business requirements to keep the strategy aligned with the business. It should state and document the business requirements as identified and stated by the stakeholders. A data quality strategy should include some guiding principles and align them with business goals or drivers. It should also take into consideration the appropriate framework, methodology, people, processes, governance, systems, and technology required to deliver value that aligns with the business objectives and priorities.

Most often, we think about vision, mission, and strategy at the enterprise level. And indeed, most successful organizations have clear vision and mission statements that address their enterprise goals. However, strategic thinking can be applied at all levels of an organization (Sebastian-Coleman 2013).

It is recommended to have a data quality strategy at an enterprise level to ensure that all the key areas of the data landscape are covered. As per the "Global Data Quality Research 2014" Experian Data Quality Market survey results, approximately 99% of companies had some kind of data quality strategy for at least some part of their overall data landscape. One in three large British organizations do not include all of their data in a data quality strategy, and this creates pockets of poor-quality data that can impact any services that depend on the underlying information (Jones 2014). While it is recommended to have a data quality strategy at the enterprise level, it can be done at the business unit level if that make more sense. In such cases the strategy defined at the business unit level should align with the enterprise strategic goals and objectives and should support the overall vision and mission of the enterprise.

It is possible for an organization to have applications or systems strategy, a data strategy, a data management strategy, a data analytics strategy, and a data quality strategy all at the same time, and they should be aligned with each other and dependencies should be identified. An organization might define these separately because different teams are charged with executing them, or in order to understand the relation between them, or to determine the work required to advance these facets of the organization's overall strategy (Sebastian-Coleman 2013). The goals in each of these different strategies should align with the organization's strategic business objectives and should not contradict or constrain each other or duplicate efforts. Aligned, they enable each other's success (Sebastian-Coleman 2013).

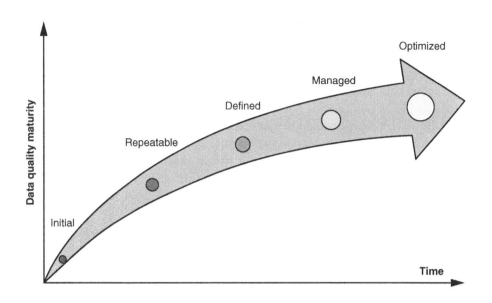

	Initial	Repeatable	Defined	Managed	Optimized
Technical	General purpose software like spreadsheet/Excel or manual processes or ad hoc routines.	Tactical tools at application level or within department silos.	Data quality tools for profiling and cleansing on a project-by-project basis, with data warehousing and business intelligence (BI) applications.	Data quality tools implemented beyond data warehousing and business intelligence (BI); advanced tools to manage metadata (repository), data quality, and databases.	Data-management tools are standardized across the organization. Platform approach to profiling, monitoring, and visualizing data.
Attitude	Data quality seen as a cost rather than ROI. Sense of apathy toward the issue of data quality.	There is awareness of the importance of managing data as a critical infrastructure asset.	Data are treated at the organizational level as critical for successful mission performance.	Data are treated as a source of competitive advantage.	Data are seen as critical for survival in a dynamic and competitive market, and data quality is viewed as a key enabler.
Approach	Firefighting mode; no strategy, tactical fixes. No root cause analysis.	Documentation of data quality steps ensuring repeatability; tactical.	DQ is part of the IT charter. Major issues are documented, but not completely rectified.	Proactive prevention.	Optimization; strategic.
People	No data-specific roles; not aware of data management practices.	Database administrator; DQ perceived as IT department's responsibility.	Data administrator and database administrator. Data stewardship and ownership emerging.	N-tiered data stewardship in place.	Central data role.
Benefits	None or limited benefits.	Few tactical gains.	Key tactical gains.	Tactical and strategic gains.	Strategic gains.

Figure 5.3   Data quality maturity model.

DATA QUALITY STRATEGY: PREPLANNING

Before you embark on the preparation of the data quality strategy, you need to do some preplanning. You need to think about, on a high level, what your data quality strategy creation process would involve, namely, resourcing, who should be on the team, when you should start this process and the approach, and the time period that you are planning for. Figure 5.4 summarizes the activities involved in preplanning.

The timing is an extremely important factor that should be kept in mind before embarking on the process of creating a data quality strategy. Devising a data quality strategy can take between two months to six months depending on what you are trying to achieve and the availability of resources and your key stakeholders. The data quality strategy should tie into the organization's planning and budget cycle, so it is advisable to start planning well in advance, say at least seven to eight months before the start of the budget planning session, so that you have enough time to do your enterprise-wide assessments, do gap analysis and build the strategy, walk through the initiatives with your stakeholders, and get executive buy-in for all the initiatives that you would be proposing during the data quality strategy development.

The next question to answer is where to start with the data quality strategy: at the enterprise level or business unit level? It is a good practice to define a data quality strategy at the enterprise level as data cross interdepartmental and business unit boundaries,

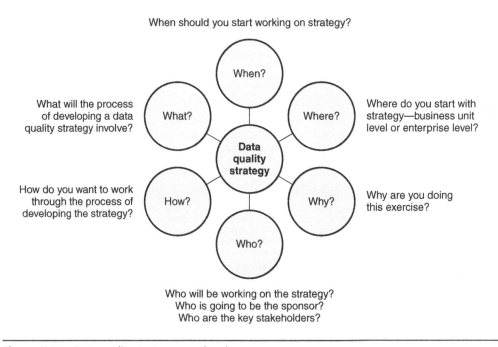

Figure 5.4   Data quality strategy: preplanning.

with data being shared and used by several business units. However, if you have a high-priority data problem to solve that is localized to a particular business unit, then you may define the data quality strategy at the business unit level.

While you will be outlining and firming up the data principles and goals and their alignment with the corporate strategic goals in the "planning and setup" phase, you need to have a vision for your data quality strategy and be able to explain how it is going to be a value-add to your organization *before* the "planning and setup" phase. You need to identify the sponsor and convince the sponsor to initially board your data quality strategy boat and be by your side in the data quality journey. The sponsor is the individual who would be there to communicate the entire value proposition to the entire organization and convince senior management and respond to their queries regarding the data quality strategy initiatives as and when they are raised. Hence, it is very important to choose your sponsor with care and get buy-in from your sponsor as well as align with him or her.

You need to have an idea of who would be working on creating the strategy. Do you have skilled resources within your organization? Are they available and have the bandwidth to work on creating the data quality strategy? If the answer to either of these questions is "no," you will need to hire consultants from outside the organization. You also need to have an idea of who your key stakeholders are going to be, and who should be communicated with and involved before the initial planning and setup phase.

You need to have an overall idea of how you want to run the process for creating the data quality strategy. An agile, iterative approach as opposed to a waterfall approach is recommended to deliver the strategy; involve stakeholders throughout the journey, set expectations and communicate what you need from them in terms of time and inputs, address their concerns, elicit feedback from them, and incorporate their feedback. Conduct brainstorming and one-to-one sessions with stakeholders. If all your stakeholders are not colocated, if possible organize a trip to the stakeholder's location for a handshake session and explain what you are trying to achieve. These approaches help your stakeholders feel valued, involved, and accountable for change so that there are no unpleasant surprises at the end and the approval process is smooth.

Once you have got a sponsor on board and have onboarded the team, you are ready to embark on the process of formulating the data quality strategy.

PHASES IN THE DATA QUALITY STRATEGY FORMULATION PROCESS

The process for formulating a data quality strategy consists of three phases, as shown in Figure 5.5:

- Planning and setup
- Discovery and assessment
- Prioritization and roadmap

Phases	Planning and setup	Discovery and assessment	Prioritization and roadmap
Activities	• Strategy goals • Stakeholder engagement • Communication plan • Activity plan finalization • Stakeholders and sponsor sign-off	• Data doman discovery • Key data issues and business function impacts • Conceptual data model • Business function—data domain mapping • Application—data domain mapping • Data maturity assessment • Initiatives and recommendations preparation	• Prioritization of initiatives • Preparation of roadmaps and financials • Preparation of executive presentations
Tools/processes	• Meetings	• Workshops, meetings, interviews • Brainstorming sessions • Data analysis and modeling • Documentation and review	• Review meetings/workshops • Presentation sessions • Documentation
Deliverables	• Activity plan • Stakeholder engagement— RACI matrix	• Current state assessment findings • Gap analysis • Business risks and issues • Initiatives and recommendations	• Roadmap and key milestones • Impact analysis • Program governance • Strategy documentation/ presentation

Figure 5.5   Phases in data quality strategy formulation.

Planning and Setup

This phase encompasses firming up the business objectives and/or guiding princi-ples, high-level scope, and need for a data quality strategy, finalizing the key stake-holders identified in the preplanning stage, and defining the schedule for delivering the data quality strategy. The RACI matrix for stakeholders' engagement is developed and shared. The communication and workshop plan is also chalked out during this phase. Plans for the following phases are firmed up and shared with the stakeholders, and the finalized work plan is approved by the stakeholders in this phase.

The business objectives and guiding principles of the data quality strategy should align with the overall enterprise strategic business objectives or drivers. Examples of strategic business drivers are operational efficiency, increased customer satisfaction, lower business risk, revenue growth, service efficiency, and regulatory compliance. The justifications and implications should be linked to each of the business objectives and/or guiding principles.

The *stakeholders* are the individuals who would be impacted by the changes proposed in the data quality strategy, and would provide inputs for the assessment and validate the contents of the strategy once it is prepared. It is essential to identify the prospective troublemakers—those who are against the objectives outlined in the data quality strategy and hence would provide resistance to part or all of the strategy—the stalwart supporters—those who will back you and the objectives of the strategy— and the natural data evangelists—who treat data as a strategic enterprise asset and believe in the power of data in making effective decisions. Knowing who they are and their motivations up front will help you plan accordingly.

Discovery and Assessment

The purpose of this phase is to find the gaps between the current state and the future desired state based on the scope, objectives, and guiding principles established in the planning and setup phase. This involves identifying all the data domains in the enterprise, and assessing the current state of the data assets and architecture, business processes, technology assets, capabilities, and policies that are impacted by the scope at a high level. Current state assessment is typically conducted through a series of workshops, one-on-one meetings, brainstorming sessions with the respective stakeholders, review of any existing models, and documentation and data analysis.

The assessment is carried out to assess data maturity and assess business functions and applications to understand the associated data issues. The mapping between the applications and data domains is used to identify gaps and issues, for example, data synchronization. The mapping between business processes and data domains helps in understanding the key data domains that are a part of different business functions and processes. The functional landscape can be elaborated further as part of the following phases to understand the use of different data entities and attributes within varied business functions and their criticality for building an enterprise data dictionary. A conceptual domain model captures the data domains within the organizational landscape and shows how the different domains interact with each other.

Based on the application and data domain mapping, and the business function and data domain mapping, different application owners and business users should be interviewed to understand their view on what data-related issues exist, the root cause of the issues, and the risks they pose to the organization. The root cause of the issues, the impact, and the severity are key to proposing appropriate recommendations.

In this phase, a data maturity assessment exercise based on an assessment framework is conducted to understand where the organization currently stands in terms of data assessment categories such as data quality, data governance, policies, standards, and metadata maturity, as per the five-level data maturity model, the target state to achieve, and the associated risks if the desired maturity level is not reached.

Table 5.1 shows the numerical mapping for the maturity levels, which is used for assigning the current and target maturity for assessment purposes.

The likelihood of risk, risk consequences, and the risk score need to be assessed. This analysis plays a major role in prioritizing and proposing initiatives. Table 5.2, Table 5.3, and Figure 5.6 illustrate the risk likelihood mapping, risk consequence mapping, and risk rating, respectively.

The risk rating is usually described in terms of red (very high), amber (high), yellow (medium), and green (low), based on risk likelihood and risk consequences, and is also indicated as risk status/RYAG status (R for red, Y for yellow, A for amber, and G for green). A screened variation of this is shown in Figure 5.6.

With the desired future state in mind, analysis should focus on identifying gaps between the current state and target state, what changes would need to be made to the processes, the technologies necessary to achieve the desired state, and the skill set and

Table 5.1	Data maturity mapping.
Level	**Numerical equivalent**
Initial	1
Repeatable	2
Defined	3
Managed	4
Optimized	5

Table 5.2	Risk likelihood mapping.
Level	**Descriptor**
1	Insignificant
2	Minor
3	Moderate
4	Major
5	Catastrophic

Table 5.3	Risk consequence mapping.
Level	**Descriptor**
1	Improbable
2	Unlikely
3	Possible
4	Likely
5	Almost certain

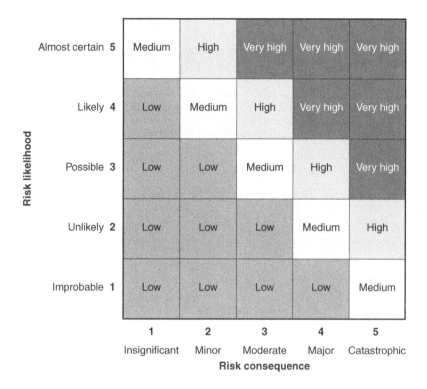

Figure 5.6   Risk rating.

training required to upskill people to adapt to the new way of doing things. The gap analysis presents multiple solution options for initiatives. The risk and success factors should also be carefully thought out in this phase.

Prioritization and Roadmap

In this phase the initiatives determined in the discovery and assessment phase are prioritized in consultation with the sponsors and stakeholders. This is typically done through presentations and workshops where the initiative options are weighed based on their alignment with strategic enterprise goals or business drivers, initiative benefits, costs, and implications if not implemented. Some of these data initiatives could be data governance, automation of system processes, and BAU (business as usual) initiatives for maintaining data quality. The cost for each initiative is also calculated during this phase, and a roadmap with implementation frames is prepared. It is very important to take into account data storage, change management, training, and technology when budgeting. The metrics for measuring the success of initiatives should also be determined to set clear expectations for how the organization will measure progress against its data quality strategy. Metrics can include data quality metrics for data quality, operational metrics, or milestone realization against the plan.

The data quality strategy formulation might span a few months. Follow an agile, iterative approach within each phase, and get buy-in from stakeholders before moving to the next phase, as output from each prior phase will drive the next phase. For example, if you do not have your objective right, then you would not carry out the right assessments and you would not have your recommendations and initiatives right. Hence, waiting until the end to validate is a huge risk. You should ideally have brainstorming sessions, meetings, and interviews with the stakeholders, and perform activities to work toward your deliverables, in each phase (this could involve any of the things to be done for creating the data quality strategy, like aligning data quality strategy goals to the strategic corporate goals, current state assessment, prioritization of initiatives, and so on) and then prepare your understanding in the form of a few presentation slides, have review sessions for addressing concerns and clarifications and eliciting feedback, present the final slide pack for endorsement, and move forward from there, as shown in Figure 5.7. This approach helps all your stakeholders feel involved and accountable for change so that there are no unpleasant surprises at the end and the approval process is smooth.

At the end of the final phase, instead of sending the data quality strategy as a Word document to the executive leaders (whose time is at a premium) for their review and approval, it is advisable to conduct a final one to two hour walkthrough session with the executive stakeholder using an executive presentation to get their approval. Since the sponsor(s) and stakeholders or their delegates have been at your side throughout the strategy preparation journey and have already viewed and endorsed bits and pieces before, they should already be familiar with the contents of the strategy, and you should have their verbal consent even before this final walkthrough session for endorsement is conducted. The walkthrough session is to get the final sign-off.

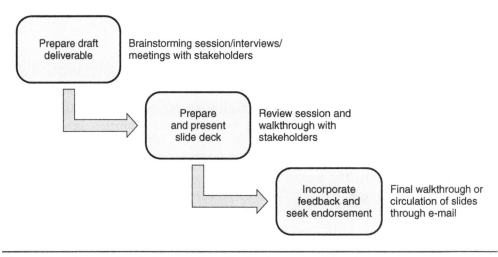

Figure 5.7 Data quality strategy—stakeholder involvement and buy-in.

DATA QUALITY STRATEGY DOCUMENT AND PRESENTATION

A data quality strategy document should have the following sections:

1. Overview

2. Assessment Approach

3. Findings and Recommendations

4. Initiative Details

5. Implementation Roadmap and Financials

Overview

This section gives a high-level overview of the data quality strategy contents, and in general consists of the following subsections:

- Background

- Strategic Objectives

- Findings Overview

- Initiatives Overview

- Roadmap and Financials Overview

Background. This section should give a brief description of what the organization does, and should concisely articulate the problem statement and need for a data quality strategy within the organization.

Strategic Objectives. The data quality strategy should clearly outline the objectives of the data quality strategy and the guiding principles, their justification, and implications, and link them to the business drivers. The main business drivers for having a data quality strategy include increased operational efficiency, reducing operational costs, and improved customer satisfaction.

Findings Overview. Typically, this section would outline the results of the data maturity assessment, and data issues discovered in the course of the business and application assessment at a high level.

Initiatives Overview. This section very briefly outlines each of the proposed initiatives and their benefits.

Roadmap and Financials Overview. The summary of financials for the various initiatives proposed is outlined in this section in a tabular form. The format shown in Table 5.4 can be used to outline the high-level financials.

Table 5.4	Format for high-level financials.				
Initiative	**\<Time frame 1>**	**\<Time frame 2>**	...	**\<Time frame *n*>**	**Total**
\<Initiative name 1>	\<Dollar value>	\<Dollar value>		\<Dollar value>	\<Total cost for initiative 1>
\<Initiative name 2>	\<Dollar value>	\<Dollar value>		\<Dollar value>	\<Total cost for initiative 2>
\<Initiative name 3>	\<Dollar value>	\<Dollar value>		\<Dollar value>	\<Total cost for initiative 3>
⋮					
\<Initiative name *n*>	\<Dollar value>	\<Dollar value>		\<Dollar value>	\<Total cost for initiative *n*>
Total	\<Dollar value in time frame 1>	\<Dollar value in time frame 2>		\<Dollar value in time frame *n*>	Total cost

Assessment Approach

This section outlines the high-level assessment plan and the assessment framework that were undertaken to build the data quality strategy. The list of stakeholders engaged by each functional area should also be listed in this section. The data domains assessed, the conceptual data domain model, application–data domain mapping, and the business function–data domain mapping should be included.

Findings and Recommendations

This section should present the results of the data maturity assessment exercise, the gaps between the current state and future state, and the associated risk (risk category, risk likelihood, and risk consequence). The template shown in Table 5.5 can be used to present the results of the data maturity assessment exercise.

The data issues by domain and their implications, and corresponding recommendations for solving or mitigating the issues, are also included in this section. The details of data issues can be captured using the format depicted in Table 5.6.

A description of the business risk, the critical business functions impacted, and the impact details linked with the data assessment categories are also presented in the this section. The table format illustrated in Table 5.7 can be used to populate this information.

Initiative Details

This section outlines all the initiatives that should be undertaken to meet the strategic goals or guiding principles of the data quality strategy. A detailed description of each initiative should be presented in this section. The total cost of each initiative, the time frame for implementation of the initiative, and the benefits, risks, success factors, and dependencies associated with each initiative should be described. The tabular format

Table 5.5 Template for data maturity assessment results.

ID	Category	Data viewpoint	Current maturity	Target maturity	Importance	Risk status (RYAG)	Risk category	Risk likelihood	Risk consequence	Comments
1	For example, data governance	For example, data policies	This is a number between 1 to 5	This is a number between 1 to 5	For example, Medium	For example, Y	For example, Regulatory compliance	For example, 2—Unlikely	For example, 3—Moderate	For example, compliance risk associated

Table 5.6   Data issues template.

ID	Data domain area	Issues/ pain points	Description	Implications	Risk status (RYAG)	Recommendations
	For example, customer	For example, missing address	For example, postal codes missing for 10K customers	For example, increased mailing costs, regulatory impact	For example, A	For example, data cleansing

Table 5.7   Business risk template.

Data category	Business risk category	Impacted audience	Business impact	Critical business functions impacted	Associated risk
<This would typically be data assessment categories, for example, data quality, data policies>	For example, compliance risk	For example, business owners, regulators	<Detailed description of the business impact>	<Names of the impacted business functions>	For example, high, medium, and so on

depicted in Table 5.8 can be used to populate a summarized version of the initiative details. Elaborate descriptions can be captured outside this table.

Implementation Roadmap and Financials

This section provides the strategic roadmap with the initiatives and their mapping to the respective timelines. Any key milestones should be mentioned. Data quality metrics or operational metrics should be outlined in this section.

The strategic roadmap would typically be depicted in a chart with the time frames along the *x*-axis and initiatives across the *y*-axis. A sample roadmap is shown in Figure 5.8.

Table 5.8	Initiative summary template.
Title	**\<Initiative Name\>**
Initiative description	
Scope/key recommendations addressed	\<Recommendation IDs\> from Table 5.6
Strategic principle supported/business drivers/strategic business goal	
Total cost of the initiative	
Benefits	
Risks	
Success factors	
Implementation time frame	
Dependencies	

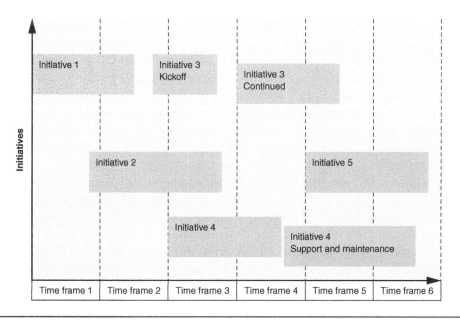

Figure 5.8   Sample roadmap.

The cost breakdown for each initiative by time frame is also presented in this section. This would typically involve software product or data technology costs, change management and training costs, human resource costs, infrastructure and hardware costs, and support and maintenance costs. All assumptions involved in the costing of each initiative should also be stated clearly.

CHARACTERISTICS OF A GOOD DATA QUALITY STRATEGY

A good data quality strategy (Casey 2017):

- Aligns the data quality strategy goals with the corporate business goals.

- Is actionable (Zaino 2017) (contains initiatives that can be implemented), measurable (Zaino 2017) (has metrics to measure progress and success) and relevant (Zaino 2017) (should align with the business goals).

- Identifies key resources, success factors, risks, and constraints.

- Is a living document and should be reviewed every six months or annually.

- Adds value to the organization.

DATA QUALITY STRATEGY IMPLEMENTATION

Once the data quality strategy formulation is complete, reviewed, and signed off, the next step is its implementation in the form of programs and projects. A data quality strategy often encompasses a greater scope than a single project, and can support the goals of an entire enterprise, numerous programs, and many individual projects (Dravis 2004). The initiatives proposed in the data quality strategy typically take the form of programs that usually comprise several projects. The implementation of a data quality strategy falls within the realm of project management.

A clear transition from strategy formulation to the detailed management of the tasks and actions (Dravis 2004) is necessary to ensure its success. Once a strategy document—big or small, comprehensive or narrowly focused—is created (Dravis 2004), it can be handed to the program managers, and the contents of the data quality strategy can be used for breaking the programs into projects, and project managers should outline project plans based on the strategy document. While the goals and initiatives have been documented in the data quality strategy, and the data domains and data entities have been established, the project manager must build the project requirements from the goals. The project manager should adhere to the sound project management principals and concepts that apply to any project, such as task formulation, estimation, resource assignments, scheduling, risk analysis, mitigation, and project monitoring against critical success factors. Few of these tactical issues are covered in a strategy-level plan (Dravis 2004).

WHO DRIVES THE DATA QUALITY STRATEGY?

Typically, the chief data officer (CDO) owns and leads the development and execution of an organization's data quality strategy. However, while the role of a CDO is becoming

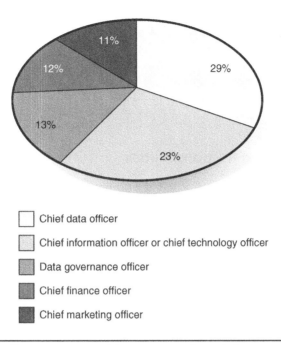

Chief data officer

Chief information officer or chief technology officer

Data governance officer

Chief finance officer

Chief marketing officer

Figure 5.9   Data quality strategy ownership—survey results statistics.

increasingly popular, not all organizations have a CDO. Gartner has estimated that one-quarter of large global organizations have already hired a chief data officer (CDO), and that by 2019 that figure will rise to 90% (Zaino 2017).

Large organizations in highly regulated industries are the most likely to employ a CDO. In smaller and data-first companies, a CDO's responsibilities may be shared among other job titles or be the domain of a single individual, such as the chief information officer (CIO) (Morgan 2016). As per survey results, Figure 5.9 depicts statistics related to the ownership of the central data quality strategy (McCafferty 2015).

CHIEF DATA OFFICER (CDO)

The chief data officer, or CDO, is a senior executive who bears responsibility for the organization's enterprise-wide data quality strategy, governance, and control, data policies, processes, and standards development, and successful use of data assets. The CDO's role will combine accountability and responsibility for data security and privacy and data governance, data quality, and data life cycle management, along with the effective utilization of data assets to create business value. A successful CDO crosses the line that divides business and technology and oversees a range of data-related functions to unleash the full power of data to drive revenue and transform the business. This role is popular in the financial services industry, where the role emerged in the aftermath of the financial collapse of 2009 (Shaw 2013).

While the first generation of CDOs was brought on to oversee data governance and data management, their role is transitioning into one focused on how to best organize and use data as a strategic asset within organizations. But many CDOs still don't have the resources, budget, or authority to drive digital transformation on their own, so the CDO needs to help the CIO drive transformation via collaboration and evangelism (Brown 2017).

CDO Capabilities and Responsibilities

The CDO's role spans the enterprise and should be aligned with the strategic goals of the organization. The CDO should be business driven to be able to attain business value using data, but at the same time have enough of an understanding and appreciation of technology to be able to make strategic decisions related to technology. The CDO should align the different business and technology teams in a common vision for their data quality strategies and platforms, to drive digital transformation and meet business objectives. This does not mean that the CDO needs to have an understanding of the nitty-gritty details of technology. CDOs should not get deeply involved in technology and systems, as they need to focus on people and processes to drive the business value of data. The CDO not only needs to be able to discuss data at a business strategy level, and be aligned to business objectives, but also needs to be able to portray initiatives or challenges in a simplistic, less technical manner to ensure that the C-suite understands the issues and/or supports the initiatives (Experian 2016).

In addition to the strategic vision, the CDO needs to work closely with the CIO to create and maintain a data-driven culture throughout the organization. This data-driven culture is an absolute requirement in order to support the changes brought on by digital transformation, today and into the future (Brown 2017).

Figure 5.10 presents a few views from different C-level executives on the role of the Chief Data Officer (CDO).

While the responsibilities of a chief data officer differ from organization to organization, the role of the CDO typically involves the following:

- Overseeing the organization's strategic data priorities and identifying new business opportunities based on the existing data

- Driving the organization's data quality strategy in alignment with the corporate business goals, and overseeing its execution

- Securing the funding necessary to execute an organization's data initiatives

- Ensuring that data are accessible to related business units and personnel across the business, and at the same time ensuring their security

- Regulating how the business captures, maintains, and presents data on a strategic level

Chief Data Officer (CDO), High Street Bank (Experian 2016)

"The CDO is not the sole individual responsible for data within an organization; he or she should be regarded as an enabler . . . Ultimately, the management of data should be a corporate-wide responsibility, with the CDO spearheading its enablement."

Deputy CDO, UK Healthcare Group (Experian 2016)

"The CDO role was implemented to address a lack of data ownership across the group, respond to increased regulation, and provide a consistent approach to data management."

Stu Gardos, CDO at Memorial Sloan Kettering Cancer Center (Brown 2017)

"My role as a CDO has evolved to govern data, curate data, and convince subject matter experts that the data belongs to the business and not [individual] departments."

Patricia Skarulis, SVP and CIO of Memorial Sloan Kettering Cancer Center (Brown 2017)

"The CDO should not just be part of the org chart, but also have an active hand in launching new data initiatives."

Steve Sacks, Chief Customer Officer (CCO), Burberry (Experian 2016)

"The role of the CDO is to use data to drive value across the business, working transversally to embed this. It's how the CDO wires data into the business to create value; I think that's the key to unlocking data and making it work."

Mike Ettling, President HR Line of Business, SAP (Experian 2016)

"This role isn't a classic profile, they need commercial sense, they need a bit of a legal background, a bit of IT, and it needs a lot of different disciplines to act in this type of role."

One CDO described the role as, "having to wear lots of different hats and regularly change his language." (Experian 2016)

Joan Dal Bianco, SVP/Head, US Office of the Chief Data Officer (OCDO), New York (INN 2016)

"Key characteristics for the role of CDO include broad business acumen along with data expertise. The CDO shouldn't be just a very technical role. The leader needs to be able to communicate well with business and control function peers, so having a broad understanding of how a business runs and the strategic direction of the organization to better align the data strategy is key."

Derek Strauss, Chief Data Officer, TD Ameritrade, Dallas, TX (INN 2016)

"A CDO needs a good understanding of business processes, enterprise architecture, and data modeling, plus the ability to tell stories (using Agile User Story format is a good place to start)."

Leandro DalleMule, Chief Data Officer, AIG, New York (INN 2016)

"Simply put, the CDO is the enabler of usable, accurate, and timely information for decision making through cleansed, standardized, and connected data, external and internal to the organization. The CDO needs the skill sets, background, and personality to be the connective tissue between the demand and capabilities of systems/technology and corporate functions/business units."

Fawad Butt, Chief Data Governance Officer, Kaiser Permanente, Oakland, CA (INN 2016)

"Today, CDOs come from diverse backgrounds and have similarly diverse experiences. The role requires individuals to have an understanding of a number of disciplines, including data management, people management, and lastly, change management. Candidates can differentiate themselves by having experiences across these disciplines and by not being one-dimensional, for example, technology experience only."

Figure 5.10   Different views of the role of the chief data officer.   *Continued*

Vincent Benita, Chief Data Officer, BNP Paribas (Experian Data Quality 2014)

"The CDO role must sit within the business and not from IT. The CDO role is around governance, monitoring, data processes, data life cycle and sourcing rather than IT, and this reflects how it should be structured."

James Platt, Chief Data Officer, Aon GRIP Solutions and CAO Aon Risk Solutions (Experian 2016)

"The CDO drives added value by innovatively combining data sets. But it's not just the data itself or the analysis, but it's the mind-set and skills of someone who can think about both the customer and product data at the same time and how this can translate into tangible value."

Figure 5.10　*Continued.*

- Overseeing cross-functional data governance while simultaneously ensuring adoption of and adherence to data quality and process governance in the relevant collaborating departments.

- Leading and driving a data-driven culture, from top to bottom in the organization, by convincing everyone of the business value of data and the importance of data quality, data security and privacy.

- Promoting the use of industry best practices, leading trends, and new data management technologies.

- Reducing costs and redundancies that result from numerous data initiatives running in silos across different lines of business.

- Although ultimate responsibility for IT security may not lie with the CDO, it's crucial that they are aware of the measures being taken and are confident that the protection is more than adequate.

In order to be successful in handling the above responsibilities, a chief data officer should have a combination of soft skills, hard skills, and business knowledge and experience as follows:

- **Soft skills:**

  - *Leadership and change management skills.* A good CDO should have good leadership and change management skills as he or she needs to drive the organization toward a data-driven culture, which would most likely be met with different levels of organizational resistance. A CDO should be a strategic thinker and a visionary when it comes to driving value from data as a product and a corporate asset.

  - *Communication and collaboration skills.* A CDO should have good communication and collaboration skills, as the CDO role spans different business units as well as the IT department in the organization.

- *Diplomacy and political clout.* The CDO role spans different business units and the IT department in the enterprise, and would have to manage conflicts related to data (for example shared data definitions and standards), and should be diplomatic and have political clout to achieve the desired outcome without imposing his or her opinion. In other words, a good CDO must have the ability to influence without authority and have good negotiating skills.

- **Technology:**

  - Familiarity with data quality tools and technologies, including data modeling tools, ETL and data integration tools, visualization tools, databases, and data storage technologies.

  - Good knowledge of data management concepts, which includes data governance, data administration, data warehousing, business intelligence, data architecture, data integration, data classification, data strategy, data quality management, data security and privacy, master data management, data mining, data standards, databases, and enterprise architecture frameworks.

  - Experience in data management projects in at least some of the above knowledge areas.

- **Business:**
  A CDO should have knowledge and preferably experience in the following:

  - Good understanding of the business domain and business processes

  - Compliance and regulatory requirements

  - Program management

  - Risk management

Reporting Structure

Ideally, the chief data officer (CDO) should report to the chief executive officer (CEO) so as to align with the enterprise business strategy, and be on the same level with the chief information officer (CIO) and chief managing officer (CMO). However, in practice, the person the CDO reports to depends on the structure of organization, the corporate politics, and the business outcomes that the organization is trying to achieve. Some of them, despite their C-level designation, may be subordinate to other C-level titles. The Forrester report has indicated that in respondent companies, one-third report to the CEO, one-third report to the CIO, and one-third report to other C-level titles (Morgan 2016). However, according to the Gartner survey, that's not how it is at most companies. Only 40% of respondents said they reported to the CEO or COO. Sixteen percent reported to the CIO, and 11% reported to a senior vice president or VP outside

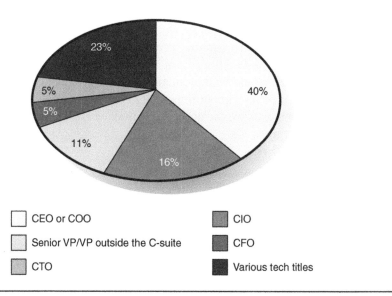

Figure 5.11 CDO reporting line survey results from Gartner.

the C-suite. Five percent report to the CFO, and another 5% report to the CTO, with the rest spread among various tech titles (Zetlin 2017). The pie chart in Figure 5.11 shows the results from Gartner's survey on reporting lines for chief data officer in different organizations.

"We were very interested to find that very few reported to the CMO," said Forrester's Bellisent. "We hear a lot about the use of data in marketing campaigns, understanding the customer, and improving customer experience, but only 2% of our survey respondents report directly to the CMO" (Morgan 2016).

"More and more, we're seeing the CDO report to a COO or CFO, but I don't want to say there's a hard-and-fast rule. Who the CDO reports to can vary quite a bit," said Chris Mazzei, chief analytics officer at professional services company Ernst & Young, in an interview.

DATA QUALITY STRATEGY—A FEW USEFUL TIPS

A data quality strategy should be at a high level and should offer organizational context and guidance to support decision making:

- The one-size-fits-all approach does not apply to data quality strategy. Every organization will have its own unique strategy depending on the organization's data and application landscape, the business impact of data issues, what value they want to derive from their data, current data maturity, and their readiness to achieve higher maturity levels.

- An organization's data quality strategy should align with the organization's overall strategy.

- A data quality strategy should have a proposed balance of defense (control) versus offense (flexibility/growth). When defining strategy, *defense* is about things like limiting risk, ensuring data security and privacy, implementing governance, and ensuring compliance, while *offense* is about improving competitive position and profitability. Achieving proper balance and flexibility is key to ensuring that the desired purpose and use of the data are met (Collibra 2017).

- Technology should not drive the development of a data quality strategy: *what problem that the organization is trying to solve using data and how the data quality strategy goals and/or data principles align with the business goals and business drivers* should form the basis for developing a data quality strategy.

  In recent years, a technology boom in the data quality and analytics area has drawn interest from both IT and business leaders, and has driven them to ask what problems they can solve with these new technologies. However, taking this path without giving meticulous thought to the desired business outcomes can result in a waste of resources, time, and money. Instead, the business and IT should first determine the problem or opportunity, quantify the benefits, understand the current state, define the desire future state, and perform an aggressive gap analysis before proposing initiatives and the technologies needed for the implementation of those initiatives. The preparation of the data quality strategy should be technology agnostic, with technology being a critical success factor in how much business value the organization reaps from data in the long run.

- A data quality strategy should be designed with inputs from the business, subject matter experts, and IT professionals. A data quality strategy that only has inputs from IT would be technology driven, without proper business focus and subject matter expert input, as IT personnel are not always aware of the business challenges and impacts due to bad data.

- Data governance should be given careful consideration as it is a key component in the delivery of the data quality strategy.

- Data architecture strengthens a data quality strategy and should have a place in the data quality strategy.

- Data quality is not a destination, but an ongoing journey. While some initiatives in the strategy would be one-off efforts followed by limited support and maintenance, there are certain data quality management activities that are required to be established as ongoing functions, for example, maintenance of data standards, business glossary, data dictionary, data governance activities, and data quality monitoring. These "business as usual" initiatives or functions should be stated in the data quality strategy.

- The key risk factors (for example, not having the right skill set and knowledge for deploying the initiatives) and success factors (for example, change management, education and training) should be explained in the strategy and clearly presented to the stakeholders.

- The strategic roadmap should be driven by business goals, not technology.

- When formulating a data quality strategy, it is necessary to take into consideration the skill sets, abilities, and culture of the organization (Dravis 2004). If the concept of data quality is new to the organization, a simple strategy addressing one critical business issue is best. This would be a good fit for a pilot project. A typical pilot project might involve one critical data element (for example, contact e-mail ID) in one table. However, the more challenging the goals of a data quality strategy, the greater the returns. An organization must accept that with greater returns come greater risks. Data quality project risks can be mitigated by a more comprehensive strategy. It should be kept in mind that the initial strategy is a first iteration that will be followed by revisions. Strategy plans are "living" work products. A complex project can be subdivided into mini-projects, or pilots. Each successful pilot builds inertia. And therein lies a strategy in itself: divide and conquer. Successful pilots will drive future initiatives. Thus, an initial strategy planning process is part of a larger repetitive cycle. True quality management is, after all, a repeatable process (Dravis 2004).

- When creating the data quality strategy, it is good practice to rest after each phase to understand what went well, what did not go so well, what went wrong, and what could be improved, in an objective manner without pointing fingers at anyone, documenting the key learnings and best practices and embedding them into the data quality strategy team.

CONCLUSION

If your organization has data quality problems, then you need a data quality strategy to improve your data; if you already have good data, then you need a strategy to maintain the data. Developing a proactive data quality strategy rather than using a reactive approach to solve data quality issues yields better results and return in the long run. However, it should be understood that data quality strategy creation and execution cannot be achieved overnight, and there is no magical software application that can solve all your data quality problems. When formulating the data quality strategy for an organization, it is important to assess the current data maturity level, be aware of the existing data quality initiatives in progress in different parts of the organization, and determine what's going well and which areas could be improved, what data initiatives should be proposed, and how these new initiatives would align with the old data initiatives. A successful data quality strategy involves understanding the organization's data landscape and the business value of your enterprise data, and how to leverage maximum benefit from the enterprise data.

6

Data Quality Management

DATA QUALITY MANAGEMENT

Data are an enterprise asset. Today's age is defined by data-driven decision making. Data and information are the facts from which conclusions are drawn and on which decisions are based on. Many projects and programs, for example, reporting and analytics, use data as their foundation. The quality of the solutions and the decisions made based on these solutions are defined by the underlying data quality. High-quality data help senior management to make more-informed strategic decisions. If the data are unreliable or inaccurate, then the analytics and reporting that run on the data cannot be trusted. Data without quality can neither contribute any value nor can they serve any purpose. Hence, high-quality data are not a "nice to have" requirement but a "must have" requirement. In order to improve data quality, a data quality improvement program can be driven with the Six Sigma approach.

Data-driven decision making, customer satisfaction, greater operational efficiencies, legal, regulatory, and compliance requirements, analytics, and high-end reporting have been the key business drivers necessitating the management of data quality to ensure good quality data. Over the past few years there have been several legal and compliance mandates that penalize companies for flawed data. Bad customer data can affect your organization's relationship with a customer, resulting in disgruntled customers or customers leaving you and enrolling in services with your competitor. Thus, data should be managed to ensure that good-quality data is captured as well as maintained. Figure 6.1 shows some of the problems faced in the absence of mature data quality management.

Data quality management (DQM) is the management of people, processes, policies, technology, standards, and data within an enterprise, with the objective of improving the dimensions of data quality that are most important to the organization. The ultimate goal of DQM is not to improve data quality solely for the sake of having high-quality data, but to realize the desired business outcomes that bank on high-quality data (Knowledgent Undated).

Six Sigma is a quality control program developed in 1986 by Motorola that advocates for qualitative measurements to improve quality. Six Sigma DMAIC (define, measure, analyze, improve, and control) methodology can be utilized to improve data quality as well as identify and develop a comprehensive data quality (DQ) framework

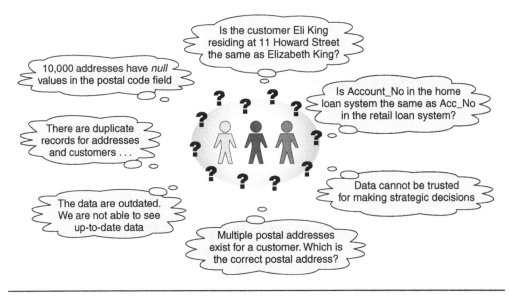

Figure 6.1 Why data quality management is needed.

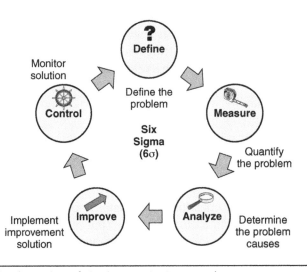

Figure 6.2 High-level overview of Six Sigma DMAIC approach.

for maintaining data quality and preventing data quality issues. The high-level overview of the Six Sigma DMAIC approach is illustrated in Figure 6.2.

This chapter starts with a discussion on the approaches to data quality management. This is followed by a section that presents in detail the application of DMAIC to data quality management, in turn followed by sections on data quality assessment, root cause analysis, data cleansing, data validation, and data quality monitoring. Next are presented detailed discussions of data quality in relation to data migration, data integration, master data management, and metadata management. These sections are followed by an example of the application of Six Sigma DMAIC methodology to data quality management, which is followed by a brief discussion on the key principles of data quality management. The chapter concludes with a summary of the main points and key definitions discussed in the earlier sections.

DATA QUALITY MANAGEMENT—REACTIVE VERSUS PROACTIVE

There are two approaches to data quality management:

- Proactive

- Reactive

While a *proactive* approach to data quality management involves eliminating data quality problems before they have a chance to appear, a *reactive* approach to data quality is based on reacting to data quality issues after they have surfaced. The difference between these two approaches is the perspective each one provides in evaluating actions and events.

It takes just one bad record to create monumental issues. This is because of the butterfly effect on data quality that we discussed in Chapter 1, and which is illustrated in Figure 6.3. As bad data travel through different systems in the organization, the bad data

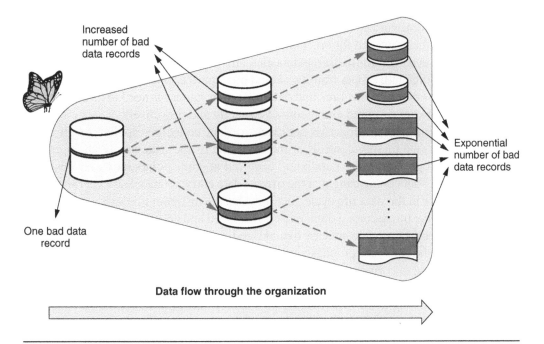

Figure 6.3   The butterfly effect on data quality.

multiplies at an alarming rate, which grows worse with time if left unattended. Therefore, the longer an organization waits to detect and correct a bad record, the more detrimental it is. Hence, taking a reactive approach to managing data quality instead of a proactive approach can be an expensive decision. Independent analysis firm SiriusDecisions notes what it calls the "1-10-100 rule," which demonstrates the benefits of proactive data quality. The rule states that it costs only $1 to verify a record upon entry and $10 to cleanse and dedupe it after it has been entered, but $100 in potential lost productivity or revenue if nothing is done (Block 2008, Taylor 2010). The old adage "prevention is better than cure" is applicable here, where prevention is proactive and cure is reactive. Also, the longer you leave a disease unattended, the more difficult and time-consuming it is to cure.

Hence, the proactive data quality approach is definitely preferable to the reactive data quality approach. For example, populating gender data on the basis of given names works correctly for a certain proportion of cases. However, some names can be used by both genders depending on the culture, race, and geography, and hence populating gender on the basis of the given name means a certain percentage of the gender data would be incorrect with no means of correcting the data without recapturing it. Hence, a proactive approach that captures the data correctly the first time during the data collection stage is highly recommended. In the case of gender, capture the gender details along with the name details correctly the first time by validating against the appropriate supporting documents, for example, passport, driver's license, or birth certificate. Names and addresses are important data elements that should be captured correctly and consistently the first time, as correcting them can be a time-consuming exercise, and having them wrong can cause lost opportunities, customer dissatisfaction, and damage to the company's reputation. The format for data capture for the data element needs to be consistent. For example, for some customers, only the first name initial is captured as opposed to the complete first names captured for other customers. This is a case of abbreviations versus full forms being captured for the same data element. Standards for data collection need to be defined beforehand, proper training should be imparted to the employees responsible for the process of data collection, and data collection standards need to be conformed to ensure that data are captured and recorded correctly and proactively.

The "first time right" proactive approach to data collection applies to all data. Applying strong data quality controls at the front end of the data supply chain can to some extent help prevent faulty data being captured at entry points into your business ecosystem. Faulty data being caught at the time of data entry is much less expensive than being caught later in the data life cycle, and prevents downstream impacts.

Some data, like transactional data, must be captured and collected correctly because amendments after the event are not easy to make and are time-consuming and very costly. For example, in the case of a purchase order made over the phone, if the wrong details are captured, trying to correct the error after the wrong goods have been delivered to the customer would require organizing the shipping of the correct item and organizing the return of the wrong item, which would be a time-consuming and costly exercise, as well as a bad customer experience and bad press for the company. When transactional data are collected right the very first time, they stay that way since the transactional data record represents a point-in-time historic event that will never change over a period of time. This also applies to static data like date of birth, gender, or place of birth, which once captured correctly will not change with the passage of time.

However, while a proactive approach to managing data quality is definitely recommended over a reactive data quality management approach that involves cleansing the data, it is not possible to rely solely on a proactive data quality approach where data quality is concerned. This is because all data do not remain static as the real-world entities that the data refer to, change. Some of these changes include people and businesses changing addresses, changing names, changing jobs, getting terminated or quitting or retiring from jobs, getting married, getting divorced and married again, changes in telephone and postal code systems, states merging or bifurcating, and new districts emerging. Hence, data related to these entities that were once correct are no longer correct. In this case, only a reactive approach to data quality will work. Hence, when considering data quality management approaches, one cannot rely on either an absolutely proactive approach or completely reactive approach. A hybrid data quality management approach is needed, employing a mix of proactive and reactive data quality management techniques and methods. The theme is to be proactive as much as possible, but be reactive too, to keep up with the data affected due to changes in the real-world entities and their attributes.

However, organizations often go ahead with implementing data quality initiatives that are designed to react to data quality issues using cleansing techniques instead of determining the root cause and addressing the root cause to prevent future data quality issues from occurring in the first place. While addressing the root causes may not always be possible—due to constraints related to legacy systems that are hard to amend, aggressive timelines for addressing business requirements, lack of skilled resources, budgetary constraints, and so on—a root cause analysis followed by multiple solution options stating the pros and cons needs to be discussed with all the stakeholders before deciding on an approach.

A mature data quality program would take into account the high-priority data quality issues—the implications of having poor-quality data, the likelihood, severity, and frequency of occurrence, the objective metrics for determining data quality levels, and the impact of data quality noncompliance—while designing an approach to ensure high levels of quality. Generally, if the data are very critical and the impact of poor-quality data is high, the approach would be to have a solution in place to cleanse and monitor the data while developing a strategic proactive data quality management solution aimed at preventing the occurrence of data quality issues, if developing such a solution is feasible. The more robust the proactive approach, the less the need for the reactive approach.

An effective data quality management approach, which is the hybrid approach, is composed of both reactive and proactive elements, with the reactive element dealing with the management of issues in the data located in existing data stores. The proactive element includes:

- Looking beyond department boundaries to trace data back to the source. *Data lineage management* with data discovery tools can help achieve this. Tracing data back to the source is important, as data issues can arise at any time the data are touched, starting from the originating point, and it is important to understand at which point the data issues are appearing in order to be able to design preventive solutions. Typically, data flow through a myriad of systems in an organization, and an error can creep in at any point where data are read, transformed, and written to a repository, as shown in Figure 6.4.

- Comprehensive and consistent data quality definitions, standards, data quality rules, data policies, and processes across the organization. This would result in data being captured consistently across the enterprise, and reduction of data issues due to inconsistency.

- Establishment of data governance across the organization, with clearly defined roles and responsibilities. Without governance, it is difficult to ensure that processes, policies, and standards are adhered to.

- Automate activities with the implementation of a technology solution, where possible, to reduce or eliminate manual intervention and facilitate business practices.

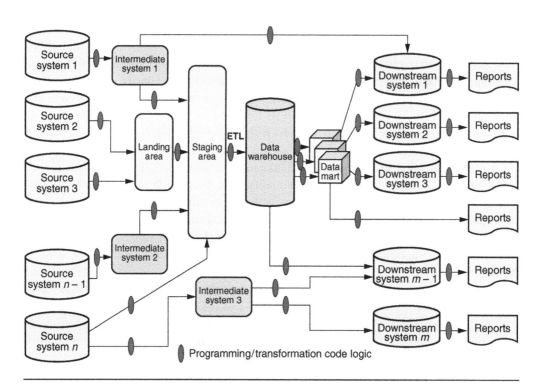

Figure 6.4 Data flow through multiple systems in organizations.

- Performing root cause analysis to understand the cause of the data issues discovered, reactively or through monitoring, at regular intervals and then working out the best way to prevent them.

DATA QUALITY MANAGEMENT— SIX SIGMA DMAIC

The Six Sigma data quality management DMAIC process is divided into the following five phases:

- Define

- Measure

- Analyze

- Improve

- Control

Figure 6.5 gives a diagrammatic view of the data quality management steps using DMAIC methodology.

Define

The *define* phase involves defining the problem statement. In the case of data quality management, this would entail defining the focus area of data quality; the data domains, data assets, and critical business processes, or a particular data quality issue that requires investigation could be the object of focus. While the data domains, data assets, and critical business processes would be uncovered in the process of formulating the data quality strategy, a data quality issue would be the result of problems reported by a data consumer or business user to the data governance team, who then do an initial analysis and populate and prioritize the data quality issue in the data quality issue log. Failure mode and effects analysis can be used to prioritize the issues.

From a data domain or data asset perspective, one approach would be to look at resolving the critical issues affecting a critical data domain or data asset. For example, in a water utility company, it is extremely important to have accurate information about underground and above-ground assets such as sites, pipes, tanks, boilers, and so on, as the performance of the assets is extremely critical to provide good service to the customer. Hence, the problem statement could look at the critical data issues affecting the asset data in the water utility company. In a retail company the product data are important, as an accurate and up-to-date list of current inventory is an essential component in managing costs, avoiding stock-outs, and impacting sales. Thus, in a retail company the problem statement could look at critical data issues affecting product data. From a business process perspective, this would involve solving critical data issues impact-

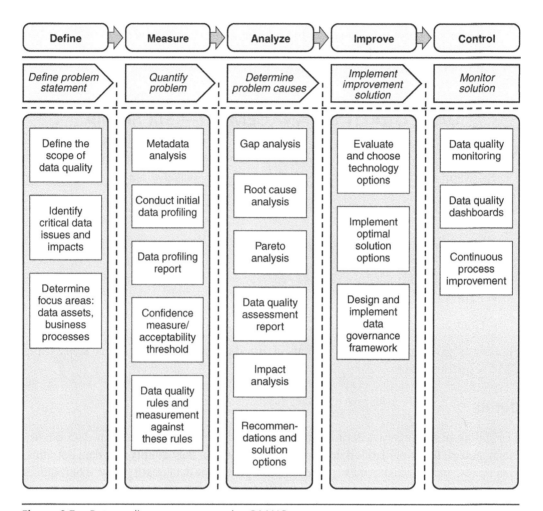

Figure 6.5   Data quality management using DMAIC.

ing critical business processes. For example, looking at the critical data issues impacting marketing processes could be a good place to start. Resolving high-priority issues in the data quality issue log maintained by data governance could also be the content of a problem statement.

In the case where the focus areas of data quality are the critical data domains/data assets or critical business processes, this would involve identifying all the concerned stakeholders, including the data consumers, in order to understand the data quality expectation, the data entities, and the critical data elements, and the range of data quality dimensions—such as completeness, validity, accuracy, and so on—to be measured at a data entity, data record, or data element level.

In the case of high-priority data issues in the data quality issue log, the concerned data steward would identify the data entities and data elements related to the data quality issue, and the respective data quality dimensions to be measured, as a starting point to solve the data quality issues.

Measure

The aim of the *measure* phase is to understand and quantify the current state of the data assets identified in the define phase. While a high-level assessment of the current state is carried out during the process of formulating the data quality strategy, a detailed assessment and in-depth analysis need to be carried out to iron out what to deliver as part of the initiatives proposed as part of the data quality strategy.

The data quality for the data entities and data elements identified in the define phase would be assessed with respect to the data quality dimensions in this phase. A data quality assessment needs to be conducted to get a comprehensive picture of the health of the data. This would begin with accessing data stored in databases or acquiring data files for data profiling purposes and assessing the metadata, that is, the information available about the data. While data quality assessment starts in the measure phase, it ends in the *analyze* phase. The acceptable threshold or confidence measure that defines the degree of conformance required for the data needs to defined and agreed on with the business. The range of data quality dimensions to be assessed would depend on the business requirements. *Confidence level,* or *acceptable threshold*, is the minimum required degree of conformance to the business rules defined for a particular data quality dimension for a data entity, data record, or data element as per the expectation of the business stakeholders. An example of acceptable thresholds or confidence level is "the asset location should be populated for at least 90% of the underground assets stored in the database." We will discuss the details of data quality assessment in the "Data Quality Assessment" section of this chapter.

In Chapter 4, "Measuring Data Quality Dimensions," we discussed in detail how to measure the data quality dimensions. Data profiling tools can be used to detect errors or anomalies in the data. The results of measurement would need to be documented in a data profiling report.

Analyze

In the *analyze* phase, the results of the measure phase are analyzed to determine the gaps, risks, occurrence, impact, and cost to business. Root cause analysis need to be performed to identify and verify potential root causes. The current controls in place also need to be investigated.

While data issues may have been uncovered at a particular point or in a particular system, the business and IT processes supporting that system may not have been responsible for the issue. This is because data flow through a number of intermediate systems before landing in the target system. The cause for the issue may be further upstream and needs to be traced back to the point, system, and business process where the error originated. Data are touched in some way when they move from one system to another system. If the data lineage is documented, then data can be traced back to the source. If not documented, data discovery tools can be used to determine the data lineage.

Pareto analysis can be used to prioritize the root causes. Both root cause analysis and Pareto analysis are discussed in detail later in this chapter in the "Root Cause Analysis" section. The data quality issue log needs to be updated with causes and implications.

Based on the results of root cause analysis and Pareto analysis, the key causes are addressed. Several high-level data quality improvement solutions with pros and cons are proposed and presented to the stakeholders and the data governance team. The solution options may comprise both reactive and proactive initiatives. The pros and cons of each solution need to be carefully weighed and a cost–benefit analysis also needs to be carried out—and the solutions need to be validated—to arrive at a decision regarding the optimal solution option.

Improve

The data quality improvement solution is built and implemented in the *improve* phase. This could be a technical solution or a process change or training employees to enter data correctly, or a combination of these options depending on the results of the root cause analysis carried out in the analyze phase. In the case of a technology solution, this would first involve evaluating the technology option and choosing the one best suited to the business requirements. A combination of reactive and proactive solutions may need to be implemented. Technical solutions should be tested properly with production-like data before being implemented in the production environment. Any business process changes need to be discussed with the impacted stakeholders, and should include proper user training and a "test and learn" phase when changes are first implemented to gauge the success of the changes. In the absence of a data governance framework, the data governance framework would typically be designed as a part of the improvement plan.

Control

The *control* phase is used to continuously improve the process and monitor the data quality delivered in the improve phase. The aim is to uncover data quality issues as early as possible. Since data quality monitoring is an expensive exercise, not all data are monitored, but only those that have maximum impact to the business. Data quality dashboards can be useful to monitor data quality.

DATA QUALITY ASSESSMENT

The *New Oxford American Dictionary* defines *assessment* as "the process of evaluating or estimating the nature, ability, or quality of a thing." ASQ defines assessment as "a systematic evaluation process of collecting and analyzing data to determine the current, historical, or projected compliance of an organization to a standard" (ASQ Undated). *Data quality assessment* is the process of profiling data and measuring the quality of data against defined business rules, documenting and analyzing the results of measurement, analyzing gaps between data quality results and expected data quality, understanding the issues and pain points, and analyzing the impacts and root causes. This would form the basis for recommendations, improvements, and devising solution approaches to fix the data quality issues.

Data quality assessment is not the same as data profiling or data quality measurement. In order to deliver value, an assessment requires measurement and comparison of the results of measurement against a benchmark, analyzing the gaps, and drawing conclusions, whereas measurement in itself does not involve comparison, analysis, or drawing conclusions. Data profiling and measurement would uncover certain facets of data in terms of counts of frequently occurring patterns, statistics (minimum, maximum, average, standard deviation, and so on), distribution of values, completeness, duplication, and so on. However, to understand exactly where you stand in terms of the quality of the data, the results obtained from data profiling need to be analyzed with the active involvement of subject matter experts to define specifics of data quality and business rules for measuring the quality of the data against the required data quality dimensions and comparing measurement results against the confidence measure or acceptance threshold defined by the business stakeholders.

Data quality assessment can be broken into the following steps, as shown in Figure 6.6.

1. Data access and preparation

2. Data profiling and analysis

3. Results and recommendations

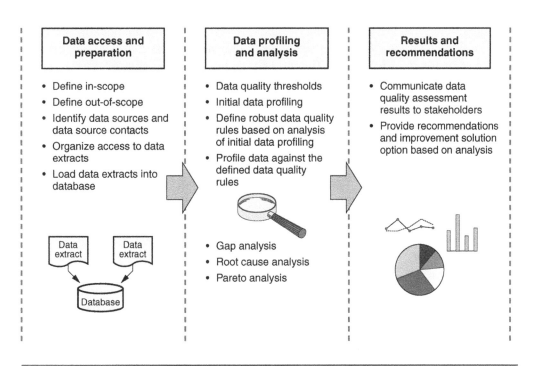

Figure 6.6 Data quality assessment.

Data Access and Preparation

Measuring and assessing the quality of the data necessitates access to the data sources containing the required data. There may be security requirements relating to the data, and appropriate approvals might be required to access and analyze the data. Acquiring data for data profiling and assessment of quality would typically involve the appropriate source system personnel who would be able extract the data or help arrange access to the data source itself. Typically, the source system contact would provide the required data extracts. A good practice is to load the data extracts into a database structure as this would provide the flexibility to write SQL queries or use data profiling tools for profiling the data.

Data profiling is a time-consuming and expensive exercise. Hence, it is essential to define what data are in scope and what are out of scope, and refine the scope by identifying the entities and critical data elements that need to be measured for quality. The number of rows or records would still be large, and hence it is advisable to start with a sample extract. However, detailed data profiling would require all rows to be extracted and profiled.

Data Profiling and Analysis

Data profiling is an important step in data quality assessment, but is not the assessment itself. Data profiling activity provides the starting point for the process of gathering data quality requirements, determining the data quality dimensions, and defining robust data quality rules to gauge the quality of data. A comprehensive data quality measurement is achieved when all the data quality requirements are captured as executable data quality rules for measuring the different data quality characteristics or dimensions. In order to define the data quality rules or business rules for measuring the different aspects of data quality, it is important to understand the context of data usage, the metadata, data types, and the allowed data formats and representations, data domain values, or range of data values, if applicable. The business stakeholders' expectations need to be clearly understood, and the business rules for data quality need to be defined in conjunction with the business stakeholders. When data are tested against the defined data quality rules, we get a true understanding of the current state of the data quality. For example, initial data profiling might reveal a large number of *null* values for certain data fields, which would give an initial impression of a large degree of data incompleteness. However, looking at the underlying data and consulting with the subject matter experts to understand the cause might reveal that some records have *null* values because of valid business scenarios. This analysis would form the basis for understanding the business requirements and expectations more clearly and defining business rules for data quality.

When defining expectations and quality requirements, it is very important to be able to quantify these expectations. If the metadata and data standards are available, these could help in understanding the expectations and defining some of the rules. However, the data system subject matter experts would be the best people to provide a clear picture of the expectations and what the data should look like, and approve the defined rules. For example:

1. Should the data field be populated in all circumstances or all business scenarios?

2. If the answer to question 1 is "no," what are the business scenarios when the data field will not be populated?

3. Does the data field need to adhere to certain formats?

4. What is the maximum length of the data field?

5. Is there any range or domain of values that the field can have? If yes, what are the business scenarios in which the data field can have these values?

6. Does the data field have any minimum or maximum threshold? (This is applicable in the case of numeric data fields.)

The above questions would typically help define specific data quality rules. However, since business scenarios might involve different attributes and entities, the rules would also have to take this into account.

Data Quality Threshold. It is necessary to understand the expectations of the business in terms of the degree of conformance, that is, acceptance threshold or confidence measure, as it is very difficult and expensive to have, achieve, and maintain 100% data quality. For example, the business stakeholders may say that if the data are 75% complete and 70% accurate, then the data would meet business requirements.

Once the data are tested against the data quality rules, the results need be compared against the acceptance threshold or confidence measure. If the results fall short of the acceptance threshold, then faulty records need to be analyzed to understand the cause. We will discuss how to conduct causal analysis in the "Root Cause Analysis" section. Understanding and prioritizing causes would help in providing recommendations and improvement solution options.

Results and Recommendations

This step involves communicating and discussing the findings and results of the data quality assessments, the inferences drawn, and proposed recommendations and solution options with the business and IT stakeholders.

Data quality assessment involves a number of activities: initial data profiling, discussing and understanding the results with the business and subject matter experts, defining data quality rules and understanding the degree of conformance required, testing against data quality rules and analysis of the gap to find the causes, and providing recommendations and improvement solution options based on the findings. These need to be documented as data quality assessment deliverables. Figure 6.7 summarizes the data quality assessment deliverables.

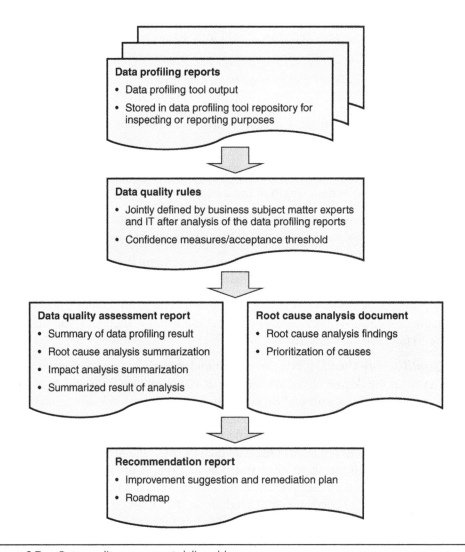

Figure 6.7   Data quality assessment deliverables.

It is wrong to assume that a data profiling tool will solve data quality issues. A data profiling tool generally uncovers characteristics of the data, including patterns and statistics; however, it is not able to draw conclusions. In order to make effective use of the tool, it is very important to understand the business expectations of the data and analyze the results of the data profiling tool to define rigorous rules for data quality.

ROOT CAUSE ANALYSIS

Root cause analysis is a method of problem solving used to identify and categorize the root causes of problems. While data profiling and measuring data quality give a picture of the health of the data and the extent of nonconformance, it is important to understand what is causing the nonconformance in order to be able to propose a viable solution. In addition, it is important to prioritize defects based on their impact and frequency of occurrence, and isolate the major contributing cause for an issue. Techniques such as the 5 whys root cause discovery process, brainstorming, and the fishbone diagram can be used to understand the causes. Pareto analysis can be used to prioritize the issues and the causes.

Once the point where the bad data are originating from has been discovered, the right business and technology subject matter experts need to be engaged and given an overview of the problem and the intent to uncover the causes. It is very important to engage the right people who have understanding and knowledge of the processes that create the data. Once stakeholders have been identified and engaged, one-on-one sessions and workshops should be organized to understand the causes.

A *fishbone diagram*, also called a *cause-and-effect diagram* or *Ishikawa diagram*, is a visualization tool for categorizing the potential causes of a problem in order to identify its root causes (Rouse Undated[2]). The design of the diagram resembles the skeleton of a fish. Fishbone diagrams are typically worked right to left from the head, which contains a clear definition of the problem, with each large "bone" of the fish having the main causal category, and branching out to include smaller bones containing more detailed causes, as shown in Figure 6.8. Some common category ideas are as follows:

- Manpower (related to humans)

- Measurements

- Machines (for example, applications, systems)

- Materials (for example, user guides, quick reference guides)

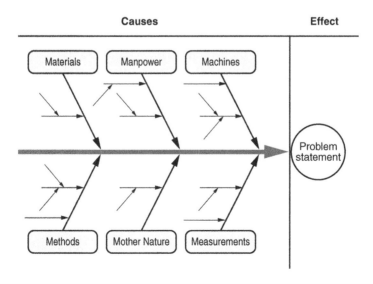

Figure 6.8 Fishbone diagram.

- Methods (for example, business processes)

- Mother Nature (for example, environmental issues)

Brainstorming can be used in the workshop sessions to identify causes in each of the major categories. Each cause is further broken down until root causes are arrived at. There might not be one single cause creating the data issue, but multiple causes. Also, you might have more-specific categories, or brainstorming might reveal additional categories. At the end of the brainstorming exercise, you would typically have a list of causes and you would need to prioritize the causes with the help of stakeholder input. Another technique used to arrive at the root cause is the 5 whys discovery process, also known as the *five Ws* (sometimes referred to as *Five Ws and How*), which uses a combination of *why, what, when, where, who,* and *how* questions to ferret out the causes.

The prioritized list of causes needs to be verified, and a plan needs to be created for verification that the causes discovered are indeed the true cause. It is good practice to obtain additional data relating to the data issue, if possible, and ensure that causes are not being uncovered through incorrect assumptions or omissions. For example, while conducting a workshop for uncovering the root cause for bad underground asset location data in a utility company, the business subject matter expert cited inadequate devices as the main reason behind underground asset workers keying in the wrong asset location data. We interviewed a few underground asset workers and also checked the devices they used to enter the data to understand whether that indeed was the problem. What we discovered was that the device keypad used to key in the asset location was too small and the keys were very close to each other, which made accurate data entry very difficult. In addition, the personnel also told us they were not aware of the importance of the data, and not all of them had undergone formal training on how to use these devices. Once the causes have been verified, it is important prioritize these causes. Pareto analysis can be used to prioritize the root causes.

The *Pareto principle* (also known as the *80/20 rule*), works under the assumption that, in all situations, 20% of causes contribute to 80% of problems. The focus should be on the 20% that cause 80% of the pain in terms of business impact. A Pareto chart, named after Vilfredo Pareto, is a type of chart that contains both bars and a line graph, where individual values are represented in descending order by the bars and the cumulative total is represented by the line (Wikipedia Undated "Pareto Chart"). The horizontal axis (x-axis) represents categories (defects or causes of defects) as opposed to a metric scale. The left vertical axis (y-axis) represents the count or percentage of defects, or their impact in terms of cost, rework, and so on, or a count or percentage of the causes. The right vertical axis is the cumulative percentage or the total of the particular unit of measure used in the left vertical axis. The bars are organized in descending order from largest to smallest. This helps reveal the categories that will create the biggest gains if resolved, and also eliminates the categories that have significantly lesser impact on the business. Because the bars are in decreasing order, the cumulative function is a concave function.

The most frequent problems may not have the biggest impacts in terms of quality, cost, or time. Construct separate Pareto charts, one using counts (for example, defects, frequency) and one that looks at impact (for example, cost or time). You can now identify the impacts that occur most frequently and that have the biggest impact (Jones 2009).

The findings of the root cause analysis and Pareto analysis need to be documented in the root cause analysis document and should be shared with stakeholders. This would form the basis for corrective, preventive, or improvement solution options. It is important to perform an impact analysis of each solution option, as there is a possibility that the solution may negatively impact other systems or even cause a system breakdown. Even if the impact analysis reveals no impact, the solution option that is considered should be rigorously tested with E2E (end to end) testing in place to reveal any issues. All the concerned stakeholders should be informed of the changes and the go-live date so that they can look for any impacts post go-live until the solution is in place for some time and no new problems have surfaced that can be attributed to the new solution. Figure 6.9 summarizes the root cause analysis steps.

DATA CLEANSING

Data cleansing, or *data cleaning*, is the process of detecting and correcting (or removing) corrupt or inaccurate records from a record set, table, or database, and refers to identifying incomplete, incorrect, inaccurate, or irrelevant parts of the data and then replacing, modifying, or deleting the dirty or coarse data (Wu 2013). Data cleansing is a reactive and costly approach to fixing data quality issues and cannot prevent issues either up or down the data chain or the data life cycle. However, it is the only option in any of the following scenarios:

- The root cause cannot be identified.

- A change to the process or system that would result in improvement of data quality not being approved because of one or more of the following reasons:

  - The impact the change might have on other processes and systems in the organization

  - Organizational politics

  - Budget constraints

  - The cost of change outweighs the benefits

- The data defects cannot be corrected or prevented at the starting point (point of capture or origination).

In the above cases, cleansing routines containing transformation logic are used to fix the data issues, which could involve correction of values of the data elements, reformatting values, elimination of irrelevant and/or meaningless data, and matching and merging of duplicate records. Cleansing the data ensures that the data meet the acceptable threshold for data quality expectation. Corrections must be socialized and synchronized with all data consumers and data suppliers, especially when the data are used in different

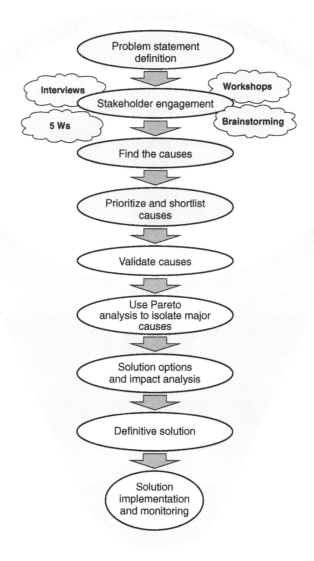

Figure 6.9　Root cause analysis steps.

business contexts. For example, there must be general agreement and supporting doc-umentation for the changes and transformational rules/business logic when comparing data in reports and rolled-up or summarized aggregate results to operational and trans-actional systems (Loshin 2009) because different numbers that have no explanation will lead to extra time spent attempting to reconcile inconsistencies. Figure 6.10 shows the various data cleansing techniques.

We will now discuss various data quality techniques involved in data cleansing.

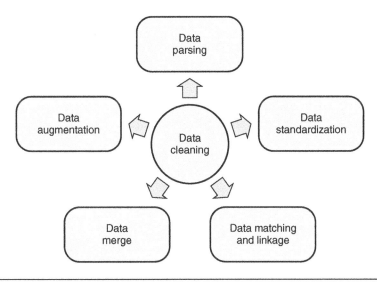

Figure 6.10   Data cleansing techniques.

Parsing and Standardization

Many data issues result from circumstances where inconsistency in representation and formatting of data values leads to duplication and ambiguity. *Parsing* is a process that involves the disintegration, conversion, and segregation of text fields and content into constituent atomic parts and the organizing values into consistent formats—based on industry standards or local standards (for example, postal authority standards for address data), user-defined business rules that involve comparison with regular expression, reference table entries, patterns, or token sets—using an assortment of techniques, including machine learning.

Parsing relies on defined formats, patterns, and structures to determine when data values conform to a common set of expectations (Loshin 2010b). Common candidate attributes for data parsing are e-mail addresses, SSNs, phone numbers, names, and addresses. Data parsing tools enable the data analyst to define patterns that can be fed into rules engines that are used to make a distinction between valid and invalid data values. When a specific pattern is matched, actions may be triggered. When a valid pattern is parsed, the distinct components may be extracted into a standard representation. When an invalid pattern is recognized, the application may attempt to transform the invalid value into one that meets expectations (Loshin 2007).

For example, parsing would break an address into street address line 1, street address line 2, city, ZIP code, and country. Consider the following address records stored in the single data field "Address," as shown in Figure 6.11.

Parsing would decompose and transform the string stored into constituent parts, and store them in separate fields, as shown in Table 6.1.

Address
12024, Swallow Falls Court, Silver Spring, Maryland 20904, United States of America
12026, Swallow Falls Ct, Silver Spring, MD 20904, USA
80, Waldo Ave, Jersey City, New Jersey 07306, NJ, USA
50, Garrison Avenue, Jersey City, NJ, 07306, United States
82, Waldo Ave., Jersey City, 07306, N.J., U.S.A.

Figure 6.11   Address records stored in a single data field.

Table 6.1   Decomposition of address.

Street address line 1	Street address line 2	City	ZIP code	State	Country
12024	Swallow Falls Court	Silver Spring	20904	Maryland	United States of America
12026	Swallow Falls Ct	Silver Spring	20904	MD	USA
80	Waldo Ave	Jersey City	07306	NJ	U.S.A
50	Garrison Avenue	Jersey City	07306	New Jersey	United States
82	Waldo Ave.	Jersey City	07306	N. J.	U. S. A.

The objective of data standardization is to build uniformity in the data. Uniformity is important when handling large volumes of data records that use numerous naming conventions. *Data standardization* involves converting data elements into forms that are uniform and standard throughout the target system or data warehouse. For example, consider the address records in the first table in Figure 6.12.

In the data field *Street Address Line 2*:

- The value "Swallow Falls Court" in row 1 is the same "Swallow Falls Ct" in row 2. In other words, "Court" and "Ct" mean the same thing, with "Ct" being the abbreviated version of "Court."

- "Ave," "Ave.," and "Avenue" mean the same thing, with "Ave" and "Ave." being abbreviated versions of "Avenue."

In the data field *State*:

- MD is the abbreviated version of the state Maryland

- NJ and N.J. are abbreviated versions of the state New Jersey

In the data field *Country*, we find the following values:

- United States of America

- USA

Street address line 1	Street address line 2	City	ZIP code	State	Country
12024	Swallow Falls Court	Silver Spring	20904	Maryland	United States of America
12026	Swallow Falls Ct	Silver Spring	20904	MD	USA
80	Waldo Ave	Jersey City	07306	NJ	USA
50	Garrison Avenue	Jersey City	07306	New Jersey	United States
82	Waldo Ave.	Jersey City	07306	N.J.	U.S.A.

Street address line 1	Street address line 2	City	ZIP code	State	Country
12024	Swallow Falls Ct	Silver Spring	20904	MD	USA
12026	Swallow Falls Ct	Silver Spring	20904	MD	USA
80	Waldo Ave	Jersey City	07306	NJ	USA
50	Garrison Ave	Jersey City	07306	NJ	USA
82	Waldo Ave	Jersey City	07306	NJ	USA

Figure 6.12   Address data records prior to and after data standardization.

- U.S.A.

- United States

Each of the above values represents the same country, that is, United States of America, with United States of America being the full name and USA, U.S.A., and United States being the abridged versions.

The possible reason for these different representations is the lack of data standards and defined data formats. Data standardization would involve converting these values to a standard format, as shown in the second table in Figure 6.12.

Table 6.2 shows the original values before standardization (from first table in Figure 6.12) and the corresponding values after standardization (from the second table in Figure 6.12) side by side for data fields: Street line address 2, State, and Country.

Parsing is used in concert with a set of standardization rules triggered to transform the input data into a form that can be more effectively used, either to standardize the representation (presuming a valid representation) or to correct the values (should known errors be identified) (Loshin 2010b). Parsing and standardization can employ a library of data domains and rules to split data values into multiple components and rearrange the components into a normalized format. Standardization can also transform full words into abbreviations, or abbreviations into full words, transform nicknames into a standard name form, translate across languages (for example, Spanish to English), correct common misspellings, and reduce value variance to improve record linkage for deduplication and data cleansing (Loshin 2010b).

Data field name	Before standardization	After standardization
Street address line 2	Court	Ct
	Ct	Ct
	Avenue	Ave
	Ave.	Ave
	Ave	Ave
State	New Jersey	NJ
	N. J.	NJ
	NJ	NJ
	Maryland	MD
	MD	MD
Country	United States of America	USA
	United States	USA
	U.S.A.	USA
	USA	USA

Table 6.2 Data values before and after standardization.

Matching, Linking, and Merging

Matching is a process of identifying similar data within and across the data sources and determining whether two records represent the same thing. Given two relational tables A and B with identical schema, we say that record "a" in table A matches record "b" in table B if they refer to the same real-world entity. *Linking*, also known as *record linkage* or *data linkage*, is necessary when joining data sets based on entities that may or may not share a common identifier (for example, database key), which may be due to differences in record sizes, data types, data models, formatting conventions, abbreviations, and storage location. Matching and linking establish connectivity between similar records, and may even *merge* a pair of records into a single surviving record in preparation for data cleansing.

Business rules need to be defined to determine what constitutes a match between two records. Data matching involves matching records in different data stores or databases. A key challenge in data matching is the absence of common entity identifiers across different systems to be matched. Hence, attributes across which matching needs to be conducted need to be determined, and business rules for matching need to be defined. Matching is usually conducted using attributes that contain partially identifying information, such as names, addresses, phone numbers, e-mail IDs, or dates of birth. However, such identifying information often suffers from frequently occurring typographical variations, and can change over time or is only partially available in the sources to be matched. Another challenge is to efficiently match a large number of records; such matching is extremely time-consuming and computationally intensive.

The aim of linkage is to determine the true match status of each record pair (Harron 2016):

- *Match*. Records belong to the same individual

- *Non-match*. Records belong to different individuals

Through the linkage methods that we use, a link status is assigned to each pair (Harron 2016):

- *Link*. Records classified as belonging to the same individual

- *Non-link*. Records classified as belonging to different individuals

In a perfect linkage, all matches are classified as links, and all non-matches are classified as non-links. If record pairs are misclassified, error is introduced (Harron 2016):

- *False match*. Records from different individuals link erroneously

- *Missed match*. Records from the same individual fail to link

Deterministic linkage is a reasonably straightforward linkage method, normally requiring exact agreement on a unique identifier (such as a national insurance number) or on a specified set of partial identifiers (for example, surname, sex, and post code) (Abrahams and Davy 2002; Mears et al. 2010; Maso et al. 2001; Muse et al. 1995; Tromp et al. 2011; Yu et al. 2010; Poluzzi et al. 2011; Harron 2016). Deterministic methods are useful when records have unique (or at least highly discriminative) identifiers that are accurate and complete (Harron 2016).

Deterministic methods are designed to avoid false matches, since it is not likely that different individuals will share the same set of identifiers, even though this can arise in the case of identifier errors (Harron 2016). On the other hand, deterministic methods requiring exact agreement on identifiers are prone to missed matches, as any recording errors or missing values can prevent identifier agreement (Grannis et al. 2002; Hagger-Johnson et al. 2015; Harron 2016).

Probabilistic methods were proposed as a means of overcoming some of the limitations of deterministic linkage, and to facilitate linkage in the presence of recording errors and/or without using a unique identifier (Harron 2016). Newcombe et al. (1959) were the first to propose probabilistic methods, suggesting that a match weight could be created to represent the likelihood that two records are a true match, given agreement or disagreement on a set of partial identifiers. Fellegi and Sunter (1969) later formalized Newcombe's proposals into the statistical theory underpinning most probabilistic linkage today (Harron 2016). An alternative form of probabilistic linkage is the Copas-Hilton method, which uses statistical models to measure the evidence that records belong to the same rather than different individuals (Copas and Hilton 1990).

In the Fellegi-Sunter approach, the contribution of each identifier to the overall match weight reflects its discriminative value so that, for example, agreement on date of birth contributes more evidence of a match than agreement on sex (Zhu et al. 2009; Blakely and Salmond 2002; Sayers et al. 2015; Harron 2016). Disagreement on an identifier contributes a forfeit to the overall match weight. To classify records as links, match weights are matched with a threshold or cut-off value. The choice of threshold values is important, since adjusting the thresholds alters the balance between the number of false matches and missed matches (Krewski et al. 2005; Harron 2016).

Probabilistic linkage is more computationally intensive than deterministic linkage, but can lead to fewer missed matches as it is more tolerant to missing values and recording errors (Grannis et al. 2003; Méray et al. 2007; Gomatam et al. 2002; Harron 2016). The computational intensiveness is directly proportional to the number of comparison pairs. In practice, linkage studies frequently use a combination of deterministic and probabilistic methods, using initial deterministic steps to decrease the number of comparison pairs for subsequent probabilistic linkage (Jamieson et al. 1995). Linkage algorithms are often developed iteratively, through trial and error, manual review, linkage error rate estimation, and evaluation of linkage quality (Harron 2016).

Common data quality problems where matching and linking procedures can help include (Loshin 2007):

- Multiple data instances that in reality refer to the same real-world entity

- The perception by an analyst or application that a record does not exist for a real-world entity, when in fact it actually does

In the first case, similar yet somewhat different representations of data values exist in the systems. For example, the following three records probably represent the same person:

Sue Terrence McKinnon 12024 Swallow Falls Court Silver Spring 20904 Maryland USA	**S. McKinnon** 12024 Swallow Falls Ct Colesville 20904 MD USA

Terrence McKinnon 12024 Swallow Falls Ct Colesville 20904 MD USA

In the second case, a small variation in representation prevents the identification of an exact match of the existing record in the data set. For example, say the analyst is searching for Sue McKinnon who lives in Silver Spring, Maryland, but the record that actually represents "Sue McKinnon" looks like the following record; it will be difficult for the analyst to identify this record.

```
Terrence McKinnon
12024 Swallow Falls Ct
Colesville
20904
MD
USA
```

Both of these issues can be addressed by the probabilistic linkage method known as *similarity analysis* in which the degree of similarity between any two records is scored, most often based on weighted approximate matching between a set of attribute values in the two records. If the score is above a specific threshold, the two records are deemed to be a match and are presented to the end client as most likely representing the same entity. Similarity analysis detects slight variations in the data values, and connects and subsequently consolidates the data values. Endeavoring to compare each record against all the other records to provide a similarity score is extremely time-consuming and computationally intensive. Most data quality tool suites use advanced algorithms for blocking records that are most likely to contain matches into smaller sets, whereupon different approaches are taken to measure similarity. Identification of similar records within the same data set probably means that the records are duplicated, and may be subjected to cleansing and/or elimination (Loshin 2007). Identifying similar records in different sets may indicate a link across the data sets, which helps facilitate cleansing and merging them into a single data set.

Quality of linkage ultimately depends on the quality of the data participating in the linkage. If data sets contained sufficiently accurate, complete, and discriminative information, data linkage would be a straightforward database-merging process. For linkage to be successful, it is important that data from different data sets are cleaned and standardized in the same way (Harron 2016).

Data Enrichment or Data Augmentation

Data enrichment, also known as *data augmentation* or *data enhancement*, is the final step in improving the quality of data. Missing or incomplete data can lead to lost business opportunities or additional expenditures. For example, incomplete address data with missing postal or ZIP code fields or states, or missing e-mail addresses, may prevent an organization from reaching out to potential customers during a marketing campaign, leading to lost sales. Data enrichment involves enhancing the value of internally held data by incorporating additional related data attributes from an organization's internal and external data sources not directly related to the base data (for example, consumer demographic attributes or geographic descriptors).

Data enrichment is common with customer data and address data, where additional information can help provide more in-depth insight into the data, reduce the manual intervention required to derive meaningful information and understanding, and considerably enhance data quality. A common example of data enhancement is using a country's postal service's master address database to append useful demographic postal data such as postal codes/ZIP codes, districts, counties, and so on. This can greatly increase address integrity, as well as provide a basis for additional applications such as geocoding, mapping, and other visualization technologies that require a valid address as a starting point (Fisher 2002).

For example, Figure 6.13 illustrates the data set field values before and after data enrichment using the US Postal Service address data. As seen in the figure, the middle name, ZIP code, and county were missing in the data set before data enrichment. After the data enrichment exercise, these fields are populated.

Some of the common techniques used in data enrichment include extrapolation, tagging, aggregation, and probability techniques, as shown in Figure 6.14. The *extrapolation* technique is based on heuristics, with the relevant fields updated or provided with values. In the *tagging* technique, common records are tagged to a group, making it easier

Before data enrichment

Field name	Field values
First name	Carol
Middle name	
Last name	Pascale
House number	80
Street name	Waldo
Street type	Avenue
City	Jersey City
Zip code	
County	
State	New Jersey
Country	United States of America

After data enrichment

Field name	Field values
First name	Carol
Middle name	Mary
Last name	Pascale
House number	80
Street name	Waldo
Street type	Avenue
City	Jersey City
Zip code	07306
County	Hudson
State	New Jersey
Country	United States of America

Figure 6.13   Data enrichment example.

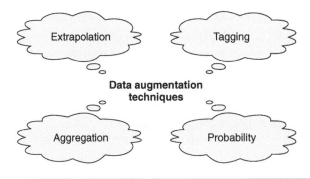

Figure 6.14   Data augmentation techniques.

to understand and differentiate for the group. The *aggregation* technique utilizes mathematical values of averages and means, where values are estimated for relevant fields if needed. The *probability* technique is based on heuristics and analytical statistics, with values being populated based on the probability of events (Technopedia Undated).

DATA VALIDATION

Data validation is a reactive approach to reducing bad data from entering the system, even though it does not address the root cause of the data quality issue. Data validation ensures that the data (whether user-input variables, read from a file, or read from a database) comply with the data quality requirements and benchmarks and that the data sent to connected systems or applications are complete, correct, valid, and consistent. Data validation is accomplished by incorporating rules and validation checks that consistently check for the validity of data by comparing the data against the predefined validation rules. Some of the types of data validation include format validation, lookup validation, data type validation, range validation, and presence check validation. The more robust the data validation checks, the less is the likelihood of bad data entering the system.

Presence Check Validation

Presence check validation is the simplest method of validation, which checks that the field has data and has not been left blank. Presence checks are used on important data fields that must have data entered into them.

Format Validation

Certain data fields like telephone number, mobile number, social security number, and UPC code have a specific input format or pattern that should be adhered to when entered and when read to assure that the right information is read from the user and written to file and table. Masked or filtered input allows only valid characters to be entered in an otherwise all-open data type, in this case, a *string*. Generally, masked input is present to give the user an indication of the type of data value required by guiding them through the process of entering the value in a field. For example, if a date is expected in a given field value, a pop-up calendar can be set up to let the user pick the date to be entered visually, thereby making it impossible for the user to enter an invalid date (Richard Undated).

Range Validation

Certain attributes can have a range or domain of values, and range validation ensures that the value entered is within the range. For example, salary and age cannot be negative numbers.

Lookup Validation

Typically, this type of validation is done when a value entered needs to be compared to a list of possible values.

Data Type Validation

Data type validation checks that the data provided through user input is of the correct data type. For example, annual income should be a numeric value.

Data validation, in order to be as successful as it can be, must be implemented at all points of the data flow chain that receive data, process the data, and save or print the results. It is important to embed data validation techniques in processes that involve data capture, migration, or integration as a part of routines reading from or writing to a file or database or exporting or importing data between different systems and applications. The different points of data validation include data entry screens and forms, and files or database manipulation routines. Any part of an application that requires the user to enter data through data fields on a data entry screen should be taken into account from a data validation perspective, as they are the most susceptible to human error.

Data validation checks can reveal specific quality problems. Depending on the problems, one of the following four options can be chosen (Geiger 2004):

- *Reject the data*. If the problem with the data is deemed to be severe, the best approach may be to reject the data and capture the data in a reject file, which would later be analyzed for a course of action.

- *Accept the data*. If the errors are within tolerance limits, the best approach sometimes is to accept the data with the error. This would usually be driven by the context of data usage.

- *Correct the data*. When different variations of a customer name are encountered, one of them could be selected to be the master so that the data can be consolidated.

- *Insert a default value*. Sometimes, it is important to have a value for a field even when we're unsure of the correct value. We could create a default value (for example, *unknown*) and insert that value in the field.

The specific validation approach taken may differ for each data element, and the decision on the approach needs to be made by the line of business or the department responsible for the data. It is also important to note that while the data quality activity improves the quality of the data that already exist, it does not address the root cause of the data problems. If the enterprise is truly interested in improving data quality, it must also investigate the reasons why the data contained the errors and initiate appropriate actions, including incentives and changes to business procedures to improve future data (Geiger 2004).

DATA QUALITY MONITORING

The data sets stored in the data repositories, databases, or data warehouses are not static, but are being continuously updated, added, archived, deleted, or purged. Data quality monitoring involves checking a set of data records in the tables against a set of defined data quality rules at regular intervals, and displaying results on a data quality dashboard. If one or more data quality rules are violated, the violation would be reflected on the data quality dashboard, and alerts would be issued in case of data quality issues. This enables detecting and investigating issues quickly, notifying the appropriate people, and initiating remediation procedures before the bad data accumulate.

Data quality monitoring provides insight into the quality of critical data elements crucial for business functions or decision making at any point in time. Data quality monitoring comes at a cost; hence, data quality monitoring is not used to track the quality of all data and systems, but only the critical data elements. Business requirements, along with the criticality of data, drive data quality monitoring requirements. The data quality monitoring requirements—including the points and frequency of the data quality monitoring, data quality rules to execute, the mode of monitoring (manual versus automated), the acceptable data quality and error thresholds, the exceptions and the required notifications and alerts, and mode of notification (for example, e-mail, phone call)—are determined by the business requirements and expectations. Figure 6.15 shows the various

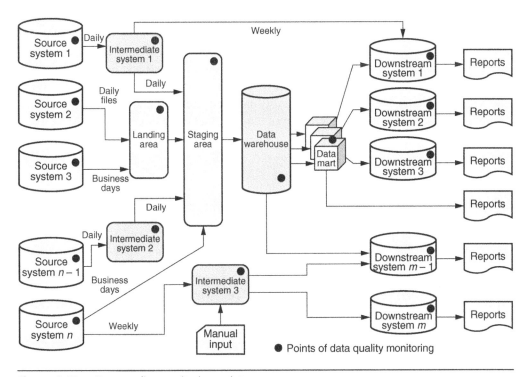

Figure 6.15 Data quality monitoring points.

possible points of data quality monitoring. Data owners and stewards are responsible for defining their data quality monitoring requirements in conjunction with IT. Generally, data sources (where the data are first captured) and target systems (critical data elements in data warehouses and master data repositories) are points for data quality monitoring. Data quality rules may be reused from the data quality assessment phase or may need to be redefined. Data quality monitoring may be automated or manual or a combination of both. Automated data quality monitoring would involve having data quality rules embedded in routines and running the routines at intervals agreed on with the business. Manual data quality monitoring may involve running SQL queries on the data tables or procuring data samples and loading them into spreadsheets for analysis purposes. Once the data quality monitoring requirements are defined, IT designs and codes the data quality rules into automated routines and deploys them in production. In the case of a tactical manual approach, the data quality rules would be implemented using Excel spreadsheets or SQL queries depending on the business requirements and complexity. Processes and accountabilities need to be defined for communicating and resolving issues discovered as a result of data quality monitoring.

DATA MIGRATION AND DATA QUALITY

Data migration or *data conversion* projects deal with the migration of data from one data structure to another data structure or transformed from one platform to another platform with a modified data structure. Figure 6.16 shows the high-level view of the data migration process. In Chapter 1, "Data, Data Quality, and Cost of Poor Data Quality" we saw that data conversion projects are one of the causes of bad data quality, with the target system often having suboptimal data quality after data conversion or migration. This is because the source data quality is not taken into consideration, and data migration is often seen as a simple chore of loading data from one system into another,

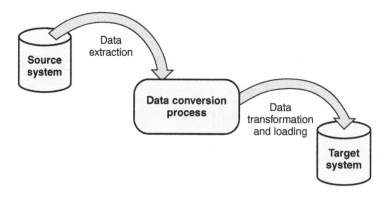

Figure 6.16   Data migration/conversion process.

without comprehending the underlying challenges. Data conversion is perceived as a purely technical exercise that just requires a good technical tool to accomplish the task.

However, data migration is complex, and complexity arises from little or no common structures between the source systems and target systems. The migration process becomes even more complicated when source systems are legacy applications. This is because source data can become corrupted in a way that is not always visible in the legacy applications. Legacy systems rarely have complete specifications, and the embedded business rules and changes are not documented well, if documented at all. There is usually a huge gap between the legacy data model and actual legacy data. Data fields are overloaded, which makes one-to-one mapping between the source and target system data elements not possible for these fields.

According to a study conducted by Experian (2017), 44% of US organizations say that data quality issues caused delays for their migration projects. Data quality issues that may not have been conspicuous in the source systems (which hold the data to be migrated) because of workarounds or system shortcomings, become obvious when trying to transfer data from the source to the new target system. Poor data quality slows down the entire migration process, and sometimes, bad data will be outright rejected by the new system as newer technologies often have stricter standards surrounding the quality of data entering the system (Experian 2017).

Usually, the target systems have different data models, data architectures, and data structures from the source systems that require data to be formatted or transformed in a certain way so as to meet the data structure and formatting requirements in the target system. Data standardization would ensure consistency and would enable data to be migrated using consistent transformation in the format acceptable by the target system. However, data in the source systems may not have data standards, so that there are multiple formats in the source data, which creates complications in data migration as a single transformation or formatting rule cannot be used when migrating a data element from the source system to the target system.

Migrating bad-quality data not only causes data quality issues in the target system, but in many circumstances also leads to all sorts of issues during the migration, preventing the data from being loaded in the target system by the automated migration software solution. The data that do not meet the minimum quality requirement of the target system will not be loaded into the target system and be rejected as error records. These records have to be dealt with manually. They either need to be manually entered into the target system or manually corrected in the source system before they can be picked up by the automated migration software solution.

As pointed out by Experian, migrating data from one system to another can be thought of in similar terms with moving from one house to another. When you move houses, you go through your stuff and see what is old and no longer of use to you, and hence would not be worthwhile taking to the new house. You might want to reorganize furniture and other items. You have two beds in one bedroom in your old house, but you might want to place them in two separate bedrooms in your new house. Your old house did not have a storeroom, and you had to store your suitcase in the wardrobe in the bedroom. But your new house has a storeroom, and you can store all the suitcases in the storeroom. You need to carefully plan and sort through your stuff and take into account the structure of your new house before moving houses. Similarly, you need to go through your data, as well as the structure and specifications of both the source and target systems, before moving the data from one system to another. Without a sufficient understanding of both source and target, transferring data into a more sophisticated application will amplify the negative impact of any incorrect or irrelevant data, perpetuate any hidden legacy problems, and increase exposure to risk (Oracle 2011). Ensuring the quality and migration readiness of the data to be migrated is essential for a data migration project to be successful and the data in the target system to be of high quality.

How to Ensure Data Quality in Data Migration Projects

The scope of the migration project and source systems and target system involved in the data migration need to be established early on in the project. This is because not all source data elements would need to be migrated, and the data that do not need to be migrated do not need to be assessed for quality purposes. Once the scope is established, the core source tables and/or files need to be identified for data profiling purposes. It is important to understand the source system data at a data field level. The source system data model, data structures, specifications, and business rules need to be understood correctly by reviewing existing documentation and validating with the technology and business subject matter experts. Often, legacy systems do not have supporting documentation, in which case subject matter experts, who are normally the business users and operational support team members, need to be actively engaged and consulted to understand the business rules and what the data actually represent. It is the subject matter experts who understand the actual meaning and value behind the data, and the operational support team who know how the data are stored in the fields and the coding logic behind the data. In legacy systems there is often overloading of fields, which means that data in a particular field is not meant for one business purpose. However, this information is not documented, hence, it is only the technology people who support the legacy system that have knowledge of these kinds of details.

Data Quality Assessment

A detailed data quality assessment of data in all the source systems involved in a data migration project needs to be carried out to understand the underlying data quality and data dependencies. This would typically involve getting access to the data first. Getting access can be an issue if data are sensitive, and hence needs to be planned and accounted for. Data profiling tools should be used to understand the data patterns, data anomalies, and errors in the source system data and the relationships between the data, as using manual methods can be time-consuming and not as effective. The source system data profiling will reveal the current state of the data assets.

The subject matter experts and system experts need to be consulted to get a true understanding of the underlying data and business scenarios that the data represent. As per Ted Friedman, an analyst with Gartner:

> What they need to do is analyze the legacy sources early in the migration effort—measure the levels of quality and identify the quality flaws that will cause the new system to experience issues. Then make the decision of whether to clean up the issues at the legacy sources or while data is being migrated from old to new.
>
> This requires heavy involvement by the business and not just its IT department, Friedman continues, explaining that the business executives know what qualifies as good enough in terms of data quality (Prince 2008).

It is also important to understand the target system data model and data structure, business requirements of the target system that will hold the migrated data, and what data are critical. Since data are migrated from the source system to the target system to support the target system business functions, the data quality needs to be assessed in line with target system data and business requirements. The detailed current state assessment at the data field level and understanding of the target system data requirements, along with input from the business stakeholders and subject matter experts should help you arrive at the following:

- Is current source systems data quality good enough for business consumption?

- What data field values are outdated and therefore will be of no use in the target system?

- Which data fields have anomalies or errors and need cleansing?

- Which data elements require enrichment?

- What is the source data formatting and representation, and how does it differ from that of the requirements of the target system?

- To what extent are data values missing?

- What data are duplicated and would need deduplication?

- Will the existing data be sufficient to support the business objectives of the data migration?

- What additional data are required?

- What are the security requirements surrounding the data?

Both technology and business subject matter experts of the source system and target system need to be actively involved in the source data quality assessments so as to have a correct and comprehensive understanding of the source data and data gaps between the source and target system to help creation of the correct data transformation rules for data migration.

Data Cleansing Approach

Data quality issues discovered would need to be documented in a data quality issues register, along with the risks and impacts. Generally, the data issues need to be fixed for the data involved in migration. In other words, data would need to be cleaned. The main objective of data cleansing is to ensure that the target systems receive data that are accurate, complete, valid, and consistent; in other words, the target data quality should be adequate and fit for purpose. There are different cleansing approaches to cleaning source system data:

- Cleanse data in the source systems
- Cleanse data during the staging process
- Cleanse data in-flight using coding logic
- Cleanse after migrating data into the target system

Cleanse Data in the Source Systems. In this approach, all the data quality issues are fixed in the source systems before migration. Solving issues in the legacy system can be highly beneficial because you're not only improving data quality for the planned target system, you're giving value back to the current users of the system (Jones 2016). However, the challenge with source system cleansing is that since data cleansing populates new values or alters existing data values in the source systems, conducting this operation without conducting an impact analysis can cause upstream or downstream process failures. Hence, a detailed impact analysis as to how data are accessed from the upstream systems, stored, and processed in the source system environments, and how the data feed into the downstream systems, needs to be carried out before taking up the approach of cleansing data in the source systems. In the case of legacy systems this is not an easy task; updating legacy systems is a manual effort requiring someone going into screens for hundreds or thousands of records. This could be a time-consuming and expensive undertaking (Novak 2015).

Cleanse Data During the Staging Process. The approach of cleansing data in the staging area relies on a kind of "halfway house" where data reside and can be preprocessed before migration (Jones 2016). It allows you to modify the legacy data into structures that closely resemble the target environment so that the final load can be validated and uploaded more easily. However, the issue here is that it is difficult to track the manual changes made in the staging area. It has always been important to track changes to legacy data, but with increasing demands for regulatory compliance, there are often legal implications around lineage and provenance of data to consider too (Jones 2016).

Cleanse Data In-Flight Using Coding Logic. In this approach, cleansing routines and lookups are embedded within the transformation logic of the migration code to handle the bad data scenarios as the data are being migrated; this is the most recommended option. The drawback of this type of cleansing is that the business focuses on what needs to happen to get the data into the target system and does not always think through the full ramifications of the automated rule. That being said, the benefits far outweigh the negative of slightly less focus from the business. The largest benefits are that logical rules are usually easy to implement and, once they're set up, the team does not need to worry about them (Novak 2015). While automated cleansing as data are being migrated is the recommended option, it is not always feasible. For example, there might be duplicate records in the source system, but a common rule cannot be set for which record to load in the target system. In this case the records that need to be loaded in the target system need to be manually loaded after confirmation from the business.

Cleanse after Migrating Data into the Target System. While some data can be cleansed in the target system, correcting all the data in the target system is definitely not a recommended approach as it would cause major business disruptions. Cleansing the data post migration can be pricier compared to cleaning the data prior to migrating the data into the target system, specifically if the target system is not designed to allow merging and deduplication. Also, trying to load the data without prior cleaning can cause a lot of records to be rejected.

An impact analysis needs to be carried out with the active participation of the target and source system business and IT stakeholders before deciding on how to proceed with cleaning the data. Generally, a combination of manual and automated routines and a combination of two or more of the cleansing approaches would be needed to cleanse the data. Figure 6.17 shows the data migration process with data cleansing options.

Solution Design—Data Mapping

In data migration, *data mapping*, or *source-to-target mapping*, involves looking at the source system data fields and comparing them to the target data fields, and then linking the fields in the source systems to the fields in the target systems, plus defining the

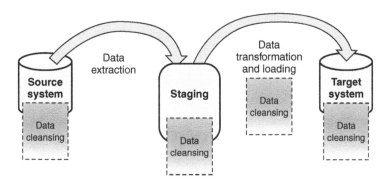

Figure 6.17   Possible data cleansing options in data migration.

mapping rules, which can be a combination of transformation logic and rules for cleansing data and data enrichment rules, if applicable. At this point, inconsistencies between legacy and target fields need to be taken into account while designing the data transformation rules for mapping between the source and target fields. For example, the lengths of string fields may not match, or the target column includes a set of domain values that are not applicable to the corresponding source system data field. However, data mapping should not be based on field names and data types alone; the data content or values should also be taken into account when creating mapping rules. Data mapping typically involves resolving discrepancies between the source data value and the format specified for its target field by transforming the source field value into a new value. For example, in the source system the gender field is a string field that can hold up to 10 characters and has any the following values:

- Male

- Female

- M

- F

However, in the target system, the gender field is a single-character field that can only hold the characters "M" or "F," "M" being indicative of *male* and "F" being indicative of *female*. The transformation rule should be designed so that the source value "Male" is transformed to "M" and "Female" is transformed to "F."

Data conversion may require splitting a source data field into two or more target data fields, or merging two or more source data fields into one target data field, depending on how data are stored in the source system and the data model in the target system. One common example where splitting is required is in the case of name and address data. The source system has the full name with the title in a single field whereas the target system has separate fields for title, first name, middle name, and last name. The source system has the entire address in one field whereas the target system has separate fields for street address, city, postal code, state, and country.

Subject matter experts and business users need to be actively consulted during the field level mapping exercise, and source-to-target mapping needs to be documented with source field names, target field names, the transformation logic rules, cleansing rule, and enrichment rules, and the reasons for the mapping. This document is called the *data mapping* document and should have the level of detail and clarity necessary to be passed to a developer for coding purposes in a data migration tool. The data mapping document should be understood, reviewed, and signed off by the business stakeholders before the coding phase.

Any interface designs that are required to extract the data from the source systems or to load the data into the target systems should be agreed on, documented, and signed off by the source system and target system stakeholders. This document is called the *interface specification* document.

Coding, Testing, and Implementation

Once requirements have been finalized and the data mapping document has been signed off, the design can be converted into code. Data migration typically consists of extraction, transform, and load programs that extract data from the source systems into the staging area, apply transformation, cleansing, and enrichment logic as defined in the data mapping document, and load the transformed data into the target system. There are two approaches to data extraction: "push" or "pull." In the *push* approach, the source system makes a copy of the data and places it on the target system servers. In the *pull* approach, specific extract routines, usually in the target system environment, are written to extract data from the source system. Most specialized extraction applications are efficient at extracting data from relational databases, either with generic SQL adapters or with specialized adapters for the particular database management system (DBMS). However, many of these tools struggle with the oddities inherent in mainframe file structures, such as a COBOL REDEFINES (a COmmon Business-Oriented Language structure in which various data attributes may be present) and other specific data storage technology structures (Reeve 2013). In such cases, the better option is to have the source system support staff create an extract and place the extract file on the target system server.

After the data migration coding is done, the code needs to be tested in development and/or testing environments before being moved into production for upload into the actual target systems. It is advisable to test the data migration by using a copy of recent production data rather than a small data set. This will result in most issues being discovered during testing and fewer problems during the data migration execution in the production environment and post-production. Once testing is completed, data are migrated in the production environment. Any data that fail to meet the validation criteria of the target system are marked as rejected and can be manually corrected and reprocessed.

Data Migration Assessment

Once data are migrated to the target system, the data quality in the target system needs to be assessed. Any data quality issues along the different data quality dimensions need to be assessed. Data quality issues in the target system may be due to coding issues, that is, issues introduced by faulty migration code or because of source system data quality issues that have not been cleansed.

Completeness is assessment of whether all the records in scope have been migrated to the target system. When data are actually loaded into the target system, there will be records that have issues and will get rejected. *Error handling* is about properly following up on errors and rejected records that could not be loaded into the target system during the data migration, and taking remediation actions to ensure that all the required data entities are migrated completely and correctly into the target systems.

Figure 6.18 summarizes the steps involved in the data migration process to ensure data quality.

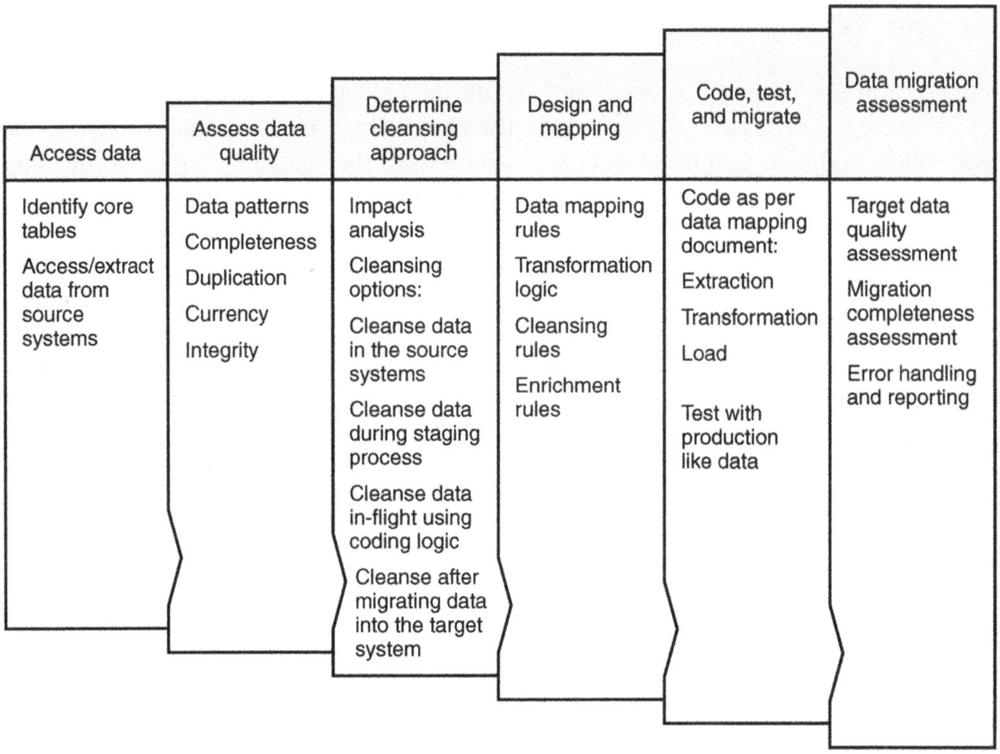

Access data	Assess data quality	Determine cleansing approach	Design and mapping	Code, test, and migrate	Data migration assessment
Identify core tables Access/extract data from source systems	Data patterns Completeness Duplication Currency Integrity	Impact analysis Cleansing options: Cleanse data in the source systems Cleanse data during staging process Cleanse data in-flight using coding logic Cleanse after migrating data into the target system	Data mapping rules Transformation logic Cleansing rules Enrichment rules	Code as per data mapping document: Extraction Transformation Load Test with production like data	Target data quality assessment Migration completeness assessment Error handling and reporting

Figure 6.18   Data migration and data quality.

Data Migration Technology

The underlying source system and target system architectures and data structures, and differences between them, the amount of cleansing required and the cleansing approach should be taken into consideration when selecting the technology or tool for data migration. The differences between the source and target systems include incongruities in terms of data types supported, data representation and format discrepancies, maximum field lengths allowed, and so on. The technology options include custom-built solutions, data integration tools, or hybrid solutions. Modern extract, transform, and load (ETL) tools are flexible and provide comprehensive data integration capabilities, making them a good technology solution option. A lot of these tools offer integrated development environments that speed up the development process and scripting/reusability for substantial customization.

DATA INTEGRATION AND DATA QUALITY

Data integration is the process of combining data from multiple heterogeneous data sources so as to provide users with an integrated and complete view of all the data. Figure

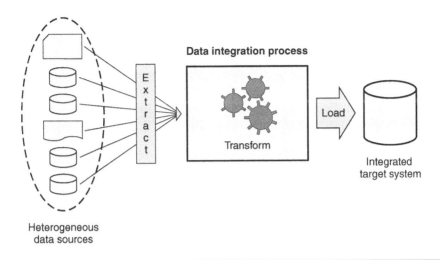

Figure 6.19   Data integration process.

6.19 provides the high-level overview of data integration. The general objective of data integration is to combine data related to different business processes that, when originally captured, may have been placed in discrete silos managed by different business units and stakeholders, that have little consistent interaction with each other, causing a lack of shared or actionable insight, which in turn can result in unexploited opportunities for the enterprise. Data integration helps to unite these information silos, thus enabling the organization to take a holistic approach when making strategic decisions. Data integration becomes increasingly important in the case of merger of two companies.

Data integration is important in building and implementing a data warehouse. Data are fed from multiple heterogeneous sources into the data warehouse, which provides users with a single physical corporate image.

Ted Friedman, a Gartner vice president and information management analyst said that "organizations cannot be successful in their data integration work unless they have a very strong focus on data quality built in. That's because it's not only about delivering stuff from here to there. You also have to make sure you're delivering the right stuff" (Miglin 2012).

Data Integration Challenges

The major issues that make integrating data difficult are heterogeneity and autonomy of data sources (Tatbul et al. 2001):

- *Heterogeneity of data sources.* Each data source might have a different data model and data structure. Integrating data represented in different data models and data structures with data of similar semantics having different terminologies across different data sources can be challenging. Data in the different data sources may be inconsistent. In addition, heterogeneity may also occur at lower levels, including access methods, underlying operating systems, and so on (Tatbul et al. 2001).

• *Autonomy of data sources.* Data sources are independent elements that are not designed for data integration. They cannot be forced to act in certain ways. As a natural consequence of this, they can also change their data or functionality unannounced (Tatbul et al. 2001).

The operational systems and applications that capture data related to different business processes serve as data sources for data integration. Data can be sourced from different sources like mainframe files, non-relational databases, relational databases, indexed flat files, proprietary tapes, and card-based systems. Usually, an organization's computing environment has a multitude of these systems. These systems were built without any consideration for integration with other data, and application and system designers made their own design decisions for the creation and enhancement of these systems. Hence, there is no consistency in encoding, naming conventions, data representations and formats, data fields, measurement of attributes, and so on, across these systems. Duplicate data may reside in multiple source systems.

While data in the individual systems might have quality issues along the different data quality dimensions discussed in Chapter 3, since data integration involves combining data from these sources and having them in a common format in the target system, schema integration and data quality issues along the inconsistency and redundancy data quality dimensions pose a significant challenge, and should be taken into consideration and analyzed before data integration. In addition, timeliness, granularity, and how the data are captured in the source systems should be taken into consideration when implementing data integration. We will discuss each of these items in detail.

Schema Integration. Heterogeneous data sources involved in data integration generally have different schemas with different naming conventions. For example, we had to integrate accounts for different products that were stored in different data sources in a financial services institution. The account number was named Account_Number in one data source, Acc_No in the second data source, Account_no in the third data source, and Account_ID in the fourth data source. Since there were no data definitions or metadata available for any of these data sources and the data representation was different in each system, we had to seek subject matter experts for each system and confirm that all these different field names actually represented the same real-world entity attribute.

Data mining algorithms can be used to discern the inherent information about the semantics of the data structures of the data sources. Often, the true meaning of a data field cannot be comprehended from its name and data type. The task of reconstructing the meaning of attributes would be optimally supported by dependency modeling using data mining techniques, and mapping this model against expert knowledge (Kalinka and Kaloyanova 2005), for example, business models and validation by subject matter experts. Association rules are suited for this purpose. Other data mining techniques, for example, classification tree and rule induction, and statistical methods (for example, multivariate regression and probabilistic networks) can also produce useful hypotheses in this context (Kalinka and Kaloyanova 2005).

Many data field values are encoded. One real-world attribute that is usually encoded is gender. In one system, *gender* might have the values "0" for *male* and "1" for *female*, respectively. In another system, the gender value *male* is represented as "Male" and *female* is represented as "Female." In another system, the gender *male* is encoded as "M" and *female* is encoded as "F." Identifying inter-field dependencies helps to construct hypotheses about encoding schemes when the semantics of some data fields are known. Also, encoding schemes change over time. Data mining algorithms are useful in identifying changes in encoding schemes, the time when they took place, and the part of the code that is affected. Methods that use data sets to train a "normal" behavior can be adapted to the task. The model can then be used to evaluate significant changes (Kalinka and Kaloyanova 2005).

Data mining and statistical methods can be used to induce integrity constraint candidates from the data. These include, for example, visualization methods to identify distributions for finding domains of attributes, or methods for dependency modeling. Other data mining methods can find intervals of attribute values that are rather compact and cover a high percentage of the existing values (Kalinka and Kaloyanova 2005).

To a certain degree, data mining methods can be used to identify and resolve different kinds of structural and semantic conflicts across different data sources. Data mining methods can discover functional relationships between different databases when they are not too complex. A linear regression method would discover the corresponding conversion factors. If the type of functional dependency (linear, quadratic, exponential, and so on) is a priori not known, model search instead of parameter search needs to be applied (Kalinka and Kaloyanova 2005).

Redundancy. Redundant data is a massive problem when integrating multiple data source systems. The same real-world entity or attribute may be present in different data source systems but named differently, as discussed in the "Schema Integration" section above. An attribute may be redundant if it is a derived attribute, that is, its value can be derived from another attribute, for example, *annual revenue*. In addition to redundancies between attributes, redundancies can be detected at the record level, where there are two or more identical records for a unique data entry case. Redundancies can be detected by correlation analysis and covariance analysis. For example, given two attributes, such analysis can measure how strongly one attribute implies the other, based on available data (Kalinka and Kaloyanova 2005).

Inconsistency. Data being redundant in the different data sources and data being represented in different formats and encoded differently in different systems results in another common data issue: data inconsistency. We have discussed data inconsistency in detail in Chapter 3, "Data Quality Dimensions." When data values are inconsistent, a decision needs to be made on which value to use when populating the target system. This is governed by the business requirements, and a subject matter expert needs to be consulted.

The absence of structure, formats, and definitions of integrated data leads to issues such as inconsistent data and data that do not meet reasonable expectations. The data integration should be governed to ensure that data formats, definitions, and standards are defined for the integrated data so as to minimize data inconsistency issues in the target system. Defining data standards can address the challenge of inconsistency, especially aligning data element definitions and semantics. When key stakeholders from across the enterprise participate in a review and approval process for proposed data standards, there is a degree of confidence that the standards will be defined so that the collected downstream data consumer requirements will be observed (Loshin 2010b).

Timeliness. The frequency and timing of data population typically varies among the different source systems, as each system has been designed to meet their own specific business requirements. Some source systems may be populated on a daily basis, some twice per day, or some on a weekly basis. The time of the day when data become available in the source systems also varies. When integrating data, the order in which data from different source systems are integrated into the target system, and their timeliness, need to be taken into consideration to avoid data quality issues in the destination. This is because while data quality in the source system may be good, failing to populate the data in the correct order and in a timely manner in the target system would cause issues in the target system. For example, loan account creation and account modification transactions (loan top-up transactions) in a financial services company reside in different source systems, respectively, that are populated at different times every day, with loan account modification transactions being available before loan account creation transactions. The loan account creation and modification transactions need to be present in the target system on the following business day by 2 p.m. for downstream systems to run reports required by the business users. However, when you integrate loan account creation and account modification transactions into the target system, the loan account creation transaction should be populated before any loan account modification transaction for a particular account, as in the real world an account cannot be modified before an account is created. Hence, the loan account creation transaction load into the target system should be scheduled prior to the loan account modification transaction load. Account modification transactions being populated before account creation transactions in the target system would not provide a correct picture of the data, even through the source data are fine. Also, what should be taken into consideration is the time window when the data should be available in the target system, and service level agreements should be established to ensure the availability of the data by the agreed-on time.

Granularity. The grain of the same entity may be different in the different source systems and target systems. This should be taken into account when analyzing source data for data integration. For example, a project that I worked on involved loan account transactions. In the case of the loan account creation and modification transactions, the business requirement was to capture the employee and account relationship information in a table in the target system on a daily basis; that is, the employee ID of the employee who created the loan account and the employee ID of the employee that created a top-up to the loan account needed to be captured for different loan products. The data source that held the loan account creation data provided the data on the employee–account creation level, with one record for each account ID and the corresponding employee who created the account and the product category, and was of the same grain as that required in the target table. However, data analysis of the source system table containing the account modification data revealed that the data were stored at a transaction level and were of a different grain when compared to that required for population in the target table, and had several records with account ID and employee ID with additional details like amount, transaction category, and transaction type. Following are two questions that needed to be addressed to populate the correct employee–account modification (top-up) relation record in the target table:

- How to identify the transaction record that was a top-up transaction?

- In the case of multiple top-up records created by different employees on the same day, which record or records would need to be extracted from the source system table for population in the target table, and what criteria would be used for extraction?

The above questions were addressed by involving the business SMEs and users who had the best knowledge as to the purpose of data usage and the best understanding of the source system data and source system IT SMEs who had a good knowledge of the source system technicalities.

Data Capture in the Source System. The manner in which the data are captured and stored in the different source system tables needs to be analyzed. Data might be incremental, or a snapshot, or might be a full load in the source system. While loading data for the first time into the target generally comprises a full load, the consecutive loads are usually *delta*, or *differential*, loads. Depending on the business requirement, transformation logic, and the technical algorithm used, a data extract might be a full or partial data extract loaded into the staging area for further processing and transformation before a subset of the data set or the entire data set is loaded into the target system. With an incremental load, usually there is a date or date-time stamp that can be used to identify the new or modified data. With snapshot data, however, the entire transaction history is stored along with the new transaction. Hence, to find the differential data, or the delta, the current snapshot needs to be compared to the previous snapshot.

Data integration, like data migration, is perceived as a technical exercise that involves extract, transform, and load (ETL) tools only. While technology and ETL tools are critical, data integration involves more than just ETL tools. Before implementing any data integration initiative, it is important to understand the different, disparate source system data models, data structures, metadata, and data content that would participate in the data integration, and the impact in terms of target data quality when the data elements from these different source systems are integrated as per the data integration business requirements.

Typical business application development considers the collection of data requirements as subsidiary to the functional requirements analysis process (Loshin 2010b). As enterprise projects such as data integration, data warehousing, and customer relationship management cross departmental and line-of-business boundaries, there is a need for a well-defined process for soliciting, documenting, and combining the collected data expectations that all downstream business users have, and then translate those expectations into data requirements to be imposed on all candidate data sources. When implementing a data integration initiative it is important to understand the business requirements of all stakeholders first, and the data requirements needed to meet these business requirements. This would typically involve understanding what data are required for data integration, and quality requirements for the data, by actively involving the business stakeholders of the source systems and target system. Not only does this impose a radical transformation in requirements gathering, it also requires the kind of oversight provided by a data governance infrastructure (Loshin 2010b).

Once the data requirements are understood and data sources are identified, it is important to locate and access the tables/files in the data sources that contain the required data for data profiling and analysis purposes. This would require active involvement of the source system IT and business stakeholders and target system stakeholders. It is essential to document all the business requirements and data requirements and link data requirements to business requirements; this document should be made available to all the stakeholders.

The source data need to be profiled to understand the current state of their quality. Most organizations take only minimal steps to understand or "profile" the data, with the result that errors are discovered much later, either just before data integration or after data integration. Figure 6.20 illustrates this situation, where you enter a never-ending vicious circle of starting data integration, then discovering data quality issues, fixing the data quality issues, and then again restarting on data integration, only to again discover issues (Mahanti 2014).

Data quality needs to be assessed across multiple source systems. The results of the data profiling need to be discussed with the source system stakeholders to understand whether there is a data quality issue or it is a valid business scenario. Sometimes data that correspond to a valid business scenario in the source system might result in data quality issues if populated in the target system tables. For example, when analyzing the employee–loan account creation relationship source data extract, we discovered a significant number of records that had a value of "00000000" for employee ID, which is not a valid employee ID. Questioning the source system subject matter experts revealed that accounts created online and not at a branch by an employee had the value "00000000" for employee ID, which was a valid scenario. However, since the target table was meant to store account–employee relationship records, the accounts not created by employees were not meant to be stored in this table and hence needed to be filtered out and not loaded into the target table.

The gap between the current data quality and the required data quality needs to be measured, and root cause analysis needs to be conducted. Data would need to be cleansed using data cleansing techniques, discussed earlier in this chapter in the "Data

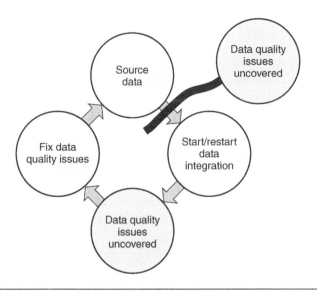

Figure 6.20 Data integration without profiling data first.
Source: Adapted from Mahanti (2014).

Cleansing" section, before data can be loaded into the target system. Since data integration is not a one-time exercise, data quality issues need to be prevented proactively, if possible. The root cause analysis results and major causes need to be analyzed with the business stakeholders, and preventive solutions need to be implemented to reduce or eliminate the data quality issue. Usually, a tactical solution involving data cleansing is put in place until the strategic improvement or preventive solution is implemented and is in place.

The data integration process must be documented from both technology and business perspectives, and reviewed by technology and business subject matter experts and made available to everyone building and using the data systems. The IT jargon, system-specific transformations, and technical details should be translated into a form and language business users can understand. A data mapping or source-to-target mapping needs to be created by documenting the mapping between source and target data elements and the transformation rules.

It is important to incorporate a standard set of data validations within the data integration process so that the constraints can be tested at specific points in the information flow process, thereby reducing the risk of inconsistency. Soliciting data quality requirements from all the downstream data consumers allows definition of standard data quality rules. Implementing validation of compliance to these rules early in the process can help ensure that the quality of the data is sufficient to meet the business needs and allow any potential issues to be identified and remediated early and consistently (Loshin 2010b).

It is important to have enough time set aside for a project plan and to perform rigorous testing to ensure that data meet the quality expectations of stakeholders as post-implementation assessment of integration.

Data Warehousing and Data Quality

Data warehousing is one of the areas that is adversely impacted by data quality issues. A data warehouse is a specific case of data integration, and as such, all the data quality issues and considerations that we discussed previously in this section applies to data warehouses too.

When building a data warehouse it is very important to understand the scope and plan for iterative delivery rather than a *"big bang"* approach. This is because a data warehouse usually stores data related to not one but multiple data domains, the data for which would be sourced from a multitude of operational or transactional systems. Usually, the data issues originate in these systems. An iterative delivery approach makes it possible to focus on data quality issues originating in specific sources rather than all the sources, and hence makes delivery more manageable.

Data quality needs to be taken into consideration at the start of the project, before designing and developing code for the data warehouse. The quality expectations of the business stakeholders in terms of acceptable thresholds should be sought early on, as they are the ones who will use the data. It is very important to understand the differences between the different data sources that will feed into the data warehouse in terms of data architecture, data representation, and metadata by organizing interviews with the source system subject matter experts. The business stakeholders who will use the data warehouse can also provide useful information about source system data quality and would be able to provide details about the data quality issues they encounter.

A detailed data quality assessment of the source systems needs to be conducted and compared with the acceptable thresholds defined by the stakeholders in order to assess the data quality gaps. The data quality gaps need to be discussed with the stakeholders, and a strategy for fixing data quality issues needs to be created. While the best approach is to fix data quality issues in the source systems, this might not always be possible. In cases where fixing data quality issues in the source system is not an option, quality rules would need to be embedded in the ETL logic. Figure 6.21 depicts the data cleansing options in the data warehouse structure.

A data warehouse attempts to provide a single version of truth; hence, it is very important to have an enterprise-wide standard definition for data elements in the data warehouse. Performance and scalability have an impact on the data quality within the ETL process since complex rules and code are involved. It is important to realistically gauge the performance that is needed and the performance that can be achieved (Dijcks Undated).

MASTER DATA MANAGEMENT AND DATA QUALITY

Master data comprise high-value, key business information that supports the transactions and plays a crucial role in the basic operation of a business. Master data are defined as the basic characteristics of instances of business entities such as customers, products, parts, employees, accounts, sites, inventories, materials, and suppliers.

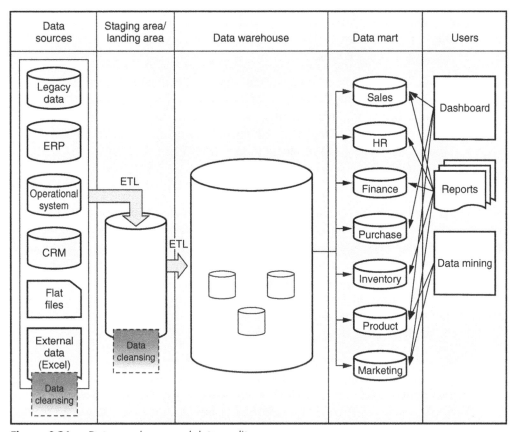

Figure 6.21 Data warehouse and data quality.

While each industry has it is own set of master data requirements and characteristics (Cleven and Wortmann 2010; Zornes 2007; Berson and Dubov 2007), three core master data domains can be identified:

- *Party.* This domain encompasses all business partner–related master data, for example, for customers, suppliers, distributors, employees, patients, vendors, or citizens. A business partner can be any kind of person or corporation. Typically, party master data contain contact information. Moreover, relationships between organizations and persons are covered; for example, employees "work for" the organization, customers "purchase from" the organization (Beasty 2008; Berson and Dubov 2007; Loshin 2008; Zornes 2007).

- *Thing.* This domain encompasses all master data that relate to the products, services, or assets an organization offers and possesses. While there is a common set of views on master data entities in this domain, the master data attributes are heavily driven by industries and their service or product characteristics. Typical views on products and services are sales (for example, prices), planning (for example, lead times), purchasing (for example, prices), or financials (for example, valuations) (Redman 2001; Snow 2008; Zornes 2007).

- *Location.* This domain encompasses all master data that relate to address, places, sites, or regions. A location can be a sales territory, a suburb, a state, a city, an office, a production facility, or a shelf in a store. Location master data are frequently used together with party or thing master data to answer questions like "Where is a product produced?" "Where is a product sold?" or "To which sales territory does a customer belong?" (Redman 2001; Zornes 2007).

Master data are usually present in more than one department or business unit in an organization, and master data objects and elements can be found in transactional data too, though master data objects are more likely to be static when compared to the transactional data. For example, in a retail company, product data are a part of purchase order, marketing, and inventory data, which are different business functions. The purchase order in itself is transactional data, with customer and product data being the master data embedded in the transactional data.

Master data have the following characteristics:

- *Independent existence* (Dreibelbis et al. 2008). In contrast to transactional data, master data objects and elements are independent of other objects. Master data objects can exist without any other object. A sales order, for example, cannot exist without a customer or product/service, whereas a customer or product does not need any other object to exist.

- *Low change frequency* (Loshin 2008). Master data objects are unchanging compared to transactional data. Most attributes of a master data object are not changed during its life cycle. While the sales order naturally changes during its life cycle (for example, status changes from "released" to "in production" to "fulfilled"), the customer master data remain unchanged during business transactions.

- *Constant data volume* (Loshin 2008). The number of master data objects (for example, products) stays relatively constant compared to transactional data objects (for example, sales order).

Master data management (MDM) is the combination of processes, policies, standards and practices, tools and technologies, needed to create, store, and maintain consolidated, consistent, contextual, complete, and accurate views of master data across multiple business processes, application systems, departments, business units, and, potentially, organizations. While transactional management systems store and process transactional data from daily operations, master data systems manage reference data and business entities. The objective of master data management is to define shared business entities and to have a single authoritative source for their master data, which can feed into other systems and applications across the organization. Master data management is more important for large corporations than small corporations, as larger corporations have a greater number of disparate systems than smaller corporations, and the disparity increases with mergers and acquisitions. This increases the difficulty in providing a single version of truth. MDM initiatives have a business focus, with emphasis on the process of entity identification and validation with the business clients (Loshin 2007).

Entity definitions based on master data provide business consistency and data integrity when multiple IT systems across an organization (or beyond) identify the same entity differently. In an Internet-based survey that TDWI ran in mid-2006, the business entity most often defined in master data is the customer (74%), followed by financials (56%) and products (54%). Other entities include business partners (49%), employees (45%), locations (41%), sales contacts (25%), and physical assets (21%) (Russom 2006). At the core of the master data management initiative is the definition of master data. *Master data management* is the discipline that endeavors to achieve a *"single version of the truth"* for core business entities and creates a single, shared reference point, known as the *"golden record,"* for the business. However, like the story of the blind men and the elephant, a "single version of the truth" is made up of various perspectives on that truth. The story of the blind men and the elephant is a classic tale of a group of blind men who each touch an elephant to discover what it is like. One man touches the trunk, another the tusk, another the tail, and another the hide, and all, of course, therefore have a different definition and perspective of what it means to be an elephant. All are correct in their own way, but the true "single version of the truth" is a superset of all of their experiences. Master data management poses a similar situation (Burbank 2016) as master data are usually present in and used by more than one department, business unit, or user group in an organization. This results in each user group or business unit having their own perspective on the data depending on what they do with the data. We will use the case of product master data to explain the perspectives of different user groups in relation to the data. While there is a comprehensive view of a "product" with a superset of attributes that supports multiple user groups across the organization, each user group has its own view of what "product" information comprises and what the context of usage of that data is. Each group along the supply chain may view, create, edit, or delete certain pieces of the information that make up the concept of "product." To make MDM successful, it is important to identify each of these stakeholder groups and work with them to understand their usage and requirements regarding the data domain in question. For example, the product development team is responsible for defining the product components and assembly instructions. When it comes to product pricing, while supply chain accounting determines the initial price, this price may be modified by marketing during the market test phase. Marketing is responsible for product naming and the description that appears in the catalog (Burbank 2016).

While it is possible to plan and implement a data quality initiative without considering MDM, it is not possible to implement MDM without careful and serious consideration being given to data quality. Irrespective of whether the MDM solution is being implemented in a single master data entity (for example, customer) or for all operational master and reference data entities, data quality needs to be taken into account. If the data quality aspect is not taken into account when implementing an MDM initiative, the MDM implementation will not realize any benefits that it was set to achieve. Hence, for every MDM implementation initiative, a data quality component consisting of identification of master data elements, profiling, and analysis and cleaning is a necessity.

There are two different approaches to implementing data quality (DQ) and master data management (MDM):

1. Data quality and MDM implementation are conducted in a sequential manner, with data quality being implemented first, followed by MDM implementation, which begins as a separate phase once data quality implementation is complete. Implementation of data quality first allows for data analysis and data cleaning to happen before MDM implementation begins, and is a common approach in many corporations.

2. Data quality implementation happens in parallel to an MDM implementation, with data analysis and cleansing being a part of the MDM initiative. This has become possible with MDM vendors providing bundled data quality tools in their suite of MDM tools. For example, SAP's acquisition of Business Objects (BO) paired SAP's MDM solution with BO's DQM tools, and IBM's InfoSphere product line combines DQM processes such as data validations and duplicate checks with a central MDM application (PricewaterhouseCoopers 2011)

Figure 6.22 shows the fundamental elements of master data management.

The first step toward master data management is to establish the data domain that needs to be mastered. This is usually a business decision. Once the data domain to master is established, it is necessary to identify data sources that hold the data related to the data domain, and the critical data objects and data attributes. If the organization has an inventory of data sources and data objects, then this can be used to identify the data sources that would be used to source data for population of the master data repository. Not all critical data elements identified would necessarily be master data elements, and it is important to isolate the master data elements.

Master Data Profiling

Once the master data sources, data objects, and data elements have been identified and isolated, the next stage is to organize access and prepare the source data for profiling and analysis purposes. Data profiling of source master data should be carried out with two objectives in mind:

• *Assessing quality of master data elements in different master data sources.* It is important to assess the quality of the source master data elements in the various data sources that will feed into the master data. It is important to understand the business user expectations of the data in terms of context of use and quality and the conformance levels required, and profile data to determine whether they will meet the quality expectations of the business users. The different profiling techniques discussed in Chapter 4 can be used for this purpose.

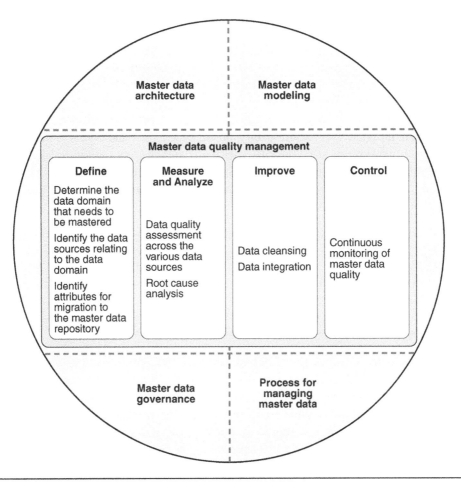

Figure 6.22 Fundamental elements of master data management.

Any quality issues discovered as a result of data profiling need to be analyzed, and root cause analysis needs to be performed to define strategies for cleansing and improving the data quality. Profiling will help reveal which data sources fall way below quality expectations and hence cannot be candidates for feeding data into the master data repository. For example, say the requirement is to create a customer master data repository, and it is found that five data sources have customer data. If on profiling customer data elements in these sources, it is found that in two of the sources the data quality is bad in terms of completeness and there are very few records, while the other three data sources have good data quality, the decision might be to source the data from these three data sources only.

• *Assessing discrepancies between different data sources.* Generally, the data sources that feed data into the master data repository are autonomous and heterogeneous. As discussed in the "Data Integration and Data Quality" section, the data objects and data elements in different sources are most likely to have different naming conventions and different representations. There are bound to be discrepancies in data types and lengths for the same data element in different systems. A classic example is the customer name and address information. One system might store the customer name as a full name in one data field and the customer address as a whole in a single data field, whereas another system may store the customer name components—first name, middle name, and last name—in different fields and customer address components—house/unit/apartment number, street address, city, postal code, state, and country—in different fields. Even if two systems store the customer name and customer address data in single data fields, the naming conventions and data representation may be different. For example, system A stores the customer name in the following format in the cust_name field, which can hold up to 55 characters:

<First Name Initial> <space> <Middle Name Initial>
<space> <Last Name>

System B may store the customer name in the following format in the customer_name field, which can hold up to 255 characters:

<First Name> <space> <Middle Name> <space> <Last Name>

Data profiling helps uncover the different patterns and representations in the different data sources, and is a starting point for analysis of which are the best data sources to source the data from and how to best consolidate these records into the master data repository. It is important to understand the underlying metadata, the data type, data lengths, semantics, formats, and representations for the source master data elements in scope for migration into the master data repository or hub, and the way the data would be represented in the master data repository. The understanding of the differences in the data standards, metadata, and data representations between the sources and target (that is, the master data repository) would drive the transformation rules needed to transform source data into target data that fit the target data model requirements. A core capability of any MDM initiative is the ability to consolidate multiple data sets representing a master data object (Loshin 2007) (such as "customer" or "product") from different data sources and resolve different representations into a single "best record," which is promoted into being the master copy for all participating applications. This capability relies on consulting metadata and data standards that have been discovered through the data profiling and discovery process to parse, standardize, match, and resolve data into that "best record." The fact that these capabilities are offered by traditional data cleansing vendors is indicated by the various consolidations, acquisitions, and partnerships between data integration vendors and data quality tool vendors (Loshin 2007).

Master Data Integration and Data Quality

Once the candidate data sources, data objects, and data elements have been identified and finalized, the next step is to integrate and consolidate data from the different sources into the master data repository. When consolidating data from different sources into the target master data repository, it is very important to keep timeliness, consistency, and synchronization aspects in mind.

Master data integration involves extraction of the required data elements from the respective data sources, and transformation rules to transform the data as per the formatting requirements in the master data repository. Transformation rules also lead to data standardization. MDM initiatives need IT and business to work closely to define data quality standards and business rules, with business driving the MDM initiative to fully reap the power of master data management. Transformation rules may be engineered directly within the data integration tool or may be alternate technologies entrenched within the tool. As data instances from heterogeneous sources are brought together, the integration tools use the parsing, standardization, linking, and matching capabilities of the data quality technologies to consolidate data into unique records in the master data model (Loshin 2007).

Once data are migrated to the master data repository, which is the target data system in the case of master data migration, the data in the target need to be profiled to assess whether the data meet quality expectations. The data quality issues may be uncovered in the master data repository, which might be due to coding issues or some data quality issues that have escaped the data source profiling assessments and are now manifest in the target systems.

Ongoing data quality monitoring may be required for the critical master data elements, and the data quality rules defined for profiling and assessing the source data can be reused. The defined data rules can contribute to baseline measurements and ongoing auditing for data stewardship and governance. In fact, entrenching the data profiling rules within the data integration framework makes the validation process for MDM reasonably transparent (Loshin 2007).

Data Governance and Master Data Management

Successful implementation of master data management requires the integration of data governance throughout the initiative. Since master data span application and business unit boundaries, master data management programs are often implemented in parallel with business data governance initiatives. There are three important aspects of data governance for master data management (Loshin 2013):

- *Managing critical data elements.* This involves ensuring agreement in identifying the master data elements associated with common business terminology, scrutinizing their authoritative sources, getting consensus on their definitions and data standards, and managing them within the master data repository as the enterprise source of truth.

- *Setting information policies and data rules.* This involves determining the critical business policies that relate to data, and formulation of information policies that comprise the specification of management objectives associated with data governance, whether they are related to risk management or common data errors.

- *Enforcing accountability.* This involves authorizing and empowering the right individuals in the organization to administer well-defined governance policies and to institute the underlying organizational structure to make it possible by defining a management structure to manage the execution of the governance framework along with the compensation model that rewards that execution. Developing a strong enterprise-wide data governance program will not only benefit the MDM program but also reinforce the ability to manage all information activities throughout the organization.

METADATA MANAGEMENT AND DATA QUALITY

Metadata (data about data) is information about data's meaning (semantics) and structure (syntax, constraints, and relationships). As per the National International Standards Organization (NISO), metadata is structured information that describes, explains, locates, or otherwise makes it easier to retrieve, use, or manage an information resource.

Metadata management includes capturing and storing metadata, integrating and publishing metadata, and maintaining and governing metadata. Figure 6.23 shows core elements of metadata management. It is imperative to ensure that metadata are properly created, stored, and controlled in order to ensure good data quality. Over time, "consistently applied metadata will yield greater and greater returns, while lack of such metadata will progressively compound retrieval issues and further stress organizational efficacy." Bad metadata management leads to unnecessary expenditures and lost opportunities. For example, on September 23, 1999, NASA lost the $125 million Mars Climate Orbiter after a 286-day journey to Mars due to a metadata inconsistency (Knight 2018).

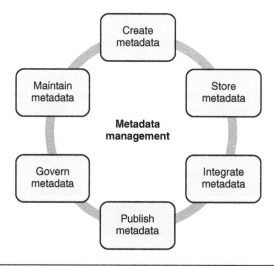

Figure 6.23   Core elements of metadata management.

Metadata management results in organizational understanding of business terms and uses, increasing the confidence in the organization's data and preventing out-of-date data or incorrect usage of those data (Knight 2018). Metadata management enables consistency of definitions, which helps reconcile variations in terminologies. Metadata aids in the resolution of ambiguity and inconsistencies when determining the relationships between entities stored throughout the enterprise data and application landscape.

Numerous applications and data systems have evolved in organizations autonomously, and an entity is likely to be stored in these applications and data systems differently and have different names. These variations give rise to inconsistencies. For example, the data field names customer_name, client_name, and cust_name are used to store customer names. Having well-defined metadata helps reconcile these differences. Metadata contain information about the origins of a particular data set and can be granular enough to define information at the attribute or data element level; metadata may contain allowed values or data ranges for a data element, its proper format, location, owner, and steward. Operationally, metadata may maintain auditable information about users, applications, and processes that create, delete, or change data, the exact timestamp of the change, and the authorization that was used to perform these activities (Berson and Dubov 2007). Through metadata management activities such as metadata stitching and tracing the data lineage, better data quality results because the right data become connected correctly (Knight 2018).

Well-designed metadata management practices can help answer the following questions:

- Who is the creator of the data element?

- What is the business description of the data element?

- Where is the data stored (table/database/file)?

- What are the data type and field length for the data element?

- What are the formatting requirements for this data element (date/numeric/ Boolean/string, and so on)?

- What are valid values and domain for the data element?

- How many data repositories—databases, legacy systems, data sources— store this data?

- If applicable, what are the default values for the data element?

- What are the specific business rules for the data?

- When does the data need to be archived/purged/deleted? For what length of time should the particular data be stored?

- What are the security and privacy requirements of the data element (confidential/public/group only, and so on)?

- Are there any regional or international privacy or security or compliance policies that regulate this data?

SIX SIGMA DMAIC AND DATA QUALITY MANAGEMENT—EXAMPLE

In this example, we will illustrate the use of the Six Sigma DMAIC methodology to improve data quality in a limited area in a small utility company as a part of the proof of concept. Because of limited inhouse data quality expertise, external consultants were hired to help with the data quality improvement program.

Six Sigma Define Phase

Engagement with different business unit stakeholders had revealed several pain points in the different data domains, and these pain points and data issues were recorded in a data issues register along with business implications. As a part of a regulatory requirement, the customer contact data needed to be complete and correct. Poor customer contact data quality was resulting in operational inefficiencies and lower productivity, and was a high-priority issue that needed to be resolved. The concerned business and IT stakeholders and subject matter experts were identified and engaged to set expectations.

Six Sigma Measure Phase

In this phase, the technology and business subject matter experts were engaged to acquire data for data profiling purposes, and any documentation related to understanding the business processes generating the data and the data fields (data field names, formats, data types, what the data field represents in the real world) was gathered and reviewed. Once a data extract was provided, the technology and business subject matter experts were engaged to identify the critical data elements that would need to be assessed. The business subject matter experts were further questioned to understand why certain data elements were critical, the data quality expectations related to these data fields, and the impact to the business if the quality expectations were not met. Discussions with the technology and business subject matter experts were conducted to determine the critical data elements whose quality would need to be assessed. Discussions revealed that the following data fields were critical:

- *Type of contact.* This data element was important because it helped distinguish new customers from current customers. The field would need to be populated for at least 90% of the records, or missing for a maximum of 10% of records, to meet the data quality expectations.

- *Customer record creation date and customer record resolution date.* Customer record creation date corresponds to the date when the customer called in with a query or to report a problem, and customer record resolution date corresponds to the date when the issue or query was resolved. Both customer record creation date and customer record resolution date needed to have valid date values, and the customer record creation would need to precede the customer record resolution, since in the real world, an issue cannot be resolved before it is created. The customer record creation date field needed to be populated for 100% of the records, and customer record resolution date would need to be populated for all the records that had a status of "closed." The customer record creation date would need to less than or equal to the customer record resolution date to be consistent, and at least 90% of the records would need to satisfy this condition, or a maximum of 10% of the records not satisfy this condition, for data quality expectations to be met.

- *High-level reason code.* This field captured the high-level reason for the customer contacting the company call center, and needed to be at least 90% complete, or a maximum of 10% incomplete, for data quality expectations to be met.

- *Detail reason code.* This field captured the detailed-level reason for the customer contacting the company call center, and needed a minimum of 90% complete or a maximum of 10% incomplete for data quality expectations to be met.

These data fields were considered critical because the company would be penalized if any of the above data were not being captured. The data extract provided was loaded into a table in a database, and SQL queries were used to profile and analyze the data.

Customer Contact Type Profiling Results. SQL queries used to analyze the count of the different contact types showed that customer contact types were either new, existing, or potential, with a total of 25% of records having missing values for customer contact type, as shown in the pie chart in Figure 6.24.

The bar chart in Figure 6.25 and Figure 6.26 shows the yearly percentages of the missing and present customer contact types. The yearly analysis of missing customer contact types showed that while in the first year (2007) the percentage of missing customer types was more than 20%, the percentage of missing customer types was considerably lower, around 10%, in the years 2008, 2009, 2010, and 2011. However, the missing customer contact types increased considerably in the years post 2011, with the percentage figure being close to 30%, which is approximately 20% higher than the confidence measure or acceptable threshold.

Customer Record Creation Date and Customer Record Resolution Date Profiling Results. The customer record creation date and customer record resolution date field values were profiled using SQL queries. Discussions with business subject matter experts revealed that customer record creation date corresponds to the date when an existing, new, or potential customer contacts customer care and reports an issue or makes an inquiry. The customer record resolution date represents the date when the

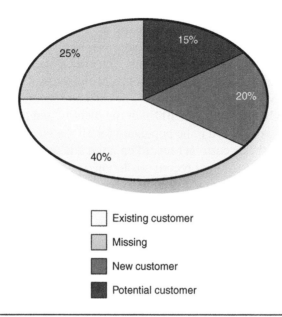

Figure 6.24   Different customer contact types and their percentages.

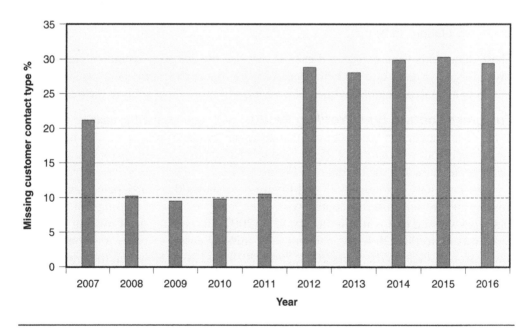

Figure 6.25   Missing contact type percentage by year.

inquiry was responded to in a satisfactory manner or the issue was resolved. Hence, the customer record creation should always precede the customer record resolution, as a query cannot be answered or an issue cannot be resolved before the event of inquiry or reporting. Issue/query can get created and resolved on the same day. The customer

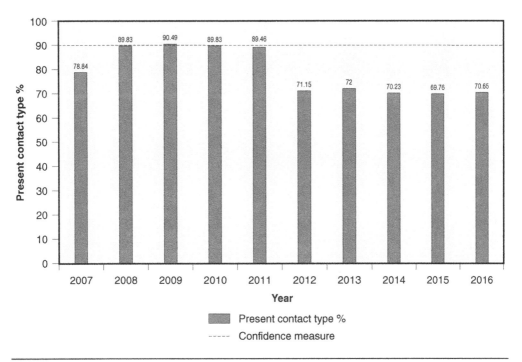

Figure 6.26   Present contact type percentage by year.

record resolution date should be populated once the matter is resolved, in which case the Status field should have a *closed* status. If the Status field has an *open* or *pending* status, then it indicates that the matter or issue has still not been resolved; hence, the customer record resolution date should not be populated for such records. On the other hand, customer record resolution date should not be missing for records with a *closed* status, and should be greater than or equal to the customer record creation date.

Figure 6.27 shows the yearly profiling results where the customer record resolution date is greater than or equal to the customer record creation date. We can see that in the years 2007 and 2011 the percentage of records for which the customer record creation date was less than the customer record resolution date was a little below the 90% confidence measure or acceptable threshold mark. However, in the years 2008 and 2009, the percentage of records for which the customer record creation date was less than the customer record resolution date was above the acceptable threshold, and in 2010 was very close to the acceptable threshold. However, from 2012 to 2016 the percentage of records for which the customer record creation date was less than the customer record resolution date was way below the acceptable threshold, as shown in Figure 6.27.

Figure 6.28 shows the yearly profiling results illustrating the percentage of records for which the customer record resolution date is missing when the status is *closed*. As seen in Figure 6.28, the percentage of missing customer record resolution dates when the status is *closed* was slightly more than the acceptable threshold of 10% in the year 2007. For the years 2007 to 2011, the percentage of records for which the customer record

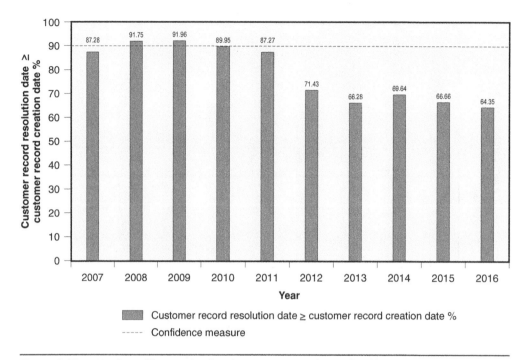

Figure 6.27   Yearly profiling results showing percentage of records with customer record resolution date ≥ customer record creation date.

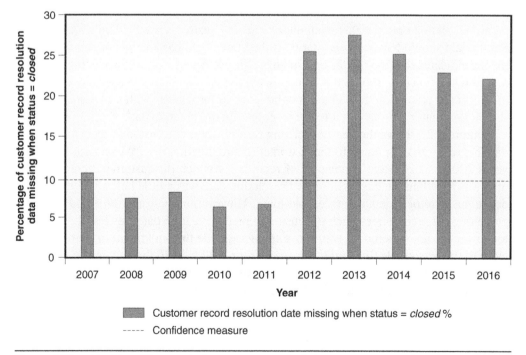

Figure 6.28   Yearly profiling results for percentage of missing customer record resolution dates when the status is *closed*.

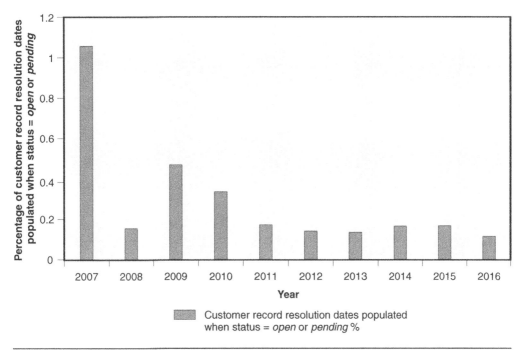

Figure 6.29 Yearly profiling results for percentage of records for which the customer record resolution date is populated when the status is *open* or *pending*.

resolution date is missing when the status is *closed* is less than the acceptable threshold of 10%, and hence meets the data quality expectations. However, for the years 2012 to 2016, the percentage of records for which the customer record resolution date is missing when the status is *closed* exceeds the acceptable threshold considerably.

Figure 6.29 shows the yearly profiling results illustrating the percentage of records for which the customer record resolution date is populated when the status is *open* or *pending*. As seen in Figure 6.29, the percentage of populated customer record resolution dates when the status is *open* or *pending* is less than the acceptable threshold of 10% in the years 2007–2016.

Reason Codes Profiling Results. Figure 6.30 and Figure 6.31 show the yearly percentages of the missing and present high-level and detailed-level reason codes, respectively. The yearly analysis of missing high-level reason codes showed that while in the first year (2007) the percentage of missing high-level reason codes was around 20%, the percentage of missing high-level reason codes was considerably lower, around 10%, in the years 2008, 2009, 2010, and 2011. However, the missing high-level reason codes increased considerably in the years post 2011, with the percentage figure being more than 25%, which is approximately 20% higher than the confidence measure or acceptable threshold. Also, as seen in the Figure 6.30, the percentage of missing detailed-level reason codes was slightly more than the percentage of missing high-level reason codes.

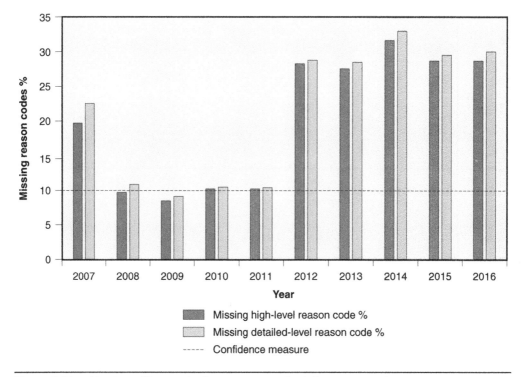

Figure 6.30   Yearly profiling results for percentage of missing reason codes.

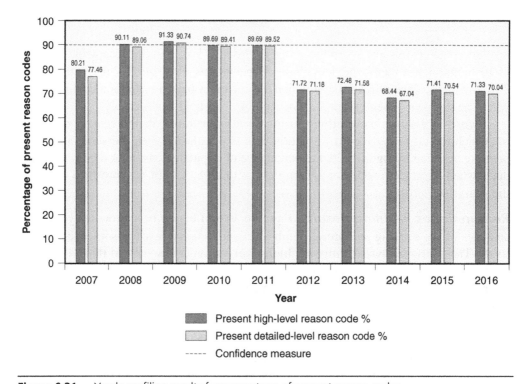

Figure 6.31   Yearly profiling results for percentage of present reason codes.

Six Sigma Analyze Phase

In this phase brainstorming sessions were conducted with the business subject matter expert, the customer care contact center team leader, and a few team members to understand the root cause behind the data issues.

As seen in the bar charts in the "Six Sigma Measure Phase" section, the issue rates were higher in the first year (2007) but were considerably less in the years 2008 to 2011. However, the issue rates shot up post 2011 in the years 2012–2016.

The brainstorming sessions revealed the following:

- In the year 2007 the online data entry system was first set up, and it took customer contact center staff a while to get trained and upskilled, which led to a lot of data entry errors. However, once the contact center staff were trained, they were able to do data entry efficiently, resulting in considerably fewer errors and data issues.

- Toward the end of 2011, two things happened:

  - A new interface was rolled out for data entry, but no training was imparted to the contact staff team members.

  - Incentives were associated with the number of calls that customer contact staff took per day.

Further investigation into system controls also revealed that the validation routines were not robust enough. These factors contributed to low-quality data.

Based on these findings, the following high-level recommendations were made:

- Revise the incentive mechanism to link to quality of data

- Train customer contact staff to use the new interface

- Automate entry of data

- Clean historical data

- Implement robust data validation routines

- Monitor data quality on a weekly basis

These recommendations were presented to the business stakeholders, along with the costing and timelines, to get buy-in.

Six Sigma Improve Phase

The incentive mechanism was revised to use quality of data entry and number of calls attended to per day for calculating incentives as opposed the number of calls only. Training sessions were conducted and quick-reference guidance and user manuals were given to the customer contact team to facilitate correct data entry. Individual projects were set up to clean historical data, automate entry of data, and implement robust data validation routines.

Six Sigma Control Phase

Customer contact record data quality was manually monitored using SQL queries to look at the number and percentage of data issues. It was found that, post training, the number of data issues went down by approximately 15%. Post implementation of automation and incorporation of robust data validation routines, defects were brought down to less than 5%.

KEY PRINCIPLES OF DATA QUALITY MANAGEMENT

Following are some of the key principles of data quality management:

- Focus on critical data elements when assessing, cleansing, or monitoring data quality.

- Apply strong data quality controls and data validation rules where data are captured, as identifying and addressing data quality issues at data entry points is easier and less costly than remediating them when they progress downstream. Automate data capture as much as possible.

- Data cleansing, while necessary, should not be solely used to fix data quality issues. Investigate the root cause behind the data quality issues, and use preventive measures and improvement initiatives, if possible, to prevent the data quality issues from occurring in the first place.

- Establish enterprise-wide data standards, if possible. For international corporations, having a universal data standard may not be possible.

- Establish a data governance framework.

- Use a centralized data quality issue log to capture, prioritize, and maintain data quality issues.

- Do not attempt to solve all the data quality issues. Solve the critical data quality issues that have the maximum business impact.

CONCLUSION

This chapter discussed the different approaches, steps, methodologies, and techniques of data quality management, and data quality aspects to consider when undertaking data-intensive projects. For any data quality management effort to bear fruit, the business and information technology departments need to work together. Business units who use the data know the context and usage of the data, and hence are best placed to define the business rules relating to the data. Information technology understands the technology and the technical environments and storage systems that store and manipulate the data. Data quality management is data, people, process, and technology intensive, with data being at the core; thus, all these elements need to work together in an integrated manner to ensure success. Advancement in one element supports progress in another, enhancing the chances of making and sustaining overall improvements in data quality. Careful consideration needs to be given to these elements when embarking on your data quality journey.

SUMMARY OF KEY POINTS

Data Quality Management

Management of people, processes, policies, technology, standards, and data within an enterprise, with the objective of improving the dimensions of data quality that are most important to the organization (Knowledgent Undated). There are two approaches to data quality management:

- *Proactive.* Eliminating data quality problems before they have a chance to appear.

- *Reactive.* Reacting to data quality issues after they have surfaced.

Six Sigma

A quality control program developed in 1986 by Motorola that advocates for qualitative measurements to improve quality. *Six Sigma DMAIC* (define, measure, analyze, improve, and control) methodology can be utilized to assess, improve, and sustain data quality:

- *Define.* Define the data quality problem statement.

- *Measure.* Quantify the data quality problem through data profiling, metadata analysis.

- *Analyze.* Analyze the data quality gaps and uncover the causes behind these gaps.

- *Improve.* Design and implement a data quality improvement solution.

- *Control.* Monitor data quality improved in the improve phase.

Data Quality Assessment

The process of profiling data and measuring the quality of data against defined business rules, documenting and analyzing the results of measurement, analyzing gaps between data quality results and expected data quality, understanding the issues and pain points, and analyzing the impact and root cause.

Root Cause Analysis

Method of problem solving used to identify and categorize the root causes of problems and can be used to uncover cause of bad data. Commonly used techniques are techniques such as the 5 whys root cause discovery process, brainstorming, and the fishbone diagram. Pareto analysis can be used to prioritize the issues and the causes.

Data Cleansing

The process of detecting and correcting (or removing) corrupt or inaccurate records from a record set, table, or database by identifying incomplete, incorrect, inaccurate, or irrelevant parts of the data, and then replacing, modifying, or deleting the dirty or coarse data (Wu 2013). The various data quality techniques involved in data cleansing include:

- *Parsing.* Involves the disintegration, conversion, and segregation of text fields and content into constituent atomic parts, and the organization of values into consistent formats based on industry standards, local standards (for example, postal authority standards for address data), or user-defined business rules.

- *Standardization.* Involves conversion of data elements to forms that are uniform and standard.

- *Matching.* Involves identification of similar data within and across the data sources and determining whether two records represent the same thing.

- *Linkage.* Involves linking data that represent or relate to the same thing.

- *Merging.* Involves merging similar records from different data sources into one record to provide a single view of data.

- *Data enrichment.* Involves enhancing the value of internally held data by incorporating additional related data attributes from an organization's internal and external data sources not directly related to the base data.

Data Validation

Reactive approach to reduce the amount of bad data entering the system, even though it does not address the root cause of the data quality issue.

Data Quality Monitoring

Involves checking a set of data records in the tables against a set of defined data quality rules at regular intervals and displaying results on a data quality dashboard.

Data Migration

Deals with the migration of data from one data structure to another data structure, or transformed from one platform to another platform with a modified data structure.

Data Migration and Data Quality

Key points to keep in mind to build data quality into data migration/conversion:

1. Establish the scope of the conversion project, and source systems and target system involved in the migration.

2. Identify the core source tables and/or files for data profiling purposes.

3. Understand the target system data model and data structure and business requirements of the target system.

4. Conduct a detailed data quality assessment of all the source systems involved in the data migration.

5. Data cleansing. There are different approaches to cleaning source system data:

   - Cleanse data in the source systems.

   - Cleanse data during the staging process.

   - Cleanse data in-flight using coding logic.

   - Cleanse after migrating the data into the target system.

6. Build data mapping or source-to-target mapping by looking at the source system data fields and comparing them to the target system data fields and then linking the fields in the source systems to the fields in the target systems. Use a combination of transformation logic and rules for cleansing data and data enrichment rules, if applicable.

7. Test the migrated data in development and test environments with production-like data or a recent copy of production data, if possible.

8. Conduct data migration assessment post-migration in production.

Data Integration

The process of combining data from multiple heterogeneous data sources so as to provide users with an integrated and complete view of all the data. A data warehouse is a specific case of data integration.

Data integration challenges:

- Heterogeneity of data sources

    - Inconsistency

    - Timeliness

    - Redundancy

    - Granularity

    - Schema integration

- Autonomy of data sources

Data Integration and Data Quality

Key points to keep in mind to build data quality into data integration:

1. Understand the business requirements of all stakeholders, and the data requirements necessary to meet the business requirements.

2. Identify data sources and profile data sources to assess the current data quality.

3. Engage stakeholders, and analyze the data quality gaps.

4. Address data quality issues.

5. Build data mapping to map source fields to target fields using transformation rules.

6. Incorporate a standard set of data validations within the data integration process.

7. Conduct testing to uncover issues.

8. Conduct a post-integration data quality assessment in the target system.

Master Data Management (MDM)

A combination of processes, policies, standards and practices, tools, and technologies needed to create, store, and maintain a consolidated, consistent, contextual, complete, and accurate view of the master data across multiple business processes, application systems, departments, business units, and, potentially, organizations.

Master Data Management (MDM) and Data Quality

There are two different approaches to implementing data quality (DQ) and master data management (MDM):

1. Data quality and MDM implementation are conducted in a *sequential manner,* with data quality being implemented first, followed by MDM implementation, which begins as a separate phase once data quality implementation is complete.

2. Data quality implementation happens in *parallel* to an MDM implementation, with data analysis and cleansing being a part of the MDM initiative. This has become possible with MDM vendors providing bundled data quality tools in their MDM suite of tools.

Key points to keep in mind to build data quality into MDM:

1. Identify critical master data elements.

2. Profile critical master data elements in different master data sources and assess discrepancies among the different sources.

3. Keep timeliness, consistency, and synchronization aspects in mind when integrating master data from different sources.

4. In the target data system (that is, the master data repository) post master data migration, the data need to be profiled to assess whether quality expectations are met.

5. Monitor ongoing data quality for the critical master data elements, if and as required.

6. Integrate data governance throughout the initiative.

Metadata Management

Involves capturing and storing metadata, integrating and publishing metadata, and maintaining and governing metadata. It is imperative to ensure that metadata are properly created, stored, and controlled in order to ensure good data quality.

7

Data Quality: Critical Success Factors (CSFs)

INTRODUCTION

Data quality is not a destination, but a journey that needs ongoing support. This is because once you have improved the quality of your data, you need processes and people to ensure that they continue to be of high quality. Implementation of data quality programs in organizations to improve, manage, and sustain high-quality data is not an easy endeavor and is fraught with challenges. It is important to understand the organizational myths related to data quality as well as the barriers and challenges faced in the implementation of data quality programs.

There are certain elements that are vital in order for an initiative or program to be successful. These elements are the *critical success factors*. A critical success factor (CSF) drives the strategy forward, or its absence pulls the strategy backward; a critical success factor makes or breaks the success of the strategy (hence the term "critical"). The concept of "success factors" was developed by D. Ronald Daniel of McKinsey & Company in 1961 (Daniel 1961). The process was refined into *critical* success factors by John F. Rockart between 1979 (Rockart 1979) and 1981 (Rockart 1986). In 1995 James A. Johnson and Michael Friesen (1995) applied it to many industry sector settings, including healthcare. CSFs are those factors that are critical to the success of any organization in the sense that if objectives associated with the factors are not achieved, the organization will fail, perhaps catastrophically so (Rockart 1979).

In order to ensure high data quality it is important to understand the underlying factors that influence data quality both from an implementation and sustenance perspective. In order for data quality strategy to be successfully implemented in an organization, knowledge of the CSFs that help in building and sustaining information systems having high data quality is desirable. In the context of a data quality initiative or data quality management, critical success factors represent the essential elements without which a data quality initiative flounders. This chapter explores the myths, misconceptions, and challenges standing in the path of achieving and maintaining high-quality data, and the factors necessary for the success of a data quality program.

DATA QUALITY MYTHS

Myths are widely held misconceptions or false beliefs or ideas.

Lightning never strikes the same place twice.

Bats are blind.

Sharks do not get cancer.

We use only 10 percent of our brains.

Bulls hate the color red.

These are some of the popular myths that are repeated and believed across the globe. Myths have an exasperating pattern of becoming established as fact if a considerable number of individuals hear them and a significant amount of time passes. There are hundreds of different myths associated with different species, food, science, geographies, space, natural phenomena, history, and so on, and often have blind acceptance. The data quality arena has not been able to escape from being a victim of myths and is surrounded by its own set of myths, which tend to mislead people when it comes to making data quality management–related decisions, or slow down, hinder, or put a stop to their data quality management efforts or deployment of data quality projects or initiatives. In this section we discuss and dispel the various data quality myths with the objective to guide you in the right direction and empower you with the ability to make the correct decisions when it comes to pursuing data quality initiatives. Figure 7.1 calls out the different data quality myths.

Myth 1: Data Has to be Absolutely Perfect

One of the biggest myths about data quality is that nothing less than absolute perfection will do, and that data have to be completely free of errors. However, the truth is that data quality is not about zero data issues, but the absence of issues that, if present, would have an adverse business impact.

Aiming for 100% clean data is a mistake. Trying to attain perfect data that is completely devoid of defects is a costly endeavor and is not always achievable. Adopting an "all or nothing" approach when it comes to data quality management is not right. In fact, appropriate data quality management is also a value proposition that should deliver more value than it costs; however, it will fail to deliver flawless data. In other words, the value of data should outweigh the cost required to achieve the level of quality of data that provides that value. Trying to improve quality beyond a certain level might consume more resources while not generating any substantial business results, resulting in costs outweighing the value derived from the underlying data.

Data quality is about striking a balance between different data quality dimensions and defining the minimum acceptable quality threshold or confidence level required for the purpose for which the data are going to be used. The minimum acceptable quality threshold or the degree of perfection varies depending on the objective of data usage

Figure 7.1 Data quality myths.

and the criticality of the data. For example, the quality threshold required for patients' historical health data used for diagnostic purposes is generally higher than the quality threshold required for customer data used for marketing purposes in a retail store. There might be different confidence levels desired of a data set by different departments in an organization. That is, the data quality threshold for a data set that is suitable for one business purpose may be unsuitable for another business purpose. For example, in a financial services organization, customer data used for regulatory reporting purposes require a higher quality threshold than customer data used for marketing purposes.

Myth 2: Data Quality Is Data Accuracy

This is one of the most common myths of data quality. The general misconception is that *data quality* is the same as *data accuracy*. This misconception stems from the fact that when people think about high quality, they think about accuracy only, and data accuracy is usually an organization's data quality improvement goal.

The reality is that while data accuracy is one of the important characteristics of data quality (also called *data quality dimensions*), there are other characteristics of data quality, like completeness, consistency, conformity, timeliness, and so on, that are also important. Please refer to Chapter 3, "Data Quality Dimensions," for details on the various data quality dimensions. For example, if data are accurate but are not delivered in time for reporting purposes, they would not be considered of high quality. As discussed in Myth 1, data quality is about striking a balance between data quality dimensions.

Myth 3: All Data across the Enterprise Need to Be of the Same Quality

Organizations often fall into the trap of the one-size-fits-all approach with this myth of all data across the enterprise needing to be of high quality. This misconception results from data not being viewed in the context of the business function and key performance indicators (KPIs) they support, and the resulting cost of quality. The high enterprise data quality and one-size-fits-all approaches are inefficient and not scalable, and are overkill for many systems, while key data needs still go unmet (Andrews 2015).

The fact is that, while data quality matters, not all data elements and data domains generate the same value or have the same degree of business impact, and hence do not need to have the same quality levels across the data quality dimensions. For example, web data need to be more timely than complete. Critical data that have high business value need to be of high quality. For example, standardized addresses for customer data are not nearly as important for a business-to-business (B2B) enterprise compared to attributes for a new product required for forecasting, manufacturing, and inventory planning. Priorities differ, and so do quality requirements; for example, automating a system process requires 97% plus data quality. However, organizations who are blinded by this myth spend a lot of time on data that look bad but may have low business value, and are prioritized over data that look much better but where higher quality is actually critical to running the business (Andrews 2015).

Myth 4a: Good Data Remain Good Forever
Myth 4b: Once Our Data Is Cleaned, It Will Remain Clean

Two similar, and similarly dangerous myths associated with data quality are that data of high quality will continue to have the same quality level, and once data quality issues have been fixed, then data will continue to remain clean. The false belief is that data quality is a one-time fix, and good data stays fresh forever.

The truth is that—while some attributes like date of birth and place of birth never change, and hence the corresponding data element values, once captured correctly or having been fixed because they had not been captured correctly in the first place, will remain correct forever—most data are time sensitive. Time in general has a negative impact on most data elements. In other words, the data decays or rots. Customer data decay at a rate of 30% per year (Herrick 2017). Individuals get married or divorced, people change names and phone numbers, identity proof like passport numbers expire and are replaced by new passport numbers, people change addresses, people change jobs, people retire—all these real-life events require related data to be updated for the data to be accurate and current.

A statistic from *Target Marketing* magazine, from a 2001 study, revealed that 70.8% of businesspeople surveyed had at least one change to their contact record data in 12 months. The breakdown of change was (Doyle 2014; Coe 2002):

- Job or title change: 65.8%

- Phone number change: 42.9%

- E-mail address change: 37.3%

- Change of company name: 34.2%

- Move from one company to another: 29.6%

- Change of name: 3.8%

As per a simulation study conducted by Hubspot, marketing databases naturally degrade by 22.5% per annum (Doyle 2014; Hubspot Undated). The misconception of data being clean forever is dangerous, because data rot silently, and the effects may not be felt immediately and hence go unnoticed for quite some time.

Also, data quality is not a one-time fix but a repetitive activity that requires periodic assessment and systems to maintain the appropriate levels of quality. In the absence of rigorous and continuous data quality processes, data quality deteriorates. Without a proactive data governance framework in place and adequate data quality processes and resources (right people and technology) to monitor and maintain data quality, data that were once accurate and current, or data that have been fixed, will become inaccurate and stale much sooner than one would envisage.

Myth 5a: Data Quality Tools Can Solve All Data Quality Issues
Myth 5b: Data Quality Tools Are Plug-and-Play

The general misconception is that data quality tools are the solution to all the data quality issues in the organization, and that they are "plug-and-play" and can clean all the data without requiring any setup (Loshin 2014). In short, this myth perpetuates the false belief that the acquisition of data quality tools is a panacea for all data quality problems. Data quality tool vendors advertise and showcase the out-of-the-box capabilities of their tools and automation as a part of their selling strategy, and people assume that tool capabilities in themselves are enough to solve all their data quality problems, and equate automation to no additional human effort being needed.

However, the fact is that data quality tools are not a magic wand that will cause all data quality problems to disappear into thin air. Data quality tools are definitely an enabler of data quality, but they cannot solve data quality problems all by themselves.

Also, data quality tools are not simply plug-and-play; they need to be configured. As the name suggests, a data quality tool is just like any other tool, and its acquisition alone will not result in clean data. For example, a hammer is a tool that can be used to drive a nail into the wall, but a hammer left to itself will not accomplish the task. An individual has to hold the nail with one hand and pound it into the wall with the other hand using the hammer. Similarly, a data quality tool is just a tool that requires people to do their own part before the tool can solve any problems. The right software environments need to be set up before any software tool can be used. There is a variety of data quality tools available from different vendors to deal with different aspects of data quality management, and these tools have varying out-of-the-box capabilities to improve the quality of data, but only if they are used, configured, and implemented in the right way. This is where the human element plays its part; in this case, the human element is skilled professionals who have knowledge of the data quality tool and the ability to correctly understand the underlying data with the help of business subject matter experts who know the data. These professionals need to work closely with the business users to understand the business rules of data quality and the associated metadata, get approvals, usually from the business and data governance team representatives (who oversee the fitness of the data elements and ensure compliance of the data with policies), and then configure the tool with these business rules and metadata and test whether the tool is delivering what it is supposed to deliver before the business can start reaping the benefits. The right approach is to build the data quality strategy and processes for managing the quality of data, chalk out the short-term and long-term goals in relation to data quality, and then proceed to acquire a data quality tool that best suits your enterprise's data landscape.

Myth 6: Data Quality Is Not My Responsibility

There is a lot of confusion and contradictory beliefs regarding who is responsible for data quality in an organization. Following are the some of the common myths related to who is responsible for data quality.

Myth 6a: The Responsibility for Data Quality Lies Solely with IT. This myth is driven by the belief that since the IT department is responsible for technology, and data quality can be achieved through implementation of data quality tools, which are technology driven, the ultimate responsibility for ensuring high data quality and fixing data quality issues lies with the IT department. However, not all data quality issues are technical, and hence cannot be fixed by even the most advanced data quality technology alone. When debunking myth 5a and myth 5b, we saw that the business rules that are electronically configured in the data quality tools are provided by business users. While IT will have to be involved in anything that touches data and is responsible for the electronic rules, the software environment, and solution architecture, and are accountable in cases where the system design is not as per business requirements specifications, holding IT alone responsible for all data quality woes would be detrimental to an organization aiming to use data for its competitive advantage.

Myth 6b: The Responsibility for Data Quality Lies Solely with the Business.
This myth has its root in the fact that since the business personnel use the data and have the knowledge of the context in which the data are used, and they are the ones who define data quality requirements and business rules, the business should be held responsible for data quality. However, anything related to data involves technology and the use of specialized tools, and since the business has little or no knowledge about the workings of the tools and technology and the software environments, they cannot be made solely responsible for data quality.

Myth 6c: The Responsibility for Data Quality Lies Solely with the Data Stewards. This myth has its root in the fact that a data steward is a role within an organization responsible for taking care of data in the organization. Data governance processes ensure fitness of data elements—both the content and metadata. Data stewards have a specialist role that incorporates processes, policies, guidelines, and responsibilities for administering all of the organization's data in compliance with policy and/or regulatory obligations (Wikipedia Undated "Data Steward"). Data stewards are more like watchdogs and caretakers: they take care of the data and ensure that others also take appropriate care of the data. And while they may have some knowledge of technology as well as business, they cannot be made solely responsible for the quality of data in an organization.

Myth 6d: The Responsibility for Data Quality Lies Solely with the Chief Data Officer. As organizations are recognizing the value of data, they are introducing senior data roles (*chief data officer* being one such role) to ensure good-quality data. The chief data officer is responsible for establishing the organization's data strategy in alignment with the organization's overall strategy, and ensuring data quality across the organization. While the chief data officer does lead the data strategy, he or she alone cannot be held accountable for data quality. The chief data officer needs the support of all the relevant teams—both IT and business—to implement the strategy successfully.

Two of the most intractable issues organizations face when dealing with data quality problems are less technical and more programmatic: funding the program and ensuring its sustainability. The conflict evolves from a difference of opinion regarding financial support and resourcing. Essentially, the intention of information technology is to drive business engagement in supporting data quality activity (Loshin 2017).

Since the business users equate data quality with data quality technology, they insist that as data quality tools can be used to clean data, the entire responsibility of funding and sustaining data quality lies with the IT department. On the other hand, the IT teams maintain their viewpoint that since poor data quality impacts the business, and the business users are the ones defining what quality means, the business users need to take ownership of data quality and absolve IT from accountability. This contradiction pits IT and the business users against each other in terms of the effort to improve data quality, thereby delaying progress rather than encouraging it (Loshin 2017).

The fact is that data quality is a shared responsibility and partnership among all the data stakeholders, with data being a strategic corporate asset that affects everyone in the organization one way or the other. Data are not restricted to a single team, department, or business unit, but cross the boundaries of teams, departments, and business units. Data get captured in the source systems and travel electronically through various intermediate systems, and are transformed, summarized, and integrated before they reach the business users, who belong to different business units, in the form of reports, as shown in Figure 7.2.

The data in the different systems are maintained by different operational teams. Hence, the responsibility for data quality cannot lie with any one individual, department, or team. The information technology department, business users, data stewards, data owners, and chief data officer are different stakeholders where data quality is concerned, and each of them have their own share of functions or activities to perform, and also work collaboratively, in order to ensure adequate data quality. Data quality is a shared responsibility across cross-functional teams and requires collaborative effort, with each stakeholder having a defined set of roles and responsibilities to ensure high data quality. For an enterprise-wide data quality initiative to be initiated, successfully implemented, and sustained on an ongoing basis once the implementation is over, requires the initiative to be a joint business and IT effort, supported by the data governance team and headed by the chief data officer.

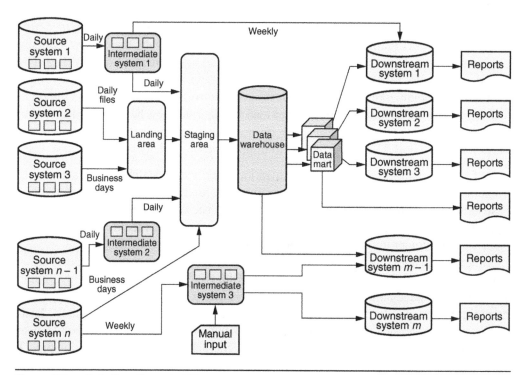

Figure 7.2   Data flow through different systems.

Myth 7: With Data, No News Is Good News

Organizations often assume that since they have not heard about any major problems related to data, the data are good and do not need to be assessed. Quite a lot of organizations take data quality for granted and mistakenly assume that their data are good, until the time comes when they crash and burn. In short, the misconception that "when it comes to data, no news is good news" is very dangerous and can have serious implications (Andrews 2015). Among the many variations of this belief are:

"Our data are good."

"If it ain't broke, don't fix it."

"If there were any major issue with the data, we would have definitely heard about it."

The following quote (Hub Designs 2009; Kumar 2014) on data quality by Ken Orr from the Cutter Consortium in "The Good, the Bad, and the Data Quality" very aptly describes the impact of this myth:

Ultimately, poor data quality is like dirt on the windshield. You may be able to drive for a long time with slowly degrading vision, but at some point you either have to stop and clear the windshield or risk everything.

The fact is that data quality issues that surface occasionally are often tactically fixed as and when they happen in a fire-fighting mode, with teams working in the background to deliver the required data by the specified deadline without senior management being any wiser, until a time when the problem becomes so big that it can no longer be ignored, resulting in chaos, and a strategic approach needs to be taken to solve the problem or risk everything. The situation can be compared to a volcano, with lava simmering beneath the surface for quite some time, with occasional, very small and quiet eruptions that are ignored until a major eruption occurs. The sudden chaos is because bad data and the cost of bad data are not always obvious, and senior management in most organizations is generally ignorant of the real costs of bad-quality data as they are removed from the actual operations relating to the data. Without formal data quality metrics tied to operational KPIs, the true data challenges and costs are hidden from view. Formal data quality metrics tied to operational KPIs would help the enterprise management to understand the hidden costs that are building and getting worse with time, and to make informed decisions.

Myth 8: Our Data Are Too Complex

Many organizations fall into the snare of assuming that since their data are very complex, the data quality tools available on the market will not able to solve their data quality problems.

The truth is that the data quality tool market is quite mature, with a wide variety of data quality tools from different vendors having varying capabilities and functional characteristics. You should be able to find a few whose capabilities would work for your data landscape and solve your data problems. Most tools employ user-defined custom logic for standard and custom fields to accurately locate and merge duplicates. Sophisticated data quality tools enable you to search using exact or fuzzy logic depending on your organization's unique data (Chinapen 2017).

Myth 9: Our Data Are Very Different from Others

Organizations often suffer from the misconception that their data are very different from other organizations' data. It is true that some companies do have data that are very different from others, but that does not apply to all data in the organization; the basic business processes are very similar across all companies in the business world (Markram Undated). To illustrate this with an example, in a water utility company, underground asset location data are stored as geospatial data, which are three-dimensional data stored in GIS systems; you would not find this kind of data in a financial services company.

As discussed in myth 8, there are sophisticated data quality tools to deal with your data landscape and data quality problems. However, the basic business processes regarding supplies, employment, buying, billing, selling, retirement, termination, taxation, inventory, and so on, will be very similar, and the underlying data captured as a part of these business process will also be similar, though the data may be organized in a different fashion in different companies. While in the case of data quality, the one-size-fits-all approach is not universally applicable, the basic data quality processes that are applicable to one organization can be tailored for other organizations as well.

Myth 10a: Data Quality Is a Luxury That Can Wait
Myth 10b: Data Quality Is a "Nice to Have"

These myths are driven by the fact that many organizations do not understand the true value of data quality and the cost of bad-quality data in dollar value, and hence think of data quality as an extravagance or a "nice to have" (Drayton 2017) that can wait, rather than as essential or a "must have," with such organizations pursuing other initiatives that they consider to be of higher priority than data quality initiatives.

The reality is that good-quality data are critical for accurate decision making, operational efficiency, compliance with regulatory requirements, customer relationships, and strategic business planning, and have a direct or indirect bearing on an organization's bottom line. Therefore, data quality is a "must have" that cannot wait. In fact, SiriusDecisions found that just by employing basic best practices for data quality, a company could generate up to 70% more revenue (Chinapen 2017). While the cost of bad data may not be obvious, as pointed out in myth 7, you do not want to wait until the point where data quality problems become so big that total chaos reigns. Taking into account the risks associated with bad data and the amount of time, money, and resources that companies spend to rectify data quality issues, it is apparent that data quality initiatives involving critical data that have a high business impact or a regulatory or compliance impact should not be postponed.

Myth 11: Return on Investment (ROI) for Data Quality Initiatives Is Difficult to Calculate

This myth stems from the fact that many companies struggle to calculate return on investment (ROI) for their data quality initiatives. This results in executives and senior management questioning whether data quality initiatives result in significant ROI and hence should be pursued.

The truth is that effective data quality initiatives generally result in substantial ROI. The specifics of the data quality initiative costs and benefits depend on the unique data landscape, processes, and challenges in determining where the value is (Andrews 2015). The first step is to find and document the relationships between data, business processes, and key performance indicators (KPIs). The functional users executing the processes also typically have a good sense of the gaps and impacts on a daily basis, for example, why it takes so long to create that report you just asked for (Andrews 2015).

Research in the area proves the ROI benefits of data quality initiatives. Experian's 2017 global research found that 69% of businesses have cited that where they have made investments in data quality solutions, they have seen a positive return on investment, and 50% of companies are using data to increase revenue (Drayton 2017). Aberdeen estimates that a typical data quality initiative saves five million hours in data cleansing time in an average company with 6.2 million records (Andrews 2015).

Myth 12: Data Quality Is Expensive

One of the myths regarding data quality is that data quality is an expensive endeavor. The perception that the current processes that produce information must be working properly (English 1999b), and myth 7, "with data, no news is good news"—plus the absence of senior management awareness of the cumulative costs of rework, data corrections, and workarounds—strengthen the acceptability of the myth that "data quality is expensive." Management accepts the costs of poor-quality data as a "normal" cost of doing business and are under the misconception that rework does not really hurt the business.

However, the truth is that the costs of rework, workarounds, data correction and cleanup, creating and maintaining proprietary databases because of inaccessibility to or non-quality data in production databases, multiple handling of data in redundant databases, and so on, take an incredible, but often transparent, toll on the bottom line. Based on numerous information quality cost analyses conducted by English, the direct costs of non-quality information in the typical organization claim 15% to 25% of its revenue or operating budget (English 1999b). Also, as discussed under myth 11, effective data quality initiatives generally result in substantial ROI.

Myth 13: Data Quality Issues Are Only Due to Data Sources or Data Entry

Data entry or the system that the data were sourced from often get blamed for data quality problems. While data entry errors and data source issues are often the cause of downstream data quality problems, they are not the sole cause. Chapter 1 discusses the details of the different causes of bad data quality.

As data travel through multiple intermediate systems in an organization, they are subject to various business transformation rules. Erroneous rules or wrong coding can introduce data quality issues in the target systems even though the original data entry and data in the source systems were correct.

Myth 14: Data Quality Checks Are a Part of the Extract, Transform, and Load (ETL) Process

Many organizations try to use the "transform" step in the ETL process to check and fix data errors (Andrews 2015) and believe that data quality checks are a part of the ETL process. While there are exceptional circumstances under which data cannot be corrected in source systems, or processes cannot be designed to prevent data errors from occurring in the first place—and in these situations data quality rules would need to be embedded in the ETL process—this should not be the norm. While using business rules to transform data obtained from the source system before loading them into the target system so that the data are loaded and displayed properly in the target system is a part of the ETL process, trying to find and fix data errors midstream by writing scripts into the ETL process should not be a part of the ETL process, as this causes more batch errors and doesn't solve the root cause of the problem, that is, bad data quality in the source systems. It also makes it impossible for business users to see, analyze, and fix exceptions as needed (Andrews 2015). When it comes to ETL, the "T" does not stand for DQ, that is, data quality (Andrews 2015).

A better approach is to validate and check model compliance and reconcile discrepancies before you send the data. This measures and improves quality in the respective systems and improves ETL process quality (Andrews 2015).

Myth 15: ETL Tools Offer Much the Same Functionality as Data Quality Tools

Some organizations mistakenly believe that ETL (extract, transform, load) tools offer much the same functionality as data quality tools. Unfortunately, ETL vendors have not gone out of their way to crush this myth (Eckerson 2002).

While ETL tools can perform some cleansing operations, such as mapping between code sets, and can apply procedural logic to catch critical data integrity problems, ETL tools do not provide many basic data quality capabilities, such as auditing, parsing, standardization via extensive reference libraries, matching, verification, and house holding.

In fact, ETL tools assume that the data they receive are clean and correct. Otherwise, their mapping and transformation programs do not output the correct data. Hence, the "code, load, and explode" phenomenon (Eckerson 2002).

Myth 16: Data Quality Is Data Cleansing

Some people have the misconception that by cleansing data they are improving the quality of the data. Data cleansing is the correction of incorrect data. While data cleansing and correction does "improve" the quality of the data product, and is one of the techniques of data quality management, it is merely information "scrap and rework." Like manufacturing scrap and rework, data cleansing is merely rework to correct defects that would not be there if the processes worked properly. Data cleansing and correction are, simply put, part of the costs of non-quality data. Data cleansing is a reactive approach to fixing data quality issues that are already present. Every hour consumed and dollar spent correcting data is an hour or dollar that cannot be spent doing something that adds value (English 1999b).

While data cleansing is required for any data warehouse migration, conversion, or integration project to succeed, quality data should ideally be produced at the source. If data in a data warehouse are of bad quality, the warehouse will fail (English 1999b).

Information quality improves processes by defining and implementing preventive measures to stop defective data from being created (English 1999b). Data cleansing attacks the symptoms of a data issue but does not treat the root cause. It fixes the results of faulty processes (English 1999b). Data quality attacks the root causes of data defects and eliminates the causes of bad data quality.

Myth 17: Data Quality Is Data Assessment

Some people have the misconception that data quality is data assessment. However, this is not true. Data assessment by itself does not result in data quality. Data audit or assessment is simply an inspection to check the health of the data and discover defects. While some data are so important that they must have regular audits and controls in place, data assessment is a costly activity that does not, all by itself, add value. Assessment of data quality has value when it is used to raise awareness of process failure and results in process improvements that eliminate the causes of defective data (English 1999b).

The ultimate goal of data assessment must be to assure that processes are creating and maintaining quality that consistently meets all information customers' requirements. Discovery of unsatisfactory data quality must lead to information process improvement and control (English 1999b).

Data quality minimizes data assessment because data quality is designed into the processes and controlled during production of data. An effective data quality function uses data assessment as a tool to uncover data issues to improve the processes that create, maintain, and deliver data (English 1999b).

Myth 18: If Data Works Well in the Source Systems, the Same Should Apply in Target Systems

If the data works well in the source system, conventional wisdom would indicate that it would work in the target systems too. However, organizations need to understand that this is a myth (Sarsfield 2017).

The reality is that data that work well in source systems may not work in the target systems. One factor is that the source systems may serve a single purpose that has less stringent data quality requirements. The unfit source system data work perfectly well because special routines may be written into the source system applications to handle data anomalies. The source application will understand the rule exceptions, but the target application will not. When data migrate to a new system, the special routines are lost, thereby causing data that do not load properly, compounded inaccuracies, time and cost overruns, and, in extreme cases, late-stage project cancellations. The data model of any source system defines which data go in what buckets, but a common data anomaly is a broken data model (Sarsfield 2017).

This is a common problem when trying to migrate data from legacy systems. During the production years, source data can become corrupted in a way that is not always visible in the legacy applications. Legacy systems rarely have complete specifications, and the embedded business rules and changes are not documented well, if documented at all. There is usually a huge gap between the legacy data model and the actual legacy data. The legacy system stores and uses data in a manner in which it should not be used. For instance, the date of birth of a customer is appended to the name of the customer and stored in a single field in the legacy system as there is no separate field for capturing the date of birth. The business rules defined in the legacy system deal with the data quality issues so that the output is as desired. However, target systems do not understand these exceptions, and data quality issues will appear in the target systems.

Tackling these types of data quality problems after the data are already loaded and operational is more difficult. When issues are identified, organizations will often undertake measures to rectify the problems, but all too often these efforts are shortsighted and only work to extinguish the fire (Sarsfield 2017). The tactic to fight this issue is not to assume that the data model is accurate. The best practice is to profile the data very early in the data migration process to completely understand the data quality challenges and ensure that there are no outliers. By profiling early, any major challenge with the data can be built into a more accurate project plan (Sarsfield 2017).

Myth 19: Data Migration Will Fix All Your Data Quality Issues

Data migration generally involves data being moved from one system to another. Many people falsely believe that data migration will fix all your data quality issues.

The truth is that a poorly executed migration can lead to worse data quality issues than you had in the first place. When migrating to a new system, planning is key (Drayton 2017). The best practice is to profile the data very early in the data migration process to completely understand the data quality challenges and ensure that there are no outliers.

By profiling early, any major challenge with the data can be built into a more accurate project plan (Sarsfield 2017).

Myth 20: Data Quality Is Too Risky

Often, people do not want to disturb the status quo for fear that they will make the situation worse. Many people hold the false belief that enforcing data quality standards is code for deleting bad data.

The truth is that improving data quality begins with normalizing all existing data, enriching blank fields, and merging records in a manner that preserves as many relevant, verified data points as possible (Chinapen 2017).

Myth 21: Data Quality Is the Same as Data Governance

There is a general misconception that data quality is the same data governance. The truth is that data quality is not the same as data governance, though they are very closely related data management disciplines, and doing one without the other is of little worth. In fact, without data governance it is very difficult to succeed in achieving and sustaining data quality throughout the enterprise due to lack of a governing framework that is rigorous in its definition and enforcement of data standards and policies, and lack of clear accountabilities, and responsibilities regarding the data.

Better-quality data is a key desired *result* from the implementation of data governance policies and processes, whereas data governance itself is the comprehensive, strategic, corporate vision of recognizing and managing data as a valued corporate asset.

DATA QUALITY CHALLENGES

With organizations having multiple data entry points and exit points, data residing in multiple systems, and huge volumes of data related to different business processes traveling through multiple systems and being massaged and transformed in many ways on its journey from source to target systems (as shown in Figure 7.2), the data environment is quite complex, and data quality management is not an easy endeavor, nor is attaining data quality an easy task. The myths and the complexity of the data environment together present some significant challenges, as shown in Figure 7.3, that discourage an organization from embarking on a data quality initiative. Some of the challenges faced by organizations are as follows.

Responsibility for Data and Data Quality, and Cross-Functional Collaboration

Data in an organization are related to different business processes, are used and shared by different business units, and flow through different systems. This poses challenges in terms of responsibility and cross-functional team collaboration. No single business unit is responsible for all the data in an organization (Geiger 2004). Also, once the data are

Figure 7.3   Data quality challenges.

transferred from the respective business unit spreadsheets to databases or systems that are maintained by the IT teams, the data are perceived as an IT responsibility, as discussed in myth 6a.

While business units and business functions within the business units align vertically, data quality management is horizontal in organizations and crosses departmental and business unit boundaries. Often, departments or business units share the same data. However, departments or business units often work in silos, making it difficult for them to align their goals and collaborate. For example, customer data are used by the sales, marketing, and financial operations departments. Effective data quality management would require these departments, along with IT, to come together and agree on common data definitions, which requires that each department take up some responsibility and give up some control at the same time, which is a challenge in itself.

Effective data quality management requires organizations to adopt a data stewardship approach, with a data steward being the person who takes care of the data. However, establishing a data stewardship program is difficult! One immediate challenge to a stewardship program is to identify the group or person responsible to care for a set of data. Usually, representatives from the business unit who use the particular data set are appointed as stewards. For example, representatives from the human resources department are appointed data stewards for employee data. The challenge in establishing data stewardship is with data sets that are shared and used by multiple business units or departments, for example, customer data that are used and shared by the different business functions of sales, marketing, and financial operations. The question would be— which business unit or department representative would be appointed as the data steward for the customer data?

Intuition-Driven Culture

Too often, organizations have a prevailing culture where intuition is valued rather than data, and there is a lack of accountability. In one survey, just 19% of respondents said that decision makers are held accountable for their decisions in their organization (Anderson and Li 2017).

Such a culture is detrimental to a data quality management program or data initiative as data, much less data quality, are not valued in such a culture, and to embark on your data quality journey, the people in the organization need to appreciate the value of data and the impact that bad quality has on realizing that value.

HiPPO, "highest paid person's opinion," a term coined by Avinash Kaushik, thrives in an intuition-driven culture (Anderson and Li 2017). They are the experts with decades of experience. They do not care what the data say, especially when the data disagree with their preconceived notions, and they are going to stick to their plan because they know best (Anderson and Li 2017). And besides, they're the boss. As the *Financial Times* explains:

> HiPPOs can be deadly for businesses, because they base their decisions on ill-understood metrics at best, or on pure guesswork. With no intelligent tools to derive meaning from the full spectrum of customer interactions and evaluate the how, when, where, and why behind actions, the HiPPO approach can be crippling for businesses (Anderson and Li 2017).

HiPPOs can be major blockers of data quality initiatives as they perceive losing their importance, position, and power in the organization with data driven decisions.

Lack of Awareness

Organizations are often in denial about their data quality problems either because they falsely believe that "with data, no news is good news," or because business executives who need to acknowledge data quality problems have their own functional responsibilities and do not have time to focus on the data related to their business functions. It sometimes takes a major catastrophe to change that attitude and to start taking serious steps to solve data quality problems. In the absence of such an event, organizations are not prone to spend money fixing something that they do not think is broken (Geiger 2004).

Resistance to Change

An effective data quality management program requires changes in operations, discipline, and behavioral changes in the organization that can be disruptive and hence lead to resistance.

Responsibilities must be assigned and formal procedures must be created and followed that require both discipline and behavioral changes on the part of everyone who handles data for the enterprise. The changes in behavior would depend on the role that the individual plays in relation to the data. Assigning responsibilities for effective data quality management means that field agents need to understand the value of the data gathered about the business function he or she are capturing so that the data are captured correctly. It also means that IT and governance must understand the quality expectations and business rules provided by the business analysts, as well as the metadata and data standards, so that the development team builds the systems to process the data correctly, and further, it means that the business analysts and users of the data understand their meaning and provide business rules correctly so that they can make well-informed decisions. Further, it means that job descriptions for individuals in these positions must reflect their data quality management responsibilities (Geiger 2004).

One of the projects that I worked on required users to query and produce reports by themselves rather than use the ready-made report being provided to them in an Excel document by the source system operational staff. Since the latter was the practice for 15 years, the users were set in their ways and were not inclined to learn something new that would cause them extra work, so they naturally resisted to the change.

Since an enterprise-wise data quality management program would impact a large number of people and require different operational behavior, training and educating people to make the change can be a big challenge.

Funding and Sponsorship

Organizations are constantly looking for ways of downsizing and cutting costs. A data quality initiative, like any other initiative, requires funding. However, this requires executives to acknowledge data quality issues and what data quality issues are doing to the bottom line. An organization has a lot of projects and initiatives for which different executives are trying to get funding and sponsorship. The question that needs to be answered is—why should data quality initiatives take priority over other projects?

A data quality management program requires skilled human resources, and it is extremely difficult to acquire endorsement for an effort that will increase the number of people on payroll. Implementing data quality management technology, however, automates manual data quality and integration projects and frees up resources who were carrying on these manual activities for other projects. Because data quality management software investment costs less than one employee (salary, benefits, and so on), implementations actually support organizational goals of increased productivity or reduced staffing (Geiger 2004). However, human resources, mostly from the business organization, will still be needed to perform certain data governance–related activities, and this cannot be automated. The effort that is avoidable is the human resources required to identify and manually fix or correct data issues on a day-to-day basis. This is an area in which data quality technology can help the organization gain an understanding of the data (data profiling), take steps to correct problems (data quality), automate some discrepancy resolution resulting from merging data from multiple sources (data integration), and add value to the data (data augmentation). To be effective, the tools need to be customizable so that they impose the rules established by the organization (Geiger 2004).

Return on Investment

Data quality management efforts require funding for which return on investment needs to be calculated—essentially the cost of bad data quality. The documentation of these costs requires recognition of data quality issues and the costs involved to fix them, and also requires managers to admit that they are wasting money or that they are not effectively utilizing resources at their disposal. Making these admissions, particularly in tough economic times, is precarious (Geiger 2004). It is a common scenario for application support personnel to use manual remediation to fix the reports periodically before sending them to the users instead of investing in a permanent fix, as it would reflect badly on the application lead or department lead to ask for budget to fix the issue. It is imperative that top management create an environment in which people are not unduly penalized for admitting to past problems (Geiger 2004).

REASONS FOR FAILURE OF DATA QUALITY INITIATIVES

Below are various reasons and situations that can contribute to or increase the probability of the failure of a data quality initiative:

- Individuals leading these initiatives have a lack of knowledge, experience (Ramchandani 2016), drive, and commitment.

- Lack of management support.

- The right individuals with the right skill sets are not involved in the execution of the initiative (Ramchandani 2016).

- The data initiative is led by IT, with limited or no business user involvement.

- Lack of clarity on expectations, accountability, and ownership (Ramchandani 2016).

- Data quality initiatives are treated as a project instead of an ongoing program (Ramchandani 2016).

- The right tools, technology, and processes are not used (Ramchandani 2016).

- Lack of a clear strategy or project plan and unrealistic expectations.

- Loss of momentum due to lack of communication and collaboration among the team.

- Lack of change management.

- The focus is on technology only and not on the business processes.

- Loss of funding.

- The initiative is perceived as an overhead expense with no defined value.

- Absence of metrics to measure and showcase return on investment.

DATA QUALITY—CRITICAL SUCCESS FACTORS

While realizing and maintaining quality data is not rocket science, it does involve a great deal of work and a significant amount of effort, time, and investment, and cultural change. Attaining and maintaining quality data is an ongoing endeavor, and implementing and sustaining the initiative is complex, challenging, and time-consuming (Southekal 2017). It is important to understand that data are part of a bigger picture where people, processes, and technology play an equally important role in ensuring its quality.

Figure 7.4 illustrates the critical success factors for achieving and sustaining data quality in an organization, and each factor will be discussed in this section. It is important to take all these factors into account when launching a data quality initiative to make sure that you achieve success in your data quality endeavors.

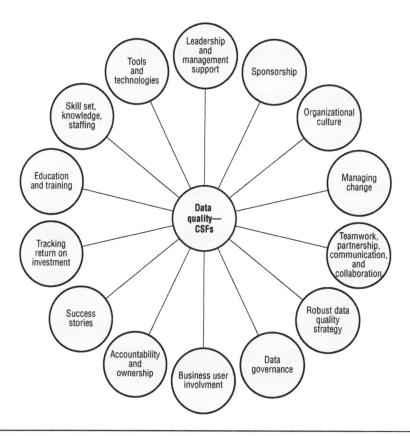

Figure 7.4 Data quality—critical success factors (CSFs).

Leadership and Management Support

Successful implementation of an enterprise-wide strategy or initiative requires leadership support, management commitment, and sponsorship, and the same applies in the case of a data quality strategy or initiative. It is important that business executives are aware of and fully understand the true cost of poor data quality and see data as an enterprise issue, and not solely as an IT or technology problem.

Providing key executives and leadership with facts and figures regarding the cost of non-quality, and estimated benefits from implementing the data quality initiative, and regular updates, and arming them with success stories will be crucial in helping to get the message disseminated across all functional teams.

Data quality initiatives often involve a massive change in the way things are done. The management group, including top management and middle management, do not actually implement change, but rather remove barriers and create an environment where responsibility is spread throughout the business (Mahanti 2011). The executives and leaders should be consistently dedicated to making the change successful. They are instrumental in creating an atmosphere conducive to fostering an organizational culture that aims to build universal commitment to the data quality initiative. Without top management's blessing, any initiative, program, project, or strategy is bound to fail, and this is no different in the case of a data quality management program.

Leadership support is the key component of a quality improvement implementation process (Meurer et al. 2002; Alexander et al. 2006; Walmsley and Miller 2007). When attempting to initiate change, one has to be mindful of the organization's emotional and political reaction quotient. Leaders play a critical role in disseminating culture and removing barriers to improve the efforts to uncover data quality issues and enhance data quality (Ababaneh 2010). Senior management must show their commitment and give full approval to the data quality initiative. Management's aim should be to create organizational awareness of data quality issues. It is the responsibility of top management to encourage and support data quality projects, and at the end, institutionalize the benefits. They should make sure resources and budget are available for implementing data quality improvement programs, and encourage data quality training and data quality awareness programs enterprise-wide. They must make it clear that data quality management is an ongoing activity.

Sponsorship

For a data quality program or strategy to be successful, sponsorship is a fundamental contributing factor. Sponsors can make or break the long-term realization of your data quality targets, and hence should be chosen with care. Sponsor support is not limited to finance but goes beyond it; you need them to articulate the core value proposition in different ways to different stakeholders, including senior executives in the organization. Therefore, a good sponsor should have a good understanding of the business impacts and benefits of data quality, the exact strategy and roadmap that is being undertaken, the short-term and long-term goals, and the systems and operational processes involved. In case the sponsors do not have this knowledge, there should be a plan to educate them. Sponsors should be committed to supporting the mission and vision for the data quality program, must invest time in the data quality endeavor, and not just pay lip service to it. Since data quality programs are long-term initiatives, it is critical to find a sponsor who will preferably back you for a considerable length of time and not leave you in limbo, trying to find the next sponsor.

Typically, the sponsor leads a function that benefits significantly from better data, and can communicate the entire value proposition to the entire organization and convince senior management and respond to their queries regarding the initiative as and when raised. For example, if the chief financial officer is the data quality sponsor, he or she should drive for consistent measurement and improvement of data quality across the information that his team consumes.

Dylan Jones, in his blog article "7 Characteristics of an Ideal Data Quality Sponsor" (2013), outlines some desirable traits that should be present in a data quality sponsor:

- Respected across the ranks (senior management)
- Possesses the right level of knowledge
- Proficient networker and introducer
- Not on a fast-track, transitory flight path
- Effective communicator at all levels
- Leads by example

Organizational Culture

Management guru Peter Drucker once said, "Culture eats strategy for breakfast" (Schein 2004). This basically means that an organization's culture can be a powerful force to counteract and resist change, no matter how good the strategy is (Southekal 2017).

A quality culture is the sum of the organization's capabilities, habits, and beliefs that enable it to design and deliver products and services that meet customer needs and be successful in the marketplace over the long term (Juran Institute 2014). The best organizations have strong cultures that encourage adaptability and continuous improvement in all areas of operation (Adams 2009). Without an understanding of the cultural facets of quality, significant and long-term improvements in quality levels are implausible.

A strong data-driven culture and mind set are necessary to sustain and maintain data quality. A data-oriented culture is characterized by viewing and valuing data as a strategic enterprise asset rather than a tactical application by-product, basing decisions on data and facts rather than assumptions, gut instincts, and experience, using KPIs to baseline the current status and to track future progress and outcomes (Southekal 2017), establishing value and responsibility for the information, and establishing processes and operations to make it easy for employees to acquire the required information while being transparent about data access restrictions and governance frameworks.

While 80% of CEOs claim to have operationalized the notion of data as an asset, only 10% say that their company actually treats it that way (Dunlea 2015). The culture of a digital enterprise—at a minimum—lies in using data for business performance, framing questions for discovery, valuing hypotheses over assumptions, and using key performance indicators (KPIs) to baseline the current status and to track future progress and outcomes. Furthermore, implementing data initiatives is not a one-time project. Becoming a digital enterprise is a continuous improvement initiative that can only be successful if every business stakeholder in the enterprise has a stake in data (Southekal 2017).

Managing Change

Managing change and overcoming individual and organizational resistance is one of the crucial factors in the successful implementation of any data quality initiative and data quality management; change management needs to be ingrained into the data quality initiative. Like any major initiative, a data quality initiative requires changes in approach, mind set, attitudes, operations, methods, and ways of doing things. Too often, organizations have a prevailing culture where intuition is valued rather than data, or there is a lack of accountability. The success of any data quality program requires a huge cultural shift. The culture needs to change from an intuition-based culture to a data-driven culture. This cultural shift takes time, and the first step is to focus on evangelizing and communicating the importance of data and data quality across all departments throughout the organization.

Executives might not trust IT to execute the needed changes, and workers (including IT) might not trust executives to create and execute a plan instead of just talking about one. In addition, each department or business unit has its own goals, agenda, jargon, and incentives, creating a virulent "us versus them" mentality. Often, data becomes a victim of organizational turf wars (Eckerson 2011).

A successful introduction and implementation of a data quality program requires adjustments to the culture of the organization and a change in the attitudes of its employees. Organizations that have been successful in managing change have recognized that the best way to deal with resistance to change is through increased and sustained communication, motivation, and education.

Change management involves identifying the teams or segments or departments that will be affected by the new program. It is important to segregate and understand the emotional and political reaction quotient of the different user constituencies when implementing a data quality program. More realistically, you need an astute understanding of what is making people nervous, what makes people tick, and what factors will help or hinder the change, a plan for selling the change to the recipients, training, education and support, details of how the change will be rolled out, and a lot of persistence and patience. Communications and training strategy should be tailored to each end user constituency. The communications plan should define which messages and operational updates get conveyed to which constituencies via which channels at what times (Eckerson 2011). Likewise, a training plan should define how and when training will be conducted, the training materials to be used, and the facilitators in place for the training. Change management tools such as change acceleration process (CAP) tools—stakeholder analysis, team charters, critical success factor analysis, threat opportunity matrix, three D's matrix, CAP profiling, and gap assessment surveys—are useful in breaking down barriers and managing change.

A data quality initiative is accompanied by technology changes and/or process changes that require employees to learn how to use the new tools and technologies and change their mode of operation. Learning to operate these new tools might require upskilling that the employees are not quite ready for. Also, people get used to the way they do things, prefer to stay in their comfort zone, and are often not open to new ways of thinking and operation. In short, people are afraid of change, and hence resist it and do not accept it. They may fear losing their status, privilege, position of power (Eckerson 2011), or job, which are often entrenched in the management of the flow of data, when a manual process or semi-automated process of processing data is replaced by an automated process for data processing. The challenge is even greater if the employees of the organization are not prone to technical thinking and find that such a change takes them out of their comfort zone, or the organization is at the lowest level of the data maturity ladder where data are viewed as a cost rather than an opportunity. It is necessary to involve stakeholders in planning workshops and set up working group meetings with team leaders as representatives of each of the impacted teams in order to give them periodic updates, resolve their concerns, and break down resistance. The more involved employees are during the planning and delivery, the more likely the change will stick.

For example, consider a scenario where the manual process of generating a monthly employee commission report in the financial operations department of a financial services organization, as depicted in Figure 7.5, is replaced by an automated process, depicted in Figure 7.6, as part of a data quality program.

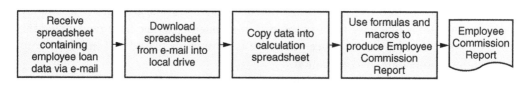

Figure 7.5 Manual process for generating the Employee Commission Report.

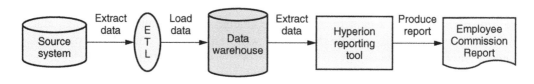

Figure 7.6 Automated process for generating the Employee Commission Report.

The manual process entailed a number of activities as follows. It started with the concerned team receiving employee and home loan data extracted from the system at the end of the month by the IT operation team via e-mail with an attached spreadsheet. This was then followed by downloading the spreadsheet containing that month's employee loan data into the local drive, and copying the data into another spreadsheet used for manually calculating the employee commission based on the number of home loan accounts opened per month by the employees, using macros and formulas embedded in the spreadsheet, and producing a monthly employee commission report. The data quality initiative replaced this set of manual activities by automating the extraction of data from the source system, loading the data into a data warehouse, and producing the reports in Hyperion. Manual manipulations for creation of the report were replaced by business rules embedded in the software code. Generation of reports involved running reports through the Hyperion front-end tool, an interface that was very different from Microsoft Excel. The process and technology changes invoked feelings of loss, mistrust, job insecurity, and discomfort in the group of employees who were involved in the creation of the report when they were first communicated about it by their managers. Workshops were organized early on during the planning phase to communicate the objectives and benefits of the change, and at the same time address the concerns of the impacted employees. These workshops were attended by representatives from the impacted business area, IT personnel, and project staff, including the project manager, change managers, and the project sponsors. Weekly working group meetings were set up to communicate progress and provide post-implementation support (consisting of training and on-site support by the analysts) for smooth rollout of the change.

Change Agents. Also known as *organizational change managers*, change agents play an important role in steering the organization toward a data-driven culture. Armed with powerful tools for problem solving, a capability to inject energy and enthusiasm, a knack for identifying patterns of resistance that can sabotage the change, and good listening and communication skills, these individuals can be the catalyst of any change initiative. Change agents get all people affected by the data quality initiative engaged, to ensure their acceptance, support, and commitment. This requires a high level of competency as the basis for acceptance, as well as soft skills, including the ability to communicate, to understand individual, team, and organizational behaviors, and to take into account the opinions and doubts of others.

Business User Involvement

It is very important for a data quality program to be driven by the business. Active business user involvement is crucial to the success of any data quality initiative. Although IT sometimes resists and wants to lead these initiatives, and even though the business team sometimes regards anything having to do with computers, databases, and information as being the responsibility of the IT department, don't make the mistake of doing a data quality initiative without the business being firmly in the driver's seat (Power 2011).

Data quality initiatives driven by IT typically fail. This is because IT does not have knowledge of business scenarios, data quality requirements, business rules governing data quality, which data are critical and have maximum business impact, and how the data will be used. For example, IT will not be able to tell a good address from a bad address, or if there are multiple customer records, which record to choose. Only the business users have business insight into their data and have knowledge of what to expect from the data. Hence, they are the ones who are aware of all the possible business scenarios and can define the requirements, tell which data entities and elements are critical, clarify ambiguous requirements, detect data issues, and make the decision as to whether data are good (that is, fit for purpose) or bad (that is, not fit for purpose). Business users should be involved in defining and signing off requirements for a data quality initiative, making sure that the test cases cover all scenarios and data used for testing have sufficient coverage, and validating the data during the test phase as well as after deployment.

Tools and Technologies

Data quality tools and technologies play a critical role in a data quality management effort. With digitization, the volume of electronic data held by organizations has increased exponentially and cannot be handled manually; specialized data quality technologies are needed to handle these large volumes of data. Studies have found that business users can spend up to 50% of their time fixing data quality errors. The right tools can help with saving time and reducing the cost of delivering data quality with a scalable platform that can be leveraged across the organization (Ramchandani 2016).

There is an abundance of established and emerging technologies that can help organizations store, manage, exploit, and access electronic data (DAMA UK 2011). Some key technology areas include databases and data warehouses, business intelligence applications, master data management (MDM) tools, data integration tools, data mining and analytic applications, metadata repositories, extract, transform, and load (ETL) tool sets, data profiling tools, data remediation/cleansing, data matching and reconciliation tools, and data monitoring and audit technologies.

It is important to keep the requirements of the entire organization in mind when choosing data quality technology. Data quality technology should be chosen based on what best suits the business objectives instead of the IT department only. Different organizations have different requirements, business practices, data quality requirements, and data complexity, as well as varied expectations from a data quality technology perspective, and different tools have different capabilities. For instance, not all data quality tools support all types of data sources. As an example, a water utility company that has data stored in a geographic information system will require more-specialized data quality tools that have the capability to read data from geographic information systems than a financial services company that has data stored in a multitude of relational databases like Oracle, DB2, Netezza, MS-SQL Server, Sybase, or Teradata or legacy systems, which are supported by most data quality tools and technologies.

The tools should support your enterprise's long-term vision and be able to scale to support current as well as future business needs. There is an abundance of data quality tools and technologies on the market by different vendors, and a cross-functional team consisting of IT and business representatives should conduct industry research and consult with industry experts before finalizing the tool assessment criteria based on their business requirements in relation to data quality and the data themselves. Some of the key evaluation criteria are the tool's out-of-the-box data quality capabilities, its ability to integrate with other applications in the enterprise, performance and scalability of the tool, mode of operation, platform supported, openness of the rules and results repositories, usability, interaction with external sources (for example USPS and other postal services for address data), auditing, consolidation, standardization, augmentation or enhancement, cleansing, matching, parsing, maturity of the product, product roadmap, total ownership cost, vendor support, and whether the product has a business user–centric tool and a developer-centric tool. A business-centric tool will enable nontechnical business users to perform data analysis tasks without the need for extensive coding.

Prioritizing the assessment criteria, allocating weights accordingly, and using a weighted scoring method will aid the selection process. The products with the top three scores can be subjected to rigorous functional and performance tests, based on your requirements, to arrive at a conclusion.

Choosing the right application to implement the processes as defined by the people is very important, and should only be done after the processes have been defined and accepted by all parties involved. The tool and technology should be chosen with the long-term benefit of the organization in mind. Furthermore, with the expansion in data volumes and new data types, the portfolio of data quality tools needs to be upgraded to be able to manage and manipulate the data.

Skill Sets, Knowledge, and Staffing

In order for a data quality program to be successful, the right people with the right skill sets, knowledge, and experience should be involved in the program.

Skill Sets and Knowledge. Data quality is an interdisciplinary area that involves business processes and functions, industry domain, technology, and data management principles and concepts. For a data quality initiative to be successful, an overlap in the variety of skill sets and knowledge areas is required to be present in the organization, as summarized in Figure 7.7.

Conceptual Knowledge. This includes conceptual and practical knowledge of information management concepts, data warehouse, database, data hierarchy, data quality concepts, and methods needed to implement data quality.

Domain Knowledge. Domain knowledge from a data quality perspective is knowledge of the data and the quality of the data in relation to the data quality dimensions and the

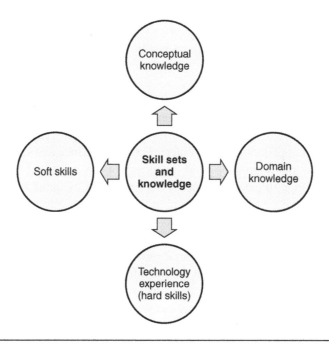

Figure 7.7   Skill sets and knowledge for data quality.

business function it supports. This knowledge usually rests with the business users in charge of the business function and process, and they are normally the subject matter experts who define the business rules related to data quality in a data quality program.

Technology Experience (Hard Skills). Technology is needed to handle the massive volume of data, and this calls for technical knowledge of and experience with the data quality tools and technologies for implementing systems. Strong information technology skill and robust programming experience are musts. Sound conceptual and technical knowledge of relational databases and file systems is necessary, as data often reside in heterogeneous sources, with relational databases (for example, Teradata, Netezza, MS-SQL Server, Oracle, DB2, and Sybase) and files being the most common sources and target systems. Downstream reporting tools (for example, Tableau, OBIEE, Hyperion, Crystal Reports, and Cognos) are used to create reports and knowledge and experience in these tools is necessary too.

Soft Skills. While achieving data quality requires technology, technology is only the enabler. Before technology can be even applied, you need articulation and presentation of the business case to get executive buy-in and sponsorship, data quality awareness, requirements to be documented clearly, and close communication among the stakeholders. The scope of work needs to be defined and agreed on, and priorities need to be set.

Success in these activities calls for strong project management, interpersonal, writing, presentation, and communication (both verbal and written) skills. Strong presentation skills are required to propagate data quality awareness within the organization and to get buy-in from stakeholders. Achieving data quality is not a one-off effort, but ongoing in nature, and requires a commitment to report program status and progress to the stakeholders on a regular basis. Communication skills play a fundamental part in keeping the importance of data quality top of mind among all levels of hierarchy in the enterprise by communicating the right amount of detail at the right time. Also, since data quality programs involve a cross-functional team, strong communication skills are necessary to avoid misinterpretation and confusion. Interpersonal skills play a critical role in building and sustaining a strong relationship.

Data quality programs result in changes to operations as well as mind sets and attitudes, and hence change management skills are required to overcome resistance to change and get people to accept the new mode of operation and not revert to their old ways of doing things.

Without these softer skill sets, a data quality initiative will not be successful.

Staffing. People are one of the essential elements in implementing and sustaining any data quality efforts. Putting a data quality program into action requires a lot of work and commitment as well as ongoing effort and support. To put forth a plan with a realistic expectation, people with the right level of knowledge and proven experience are needed to guide and sustain the ongoing efforts. Long-term improvements will not materialize unless the data quality program is fully staffed and the right people with the right skill sets and experience are hired. This is because data quality management typically involves changes to processes or the introduction of new processes to improve data quality, technology to improve the standard of data quality, and ongoing data governance. People support business processes and IT systems (databases, data warehouses, ETL processes), filling the gaps where necessary and addressing data exceptions as and when they occur.

Data quality programs require a cross-functional team with individuals or groups of individuals playing different roles and shouldering responsibilities to achieve the program goals. Different roles and responsibilities might call for a combination of hard and soft skills. For example, a technical business analyst working on a data integration project needs to have a good understanding of data quality, database concepts, SQL knowledge, and overall understanding of the data quality technology, a logical and analytical mind set, as well soft skills—stakeholder management skills, good communication skills, documentation skills, and presentation skills. For example, I was working as an analyst on a project that involved sourcing additional data from legacy and SAP Operational Data Store (ODS) into an existing table in the data warehouse in a financial services organization. The data flowed through several intermediate system environments before landing in the data warehouse. For this exercise, I had to understand the business, profile legacy data in Excel and SAP ODS data using SQL queries, interpret the results with the help of subject matter experts as to what constituted an anomaly and what was a valid business scenario, understand the current mapping document and liaise with the developers to confirm that the code indeed reflected the current mapping requirements, understand the current target table data by running SQL queries, and determine the impacts that adding the new data could have on other applications and downstream systems extracting data from this table. Since the immediate upstream system, SAP ODS, had no transformational rules, and SAP ODS subject matter experts could not provide clarifications related to the data, I had to engage with further upstream system (that is, SAP) stakeholders and subject matter experts to understand the data, which involved viewing the SAP interfaces and communicating the findings to the target stakeholders and subject matter experts. When target system stakeholders were satisfied with the source data quality, I had to modify the existing mapping document with transformation rules, explain the rules to the developers, and design test cases and validate the final results in the data warehouse post testing and implementation.

While there should not be a lack of domain knowledge in the organization, with different business units and departments having their own subject matter experts, there is a strong possibility that the organization might not have people with the right level of experience in managing the data. In case of a lack of in-house technology talent, it is recommended to use external information management consultants with the required skill set and a proven track record when the organization initially deploys a data quality program, while concomitantly organizing training for internal staff to upskill them so that at a given point in time the internal staff can take over as part of business-as-usual activity.

Accountability and Ownership

For a data quality program or initiative to be successful, a clear definition and assignment of ownership, accountability, roles, and responsibilities in relation to implementation of data quality is required. There should be a clear segregation of duties between business and IT organizations to avoid a duplication of effort, potential confusion, ambiguity of roles and responsibilities, ownerships issues, and inevitable chaos.

IT has a better understanding of the technical aspects of data and what happens to them as they are stored in systems, extracted from data stores, and transferred between applications and systems, as well as how they are stored and transferred and the software and database environments. The business team has a better understanding of the business function related to the data, the process that generates them, and the data usage. Hence, IT should be accountable for the technology delivery aspect, and business users should be accountable for the quality improvement aspect: business rules for data quality. Governance team representatives should be responsible for compliance with policies, standards, and guidelines and support their enforcement.

IT can focus on enabling and supporting the business with proactive data profiling and implemention of tools and processes, as well as on training business stewards on the usage of tools and data lineage. On the other hand, the business can focus on the actual improvements in the data by fixing the data in the source system, monitoring the trends in quality, identifying the root causes of issues, and recommending process and system improvements (Ramchandani 2016).

Industry experts outline numerous data quality positions. If the organization is not large enough to dedicate individuals to each of these positions, it's important that someone assumes the responsibilities described. In small or mid-sized organizations or departments, a single individual may assume responsibility for multiple roles (Eckerson 2002):

- *Chief data officer.* A business executive who oversees the organization's data stewardship, data administration, and data quality programs.

- *Data steward.* A businessperson who is accountable for the quality of data in a given subject area (Eckerson 2002).

- *Subject matter expert (SME).* A business analyst whose knowledge of the business and systems is critical to understand data, define rules, identify errors, and set thresholds for acceptable levels of data quality (Eckerson 2002).

- *Data quality leader.* Oversees a data quality program that involves building awareness, developing assessments, establishing service level agreements, cleaning and monitoring data, and training technical staff (Eckerson 2002).

- *Data quality analyst.* Responsible for auditing, monitoring, and measuring data quality on a daily basis, and recommending actions for correcting and preventing errors and defects (Eckerson 2002).

- *Tools specialists.* Individuals who understand either ETL or data quality tools, or both, and can translate business requirements into rules that these systems implement (Eckerson 2002).

- *Process improvement facilitator.* Coordinates efforts to analyze and reengineer business processes to streamline data collection, exchange, and management, and improve data quality (Eckerson 2002).

- *Data quality trainer.* Develops and delivers data quality education, training, and awareness programs (Eckerson 2002).

Teamwork, Partnership, Communication, and Collaboration

Teamwork and partnership are essential for the success of a data quality initiative. Depending on the subject area, source data are managed by cross-functional teams consisting of IT, business, and governance personnel, which necessitates partnership, communication, cooperation, and collaboration between these teams. Data are an enterprise asset, and as such, cross business unit and departmental boundaries in an organization. Data from the source systems generally traverse various intermediate systems before the data are available in the target systems. All these systems are supported by different information technology and data management groups. Data quality programs are collaborative in nature and involve the combined efforts of a number of teams drawn from information technology groups and various business units in the organization. Implementing such a program calls for very close collaboration between IT teams and senior business executives, as well as the involvement of business users.

Alliance is needed among multiple data management teams that exist within the organization, as these teams need to collaborate and agree on common standards for defining and modeling business entities (such as customers, products, assets, and financials) and how data about these can be improved and shared across IT systems. Collaboration is necessary between large data management teams, ranging from business data stewards to data analysts to the technical application teams, in order to enable the complete data management life cycle, from data standards and definitions, data capture, and data transformation to data quality deployment, data quality monitoring, and issue resolution. For example, consider a data quality improvement project in a utility company involving customer and asset data that touch processes to maintain assets based on customer complaints. With multiple source systems for these data and data being integrated in a data warehouse and used for downstream reporting, multiple cross-functional teams—including both business (asset department, performance monitoring department, customer contacts department) and different IT teams—needed to be involved, and collaboration and agreement were needed across the teams in order to be successful.

Therefore, interdependence and harmonization among the cross-functional teams becomes crucial to the success of a data quality program. The success of a project depends on this factor (Bunse et al. 1998; Li et al. 2000). Information technology groups must partner with each other, and business groups should also partner with one another. What is required to succeed is striking the right balance of business and IT alignment, where the business takes the lead but has strong support from and is aligned with leadership from IT (Power 2011).

The value of teamwork formed by cross-functional teams will launch a sense of ownership, better communication, team working value, and an overall view of the organization (*Aviation Week* 1998).

Education and Training

Education and training are prerequisites to the implementation and success of any initiative or program, and this applies in the case of data quality too. Education and training bring about an enhancement in knowledge and skills and a transformation in the behavior and outlook of personnel.

Human nature tends to resist that which is new and not understood. There will be considerably less resistance to a data quality initiative and better backing from the key stakeholders if they understand data quality management and are committed to its deployment. Data quality awareness training should be conducted throughout the organization so that employees are able to comprehend the importance of data quality and the need for data quality management and improvement. Training should be regarded as an investment necessitating funding, with a return on that investment. There is no substitute for a well-trained staff of data entry operators, process analysts and specialists, developers, designers, architects, analysts, leaders, and so on.

Depending on the roles and responsibilities of the user constituencies, they would be required to learn different skills to adapt to the new way of doing things, which would in turn necessitate diversified training requirements, and this should be taken into consideration when devising the training plan and strategy. In general, data quality tasks will fall into one or more of the following categories:

1. Data entry

2. Process design and control

3. IT application design, implementation, and support

Data Entry. Since a lot of errors occur at the point of data entry, users need to be adequately trained to minimize the potential for errors. Data entry involves responsibility for the accuracy and completeness of data as they are entered into a system or are processed by a system. Users need to be educated on data standards, the business scenarios, and exception cases, and what action they need to take in different exception cases, for example, if a piece of information is missing, under which conditions they need to enter a default value, or when they should not proceed with the data entry until a particular data field value is present. For example, for banks, it is important to have the date of birth when they enroll a customer, and they cannot proceed until they know this value, so data entry should not proceed without this information. However, a work telephone number is optional, and hence data entry can proceed without this information. Usually, data quality improvement involves modern, interactive data entry screens replacing a completely manual system, or the redesign of an existing data entry screen. Data entry professionals would need to be adequately trained in order to realize their potential for minimizing data issues resulting from data entry. They need to understand the data quality standards and what characters are allowed and not allowed in the fields, and have the ability to recognize junk data.

Process Design and Control. Data quality improvement is often accompanied by changes in the business process design and an increase in controls to ensure better quality. This might involve reducing data touchpoints or increasing data touchpoints depending on the situation. The impacted teams need to be made aware of the change, and trained and educated in the to-be processes—what would change for them. For example, implementation of an in-house tool to process lending applications in a financial services organization resulted in business process changes necessitating an increase in data touchpoints where certain teams needed to record comments in the web-based tool after commencement of a particular activity and read comments before commencing particular activities. This was clearly communicated through training, and quick-reference guidance and user manuals with illustrations were used to educate and assist the users.

IT Application Design, Implementation, and Support. IT application design and implementation are characterized by the design and implementation of new systems, or upgrading existing applications, with data quality management as a primary goal. Once these applications are implemented, they would also need to be supported by the operational or production support teams in case of problems. IT staff need to be trained in data quality tools and technologies and data quality standards. This education needs to consist of a combination of the data quality and information management concepts, data quality case studies and success stories from other organizations, and specific issues within the organization's data.

While many organizations have already implemented data warehouses, there are still organizations who are going through the discovery process of implementing a data warehouse. In addition, depending on the data quality requirements, organizations may need to purchase and implement data quality tools and technologies. There are a plethora of data quality tools available in the market, and while all of them are based on the common theoretical concepts of data quality, data warehouses, master data management, and so on, the technical knowledge required to use the tools differs and necessitates specialized training.

Generally, the IT development team consists of a combination of designers, analysts, developers, and testers headed by the team lead and project manager, and each needs to be trained in the appropriate tools and technologies as per their roles and responsibilities. For example, for a data warehouse implementation, while all the stakeholders would need to be educated in data quality, data warehouse, and database concepts, there would be additional training needed for the IT development team depending on their roles and responsibilities. For example, a data designer would need to be trained in data modeling concepts and the data modeling tool that he or she is going to use, and a developer should be trained in database technologies, data quality tools, and ETL tools.

In addition, the system users across the organization should be trained in data quality audit and monitoring technologies to be able to audit and monitor the performance of their systems in relation to data quality management.

While the IT team would require deeper conceptual and technical knowledge and hence more-rigorous training relating to information management concepts and technologies, their business counterparts would need only a basic understanding of information management and technologies, hence, less-rigorous training.

Success Stories

Success stories have a great impact on the prevailing culture. Success stories help in instilling individuals' faith and confidence in the data quality approach as well as boosting the employees' morale. It will be much easier to garner support for the data quality initiative if people recognize that the enterprise is either spending more money or is losing business opportunities due to data quality management deficiencies.

Robust Data Quality Strategy

As discussed in Chapter 5, "Data Quality Strategy," without a data quality strategy, initiatives that should have been a part of a comprehensive strategy are addressed piecemeal, without assessing the enterprise-level implications, the risks, and alignment or lack of alignment with the organization's strategic objectives. This results in implementation of suboptimized solutions, introduction of initiatives or programs that may have an adverse effect on the overall enterprise, inconsistencies, or development of systems that cannot be easily integrated.

There is a correlation between the sophistication of a data quality strategy and the quality of data within the data stores and systems. Organizations who have a robust data quality strategy tend to experience fewer data issues, waste less revenue due to data problems, have fewer compliance issues, and, overall, are more lucrative. A good data quality strategy is a key to greater success in terms of data quality. It is essential that organizations manage and maintain data over time. Organizations have to become more sophisticated in their data management in order to stay competitive. However, improving these processes can be overwhelming for organizations. Determining the right data initiatives that will provide the maximum benefit to the organization requires speaking to the right people across the business area and IT, aligning the data quality strategy to the corporate business strategy, determining the current state and establishing the future state, doing gap analysis and prioritizing data initiatives, performing a cost–benefit analysis, outlining the risk and success factors, and preparing a strategic roadmap; all these activities are a part of the strategy formulation process. The more rigorous the data quality strategy formulation process, the more robust the data quality strategy, leading to better processes for delivering better-quality data.

Data Governance

Data governance plays a fundamental role in enterprise data quality management efforts and data quality, and a carefully designed framework for enterprise-wide data governance is crucial to ensure the long-term success of data quality management efforts in an organization. Data governance is essential for providing clarity on data access, integration, usage, and management, and ownership of enterprise data. Data governance provides a forum in which the business and IT can reach agreement on data that are shared across the enterprise. Data governance refers to the policies, processes, rules, standards, and procedures geared toward the overall management of data quality. Data governance is about how decisions are made on data-related matters and who has what authority to make those decisions. Data governance incorporates organizational bodies, rules (policies, standards, guidelines, and business rules), processes, decision rights (including guidance on "deciding how to decide"), accountabilities, and enforcement (Innovit Undated). We will discuss the data governance framework in detail in Chapter 8, "Data Governance and Data Quality."

One of the unique characteristics of data is that they're an enterprise, departmental, and individual resource. However, without strong governance, data always default to the lowest common denominator, which is, first and foremost, an analyst armed with a spreadsheet, and second, a department head with his or her own IT staff and data management systems (Eckerson 2011).

Governance provides oversight and standards to the data quality program. The data standards and data definitions may already exist within the organization, but a successful data quality program requires formalized governance that centralizes these standards from all areas of the organization, including business, legal, and operational levels. Governance involves more than oversight; it's also about process management that supports the people at all levels who fix the data. Data governance helps create sustainable processes that ensure appropriate levels of data quality.

In addition to providing the blueprint for data quality within an application, governance plays a key role in defining the data policies that help sustain a data quality program. The data governor will typically help define survivorship rules that determine how to construct the "single source of truth" record following a match. Moreover, data edits and rules (beyond data architecture) are specified by data governance. Governance also helps determine the severity of exceptions to these business rules, and defines ways to resolve data errors. Finally, data governance formulates these policies in a cohesive manner that takes cross-project or cross-system dependencies into account. Data governance vertically supports a data quality program as a platform for sound data architecture and data policies (Collaborative Consulting 2014). Data governance is an ongoing program or function, and when the data quality program is successfully finished, the organization must take ownership of the data as an "asset."

Data governance involves defining consistent processes, policies, rules, and standards, and assignment of roles and responsibilities to ensure success of data quality management efforts. One such role is the *data steward*, who is responsible for taking care of the data assets of an enterprise and ensuring their fitness for purpose. Gartner says, "Organizations striving to improve data quality must consider appointing data stewards." Data stewards are critical components of a data quality initiative. According to Andreas Bitterer, research vice president at Gartner:

> Appointing data quality stewards help organizations achieve data quality improvement goals. Such individuals should be considered subject-matter experts for their departments and act as trustees of data, rather than owners of it. They will ensure that quality is maintained to make the data support business processes. (MyCustomer 2008)

To achieve the greatest benefit, enterprises must properly define the data steward role, select the right individuals to fill the role, and guide the stewards' behavior in accordance with best practices (Friedman 2007). We will discuss the roles and responsibilities and different types of data stewards in Chapter 8, "Data Governance and Data Quality."

Track Return on Investment

Achieving data quality takes time and effort, which in turn requires investment. Any investment raises the question of quantification justification of the investment and returns on the investment. While the initial business case containing the problem statement and proposed benefits would result in the initial investment, continuous investment would require proof of benefit. Without metrics for calculating return on investment, there is no way of being certain about the effectiveness of the data quality initiative and proving the benefits and value. Without metrics, value is driven by perception and beliefs. Not tracking return on investment can result in the following challenges:

- In the absence of proof of return on investment, budget allocated to the initiative may be cut, or the initiative may be stopped altogether if limited or no value is perceived.

- Poor solutions that do not benefit the enterprise could continue to receive investment rather than opening up budget for other promising initiatives.

Organizations not only need to measure the cost of bad data quality but also the immediate benefits of improved data quality as a result of data quality initiatives. It is essential to be able to define metrics and key performance indicators. In the absence of metrics, what we have is perceived value driven by gut instincts and experience. However, perceived value is different from calculated value. The perceived value alludes to a positive perception of the data quality initiative, but that can dwindle as staffing changes or organizations restructure. The only way to actually prove return on investment over time is by calculating it with hard figures. Metrics can range from shorter processing time, reduced hardware costs, shorter sales cycles, and more accurate analytics, to reduced telemarketing costs, increased return on existing technology investments, and higher cross-sell and upsell volumes, and can be used to reveal the benefits of improved data quality (Shivu 2017).

For example, before the start of the data quality initiative, there were 160,000 duplicate customer records and 100,000 inaccurate customer records in a customer database containing 600,000 customer records. In terms of money, if the mailing cost per customer is $2, then total loss in mailing cost is the sum of mailing costs due to inaccuracy and duplication, that is, $520,000, as per the following calculation:

$$\text{Total duplicate customers mailing cost}$$
$$= \text{Unit cost} \times \text{Number of duplicate customer records}$$

$$= \$2 \times 160{,}000$$

$$= \$320{,}000$$

$$\text{Total inaccurate customers mailing cost}$$
$$= \text{Unit cost} \times \text{Number of duplicate customer records}$$

$$= \$2 \times 100{,}000$$

$$= \$200{,}000$$

$$\text{Total mailing costs due to inaccuracy and duplication}$$
$$= \text{Total duplicate customers mailing cost} + \text{Total inaccurate customers mailing cost}$$

$$= \$320{,}000 + \$200{,}000$$

$$= \$520{,}000$$

A data cleansing program was initiated to solve the duplicate customer data issue in the first release and the inaccuracy problem in the second release. After the first release, the number of duplicate customers came down to 10,000 records, which when converted to savings in terms of mailing costs was $(160,000 - 10,000) \times \$2 = \$300,000$.

After the second release, the number of inaccurate records came down to 10,000 records, resulting in a cost saving of $(100,000 - 10,000) \times \$2 = \$180,000$.

The total cost savings
= Cost savings from reduction in duplicate customers records
+ Cost savings from reduction of inaccurate customer records

$$= \$300,000 + \$180,000$$

$$= \$480,000$$

Tracking return on investment reduces or eliminates the risk of moving forward with the implementation of a bad solution in the case of a lack of substantial benefits, and provides the opportunity to revise the solution approach. In the case of substantial benefits, it serves as a motivating factor.

KEY CONSIDERATIONS WHILE ESTABLISHING A DATA QUALITY PROGRAM

Following are certain things that you might want to take into consideration when embarking on a data quality program.

Think Big, Start Small

An enterprise-wide data quality initiative can be huge and overwhelming from an implementation and change perspective. The sayings "Do not attempt to boil the ocean at once" and "You wouldn't eat an elephant in one bite," also apply to the rollout of a data quality initiative. "Think big, start small" means laying out the complete data quality roadmap and future state vision, but starting small. It is recommended to implement data quality initiatives in a staggered and incremental fashion by breaking them into smaller, meaningful deliverables (implemented in the order of business priority) rather than use the "big bang" approach.

A cornerstone of successful deployment of data quality initiatives is the usage of iteration in implementation and delivery to provide incremental benefits and then expand. As opposed to the big bang approach, an iterative approach in deployment results in breaking the bigger scope work into smaller, manageable chunks or projects deployed in a series of subsequent phases. The most critical functions and areas of business where having good data matters the most, or lend themselves to quick wins, should be targeted first for implementation. Dividing the program into phases is advantageous in the following ways:

- Risk is reduced as issues discovered in the earlier phases can be fixed in the next phase, and skills and experience are gained with each phase, which can help smooth the process as you get further along. Lessons learned in the first phase can smoothe the data quality journey in the subsequent phases.

- Doubt and insecurity are reduced when data quality is implemented successfully in one business unit, module, or department.

- The changes and new knowledge are embedded gradually; the organization has more time to train employees, and employees have more time to adjust to the new system, as opposed to the big bang approach where change impacts a huge number of people at once and can be quite overwhelming. Since the implementation occurs over a prolonged period, staff are able to concentrate and adapt to changes in a single module or department at a time rather than the system as a whole.

Balancing the Extremes

One of the key elements in managing data is reconciling enterprise and local requirements for data (Eckerson 2011). Most organizations whipsaw between these two extremes, but astute managers foster a dynamic interplay between the two polarities, embracing both at the same time without getting stuck at either end (or somewhere in the middle.) Organizations with highly centralized approaches to data management need to distribute development back to the departments or business units while maintaining high standards for data integrity and quality; organizations with fragmented data and lots of analytic silos need to implement initiatives, processes, and controls to standardize shared data across functional areas in the organization (Eckerson 2011).

Set Expectations

Data quality programs are time-consuming endeavors and require participation of cross-functional teams to bring about change. From the beginning, all the stakeholders should be made aware of the time commitment involved, the expectations of the program of them, the change involved, and the communication requirements. The individual roles and responsibilities of the stakeholders with respect to the program need, and what specifically is needed from the stakeholders in order for the program to be a success, need to be clearly communicated and agreed on by those involved.

Get a Few Quick Wins

Demonstrating the value of data quality to an extensive audience by resolving a data quality issue or fixing a critical problem with extensive visibility and significant impact in the organization will get people motivated and committed to the initiative and win the confidence of the skeptics. As data quality initiatives involve significant changes in culture and the way people do things, showing benefits early on can go a long way in gaining acceptance and buy-in, reducing the resistance to change, and providing justification for continued sponsorship.

Acknowledge That It Will Not Be Easy

Achieving data quality is not an easy undertaking, and it is imperative to acknowledge this up front and be prepared for the challenges. As with any initiative, sizing up the difficulty of the data quality journey in terms of risks, blockers, and resistance, having a plan in place to overcome these hurdles, setting expectations, and uniting to work together as a team can make the data quality journey a whole lot easier.

Buy Data Quality Software after Understanding the Business Process and Related Data

While technology is a key enabler of data quality, it is important to understand the data quality issues, their impact, and the root causes of data quality issues prior to spending money on data quality software. David Loshin seconded the idea that companies should avoid purchasing data quality software until they have a clear understanding of their data shortcomings and a plan for addressing the problems, including changes in business processes to minimize data errors (Earls 2013).

It is important to do a cost–benefit analysis when implementing a data quality tool. This includes the long-term benefits of buying the data quality tool. As per David Loshin, president of Knowledge Integrity Inc. consultancy in Silver Spring, Maryland, data quality is largely a process improvement activity that can be enhanced by using tools, not the other way around (Earls 2013). Data quality software can treat the symptoms, but cannot eliminate the root cause. The root cause may be faulty business processes, and while data cleansing software can be used to clean the existing data, it cannot correct or change the business process to reduce or prevent bad data from being created in the first place. In large organizations process change can be expensive and resource-heavy, and once set up, it tends to require ongoing control and assurance. Data quality technology might be essential, as the control can be manually intensive and resource-hungry to implement, especially in larger organizations. Also, not all data quality issues are due to faulty business processes, and data quality technology might be the only option. Whatever the case, it is important to understand the data issues before choosing and purchasing data quality software.

Multiple Solution Options

Data generally course throughout an organization from multiple source systems, through various intermediate systems, and into many target systems. Data quality issues can creep in at any point in the data trajectory. Data quality can be managed at any point in the data trajectory and in a number of ways depending on data governance policies, data quality requirements, business usage, compliance and regulatory requirements, data ownership, costs involved, system architectures, and so on. The pros and cons of the various solution options need to be weighed, and the optimal solution should be chosen.

Monitor Progress

Data quality efforts are not one-time projects; they are ongoing in nature and require support from management and sponsors. Ways to ensure this support are to break the big work into smaller chunks, execute the high-priority chunks that are most critical, use metrics to calculate return on investment, communicate continued progress, showcase continuous results, and establish incremental value at regular intervals to the stakeholders.

Commitment to Continuous Improvement

Data quality is not a project with a fixed start date and end date. With the changing data landscape, increasing volumes of data, new data types, and new processes, new issues will be uncovered that could result in a dip in data quality and would need changes in behaviors or changes in business processes to improve the quality of the data.

CONCLUSION

Data quality is not a destination but a journey. To achieve and sustain data quality requires a combination of a number of contributing elements: people, processes, technology, robust and sustainable strategies, sponsorship, leadership and management support, "soft" skills required to get executive buy-in and rollout and manage change, and "hard" skills—mastering a portfolio of technologies, tools, and techniques to ensure the delivery of consistent, high-quality data that's aligned with business strategies and initiatives. Recognizing the prevailing data quality myths and debunking them is also crucial to pave the way toward achieving success in data quality efforts. It is necessary to understand the challenges, organizational culture, mind set of the people and their skill sets, current state and future state (after implementation of a data quality initiative), and pockets of resistance, and based on this understanding, devise the best way to manage change. Following is a summary of the challenges and critical success factors for achieving data quality and the key considerations to keep in mind when establishing a data quality program in your organization.

SUMMARY OF KEY POINTS

Challenges

- Responsibility for data and data quality and cross-functional collaboration

- Intuition-driven culture

- Lack of awareness

- Resistance to change

- Funding and sponsorship
- Return on investment (ROI)

Key Considerations

- Think big, start small
- Get a few quick gains
- Balance the extremes
- Set expectations
- Multiple solution options
- Acknowledge that it will not be easy
- Buy data quality software after understanding business processes and related data
- Monitor progress
- Commitment to continuous improvement

Critical Success Factors

- Leadership and management support
- Sponsorship
- Organizational culture
- Managing change
- Business user involvement
- Tools and technologies
- Skill set, knowledge, and staffing
- Accountability and ownership
- Teamwork, partnership, communication, and collaboration
- Education and training
- Success stories
- Robust data quality strategy
- Data governance
- Track return on investment

8

Data Governance and Data Quality

INTRODUCTION

As discussed in Chapter 7, "Data Quality: Critical Success Factors (CSFs)," data governance plays a crucial role in ensuring the success of data quality management efforts in an organization. In principle, data only has value when it is used (Otto and Osterle 2015) and data is used only when it is fit for use. Data's fitness for use is referred to as *data quality*. In contrast to other tangible assets, such as money, buildings, clothes, machinery, or furniture, which have a finite life, are subject to wear and tear, and whose life diminishes as you use them more and more until a point in time when they are beyond repair, data assets become more valued when they are used more and more. Data governance pursues the objective of maximizing the value of the data (Otto 2011) in an organization by putting processes, rules, and practices in place to oversee the proper management of data. The instant data are shared across teams, business units, and departments, they become an enterprise asset, and data governance is necessary for securing and protecting the data and reducing the costs of managing the data, in addition to maximizing their value.

Even without a formal data governance function, departments and business units use data. Individuals within these departments have responsibility for their data, with different individuals having different roles, namely, operational, tactical, strategic, and support roles relating to the data. Different individuals have varied knowledge about the data, metadata, and how the data relate to the business process. All these are indicative of the fact that data are being governed informally in silos, though the effectiveness and efficiency of such governance is questionable. With silos, data inconsistency is a common problem. However, data are not a departmental asset only, but an enterprise asset, and, therefore, an enterprise view and responsibility for data that slashes across the silos in your organization and manages data as a shared resource (Seiner 2014) is essential to leverage maximum data value. This can only be achieved through a formal data governance program and function. While all organizations make decisions about data, regardless of whether they have a formal data governance function in place, those that establish a formal data governance program exercise authority and control with greater intentionality (Seiner 2014) and more holistically.

This chapter starts with a section on the evolution of data governance, followed by sections on data governance, data governance misconceptions, the difference between IT governance and data governance, reasons behind data governance failures, data governance and data quality, and data governance framework. This is followed by a brief section on the data governance approach. The chapter concludes with a summarization of key points.

EVOLUTION OF DATA GOVERNANCE

The concept of data governance has been around for decades. The 1980s saw the evolution of technologies designed to tackle data quality and metadata management, often on a departmental basis to support database marketing or data warehousing efforts. While pockets of "data governance" emerged—and sometimes grew as a grassroots effort—it was rarely a hot topic in the IT community (SAS 2018).

By the early 2000s, data governance started to get more attention. Many of the early drivers for data governance came about as directives from the compliance, risk, and audit departments. These "demands" were observed by other groups as an indispensable overhead to meet regulatory and audit commitments, with little or no intrinsic value to the organization as a whole (SAS 2018). The collapse of companies like Enron led the US federal government to establish rules to improve the accuracy and reliability of corporate information. Data governance was a key component of these efforts. For example, the Sarbanes-Oxley Act required executives to know—and be personally responsible for—the data driving their businesses (SAS 2018). In recent years there has been a large increase in regulatory oversight as a result of prior corporate transgressions. New legislation enacted includes Gramm-Leach-Bliley, Sarbanes-Oxley (SoX), and the newly enacted Dodd-Frank Wall Street Reform and Consumer Protection Act, Current Expected Credit Losses (CECL) accounting standard, and the General Data Protection Regulation (GDPR). GDPR is the most popular example of data sovereignty regulations that are being propagated across jurisdictions, which include Australia's Privacy Act, Canada's Anti-Spam Law, the People's Republic of China's Cybersecurity Law, and Russia's Personal Data Localization law (Soares and Franco 2017). With the enforcement of the European Union's General Data Protection Regulation (GDPR) on May 25, 2018, which focuses on protection of personally identifiable information (PII), organizations need to have adequate data governance practices in place to be in line with its mandates on handling and securing personal data or protecting the privacy of personal data. For multinational organizations, a myriad of additional regulations exist, such as the EU-backed Basel II and Solvency II proposals. In the face of such industry drivers, data governance matured rapidly. Technology that grew out of data quality or business process management tools began to offer automated creation and management of business rules at the data level. To keep pace with technologies, trends, and new regulations, data governance continues to evolve (SAS 2018).

DATA GOVERNANCE

According to the *Oxford Dictionary*, *governance* is defined as "the act of controlling, influencing, or regulating a person, action, or course of events." When applied to data governance, the definition should be "the act of controlling, influencing, or regulating data."

Data governance comprises a group of people from business and information technology streams with a common objective to improve the quality of data within the organization and develop policies, processes, procedures, and standards to be followed within the enterprise for improving the organization's operational efficiency. Data governance ensures maintenance of data quality, proper use of data and available resources, and standardized management and mastering of data within the organization.

The *DAMA Dictionary of Data Management* (2011) defines *data governance* as:

> The exercise of authority, control, and shared decision making (planning, monitoring, and enforcement) over the management of data assets.

According to Jill Dyché, partner and cofounder of Baseline Consulting Group Inc., data governance does the following things (Eckerson 2011):

- Establishes business stakeholders as information owners
- Positions enterprise data issues as cross-functional
- Aligns data quality with business measures and acceptance
- Removes IT from business/data conflict ownership
- Ensures that data are managed separately from applications
- Expands change management to include data
- Requires monitoring and measurement

To promote desirable behavior, data governance develops and implements corporate-wide data policies, guidelines, and standards that are consistent with the organization's mission, strategy, values, norms, and culture (cp. Weill 2004) (Weber and Otto 2007).

DATA GOVERNANCE MISCONCEPTIONS

Organizations have different perceptions and misconceptions related to data governance. The misconceptions are described in Figure 8.1. We will discuss each of the misconceptions in detail and provide clarification for each of them.

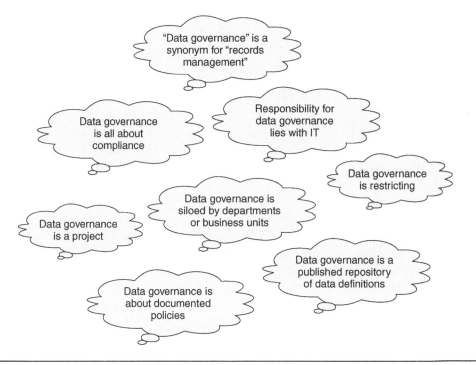

Figure 8.1   Data governance misconceptions.

Misconception #1: Responsibility for Data Governance Lies with IT

Many people have the misconception that IT is responsible for data governance and that an organization's chief data officer (CDO) spearheads the IT's data governance program.

While IT is responsible for the technology facet of data quality implementation, they are not aware of the business rules that define data quality as well as the users of the data. Hence, data governance frameworks should be primarily driven by the business, with IT in a supporting role. The responsibility for deploying data governance is split: the business owns the policies and processes, but IT owns the implementation (Loshin 2017).

Although the role and the list of responsibilities of the CDO are still evolving, there is a greater risk of failing to properly institute sustainable practices for data governance when the CDO's mandate is designated within the information technology silo. The most effective chief data officer will report directly to the CEO, and be empowered to implement data governance by leveraging a partnership between the business and IT. That way, the organization can inaugurate a sustainable data governance program that directly integrates data policy compliance within defined business processes (Loshin 2017).

Misconception #2: Data Governance Is Restricting

Data governance has a propensity to be regarded as barring people from what they can do and limiting accessibility and opportunities for the user (Chen 2017).

However, true data governance should lead to enablement, unlocking the creativity and ingenuity of the users. While control is important, good governance must balance security, protection, accessibility, and enablement (Chen 2017).

Misconception #3: Data Governance Is a Project

Some people have the misconception that data governance is a project. However, a project has a definite start date and an end date, and while data governance has a start date, it does not have an end date.

The fact is that data governance is an ongoing process that involves people, processes, rules, procedures, and policies to handle an organization's data in a secured and controlled way, and does not have an end date. Data governance can never, ever be a project. Its life is as long as a business is running and technology is supported to run that business. Data governance programs should be a systematic and continuous investment in the enterprise. This is very important because change is the only constant in any business, and so data governance initiatives should be able to dynamically adapt to those changes coming from the business initiatives and technology practices (Chikkatur Undated).

Misconception #4: "Data Governance" Is a Synonym for "Records Management"

There is a misconception that data governance is the same as records management. However, the fact is that records management is a key component of data governance. Data governance is the overarching framework ensuring appropriate behavior in the valuation of an organization's data. Data governance defines the roles, policies, processes, and metrics for managing the information life cycle (Iron Mountain Undated).

Misconception #5: Data Governance Is All about Compliance

There is a misconception that data governance is only about compliance. While regulatory compliance is critical, and is often a trigger for implementation of data governance in an organization, and has a clear place in the process, it is not the only reason for data governance. Data governance results in increased operational efficiency, improved data understanding and lineage, better decision making, and higher data quality. Implementing data governance effectively results in an organization being able to comply with what is asked for by the regulators by ensuring greater data transparency, with compliance becoming the byproduct of the ongoing data governance process.

Misconception #6: Data Governance Is about Documented Policies

There is also a common misconception that data governance is all about documented policies. While data governance does have documented policies, it is not only about documented policies. The truth is that data governance programs are active and ongoing. They consist of systematic audits, reconciliations, compliance reviews, and quality control activities.

Misconception #7: Data Governance Is Siloed by Business Units or Department

Another misconception is that data governance should be siloed by business units or departments. However, this is not true. Data are an enterprise asset, and certain data entities will be used by multiple business units. The most common example of cross–business unit data is customer data. Hence, data governance should not be restricted to one department or business unit. To provide maximum efficiency, data governance processes should be implemented in a similar manner across business units or departments in the organization. Taking effective processes incorporated into one business unit or department and extending them to others is often the best approach. A coordinated data governance approach should be established among the different business units and departments across the organization, which will help provide a broader perspective on the business.

Misconception #8: Data Governance Is a Published Repository of Common Data Definitions

While data governance professionals are, in general, fixated on common data definitions for the enterprise, and common data definitions are an essential component of data governance, data governance is not only about a data definition repository. A data definition repository without ownership and processes to maintain it will soon be outdated and of no use. Data governance is also about having people and processes to not only maintain a common data repository but to maximize the value of the data.

DATA GOVERNANCE VERSUS IT GOVERNANCE

Data governance is not the same as IT governance. *IT governance* makes decisions about IT investments, the IT application portfolio, and the IT project portfolio, in other words, hardware, software, and overall technical architecture. IT governance aligns the IT strategies and investments with enterprise goals and strategies. The COBIT (Control Objectives for Information and Related Technology) framework provides standards for IT governance, but only a small portion of the COBIT framework addresses managing data and information. Some critical topics, such as Sarbanes-Oxley compliance in the United States, span the concerns of corporate governance, IT governance, and data governance.

In contrast, data governance focuses exclusively on the management of data assets, and of data as an asset (DAMA International 2017).

WHY DATA GOVERNANCE FAILS

There are many reasons why data governance fails, or at least underperforms. Following is a list of reasons that can be contributory factors to the failure of a data governance implementation in an organization:

- Data governance is not well defined (SAS 2018).

- Business executives and managers consider data "an IT issue," and business units and IT don't work together (SAS 2018).

- The organization's unique culture isn't taken into account (SAS 2018).

- Organizational structures are too fragmented, the culture doesn't support centralized decision making, or decision-making processes are not well understood or designed (SAS 2018).

- Data governance is viewed as an academic exercise, or is treated like a finite project (SAS 2018).

- Existing steering committees with knowledge and clout are overlooked (SAS 2018).

- Execution is lacking; data are not managed in a structured, tactical, and repeatable way (SAS 2018).

- The return on investment (ROI) isn't clear, and it's hard to link data governance activities to business value (SAS 2018).

- Key resources are already overloaded and can't take on governance activities (SAS 2018).

- Data governance is a human-intensive process and a time-consuming exercise. Lack of proper planning, prioritization, and assignment of responsibilities, and trying to implement too much in one go, leads to failure.

- Communication gaps and absence of change management.

- Lack of metrics to track progress and measure success and failures.

DATA GOVERNANCE AND DATA QUALITY

Data governance and data quality are closely related disciplines. Data quality requires sustained discipline in the management and production of data. Data governance is a large part of that discipline. High-quality data cannot be attained without active data governance (Smith 2016). How well the data are governed has a direct influence on the quality of the data. In other words, good governance is a key to good data.

Data governance coach Nicola Aksham (2014) describes the relationship between data governance and data quality as symbiotic since their relationship is based on mutual interdependence, adding that "You would not want to do one without the other if you want to successfully manage and improve the quality of your data in a sustainable manner."

Content marketing manager at Experian Data Quality Stephanie Zatyko uses the example of water to illustrate the relationship between data governance and data quality. She says that if data were water, then data quality would ensure that the water is pure and uncontaminated, and data governance would ensure that the right people with the right tools are responsible for the right parts of the water system (Zatyko 2017).

High-quality data require high-quality data definitions, high-quality data capture and creation, and high-quality data usage (Smith 2016). Data governance is the practice of applying formal accountability and behavior—through a framework of roles and responsibilities (assigned to the right people), standards, policies, and processes—to business processes to assure that data definitions, data capture and creation, and data usage improve regulatory compliance, privacy, data security, and data quality. Figure 8.2 shows the components of data governance at a high level.

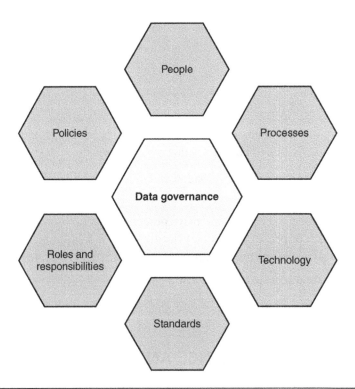

Figure 8.2   Data governance components.

Quality data definition requires that the right people in the organization are responsible for creating and managing the data definitions, and that the right people approve the data definitions. In addition, these definitions need to have context and consistency, and be recorded in a physical format that is accessible in order to qualify as being of high quality. Improving data definition quality eliminates or reduces duplication of data, improves knowledge of the existing data, and improves consistent understanding and usage of data. Data governance establishes formal accountabilities for managing data definitions and standards, and procedures for creating consistent data definitions.

High-quality data capture and creation requires people to understand the impact of the data they capture, and that they are trained to create quality data, with automated mechanisms for capture of data whenever possible, multifaceted data validation to minimize data entry errors, and timely availability of the data. Improvement in data capture and creation process results in increased formality of data capture, greater confidence in the data, and improvement in the efficiency and effectiveness of data usage. Data governance outlines the processes and rules for data entry.

High-quality data usage requires that the right data are used for the right purpose, that data are shared appropriately based on security classification, and only the right people have access to the data, and only they know where to retrieve the data from. People should have a knowledge of the rules for data handling and "do's and don'ts" related to data usage, and ensure that the rules are adhered to and data are reported compliantly. Data governance outlines the policies for usage based on security classification, procedures and rules for access, and standards and processes for data handling.

Data governance also provides a structure for assignment of roles and responsibilities for undertaking and defining policies, procedures, and standards for various data management activities, including the measurement and improvement of data quality across the organization.

Data Governance, GDPR, and Data Quality

The GDPR applies to the handling of the personal data of all European Union (EU) data subjects: customers, employees, and prospects. Any organization that processes the personal data of individuals who live in the European Union also falls under its purview. For example, GDPR would apply for an employee who lives in France but works for a company in the United States, or a supplier or buyer in Germany doing an online transaction with a retailer in China. TDWI analyst Philip Russom wrote in a March 2018 report on the compliance issues that GDPR and other regulations create for data management teams that:

> There's a balancing act between complying with regulations and extracting business value from the customer data that companies collect. Targeted improvements to data management practices can help with GDPR, compliance without hamstringing the use of data, listing things such as the creation of data catalogs, the tracking of data lineage and an increased focus on data quality. Without such

governance controls, data can be a source of risk instead of value. (Stedman Undated)

The GDPR provides for a specific use case relating to data quality. Article 16 of the GDPR requires organizations to rectify inaccurate personal information and to complete any missing personal data without undue delay (Soares and Franco 2017). Data governance should involve the establishment of appropriate controls to address any data quality issues relating to the personal information of customers, employees, and other data subjects in a timely manner. Data reconciliation is also another important aspect to consider, as customer and employee data might be fragmented in many places and systems within the organization. The GDPR mandates that this information should be reconciled into a consistent and complete view that can be exposed to data subjects on request (Soares and Franco 2017).

Data Governance and PII

Since data governance operates throughout an organization, crossing business unit and departmental boundaries, data governance is best positioned to be aware of and facilitate an ability to locate all the personally identifiable information (PII) the organization holds, as well as get agreement from all the concerned stakeholders. Data governance should ensure that standards, policies, processes, and accountabilities are in place regarding access, usage, and protection of PII and sensitive data, compliance monitoring, and resolution of privacy and security issues related to the data.

DATA GOVERNANCE FRAMEWORK

A data governance framework is a framework that is designed so that organizations can proactively manage the quality of their data.

The *DAMA Dictionary of Data Management* (2011) defines *data governance framework* as:

> An organization's approach to managing the quality of its data, that is, what they are going to do, who is going to do it, and how they intend to achieve it.

WHY IS A DATA GOVERNANCE FRAMEWORK NEEDED?

Often, companies deploy data quality initiatives without having a data governance framework in place to support them. However, this results in many data quality initiatives ending up being tactical solutions with short-term results only, without resulting in any significant benefits when compared to the financial investment that went into the data quality initiative. The reason for this situation is that without a data governance framework, roles and responsibilities often are not set up and agreed on, hence, there is no clear accountability and ownership, there is no escalation path for data quality problems, and there are no organizational processes in place to proactively manage data quality.

For example, let us consider the scenario of setting up data quality reporting without a data governance framework. Who is responsible for any corrective activity if the reports reveal that the data are not up to the mark? In some cases the initial recipient of such reports may be interested in the results and may even take action to improve the quality of the data as a result, but he would definitely not be bound to do it if he is not accountable for it. If the task has not been allocated as a definite role responsibility, how can you guarantee this will continue when their priorities change or when the person leaves the organization? What are the chances that they will remember to tell their successor about the reports if they change roles? As noted by Nicola Askham (2014), "On many occasions, I have come across data quality reports disappearing into a black hole because the person who originally requested them has moved on, rendering a valuable insight into the health of an organization's data as useless, time-consuming, and costly."

Also, without data governance in place, a department or user group might not have any idea about an existing data set or report that is already in use in another department or business unit, and end up reproducing the same report, causing duplication of effort.

Over the years, there has been a transition from applying quick, tactical, one-time fixes to correct data issues to well-defined approaches to evaluating data sets to identify problems and sophisticated techniques for cleaning and enrichment of the data. However, despite the maturity of these techniques, they need to be constantly and frequently repeated to maintain lasting quality. The reason that the data do not stay fixed is a lack of governance or control over the data. In order to maintain a consistently good level of data quality, it must be proactively managed, ensuring that data are captured accurately and that deterioration in their quality is prevented (Askham 2014), which is only possible with an organized data governance framework in place.

Certain data are shared and used by multiple business units, which requires input and agreement from all these business units when creating a data definition and interdependent rule. Also, though data are used by business, the storage systems and transfer of data between systems are handled by IT. A data governance framework is necessary to bring together cross-functional teams to make interdependent rules and agree on data definitions, and in cases of conflict, resolve them. Since data governance activities require coordination across functional areas, the data governance program must establish a framework that defines roles, responsibilities, and collaborations.

Planning and applying the right data governance framework in an organization supports its data quality activities, including data quality issue resolution, and aids in entrenching these activities into "business as usual," and is vital for the long-term success and sustainability of these data quality activities. It is only through using the right data governance framework, where data quality and data governance become intertwined, that sustainable benefits begin to appear (Askham 2014).

DATA GOVERNANCE FRAMEWORK COMPONENTS

A data governance framework is the best way to proactively manage data quality, by making sure that the right people, processes, and technology are in place to continuously monitor and sustain the quality of your data. For a data governance framework to work, it must fit with the organization's culture, environment, structure, and practices. Hence, an organization would have different data governance frameworks depending on the environment, culture, focus, and level of formality needed. However, there is no one-size-fits-all approach where the data governance framework is concerned. The basic components of a data governance framework are:

- Rules and rules of engagement

- Data policies

- Processes

- People

- Roles and responsibilities

- Technology

Rules and Rules of Engagement

Rules and rules of engagement include the following:

Principles. At its highest level, a data governance program should define what it is set to achieve and the rationale behind it. A *principle* is a statement that articulates shared organizational values, strategic mission, and vision, and serves as a basis for integrated decision making. A key aspect of creating data governance principles is to keep them crisp and concise. Principles are more basic than policies and the data culture, and drive desired outcomes. Robert Seiner (2017b) outlines the core principles of data governance, which are shown in Table 8.1.

Data Rules and Definitions. Data rules and definitions refers to data-related standards, business rules, and data quality rules and data definitions. Data governance professionals set rules for managing data assets in the organization. All the business units and departments follow and carry out these rules.

Standards. Standards contain specific, low-level mandatory controls for supporting and enforcing data policies, and can take different forms depending on what they describe: assertions about how data elements/fields must be populated, naming conventions in data models, rules governing the relationships between fields, detailed documentation of acceptable and unacceptable values, format (DAMA International 2017), whether a field is optional or mandatory, whether null values are acceptable or not, data security standards, data modeling naming conventions, standard abbreviations, standards for data transfer, and so on. Data standards should be reviewed, approved, and

Table 8.1	Core principles of data governance.
Data principles	**Rationale/justification**
Data must be recognized as a valued and strategic enterprise asset.	Data are a valuable corporate resource and have measurable value. Data are the foundation of decision making and customer service, so data should be carefully managed to ensure their accuracy and timeliness.
Data must have clearly defined accountability.	Most data have value to the organization beyond the uses of any one specific application or business function. A company requires that data be shared and integrated at the enterprise level, consistent with information security and privacy policies. Data must be well defined to be shareable. Enterprise-shareable data must be defined consistently across the enterprise, with understood definitions available to all users.
Data must be managed to follow internal and external rules.	Current legislation and regulations require the safeguarding, security, and privacy of personally identifiable information. Open data sharing, managed accessibility, and the release of data and information must be balanced against the need to restrict the availability of restricted, proprietary, or sensitive information.
Data quality must be defined and managed consistently across the data life cycle.	The quality standards for data must be well defined in order to be able to identify, record, measure, and report the quality of the data. The quality standards will focus on measuring business process and decision-making improvements from complete, relevant, and unique data. Enterprise-critical data must be tested against the standards consistently across the enterprise, with understood standards available to all data definers, producers, and users.

adopted by the data governance council (DAMA International 2017). The level of detail in data standards documentation varies from one organization to another, and is partly driven by the organizational culture.

By embracing a standard, an organization makes a decision once and codifies it in a set of assertions (the standard). It does not need to make the same decision all over again for each project. Enforcing standards should promote consistent results from the processes using them. It is important to keep in mind that documenting data standards presents an opportunity to capture details and knowledge that otherwise may be lost. Recreating or reverse engineering to access this knowledge is very expensive compared to documenting it up front (DAMA International 2017).

Data standards must be effectively communicated across the organization, monitored, and periodically reviewed and updated. Data standards help ensure that all the business units and departments using the data have the same understanding. Most importantly, there must be a means to enforce them (DAMA International 2017). Data can be measured against standards, hence, data standards can help measurement of data quality.

Business Rules and Data Quality Rules. Expectations used to define high-quality data are often formulated in terms of rules rooted in the business processes that create or consume data. Stewards help surface these rules in order to ensure that there is consensus about them within the organization and that they are used consistently (DAMA International 2017).

Business Glossary. It is important that people across the organization have a common understanding of the enterprise data and the business terms that represent the data. A survey done in 2007 identified that 42% of the managers participating in the survey acknowledged that they had recently made erroneous business decisions due to misunderstanding of terminology and data usage (Fryman 2012). Data are representations of real-world entities, events, phenomena, and their attributes. Thus, it is crucial to have clear standards, definition of the data in terms of what they represent and the business context, and a note of any exceptions, synonyms, and variants. A *business glossary*, also known as a *data glossary*, is a repository that has definitions of terms used across business domains, specific to the industry and organization, that is shared across the organization. A business glossary is not merely a list of terms and definitions. Each term will also be associated with other valuable metadata: synonyms, metrics, lineage, business rules, the steward responsible for the term (DAMA International 2017), data owners, and descriptions of any exceptions, variations, and so on.

A business glossary reduces ambiguity, improves communication, reduces data issues, speeds up project delivery cycles, and facilitates the distribution and availability of trusted data in support of informed business decisions and processes. A business glossary increases the return on data by providing a common vocabulary of business terms across the enterprise.

Data stewards are generally responsible for business glossary content. A glossary is necessary because people use words differently. Approvers of terminology should include representatives from core user groups (DAMA International 2017).

While building a business glossary it is possible to come across identical terminologies used in different parts of the organization with completely different definitions and meanings, and conversely, cases where a number of different terms have the same definition. The lesser the data maturity of the organization, the more likely is the probability of this occurrence. These situations need to be analyzed. In the former case, if there is a valid business reason for the same term to have different meanings, the terms should be renamed in agreement with the user groups so that they have unique names to avoid confusion. In the latter case, since different terms have the same definition, it is the perfect opportunity for the different stakeholders to agree on standardizing the name so as to have a single name instead of multiple names for the same business term. This helps in preventing or solving data quality issues due to lack of understanding of what the data mean. This can cause issues in three ways:

- The data producers do not understand what a field should be used for and enter something similar, but slightly different (Askham 2016).

- Misuse of data by data consumers due to inconsistent understanding of the business concepts.

- Data consolidation and inconsistency issues (Askham 2016).

Let us illustrate business terminology name and definition inconsistencies with the following scenarios:

Scenario 1. *The same business terms have different definitions.* In a financial organization, the term *party* can indicate any of the following, depending on the business function:

- Employee
- Customer
- Vendor
- Contractor
- Supplier
- Broker

To eliminate ambiguity and promote consistency, it makes sense to have a different term for each of these entities across the different business functions.

Scenario 2. *Different business terms have the same definitions and meanings.* Different business functions in a retail company have the following different terminologies for *customer*—someone who purchases items from the physical or online retail store:

- Buyer
- Client
- Purchaser
- Consumer

All the above terms have the same definition: someone who purchases items from the physical or online retail store.

To eliminate ambiguity and promote consistency in understanding, it makes sense to have a common term for this entity across all business functions.

Decision Rights. Without governance, decision making is ad hoc. Decisions often get stuck because of a lack of agreement among the parties having a stake in the data due to the absence of a data policy and process that provide guidelines on decision making.

Before any rule is created or any data-related decision is made, a prior decision must be addressed: who gets to make the decision, and when, and using what process? It is the responsibility of the data governance program to facilitate (and to sometimes document and store) the collection of decision rights that are the "metadata" of data-related decisions (Thomas Undated).

Accountabilities. Once a rule is created or a data-related decision is made, the organization will be ready to act on it (Thomas Undated). Who should do what, and when? For activities that do not neatly map to departmental responsibilities, the data governance program may be expected to define accountabilities that can be baked into everyday processes and the organization's software development life cycle (SDLC) (Thomas Undated).

RACI (that is, responsible, accountable, consulted, informed) is a responsibility charting concept of people and things defined as a matrix. RACI categorizes processes and lines up resources by way of process mapping. All relevant processes are added to one section, and related responsibilities and roles are associated.

In terms of data management, the term *RACI* stands for the following:

- *Responsible*. The individual who has the delegated responsibility to manage a data-related activity or attribute. There may be multiple responsible teams for an attribute or activity.

- *Accountable*. The individual who has ultimate accountability for a data-related activity or attribute. The accountable individual may delegate the responsibility to a party that has the right authorities. There should only be one accountable party.

- *Consulted*. The individual or individuals who are consulted via bidirectional communications.

- *Informed*. The individual or individuals who are kept informed via unidirectional communications.

Clinton Jones, product manager at Experian, outlines the alignment between data governance roles and RACI (Jones 2014) as shown in Table 8.2.

Metrics and Success Measures. It is essential to define the measurement strategy for data quality improvement that is effected by data governance. It is extremely important to be able to measure progress and display success. The extent of adoption of enterprise data standards, degree of improvement in data quality and metadata quality, performance of data stewards and stewardship teams, and cash flow are some examples of metrics used when measuring the progress of a data governance program.

Table 8.2   Data governance roles and RACI.

Roles	RACI
Data owner	*Accountable* for the quality of a defined data set
Data steward	*Responsible* for the quality of a defined data set
Data producer	*Responsible* for creating or capturing data according to the data consumer's requirement
Data consumer	*Responsible* for defining what makes the data they use of sufficient quality to use
Data custodian	*Responsible* for maintaining the data on IT systems in accordance with business requirements
Data quality team	*Responsible* for undertaking and supporting data quality activities across the organization

Controls. It's well established that data are constantly at risk. With the proliferation of breaches of sensitive data—and the consequences for those who were entrusted with the data—it is becoming clear that data can also represent risk. How do we deal with risk? We manage it, preferably by preventing the events that we don't want to occur. Those we can't be sure of preventing, we at least detect, so we can then correct the problem. An organization's risk management strategies are made operational through controls. Often, the data governance program is asked to recommend data-related controls that could be applied at multiple levels of the controls stack (network/operating system, database, application, user processes) to support governance goals. Data governance may also be asked to recommend ways that existing general controls (change management, policies, training, SDLCs, and project management, and so on) could be modified to support governance goals or enterprise goals (Thomas Undated).

Data Policies

Data policies are a set of documented guidelines, principles, and rules for ensuring proper management and use of metadata and data during the life cycle of the data, including data creation, data acquisition, data integrity, data security, data quality, data retention and disposal, and data privacy.

Data policies are global. They support data standards, as well as expected behaviors related to the key aspects of data management and data use. They are defined keeping in mind the context of the people, business processes, data, and systems. Data policies vary widely across organizations. Data policies describe the "what" of data governance (what to do and what not to do) and "who" of data governance, while standards and procedures describe "how" to do data governance. Effective data policies require a cross-functional approach to data, and input from business units and the IT department within the organization.

There should be relatively few data policies, and they should be stated briefly and directly (DAMA International 2017). The policies should be designed with the goals of data quality in mind, for example, prohibition of manual data entry whenever an automated solution can be used instead.

Processes

Processes or procedures describe the methods, techniques, and steps that need to be followed to govern data and manage their quality. Processes include step-by-step activities to implement policies, including requirements and monitoring. Ideally, these processes for managing the data across the organization should be standardized and documented, as well as be consistent, and repeatable and should support regulatory and compliance requirements for data management, privacy, security, and access management. While the structure and formality associated with the process of governing data are to be decided by the organization, it is recommended to have formal, documented, consistent, and repeatable procedures for (Patel 2013):

- Aligning policies, requirements, and controls
- Establishing decision rights
- Establishing accountability
- Performing stewardship
- Defining data
- Resolving issues
- Specifying data quality requirements
- Building governance into technology
- Communications
- Measuring and reporting value

Like policies and standards, procedures vary extensively across organizations. As is the case with data standards, procedural documents capture organizational knowledge in an explicit form (DAMA International 2017).

Procedures formalize the declarations of the policy, and are specific and concrete. Therefore, multiple processes may be required to enact a single policy or a set of policies. Processes are required for the effective management and valuation of data, ensuring consistency of data, and ensuring conformity to established data standards. Processes may involve the profiling and analysis of information, determining the classification and characteristics of information, the integration of reference data, or issue reporting and resolution.

People

People are at the heart of the data governance function. It is essential to clearly define their roles and responsibilities, as these people will be in charge of managing all aspects of the enterprise data. Usually, a data governance framework will have several layers and organization bodies. The different layers or levels are as follows:

- The executive level
- The strategic level
- The tactical level
- The operational level
- The support level

The Executive Level. At the executive level is the *steering committee*, which consists of cross-functional senior management who are responsible for sponsoring, approving funding, and resource allocation for the lines of business, championing the strategy for the overall data products, communicating expectations and requirements for data governance to the lines of business, and prioritization of data quality initiatives.

The Strategic Level. At the strategic level is the *data governance council*, which consists of business data owners who are the business authority for the data they own, and make decisions at a strategic level. They are responsible for approving data policies, the data role framework, tools, and so on, and pushing data governance into their areas by actively promoting improved data governance practices. They are responsible for identifying and approving pivotal data governance roles, including cross-enterprise domain stewards and coordinators, and advising the data governance council owner on applying data governance to risk management, compliance, and business unit–specific governance interests (Seiner 2017a).

The Tactical Level. At the tactical level is the *data steward council*, which consists of *data domain stewards* and *data steward coordinators*.

The data domain stewards focus on the quality of data for their respective data domains or subject area, facilitate cross–business unit resolution of data definition, production, and usage issues, escalate well-documented issues to the strategic level with or without recommendation, document data classification rules, compliance rules, and business rules for data in their domain, and ensure that the rules are communicated to all stakeholders of data in that domain. They participate in tactical groups (with other domain stewards, steward coordinators, and operational stewards) for finite periods of time to address specific issues and projects related to their domain and business unit (Seiner 2017a).

The data steward coordinators act as the point communications person for distributing rules and regulations per domain of data to the operational stewards in their business unit (and ensure that the operational data stewards understand the rules and risks). They also act as the point communications person for their business unit to document and communicate issues pertaining to specific domains of data to the proper data domain steward, and act as the point of contact for the regular change control process. They are responsible for identifying the operational stewards of data per domain for their business unit. This typically requires research and inventory time for the data steward coordinator (Seiner 2014). They work with the data domain stewards and operational data stewards on specific tactical data steward teams that are set up for the duration of issue resolution or project-focused task. The data steward coordinator typically has no decision-making authority but plays a pivotal role in data governance and data stewardship success (Seiner 2017a).

The Operational Level. At the operational level are the *data stewards*, who are responsible for defining the data that will be used by the organization, how the data will be used, and how the data will be managed; producing, creating, updating, deleting, retiring, and archiving the data that will be managed; using data to perform their job and processes and maintaining the integrity of data usage; creating, reviewing, and approving data definitions; ensuring the quality of data definition; identifying and classifying data access levels; identifying and documenting regulatory and legal/risk issues, including data retention requirements; supporting and sharing knowledge with other stewards; communicating new and changed business requirements to individuals who may be impacted; and communicating concerns, issues, and problems with data to the individuals that can influence change (Seiner 2017a).

The Support Level. The support level consists of the following groups, and supports all of the above groups:

- Data governance office

- Information technology partners

Data Governance Office. The data governance (DG) office, or *data governance team*, works with all business units and IT to develop and implement data governance solutions throughout the organization. They also coordinate integration among multiple data governance disciplines, as well as administrate, monitor, and report data governance activities. The DG office operates at the tactical level but needs to be comfortable managing up (to the strategic level) and down (to the operational level).

Roles include the *data governance lead* (DGL), *IT representatives*, and *data governance coordinator*. The DGL must be a leader, have political acumen, and know who the key influencers are. They should also be adept in data governance as well as industry practice. The DGL should be someone who has been in the organization for a number of years and who already knows the objectives of the company and the political landscape. The IT representative is a partner who manages technology-related issues part time. The data governance coordinator schedules meetings, workshops, and conference calls, records and circulates meeting minutes, updates data issue logs, and performs administrative duties. The DG office has *chief data stewards*, *executive data stewards*, *coordinating data stewards*, *data owners*, *data analysts*, *business stewards*, and *data stewards*, or *subject matter experts* (Ott 2015).

The DG office is critical to having a successful data governance initiative. Creating the right data governance office can make or break your entire effort.

Information Technology Partners. Information technology partners consist of *technical stewards*, *data stewards*, *data subject matter experts* and *system subject matter experts*, *designers*, *data administrators*, and *data architects*. They focus on consistent protection/classification of data by data classification (confidential, public, internal use, and so on), technical handling of data to meet data classification requirements, securing IT infrastructure on behalf of the business units that own or have responsibility for data, and assuring that sensitive data, regardless of format, is protected at all times by only using approved equipment, networks, and other controls, championing the integration of data governance within the standard project methodology, ensuring that standard project methodology is followed and that policies, procedures, and metrics are in place for maintaining/improving data quality and ensuring the creation, capture, and maintenance of metadata, as well as ensuring that all "strategic" data are modeled, named, and defined consistently. They provide technical support for ensuring data quality, for data governance, and data cleansing efforts where required. They also ensure that metadata critical to data governance are included in the metadata resource and are accessible (Seiner 2017a).

Roles and Responsibilities

Roles and responsibilities are essential for accountability and sustaining data quality, and are a vital component of data governance.

Data Producer. The data producer is a person, organization, or software application responsible for creating, capturing, or providing data according to the data consumers' requirements.

Data Consumer. The data consumer is a person or group who receives or accesses the data and uses the data. The data consumer is responsible for defining what makes the data they receive of sufficient quality to use (Askham 2014).

Data Custodian. Data custodians typically belong to the information technology or operations area and manage access rights to the data they oversee. In addition, data custodians implement controls to ensure the integrity, security, and privacy of their data (Zaidi 2012).

Data stewards and data custodians work closely to ensure that their organization complies with the enterprise data management standards and policies and that critical data-related issues are escalated to the appropriate data governance boards in a timely manner (Zaidi 2012).

Data Steward. As per the *Oxford Dictionary*, a *steward* is a person whose responsibility is to take care of something. In this light, a data steward is a person whose responsibility is to take care of organizational data assets.

A data steward is a role within an organization responsible for applying an organization's data governance processes to ensure fitness of data elements, both from content and metadata perspectives. Data stewards have a specialized role that incorporates processes, policies, guidelines, and responsibilities for administering all of an organization's data in compliance with policy and/or regulatory obligations (Wikipedia Undated "Data Steward").

The overall objective of a data steward is data quality—in regard to the key or critical data elements existing within a specific enterprise operating structure—of the elements in their respective domains (Wikipedia Undated "Data Steward"). Data stewards represent the interests of all stakeholders and must take an enterprise perspective to ensure that enterprise data are of high quality and can be used effectively. Effective data stewards are accountable and responsible for data governance activities and have a portion of their time dedicated to these activities (DAMA International 2017).

Ted Friedman, research vice president at Gartner, recommends that each major business function have data stewards, including sales, marketing, service, production, finance, HR, and IT. As per Friedman, "Successful and effective data stewards reside in the business, are visible, respected, and influential—they must have the vision to understand the importance of data quality to the overall business objectives, as well as the impact of quality issues on downstream business processes" (Gartner 2008). Gartner cites the example of a marketing specialist from the company's marketing department acting as the data steward in the data quality improvement program by keeping marketing data complete, correct, consistent, honest, and not redundant. In this role they would have responsibility for ensuring that marketing-relevant information adheres to the corporate data quality standards (Gartner 2008). Similarly, in a financial services organization the data standards and business rules for the quality of the general ledger data would reside with the financial operations department, who are closest to the subject area, and not any other department.

Data stewards begin the stewarding process with the identification of the critical data elements that they will steward, with the ultimate result being definitions, standards, controls, and data entry. The steward works closely with business glossary standards analysts (for standards), data architects or modelers (for standards), DQ analysts (for controls), and operations team members (for good-quality data going in as per business rules) while entering data (Wikipedia Undated "Data Steward").

Data Stewardship

According to *The Data Governance Institute*:

> Data stewardship is concerned with taking care of data assets that do not belong to the stewards themselves. Data stewards represent the concerns of others. Some may represent the needs of the entire organization. Others may be tasked with representing a smaller constituency: a business unit, department, or even a set of data themselves. (The Data Governance Institute Undated; Knight 2017)

According to the *DAMA Body of Knowledge* (DMBOK):

> Data stewardship is the most common label to describe accountability and responsibility for data and processes that ensure effective control and use of data assets. Stewardship can be formalized through job titles and descriptions, or it can be a less formal function driven by people trying to help an organization get value from its data. (DAMA International 2017)

The focus of stewardship activities will differ from organization to organization depending on organizational strategy, culture, the problems an organization is trying to solve, its level of data management maturity, and the formality of its stewardship program (DAMA International 2017). Generally, data stewardship activities include:

- Creation and management of the organization's core metadata (DAMA International 2017), including the business glossary

- Definition and documentation of business rules, data quality rules, and data standards, and ensuring they are agreed on by all the stakeholders to ensure consistent usage

- Data quality issue management

- Execution of operational data governance activities, including influencing decisions to ensure that data are managed in ways that support the overall goals of the organization, and ensuring that data governance policies and initiatives are adhered to on a day-to-day and project-to-project basis (DAMA International 2017)

The success of data stewardship involves organizations moving toward a culture that views data as a competitive asset rather than a necessary evil, and defining clear goals for data quality improvement (Gartner 2008).

Types of Data Stewards

Depending on the complexity of the organization and the goals of the data governance function, formally appointed data stewards may be differentiated by their place within an organization, by the focus of their work, or by both (DAMA International 2017).

Different types of data stewards include the following.

- *Chief data stewards.* Chief data stewards may chair data governance bodies in lieu of the chief data officer or may act as a chief data officer in a virtual (committee-based) or distributed data governance organization. They may also be *executive sponsors* (DAMA International 2017).

- *Executive data stewards.* Executive data stewards are senior managers who serve on a data governance council (DAMA International 2017).

- *Enterprise data stewards.* Enterprise data stewards have oversight of a data domain across business functions (DAMA International 2017).

- *Business data stewards.* Business data stewards are business professionals, most often recognized subject matter experts, accountable for a subset of data. They work with stakeholders to define and control data (DAMA International 2017). Business data stewards are the authorities on their data in that they know what the data are supposed to represent, what they mean, and what business rules are associated with them (Plotkin 2013). Business data stewards are usually assigned to data domains but identified with the data element level. This is because there might be more than one business data steward assigned to a specific data domain, in which case some of the data elements in a data domain are the responsibility of one business data steward, while other data elements in the domain are the responsibility of the other business data stewards.

The people chosen to be business data stewards need to have a good understanding of the data they are accountable for, how the data are used, and the data problems. They should be aware of where the data are not meeting business needs, as well as data elements whose meaning is not well understood or is ambiguous. Most business areas have people who care about the data and can even be said to have a passion for the data. These people are good candidates for the role (Plotkin 2013).

- *Doman data stewards.* There are data domains that are shared by multiple business functions. A customer data domain is a good example of such a data domain. In such cases, a *domain data steward* is designated as the official steward of the shared data. The domain data steward is also responsible for keeping track of which business functions have a stake in the shared data and reaching agreement with the other relevant stewards on any proposed changes. The domain data steward must document the list of consulted business functions, and is responsible for convening meetings or finding other ways to reach consensus on changes, then recording those changes just as any business data steward would do (Plotkin 2013).

- *Project data steward.* With multiple projects running in an organization simultaneously, it is not feasible for a business steward to be in every meeting and work session. A *project data steward* is an individual who is trained to understand the project issues and questions that require input from the business data stewards, and who brings that information to the appropriate business data steward. The business data steward then provides input and answers to questions, which the project data steward brings back to the project. The project data steward is not responsible for the decisions about the data. The project data steward is simply the messenger between the project team and the business data steward. Project data stewards are assigned to projects, and depending on the project's size, may cover multiple projects (Plotkin 2013).

- *Data owner.* A *data owner* is a business data steward who has approval authority for decisions about data within their domain (DAMA International 2017).

- *Technical data stewards.* Technical data stewards are IT professionals operating within one of the knowledge areas, such as data integration specialists, database administrators, business intelligence specialists, data quality analysts, or metadata administrators (DAMA International 2017). Technical data stewards provide support and are associated with specific systems, applications, data stores, and technical processes, such as identity resolution (for master data management), data quality rule enforcement, and ETL jobs (Plotkin 2013). Technical data stewards have the knowledge of—or can find out—*how* the data are created, manipulated, stored, and moved in technical systems. They can answer questions about how data got to be a certain way (Plotkin 2013). For example, an account database storing details of loan accounts created by employees had significant anomalies in the employee ID field. There were 1000 records that had the value "FNS29012012." The technical data steward for the data system explained that the previous system from which the data were migrated did not have values populated in the employee ID field. During the migration to the new system, since employee ID could not have *null* values, and in order to enable traceability, the employee ID was populated with the previous system initials appended with the date of migration.

- *Coordinating data stewards.* Coordinating data stewards lead and represent teams of business and technical data stewards in discussions across teams and with executive data stewards. Coordinating data stewards are particularly important in large organizations (DAMA International 2017).

- *Operational data stewards.* Operational data stewards are "helpers" who assist the business data stewards. They can step in on some of the duties that mesh with their jobs. For example, they can help ensure that data creation rules are followed, or assist with researching issues. Business data stewards can designate operational data stewards to help them, though the business data stewards remain responsible for the data owned by their business area (Plotkin 2013).

Technology

Technology alone does not ensure data governance, but it is an enabler. While it is not impossible to manage a data governance program using documents, spreadsheets, and database-embedded data quality validation routines, this method is extremely manpower-intensive and challenging to manage, as data governance has a large number of components, and the data landscape of an organization can be complex. Typically, master data management and big data initiatives may need governance of a large number of data elements, which when done manually can be extremely cumbersome. Most organizations start with Microsoft Excel and Sharepoint to maintain data definitions and information on data lineage and reference data relationships, and Microsoft Word and Sharepoint to document policies and procedures; however, the complexities of their data landscape result in an unmanageable set of standards, policies, procedures, definitions, and workflows that cannot be easily managed in spreadsheets and documents (Ladley 2016). Hence, organizations should leverage solutions that will help with your governance initiatives. Examples include technology that will help enforce business rules, monitoring and reporting software, and data quality solutions (Experian Undated). Tools and technology not only accelerate the adoption and execution of the roles and responsibilities in data governance, they also make these roles and responsibilities clear, and show the progress and results of data quality improvement. For instance, tooling that automatically updates a data steward on the requested improvement of a data quality issue, for example, data definition improvements, makes the role of that data steward come alive. In turn, this increases the acceptance and adoption of the data steward's role. With the appropriate tooling, data quality issues and ownership of these issues are made visible, and even more importantly, the progress and results of resolving data quality issues are made visible, too, so that employees see the benefits of their effort. Finally, it enables data quality improvements on each organizational level, and it provides more transparency on how the different roles in the data governance structure are functioning (Deloitte Undated).

While there is some overlap of functionality between data governance tools and data management tools, they are not the same. Data management tools are focused on the actual management of data and have functionality to support this activity, and typically create executables and data layouts, whereas, data governance tools are focused on oversight of data management, and do not create executables or data layouts. Instead, data governance tools support the various artifacts and moving parts of a program, such as sophisticated administration of rules and policies. Nevertheless, many data management tools that an organization already uses can assist with data governance. For example, a data dictionary tool or data modeling software can be adapted to handle a data glossary that manages the definition of business data elements (Ladley 2016).

However, tools built to exclusively support data governance are simpler and have better productivity when compared to data management tools adapted to support data governance. Depending on the functionality needed for the data governance program, a data governance program should have the capability to support one or more of the following functions: program and policy management, data lineage tracking, data repository, semantics, and business glossary management, business rules governance, reference and master data management, and data quality issue management and remediation.

DATA GOVERNANCE—TOP-DOWN OR BOTTOM-UP APPROACH

A combination of top-down and bottom-up approaches needs to be used while implementing data governance. If a particular data governance rule or metric applies to all the business units in the organization, a top-down approach makes more sense. On the other hand, if a particular data governance rule or metric only applies to a single business unit, it makes sense to use a bottom-up approach.

CONCLUSION

Data governance is not a one-off exercise. Data governance, like data quality, is a journey. It is a repeatable process for ensuring ongoing compliance with business standards and requirements. Although there may be a set of generic governance organizational structures, roles, and associated responsibilities, the way that data governance is implemented in different organizations is heavily dependent on the context of each organization and the organization culture. In other words, there is no one-size-fits-all approach when implementing data governance in organizations (Mahanti 2018). Decisions on centralized versus decentralized roles, the number of forums, the percentage of effort from existing full-time employees to support data governance activities, the level of an organization's maturity, the extent of the pain, and the volume of the data being governed all contribute to the design of an appropriate governance framework that is suitable for the needs of the organization (Zaki Undated).

In relation to data governance, organizations usually never start from zero. Groups exist in your organization that have varying levels of governance maturity. As you develop your long-term data governance plan, the framework can help you understand how the individual components can be used as a part of the whole, thus enabling you to achieve a sustainable program for data governance.

SUMMARY OF KEY POINTS

Data Governance

The exercise of authority, control, and shared decision making (planning, monitoring, and enforcement) over the management of data assets (DAMA International 2011)

Data Governance Misconceptions

- Responsibility for data governance lies with IT.
- Data governance is restricting.
- Data governance is a project.
- *Data governance* is a synonym for *records management.*
- Data governance is all about compliance.
- Data governance is about documented policies.
- Data governance is siloed by business units or department.
- Data governance is a published repository of common data definitions.

Data Governance Framework

An organization's approach to managing the quality of its data, that is, what they are going to do, who is going to do it, and how they intend to achieve it (DAMA International 2011).

The basic components of a data governance framework are:

- Rules and rules of engagement—principles, data rules and definitions (standards, business rules, business glossary), decision rights, accountabilities, metrics and success measures, controls.
- Data policies.
- Processes.
- People—usually a data governance framework will have several layers and organization bodies.

    The different layers or levels are as follows:

    - *The executive level.* The steering committee

    - *The strategic level.* The data governance council

– *The tactical level.* The data steward council, which consists of data domain stewards and data steward coordinators

– *The operational level.* The data stewards

– *The support level.* Data governance office and information technology partner.

- Roles and responsibilities. Data producer, data consumer, data custodian, data steward.

- Technology.

Data Stewardship

Term used to describe accountability and responsibility for data and processes that ensure effective control and use of data assets (DAMA International 2017). Different types of data stewards are as follows:

- Chief data stewards

- Executive data stewards

- Enterprise data stewards

- Business data stewards

- Domain data stewards

- Project data steward

- Data owner

- Technical data stewards

- Coordinating data stewards

- Operational data steward

Data Principles

- Data must be recognized as a valued and strategic enterprise asset.

- Data must have clearly defined accountability.

- Data must be managed to follow internal and external rules.

- Data quality must be defined and managed consistently across the data life cycle.

Appendix A
Data Quality Dimensions: A Comparison of Definitions

ata quality dimensions are the fundamental measurement elements in the data quality domain, and hence are crucial to the management of data quality. Several experts and researchers have used different definitions for the different data quality dimensions, and in this section, I have presented the definitions used by different researchers and experts for the most commonly used data quality dimensions—completeness, conformity, uniqueness, consistency, accuracy, integrity, and the time-related dimensions (timeliness, currency, and volatility)—in tabular form and have tried to compare the different definitions to show similarities and differences in the different suggestions.

COMPLETENESS

Table A.1 records the different definitions of the *completeness* dimension by different authors. All the authors share the same overall view when defining completeness, that is, the extent of the presence of data, except for a few nuances. DAMA's and Naumann's definition of *completeness* is inclined toward a measurement angle. Naumann's definition also specifies non-*null* values to be complete. Southekal's definition is more oriented to the usage of data elements. While Wang and DAMA define completeness of data without specifically mentioning the level or granularity, Bovee et al. define completeness in relation to entities, Wand and Wang define completeness at the information system level, Jarke et al. at the data source and data warehouse levels, Naumann at the data source and relation levels, Jugulum, English, and Liu and Chi, Loshin and Redman at the data element or data field level, in relation to data sets, and Sebastian-Coleman at the attribute and record levels.

Table A.1   Different definitions for the *completeness* dimension.

Authors/references	Completeness definition
Wang and Strong 1996	The extent to which data are of sufficient breadth, depth, and scope for the task at hand.
Loshin 2006	The expectation that certain attributes are expected to have assigned values in a data set.
Redman 1996	The degree to which values are present in a data set.
English 1999	Refers to the characteristic of having values for the data fields.
Jarke et al. 2000	Percentage of the real-world information entered in the sources and/or the data warehouse.
Wand and Wang 1996	The ability of an information system to represent every meaningful state of the represented real-world system.
Naumann 2002	The quotient of the number of non-*null* values in a source and the size of the universal relation.
Liu and Chi 2002	All values that are supposed to be collected as per a collection theory.
Bovee et al. 2001	Information having all required parts of an entity's information present
DAMA International 2013	The proportion of stored data versus the potential of "100% complete"
Sebastian-Coleman 2013	The degree that it contains required attributes and a sufficient number of records, and to the degree that attributes are populated in accord with data consumer expectations.
Southekal 2017	The degree of usage of the attributes of a specific data element. Data element population and management should be based on usage of the attributes.
Jugulum 2014	The measure of the presence of core source data elements that, exclusive of derived fields, must be present in order to complete a given business process.

CONFORMITY

Table A.2 records the different definitions of the *conformity* dimension by different authors. While DAMA, Southekal, and Jugulum emphasize conformance to specifications or format or syntax as per the data definition, Loshin emphasizes formats consistent with the domain values, Sebastian-Coleman emphasizes conformance to business rules, and English emphasizes conformance to business rules or domain.

UNIQUENESS

Table A.3 records the different definitions of the *uniqueness* dimension by different authors. There is a general agreement among all authors on the definition of uniqueness, except for minor nuances related to granularity. While English defines uniqueness at the

Table A.2	Different definitions for the *conformity* dimension.
Authors/references	**Conformity definition**
English 1999	A measure of conformance of data values to a domain or to a business rule.
DAMA International 2013	A measure of conformance to the syntax (format, type, range) of its definition.
Sebastian-Coleman 2013	The degree to which data conform to a set of business rules, sometimes expressed as a standard or represented within a defined data domain.
Southekal 2017	Adherence to specifications, standards, or guidelines, including data type, description, size, format, and other characteristics.
Loshin 2006	Refers to whether instances of data are either stored, exchanged, or presented in a format that is consistent with the domain of values, as well as consistent with other similar attribute values.
Jugulum 2014	The measure of a data element's adherence to required formats (data types, field lengths, value masks, field composition, and so on) as specified in either metadata documentation or external or internal data standards.

Table A.3	Different definitions for the *uniqueness* dimension.
Author	**Uniqueness definition**
English 1999	The degree to which there is a one-to-one correspondence between records and what they represent.
DAMA International 2013	Nothing will be recorded more than once based on how that thing is identified.
Southekal 2017	There are no duplicate values for a data element.
Loshin 2006	Refers to requirements that entities modeled within the enterprise are captured and represented uniquely within the relevant application architectures. Asserting uniqueness of the entities within a data set implies that no entity exists more than once within the data set and that there is a key that can be used to uniquely access each entity (and only that specific entity) within the data set.

record level, Southekal defines it at the data element level, DAMA does not specify any level of granularity, and Loshin defines uniqueness in terms of entity data set and key.

CONSISTENCY

Table A.4 records the different definitions of the *consistency* dimension by different authors. Southekal defines consistency at the lowest level of granularity, that is, the data element level, Batini et al. define consistency at the higher level of the data record, and Loshin defines consistency at the data set level, while DAMA, Sebastian-Coleman, and Redman define consistency at a generic level.

Table A.4	Different definitions for the *consistency* dimension.
Author	**Consistency definition**
Redman 1996	Two things being compared do not conflict.
Batini et al. 2009	Refers to the violation of semantic rules defined over (a set of) data items, where items can be tuples of relational tables or records in a file.
DAMA International 2013	The absence of difference when comparing two or more representations of a thing against a definition.
Sebastian-Coleman 2013	The degree to which data conform to an equivalent set of data, usually a set produced under similar conditions or a set produced by the same process over time.
Southekal 2017	Data values across all tables and databases for a specific data element within the enterprise system landscape (or outside the enterprise system landscape) are the same.
Loshin 2006	Refers to data values in one data set being consistent with values in another data set. A strict definition of consistency specifies that two data values drawn from separate data sets must not conflict with each other.

In essence, while all authors in effect agree on the absence of conflict, Batini et al. are more specific in stating violation of semantic rules over data items. Sebastian-Coleman is more specific in that she compares data sets produced under similar conditions or by the same process.

ACCURACY

Table A.5 records the different definitions of the *accuracy* dimension by different authors. English and DAMA define accuracy in relation to real-world objects or events. McGilvray, Batini and Scannapieco, Redman, Loshin, and Jugulum define accuracy in comparison of data to a reference that is supposed to hold the true value. Southekal defines accuracy in relation to real-world objects or events as closeness to a reference that is supposed to be the true value. Olson, Wang and Strong, and Sebastian-Coleman define accuracy in terms of the data's correctness. Except for Jugulum and Redman, who explicitly mention data elements and attributes, respectively, in their definitions of accuracy, the other authors define accuracy in terms of data value or data in general.

INTEGRITY

Table A.6 records the different definitions of the *integrity* dimension by different authors. While all three authors—Sebastian-Coleman, Southekal, and Jugulum talk about connectivity and traceability between different data, Sebastian-Coleman uses the term "data relationship rules" and Jugulum uses the concept of primary key and foreign key to

Table A.5	Different definitions for the *accuracy* dimension.
Author	**Accuracy definition**
English 1999	The degree to which data accurately reflect the real-world object or event being described.
McGilvray 2008a	A measure of the correctness of the content of the data (which requires an authoritative source of reference to be identified and accessible).
DAMA International 2013	The degree to which data correctly describe the real-world object or event being described.
Redman 1996	The accuracy of a datum <e, a, v> refers to the nearness of the value v to some value v' in the attribute domain, which is considered the correct one for entity e and attribute a. If the value v = value v', the datum is said to be correct.
Batini and Scannapieco 2006	The closeness between a value v and a value v', considered as the correct representation of the real-life phenomenon that v aims to represent.
Olson 2003	Whether data values are correct.
Wang and Strong 1996	The extent to which data is correct, reliable, and certified.
Sebastian-Coleman 2013	Data's correctness or truth in representation.
Southekal 2017	Closeness of a measured value to a standard or true value. The degree to which data truly reflect the business category, entity, or event.
Loshin 2006	The degree to which data values agree with an identified source of correct information.
Jugulum 2014	A measure of whether the value of a given data element is correct and reflects the real world as viewed by a valid real-world source (SME, customer, hard copy record, and so on).

Table A.6	Different definitions for the *integrity* dimension.
Author	**Integrity definition**
Sebastian-Coleman 2013	The degree to which data conform to data relationship rules (as defined by the data model) that are intended to ensure the complete, consistent, and valid presentation of data representing the same concepts.
Southekal 2017	Ensures that data remain intact and unaltered. It also describes data that can be traced and connected to other data, and ensures that all data are recoverable and searchable.
Jugulum 2014	An entity-level measure of the existence of a unique primary key field, as well as a measure of whether foreign keys in one table reference a valid primary key in the respective parent table

illustrate the same. While Coleman's definition emphasizes the completeness, consistency, and valid presentation of data representing the same concepts, Southekal's emphasis is on data being unaltered, searchable, and recoverable.

TIME-RELATED DIMENSIONS

The time-related dimensions are *timeliness*, *currency*, and *volatility*. Tables A.7, A.8, and A.9 record the different definitions of the timeliness, currency, and volatility dimensions, respectively, by different authors. There are overlaps in the dimension definitions by different authors, and there is no substantial agreement on the name to use for the time-related dimensions. For example, as indicated in Table A.7. Bovee et al. define timeliness in terms of currency and volatility. Naumann's definition for timeliness is in line with Bovee et al.'s and Southekal's definition for currency. Liu and Chi's and Batini and Scannapieco's definition for timeliness is in line with Redman's definition for currency. Jarke et al., Bovee et al., and Batini and Scannapieco provide very similar definitions for volatility. Batini and Scannapieco's definition for currency is very similar to the definition of timeliness furnished by English and Wand and Wang.

From the definitions of the time-related dimensions we can see that:

- Authors provide different definitions for the same dimension, with disagreement on the semantics of a specific dimension. This is more pronounced in the cases of timeliness and currency, where *timeliness* and *currency* have a different meaning for different authors.

- Authors provide very similar definitions for different dimensions.

Table A.7	Different definitions for the *timeliness* dimension.
Author	**Timeliness definition**
English 1999	The length of time between when data is known and when it is available for use.
Wand and Wang 1996	The delay between a change of the real-world state and the resulting modification of the information system state.
Loshin 2006	Refers to the time expectation for accessibility of information.
Naumann 2002	The average age of the data in a source.
Liu and Chi 2002	Refers to the extent to which data are sufficiently up-to-date for a task.
Batini and Scannapieco 2006	Refers to how current data are for the task at hand.
Bovee et al. 2001	Timeliness has two components: age and volatility. Bovee et al. use currency and age interchangeably.
Southekal 2017	Refers to whether the most current data value is readily available when it is needed.
DAMA International 2013	The degree to which data represent reality from the required point in time.
Jugulum 2014	A measure of current data available for business use as defined by established service level agreements (SLAs) for delivery/receipt.

Table A.8   Different definitions for the *currency* dimension.

Author	Currency definition
Redman 1996	Refers to time-related changes in data. The degree to which a datum is up-to-date. A datum value is up-to-date if it is correct in spite of possible discrepancies caused by time-related changes to the correct value
Jarke et al. 2000	Describes when the information was entered in the sources and/or the data warehouse
Loshin 2006	The degree to which information is current with the world that it models
Batini and Scannapieco 2006	Refers to how promptly data are updated.
Bovee et al. 2001	Age or currency is a measure of how old the information is, based on how long ago it was recorded.
Southekal 2017	Refers to how "stale" the data is, and how much time has elapsed since it was created or last changed at the data source.

Table A.9   Different definitions for the *volatility* dimension.

Author	Volatility definition
Sebastian-Coleman 2013	The degree to which data is likely to change over time.
Jarke et al. 2000	Describes the time period for which information is valid in the real world.
Bovee et al. 2001	A measure of information instability-the frequency of change of the value for an entity attribute.
Batini and Scannapieco 2006	The frequency with which data vary over time.

Appendix B
Abbreviations and Acronyms

BAU—business as usual

BI—business intelligence

CAP—change acceleration process

CDO—chief data officer

CECL—current expected credit loss

CEO—chief executive officer

CFO—chief financial officer

CIO— chief information officer

CMM—capability maturity model

CMO—chief managing officer

COBIT—Control Objectives for Information and Related Technology

COBOL—COmmon Business Oriented Language

CODASYL—COnference on DAta SYstems Languages

COO—chief operating officer

COQ—cost of quality

CPU—central processing unit

CRM—customer relationship management

CSF—critical success factor

CTO—chief technology officer

DBA—database administrator

DBMS—database management system

DG—data governance

DGL—data governance lead

DMAIC—define, measure, analyze, improve, and control

DoD—Department of Defense

DQ—data quality

DQM—data quality management

DW—data warehouse

EDW—enterprise data warehouse

EHR—electronic health record

ERP—enterprise resource planning

ETL—extract, transform, load

EU—European Union

FK—foreign key

GAO—Government Accountability Office

GDPR—Global Data Protection Regulation

GIS—geographic information system

HiPPO—highest paid person's opinion

HR—human resource

ISO—International Organization for Standardization

IT—information technology

KPI—key performance indicator

MDM—master data management

MDX—multidimensional expression

NISO—National International Standards Organization

ODS—operational data store

OLAP—online analytical processing

PHI—protected health information

PII—personally identifiable information

PK—primary key

RACI—responsible, accountable, consulted, informed

RDBMS—relational database management system

ROI—return on investment

SDLC—software development life cycle

SIC—standard industrial classification

SIM—service incentive mechanism

SME—subject matter expert

SoX—Sarbanes-Oxley Act

SQL—structured query language

SSN—Social Security number

TDQM—total data quality management

TDWI—The Data Warehousing Institute

UNF—unnormalized form

VP—vice president

Bibliography

Ababaneh, Raed Ismail. 2010. "The Role of Organizational Culture on Practicing Quality Improvement in Jordanian Public Hospitals." *Leadership in Health Services* 23 (3): 244–59.

Abrahams, Carole, and Kevin Davy. 2002. "Linking HES Maternity Records with ONS Birth Records." *Health Statistics Quarterly* 13: 22–30.

Actuate. 2010. "Seven Dimensions: Conformity (Part 5 of 8)." Data Quality Blog. Accessed October 8, 2018. Available at http://www.blog.acuate.com/2010/08/seven-dimensions-conformity.html.

Adams, Laura L. 2009. "The Role of Health Information Technology in Improving Quality and Safety in RI: Can New Money Solve Old Problems?" *Medicine and Health, Rhode Island* 92 (8): 267–8.

Adamson, Georgina. 2014. "The Well-Oiled Data Machine." Experian Data Quality. Accessed May 15, 2015. Available at https://www.edq.com/uk/blog/the-well-oiled-data-machine/.

Adelman, Sid, Larissa Moss, and Majid Abai. 2005. *Data Strategy*. Upper Saddle River, NJ: Pearson Education.

Agarwal, Nitin, and Yusuf Yiliyasi. 2010. "Information Quality Challenges in Social Media." The 15th International Conference on Information Quality. Accessed October 8, 2018. Available at https://www.researchgate.net/publication/260337476_Information_quality_challenges_in_social_media.

Alexander, Jeffrey A., Brian J. Weiner, Stephen M. Shortell, Laurence C. Baker, and Mark P. Becker. 2006. "The Role of Organizational Infrastructure in Implementation of Hospitals' Quality Improvement." *Hospital Topics* 84 (1): 11–20.

Alshawi, Sarmad, Farouk Missi, and Zahir Irani. 2011. "Organisational, Technical and Data Quality Factors in CRM Adoption—SMEs Perspective." *Industrial Marketing Management* 40 (3): 376–83.

Anderson, Carl, and Michael Li. 2017. "Five Building Blocks of a Data-Driven Culture." Crunch Network. Jun 23. Accessed December 6, 2017. Available at https://techcrunch.com/2017/06/23/five-building-blocks-of-a-data-driven-culture/.

Andrews, Mark. 2015. "Data Quality Myths Part 10: Reality Checks and a Better Way." LinkedIn. August 27. Accessed December 16, 2017. Available at https://www.linkedin.com/pulse/part-10-data-quality-myths-mark-andrews.

Anokhin, Philipp. 2001. "Data Inconsistency Detection and Resolution in the Integration of Heterogeneous Information Sources." Doctoral dissertation. School of Information Technology and Engineering, George Mason University.

Askham, Nicola. 2014. *Squaring the Circle: Using a Data Governance Framework to Support Data Quality.* Experian white paper. Dublin: Experian. Accessed December 23, 2017. Available at https://www.edq.com/globalassets/au/papers/squaring_the_circle.pdf.

———. 2016. "Ask the Data Governance Coach: What Is a Data Glossary?" The Data Administration Newsletter. May 1. Accessed December 14, 2017. Available at http://tdan.com/ask-the-data-governance-coach-what-is-a-data-glossary/19752.

ASQ (American Society for Quality). Undated. "Quality Glossary—A." Accessed October 18, 2018. Available at https://asq.org/quality-resources/quality-glossary/a.

Aviation Week. 1998. "Success with Six Sigma after an Elusive Goal." *Aviation Week* 149 (20): 53.

Ballou, Donald P., and Harold L. Pazer. 1985. "Modeling Data and Process Quality in Multi-Input, Multi-Output Information Systems." *Management Science* 31 (2): 150–62. Available at https://www.researchgate.net/publication/227445587_Modeling_Data_and_Process_Quality_in_Multi-Input_Multi-Output_Information_Systems.

Batini, Carlo, and Monica Scannapieco. 2006. *Data Quality: Concepts, Methodologies and Techniques.* New York: Springer-Verlag.

Batini, Carlo, Cinzia Cappiello, Chiara Francalanci, and Andrea Maurino. 2009. "Methodologies for Data Quality Assessment and Improvement." *ACM Computing Surveys* 41 (3): 1–52. Available at https://dl.acm.org/citation.cfm?id=1541883.

Beasty, Colin. 2008. "The Master Piece." *CRM Magazine* 12 (1): 39–42.

Becker, Jörg, Ralf Knackstedt, and Jens Poeppelbüss. 2010. "Developing Maturity Models for IT Management? A Procedure Model and Its Application." *Business & Information Systems Engineering* 1 (3): 213–22. Available at https://www.researchgate.net/publication/272006210_Developing_Maturity_Models_for_IT_Management.

Bell, Royce, and Davis Frank. 2006. *Is Your Data Dirty? (And Does That Matter?).* Accenture white paper. Dublin: Accenture. Accessed August 20, 2014 at http://www.accenture.com/SiteCollectionDocuments/PDF/ACN_DataQuality2.pdf.

Berson, Alex, and Lawrence Dubov. 2007. *Master Data Management and Customer Data Integration for a Global Enterprise.* New York: McGraw-Hill.

Betts, Mitch. 2002. "Data Quality: 'The Cornerstone of CRM.'" *Computerworld.* February 18. Accessed June 17, 2015. Available at https://www.computerworld.com/article/2585776/crm/data-quality---the-cornerstone-of-crm-.html.

BI. 2018. Business Intelligence. Accessed February 28, 2018. Available at https://businessintelligence.com/dictionary/historical-data/.

Bitterer, Andreas. 2007. "Gartner's Data Quality Maturity Model." Gartner. Available at https://www.gartner.com/doc/500906/gartners-data-quality-maturity-model.

Blakely, Tony, and Clare Salmond. 2002. "Probabilistic Record Linkage and a Method to Calculate the Positive Predictive Value." *International Journal of Epidemiology* 31 (6): 1246–52.

Block, Jonathan. 2008. *The Impact of Bad Data on Demand Creation.* Wilton, CT: SiriusDecisions.

Blosser, Dave, and Paul Haines. 2013. *Data Governance at Chevron GOM: A Case Study.* PNEC 17th International Conference on Petroleum Data Integration, Data and Information Management. Accessed June 23, 2015. Available at http://www.noah-consulting.com/experience/papers/DG%20at%20Chevron%20GOM%20-%20PNEC17.pdf.

Bobrowski, Monica, Martina Marré, and Daniel Yankelevich. 1970. "A Software Engineering View of Data Quality." Accessed November 8, 2018. Available at http://citeseerx.ist.psu. edu/viewdoc/download?doi=10.1.1.41.5713&rep=rep1&type=pdf.

Boeing, Geoff. 2016. "Visual Analysis of Nonlinear Dynamical Systems: Chaos, Fractals, Self-Similarity and the Limits of Prediction." *Systems* 4 (4): 37–54.

Bovee, Matthew, Rajendra P. Srivastava, and Brenda Mak. 2001. "A Conceptual Framework and Belief-Function Approach to Assessing Overall Information Quality." In *Proceedings of the Sixth International Conference on Information Quality (ICIQ 01)*. Boston, Massachusetts. Accessed October 24, 2018. Available at https://pdfs.semanticscholar. org/036e/d018847901a8d308fc3a740e36e95170155d.pdf.

Brown, Eric D. 2017. "You Need a Chief Data Officer. Here's Why." CIO from IDG. Accessed December 7, 2018 at https://www.cio.com/article/3202647/analytics/you-need-a-chief-data-officer-heres-why.html.

Bunse, Christian, Martin Verlage, and Peter Giese. 1998. "Improved Software Quality through Improved Development Process Descriptions." *Automatica* 34 (1): 23–32.

Burbank, Donna. 2016. "The Business of Data: The Importance of Business Process in Data Management," The Data Administration Newsletter. November 16. Accessed November 17, 2017. Available at http://tdan.com/ the-business-of-data-the-importance-of-business-process-in-data-management/20547.

Burns, Rebecca. 2012. "Poor Data Quality Proving Costly to UK Businesses." Fourth Source. April 11. Accessed November 9, 2018. Available at http://www.fourthsource.com/news/ poor-data-quality-proving-costly-to-uk-businesses-7722.

Business Data Quality. 2010. "Data Profiling: Underpinning Quality Data Management." Available at http://www.businessdataquality.com/BDQ%20-%20The%20case%20for%20 Data%20Profiling%20v1.7.pdf.

Capgemini. 2008. *The Information Opportunity Report: Harnessing Information to Enhance Business Performance.* Paris: Capgemini.

Cappiello, Cinzia, Chiara Francalanci, and Barbara Pernici. 2003. "Time-Related Factors of Data Quality in Multichannel Information Systems." *Journal of Management Information Systems* 20 (3): 71–92.

Casey, Micheline. 2017. "Developing a Data Strategy: Ensuring Alignment and Prioritization with Business Strategy to Drive Value." CDO Vision presentation. Data Strategy and Innovation, April 4–5, 2017. Produced by DataVersity.

Chen, Angie. 2017. "Breaking Data Myths—Highlights from Tableau CEO's Keynote at #Data17." Centric. October 11. Accessed December 26, 2017. Available at https://centricconsulting.com/blog/breaking-data-myths-by-tableau-ceo-data17-keynote_cincinnati/.

Chikkatur, Lalitha. Undated. "Information Management Part 1: Myths and Facts." Accessed December 25, 2017 at https://www.melissadata.com/enews/articles/010809/1.htm.

Chinapen, Rachel. 2017. "5 Data Quality Myths Debunked." RingLead. June 19. Accessed December 19, 2017. Available at https://www.ringlead.com/5-data-quality-myths-debunked/.

Chisholm, Malcolm. 2014. "Data Credibility: A New Dimension of Data Quality?" Information Management. Accessed August 8, 2017. Available at https://www.information-management. com/news/data-credibility-a-new-dimension-of-data-quality.

Cleven, Anne, and Felix Wortmann. 2010. "Uncovering Four Strategies to Approach Master Data Management." In *Proceedings of the 43rd Hawaii International Conference on System Sciences.*

Codd, Edgar F. 1970. "A Relational Model of Data for Large Shared Data Banks." *Communications of the ACM* 13 (6): 377–87. Available at https://dl.acm.org/citation. cfm?id=362685.

Coe, John M. 2002. "B-to-B Data Decay: The Untold Story." *Target Marketing.* July 1. Accessed December 16, 2017. Available at http://www.targetmarketingmag.com/ article/b-to-b-data-decay-the-untold-story-27870/.

Collaborative Consulting. 2014. *Four Elements of a Successful Data Quality Program.* Collaborative white paper series. Accessed December 23, 2017. Available at https://azslide. com/queue/four-elements-of-successful-data-quality-programs_5993ef3b1723dd232b0 00a20.html.

Collibra. 2017. "How to Build Data Strategy: The Balance of Control versus Flexibility." Collibra blog. Accessed December 10, 2017. Available at https://www.collibra.com/blog/ build-data-strategy-balance-control-versus-flexibility/.

Committee on Innovation in Computing and Communications: Lessons from history, National Research Council. 1999. *Funding a Revolution: Government Support for Computing Research.* Washington, DC: The National Academies Press. Retrieved from http://www. nap.edu/openbook.php?record_id=6323&page=1.

Connecting for Health (CFH). 2006. *Background Issues on Data Quality.* United Kingdom: National Health Service. Accessed August 21, 2018. Available at https://library.ahima.org/ PdfView?oid=63654.

Copas, J. B., and F. J. Hilton. 1990. "Record Linkage: Statistical Models for Matching Computer Records." *Journal of the Royal Statistical Society Series A (Statistics in Society)* 153 (3): 287–320.

Couture, Nancy. 2016. "How to Implement a Robust Data Quality Solution." The Data Download. Data Source Consulting. Accessed December 2, 2017. Available at http:// ds.datasourceconsulting.com/blog/how-to-implement-a-robust-data-quality-solution/.

Crosby, Philip B. 1979. *Quality Is Free: The Art of Making Quality Certain.* New York: McGraw-Hill.

The Daily Mail. 2011. "Mother with Young Son Dies of Cancer at 38 after Hospital Typing Error Sent Urgent Letters to the Wrong Address." March 14. Accessed November 9, 2018. Available at www.dailymail.co.uk/news/article-1366056/Mistyped-address-leavesmother-dead-cancer-son-8-orphan.htm.

DAMA International. 2010. *DAMA Guide to the Data Management Body of Knowledge.* Bradley Beach, NJ: Technics.

———. 2011. *The DAMA Dictionary of Data Management.* Edited by Susan Earley. Bradley Beach, NJ: Technics.

———. 2013. "The Six Primary Dimensions for Data Quality Assessment: Defining Data Quality Dimensions." DAMA UK Working Group white paper. Accessed August 8, 2017. Available at https://www.whitepapers.em360tech.com/wp-content/files_mf/ 1407250286DAMAUKDQDimensionsWhitePaperR37.pdf.

———. 2017. *DAMA-DMBOK: Data Management Body of Knowledge.* 2nd ed. Basking Ridge, NJ: Technics.

DAMA UK. 2011. "The Four Primary Approaches to Data Quality Management." V1.1. Accessed December 25, 2017 at http://www.damauk.org/RWFilePub.php?&cat=403&dx=1&ob=3&rpn=catviewleafpublic403&id=104839.

Daniel, D. Ronald. 1961. "Management Information Crisis." *Harvard Business Review* 39 (5): 111–21.

Danielsen, Asbjørn. 1998. "The Evolution of Data Models and Approaches to Persistence in Database Systems." Accessed Nov 30, 2017. Available at https://www.fing.edu.uy/inco/grupos/csi/esp/Cursos/cursos_act/2000/DAP_DisAvDB/documentacion/OO/Evol_DataModels.html.

The Data Governance Institute. Undated. "Governance and Stewardship." Accessed November 9, 2018. Available at http://www.datagovernance.com/adg_data_governance_governance_and_stewardship/.

DataFlux Corporation. 2003. *Data Profiling: The Foundation for Data Management.* DataFlux white paper. Cary, NC: DataFlux Corporation.

Davis, Ben. 2014. "The Cost of Bad Data: Stats." Econsultancy blog. March 28. Accessed November 9, 2018. Available at https://econsultancy.com/the-cost-of-bad-data-stats/.

Deloitte. Undated. "Data Governance Structure: Key Enabler for Data Quality Management." Accessed December 14, 2017 at https://www2.deloitte.com/nl/nl/pages/financial-services/articles/data-governance-structure-key-enabler-for-data-quality-management.html.

Department of Defense. 2001. *DOD Guidelines on Data Quality Management (Summary).* Accessed October 4, 2018. Available at https://pdfs.semanticscholar.org/c353/a0b55fd87e6452597afb3142d63e2d171315.pdf.

Dijcks, Jean-Pierre. Undated. "Integrating Data Quality into Your Data Warehouse Architecture." Business Intelligence Best Practices. Accessed January 31, 2018. Available at http://www.bi-bestpractices.com/view-articles/5826.

Dorr, Brett, and Rich Murnane. 2011. "Using Data Profiling, Data Quality, and Data Monitoring to Improve Enterprise Information." *Software Quality Professional* 13 (4): 9–18.

Doyle, Martin. 2014. "The Longer You Delay, the More the Data Decay." DQ Global Blog. September 30. Accessed December 16, 2017. Available at https://www.dqglobal.com/2014/09/30/delay-the-more-data-decay/.

Dravis, Frank. 2004. "Data Quality Strategy: A Step-by-Step Approach." In *Proceedings of the Ninth International Conference on Information Quality* (ICIQ-04). Accessed on December 10, 2017. Available at https://pdfs.semanticscholar.org/5b5b/a15e8ea1bd89fe4d14d5e97ce456436291e0.pdf.

Drayton, Scott. 2017. "5 Common Data Quality Myths—Setting the Record Straight. Experian. May 18. Accessed December 19, 2017. Available at https://www.edq.com/uk/blog/five-common-data-quality-myths-setting-the-record-straight/.

Dreibelbis, Allen, Eberhard Hechler, Ivan Milman, Martin Oberhofer, Paul van Run, and Dan Wolfson. 2008. *Enterprise Master Data Management: An SOA Approach to Managing Core Information.* Boston: IBM Press/Pearson.

Dun & Bradstreet. 2012. *The Big Payback on Quality Data—Five Tenets Companies Embrace to Realize ROI.* Short Hills, NJ: Dun & Bradstreet. Accessed November 9, 2018. Available at https://www.dnb.com/content/dam/english/dnb-data-insight/big_payback_on_quality_data_2012_05.pdf.

Duncan, Karolyn, and David L. Wells. 1999. "Rule-Based Data Cleansing." *The Journal of Data Warehousing.* Fall.

Dunlea, Elizabeth. 2015. "The Key to Establishing a Data-Driven Culture." Gartner. November 30. Accessed December 12, 2017. Available at https://www.gartner.com/ smarterwithgartner/the-key-to-establishing-a-data-driven-culture/.

Dyché, Jill, and Evan Levy. 2006. *Customer Data Integration: Reaching a Single Version of the Truth.* Hoboken, NJ: John Wiley & Sons.

Dynamic Markets. 2005. International DQ Research. September.

Earls, Alan R. 2013. "Better Data Quality Process Begins with Business Processes, Not Tools." TechTarget. June. Accessed December 23, 2017. Available at http://searchdata management.techtarget.com/feature/Better-data-quality-process-begins-with-business-processes-not-tools.

Eckerson, Wayne W. 2002. *Data Quality and the Bottom Line: Achieving Business Success through a Commitment to High Quality Data.* Seattle: The Data Warehousing Institute. Accessed October 4, 2018. Available at http://download.101com.com/pub/tdwi/Files/ DQReport.pdf.

———. 2011. *Creating an Enterprise Data Strategy: Managing Data as a Corporate Asset.* BeyeNetwork/TechTarget. Accessed October 22, 2018. Available at http://docs.media. bitpipe.com/io_10x/io_100166/item_417254/Creating%20an%20Enterprise%20Data%20 Strategy_final.pdf.

Elmasri, Ramez, and Shamkant B. Navathe. 2007. *Fundamentals of Database Systems.* 5th ed. Arlington: University of Texas.

English, Larry P. 1999. *Improving Data Warehouse and Business Information Quality: Methods for Reducing Costs and Increasing Profits.* New York: John Wiley & Sons.

———. 1999b. *7 Deadly Misconceptions about Information Quality.* Brentwood, TN: Information Impact International.

———. 2000. "Plain English on Data Quality: Information Quality Management: The Next Frontier. *DM Review Magazine,* April.

———. 2004. "Information Quality Management Maturity: Toward the Intelligent Learning Organization." The Data Administration Newsletter. June 1. Accessed November 9, 2018. Available at http://tdan.com/information-quality-management-maturity-toward-the-intelligent-learning-organization/5409.

———. 2009. *Information Quality Applied: Best Practices for Improving Business Information, Processes, and Systems.* Indianapolis, IN: Wiley.

Ernst & Young. 2008. *Raising the Bar on Catastrophe Exposure Data Quality: The Ernst & Young 2008 Catastrophe Exposure Data Quality Survey.* London: Ernst & Young.

European Commission. 2012. "Proposal for a Regulation of the European Parliament and at the Council on the Protection of Individuals with Regard to the Processing of Personal Data and on the Free Movement of Such Data (General Data Protection Regulation)." Brussels: European Commission.

Experian. 2015. *Data Quality Management Software: Experian Pandora.* Experian white paper. Dublin: Experian. Accessed November 8, 2018. Available at http://www.experian. com.au/wp-content/uploads/2018/01/data_quality_management_software.pdf.

———. 2016. "The Rise of the Data Force." Experian Research Paper.

———. 2017. *Data Migrations Begin (and End) with Data Quality.* Experian white paper. Boston: Experian. Accessed December 1, 2017. Available at https://www.edq.com/ globalassets/white-papers/data-migrations-begin-with-data-quality-whitepaper.pdf.

————. Undated. "Data Governance." Experian data quality glossary. Accessed December 14, 2017. Available at https://www.edq.com/glossary/data-governance/.

Experian Data Quality. 2014. *Dawn of the CDO Research*. London: Experian. Accessed November 9, 2018. Available at www.edq.com/cdo.

Faltin, Frederick W., Ron S. Kenett, and Fabrizio Ruggeri. 2012. *Statistical Methods in Healthcare*. Chichester, West Sussex, UK: John Wiley & Sons.

Fan, Wenfei, Floris Geerts, and Xibei Jia. 2009. "Conditional Dependencies: A Principled Approach to Improving Data Quality." Accessed November 9, 2018. Available at http://homepages.inf.ed.ac.uk/fgeerts/pdf/bncod.pdf.

Fellegi, Ivan P., and Alan B. Sunter. 1969. "A Theory for Record Linkage." *Journal of the American Statistical Association* 64 (328): 1183–1210.

Ferriss, P. 1998. "Insurers Victims of DBMS Fraud." *Computing Canada* 24 (36): 13–15.

Fisher, Craig, Eitel Lauria, Shobha Chengalur-Smith, and Richard Y. Wang. 2011. *Introduction to Information Quality*. Cambridge, MA: MIT Information Quality Program.

Fisher, Craig W., InduShobha Chengalur-Smith, and Donald P. Ballou. 2003. "The Impact of Experience and Time on the Use of Data Quality Information in Decision Making." *Information Systems Research* 14 (2): 170–188.

Fisher, Tony. 2002. "Data Quality—The Fuel that Drives the Business Engine." In *Conference Proceedings* SUGI 27. Cary, NC: DataFlux Corporation.

————. 2009. *The Data Asset: How Smart Companies Govern Their Data for Business Success*. Hoboken, NJ: John Wiley & Sons.

Foote, Keith D. 2017. "A Brief History of Database Management." Dataversity. Accessed October 5, 2018. Available at http://www.dataversity.net/brief-history-database-management/.

Foote, Kenneth E., and Donald J. Huebner. 1995. "The Geographer's Craft Project." Department of Geography, University of Colorado–Boulder. Accessed August 6, 2017 at http://www.colorado.edu/geography/gcraft/notes/error/error_f.html.

Forbes, James. 2014. "Bad Data Is Costing Your Business; Don't Rely on IT to Fix It." CMO from IDG. August 5. Accessed November 9, 2018. Available at https://www.cmo.com.au/article/551539/bad_data_costing_your_business_don_t_rely_it_fix_it/.

Fraser, P., J. Moultrie, and M. Gregory. 2002. "The Use of Maturity Models/Grids as a Tool in Assessing Product Development Capability." IEEE International Engineering Management Conference. *Proceedings of the 2002 IEEE International Engineering Management Conference* 1: 244–49. Available at https://www.tib.eu/en/search/id/BLCP%3ACN045609509/The-Use-of-Maturity-Models-Grids-as-a-Tool-in-Assessing/.

Friedman, Ted. 2007. "Overview: Best Practices for Data Stewardship." Gartner. December 13.

————. 2009. *Findings from Primary Research Study: Organizations Perceive Significant Cost Impact from Data Quality Issues*. Stamford, CT: Gartner Group.

Friedman, Ted, and Michael Smith. 2011. *Measuring the Business Value of Data Quality*. Stamford, CT: Gartner. Accessed October 4, 2018. Available at https://www.data.com/export/sites/data/common/assets/pdf/DS_Gartner.pdf.

Friesen, Michael E., and James A. Johnson. 1995. *The Success Paradigm: Creating Organizational Effectiveness through Quality and Strategy*. New York: Quorum Books.

Fryman, Lowell. 2012. "What Is a Business Glossary?" BeyeNetwork. September 13. Accessed October 23, 2018. Available at http://www.b-eye-network.com/view/16371.

GAO (General Accounting Office). 2009. "Assessing the Reliability of Computer-Processed Data." GAO-09-680G. External Version I. Accessed October 9, 2018. Available at http://www.gao.gov/assets/80/77213.pdf.

Gartner. 2008. "Gartner Says Organisations Must Establish Data Stewardship Roles to Improve Data Quality." Gartner press release. January 22. Accessed December 24, 2017. Available at https://www.gartner.com/newsroom/id/589207.

Gartner Group. 2010. *Findings from Primary Research Study: Data Quality Issues Create Significant Cost, Yet Often Go Unmeasured.* Stamford, CT: Gartner Group.

Geiger, Jonathan G. 2004. "Data Quality Management: The Most Critical Initiative You Can Implement." Paper 098-29. In *Proceedings of SUGI 29.* Boulder, CO: Intelligent Solutions. Accessed December 10, 2017. Available at http://www2.sas.com/proceedings/sugi29/098-29.pdf.

Gibson, Cyrus F., and Richard L. Nolan. 1974. "Managing the Four Stages of EDP Growth." *Harvard Business Review* 52 (1): 76–88. Accessed October 16, 2018. Available at https://hbr.org/1974/01/managing-the-four-stages-of-edp-growth.

Golfarelli, Matteo. "Data Warehouse Architectures, Concepts and Phases: What You Need to Know." TechTarget. Accessed November 29, 2017. Available at http://searchdata management.techtarget.com/feature/Data-warehouse-architectures-concepts-and-phases.

Gomatam, Shanti, Randy Carter, Mario Ariet, and Glenn Mitchell. 2002. "An Empirical Comparison of Record Linkage Procedures." *Statistics in Medicine* 21 (10): 1485–96.

Grady, Denise. 2003. "Donor Mix-Up Leaves Girl, 17, Fighting for Life." January 19. *New York Times.* Accessed October 4, 2018. Available at https://www.nytimes.com/2003/02/19/us/donor-mix-up-leaves-girl-17-fighting-for-life.html.

Grannis, Shaun J., J. Marc Overhage, and Clement J. McDonald. 2002. "Analysis of Identifier Performance Using a Deterministic Linkage Algorithm." *Proceedings of the AMIA Symposium*: 305–9.

Grannis, Shaun J., J. Marc Overhage, Siu Hui, and Clement J. McDonald. 2003. "Analysis of a Probabilistic Record Linkage Technique without Human Review." *AMIA Annual Symposium Proceedings*: 259–63.

Greengard, Samuel. 1998. "Don't Let Dirty Data Derail You." *Workforce* 77 (11). Accessed July 29, 2017. Available at https://www.workforce.com/1998/11/01/dont-let-dirty-data-derail-you/.

Hagger-Johnson, Gareth, Katie Harron, Tom Fleming, and Roger C. Parslow. 2015. "Data Linkage Errors in Hospital Administrative Data When Applying a Pseudonymisation Algorithm to Paediatric Intensive Care Records." *BMJ Open* 5 (8)

Harron, Katie. 2016. *Introduction to Data Linkage.* Colchester, Essex, UK: Administrative Data Research Network. Accessed October 18, 2018. Available at https://adrn.ac.uk/media/174200/data_linkage_katieharron_2016.pdf.

Haug, Anders, and Jan Stentoft Arlbjørn. 2011. "Barriers to Master Data Quality." *Journal of Enterprise Information Management* 24 (3): 288–303.

Haug, Anders, Frederik Zachariassen, and Dennis van Liempd. 2011. "The Cost of Poor Data Quality." *Journal of Industrial Engineering and Management* 4 (2): 168–93. Accessed November 9, 2018. Available at http://www.jiem.org/index.php/jiem/article/view/232/130.

Hempfield Jr., Clarence W. 2011. *Data Quality? That's IT's Problem Not Mine: What Business Leaders Should Know About Data Quality.* Pitney Bowes white paper. Stamford, CT: Pitney Bowes. Accessed June 16, 2015. Available at http://www.pbinsight.com/files/resource-library/resource-files/dirty-data-not-my-problem-wp.pdf.

Herrick, Jonathan. 2017. "How to Prevent Data Decay from Ruining Your CRM System." Business.com. September 27. Accessed December 16, 2017. Available at https://www.business.com/articles/prevent-data-decay-from-ruining-your-crm/.

HIMSS (Healthcare Information and Management Systems Society). 2017. *HIMSS Dictionary of Health Information Technology Terms, Acronyms, and Organizations.* 4th ed. Boca Raton, FL: CRC Press.

Howles, Trudy. 2014. "Data, Data Quality, and Ethical Use." *Software Quality Professional* 16 (2): 4–12.

Huang, Kuan-Tsae, Yang W. Lee, and Richard Y. Wang. 1999. *Quality Information and Knowledge.* Upper Saddle River, NJ: Prentice Hall.

Hub Designs. 2009. "New Columns in Information Management." Hub Designs Magazine. Accessed November 9, 2018. Available at https://hubdesignsmagazine.com/2009/04/09/new-columns-in-information-management/.

Hubspot. Undated. "Database Decay Simulation: How Inbound Marketing Helps Overcome Database Decay." Accessed December16, 2017. Available at https://www.hubspot.com/database-decay.

IBM. 2007. *The IBM Data Governance Blueprint: Leveraging Best Practices and Proven Technologies.* Accessed June 23, 2015. Available at http://www-935.ibm.com/services/au/cio/pdf/data-governance-best-practices.pdf.

———. https://www.ibm.com/support/knowledgecenter/en/SS6RBX_11.4.2/com.ibm.sa.sadata.doc/topics/r_Data_Element.html. Accessed December 10, 2017.

———. 2011. "Identifying Keys and Analyzing Relationships." IBM Knowledge Center. Accessed December 10, 2017. Available at https://www.ibm.com/support/knowledgecenter/en/SSZJPZ_8.7.0/com.ibm.swg.im.iis.ia.profile.doc/topics/t_nk_pk_fk.html.

IBM Software. 2012. *Getting Started with a Data Quality Program.* IBM Software white paper. Somers, NY: IBM Corporation. Accessed November 9, 2018. Available at http://alpineinc.com/wp-content/uploads/2014/04/IMW14623USEN.pdf.

Inmon, William H. 2005. *Building the Data Warehouse.* 4th ed. Indianapolis, IN: Wiley.

———. 2008. "How Much Historical Data Is Enough?" TechTarget.com. July 10. Accessed February 28, 2018. Available at http://searchdatamanagement.techtarget.com/news/2240034112/How-much-historical-data-is-enough.

———. 2009. "Data Degradation." BeyeNetwork. Accessed May 25, 2015. Available at http://www.b-eye-network.com/view/10142.

Inmon, William H., Derek Strauss, and Genia Neushloss. 2008. *DW 2.0: The Architecture for the Next Generation of Data Warehousing.* San Francisco: Morgan Kaufmann.

INN (Insurance Networking News). 2016. "19 Tips for Becoming a Chief Data Officer." Scyllogis. Accessed December 10, 2017. Available at https://www.scyllogis.com/media/market-news/19-tips-becoming-chief-data-officer/.

Innovit. Undated. "Data Quality and Governance." Accessed December 23, 2017 at http://www.innovit.com/knowledge-center/mdm-faq.

Inserro, Richard J. 2002. "Credit Risk Data Challenges Underlying the New Basel Capital Accord." *The RMA Journal* 84 (7).

Institute of International Finance (IIF) and McKinsey & Company. 2011. *Risk IT and Operations: Strengthening Capabilities.* New York: McKinsey & Company. Accessed November 9, 2018. Available at https://www.mckinsey.com/~/media/mckinsey/dotcom/client_service/risk/pdfs/iif_mck_report_on_risk_it_and_operations.ashx.

Insurance Data Management Association (IDMA). Undated. *Data Management Value Propositions.* Jersey City, NJ: IDMA. Accessed August 21, 2018. Available at https://s3.amazonaws.com/amo_hub_content/Association352/files/IDMA%20Data%20Management%20Value%20Proposition--LATEST.pdf.

Iron Mountain. Undated. "Information Governance: Puncturing The Myths." Accessed
December 25, 2017. Available at http://www.ironmountain.com/resources/
general-articles/i/information-governance-puncturing-the-myths.

Jamieson, E. Norman, Jennifer Roberts, and Gina Browne. 1995. "The Feasibility and
Accuracy of Anonymized Record Linkage to Estimate Shared Clientele among Three
Health and Social Service Agencies." *Methods of Information in Medicine* 34 (4): 371–77.

Jarke, Matthias, Maurizio Lenzerini, Yannis Vassiliou, and Panos Vassiliadis. 2000.
Fundamentals of Data Warehouses. Heidelberg: Springer-Verlag.

Jones, Clinton. 2014. "Getting RACI with Your Data Governance." Toolbox. Accessed
December 14, 2017. Available at https://it.toolbox.com/blogs/africanoracle/
getting-raci-with-your-data-governance-092514.

Jones, Dylan. 2009. "10 Techniques for Data Quality Root-Cause Analysis." Data
Quality Pro. Accessed November 20, 2017. Available at https://www.dataqualitypro.
com/10-techniques-for-data-quality-root-cause-analysis/.

———. 2012. "3 Tips for More Effective Data Profiling." SAS blog. Accessed October 9,
2018. Available at http://blogs.sas.com/content/datamanagement/2012/11/30/
3-tips-for-more-effective-data-profiling/.

———. 2013. "7 Characteristics of an Ideal Data Quality Sponsor." Data Quality Pro.
April 22. Accessed October 22, 2018. Available at https://www.dataqualitypro.
com/7-characteristics-of-an-ideal-data-quality-sponsor/.

———. 2014. *How to Create a Comprehensive Data Quality Management Strategy.* Experian
white paper.

———. 2016. "How to Tackle the Data Migration Cleansing Challenge." Experian UK
Blog. Accessed December 10, 2017. Available at https://www.edq.com/uk/blog/
how-to-tackle-the-data-migration-cleansing-change/.

Jugulum, Rajesh. 2014. *Competing with High Quality Data: Concepts, Tools, and Techniques
for Building a Successful Approach to Data Quality.* Hoboken, NJ: John Wiley & Sons.

Juran, Joseph M., and A. Blanton Godfrey. 1999. Juran's Quality Handbook. 5th ed. New York:
McGraw-Hill.

Juran Institute. 2014. "The New Quality Culture: What's Wrong with Yours?" Accessed
February 28, 2014 at http://www.asqlongisland.org/seminars/The_New_Quality_Culture.
pdf.

Kahn, Beverly K., Diane M. Strong, and Richard Y. Wang. 2002. "Information Quality
Benchmarks: Product and Service Performance." *Communications of the ACM* 45 (4):
184–192. Accessed November 9, 2018. Available at http://citeseerx.ist.psu.edu/viewdoc/
download?doi=10.1.1.5.4752&rep=rep1&type=pdf.

Kaila, Isher, and Matthew Goldman. 2006. *Eight Steps to Implementing a Successful CRM
Project.* London: Gartner Group.

Kalinka, Mihaylova, and Kalinka Kaloyanova. 2005. "Improving Data Integration for Data
Warehouse: A Data Mining Approach." ResearchGate. Accessed October 19, 2018.
Available at https://www.researchgate.net/publication/228938054_Improving_data_
integration_for_data_warehouse_a_data_mining_approach.

Kantardzic, Mehmed. 2011. *Data Mining: Concepts, Models, Methods, and Algorithms.* 2nd
ed. Hoboken, NJ: IEEE Press/John Wiley & Sons.

Kelly, Jeff. 2009. "Gartner: Open Source Data Quality Software Focuses on Data Profiling." TechTarget. Accessed August 20, 2014. Available at http://searchdatamanagement.techtarget.com/news/1374227/ Gartner-Open-source-data-quality-software-focuses-on-data-profiling.

Kempe, Shannon. 2012. "A Short History of Data Warehousing." Dataversity. Accessed October 5, 2018. Available at http://www.dataversity.net/a-short-history-of-data-warehousing/.

Kenett, Ron S., and Galit Shmueli. 2016. *Information Quality: The Potential of Data and Analytics to Generate Knowledge.* Chichester, West Sussex, UK: John Wiley & Sons.

Kimball, Ralph. 1996. *The Data Warehouse Tool Kit.* New York: John Wiley & Sons.

———. 1998. "Is Data Staging Relational?" *Wayback Machine.*

———. 2004. "Kimball Design Tip #59: Surprising Value of Data Profiling." Kimball Group, Kimball University. Accessed October 15, 2018. Available at http://www.kimballgroup.com/wp-content/uploads/2012/05/DT59SurprisingValue.pdf.

Kimball, Ralph, and Margy Ross. 2002. *The Data Warehouse Toolkit: The Complete Guide to Dimensional Modeling..* 2nd ed. New York: John Wiley & Sons.

Kimball, Ralph, Margy Ross, Warren Thornthwaite, Joy Mundy, and Bob Becker. 2008. *The Data Warehouse Lifecycle Toolkit.* 2nd ed. Indianapolis, IN: Wiley.

Kimball Group. Undated. *Kimball Dimensional Modeling Techniques.* Accessed December 4, 2017. Available at http://www.kimballgroup.com/wp-content/uploads/2013/08/2013.09-Kimball-Dimensional-Modeling-Techniques11.pdf.

Kisubika, Priscilla. 2011. "Assessing and Enhancing the Information Quality Maturity Model in an Organization: The Case of Shell Global Functions IT." Master thesis. University of Twente, Enschede, Netherlands. Accessed October 16, 2018. Available at http://essay.utwente.nl/61746/1/MSc_P_Kisubika.pdf.

Kitagawa, Hiroyuki, and Tosiyasu L. Kunii. 1989. *The Unnormalized Relational Data Model: For Office Form Processor Design.* Tokyo: Springer-Verlag.

Knight, Michelle. 2017. "What Is Data Stewardship?" Dataversity. November 6. Accessed November 9, 2018. Available at http://www.dataversity.net/what-is-data-stewardship/.

———. 2018. "Metadata Management vs. Master Data Management." Dataversity. January 16. Accessed January 20, 2018. Available at http://www.dataversity.net/ metadata-management-vs-master-data-management/.

Knolmayer, Gerhard F., and Michael Röthlin. 2006. "Quality of Material Master Data and Its Effect on the Usefulness of Distributed ERP Systems." In *Advances in Conceptual Modeling—Theory and Practice*, edited by J. F. Roddick, et al. ER 2006 Workshops. Lecture Notes in Computer Science 4231. Berlin, Heidelberg: Springer-Verlag.

Knowledgent. Undated. "Building a Successful Data Quality Management Program." Knowledgent Group. Accessed on January 2, 2017. Available at https://knowledgent.com/ whitepaper/building-successful-data-quality-management-program/.

Krewski, D., A. Dewanji, Y. Wang, S. Bartlett, J. M. Zielinski, and R. Mallick. 2005. "The Effect of Record Linkage Errors on Risk Estimates in Cohort Mortality Studies." *Survey Methodology* 31 (1): 13-21.

Kumar, Girish. 2014. "Data Governance." Data Design blog. Accessed August 10, 2018. Available at http://www.data-design.org/blog/data-governance.

Ladley, John. 2016. "How Data Governance Software Helps Ensure the Integrity of Your Data." TechTarget. Accessed June 1, 2018. Available at https://searchdatamanagement.techtarget.com/feature/How-data-governance-software-helps-ensure-the-integrity-of-your-data.

Lake, P., and Paul Crowther. 2013. *Concise Guide to Databases: A Practical Introduction.* London: Springer-Verlag.

Lederman, Reeva, Graeme Shanks, and Martin R. Gibbs. 2003. "Meeting Privacy Obligations: The Implications for Information Systems Development." In *Proceedings of the 11th European Conference on Information Systems (ECIS)*, Naples, Italy, June 16–21. Accessed October 4, 2018. Available at https://pdfs.semanticscholar.org/81b0/44fa4d96e1806bc16200657efd61c858ef92.pdf.

Lee, Sang Hyun. 2014. "Measuring Correlation of Information Quality Dimensions Using Six Sigma Based Product Perspective." Doctoral dissertation. University of South Australia. Accessed November 10, 2017. Available at http://search.ror.unisa.edu.au/media/researcharchive/open/9915885211501831/53111889120001831.

Levitin, Anany V., and Thomas C. Redman. 1998. "Data as a Resource: Properties, Implications, and Prescriptions." *Sloan Management Review* 40 (1): 89–101. Accessed October 4, 2018. Available at https://sloanreview.mit.edu/article/data-as-a-resource-properties-implications-and-prescriptions/.

Levy, Evan. 2018. *The 5 Essential Components of a Data Strategy.* SAS White paper. Cary, NC: SAS Institute. Accessed May 28, 2018. Available at https://www.sas.com/content/dam/SAS/en_us/doc/whitepaper1/5-essential-components-of-data-strategy-108109.pdf.

Li, Eldon Y., Houn-Gee Chen, and W. Cheung. 2000. "Total Quality Management in Software Development Process." *The Journal of Quality Assurance Institute* 14 (1): 4–6, 35–41.

Liddell, Henry George, and Robert Scott. 2007. *Liddell and Scott's Greek-English Lexicon.* Abridged. Simon Wallenburg.

Liu, Liping, and Lauren N. Chi. 2002. "Evolutionary Data Quality: A Theory-Specific View." In *Proceedings of the Seventh International Conference on Information Quality (ICIQ-02)*. Boston: Massachusetts Institute of Technology. Accessed October 24, 2018. Available at https://pdfs.semanticscholar.org/cd84/74a22c554b60ba975af93b99e0c0cdc9893f.pdf.

Loshin, David. 2001. *Enterprise Knowledge Management: The Data Quality Approach.* San Francisco: Morgan Kaufmann/Academic Press.

———. 2004. "Data Profiling Techniques for Your BI Program: Taking a Look at Data Profiling." TechTarget. Accessed October 15, 2018. Available at http://searchdatamanagement.techtarget.com/news/2240036409/Data-profiling-techniques-for-your-BI-program.

———. 2006. *Monitoring Data Quality Performance Using Data Quality Metrics.* Informatica white paper. Redwood City, CA: Informatica. Accessed August 8, 2017. Available at https://it.ojp.gov/documents/Informatica_Whitepaper_Monitoring_DQ_Using_Metrics.pdf.

———. 2007. "Data Profiling, Data Integration and Data Quality: The Pillars of Master Data Management." White paper. BeyeNetwork. Accessed October 28, 2018. Available at http://www.b-eye-network.com/view/11239.

———. 2008. *Master Data Management.* Burlington, MA: Morgan Kaufmann/Elsevier.

———. 2009. *Five Fundamental Data Quality Practices.* Pitney Bowes white paper. Stamford, CT: Pitney Bowes. Accessed January 10, 2018. Available at http://www.pbinsight.com/files/resource-library/resource-files/five_fundamental_data_quality_practices_WP.pdf.

———. 2010a. *The Practitioner's Guide to Data Quality Improvement.* Burlington, MA: Morgan Kaufmann/Elsevier.

————. 2010b. *Data Integration Alternatives—Managing Value and Quality: Using a Governed Approach to Incorporating Data Quality Services within the Data Integration Process.* Pitney Bowes white paper. Stamford, CT: Pitney Bowes. Accessed December 20, 2017. Available at http://www.pbinsight.com/files/resource-library/resource-files/data_integrate_alt_wp_us_0910.pdf.

————. 2011a. "Evaluating the Business Impacts of Poor Data Quality." *IDQ Newsletter.* International Association for Information and Data Quality. Available at http://www.sei. cmu.edu/measurement/research/upload/Loshin.pdf"www.sei.cmu.edu/measurement/research/upload/Loshin.pdf.

————. 2013. *Data Governance for Master Data Management and Beyond.* SAS Institute white paper. Cary, NC: SAS Institute. Accessed January 20, 2018. Available at https://www.sas.com/content/dam/SAS/en_us/doc/whitepaper1/data-governance-for-MDM-and-beyond-105979.pdf.

————. 2014. "Busting 7 Myths about Data Quality Management." Information Builders. Accessed December 10, 2014. Available at http://www.informationbuilders.com.au/about_us/analyst_reports/12746.

————. 2017. *Busting 10 Myths About Data Quality Management.* Washington, DC: Knowledge Integrity Incorporated.. Accessed December 18, 2017. Available at https://www.informationbuilders.com/sites/default/files/pdf/about_us/whitepapers/wp_busting_10_myths_dq_management_2017.pdf.

Mahanti, Rupa. 2011. "Software Six Sigma and Cultural Change: The Key Ingredients." *Software Quality Professional* 13 (2): 38–47.

————. 2014. "Critical Success Factors for Implementing Data Profiling: The First Step toward Data Quality." *Software Quality Professional* 16 (2): 13–26.

————. 2015. "Data Profiling Project Selection and Implementation—the Key Considerations." *Software Quality Professional* 17 (4): 44–52. Available at http://asq.org/qic/display-item/index.html?item=38149.

————. 2018. "Data Governance Implementation—Critical Success Factors." *Software Quality Professional* 20 (4): 4–21.

Markram, Ian. Undated. "Five Data Myths." Seed Analytics Group. Accessed December 19, 2017. Available at http://seedanalyticsgroup.com/five-data-myths/.

Marsh, Richard. 2005. "Drowning in Dirty Data? It's Time to Sink or Swim: A Four-Stage Methodology for Total Data Quality Management." *Journal of Database Marketing & Customer Strategy Management* 12 (2): 105–12.

Maso, Luigino Dal, Claudia Braga, and Silvia Franceschi. 2001. "Methodology Used for 'Software for Automated Linkage in Italy' (SALI)." *Journal of Biomedical Informatics* 34 (6): 387–95.

Maydanchik, Arkady. 2007. *Data Quality Assessment.* Bradley Beach, NJ: Technics.

McCafferty, Dennis. 2015. "Why Organizations Struggle with Data Quality." CIO Insight. Accessed December 10, 2017. Available at https://www.cioinsight.com/it-strategy/big-data/slideshows/why-organizations-struggle-with-data-quality.html.

McGilvray, Danette. 2008a. *Executing Data Quality Projects: Ten Steps to Quality Data and Trusted Information.* Burlington, MA: Morgan Kaufmann/Elsevier.

————. 2008b. "The Information Life Cycle." BeyeNetwork. Accessed October 4, 2018. Available at http://www.b-eye-network.com/view/7396.

Mears, Greg D., Wayne D. Rosamond, Chad Lohmeier, Carol Murphy, Emily O'Brien, Andrew W. Asimos, and Jane H. Brice. 2010. "A Link to Improve Stroke Patient Care: A Successful Linkage between a Statewide Emergency Medical Services Data System and a Stroke Registry. *Academic Emergency Medicine* 17 (12): 1398–1404.

Méray, N., Johannes B. Reitsma, Anita C. J. Ravelli, and Gouke J. Bonsel. 2007. "Probabilistic Record Linkage Is a Valid and Transparent Tool to Combine Databases without a Patient Identification Number." *Journal of Clinical Epidemiology* 60 (9): 883–91.

Mettler, Tobias. 2010. "Maturity Assessment Models: A Design Science Research Approach." *International Journal of Society Systems Science* 3 (1): 81–98. Accessed October 16, 2018. Available at https://www.alexandria.unisg.ch/214426/1/IJSSS0301-0205%2520METTLER.pdf.

Meurer, Steven J., Doris McGartland Rubio, Michael A. Counte, and Tom Burroughs. 2002. "Development of a Healthcare Quality Improvement Measurement Tool: Results of a Content Validity Study." *Hospital Topics* 80 (2): 7–13.

Mierzejewski, Steve. 2017. "Hacker Corruption of Data May Be the Next Major Attack Vector." Workplacetablet.com. March 28. Accessed October 4, 2018. Available at https://workplacetablet.com/2017/03/28/hacker-corruption-of-data-may-be-the-next-major-attack-vector/.

Miglin, Karen. 2012. "Gartner Says Data Quality before Data Integration." Bardess. Accessed January 23, 2018. Available at http://www.bardess.com/gartner-says-data-quality-before-data-integration/.

Mojsilovic, Aleksandra (Saška). 2014. "The Age of Data and Opportunities." IBM Big Data and Analytics Hub. Accessed July 29, 2017. Available at https://www.ibmbigdatahub.com/blog/age-data-and-opportunities.

Morgan, Lisa. 2016. "Rise and Fall of the Chief Data Officer." InformationWeek. Accessed December 10, 2017. Available at https://www.informationweek.com/strategic-cio/it-strategy/rise-and-fall-of-the-chief-data-officer/a/d-id/1324280?

Morgan, Stephen L., and Colleen G. Waring. 2004. *Guidance on Testing Data Reliability.* Austin, TX: Office of the City Auditor. Accessed April 10, 2018. Available at http://www.auditorroles.org/files/toolkit/role2/Tool2aAustinCityAud_GuidanceTestingReliability.pdf.

Mullins, Craig. 1997. "Capability Maturity Model from a Data Perspective." The Data Administration Newsletter. Accessed October 16, 2018. Available at http://tdan.com/capability-maturity-model-from-a-data-perspective/4205.

Muse, Alison G., Jaromir Mikl, and Perry F. Smith. 1995. "Evaluating the Quality of Anonymous Record Linkage Using Deterministic Procedures with the New York State AIDS Registry and a Hospital Discharge File." *Statistics in Medicine* 14 (5–7): 499–509.

MyCustomer. 2008. "Businesses Need Data Stewards for Quality." MyCustomer Newsdesk. January 23. Accessed December 28, 2017. Available at https://www.mycustomer.com/businesses-need-data-stewards-for-quality.

Myler, Larry. 2017. "Better Data Quality Equals Higher Marketing ROI." *Forbes,* July 11. Accessed August 8, 2017. Available at https://www.forbes.com/sites/larrymyler/2017/07/11/better-data-quality-equals-higher-marketing-roi/#187d034c7b68.

National Information Standards Organization (NISO). 2007. *A Framework of Guidance for Building Good Digital Collections.* 3rd ed. Baltimore, MD: NISO.

Naumann, Felix. 2002. *Quality-Driven Query Answering for Integrated Information Systems.* Berlin, Heidelberg: Springer-Verlag.

Neubarth, Michael. 2013. "Good Addresses Go Bad: Keeping Pace with Email Data Decay Gets Harder." Towerd@ta. Email Solutions Blog. Accessed October 4, 2018. Available at http://www.towerdata.com/blog/bid/117701/Good-Addresses-Go-Bad-Keeping-Pace-with-Email-Data-Decay-Gets-Harder.

Newcombe, Harold B., John M. Kennedy, S. J. Axford, and A. P. James. 1959. "Automatic Linkage of Vital Records." *Science* 130 (3381): 954–59.

Nguyen, Tho. Undated. *The Value of ETL and Data Quality.* SUGI 28. Paper 161-28. Data Warehousing and Enterprise Solutions. SAS Institute. Accessed October 4, 2018. Available at http://www2.sas.com/proceedings/sugi28/161-28.pdf.

Nolan, Richard L. 1973. "Managing the Computer Resource: A Stage Hypothesis." *Communications of the ACM* 16 (7): 399–405. Available at https://dl.acm.org/citation.cfm?id=362284.

Novak, May. 2015. "Three Approaches to Data Cleansing." Data Migration Fundamentals blog. April 6. Accessed August 10, 2018. Available at https://www.datamigrationfundamentals.com/posts/three-approaches-to-data-cleansing.

Office of the National Coordinator for Health Information Technology (ONCHIT). 2013. *Capturing High Quality Electronic Health Records Data to Support Performance Improvement: A Learning Guide.* HealthIT.gov. Accessed August 21, 2018. Available at https://www.healthit.gov/sites/default/files/onc-beacon-lg3-ehr-data-quality-and-perform-impvt.pdf.

Ofner, Martin H., Boris Otto, and Hubert Österle. 2012. "Integrating a Data Quality Perspective into Business Process Management." *Business Process Management Journal* 18 (6): 1036–67.

Olson, Jack E. 2003. *Data Quality: The Accuracy Dimension.* San Francisco: Morgan Kaufmann/Elsevier.

1Key Data. Undated. "Data Modeling: Conceptual, Logical, and Physical Data Models." Accessed October 5, 2018. Available at https://www.1keydata.com/datawarehousing/data-modeling-levels.html.

Oracle Corp. Undated. *Oracle 9i Data Warehousing Guide.* Data Warehousing Concepts. Oracle.

———. 2011. *Successful Data Migration.* Oracle white paper. Redwood Shores, CA: Oracle. Accessed December 10, 2017. Available at http://www.oracle.com/technetwork/middleware/oedq/successful-data-migration-wp-1555708.pdf.

Ott, Michael. 2015. "A Ten-Step Plan for an Effective Data Governance Structure." The Data Administration Newsletter. December 1. Accessed December 24, 2017. Available at http://tdan.com/a-ten-step-plan-for-an-effective-data-governance-structure/19183.

Otto, Boris. 2011. "Data Governance." *Business & Information Systems Engineering* 3 (4): 241–44.

Otto, Boris, and Österle, Hubert. 2015. *Corporate Data Quality: Voraussetzung erfolgreicher Geschäftsmodelle.* Heidelberg: Springer Gabler.

Pandey, Rahul Kumar. 2014. "Data Quality in Data Warehouse: Problems and Solution." *IOSR Journal of Computer Engineering* 16 (1): 18–24. Accessed November 9, 2018. Available at http://www.iosrjournals.org/iosr-jce/papers/Vol16-issue1/Version-4/D016141824.pdf.

Park, Jung-Ran. 2009. "Metadata Quality in Digital Repositories: A Survey of the Current State of the Art." *Cataloguing & Classification Quarterly* 47 (3-4): 213–28.

Parker, Glenn. 2007. "The Cost of Poor Data Quality in the Banking and Financial Sectors." *The Journal of Financial Services Technology* 1: (1): 17–20. Accessed October 9, 2018. Available at https://www.fsprivatewealth.com.au/media/library/CPD/PDFs/Journals/ Financial%20Services%20Technology/Volume%201/Number%201/JFST-v1n01-07_ parker.pdf.

Patel, Priyal. 2013. "Establishing Data Governance, Part 2: 10 Universal Components." Perficient blog. April 22. Accessed July 10, 2018. Available at https://blogs.perficient. com/2013/04/22/establishing-data-governance-part-2/.

Paulk, Mark C., Charles V. Weber, Suzanne M. Garcia, Mary Beth Chrissis, and Marilyn Bush. 1993. "Key Practices of the Capability Maturity Model, Version 1.1." Technical Report CMU/SEI-93-TR025; ESC-TR-93-178. Software Engineering Institute. Carnegie Mellon University. Accessed October 16, 2018. Available at https://resources.sei.cmu.edu/asset_ files/TechnicalReport/1993_005_001_16214.pdf.

PC Magazine. Undated. "Data Element." Accessed October 5, 2018. Available at https://www. pcmag.com/encyclopedia/term/40771/data-element.

Pipino, Leo L., Yang W. Lee, and Richard Y. Wang. 2002. "Data Quality Assessment." *Communications of the ACM* 45 (4): 211–18.

Plotkin, David. 2013. *Data Stewardship: An Actionable Guide to Effective Data Management and Data Governance.* Waltham, MA: Morgan Kaufmann/Elsevier.

Poluzzi, Elisabetta, Carlo Piccinni, Paolo Carta, Aurora Puccini, Monica Lanzoni, Domenico Motola, Alberto Vaccheri, Fabrizio De Ponti, and Nicola Montanaro. 2011. "Cardiovascular Events in Statin Recipients: Impact of Adherence to Treatment in a 3-Year Record Linkage Study." *European Journal of Clinical Pharmacology* 67 (4): 407–14.

Ponniah, Paulraj. 2001. *Data Warehousing Fundamentals: A Comprehensive Guide for IT Professionals.* Hoboken, NJ: Wiley Interscience.

Power, Dan. 2011. *All the Ingredients for Success: Data Governance, Data Quality and Master Data Management.* Oracle white paper. Hingham, MA: Hub Designs. Accessed December 23, 2017. Available at http://www.oracle.com/us/products/middleware/data-integration/odi-ingredients-for-success-1380930.pdf.

PricewaterhouseCoopers (PwC). 2011. *Hidden Treasure: A Global Study on Master Data Management.* Hamburg: PwC. Accessed August 10, 2018. Available at https://www.pwc. de/de/prozessoptimierung/assets/studie_mdm_englisch.pdf.

Prince, Brian. 2008. "Don't Let Data Quality Concerns Stop a Data Migration Project." eWeek. Accessed Dec 10, 2017. Available at http://www.eweek.com/database/ don-t-let-data-quality-concerns-stop-a-data-migration-project.

Ramchandani, Purvi. 2016. "10 Reasons Why Data Quality and Data Governance Initiatives Fail." Data Quality Pro Blog. November 15. Accessed December 25, 2017. Available at https://www.dataqualitypro.com/10-reasons-data-quality-fail/.

Redman, Thomas C. 1996. *Data Quality for the Information Age.* Norwood, MA: Artech House.

———. 1998. "The Impact of Poor Data Quality on the Typical Enterprise." *Communications of the ACM* 41 (2): 79–82.

———. 2001. *Data Quality: The Field Guide.* Boston: Digital Press.

———. 2004. "Barriers to Successful Data Quality Management." *Studies in Communication Sciences* 4 (2): 53–68.

————. 2012. "Make the Case for Better Quality Data." *Harvard Business Review*, August 24. Accessed November 9, 2018. Available at https://hbr.org/2012/08/make-the-case-for-better-qua.

Reeve, April. 2013. *Managing Data in Motion: Data Integration Best Practice Techniques and Technologies*. Waltham, MA: Morgan Kaufmann/Elsevier.

Reid, Andrea, and Miriam Catterall. 2005. "Invisible Data Quality Issues in a CRM Implementation." *Journal of Database Marketing & Customer Strategy Management* 12 (4): 305–14.

Richard, Stéphane. Undated. "The Art of Data Validation." Accessed October 18, 2018. Available at http://www.petesqbsite.com/sections/express/issue10/datavalidation.

Rockart, John F. 1979. "Chief Executives Define their Own Data Needs." *Harvard Business Review* 57 (2): 81–93.

————. 1986. "A Primer on Critical Success Factors." In *The Rise of Managerial Computing: The Best of the Center for Information Systems Research*, edited by John F. Rockart and Christine V. Bullen. Homewood, IL: Dow Jones-Irwin.

Rogova, Galina L., and Eloi Bosse. 2010. "Information Quality in Information Fusion." Conference paper presented at the 13th International Conference on Information Fusion. Accessed October 8, 2018. Available at http://citeseerx.ist.psu.edu/viewdoc/download?doi=10.1.1.1006.3323&rep=rep1&type=pdf.

Ross, Joel E. 1993. *Total Quality Management: Text, Cases, and Readings*. Boca Raton, FL: St. Lucie Press.

Rouse, Margaret. Undated [1]. "Historical Data." TechTarget. Accessed February 28, 2018. Available at http://whatis.techtarget.com/definition/historical-data.

————. Undated [2]. "Fishbone Diagram." TechTarget. Accessed October 10, 2018. Available at https://whatis.techtarget.com/definition/fishbone-diagram.

Russom, Philip. 2006. *Master Data Management: Consensus-Driven Data Definitions for Cross-Application Consistency*. The Data Warehousing Institute (TDWI) best practices report. Renton, WA: TDWI. Accessed January 10, 2018. Available at http://download.101com.com/pub/tdwi/Files/TDWI_MDM_Report_Q406REVISED.pdf.

Ryu, Kyung-Seok, Joo-Seok Park, and Jae-Hong Park. 2006. "A Data Quality Management Maturity Model." *ETRI Journal* 28 (2): 191–204. Accessed October 4, 2018. Available at https://onlinelibrary.wiley.com/doi/pdf/10.4218/etrij.06.0105.0026.

Samitsch, Christoph. 2015. *Data Quality and Its Impacts on Decision-Making: How Managers Can Benefit from Good Data*. Berlin/Heidelberg: Springer Gabler.

Sarsfield, Steven. 2017. "Six Myths about Data Quality." Data Management University. January 28. Accessed December 18, 2017. Available at https://www.ewsolutions.com/six-myths-data-quality/.

SAS Institute. 2012. *The Practitioner's Guide to Data Profiling*. SAS white paper. Cary, NC: SAS Institute. Accessed November 18, 2017. Available at http://resources.idgenterprise.com/original/AST-0087746_PractitionersGuideToData.pdf.

————. 2018. *The SAS® Data Governance Framework: A Blueprint for Success*. SAS white paper. Cary, NC: SAS Institute. Accessed December 14, 2017. Available at https://www.sas.com/content/dam/SAS/en_us/doc/whitepaper1/sas-data-governance-framework-107325.pdf.

Sayers, Adrian, Yoav Ben-Shlomo, Ashley W. Blom, and Fiona Steele. 2015. "Probabilistic Record Linkage." *International Journal of Epidemiology* 45 (3): 954–64.

Scannapieco, Monica, Paolo Missier, and Carlo Batini. 2005. "Data Quality at a Glance." *Datenbank-Spektrum* 14 (14): 6–14. Accessed August 3, 2017. Available at http://dc-pubs. dbs.uni-leipzig.de/files/Scannapieco2005DataQualityata.pdf.

Scarisbrick-Hauser, AnneMarie, and Christina Rouse. 2007. "The Whole Truth and Nothing But the Truth? The Role of Data Quality Today." *Direct Marketing: An International Journal* 1 (3): 161–71. Available at https://doi.org/10.1108/17505930710779333.

Schein, Edgar H. 2004. *Organizational Culture and Leadership*. 3rd ed. San Francisco: Jossey-Bass.

Scottish Qualification Authority (SQA). 2007. "Entity." Accessed October 5, 2018. Available at https://www.sqa.org.uk/e-learning/MDBS01CD/page_06.htm.

Sebastian-Coleman, Laura. 2013. *Measuring Data Quality for Ongoing Improvement: A Data Quality Assessment Framework*. Waltham, MA: Morgan Kaufmann.

Seiner, Robert S. 2014. *Non-Invasive Data Governance: The Path of Least Resistance and Greatest Success*. Basking Ridge, NJ: Technics.

———. 2017a. "Complete Set of Data Governance Roles & Responsibilities." The Data Administration Newsletter. June 21. Accessed December 24, 2017. Available at http://tdan. com/complete-set-of-data-governance-roles-responsibilities/21589.

———. 2017b. "Defining Data Governance Core Principles." The Data Administration Newsletter. March 1. Accessed December 10, 2017. Available at http://tdan.com/ defining-data-governance-core-principles/17087.

Sellar, S., 1999. "Dust off That Data." *Sales and Marketing Management* 151 (5): 71–73.

Shaw, Tony. 2013. "The Evolution of the Chief Data Officer." Dataversity. Accessed December 10, 2017. Available at http://www.dataversity.net/the-evolution-of-the-chief-data-officer.

Sheina, Madan. 2010. "Best Practices for Evaluating Data Quality Tools." *Ovum*, August 24.

Shepard, Martin G. 1997. *Paper 1050—Customer Data Quality: Building the Foundation for a One-to-One Customer Relationship*. LaCrosse, WI: i.d.Centric. Accessed October 9, 2018. Available at www.openmpe.com/cslproceed/HPW97CD/PAPERS/1050/1050.pdf.

Shivu, Sagar. 2017. "Five Steps to Ensure Data Quality Success." Quora. January 19. Accessed October 28, 2018. Available https://www.quora.com/How-do-you-ensure-data-quality.

Silberschatz, Abraham, Henry F. Korth, and S. Sudarshan. 2006. *Database System Concepts*. 5th ed. McGraw-Hill.

Silvola, Risto, Olli Jaaskelainen, Hanna Kropsu Vehkapera, and Harri Haapasalo. 2011. "Managing One Master Data: Challenges and Preconditions." *Industrial Management & Data Systems* 111 (1): 146–62. Available at https://doi.org/10.1108/02635571111099776.

Smith, Harald. 2016. "Achieving Data Quality through Data Governance." RWDG webinar. Dataversity. October 24. Accessed December 14, 2017. Available at https://www.slideshare. net/Dataversity/achieving-data-quality-through-data-governance.

Snow, Colin. 2008. "Embrace the Role and Value of Master Data Management." *Manufacturing Business Technology* 26 (2): 38–40.

Soares, Sunil, and Jean-Michel Franco. 2017. *Data Governance & Privacy Compliance: 16 Practical Steps towards GDPR Compliance with Talend*. Talend white paper. Redwood City, CA: Talend. Accessed May 25, 2018. Available at https://info.talend.com/rs/talend/ images/WP_EN_TLD_Talend_Outlining_PracticalSteps_GDPR_Compliance.pdf.

Southekal, Prashanth H. 2017. *Data for Business Performance: The Goal-Question-Metric (GQM) Model to Transform Business Data Into an Enterprise Asset*. Basking Ridge, NJ: Technics.

Stedman, Craig. Undated. "GDPR Data Protection Edicts Make Good Data Governance a Must." TechTarget. Accessed June 1, 2018. Available at https://searchdatamanagement. techtarget.com/ehandbook/GDPR-data-protection-edicts-make-good-data-governance-a-must.

Strong, Diane M., Yang W. Lee, and Richard Y. Wang. 1997. "Data Quality in Context." *Communications of the ACM* 40 (5): 103–110.

Studytonight. Undated. "Normalization of Database." Accessed October 5, 2018. Available at https://www.studytonight.com/dbms/database-normalization.php.

Tatbul, Nesime, Olga Karpenko, Christian Convey, and Jue Yan. 2001. *Data Integration Services*. Technical report. Providence, RI: Brown University.

Tay, Liz. 2011. "Actuaries Count Cost of Poor Data Quality." IT News. September 23. Accessed November 9, 2018. Available at https://www.itnews.com.au/news/actuaries-count-cost-of-poor-data-quality-272638.

Tayi, Giri Kumar. 1998. Research Seminar on Data Quality Management. July 22. Universidad de Buenos Aires.

Tayi, Giri Kumar, and Donald P. Ballou. 1998. "Examining Data Quality." *Communications of the ACM* 41 (2): 54–57.

Taylor, John "JT." 2010. "Lesson—The Need for Proactive Data Quality Management." The Data Warehousing Institute. May 6. Accessed August 10, 2018. Available at https://tdwi.org/articles/2010/05/06/the-need-for-proactive-data-quality-management.aspx.

Technopedia. Undated. "Data Augmentation." Accessed October 18, 2018. Available at https://www.techopedia.com/definition/28033/data-augmentation.

Thomas, Gwen. Undated. *The DGI Data Governance Framework*. The Data Governance Institute.

Thorp, Adam. Undated. "The High Cost of Bad Data." TRED International. Latest Thinking. Accessed October 4, 2018. Available at http://tredinternational.com.au/bad_data-186.

Tress, Florian. 2017. "What Is Data Quality?" Norstat. Accessed August 10, 2017. Available at https://norstatgroup.com/blog/articles/news/detail/News/what-is-data-quality-part-22/.

Trillium Software. 2007. *Solving the Source Data Problem with Automated Data Profiling*. Harte-Hanks/Trillium white paper. San Antonio, TX: Trillium Software. Accessed October 9, 2018. Available at http://static.progressivemediagroup.com/uploads/whitepaper/31/34fcaf18-a5de-44f5-9ddb-d8493dcaf056.pdf.

Tromp, Miranda, Anita C. J. Ravelli, Gouke J. Bonsel, and Johannes B. Reitsma. 2011. "Results from Simulated Data Sets: Probabilistic Record Linkage Outperforms Deterministic Record Linkage." *Journal of Clinical Epidemiology* 64 (5): 565–72.

Vosburg, Jodi, and Anil Kumar. 2001. "Managing Dirty Data in Organizations Using ERP: Lessons from a Case Study." *Industrial Management & Data Systems* 101 (1): 21–31.

Walker, Jim. 2011. *The Butterfly Effect on Data Quality: How Small Data Quality Issues Can Lead to Big Consequences*. Talend white paper. Redwood City, CA: Talend. Accessed March 3, 2018. Available at https://www.datatechnology.co.uk/wp-content/uploads/2014/08/WP_Talend_Butterfly_Effect_DQ-EN-11Q2.pdf.

Walmsley, Jan, and Karen Miller. 2007. "Building Capacity for Quality Improvement through Leadership Development: Lessons from the Health Foundation's Leadership Programme." *The International Journal of Leadership in Public Services* 3 (2): 4–17.

Wand, Yair, and Richard Y. Wang. 1996. "Anchoring Data Quality Dimensions in Ontological Foundations." *Communications of the ACM* 39 (11): 86–95. Available at https://dl.acm.org/citation.cfm?id=240479.

Wang, Richard Y., Veda C. Storey, and Christopher P. Firth. 1995. "A Framework for Analysis of Data Quality Research. *IEEE Transactions on Knowledge and Data Engineering* 7 (4): 623–40. Accessed November 9, 2018. Available at http://mitiq.mit.edu/Documents/ Publications/TDQMpub/SURVEYIEEEKDEAug95.pdf.

Wang, Richard Y., and Diane M. Strong. 1996. "Beyond Accuracy: What Data Quality Means to Data Consumers." *Journal of Management Information Systems* 12 (4): 5–33.

Watts, Stephanie, Ganesan Shankaranarayanan, and Adir Even. 2009. "Data Quality Assessment in Context: A Cognitive Perspective." *Decision Support Systems* 48 (1): 202–211.

Weber, Kristin, and Boris Otto. 2007. "A Contingency Approach to Data Governance." Conference paper. 12th International Conference on Information Quality (ICIQ-07), Cambridge, Massachusetts.

Weill, Peter. 2004. "Don't Just Lead, Govern: How Top-Performing Firms Govern IT." *MIS Quarterly Executive* 3 (1), 1–17.

Weise, Elizabeth. 2005. "Medical Errors Still Claiming Many Lives." *USA Today*, May 18, 1A. Accessed November 9, 2018. Available at https://health.maryland.gov/newsclippings/ archives/2005/may05/051805.htm.

Wikipedia. Undated. "Butterfly Effect." Accessed October 4, 2018. Available at https:// en.wikipedia.org/wiki/Butterfly_effect.

———. Undated. "Data Management." Accessed October 5, 2018. Available at http:// en.wikipedia.org/wiki/Data_management.

———. Undated. "Data Steward." Accessed October 22, 2018. Available at https:// en.wikipedia.org/wiki/Data_steward.

———. Undated. "Database Model." Accessed October 5, 2018. Available at https:// en.wikipedia.org/wiki/Database_model.

———. Undated. "Dimension Modeling." Accessed October 5, 2018. Available at https:// en.wikipedia.org/wiki/Dimensional_modeling.

———. Undated. "Metadata." Accessed October 4, 2018. Available at https://en.wikipedia.org/ wiki/Metadata.

———. Undated. "Pareto Chart." Accessed October 18, 2018. Available at https://en.wikipedia. org/wiki/Pareto_chart.

———. Undated. "Reference Data." Accessed October 4, 2018. Available at https:// en.wikipedia.org/wiki/Reference_data.

———. Undated. "Social Security Number." Accessed October 10, 2018. Available at https:// en.wikipedia.org/wiki/Social_Security_number.

———. Undated. "Staging (Data)." Accessed October 5, 2018. Available at https:// en.wikipedia.org/wiki/Staging_(data).

———. Undated. "Unnormalized Form." Accessed October 5, 2018. Available at https:// en.wikipedia.org/wiki/Unnormalized_form.

Willcocks, Leslie, and Stephanie Lester. 1996. "Beyond the IT Productivity Paradox." *European Management Journal* 14 (3): 279–90.

Witten, Ian H., Eibe Frank, and Mark A. Hall. 2011. *Data Mining: Practical Machine Learning Tools and Techniques*. 3rd ed. San Francisco: Morgan Kaufmann.

Wu, Shaomin. 2013. "A Review on Coarse Warranty Data and Analysis." *Reliability Engineering and System Safety* 114: 1–11. Accessed October 18, 2018. Available at https://www.researchgate.net/publication/257391984_A_review_on_coarse_warranty_ data_and_analysis.

Yu, Ning, Peter T. Donnan, and Graham P. Leese. 2010. "A Record Linkage Study of Outcomes in Patients with Mild Primary Hyperparathyroidism: The Parathyroid Epidemiology and Audit Research Study (PEARS)." *Clinical Endocrinology* 75 (2): 169–76.

Zaidi, Jay. 2012, "Data Governance Demystified–Lessons from the Trenches." Dataversity. January 19. Accessed December 10, 2017. Available at http://www.dataversity.net/data-governance-demystified-lessons-from-the-trenches/.

Zaino, Jennifer. 2017. *"A Chief Data Officer Challenge: Build Your Data Strategy."* Dataversity. Accessed December 10, 2017. Available at http://www.dataversity.net/chief-data-officer-challenge-build-data-strategy/.

Zaki, Amir. Undated. "Making Data Governance Successful—5 Key Principles." Altis. Accessed December 14, 2017. Available at http://altis.com.au/making-data-governance-successful-5-key-principles/.

Zatyko, Stephanie. 2017. "Data Quality vs. Data Governance." Experian. June 7. Accessed December 14, 2017. Available at https://www.edq.com/blog/data-quality-vs-data-governance/.

Zaveri, Amrapali, Anisa Rula, Andrea Maurino, Ricardo Pietrobon, Jens Lehmann, and Sören Auer. 2012. "Quality Assessment Methodologies for Linked Open Data: A Systematic Literature Review and Conceptual Framework." *IOS Press*. Accessed October 16, 2017. Available at http://www.semantic-web-journal.net/system/files/swj414.pdf.

Zeiss, Geoff. 2013. "Estimating the Economic and Financial Impact of Poor Data Quality." Between the Poles blog. May 7. Accessed November 9, 2018. Available at http://geospatial.blogs.com/geospatial/2013/05/estimating-the-economic-impact-of-poor-data-quality.html.

Zetlin, Minda. 2017. "What Is a Chief Data Officer? A Leader Who Creates Value from All Things Data." CIO from IDG. Accessed December 7, 2018. Available at https://www.cio.com/article/3234884/leadership-management/chief-data-officer.html.

Zhu, Vivienne J., Marc J. Overhage, James Egg, Stephen M. Downs, and Shaun J. Grannis. 2009. "An Empiric Modification to the Probabilistic Record Linkage Algorithm Using Frequency-Based Weight Scaling." *Journal of the American Medical Informatics Association* 16 (5): 738–45.

Zornes, A. 2007. "The Fourth Generation of MDM." *DM Review* 17 (10): 26–37.

Index

WHY ASQ?

ASQ is a global community of people passionate about quality, who use the tools, their ideas and expertise to make our world work better. ASQ: The Global Voice of Quality.

FOR INDIVIDUALS

Advance your career to the next level of excellence.

ASQ offers you access to the tools, techniques and insights that can help distinguish an ordinary career from an extraordinary one.

FOR ORGANIZATIONS

Your culture of quality begins here.

ASQ organizational membership provides the invaluable resources you need to concentrate on product, service and experiential quality and continuous improvement for powerful top-line and bottom-line results.

www.asq.org/why-asq

ASQ
The Global Voice of Quality

BELONG TO THE
QUALITY COMMUNITY

JOINING THE ASQ GLOBAL QUALITY COMMUNITY GIVES YOU A STRONG COMPETITIVE ADVANTAGE.

For people passionate about improvement, ASQ is the global knowledge network that links the best ideas, tools, and experts — because ASQ has the reputation and reach to bring together the diverse quality and continuous improvement champions who are transforming our world.

- 75,000 individual and organizational members in 150 countries
- 250 sections and local member communities
- 25 forums and divisions covering industries and topics
- 30,000+ Quality Resources items, including articles, case studies, research and more
- 19 certifications
- 200+ training courses

ASQ
The Global Voice of Quality®

For more information, **visit asq.org/communities-networking.**